PRAISE FOR *THE SECRET LIFE OF MONEY*

"In this illuminating and captivating book, Crawford relates myths and stories from various cultures throughout history that illustrate money's hidden nature . . . Crawford's discussion leads us to understand what money is and how it functions in our minds and histories."

—*Minneapolis Star Tribune*

"This fascinating account reads like a novel and contains the information of a small encyclopedia. . . . Crawford's style is anecdotal and easy reading, yet his subject matter is so powerful it borders on the taboo. *The Secret Life of Money* will lead readers on a spiraling journey into their own psyches, revealing monetary desires and fears."

—*Whole Life Times*

"If you want to learn more about the psychological and spiritual effects of money in our lives and throughout history, Crawford can offer compelling insight. . . . He is an excellent weaver of tales, and his compelling style makes this book fascinating reading. From ancient myths to modern illustrations, Crawford reveals the ways in which money can impact our lives both for good and for evil."

—*Small Press*

"*The Secret Life of Money* is a captivating book in which Crawford explores myths and stories about money and the power it has always held over people. . . . It will lead readers on a fascinating journey to uncover the sources of their monetary desires and reveal how they can free themselves from the powerful obsession with money that can control their lives."

—*Common Ground*

"We can change our relationship with money by 'spending' a little time getting to know why we have the attitude we do have about it. I recommend this book to anyone who has ever felt frustrated with their boring and unimaginative relationship with the Almighty dollar."

—*Infinitum*

PRAISE FOR THE SECRET LIFE OF MONEY

"In this illuminating and captivating book, Crawford refers to films and stories from various cultures throughout history that illustrate money's hidden nature . . . Crawford's discussion leads us to understand what money is and how it functions in our minds and histories."
—Minneapolis Star Tribune

"This fascinating account reads like a novel and contains the informa- tion of a small encyclopedia . . . Crawford's style is anecdotal and easy reading, yet his subject matter is so powerful it borders on the taboo. The Secret Life of Money will lead readers on a spanking journey into their own psyches, revealing monetary desires and fears."
—Whole Life Times

"If you want to learn more about the psychological and spiritual effects of money in our lives and throughout history, Crawford can offer com- pelling insight . . . He is an excellent weaver of tales and his compelling style makes this book fascinating reading. From ancient myths to mod- ern illustrations, Crawford reveals the ways in which money can impact our lives both for good and for evil."
—Small Press

"The Secret Life of Money is a captivating book in which Crawford ex- plores myths and stories about money and the power it has always held over people . . . It will lead readers on a fascinating journey to uncov- er the sources of their monetary desires and reveal how they can free themselves from the powerful obsession with money that can control their lives."
—Common Ground

"We can change our relationship with money by spending a little time getting to know why we have the attitude we do have about it. I recom- mend this book to anyone who has ever felt frustrated with their boring and unimaginative relationship with the Almighty dollar."
—Inspireum

The
Secret Life
of
Money

The
Secret Life
of
Money

ENDURING TALES OF DEBT,
WEALTH, HAPPINESS, GREED, AND CHARITY

TAD CRAWFORD

SECOND EDITION WITH NEW INTRODUCTION

ALLWORTH PRESS
NEW YORK

25 24 23 22 21   5 4 3 2 1

Published by Allworth Press, an imprint of Skyhorse Publishing, Inc. 307 West 36th Street, 11th Floor, New York, NY 10018. Allworth Press® is a registered trademark of Skyhorse Publishing, Inc.®, a Delaware corporation.

www.allworth.com

Cover design by Mary Belibasakis

Library of Congress Cataloging-in-Publication Data is available on file.

Print ISBN: 978-1-62153-804-2
eBook ISBN: 978-1-62153-815-8

Printed in the United States of America

With Love
For Susan and Chris

CONTENTS

CONTENTS

2022
INTRODUCTION

THE SECRET LIFE OF MONEY explores how we can deepen our self-awareness and relationship to money. It is unlike the numerous money books offering practical advice. Instead, it uses tales from many cultures and times, insights of spiritual leaders, economic history and more to unlock what is secret about money.

The richness sought in these pages is inner richness, the expansive supply of a life fully lived. The ability to give thanks and feel gratitude for the mystery of our lives and the bounty of nature.

Psychologist C. G. Jung speaks of individuation, the process by which people can develop to become more fully themselves. Part of this process is working to reveal what is hidden in the unconscious and becoming aware of what previously was unknown. *The Secret Life of Money* seeks to play a role in that self-discovery.

Early peoples expressed gratitude and thanksgiving for what was hunted, foraged, or grown. They created a circulation between what nature offered and what we could offer in return. What nature gave was concrete, but what we offered in return—rituals, prayers, and sacrifices—was spiritual, a recognition of the divine source from which this abundance flowed.

Eventually, to replace barter and facilitate exchanges among people, money sprang into being in innumerable forms. The limits of what money can be are the limits of the human imagination. From the teeth of dogs and dolphins to paper and coins saying "In God We Trust" to Bitcoin and the many digital currencies—money is a creation of the human mind.

Side by side with its secular use, money could also be used for spiritual circulation. The ancient Greeks built treasuries at shrines like Delphi. The treasuries contained wealth for dedication to the gods. Later, the Romans made the fertility goddess Moneta the goddess of money. From her mint flowed the abundance of money. In the roots of the name Moneta are thought, measurement, memory, spirit, courage, warning, and mania.

Midas who can turn all to gold, fishermen who will not share their catch, Dorothy and her companions on the golden road to the Emerald City, Scrooge who cannot give, the hunter who shares not only food but also debt, money that falls from the skies, buried treasures that can be spiritual wealth or be stolen, how debt can be like inheritance, the impact of inheritance on families, the symbolism of the bulls and bears of Wall Street, the golden bough that leads us from the world we know to the unknown underworld, credit cards, the Consumer Confidence Index, the New York Stock Exchange, the all-seeing eye on the back of the dollar bill—all these and so much more fill the pages of *The Secret Life of Money* to illustrate the meanings rooted in the words Moneta and money.

More than a quarter century has passed since the original publication of *The Secret Life of Money*. As money becomes more and more abstract (paper that lacks the backing of precious metals or digital currencies backed by unseen blockchains), we move farther and farther from the natural abundance that led to exchange and, eventually, money. To better understand money in our depths cannot help but affect practical, day-to-day issues with money as well. Beyond this, our relationships to ourselves and others are deepened. With the hope of offering aid and insight to a new generation, I welcome this new life for *The Secret Life of Money*.

—Tad Crawford

INTRODUCTION

ONCE UPON A TIME there was a man who prayed to a wooden idol, which he had enshrined in his home. He beseeched the idol to give him money and make him prosper in the world. But even if he had knelt until his knees ached and his muscles cramped, the idol would have given him no reward. In fact, with each passing day, the winds blew ill for this man's fortunes. He had less money; prosperity eluded him.

At last, the man was awakened by a terrible rage to have prayed so long and so hard to so little purpose. He seized the wooden idol and smashed its head to pieces against the wall. Suddenly, as if a magic key had turned in a lock, a fortune in shining gold poured from the idol's broken head.

This ancient tale captures the paradox of money. To pray for money brings frustration and despair. Our fervent petition gives life to the wooden idol, as if the idol knows the secret way to make us prosper. But if we can shatter our ideas about how money has the power to be our salvation, often we will find wealth in places and forms that we would never have imagined, even hidden in what seems most familiar to us.

The Secret Life of Money is an exploration of why

money is so much more than the useful tool we think it is. To understand money we must see its symbolic value. This book gathers together stories and myths from around the world, from the present and the past, that reveal money as a marker of issues of the human heart and soul. The subjects of the stories revolve around money, or sometimes gold or even food, but the themes are about our nature, our inner richness, and our connection to other people and to community.

This is not a book about finance. It does not tell how to earn more, balance a budget, play the stock market, or hide money in foreign bank accounts. Many books give practical advice about money; this book does not cover that familiar territory. And, emphatically, this is not a book about how certain spiritual practices might enable one to "manifest" divine favor in the form of money.

In this book the quest for money is not a quest for acquisition, but for understanding. We have to seek the origins of money if we want to know why it has the power to captivate our minds. When we understand these origins, we see that money speaks to us of life and death, of the fertility of the natural world, and of our own natures.

We deal constantly with money in our daily lives, so much so that money may seem too familiar to merit our curiosity. What can we learn from money? Its rules look so simple. If you have it, you can buy what you want. If you don't have it, you must either get it or suffer deprivation.

If we are literal-minded when we approach money, we may love money and want to possess it whatever the cost. It is this love, or attachment, rather than money itself, that is corrupting to us. But if we see money as a symbol, we may feel a deepening connection to others and a desire to express and share an ever-increasing inner richness.

Keeping the symbolic value of money firmly in mind, we can understand how inheritance may raise emotional issues that have little to do with the money and property we receive. We can gain a new view of debt, seeing it not merely as an obligation that must be repaid but also as a statement about how our inner richness will be expressed in the future. We become able to contrast the symbolism of money with the seductive symbolism of bank credit cards that rely on the creation of debt for profits. We can better comprehend why in the last hundred years we have seen the invention and widespread use of credit cards, changes in bank architecture, the growth of debt, and a dramatic transformation in the very nature of United States money.

We refer so frequently to money in our everyday lives that we forget how taboo a subject money truly is. Of course, we feel comfortable chatting about prices, bargains, and news stories about the wealthy. But how often do we dare ask how much someone else earns, has in the bank, has inherited, or owes? Inquiries like these violate boundaries of privacy about which we feel strongly. But we can only understand why we feel so strongly if we understand money's secret life and symbolic value.

This book is titled *The Secret Life of Money* because it seeks to see beyond and beneath the usefulness of money and understand the ways in which money lives in our imaginations. It seeks to present money as a challenge, a door to a path on which we journey in search of greater knowledge of ourselves. If we do not go through this door, we risk losing our inner richness and our vital connection to family and community. Knowing the secret life of money—why, for example, "In God We Trust" appears on our bills and coins—may help us find an inner richness that is certainly wealth, but not the wealth that money can measure.

CHAPTER ONE

THE MANY FORMS OF MONEY

Understanding Its Symbolic Value

In THIS ERA of extraordinary inventions, many of our grandparents knew a world where horses reared at the first glimpse of an automobile, recordings of sound were a new marvel, airplanes realized the dream of flight, and radio, television, nuclear bombs, computers, and genetic engineering were obscured in the mysteries of the future.

But who, even among the eldest of us, can remember a time without money? Many believe that in an era of immense change, money is our North Star, the one reference we can trust to be stable and unchanging. We may have to worry about inflation, debt, and where the interest rate is pegged, but few people question whether we should have money. Checks, credit cards, electronic fund transfers, and automatic teller machines merely enhance the ease with which money is used. Money feels to us like language, a great invention whose date of origin is lost in prehistory. And like language, money can be translated and exchanged from one currency to another.

The ubiquity of money, its easy flow through our hands and the world around us, allows us to link our identity to money. We allow our self-worth to depend, at least in part, on whether we succeed in gaining money. In this chapter, we will take a step back from the everyday pursuit of money. We will see how dreams of having more money can be symbolic and serve us whether or not we in fact get the money. By looking at the innumerable forms that money has taken in different societies and at different times, we will see that the value of money rests, for the most part, in its power over our minds. Money is a potent symbol, but of what? To answer that question, we will meet a goddess named Moneta and see how money is rooted in challenges to each of us and our society to be fertile and productive.

THE POWER OF MONEY AS A SYMBOL

"If only I had more money, I would . . ."

We can find an infinite variety of ways to complete that sentence: Take a trip. Buy clothing. Have a nicer home. Help the poor. Continue our education. The list flows on and on, as endless as the needs and dreams of human beings.

When we fantasize about what more money would bring us, we rarely distance ourselves so that we can see the fantasy as distinct from the money that would be needed to realize the fantasy. But which is more important—the money or the fantasy? The fantasy is within us, the money outside us. Because of this, the fantasy tells us what we desire. The money is neutral, silent as to who we are or what we desire.

An examination of money fantasies reveals our minds to us, the inmost workings of ourselves. For example, a man of thirty-five yearns to leave his work and go to live on a tropical island. If only he had the money, he would go. If he forgets about the absence of money and welcomes the opportunity to explore his own thoughts, he may discover any number of truths: He fears the duties that he will have to perform if he is promoted; he is worried about his marriage but feels unable to confront his spouse; or even the banal possibility that he needs a vacation.

If the man stalls this self-examination by saying that he doesn't have enough money, he loses the opportunity to see into himself. He goes through his days dreaming of another life, an unlived life filled with equatorial passion and spent on the sandy shores of exotic islands. He does not recognize that this other life, this island life, is illusory, a flight from his reality. He sees money as an adversary and chooses to live with his feelings of deprivation. However, his deprivation is not of money but of self-exploration.

We seldom think of the power that we mentally give to money. We are aware that we feel limited by the absence of money, or that we feel strengthened by possessing it. Yet money is truly powerless until we vivify it through the power of our minds. Money itself has never built a building, manufactured a product, performed an operation to save a life, or given sound investment advice. Especially in today's world, money is valueless paper—valueless except for the consensual value that we give it.

THE STONE MONEY OF YAP

To illustrate the power our minds give to money—and then money's power over our minds—let us take an example that seems far away in time and place. In the nineteenth century, the islanders on Yap (one of the Caroline Islands in the Pacific) used money in the form of quarried stones. These stones were one foot to twelve feet in diameter with a hole drilled in the center of each stone. The hole allowed this very heavy money to be slung on poles and carried.

The money, called *fei*, was quarried on an island four hundred miles to the south of Yap. The stone had to be a close-grained, white limestone. Assuming the stone was of the proper quality, size was the most important factor in determining value. After the sea voyage to transport the money to Yap, many of the pieces of currency were too large to be moved easily around the island. This led to transactions in which the ownership of the fei would be transferred, but the actual stone would not be moved. The old owner would merely give a verbal acknowledgment of the change of ownership without even a mark of any kind being put on the stone. The stone itself might remain on the property of the old owner, but everyone understood that the ownership of the fei had changed hands. (Even the term "changing hands" is so much better suited to our contemporary bills and coins than to this majestic stone money which, when moved, had to be "shouldered" by many men.) To serve as "coins" with the fei, the islanders used coconuts, tobacco, and strings of beads.

If ownership of the fei could change simply by agreement, a meeting of minds and nothing more, why was it necessary to move it from one island to another? If everyone agreed that someone owned a certain stone, it shouldn't matter where the stone rested. This supposition is borne out by a fascinating story about a stone of immense proportions.

This stone endowed the wealth of a certain family on Yap, yet the stone had not been seen for several generations. Everyone agreed that the family was indeed wealthy, but this particular stone had been lost at sea on the long voyage home from the island where it was quarried. In the face of a violent storm, the raft bearing the stone was cut free and the stone slipped into the depths. It certainly could not be recovered. However, when the adventurers told of the size and beauty of the stone and the fact that its owner could not be faulted for its loss, everyone agreed that its value should not be affected by its position on the bottom of the sea. Nor did the passage of several generations diminish the value of this legendary stone. It might as well have been in the family's front yard as lost at sea, since its value as money remained undiminished in the minds of living men and women.

This is a remarkable illustration of the connection between mind and money. In essence, the islanders decided that the money did not have to be in their immediate possession, or even visible, to have value and be owned. By this communal assent, the life of money was conferred on inanimate (and invisible) stone. By giving life to stone, the islanders also gave it power. And, like the sculptor whose beautiful statue became a living woman, the islanders found that stone transformed to life can be the source of great anguish.

In 1898, the German government acquired the Caroline Islands from Spain. Since Yap had no roads and the paths were in poor condition, the islanders were ordered to improve the condition of the paths. However, the islanders had walked these paths for generations with fei hanging from their shoulder poles. They neither needed nor wanted to improve the paths.

Faced with the passive resistance of the people of Yap, the German authorities pondered how to force compliance. The wealth of the islanders dotted the landscape in the form of fei, but it would require far too much work to confiscate this money. And if it could be moved, where would it be stored? At last the Germans came up with a diabolic plan. A single man was dispatched around the island with a can of black paint. On the most valuable pieces of fei he painted a small black cross. That was all.

The Germans then announced that the black crosses symbolized the fact that the stones were no longer money. The people of Yap, who had floated tons of stone on unruly seas, were impoverished by a paintbrush. Immediately the islanders set to work improving the paths. When their work had been completed to the satisfaction of the authorities, the Germans sent another man to remove the black crosses from the fei. The islanders rejoiced to have their wealth restored.

Of course, nothing had changed on the island except for paint being applied and removed and the thoughts in people's minds changing. The brilliant stratagem of the German authorities placed the fei under the power of the German mind. This led directly to their gaining power over the islanders, since they gave the fei itself power over their own minds.

We may feel that the minds of the islanders of Yap are nothing like our own minds, but, for a moment, let us imagine a science fiction scenario somewhat like *War of the Worlds* by H. G. Wells. Alien spacecraft begin landing all over the Earth. The aliens' technology is far more advanced than ours. Fortunately, the aliens are benevolent. Their only demand is that we improve our highway system.

We are happy with our highway system as it is and do nothing. The aliens then issue an ultimatum. If we do not repair the highway system within thirty days, all the currencies of Earth will lose their status as money. To demonstrate their power, the aliens use an electromagnetic pulse to void all credit cards, making reliance on cash all the more necessary.

Suddenly we seem far more like the people of Yap than we might have imagined (or wanted). Most of our money is simply paper and obviously valueless except for the value we give it. If the aliens are to void our money, surely we can change to some new system. Isn't it merely a matter of agreeing to call something else money? All things considered, however, who can doubt that we would immediately improve our highways and hope for an early departure by the aliens?

Life is never the same after the aliens visit. On Yap, fei remained in use until the outbreak of World War II. Although the islanders changed to using American and Japanese money, they did so with reluctance. The white spheres of stone that had once been money became ornaments, their value as currency a memory.

THE MANY FORMS OF MONEY

Economists usually define money by its functions: (1) Money must serve as a means of exchange and be freely accepted for goods and services; (2) Money must offer a measuring device, like a ruler, so that goods and services can be evaluated in relation to one another; and (3) Money must be in a form in which wealth can be stored.

How dry this definition is compared to the variety of money itself! For money can take almost any form and still meet these functions. Stones, coconuts, tobacco, and strings of beads only suggest how money, like the god Proteus, can assume innumerable forms.

One haunting example is of Chinese skin money. First used in the reign of Wu-ti (circa 140 B.C.), skin money was made of white stag skin. Each piece was square and represented significant wealth. In the white deer the Chinese had money with a life of its own and a propensity to breed more! The Chinese solution to inflation was to limit the imperial herds of white deer.

This process of limitation had unforeseen and unfortunate consequences. In their zeal to control inflation, the Chinese authorities restricted the herds too greatly. Ultimately, the white deer became extinct. Now the powerful white stag, leaping through ancient forests, is simply an image that flickers in our minds. It has no reality, for the stag and much of the forest have been consumed. It is as if money can be vampiric and take the beauty, and the very life, of nature.

This sacrifice of life for money has been reenacted in numerous societies. Porpoise teeth served as money for the islanders of Malaita (in the Solomons). A school of porpoises would be driven into the shallows, slaughtered, and their teeth extracted for use as money. On Fiji, whale's teeth served as currency, with the rarer red teeth worth twenty times the value of the white teeth. On the island of San Cristobel, thousands of dogs were reared and killed so that their teeth could be harvested as money. In parts of New Guinea, the tusks of boar were used as money. In the Santa Cruz Islands, the young men made money from the red feathers that crested the head of a tiny jungle bird. By filling a shell with sticky sap and imitating the bird's call, they would lure the bird to its death. In the Pacific Northwest, beaver skins were commonly used as currency along with the shells of snails and abalone, blankets, other skins, and even human slaves. These slaves were fortunate, however, to remain alive, when compared to the money of Borneo that was made of human skulls. This skull money is certainly the most literal (and gruesome) example of the triumph of money over mind.

Money often evolved from what was either nourishing or beautiful. The ancient Egyptians used grain as money, while cattle were the prevalent form of money in the Mediterranean countries. Many coastal and island peoples made beautiful strings of shells, especially cowrie shells, which are about an inch long and white or straw colored. These shells may have been the first money. They circulated for thousands of years before Christ in India, China, and the Middle East, and were later used in Africa, Asia, and throughout the Pacific Islands. In fact, when the Japanese military handed out large quantities of cowrie shells in New Guinea in 1942, the value of the cowries tumbled and the financial system of the island was threatened.

Settlers in the New World found that the Indians made wampum from seashells. Wampum became the first local currency of New Netherland. In a 1648 law, Connecticut set a standard that wampum should be "strung suitable and not small and great uncomely and disorderly mixt as formerly it hath been." This has the ring of a law against counterfeiting, which indeed was a serious problem with wampum. The white beads, four to eight of which equalled a penny, were often dyed to simulate the more valuable black beads. Massachusetts allowed the payment of small debts with wampum, but would not allow it to be used in payment of taxes.

The first money in the modern sense, that is, a currency minted for the specific purpose of serving as money, was created in China, where agricultural tools had been used as money over a long period of time. In about the twelfth century B.C., the Tchou rulers substituted miniatures of tools to act as currency in place of the actual tools. Over nearly a thousand years, one of these "coins"—the knife—evolved so that its blade disappeared and only its round handle with a hole in it remained. The hole had originally allowed the knives to be strung together.

The first coins in the West were minted by the Greeks in about 750 B.C. and were made from electrum, an alloy of gold and silver. Because this alloy was easily debased, Croesus, the sixth-century king of Lydia, minted coins of pure gold and silver. His legendary wealth is why we still say today, "As rich as Croesus."

What we receive for our employment, which determines the use of so much of our energy and time, is not only money but salary. The word salary comes from the Roman word *salarium*, which means salt, and reflects the Romans' use of salt to pay the wages of workers.

TOBACCO AS MONEY IN THE COLONIES

The colonial governments fixed the values of various farm products for use as currency. Taxes could be paid in such produce, and the taxing authorities struggled to avoid taking lean cattle (since the best cattle were "hoarded" and not used to pay taxes) and to dispose of surpluses. It was only in 1670 that Massachusetts repealed the law that fixed a value for the use of corn and cattle as money. South Carolina's legislature fixed a value for rice as money as late as 1720.

Tobacco, in particular, offers a fascinating history of the power of money over the minds of its inventors. By 1619, tobacco was already a local currency in Virginia, and the legislature declared tobacco to be money with a pound of the best tobacco equal to three shillings. Production increased very rapidly, so that by 1631 the value of tobacco had tumbled in relation to minted money. To raise the value of tobacco, laws were enacted forbidding certain people (such as carpenters and other crafts workers) from growing tobacco, restricting the amount that could be grown by those allowed to grow it, and raising standards for the quality of the crop. In 1640 and 1641, the legislature set the value of tobacco as currency, but fixed it at about five times the value in the marketplace. Growers were forbidden to sell their tobacco for less than the official rate. Not only were these laws ineffective, but they created serious inequities between debtors and creditors.

When these laws failed to halt the increasing cultivation of tobacco and its decline in value in relation to money, in 1642 the legislature took the remarkable step of enacting a law requiring that contracts be payable in tobacco. This virtually made tobacco the sole currency, so, of course, people wanted all the more to grow money. By 1666, Maryland, Virginia, and Carolina had to enter into a treaty in which they agreed to grow no tobacco during that year. By 1683, the falling price of tobacco caused vigilante groups to go about burning the tobacco crops. The legislature viewed this destruction of currency as subversion and made it punishable by the death penalty.

Once given the magical designation of money, tobacco

became far more than a crop. Its seeds were no longer rooted in the earth alone but in the minds of the people as well. Its power as money caused far more tobacco to be planted than the price of tobacco could have justified. The authorities refused to accept the prices set in the market-place, but instead believed they could legislate the value that tobacco as money should have. Crops were not planted and fields were burned, but the powerful lure of money was such that the supplies of tobacco/money increased nonetheless.

MONEY AS AN ARCHETYPE

We have seen the innumerable, often surprising, forms that money has taken. If we *believe* in money, it doesn't matter whether the money is shaped as minted coins, printed paper, giant wheels of stone, grain, tobacco, the teeth of dogs and porpoises, or the feathers of exotic birds.

The key point is that money must have power over us inwardly in order to have power in the world. We must believe in its value before we will change our conduct based on whether or not we will receive it. In the broadest sense, money becomes a vehicle of relationship. It enables us to make choices and cooperate with one another; it signals what we will do with our energy.

It is this flow of our energy into the world that demands exchange, whether of conversation, love, bartered goods, or money. In fact, another definition of money is simply that it is energy, the potential for action.

The life of money comes mainly from its hidden nature.

Money is not only about the financial transactions of individuals, corporations, or even nations. It is also about the deeper questions of how life energy will be spent, how people live in relation to one another, and how culture and community survive and grow. Our daily striving for our salt obscures the deeper meanings of money and the way in which, whether we realize it or not, money confronts us with the meaning of our existence and our actions.

Because money is about relationship and exchange, which are fundamental issues of the human condition, it is archetypal. An archetype is a pattern inherited from ancient human experiences and present in each of us. Often we are not aware of these patterns, but they exist in us nonetheless. So these patterns are unconscious, living in the part of us that is separate from our everyday awareness and identity. Yet we are influenced by these patterns. And we may have a desire to understand the archetypes so that we can better understand ourselves.

This realm of the archetypes is timeless and transcends the individual. It is truly the realm of the gods. Our contemporary fascination with ancient gods is largely because they express archetypes. To use some of the Greek gods for examples: Zeus is the chief god who integrates and organizes all the aspects of life; Hera, the wife of Zeus, is concerned with marriage and the family; Hermes plays many roles, including the god of commerce who helps us to exchange among ourselves.

When a corporate president reorganizes a company to increase profits, he or she is operating with the archetypal energy of Zeus. A husband or wife's concern that there be enough money for the family to prosper comes from the archetypal pattern of Hera. Every step that brings a product to the consumer is influenced by the archetype of Hermes who governs commerce: the market research, the product design, the packaging, the advertising campaign, and the determination of the price to charge. The study of gods lets us see the larger patterns that operate within us. We learn of the forces that shape the destiny of the human race and sometimes make the individual feel overwhelmed and at a loss to understand his or her experiences.

THE GODDESS MONETA

What are the origins of the word *money*? If we search in this direction, we meet a goddess. She lives in the world of archetypes, the larger patterns that shape us and await our discovery. Often such a goddess can help us in our efforts to become aware of these patterns.

The word "money" derives from the Roman goddess named Moneta. Coins minted in her temples were issued to the far reaches of the empire. In fact, the Latin word *moneta* (meaning mint or coins) evolved into the Old English word *mynet* (meaning coins or money), which became the English word "mint."

To understand Moneta, we have to speak of Juno, the mother goddess of Rome. Juno is a fertility goddess whose origins are with the Mother Goddesses who imbue fertility and make harvests abundant. June, the month named for Juno, is a favored month in which to marry. In her role as the preeminent goddess, Juno is the protectress of the city of Rome, her favorite city and the capital of the empire. In a more personal role, Juno is the protectress of women and so presides over marriage (as Juno *Jugalis*), childbirth (as Juno *Lucina*), and motherhood (as Juno *Matronalia*).

Ancient gods and goddesses often had more than a single name. Each name revealed an aspect of their nature. Like Juno, a goddess might preside over marriage, childbirth, and motherhood, and possess a different name for each of these roles. If she made the earth fertile, she would have a name to match that role. Moneta is the name of Juno in her role as the mother of money. She is Juno Moneta from whom money plentifully issues forth.

It will help us to have an image of a fertility goddess like Juno, because such fertility goddesses will play an important role in our exploration of money. Let us imagine Juno Moneta standing before us as a radiant, tall, and full-figured woman. She is mature, no longer a girl and not yet old. Her face is powerful and serene. She wears a flowing gown not from modesty but to protect us from being blinded by her overpowering radiance. On her head she carries a basket filled to overflowing with wheat, corn, and all the foods which nourish humanity. She holds an infant in each arm, a girl and a boy, and has lowered the top of her gown to let them suckle at her full breasts. Wild and domesticated animals rub against her flanks to gain her gift of fertility. At her feet are measureless piles of gold and silver coins that flow from her like water from an unending spring. In everything she is abundant, cornucopic, rich beyond measure or imagining.

Let us fix this image of Moneta in our minds. She symbolizes the pattern or archetype to which we will return as we examine the meaning of money. It would be natural to assume such a goddess is wise. In the case of Moneta, wisdom is rooted in her very name.

The Latin word *moneta* derives from the Indo-European root *men-*, which meant to use one's mind or think. The goddess Moneta is modelled on the Greek goddess of memory, Mnemosyne. Contained in the power to remember is the ability to warn, so Moneta is also considered to be a goddess who can give warnings. To suggest how money can affect us in different ways, we might remember that the Greek words *menos* (which means spirit, courage, purpose) and *mania* (which means madness) come from the same root as memory and Moneta. Measurement, from the Indo-European root *me-*, also relates to mental abilities and is a crucial aspect of money.

Measurement, memory, and warning are important concepts that will figure in our explorations, but the theme of this chapter has been the power of money over our minds. In one form or another, we all worship wooden idols. Moneta draws our attention to this fact. Because the derivation of her name reveals the deep connections between money and mind, she alerts us to the likelihood of confusion and illusion. Even more, she suggests the necessity of using our minds to bring light to the subject of money, to remove the obscurity and mystery which surrounds what we do not think about and do not understand.

THE RABBI'S ADVICE

A folktale from the Jewish tradition tells of a poor man who comes to his rabbi for advice. It is a few days before Passover and the man complains bitterly that he hasn't any money for matzos, meat, and sacramental wine. He feels that he and his family cannot come to the synagogue in their tattered clothes.

The rabbi tries to relieve the man's fears by saying, "God will help you. Don't worry."

The poor man cannot let go of his fears. Finally the rabbi asks him to list the items that he needs and what each would cost. The total for the matzos, meat, wine, and new clothing is fifty-two rubles.

"So you need fifty-two rubles," the rabbi says. "Now there's no need to worry about matzos, meat, wine, or clothing. You'll have only one worry: How to get fifty-two rubles."

Is this rabbi cruel or wise? He has offered this poor man the solace of God. If the man cannot trust that God will help him, then, in a sense, he is not ready to enter the synagogue and worship. He has a task to perform. He must worry about money. If he worries deeply enough and long enough, perhaps his worries will transform his understanding of money. He may see money in a new and brilliant light, transfigured, something quite other than he might ever have imagined.

The story doesn't tell us whether the poor man finally worshipped in the synagogue. But for Christian, Hindu, Moslem, Buddhist, polytheist, animist, atheist, or agnostic, money holds the same mysteries, the same secret life. Why do we so frequently set up wooden idols? Why are we so seldom awakened by a rage that allows us to smash their heads to smithereens? Why do people of goodwill lament that we worship money or accuse us for losing ourselves in pursuit of the almighty dollar?

If we had the memory of Moneta, we might answer these questions and more. One image of Moneta shows her head tilted to one side and a hand cupped to her listening ear. What she hears, she remembers. When she speaks to us, she is like a woman we meet in a dream. Our task, our challenge, is not only to hear her, but to remember her words when we wake.

CHAPTER TWO

THE ALMIGHTY DOLLAR
Why Money Is So Easily Worshipped

WE OFTEN HEAR condemnations of the worship of money. These critics—whether of a society driven by consumption, of the inordinate millions made by stock market manipulators, or of the crass ostentation of certain of the wealthy—miss a fundamental point. The reason that so many people worship money is because money, in its origins, was divine. It is no accident that the Roman mint was in a temple sacred to Moneta.

If we simply complain of the evils of money, we miss the opportunity to explore its symbolic richness. Certainly the Bible does not condemn money, but warns: "The love of money is the root of all evils." Not money, but the love of money, is the root of evil. If we love money, we are likely to lose sight of its deeper significance. If we literalize money as our goal, we fail to see it as a symbol of life forces that could connect us more deeply to ourselves, our families, and our communities. So the evil that flows from an attachment to money is done not only to ourselves but also to those we most hope to love. In a sense, money challenges us to learn what is truly worthy of our love. If we understand the origins of money, we can direct our love away from money as we develop the potentials that it symbolizes.

This chapter will explore how, thousands of years ago, the divine origins of money were lost to sight, lost to consciousness. We are left only with the device of money and its practical applications in the world. Of its sources and first purposes, we know nothing. Yet the initial religious fervor which forged money remains within us. It animates us and gives money a mystical allure. Mystical because we are unaware that in our imaginal world the touch of money can be experienced as contact with the divine.

Hints and vestiges of money's divine origins are present on money today—in some cases quite visible, in other cases more hidden. The coins and bills of the United States firmly pledge "In God We Trust." This is remarkable in a country whose Constitution guarantees the separation of Church and State. The First Amendment states that "Congress shall make no law respecting the establishment of religion, or prohibit the free exercise thereof. . . ." The Supreme Court has interpreted this clause to forbid the federal government, states, and agencies of the states (such as school boards) from enforcing regulations or "laws which aid one religion, aid all religions, or prefer one religion over another." So no one can be punished for going to church or refusing to go to church, and prayers in schools, even interdenominational prayers, violate this Constitutional safeguard.

If a school board required students in public school to say "In God We Trust" each morning, the board would transgress the First Amendment. But the Treasury, as required by federal law, must place the phrase "In God We

Trust" on all coins and bills. Each day hundreds of millions of people hand this phrase back and forth when they exchange money. If the phrase means nothing, perhaps it should be changed to "In the Federal Reserve We Trust." Of course, that wouldn't have the same ring or the same profound meaning. The reason that we accept "In God We Trust" on our coins but not in our schools probably has to do with the most ancient origins of money.

To delve into these ancient origins, we will look first at societies that had no money. Money did not suddenly appear, fully imagined and realized, in the world. Rather, it came gradually and in response to the evolution of human needs. To understand the origins of money, we must imagine worlds without money. We have to see how cycles of exchange came to connect both hunting and agricultural societies to their gods, and how money and markets evolved from these cycles of exchanges.

HOW HUNTERS INFLUENCED THE SPIRIT WORLD

Early tribal peoples attempted to influence nature by entering into a proper relationship with it. This proper relationship is, fundamentally, a relationship of exchange. If nature gives its abundance today, what will make it willing to give its abundance tomorrow? Early peoples found the answers to this question in numerous rituals of prayer and sacrifice. These rituals forged a bond of spirit between the people and the world in which they lived. The very word "sacrifice" derives from the Latin *sacrum facere*, which means to make sacred, to perform a sacred ceremony. So a sacrifice is a sacred giving to the gods. The rationale offered for sacrifice was *do ut des:* I give to you so that you will give to me. Nor was this a crass exchange, like merchants bickering in a bazaar. Because the power of nature could not be contested, the sacrifice had to be made with reverence, humility, and, at most, hope for an auspicious outcome.

For example, the American Indians sought to honor the spirits of the game that nourished them. In the Pacific Northwest, the Tlingit, Haida, Tsimsyan, and other tribes lived off their stocks of dried and smoked salmon through the long winters. The annual migratory return of the salmon was eagerly awaited, and a tale was told of how a young boy went to the land of the salmon people. There he learned of the rituals that would cause the salmon consumed by the tribe to be given flesh again in the spirit world and return with the annual migration. From the boy's experience, the Indians came to show their respect for the spirits of the salmon by burning any parts that were not eaten. These offerings restored the salmon, who in turn nourished the Indian tribes.

Even inland tribes held great feasts to honor the first salmon. At these feasts the chief, or shaman, would ask for the continued blessings of the Sky Chief. Then each person present would be given a small piece of the salmon to eat, so that the first fruits of the salmon harvest were shared by everyone. After the bones of the salmon were burned or, in some cases, buried or returned to the stream with proper invocations, the Indians believed that the bones found their way back to the home of the salmon people. There the bones became whole salmon, ensuring the fertility that would again bring the spawning salmon to the nets of the Indian fishermen in the annual cycle of

These Native American ceremonies exemplify the universal belief that prayers and offerings help ensure the abundance of nature. For example, the bear festival among tribes in Finland required that the bones of a slain bear be placed in a tomb with useful objects such as a knife and skis. The bear was honored, treated as a friend, and asked to tell the other bears about the honors paid to it by man. This ensured that the bear spirits would want to return in the form of the fully fleshed bear.

This festival is similar to the worship of the bear by the Ainu of Japan. If the Ainu captured a bear cub in the mountains, the cub would be brought to the village and treated like a visiting god. Nursed at a woman's breast until the cub became too large, even its caging would be gentle until the time came to send the bear to its spirit home. After the killing of the bear by arrow and ritualized strangulation, the bear's head and pelt would be arranged at the feast in its honor. This worshipful respect encouraged the bear spirits to return and share their renewed flesh with the Ainu in unending cycles of fertility.

HOW AGRICULTURAL SOCIETIES SOUGHT GOOD HARVESTS

Nor was it only hunting-and-gathering societies around the world which shared these beliefs. The development and evolution of agriculture, beginning nearly ten thousand years ago, was accompanied by immense changes in human behavior. The farmer became attached to the land. At the same time, the abundance of food encouraged the specialization of labor, the growth of cities, and the armies that built empires. Yet the priests, who had become a larger and more organized group, offered prayers and sac-rifices so the spirits and gods would make the fields fer-tile. The failure of the crops threatened the farmers, and the rulers, priests, soldiers, and artisans, with the very real danger of starvation.

Fertility rituals are universal among agricultural socie-ties. For example, the rain dance of the Hopi Indians is well known to tourists who have visited the parched mesas of Arizona in August. Their faces dark with soot and chins bright with white clay, one by one the priest-dancers of the Snake Society clamp live rattlesnakes be-tween their teeth and circle the plaza of the pueblo. Other priests guide the dancers and soothe the snakes with feathered wands. All the while a chant reverberates that seems to come from within the Earth. Songs are sung about clouds gathering and rain falling. At the end of the dancing, the priests seize as many snakes as they can and carry them into the desert: to the east, the west, the north, and the south. The snakes are blessed and released to carry a message of renewal across the land and to crawl into the underworld depths, the womb of the world, and intercede with the spirits for life-nourishing rain.

This snake-dancing ceremony alternates each year with the flute ceremony, which also seeks to ensure the matur-ing of the crops and rainfall at the end of summer. These sixteen-day ceremonies are at the heart of a year-round procession of rituals. Beautiful and complex in their my-thology and symbolism, many of the rituals seek to ensure that the nourishing rains will come and bring fertility to the land.

The annual round of ceremonies is not only about fertil-ity but also about the relationship of humans to nature and the universe. This is shown in the marriage of the

Snake Maiden, a young virgin who is the living representation of two sacred statues of Snake Maidens, to the Antelope Youth, a young boy who has undergone purification. This marriage ritual, part of the sequence of ceremonies that culminate in the snake dance, uses corn, vegetables, seeds, and the milky fluid derived from the yucca root to symbolize the hoped-for fertility.

After the wedding, the young couple, married for this one night, sit together as sacred songs are sung and, at last, are taken home by their godparents. This ritual seeks fertility in its many unions: the joining of the Snake Society and Antelope Society in the ritual, the connection between the antelope whose horn rises to the sky and the snake which is capable of penetrating the earth, the joining of people with the natural world, and the merging of the masculine and feminine forces in nature.

To illustrate the universality of these rituals, we can compare the Hopi ceremonies to those practiced by the Greeks more than two thousand years ago. The Greek rituals were celebrated in cycles called the Lesser Mysteries (held in February) and the Greater Mysteries (held in September). These Mysteries were considered so sacred that death was the punishment for even speaking of them to the uninitiated.

What we know of the Mysteries suggests that the initiates, after a rigorous purification (which would include bathing and fasting), experienced a union with the Goddess Demeter. In the ecstasy of the rituals, the initiates felt themselves carried to Mount Olympus, the abode of the Gods, where they witnessed the sacred marriage of Demeter and Zeus, the highest of the gods. This divine union offered salvation. A voice thundered "A sacred child is born" and spoke of the "ear of corn in silence reaped." To these symbols of the ever-regenerating and life-giving Earth, the initiates shouted their thanksgiving *"Ye"* (for rain) and, kneeling, *"Kye"* (for giving birth).

The similarity between the rituals of these agricultural societies, separated by thousands of miles, and years, reveals the universality of the prayers and sacrifices adopted by agricultural peoples to placate and win the favor of the gods and spirits. To give a final example, in the nineteenth century each clan on the East Indian island of Buru concluded the rice harvest with a feast. All of the members of the clan had to contribute a small amount of their rice to this shared meal, and a portion of the rice was offered to the spirits. Called "eating the soul of the rice," this meal nurtured the clan with the vitality of nature. Our wedding ceremonies today contain a hint of such ritual practices; the throwing of the rice at the bride and groom is a vestige of ancient fertility rituals.

THE RAINMAKER IN BUSINESS

Today, in business, a rainmaker is someone who can put deals together and generate money for the other participants, who may not have the same access to powerful connections and financial resources. Such a rainmaker creates prosperity, not in the form of crops but as money. The rainmaker's exchanges are not with spirits or gods but with banks, investors, stockholders, clients and others who will benefit. These transactions are memorialized with agreements, such as promissory notes and limited partnerships, which connect the parties in the world of business.

What is missing, of course, is the beauty of the rituals which connect the tribal rainmakers to their gods and their own natures. What would it be like if every business transaction were celebrated like a wedding with the divine? If we could understand the origins of money and the marketplace, we might recapture at least a sense of the sacred rituals that once played so crucial a role in the creation of prosperity.

MONETA, MONEY, AND THE MARKETPLACE

What is the connection of these sacred exchanges between the human and the divine and the evolution of marketplaces and money? The Goddess Moneta offers us the key. Money is minted in her temples. She is also a representation of one of the many aspects of the Goddess Juno. This evolution of Moneta from Juno, who herself had evolved from earlier and more powerful Earth Goddesses, informs us that money evolves as an aspect of fertility. When the riches of the hunt and the fields were first offered back to the spirit world to ensure further renewal, there could be no doubt that this natural bounty was sacred. As cultures became more complex and specialized, this sacred bounty came to be traded outside of the sacrificial rituals binding human to god. It became a commodity, bartered at first and, later, either became money proper or was exchanged for money. So, inevitably, whatever the shape of money, it originated in the exchange between the human and spirit worlds.

But why did the sacred bounties of nature come to enter the marketplace as commodities? Why did money evolve out from religious ceremonies? Certainly money and market exchange had no place in the family, where food was shared because of love and familial responsibilities. This love feast served as the basis for sharing food in the larger community that developed from the family—that is, the clan or kinship group.

The saying of grace before a meal captures the feeling of the love feast. One form of grace, for example, is: "Bless us, O Lord, and these thy gifts which we are about to receive from thy bounty through Christ our Lord. Amen." This is a thanksgiving to God and a prayer that both family and food will be blessed.

The importance of circulating food is stressed in a passage from the *Rig-Veda:* "The man without foresight gets food in vain. . . . The man who eats alone brings troubles on himself alone." *The Bhagavad Gita* makes the distribution of food an essential element of the ritual of sacrifice: "The sacrifice contrary to the ordinances, without distributing food, devoid of words of power and without gifts, empty of faith, is said to be of darkness."

The sharing of food, its bestowal on others, is a way of circulating the divine essence in the human world. *The Bhagavad Gita* suggests the close relationship between the eater and the food, since it views both people and food as part of a cycle that requires sacrifice to connect with the divine. "From food creatures become; from rain is the production of food; rain proceedeth from sacrifice; sacrifice ariseth out of action."

On a practical level, sharing is also a way of trusting in one's family and community. If all will share, times of hardship will be far more bearable and scarcity will be less difficult to endure and survive. Eating alone makes one guilty, for it violates the trust, the love feast, that underlies the community.

In the Lord's Prayer there is a recognition of God as the source of our daily bread. "Bread," symbolizing nourishment for the body and the spirit, is also slang for money, as is the word "dough." But bread and dough are food, while money is neither food nor fertility. The origins of money are in fertility rituals, yet money is far more ambiguous than food in what it means to us.

MONEY, STRANGERS, AND THE LOVE FEAST

A story from *Aesop's Fables* suggests how money brings into the family circle strangers who lack the family's shared concerns. In "A Woman and Her Two Daughters," one daughter has died and the burial is arranged, including the hiring of mourners. The woman's surviving daughter is shocked to see strangers weeping and crying out with such grief over the death of her sister, while her own relatives show far less feeling. The daughter asks her mother how this can be. The mother answers that the kin are never the better for grieving, but the strangers gain money by it. So money can create the outward appearance of a feeling but not its inner reality.

A Jewish folktale also speaks of how money can distort our view of the world. Once a miser of great wealth came to the home of his rabbi and asked for his rabbi's blessing. The rabbi made the miser stand before a window and look at the people in the street. The rabbi asked the miser what he saw, and the miser answered, "People." Then the rabbi placed a mirror in front of the miser and asked again what he saw, and the miser answered, "Myself." The rabbi then explained that both the window and the mirror are made of glass, but the mirror also has a veneer of silver. Glass by itself allows us to see people, but glass covered by silver makes us stop seeing others and see only ourselves.

The danger of money, that we will be blinded by it and no longer see others, suggests how different a role money can play when compared to food. The love feast joins family and kinship group together in the sharing of food which is clearly seen as nature's gift. Money is needed to deal with strangers. In fact, money may encourage us to see others as strangers.

As societies became more complex, the likelihood of having to deal with strangers increased. Within the society itself, larger populations and specialized tasks meant that however large the family group, there would still have to be dealings with outsiders. Also, these complex societies developed the knowledge and the resources to send explorers, traders, and armies to new lands whose inhabitants were certainly strangers. At what point of blood relationship or geographic distance a person would be viewed as a stranger might vary greatly, but the love feast of the family at some point excludes the other, the stranger.

Unlike sacrifices and the intrafamily giving that connects the giver and ancestors to the renewing spirit world, exchanges with strangers promise no such renewal. Barter and trading are the way strangers deal with one another; when strangers meet, sacred circulation changes into the exchange of commodities in the marketplace. And, eventually, money in its many shapes came to be used to facilitate the circulation of these commodities.

Some scholars speculate that religious pilgrimages may have been one of the more important ways in which strangers came into contact with each other and served as an impetus to the creation of money. Far from home, the pilgrim would have to obtain food and other supplies, both to survive and make the required sacrifices. So traders would be encouraged to root themselves beside the temples, and pilgrims would bring various forms of wealth. Protected by the sacred association with the temples, fairs developed for the purpose of exchange. In fact, the German word for Mass—*Messe*—also means fair.

HOW THE TEMPLE AT DELPHI CAME TO MINT MONEY

One goal of pilgrims in the ancient world was to visit the famed oracle at Delphi in Greece. As early as 1400 B.C., a sanctuary of Gaia, goddess of the Earth and mother of the gods, existed on this mountainous site with its natural spring and panoramic views of Mount Kirfis and the Gorge of Pleistos running to the Gulf of Corinth. The myths tell of Apollo's killing of the female serpent that guarded the prophetic spring. Thus a male deity displaced Gaia, and from the eighth century onward Apollo, a culture-giving god of intellect, the arts, and prophecy, was worshipped there.

From all over the known world people came to consult the Delphic oracle for information from the gods. After paying a fee and sacrificing animals, the suppliant was brought into the inner shrine of the temple. Separated by a curtain from the priestess, who sat on a sacred tripod and breathed intoxicating fumes rising from the rocks, the suppliant could hear her incomprehensible words and shouts. Male priests interpreted these utterances in the form of brief verses.

It is surprising when visiting Delphi today to find the ruins of treasuries beside the ruins of temples. Corinth built the first treasury at the beginning of the sixth century B.C. The most powerful city-states followed suit until twenty treasuries lined the Sacred Way that ran through the sanctuary and past the Temple of Apollo. The word "treasury" comes from the same root as the word "thesaurus." It refers to a gathering of things, a repository. In addition to contributing to the support of the Temple of Apollo, the city-states also dedicated riches to their treasuries. These elegant marble buildings filled with gold, silver, and art, offerings that represented immense wealth. If necessary, especially in the event of war, the city-states could use these treasures as security for borrowing. In fact, the templelike architecture of many banks is a tribute to these ancient, and sacred, treasuries.

Delphi issued its first silver coins in the fifth century B.C., and temples which had the precious metal to mint coins facilitated trade by placing some of their silver in circulation as coinage. In this way, wealth offered as sacred treasure moved into the world of trade.

Many of the earliest Greek coins visibly show their origins in the temples. Gods, symbols for gods, mythological beasts and stories, and objects for sacrifice are the images most frequently selected for these coins. The busts of Olympian gods such as Zeus, Poseidon, Athena, and Apollo conferred trustworthiness on the new invention of money. We see the thunderbolt of Zeus, the trident of Poseidon, the owl of Athena, and the lyre of Apollo. Griffins, sphinxes, and the winged horse Pegasus show their fantastic forms and connect the spirit world to the realm of coins. Wheat, tuna, tripods (which first contained sacred offerings and later were themselves used as offerings), and double-headed axes are all sacrificial offerings that are portrayed on coins.

Of course, even the earliest coins are a recent, indeed a modern, development compared to the fertility rituals and offerings that originated with prehistoric peoples. Just as food and other offerings ultimately left the realm of the sacred to be traded with strangers, so coins left the temples to serve for trade. Scholars debate whether every early Greek coin came from religious sources, but most of these coins clearly do. These early coins are memorable not only for their religious types but also for the exquisite beauty of so many of the images. The busts of Arethusa (goddess of rivers and streams), Medusa (the snake-headed goddess), and Persephone (the daughter of Demeter and goddess of the underworld) are only a few of the aesthetic triumphs of the artists who created these coins.

One of the most important of these coins began to be minted in the temples of Athens in 525 B.C. Picturing a head of Athena on one side and her owl on the reverse, the preeminence of Athens made the Athenian tetradrachm widely and readily accepted. This facilitated trade across the Mediterranean world and beyond. On the tetradrachm, Athena's characteristic helmet symbolizes her role as protectress of the freedom of Athens. Many coins of the United States used images of Liberty or Standing Liberty that owe a debt to the images of Athena guarding the city of Athens. And, as Athena Medusa, Athena served as a goddess of fertility as well.

Today we feel a concern for the separation of Church and State which the ancient Greeks did not share. The divine and secular authorities in the city-states worked in unison. Despite the fact that coins in ancient Greece were minted in the temples, control of the mints either began with the rulers of the city-states or quickly passed into their hands. Nonetheless, several centuries passed before the face of a mortal as opposed to that of a god or goddess appeared on a coin. This first portrait, that of Alexander the Great, dates to approximately 300 B.C., about twenty-three years after Alexander's death. Alexander had declared himself a living god but was not officially deified until after his death. The use of his image reflected this deification and opened the way for living rulers to make godlike portrayals of themselves on coins.

WHY OUR MONEY SAYS "IN GOD WE TRUST"

Viewed against this background, many aspects of our coins and bills reflect the sacred origins of money. The Founding Fathers preferred simple busts of Liberty on the coinage of the Republic. Today the motto "In God We Trust" on all our coins and bills is accepted almost without question. We may not consider why such a motto appears on our money or realize that its first use was in 1864 during the agony of the Civil War.

On November 13, 1861, N. R. Watkinson, a minister from Ridleyville, Pennsylvania, wrote to Salmon P. Chase, Secretary of the Treasury, as follows:

> One fact touching our currency has hitherto been seriously overlooked. I mean the recognition of the Almighty God in some form in our coins.
>
> You are probably a Christian. What if our Republic were now shattered beyond reconstruction. Would not the antiquaries of succeeding centuries rightly reason from our

past that we were a heathen nation. What I propose is that instead of the goddess of liberty we shall have next inside the 13 stars a ring inscribed with the words "perpetual union"; within this ring the allseeing eye, crowned with a halo; beneath this eye the American flag, bearing in its field stars equal to the number of the States united; in the folds of the bars the words "God, liberty, law."

Secretary Chase advised the Director of the Mint: "No nation can be strong except in the strength of God, or safe except in His defense. The trust of our people in God should be declared on our national coins." A variety of mottos: "Our country, our God," "God, our Trust," "Our God and our country," led finally to the adoption of "In God We Trust," which first appeared in 1864 on the newly created two-cent piece.

Subsequent coinage acts allowed the use of "In God We Trust" on other coins. When, in 1907, President Roosevelt did not include this motto on the beautiful eagle ($10) and double eagle ($20) gold coins that he had commissioned Augustus Saint-Gaudens to design, a public outcry protested "Roosevelt's Godless Coins." In 1908, Congress passed a law requiring that "In God We Trust" appear on all coins of the United States.

An irony is that Roosevelt hardly had a godless motive in removing the motto; rather, he felt the very mention of God in the motto to be a sacrilege. It is interesting that the suggested motto of "God, liberty, law," which says nothing about trusting, became "In God We Trust." The Secretary of the Treasury added the concept of trust. It almost seems that we are being asked to trust in God when, in fact, the government really wants us to trust in the currency and the government which issues it. This might explain Roosevelt's feelings. Also the currency was not trustworthy when the phrase first appeared, since the Civil War was financed by debt and inflation rather than taxes. In any event, President Eisenhower signed legislation in 1955 extending use of the motto to paper currency, and since 1957 "In God We Trust" has appeared on bills as well as coins.

The all-seeing eye did not appear on coins of the United States, as N. R. Watkinson wished, but we are all familiar with its presence today on our currency. The Great Seal of the United States, adopted in 1782, has both its front and reverse portrayed on the back of the one-dollar bill. The reverse of the Great Seal shows an unfinished pyramid with the all-seeing eye contained in a triangle floating above it. This all-seeing eye is, of course, the eye of God contained in a triangle representing the Christian Trinity. Its presence on the Great Seal represents the desire of the Founding Fathers to have God oversee the continued building of the unfinished pyramid (nation) which they had begun. Not only was God's favor sought for the future, but His support for their efforts was unequivocally stated in the Latin phrase *"annuit coeptis,"* which translates "He [God] has approved our undertakings."

The color and motifs of United States paper money also arouse, at least unconsciously, associations with fertility cycles. The money is green on its reverse side and the decorative motifs are unfailingly of vegetation. This reminds me of an artist who told of his shock when he saw the Grim Reaper on the back of a Swiss thousand-franc bill. He had difficulty connecting money with the Grim Reaper, a death figure who scythes down humanity like a crop in the field. It jarred him, and yet he found it compelling. To give himself a feeling of financial security, he didn't spend that bill for a long while. Its value, about $500 at the time, could hardly explain why this image connecting money to cycles of life resonated with such strength for him.

More recently, when the Swiss government sponsored a competition for new designs for its currency, the winning entry portrayed photographs of famous Swiss artists in boldly colorful and contemporary designs. The idea of such new money outraged the public. Critics decried the designs as macabre, repulsive, like theater tickets, and suggestive of national decline. But how can pictures of artists be more macabre or repulsive than the Grim Reaper? Or does the Grim Reaper, by some paradox, speak to us of the ancient cycle of life and death, a cycle that promises fertility and prosperity in the very image of death? In any event, the outcry suggests that some sense of sacred propriety had been touched, and to this day the currency has not been modernized.

THE BIRTH OF THE DOLLAR

The very word "dollar" has a curious history that connects it with the name of a shepherd, Joachim, later St. Joachim. According to nonbiblical tradition, St. Joachim was father to Mary and grandfather to Jesus.

The expansion of trade in the sixteenth century increased the need for internationally accepted coinage. A valley, Joachimsthal (which means St. Joachim's valley) in what is now the Czech Republic, proved rich in silver. In 1518, the first coins minted from mines in Joachimsthal began to circulate. These coins quickly gained international popularity and took their name, Joachimsthalers, from their place of origin. Soon the name was abbreviated to the easier-to-say *taler* (or *thaler*). For more than three centuries, the taler and its many imitations, including England's crown, France's écu, Russia's ruble, and Spain's peso, became the standard for international trade.

In English-speaking countries, taler soon transformed to a more easily spoken word—dollar. Shakespeare made one of the earliest references to the dollar in *Macbeth*, in which a character speaks of a Norse king who had to pay "ten thousand dollars." In his 1782 proposal that the dollar be the currency unit for the United States, Thomas Jefferson wrote that the "dollar is a known coin and the most familiar of all to the mind of the people. It is already adopted from south to north." The dollar to which Jefferson referred was actually the Spanish peso (or piece of eight). Pesos remained legal tender in the United States until 1857, when more than 2,000,000 of them were redeemed.

THE SIGN OF THE DOLLAR

If the word for dollar traces back to St. Joachim, the sign for the dollar may have an equally surprising connection to religion. The origin of the dollar sign has been a subject of debate among numismatic experts. Since the dollar and its symbol existed before the United States, the popular belief that the dollar symbol evolved from the drawing together of the *U* and *S* in U.S. must be incorrect.

Another theory is that the dollar symbol evolved from the plural of the sign for pesos. This theory posits that *P* (for peso) and *s* (for the plural) gradually became superimposed in the late eighteenth century, but the graphic proof offered for this evolution is not fully persuasive.

The most intriguing explanation traces the roots of the taler itself. In the sixteenth century, Charles V not only ruled Germany but also Spain and its American possessions. On the reverse of his taler he placed two pillars to show his connection with Spain and entwined these pillars with scrolls. The ancient Phoenicians, famed for their explorations, built such pillars in Gibraltar when they erected a temple to Herakles near present-day Cadiz. These pillars derived from ancient coins from Tyre (in modern-day Lebanon) depicting the pillars of the temple of Solomon. Solomon's pillars had names: Jachin, which means "He shall establish," and Boaz, which means "In it is strength." So the dollar symbol is formed by the scrolls added by Charles V to the image of Solomon's pillars shown on the coins of Tyre. If this theory is correct, the upright of the dollar sign is a pillar with a meaning similar to that expressed on the reverse of the Great Seal and the dollar bill: "He [God] has approved our undertaking."

WHAT WE MIGHT LEARN FROM THE WORSHIP OF MONEY

We are taught to think of money in practical terms. Can we afford to buy a car or a dinner at a nice restaurant? Can we risk starting a small business or making an investment? Does our budget balance or must we cut our expenses or work harder to earn more? Are we threatened by bankruptcy or homelessness? Our hopes and fears constantly revolve around whether we will have enough or too little.

But Moneta does not speak only in terms of the everyday; she is not only a figure of our conscious lives, of the lives that we are aware we lead. She is also the wise woman in a dream that we struggle to remember. If her words remain with us when we wake, then we know that money speaks to us of cycles far larger than our own lifetimes. These cycles of birth, death, and rebirth are as true for the crops in the fields as for the farmers, the hunters, and even the urbanites.

Moneta's words imply that we might learn from the mysteries that make nature fertile. She reminds us of the love feast, the thankful sharing of the bounties of nature. In this we are made aware again of our desire for community and sharing. Ultimately, whether in a slogan like "In God We Trust" or simply by money's forgotten origins in religious ritual, Moneta arouses energies that once connected us to a higher realm, energies related to what is transcendent in the world and in ourselves.

Understanding the origins of money may let us be more forgiving of our desires to worship money. The adoration of money may have devastating consequences, as we shall see, but these consequences come from misdirected energy that, channeled differently, could have served us well. Gurdjieff spoke of harnessing the energy of a demon to do the work of an angel. If we can remember Moneta's words and bring her wisdom to our daily lives, perhaps we can regain and redirect these energies to more appropriate purposes.

But our quest has a fearsome aspect as well. The Grim Reaper is a reality: The abundance of nature flows always from death in endless cycles. This is another face of

Moneta, or any fertility goddess. To remember Moneta's dream words we may have to endure a journey through the underworld, the realm of the Grim Reaper. In this passage we may find in our own natures the richness and fertility that the shamans and priests sought by sacrifices to their gods.

CHAPTER THREE

MONEY AND SACRIFICE
When Money Feels More Important Than Life

THE CONNECTION OF MONEY to ancient rituals of fertility is lost to our conscious awareness today. However, an implication of this connection is everpresent: money issues can make us feel that our very lives are at stake. Almost all of us have struggled at one time or another with money shortfalls and found ourselves face to face with overwhelming fears. Our self-worth vanishes as we feel despair and see the future as futile. These feelings may not be a response to actual hunger or homelessness or an untended injury. Rather, they are a response to ideas about money, ideas that flow up from our unconscious and overwhelm our ability to reason and see reality.

The power of money to meet material needs, acquire status and power, and free us of many constraints does not explain why money can make us feel that our lives hang in the balance. As we shall see, the stories that begin this chapter, "The Rocking-Horse Winner," by D. H. Lawrence and the tale of King Midas, offer insights into how money arouses energies that once connected us to a higher realm. If these energies are misdirected, we risk losing our inner richness and our vital connection to family and community. We may gain wealth but at the cost of all that makes life worth living and, in some cases, at the cost of life itself.

To understand why this should be so, this chapter will explore an aspect of the ancient fertility rituals that is shocking today: human sacrifice. If we see that the exchange of our time and energy for money is a form of sacrifice that echoes ancient rites of human sacrifice, then we may be freed from a fearful attachment to money and be able to seek the deeper values which it symbolizes.

WHEN LIFE IS SACRIFICED FOR MONEY

In the short story titled "The Rocking-Horse Winner," D. H. Lawrence offers a penetrating look at the damage caused by the love of money. A boy named Paul knows that his mother does not love him or anyone, despite her appearance of being a loving mother. Although the family lives in a nice house and has servants, both father and mother have expensive tastes that they can't afford. Soon Paul and his sisters hear the house speaking to them, whispering "There must be more money! There must be more money!"

Paul's mother tells him that his father has no luck, and Paul confuses the word luck with lucre, "filthy lucre," as his Uncle Oscar once said. When his mother distinguishes luck from lucre, Paul tells her that he has luck. His mother doesn't believe him; Paul insists, saying, "God told me."

The family's gardener, Bassett, gambles on the horse

races. Paul is growing too old to ride his rocking horse but finds that when he rides the rocking horse with a frenzied, mad strength he somehow learns the names of the horses that will win the races. He and Bassett become partners in betting on the races, and Paul accumulates five thousand pounds. Hoping to silence the voices in the house that always whisper of money, Paul arranges through his Uncle Oscar to give to his mother one thousand pounds a year for five years as if it were a gift from an anonymous relative.

Paul is terribly hopeful that this money will quiet the voices in the house. Instead, his mother shows no pleasure in receiving the money. She goes to the lawyer who has served as intermediary and asks if the entire amount cannot be advanced to her. Hoping this will quiet her, Paul (through his uncle) agrees. But the voices grow louder and more insistent in demanding money, "More than ever!"

Paul knows that his mother does not love him. His primary reason for seeking the money is not to gain her love but rather to quiet the voices in the house, to quiet her insatiability. Such a child's effort to save a parent so the child's needs can be met is doomed to failure, especially if the parent is addicted and insatiable. Paul cannot change his mother's nature; his superhuman efforts only feed her yearning for more and more.

Lawrence suggests in several ways that Paul, in the grip of his obsession, is connecting to divine energies. Not only does Paul say that he knows he has luck because "God told me"; but Bassett, when telling Uncle Oscar of Paul's ability to name the winners, looks, "as if he were speaking of religious matters." Later Basset says to Uncle Oscar, "It's as if he had it from heaven," and Uncle Oscar replies, "I should say so!" This divine energy allows Paul to transcend what is normal. He becomes psychic, a word derived from Psyche, goddess of the Soul or Spirit; he is able to know what no ordinary human could know.

When we cross the boundaries between our material world and the higher realms, we expose ourselves to grave dangers. Shamans and priests perform rituals to give a form, a container, that allows for a transformative encounter with these higher energies and a safe return. The blind pursuit of money, even with the best motives, touches energies that can easily destroy us. Paul gives what is most precious and most powerful in himself, but he has no guide to help him on his journey. Even Basset and Uncle Oscar, good enough men themselves, become his fellow conspirators in using the uncanny information Paul has gleaned.

Finally, riding his rocking horse with superhuman force, Paul calls out the name of another winner. Then he collapses, unconscious, with a fever of the brain. He regains consciousness to learn that he has won over eighty thousand pounds for his mother. But he has sacrificed his very life for this money, and soon dies of the fever.

"The Rocking-Horse Winner" has many parallels with the well-known story of King Midas and the golden touch. While details vary from one version to another, Midas is always a lover of gold. In Nathaniel Hawthorne's retelling of the tale, Midas loves both gold and his daughter, Marygold. Unfortunately, Midas entwines these two loves and longs to bequeath to his daughter the largest pile of gold that has ever existed in the world. Midas loses his love of flowers (unless golden) and music (except for coins clinking together) and spends most of his time in the miserable underground vault—"little better than a dungeon"— where he plays with his gold and whispers to himself of his happiness.

One day a handsome stranger appears in the vault. Midas, certain that he turned the key in the lock, knows that this radiant young man must be a god. Soon the visitor, who is never named in the story, learns that Midas is not satisfied to have more gold than anyone else in the world. What, asks the beneficent stranger, would make Midas happy? Midas cannot imagine a large enough pile of gold, but at last conceives that his touch might turn everything to gold. The god asks if anything might ever make Midas regret having the golden touch. When Midas says that the golden touch will make him "perfectly happy," the god replies that the next morning Midas shall indeed possess this power. And the god, becoming brighter and brighter, at last vanishes like a sunbeam.

We are all familiar with how Midas's greedy joy soon disappears when he learns that he cannot eat or drink, for his food turns to gold in his mouth. Worse, he kisses his daughter, thinking that she is worth one thousand times more than the golden touch, only to have her turn to gold. Midas had liked to say his daughter was worth her weight in gold, but now this has literally become true. Stricken with misery, Midas suddenly discovers the god once again before him. When questioned by the god, Midas answers that a glass of water, a crust of bread, and certainly his daughter Marygold are all worth far more than the golden touch.

"You are wiser than you were, King Midas!" says the god, adding that Midas appears "to be still capable of understanding that the commonest things, such as lie within everybody's grasp, are more valuable than the riches which so many mortals sigh and struggle after."

The god tells Midas to wash himself in the river and pour water over all that he has turned to gold. If he is fortunate, everything, including Marygold, will return to what it was. And he is fortunate, for the story finishes many years later with Midas dandling his grandchildren on his knees and telling them how he came to hate the sight of gold, except for the golden hair of his daughter.

Paul's mother in "The Rocking-Horse Winner" has a great deal in common with King Midas. She is insatiable for money; he is insatiable for gold. She gains the golden touch in the form of her son's psychic powers; while Midas gains it directly as a gift from the god. She cannot save her son from death, and Midas cannot save his daughter from the death of becoming gold. Paul's mother is starving inwardly in a way that can never be satisfied; Midas's similar inner starving is reflected outwardly when his golden touch denies him the normal human joys of eating and touching.

But here the stories diverge. Paul's mother cannot love; she does not relate to her son and her family from an inner richness. Midas, while he is foolish and wrongheaded in asking for what will give him misery rather than happiness, does love his daughter. From this love, he is able to gain the wisdom that his love is far superior to acquiring gold. He is also able to see quite plainly his starvation and recognize that, for him, gold has become life-denying. He becomes richer within, richer in love and wisdom, because he learns from his experience and, according to Hawthorne's story, overcomes his obsession with gold.

THE GODS OF HUMAN SACRIFICE

Who is this golden god that visits Midas? Why does he come to that underground vault with such good will toward a mortal? And, having granted Midas one wish, why is he willing to intervene and save the foolish king from the folly of having wished for the golden touch?

King Midas, while probably a figure of myth rather than history, is said to have ruled the kingdom of Phrygia (in what is now western Turkey) at the beginning of the seventh century B.C. To show his piety, he is reputed to have sent his golden throne as an offering to the sanctuary at Delphi. He lived only a few generations before King Croesus, whose wealth we know to have been historical fact. The original story of Midas is Greek and, like so many Greek myths, was retold by a Roman poet, Ovid, in *The Metamorphoses*. As Ovid tells the story, Midas had no daughter at all, and Midas's gaining the golden touch is only one episode among many involving the golden god whom Hawthorne never named.

Ovid tells us that the god's name is Dionysus, lord of the vine and intoxication. Dionysus, or Bacchus as the Romans called him, had many drunken worshippers. One such worshipper was an old satyr named Silenus who weighed nearly half a ton from all his drinking. Trapped by peasants, Silenus is taken to their king—none other than Midas! Midas knows the drunken joys of Dionysus and has been inebriated with Silenus many times. So Midas treats his old friend to a drinking binge that lasts for ten days and nights. Then Midas takes Silenus home to Dionysus. The god, delighted by this, offers Midas a boon: any wish that Midas makes will come true. The balance of Ovid's tale about Midas is similar to Hawthorne's, so we will leave Midas to focus on the generous god Dionysus.

Son of Zeus and a mortal woman, Dionysus is plagued by madness. He wanders from kingdom to kingdom, from Egypt to Syria to Phrygia, and introduces in each place knowledge of how to cultivate the vine and make wine. In

Phrygia, Dionysus is initiated into the mysteries of the cult of the goddess Cybele. This goddess exemplified many of the terrifying aspects of fertility goddesses. As mother of the crops, the animals, and human offspring, the fertility goddess is endowed with immense powers. The cycles of life and death are the realm of Cybele or the very similar Mother Goddesses of neighboring lands.

As ruler over life and death the goddess herself must sacrifice. For Cybele, this sacrifice was Attis, the young shepherd whom she loved and, perhaps, had even mothered. Attis is slain by a wild boar or, in some versions of the myth, castrates himself and bleeds to death beneath the pine tree which is sacred to Cybele. After Attis dies, he is transformed into a pine tree and so finds new life.

The death of Attis led to the renewal of the land, the life of the new crops. This death was re-enacted each year in a great festival held around the spring equinox in March. On the third day, known as the Day of Blood, the high priest drew blood from his arms and offered this blood as a sacrifice. To the wild music of cymbals, drums, horns, and flutes, the worshippers danced to intoxication and gashed themselves so their blood flowed on the altar. In this frenzied state, some of the worshippers lifted their robes and castrated themselves, flinging their genitals on the statue of Cybele as an ultimate offering.

What purpose could be served by these terrible mutilations? Apparently the power of the male genitals was felt to be transformed by being sacrificed. No longer capable of impregnating mortal women, these genitals could be buried to impregnate the earth herself. So like the sacrifices of human blood, the severed genitals would serve to move life's great wheel from the season of death to that of birth.

From this description, it can be easily understood why Cybele was served by eunuch priests. Cybele had to sacrifice Attis, whom she most loved, to fulfill her role in making the land fertile. Likewise her worshippers at times sacrificed what was most precious to them—their manhood, their generative powers—to amplify her powers of fertility. In fact, the death of Attis strongly suggests that human sacrifice had been part of these fertility rituals. Not only the power of the genitals but the power of life itself would be offered in service to the goddess.

King Midas's benefactor, Dionysus, learned well from the frenzied rites of Cybele. As the cult of Dionysus spread, his worshippers would also aspire to a divine intoxication (often through the consumption of wine). In this frenzied state, they might see loved ones as beasts and tear them limb from limb. That his worshippers were often bands of women called maenads and their victims men (such as Penteus in *The Bacchae* by Euripides) suggests a re-enactment of the violent moments when the fertility goddess brings life from death by sacrifice.

The implication of human sacrifice in the death of Attis is made explicit in what we know of many fertility goddesses (and gods). The Old Testament is filled with references to the long struggle to end human sacrifice, often portrayed as part of the struggle between Yahweh and the pagan gods. We are told of King Ahaz who "did not do what was right in the eyes of the Lord [but] . . . even made molten images for the Ba'als; and . . . burned his sons as an offering, according to the abominable practices of the nations whom the Lord drove out before the people of Israel." Ba'al was a Phoenician god with power over the rain and thus over the fertility of the land. Often worshipped in the form of a calf or bull, the human sacrifices to Ba'al sought to make the land fertile. Human sacrifice was used to forge a connection to the divine by King Ahab, the warrior Jephthat, and perhaps even the prophet Elijah.

The worship of Ba'al and similar gods spread with the explorations of the ancient Phoenicians, who established colonies in many parts of the Mediterranean. In Carthage, founded by the Phoenicians, innumerable children were offered as sacrifices. As worshippers danced to timbrels and flutes that drowned the victims' screams, the children were placed in the hands of a bronze idol with a calf's head. From here they slid inexorably down into ovens filled with fire. Archeologists have found urns containing the remains of as many as twenty thousand infants who served as sacrificial victims.

Religious rites involving human sacrifice appear in many cultures around the world, cultures quite unrelated to each other. So the practice of human sacrifice was certainly not limited to the tribes and times of the Old Testament. When Julius Caesar conquered Gaul, he wrote of the fertility sacrifices of the Celts. At a great festival held every fifth year, condemned criminals would be sacrificed by the Druids (priests). The Celts believed that the more humans sacrificed, the greater the fertility of the land.

No culture made human sacrifice more central to its existence than that of the Aztecs. In the mythology of the Aztecs, the gods had sacrificed themselves to nourish the Fifth Sun. So the Aztecs believed their practices of human sacrifice came from the gods and that the continued existence of their universe depended on such sacrifice. Blood kept the sun in the heavens; and innumerable methods of bloodletting let the Aztecs put off the dread day when the sun would cease its movement through the sky.

The preferred sacrifice was of the human heart, for the

heart symbolized life to the Aztecs. They believed that the heart contained vital fluids that made it move and, through sacrifice, would make the sun continue to move and ascend the heavens each day. So priests would often pull the pulsating heart from the victim and hold it aloft to feed the sun. This tearing out of the heart also symbolized the husking of the corn; lifting the heart to the heavens aided the new corn to grow ever higher.

The Aztecs institutionalized a system of recurring warfare that allowed the taking of prisoners for the purpose of sacrifice. Although the sixteenth-century estimates of the sacrificial slaughter made by the Spanish conquerors are unreliable, such sacrifices were clearly widespread and systematic. Thus a mother who gave birth was said "to make a prisoner." One of the songs of Xipe, the Aztec god of the sun and the corn, speaks of his transformation into the war god Huitzilopochtli. So the blood of sacrificed prisoners feeds the growth of the corn.

Some sacrificial victims were actually made to act the role of a god or goddess. By doing so, these victims were given the sacred duty of representing the god or goddess. For example, each September there was a festival to celebrate the Maize Goddess Chicomecohuatl. After a strict fast lasting seven days, a beautiful slave girl, twelve or thirteen years old, would be dressed in the robes of the goddess with maize cobs about her neck and a green feather upright on her head. This feather symbolized the ripening maize which, at the time of the festival, would be almost ready to be harvested.

After a series of rituals, including perhaps a marriage of the girl to the war god Huitzilopochtli, each person had to come before the girl, squat (the equivalent of kneeling), and offer her a cup containing blood drawn from their ears as penance during the seven days of the fast. Later that day the priests would sacrifice the girl so that her blood soaked an altar piled with maize, vegetables, and seeds of every type. The body of the girl was flayed and her skin worn by a priest, who also dressed in the robes of the goddess. As the procession left the temple, this priest danced to the front to show the resurrection of the goddess.

If these examples of human sacrifice in fertility rituals seem far removed from contemporary life, we might consider how many people today are willing to kill for money. Listening to the news brings us endless varieties of this life sacrifice: cabbies killed for a few hundred dollars; shopkeepers shot down even after surrendering their money; and a tourist knifed to death for enough money to spend an evening at a disco. In his book *The Highest Altar*, journalist Patrick Tierney argues persuasively that human sacrifice actually takes place today in Peru. As remarkable as the fact of this sacrifice is its purpose: the murderers pray not for rain or good harvests, but for money.

When we first encountered Moneta, the Roman goddess of money, we spoke of the meanings hidden within her name. She is a goddess who warns, but what does she warn us against? Now we can understand Moneta far better, for we see her among her sister fertility goddesses. We know the sweetness of the Hopi ceremony which weds the Snake Maiden to the Antelope Youth in worshipping the Corn Mother. And we know the violence of the human sacrifices of the Aztecs in serving the very same goddess, the Maize Goddess Chicomecohuatl. Moneta promises us the new life that flows from the sacred marriage and warns us of the death that is inevitable in her endless cycles of fertility. In her most violent aspect, she demands human sacrifice to ensure her own rebirth, the annual renewal of the natural world, and the survival of humanity.

Moneta's message is difficult to hear, because our mortality is a painful and inscrutable truth. Yet neither the sacrifice of human victims nor the accumulation of vast amounts of wealth will allow us to escape from the cycles of life and death. When we contemplate money in this way, we may feel far greater sympathy for Paul's mother in "The Rocking-Horse Winner" or King Midas in "The Golden Touch." A son dead of brain fever or a daughter turned to lifeless gold are the sacrificial victims of parents who have no idea why they yearn for ever greater wealth. They know nothing of Moneta, much less Chicomecohuatl. They have not plumbed the depths to learn the origins of their own passions and fears. Having failed to do this, they cannot see the paradox of wealth. For while money symbolizes the life force and abundance, it must be recognized as a symbol. To possess money without possessing the vitality and abundance that money symbolizes is to make money a dangerous illusion.

When people lived without money and hunted or farmed for their livelihood, abundance needed far less interpretation. But in recent centuries a worldwide migration of people to cities has separated us from the cycles of nature. Without trees we no longer witness leaves tumbling in autumn, the bare limbs of winter, and the green renewal of spring. Without crops we forget the plowing and planting of fields, the sprouting and ripening, and the harvest. Without wildlife or farm animals we divorce the meat filling the refrigerated bins of our supermarkets from the living animals that are the source of this nourish-

In a way, cities are like the sacred grove at the ancient Greek center of healing in Epidaurus. Neither birth nor death was permitted within this sacred grove, making life the eternal constant. For someone who is ill, it must be profoundly healing to escape for a while the endless turning of the wheel of life and death. An important aspect of the cures at Epidaurus was a healing of the mind. After cleansing rituals and prayers, an ill person would sleep in a special chamber and hope to receive a dream from the gods. For the dream itself might heal or give an understanding of what course the cure should take.

Healing though it may be to enter the sacred grove where life neither begins nor ends, we cannot remain in such a timeless place. Both Paul's mother and Midas fail to understand the limitations of mortal women and men. They imagine that they can accumulate an infinite amount of the substance (money or gold) that symbolizes the life force.

Why can't Paul's mother or Midas evaluate money or gold and know when each has gained enough? They are grappling with the secret life of money. Unless they bring this secret life into the light of consciousness, they cannot possibly inhibit their compulsions and redirect their life energies. On one level, they are unaware that beneath money issues are fears and hopes about the fertility of nature, a fertility which is largely outside of their control. On another level, they are unaware of the sacrifices demanded in the cycles of fertility, sacrifices that would make all of us tremble if we allowed them to rise to consciousness. Yet that which we leave hidden from sight will always possess immense, destructive power. If we fail to face inner issues of fertility, sacrifice, and mortality, we risk losing what is most dear to us and receiving nothing in return.

The issue of sacrifice is embedded in money. This is true for all people and all cultures, because nature's cycles of life and death are universal. If we had been born as Aztecs and had to sacrifice our own blood to the Maize Goddess, we would recognize how we and our culture ritualized the attempt to offer our life energy in exchange for the divine energy that brings the richness of nature. Living in modern cultures that abhor such sacrifices of life, we have no easy way to see the connection between money and our aspiration to be blessed by the richness of the divine.

Such an aspiration, like so much touched by money, is paradoxical. On the one hand, we have the understandable hope that proper handling of money will bring well-being and prosperity for ourselves, those we love, and perhaps even the society of which we are a part. On the other hand, we hope that the accumulation of sufficient amounts of money will give us an excess of the life force. If we could gain such an excess, we could be like the gods, immortal, no longer subject to the rule of nature that decrees death as both the precursor and end of life.

Of course, we would ridicule anyone who expressed such a fantasy of living forever. In the conquest of the New World, the Conquistadors searched for two fabled sites: El Dorado (the city of gold) and the Fountain of Eternal Youth (which conferred immortality on those who drank its waters). Viewed through our lens of fertility goddesses who are the source of wealth (symbolized by money or gold) and also the source of life, we know that El Dorado and the Fountain of Youth are parts of the same mythical landscape. So Dionysus, the vegetative god of the vine, is capable of conferring infinite amounts of gold on Midas; indeed, capable of giving Midas the very power to create gold. What Midas risks losing in return is life it-self, whether his daughter's life or his own.

THE COLLECTIVE UNCONSCIOUS AND THE BUSINESS CYCLE

Money, life, and sacrifice are not only connected in the un-conscious of the individual but in the collective uncon-scious of the culture as well. This collective unconscious is the home of the archetypes, the larger patterns devel-oped during human evolution and affecting each of us. During recessionary times we may read in the newspapers of some bureaucrat who declares that lowering the inter-est rate will pump new lifeblood into the economy. These are not the words of an Aztec priest who has pierced his genitals to let his blood nourish the earth and sustain the Fifth Sun in the heavens. These are the words of a secular official, perhaps a member of the Federal Reserve Board, who is unconsciously making the ancient connection be-tween blood and abundance. In this case, however, the abundance is not of the fields alone but of a more compli-cated modern economy.

This economy depends, in large part, on the willingness of the people to consume. We have even developed mea-surements of Consumer Confidence. If Consumer Confi-dence rises, we can expect more consumer spending. This will have what the economists call a multiplier effect, since each dollar spent will be received by others who will be encouraged to spend more. Soon money will be flow-ing like life-giving blood through the system. But if the Consumer Confidence falls, people will be fearful about prosperity in the future and will spend less. The decreasing circulation of money-blood will ensure contraction of the economy with ensuing recession or depression.

Of course, the full complexities of the modern economy are beyond the focus of this book, but I would like to pose a simple question: Why are there recessions or depressions at all? Assuming for a moment that consumer spending is the key to boom and bust, what makes the consumer fearful or optimistic about the future? What animates this statistical consumer stitched together from the information contained in the index of Consumer Confidence? Where does he or she discover the facts that make prosperity seem more or less likely? What is the first cause, the prime mover, of this economic system?

Our consumer might ask someone else what is likely to happen. Based on the answer, our consumer might have soaring or plummeting confidence. But how did the second person have any information to give the first? Perhaps the second person has been laid off by a business. Then we would ask why did the business lay off the second person and cause panic about the future? If the answer is that the business is not selling as much as it used to because Consumer Confidence is low, then we have come full circle. How did the confidence of this business's consumers fall in the first place?

If someone answered that a drought has destroyed the crops in the fields and we need a prophet like Elijah to bring rain, then it would be easy to understand a low level of the index of Consumer Confidence. But in the world economy, such natural events rarely are the cause of economic contractions. In fact, the natural resources, the factories, and the skilled labor are all as available for use when the economy contracts as when it expands. What differs is our willingness to make use of these resources, which include ourselves, our life energy.

In an ideal world, perhaps a band of courageous people would agree to go against the trend. When the index of Consumer Confidence fell, they would begin a holy crusade of consumption by buying houses, lavish meals, clothing, and gifts until everyone around them would be employed as a natural result of their largesse. The multiplier effect would send waves of money through the economy, until the money inevitably returned to the very consumers who had originally banded together. Prosperity would ensue for all, even those who initially risked their assets (or perhaps went into debt) in order to consume.

We might call our hardy band the Consumers of the Round Table and reward the most prodigious among them with medals and feasts in their honor. In our Consumer Hall of Fame, we would enshrine golden statues of heroes and heroines—those who consumed not from self-love but in loving service to others. After several prosperous generations passed, with all the indexes of Consumer Confidence remaining at the highest possible levels, some misguided souls might begin to pray to these golden statues as gods and burn money on their altars to ensure that more money would be sent from the divine world back into our own.

What a grotesque fantasy! But let us use it for a moment to examine what the individual misses when facing the secular life of the modern economy. Basically, there is no way for the individual to make a meaningful sacrifice. We are not going to squat in front of some wooden idol and give it blood drawn from our ears. Yet if we fail to have some ritual by which the economy is positioned in the natural world, as well as in the artificial worlds of our industrial and informational revolutions, we may sense that a crucial link with the life-and-death reality of humanity has been lost.

That lost link condemns us to a statistical world. In such a world we cannot use sacrifice to re-establish our connection to the richness of nature and to re-establish our confidence. Instead of being active participants in rituals that strengthen the will of the society to survive, we become the victims whose lack of productivity is reflected in the unemployment figures. No goddess is sacrificed, but six or ten or fourteen percent of the work force is unemployed. Our sacrifices are hidden behind our statistics. Even these statistics do not suggest the full extent of the sacrifice. For example, the unemployment statistics do not include people who have given up looking for employment, who are underemployed, who are temporary workers but wish they were permanently employed, or who have started their own businesses from desperation when they were unable to find work. Those who are statistics, and those who are not even counted in the statistics, cannot make the community perceive any value in their sacrifices. They are left with no way to commune with the gods or their own natures.

Inevitably the people call for the sacrifice of the leader believed to be responsible for the recession, usually the president. Fearing to be voted out of office, he (or, someday, she) soon selects a trusted aide, usually a key advisor on economic policy, and, to use a common expression, gives this aide the ax. This scapegoating, a phrase which also comes from the lexicon of human and animal sacrifice, allows the president to blame the aide for sins (the recession or depression) that probably were not the fault of anyone. It is a secular counterpart of the Aztec priest sacrificing the goddess to renew the natural world.

However, the Aztec priest had the advantage of making the people believe that they were giving of themselves to nourish their gods. They were active participants in restoring the divine order that let the sun rise in the sky and the corn grow to be husked and devoured. Without recognition of this cycle of nature, a cycle which includes death as well as life, we are living in a culture out of touch with psychic realities as true for us as for the first man and woman who lived eons ago. We are denying our unconscious knowledge that there must be death, there must be a time when activity lessens or ceases. If unending growth is truly a goal that we desire, we must bring to the light of awareness our secret belief that such growth is as impossible for us as immortality. Only then can we evaluate whether such growth would be possible and wise.

No wonder "In God We Trust" appears on all of our coins and bills. In times of recession or depression, this slogan offers a way to understand why money fails us. Money, although a secular tool, requires our trust in the richness of a divine power. If we feel a constriction in the flow of money-blood, we will yearn for more life energy. If we feel that our political leaders are sacrificing us, then we (living in a democracy and not a theocracy) will demand their sacrifice. If a credible leader tells us that he or she can create more money and save us from the incompetents in power, that leader will find followers whose fervor seems religious.

Let us return to the Civil War, when, as we discussed in the last chapter, "In God We Trust" first appeared on a coin. Until 1862, the dollar had been defined as being worth a certain amount of silver or gold. The government would buy gold or silver at fixed official rates (which also created an official ratio between the value of gold and silver) for conversion into coins. However, the difficulties of financing the Civil War forced the issuance of paper money. Called greenbacks, these paper bills were not backed by gold or silver and quickly inflated the money supply. An ounce of gold rose to be worth twice as many greenbacks as the government's official rate provided. The marketplace determined the shifting relationship between gold and greenbacks by a floating exchange rate.

The desire for a more sound currency prompted enactment of laws in 1873, 1874, and 1875 that caused the United States Mint to resume purchasing gold in 1879 at the official exchange rate that had prevailed before the Civil War. However, the Coinage Act of 1873 failed to include a requirement that the government purchase silver for conversion into dollars. This omission meant that the United States had abandoned the bimetallic standard that had existed from 1792 through 1862 in favor of a gold standard. While I am omitting to discuss the complexities of the effect of the relationship between the prices of gold and silver established in the marketplace (which caused only one metal to be sold to the government during any given period, since the other metal would best be sold in commerce), many people believed that the failure to commit the government to purchasing silver as well as gold caused a continuation of the serious deflation that began in 1869 and reached its lowest point in 1896. That is why the Coinage Act of 1873 came to be called the Crime of '73 by supporters of bimetallism.

By 1896, deflation made goods cost only sixty-one percent of what they had cost in 1869. The effect on farm prices had been even more severe. In 1896, farm products cost forty-four percent of what they had cost in 1869. This deflation hurt debtors who had to pay back their debts with dollars worth more than when they had been borrowed. Farmers and small businesses, especially in rural areas in the South and West, sought a rainmaker who would relieve them of the onerous burdens caused by deflation. As banks failed (496 failed in 1893) and the unemployment rate rose rapidly after the Panic of '93—to 18.4 percent in 1894 and the still unacceptably high 14.4 percent in 1896—the nation languished in a depression, the like of which had not been seen since the 1830s and would not be seen again until the 1930s.

The Democrats came to their 1896 nominating convention divided into two wings, one which favored the gold standard and the other which favored a return to a gold and silver standard. Repudiating President Grover Cleveland, who had presided over four years of depression and favored a gold standard, the convention turned to a thirty-six-year-old newspaperman and former congressman from Nebraska named William Jennings Bryan. When Bryan gave his famous "Cross of Gold" speech and ultimately won the nomination, he framed this money issue with striking religious metaphors:

"I come to speak to you in defense of a cause as holy as the cause of liberty," Bryan said early in his speech, "the cause of humanity." Pointing out that his cause was not a dispute over personalities but over principles, he touched on human mortality: "The individual is but an atom; he is born, he acts, he dies; but principles are eternal; and this has been a contest over a principle."

This is marvelous oratory, but what eternal principle does Bryan refer to here? On one level, he is speaking of bimetallism, but in a deeper sense he is speaking of the prosperity that he believes would result from increasing the quantity of money in circulation. This eternal principle of prosperity flows from the confluence of death and re-birth over which fertility goddesses such as Moneta rule.

"With a zeal approaching the zeal which inspired the crusaders who followed Peter the Hermit, our silver Democrats went forth from victory unto victory . . ." Bryan continued, placing himself on the side of the "plain people of this country" whom he extolled: "The farmer who . . . by the application of brain and muscle to the natural resources of the country creates wealth, is as much a business man as the man who goes upon the board of trade and bets upon the price of grain; the miners who go down a thousand feet into the earth . . . and bring forth from their hiding places the precious metals to be poured into the channels of trade are as much business men as the few financial magnates who, in a back room, corner the money of the world."

In distinguishing those who labor to bring forth the riches of nature from those who are manipulators of money, Bryan glorifies the "hardy pioneers who have braved all the dangers of the wilderness, who have made the desert to blossom as the rose. . . ." Condemning the effect of monometalism, he speaks of how "the gold standard has slain its tens of thousands."

In contrast to the idea that "if you will only legislate to make the well-to-do prosperous, their prosperity will leak through on those below," Bryan avows that "the democratic idea, however, has been that if you legislate to make the masses prosperous, their prosperity will find its way up through every class which rests upon them."

This leads him to an interesting observation about the farms and the cities, the city voters having been generally supportive of the gold standard.

"Burn down your cities and leave our farms," he says, "and your cities will spring up again as if by magic; but destroy our farms and the grass will grow in the streets of every city in the country." So, as if Moneta herself stood behind him, he refers again to the necessity of natural fruitfulness. Like a shaman who can bring rain in the form of an increased money supply, he claims a superior knowledge of the secrets of fertility. He knows as well, therefore, that fertility demands sacrifice. He has stated clearly that he will sacrifice the interests of the capitalists and protect the interests of the working masses. This leads to the famous finish of his speech, a thunderous ending worthy of any god of rain-bringing storms.

"Having behind us the producing masses of this nation and the world, supported by the commercial interests, the laboring interests, and the toilers everywhere, we will answer their demand for a gold standard by saying to them: You shall not press down upon the brow of labor this crown of thorns, you shall not crucify mankind upon a cross of gold."

Bryan's fervent crusade for "the plain people" did not win him the presidency, but his imagery suggests the strong connection between money issues, productivity, and sacrifice. We may not keep this connection in our awareness, but an orator like Bryan, speaking in a time of crisis, can bring to light the ancient roots from which our economies have grown. When he speaks of sacrifice, he lets us glimpse our nature as individuals and, collectively, as a society. He may or may not have been correct in his beliefs about bimetallism (that debate continues), but his metaphor exposes truths of how we feel and experience money.

In a larger sense, the Cross of Gold is the power of money to create illusion. King Midas nearly lost his life, and his daughter's, on the Cross of Gold; Paul was indeed crucified, the madness of money too great a fever for his brain. Illusion is ever-present when dealing with money; our struggle is to find a microscope or telescope that will allow us to pierce the veil of illusion. Understanding the fertility myths with their legacy of sacrifice is one step toward deepening our understanding.

Looking back a century, Bryan himself seems transfigured. Running for president at the age of thirty-six, he conjures up the image of Attis, the shepherd boy loved by the goddess, the vegetative god sacrificed for the renewal of nature and productivity. In the election of 1896, Bryan was abandoned by the conservative eastern Democrats. His support in the Rocky Mountain states and the Great Plains could not overcome Republican William McKinley's success in the East and Middle West. McKinley won 271 electoral votes to Bryan's 176, and also won a decisive plurality of 600,000 votes.

Prosperity quickly returned to the nation. Deflation halted. The supply of gold increased both from new sources in the Klondike, South Africa, and Australia, and from the discovery of an inexpensive cyanide process to extract gold from low-grade ore. Harvests improved at home, while crop failures in Europe helped to keep farm prices high. On March 14, 1900, the Republicans passed the Gold Standard Act of 1900 which made the gold dollar the standard unit of value and required that all paper currency be redeemable in gold. Resurrected like Attis, Bryan ran for president again in 1900 but lost by an even larger margin. President McKinley could point to four years of Republican prosperity. Moneta had blessed him, answering not only his prayers but those of the "plain people" as well.

Yet Bryan, when writing his memoirs in 1925, sought to have the final word. He had fought for silver not for its own sake, but as a method of achieving an increased quantity of money. So he posed his question as follows: "Suppose the citizens of a town were divided, nearly equally, on the question of water supply, one faction contending that the amount should be increased, and suggesting that the increase be piped from Silver Lake, the other faction insisting that no more water was needed; suppose that at the election the opponents of an increase won (no matter by what means); and suppose, soon after the election, a spring which may be described as Gold Spring, broke forth in the very center of the city, with a flow of half as much water as the city had before used; and suppose the new supply was turned into the city reservoir to the joy and benefit of all the people of the town. Which faction would, in such a case, have been vindicated?"

Water, which Midas sprinkled on his possessions and his daughter to return them to their true reality, offers an apt metaphor for the flow of money. The very word currency comes from the Latin *currens*, which means to run or flow. And this flowing water has a deep source in the Cross of Gold, at once the symbol of sacrifice and of the tree of life. For the ancients sacrificed to bring the rainfall, to bring the inseminating and life-nurturing water. They offered blood in exchange for water; sometimes, in fact, their own blood and the blood of their loved ones. In Christianity, in the baptismal rituals, the sprinkling of or immersion in water is believed to bring about the most profound reality: the entry of spirit into flesh.

These are not ancient images fit only for academic study, but living images for us today. If we speak of King Midas instead of the fallen financiers of Wall Street's scandals, it is because the story of Midas is so obviously universal—as true in Phrygia seven centuries before Christ as on Wall Street during the junk-bond-financed mergers and acquisitions of the 1980s.

The connection of money to water, blood, and spirit can be ignored only at our peril. Money offers us illusions because of its own origins in temples and sacrificial offerings. It speaks to us of the inseminating power of water, the sacrificial efficacy of blood, and the eternal life of spirit. This is all implicit in the paycheck we carry home each Friday, the profit of our small business, the dividend on our stock, and the interest on our loan.

If we understand this, then we understand that our task is to dispel the illusions of money, so that we can see beneath and beyond money to the deeper truths of our lives. Money itself can then be placed in service to those truths, rather than to illusions. If we succeed in this process, Moneta will have served us well indeed.

CHAPTER FOUR

HOARDING MONEY
Why the Life Energy of Misers Is Stolen

ONCE THERE WAS a miller who loved gold. This love so possessed him that he sold everything he owned to buy what he loved. Then he melted all this gold into one large piece which he buried in his field. Each daybreak he would hurry to his field and dig up his glorious treasure.

But a thief must have watched the miller's furtive visits, for one night someone unearthed the miller's hoard and carried it away.

The next morning the miller dug and dug but found nothing. He howled with such anguish that at last a neighbor came to find out what terrible thing had happened.

When he heard that the gold had been stolen, the neighbor spoke to the miller as follows: "Why are you so upset? You had no gold at all, so you haven't lost any. You merely imagined that you had it, and you may as well imagine that you have it still. Simply bury a stone where you buried your money. Imagine that stone to be your treasure, and you'll have your gold again. After all, you didn't use the gold when you had it; and you will never miss it as long as you are determined not to use it."

The miller had a wise neighbor, but this hardly makes the neighbor's advice any easier to hear. The miller, like Midas, had fallen in love with gold. Misers are notorious for refusing to allow their great wealth to benefit anyone. If the neighbor acted more conventionally and sympathized with the miller over the theft of the gold, then an important truth would be lost. The mere possessing of something does not confer wealth; rather the wealth is conferred in the using of what is possessed. So money must circulate if it is to have meaning as money. Like blood, water, and spirit, money's circulation is a key to finding the wealth it measures.

Burying money in the earth symbolizes the removal of life energy from the human community. In fact, money is the least of what the miser withholds from the world, for it is a mere symbol of what might have been shared—love, kindness, joy, and creativity. The neighbor speaks for the community which the miller has denied and retreated from by being so miserly. This neighbor has no sympathy to give, but offers the miller a chance to see the illusory nature of wealth that is not used.

In this chapter we will explore the ways in which money symbolizes life energy. If we imagine gaining money to be the goal of any endeavor (or of our lives), then for a moment we lose sight of the underlying relationships that money was created to serve. Certainly in the context of the family, the using of money can be like the sharing of food or of love; in business, the flow of money can facilitate productivity and the creation of well-being for the whole community. If we hoard our energy and the fruits of our productivity, we gain little, and we steal from ourselves the connection to others and to community that makes life meaningful.

In each of the four stories in this chapter, there is an intervention from the spirit world. A boy becomes an eagle; a miser is visited by ghosts and spirits; the god of luck helps a peasant; and a king's wife proves to be a goddess in disguise. We might think of such interventions as thoughts or powers of imagination that live within each of us. At moments of crisis, we may suddenly encounter a new way of seeing an issue, a new way of thinking about money and possessions. If we are fortunate enough to have this spiritual intervention, what we experience is truly the power of self-healing.

THE PUNISHMENT OF THE STINGY

Our first story, from the Chinook tribe of the Northwest, is titled "The Punishment of the Stingy." It illustrates how damaging it can be to refuse to circulate wealth—in this case, the wealth of food. By looking at the failure to circulate food, we see a concrete example of the social damage that results from refusing to circulate what is life-sustaining. In our culture, in which food can so easily be purchased, the equivalent would be the hoarding of money.

In the story, a harsh winter has brought hunger to the many people who live in their village built above a wave-swept beach. The chief has died and his only son is growing up to be a man. No food washes up from the sea, and the people eke out a meager sustenance from mussels and roots.

One day a hunter says the men should go to sea. Even if

they can't find anything to eat, at least they can gather more mussels. So all the men pile into two canoes and paddle until the village disappears from sight. When they reach a small island, they sight sea lions, spear one, and drag it ashore.

Now Bluejay, one of the hunters, says they should eat all of the sea lion and take nothing home to share with the women and children. None of the hunters argues with Bluejay, so the sea lion is boiled and eaten on the island. When another hunter, Raven, tries to hide a piece of meat in his mat to take home for the people who are hungry, Bluejay finds the meat and burns it in the fire. Then the hunters gather mussels to give to the women in the village.

The next day the chief's son wants to join the hunters, but Bluejay says the waves will carry the boy away and forces him to stay in the village. Again the hunters spear a sea lion. Again Bluejay says they should bring nothing back to the village, because it will make the chief's son want to come with them. The other hunters do not question this decision or the reason given for it, but Raven ties a piece of meat in his hair to bring back for the people. Bluejay discovers the meat and throws it into the fire. Before leaving the island, the hunters look for mussels, which they bring back to the women in the village.

On the third morning, the chief's son wants to go again, but Bluejay refuses to take him. Once again, Raven tries to conceal meat for the village but is discovered. The hunters feast on sea lion and bring back mussels for the villagers. The fourth morning these same events are repeated, and on the fifth morning, too.

On the fifth morning, the chief's son holds the side of the canoe until Bluejay hits his hands and makes him let go. Then the boy takes his bow and arrows and walks on the beach. When he sees a black eagle, he shoots and skins it and tries to put the skin on his body. However, it is too small to fit him, as is the skin of the second eagle that he shoots and skins. Then he shoots a bald-headed eagle and squeezes himself into its skin.

Soon the chief's son is flying and smells the smoke of fat cooking. He follows this scent to the island where the hunters are feasting on the meat of a sea lion. First the boy lands on a branch, but then he wants Bluejay to see him and circles the fire five times. Bluejay throws a piece of meat to the eagle, surprised that the bird has feet like a human (because the skin was too small to fit over the boy's feet).

The next morning, the sixth day, the hunters haul their canoes into the water, but the chief's son makes no effort to go with them. Once the hunters are gone, the boy calls together all the women and children in the village. He shows them the meat which Bluejay gave him and uses the meat to grease the heads of everyone left in the village. Then he pulls down all the houses but the one belonging to Raven. Sharpening the planks from the houses, he fastens a plank to the back of each woman.

Swim to the island and circle it five times, the chief's son tells the women, and you will become killer whales and always be able to kill sea lions for yourselves. But give nothing to stingy people.

As for the children, the chief's son says they will become seabirds. Lastly he splits sinews and ties the mussels to the rocks so that Bluejay and the others will always have the painful task of prying the mussels free.

Then the women swim to the island where their husband-hunters feast. The women-whales leap from the water as they circle five times around the island before heading out to the sea. Soon seabirds with blood-red beaks fly five times around the island until they, too, disappear from sight. Only Raven recognizes these birds as the children of the village.

Bluejay fears that he and the hunters have seen evil spirits. Now they not only gather mussels, but load their meat into the canoes as well. They rush home to the village, but the houses (except for Raven's) are all tumbled down and the women and children have vanished.

Bluejay laments until one of the hunters tells him to be silent. If you had not been bad, the hunter says, our chief would not have done this to us.

The women and children do not return. Instead the hunters live without shelter and scavenge for food on the beach. They eat roots and have to break the mussels from the stones. Bluejay is the most unfortunate of all, for he seldom finds food, and often hailstones cascade on him from the skies above. Only Raven, who had been kind-hearted, finds a seal or a sturgeon on the beach and has a shelter in which to live. But those who did not bring food to their families lose everything. This is how their chief punished them for their stinginess.

HOW THE REFUSAL TO SHARE AFFECTS THE COMMUNITY

We are often caught in the struggle over whether to follow a Bluejay or a chief's son. They are like our inner voices, one stingy and one generous. Sometimes, like the hunters, we nod assent and follow the wrong leader. Perhaps a voice like Raven's offers an opportunity to change our course, but such a voice can be difficult to hear.

Clearly the death of the chief has left its mark. Without good leadership, the hunters are unable to perform right actions. Bluejay benefits himself, for he and the men feast heartily. But he fails to circulate the wealth of food that should be shared with the villagers. This failure is immensely disturbing to the social order. When we looked at the roots of money, we saw its distant origins in sacrifices offered to ensure the abundance of nature. The story implies that there may be retribution from the world of nature, which is the source of richness, when wealth is not shared properly. Thus Bluejay's succulent feasts become the cause of life-long deprivation for the hunters.

The chief's son yearns to take part in several aspects of communal life. By seeking to join the hunters, he readies himself to be initiated as one of the men of the village. By his willingness to share the wealth of the hunt with the entire village, he shows his awareness of his duties to the community.

Bluejay's repeated rebuffs drive the boy to seek a higher justice. He slays three eagles and at last attires himself in the bald eagle's skin and gains its power of flight. The eagle symbolizes spiritual aspirations, the connection of the human to the realm of the spirit world. The eagle has the strength to rise above and destroy all the other birds (including the bluejay), so the eagle possesses the power to destroy what is base and evil. Kings, emperors, and nations have taken the eagle as their symbol, both to show their divine blessing and to manifest their power. When the boy draws on the skin of the eagle, he seeks the role and power of the father and the chief.

Drawing his strength from the supernatural world, the

THE SECRET LIFE OF MONEY

chief's son sits in judgment of his fellow men. Since the men will not care for the women and children, the natural order of the tribe no longer functions. If the weak cannot rely on the strong, the chief's son will free them from their dependence. He transforms them into killer whales and seabirds that are capable of capturing prey. The men did not give the loyalty and love that would have been symbolized by sharing their wealth, so the women and children are freed from the social contract which made the village thrive.

A key aspect of the story is timing. The gifts of nature must be used when given; we must live in the moment. As each day passes, it becomes more and more difficult for the hunters to make amends. Five is a magical number, repeated numerous times in the story, and on the sixth day the village—and all that it represents, including the value of human connection—is destroyed. At last Bluejay and the others pile the meat into their canoes, but giving from fear or compulsion is not true generosity. By the time they are willing to give, their stinginess has been ruinous. Once the women and children have been transformed, it is too late to bring the wealth to the village.

Those who do not circulate lose what would have been circulated to them in return. The very word "circulation" implies this outcome, for it shares its root with circularity and circle. Circularity suggests that the energy given will return in some form to the giver, while a circle is a symbol of the connection of all things in the whole. Bluejay and the hunters deny this principle of circulation. They deny their connection to the whole. Only Raven, who was kind, is spared in some measure from the cataclysm that follows.

Repetition is like habitual thought. Bluejay and the

hunters do not fail once; they fail five times. Bluejay is not only stingy in refusing to share the food, but he also refuses to give the chief's son a proper role as a hunter and a man in the village. As the story repeats itself, so the habitual thinking of the miser is repeated. The miser must withhold; the miser fears what will happen if life's energies flow freely. But the miser cannot control the powers of richness that reside in nature. So the chief's son becomes a powerful man and, at the very end of the story, is acknowledged as the chief because of the wealth and rightness of his nature.

A CHRISTMAS CAROL

If these hunters lived in a more modern society, Bluejay would have convinced them not to share their paychecks with their families. Whether the substance not shared is food or money, the human issues remain the same.

The most famous tale of stinginess may well be *A Christmas Carol* by Charles Dickens. Set in the middle of the nineteenth century in London, this story's portrait of the miser Scrooge is even harsher than the portrait of Bluejay.

The hunter Bluejay and the money-lending miser Scrooge have one point in common: their refusal to circulate wealth to the less fortunate. Even at Christmas, Scrooge cannot overcome his miserly nature and join in the celebratory spirit of the season. Scrooge's nephew comes to wish a merry Christmas to his uncle, only to be rebuffed as always by Scrooge's famous "Humbug." The nephew tries to move Scrooge, speaking of how Christmas is "a good time: a kind, forgiving, charitable, pleasant time: the only time I know of, in the long calendar of the year, when men and women seem by one consent to open their shut-up hearts freely, and to think of people below them as if they really were fellow-passengers to the grave, and not another race of creatures bound on other journeys."

This speech moves Scrooge's clerk, who suffers from the cold in the office and dreadfully low wages and the fact that Scrooge begrudges him the day off for the Christmas holiday. But it does not affect Scrooge at all. Instead, Scrooge berates his nephew for marrying for love, refuses the invitation to come to Christmas dinner, and shows his nephew the door.

Next Scrooge is visited by two businessmen, who have formed a committee to make "provision for the poor and destitute, who suffer greatly at the present time."

In words that will later haunt him, Scrooge demands, "Are there no prisons? . . . And the Union workhouses? . . . Are they still in operation?" So Scrooge expresses his belief that he has no obligation to the poor, who can either go to prison or the workhouse.

One of the gentlemen speaks of how, especially at Christmas, "Want is keenly felt, and Abundance rejoices," and asks Scrooge what he will contribute, but Scrooge replies, "Nothing!"

When told that many would rather die than go to prison or the workhouse, Scrooge answers, "If they would rather die, they had better do it, and decrease the surplus population." So, with this pitiless reference to Malthus's *Essay on the Principle of Population*, Scrooge shows the gentlemen out.

Unable to give to others or care for them, Scrooge is

also unable to give to himself. He makes his clerk freeze by a tiny fire, but he does not allow himself very much more. At home, in fact, he must sit close to the fire and brood over it before he can feel the least sense of warmth. He does not feast for his dinner, but eats in "a melancholy tavern." His lodgings are a gloomy suite of rooms. He saves money by using only a candle for light and makes money by renting the other rooms in the house as offices (so he is alone at night). The miserly face that he shows to the world is the face that he shows to himself. If he yearns for warmth, a loving family, a Christmas feast, a brightly lit home, he can have none of it. He can no more give to himself than he can give to the poor.

In fact, the miser Scrooge suffers a living death; he has died to the joys that make human life worthwhile. To be saved, he must connect again to the source of richness. For Scrooge, this possibility of salvation comes in the form of a ghost and three spirits.

Scrooge once had a partner named Jacob Marley, who died seven years earlier. Scrooge has never removed his partner's name from the office sign, which read Scrooge and Marley. When Marley died, Scrooge was his "sole residuary legatee, his sole friend and sole mourner," for Marley had been as much a miser and just as unpopular as Scrooge. Now, on Christmas Eve in the dark, cold, and cavernous house that Scrooge inherited from Marley, Scrooge is rudely interrupted by the appearance of the ghost of Marley. His partner looks as he did in life, except that his body is transparent, and clasped about his middle is a chain "of cash-boxes, keys, padlocks, ledgers, deeds, and heavy purses wrought in steel."

This ghost terrifies Scrooge and warns that if a "spirit goes not forth in life, it is condemned to do so after death . . . and witness what it cannot share, but might have shared on earth, and turned to happiness!" Marley's ghost then says that Scrooge's own chain equalled Marley's in length, and that was seven years ago.

Scrooge is terrified and implores the ghost for some comfort. " 'I have none to give,' the Ghost replied. 'It comes from other regions, Ebenezer Scrooge, and is conveyed by other ministers, to other kinds of men.' " The ghost regrets that, when alive, his "spirit never walked beyond our counting-house" and says that "no space of regret can make amends for one life's opportunity misused."

Scrooge's only hope of a better fate, the ghost tells him, will come from the haunting intervention of three spirits. So Scrooge must face these forces from other regions in order to deal with issues of wealth and its circulation.

The Ghost of Christmas Past

The first spirit, arriving at one o'clock in the darkness of night, is the Ghost of Christmas Past—more especially, the ghost of Scrooge's own past Christmases. The Ghost transports him to visions of the characters in the books that he joyously read as a boy. He sees himself as a youth when his beloved sister, Fan, comes to bring him home from exile at school to live again with his family. The ghost reminds him that Fan died, but had a child— Scrooge's nephew.

Next Scrooge sees himself as a young man working for Old Fezziwig, a jovial and benevolent man who hosts a joyous celebration of Christmas. The young Scrooge and another apprentice speak of how they admire Fezziwig, but the ghost points out how little this party cost. Scrooge, forgetting the miser he has become, retorts, "The happiness he gives, is quite as great as if it cost a fortune." In saying this, Scrooge suddenly wishes that he could speak to his own clerk, Bob Cratchit, who is raising a large and happy family on a meager wage.

Lastly the Ghost of Christmas Past takes Scrooge to see the scene at which he parted from Belle, the woman whom he might have married. "Another idol has displaced me," Belle says to the young Scrooge, ". . . a golden one. . . . I have seen your nobler aspirations fall off one by one, until the master-passion, Gain, engrosses you." Saying that the man he has become would not choose a dowerless girl, she releases him from his promise to marry her.

Scrooge begs the ghost to show him no more, but nonetheless he sees Belle and her husband with their children. It is the Christmas that Marley died, seven years earlier, and the husband says how he passed Scrooge's office and saw Scrooge "quite alone in the world . . ."

Scrooge cries out to be removed from these scenes and tries vainly to extinguish the ghost's haunting light. At last he falls into an exhausted sleep. While he sleeps, we begin to see Scrooge in a new light. His encounter with the Ghost of Christmas Past has revealed that Scrooge was not always a miser. Once he had been a lonely schoolboy who loved his sister and yearned to go home to his family; once he had admired the joyful vitality and benevolence of his employer; once he had loved and been loved. Whatever hardened and limited him had come gradually, and had appeared to be a reasonable effort to lift himself from poverty. Scrooge, by his pain in what he sees in his past, reveals that he possesses the potential to change. He is not beyond salvation, but he has lost his way. Will these haunting ghosts, conjured from the redemptive depths of his own imagination, succeed in returning him to the loving exchanges that give life value?

The Ghost of Christmas Present

Scrooge sleeps twenty-four hours and wakes just in time to meet the next spirit, the Ghost of Christmas Present. This ghost transforms Scrooge's room, filling it with the light of a roaring fire and decorating it with so many leaves of holly, mistletoe, and ivy that the room seems "a perfect grove." A throne is formed by an abundant mound of different foods fit for holiday feasting, and on this throne sits "a jolly Giant."

This giant is the ghost, a striking figure with none of the spectral qualities that we would ordinarily ascribe to ghosts. He is dressed in a green robe, his chest bare as if he disdains artifice or concealment. The torch that he holds aloft is shaped like "Plenty's horn." He is joyous and unconstrained, and a green wreath of myrtle sits atop his flowing curls of hair. Around his middle is an antique sheath for a sword, but the sheath is rusted and empty.

This remarkable ghost is clearly a vegetation or fertility god. With his green robe, the wreath in his hair, his cornucopic flame, and his spontaneous vitality, he might be a brother to Attis or Dionysus. So the miser Scrooge is confronted by an image of the renewing richness of nature, the feast which calls out to be shared with others. The ghost takes Scrooge across the city and the countryside and far out on the ocean. Everywhere Scrooge witnesses people joyous and celebratory in the spirit of the season. The ghost brings him to see his clerk, Bob Cratchit, celebrating a dinner of goose with his large family. Cratchit's tight finances and fears for his ill son, Tiny Tim, don't lessen the family's joy in this feast.

Scrooge feels concern for Tiny Tim and asks the ghost if the boy will live. Unless the future is altered, the ghost answers, Tiny Tim will die. When Scrooge begs the ghost to say that Tiny Tim will be spared, the ghost quotes Scrooge's own words back to him, "If he be like to die, he had better do it, and decrease the surplus population."

Scrooge is overcome with grief and a feeling of penitence to hear his own words. The ghost tells him not to use such words until "you have discovered What the surplus is, and Where it is."

The ghost brings Scrooge to the home of his nephew, Fred, who is celebrating with his wife and in-laws. Fred laughs as he recounts his meeting with Scrooge and says, ". . . his offenses carry their own punishment . . . His wealth is of no use to him. He doesn't do any good with it. He doesn't make himself comfortable with it. . . . Who suffers by his ill whims? Himself, always."

Fred's wife plays the harp and Scrooge softens to hear music that he loved as a boy. He wishes that he could have heard this music years earlier and "cultivated the kindnesses of life for his own happiness. . . ." He finds himself enjoying the blind-man's buff and other games the party-goers play. When the ghost wants to leave, Scrooge begs like a boy to be allowed to watch until the guests go home.

The ghost allows him one more game, then carries him again across the world. Everywhere the ghost brings the rich joy of the season, but the ghost grows visibly older and his hair becomes gray as midnight approaches. When Scrooge inquires about this, the ghost replies, "My life upon this globe is very brief. . . . It ends to-night."

Now Scrooge sees something beneath the ghost's robe and asks what it is. In reply, the ghost pulls open its robe to reveal two children—"wretched, abject, frightful, hideous, miserable" as well as "yellow, meagre, ragged, scowling, wolfish; but prostrate, too, in their humility."

Scrooge asks if these children are the ghost's, but the ghost replies, "They are Man's. . . . This boy is Ignorance. This girl is Want."

"Have they no refuge or resource?" cries Scrooge.

Again Scrooge's earlier words are used against him, as the ghost replies, "Are there no prisons? . . . Are there no workhouses?"

These are the ghost's last words, for midnight comes and the Ghost of Christmas Present is gone—only to be replaced by the third and last of the spirits, the Ghost of Christmas Yet to Come.

The Ghost of Christmas Yet to Come

This phantom is "shrouded in a deep black garment" which conceals everything except a single outstretched hand. Scrooge trembles before this "dusky shroud," but tells the silent phantom that "I know your purpose is to do me good. . . . Lead on, Spirit!"

In several scenes it becomes apparent to the reader, but not to Scrooge, that Scrooge has died before the next Christmas. First a group of businessmen speak of a wealthy man who has died, but whose funeral will be cheap because no one is likely to go to it. Then, in a part of the city reeking with crime, several people come to sell booty that they looted from the dead man. Next Scrooge is in a room where the corpse lies on a bed beneath a ragged sheet. The ghost motions for Scrooge to draw back the sheet, but he cannot.

Scrooge begs the phantom to show him anyone in the city "who feels emotion caused by this man's death."

Two scenes follow. In one, a young couple is thankful because the man's death will allow them time to find the money needed to repay a debt that they owed him. But even if they cannot gather that money, the husband believes that they "will not find so merciless a creditor in his successor."

The second scene brings Scrooge again to the home of his employee, Bob Cratchit. The little boy, Tiny Tim, has died and the family is in mourning.

Scrooge demands to know who the dead man had been. At last the ghost brings him to a graveyard where Scrooge sees a neglected grave. On the stone is Scrooge's own name.

Pleading with the ghost, Scrooge says that he will live an altered life and begs for assurance that the future he has seen can alter too. "I will honour Christmas in my heart, and try to keep it all the year," Scrooge promises, only to see the dread phantom dissolve and dwindle into a bedpost.

Joyous to be alive, Scrooge leaps from his bed and celebrates with splendid laughter. He flings open his windows and learns from a boy that it is Christmas Day, so the three spirits actually visited him during a single night. He has the boy take a plump turkey to the Cratchits, then dresses himself in his best clothes. Meeting one of the gentlemen who asked him for funds to help the poor, he promises a munificent amount. He goes to church, talks to beggars, and pats children on their heads. He finds "wonderful happiness" at his nephew's Christmas dinner. The next morning he gives Cratchit a raise and promises to help the clerk's family.

Tiny Tim lives and Scrooge, we are told, "became as good a friend, as good a master, and as good a man, as the

good old city knew. . . ." and ". . . had no further inter-
course with Spirits. . . ."

TO RECOGNIZE MONEY'S ILLUSORY ASPECTS

The spirits bring the possibility of profound change to
Scrooge. He is placed in the age-old drama between the
human and spirit worlds, a drama of sacrifice and exchange. The renewing richness of nature is symbolized by
the Ghost of Christmas Present. But as we well know,
such a fertility god is caught up in endless cycles of life
followed by death. The empty scabbard that the Ghost of
Christmas Present wears about his waist suggests the
bond between fertility and death. This bond quickens our
awareness that there is only the present in which to live;
only the present moment, only the present lifetime. For
Scrooge, Death comes robed as the dark phantom whom
Scrooge welcomes as a messenger of good will, the Ghost
of Christmas Yet to Come.

In seeing this struggle of elemental forces, this struggle
which he experiences in his own life, Scrooge realizes
how money has become illusory for him. He has pursued
money for its own sake but has forgotten the richness of
which money is but a symbol. When he dies, money will
be of no value at all; it will bring no mourners to his grave-
side. On Christmas Day, a day of birth (for both the sun
and the light of the Christ), Scrooge himself is born into a
new life. His only alternative is death, whether the literal
death shown by his name on a grave marker or the metaphoric death of a man who cannot offer his own vitality to
the world.

It is a paradox, of course, that Scrooge must die to his old self in order to avoid the death that he has been living and the grave that awaits him. Once he is able to free the money that he has accumulated, his energy flows into the world and connects him to other people. And once he can give to others, he is far more generous with himself.

Scrooge is brought by spiritual trials to a realization of his proper role in relation to the world and himself. However, each person must experience their own spiritual journey in relation to the handling of money or material possessions. Thoreau, for example, would argue that he wanted nothing of ownership, since property can easily own people by the cares and worries that it imposes. Scrooge couldn't share this attitude, because his early poverty had raised the value of wealth above everything else. In fact, many community leaders in the nineteenth century believed that poverty served as a school where people learned the reward of hard work. Even if this were true, Scrooge failed to learn how to use what he possessed, both for himself and for others.

Scrooge at least was quite open about being a miser. Other stories illustrate how sharing wealth, or even renouncing the acquisition of wealth, may conceal inner feelings that are quite the opposite of generosity and loving connection to community. A folktale from China illustrates how stinginess may disguise itself as generosity.

MONEY MAKES CARES

Titled "Money Makes Cares," the story tells of two neighbors, one rich and one poor. The rich man, Ch'en Po-shih, spends all of his time busy with his money: making investments, giving loans, paying taxes. He hardly has time to eat, because dealing with the money fills his days and nights. His wife begs him not to slave himself to death, but he knows of no way to lessen his tasks.

The poor neighbor, Li the Fourth, works as a laborer. Despite being a hard worker, he earns very little and has no savings. When he comes home in the evening he gives his wages to his wife. Combined with what she earns, they have barely enough to survive. Nonetheless, Li and his wife are happy, and after dinner Li often plays the mandolin and sings.

The rich neighbor never hears this music and singing, because he is buried in calculating rent and interest. However, his wife does hear, and the happy music makes her sad. She says to her husband that their wealth gives them no happiness, while their poor neighbors are joyous.

Ch'en says that Li is only happy because he is poor and, according to a proverb, the poor have plenty of time. The way to make him stop singing, according to Ch'en, is to give Li some money. Ch'en's wife argues that having money will only make Li and his wife happier, but Ch'en is certain that he is right.

The next day Ch'en invites Li to visit. When Li arrives, Ch'en says that as old neighbors they share a common bond. Ch'en observes that Li will never earn very much being a laborer and offers to give him five hundred pieces of silver. He suggests that Li use it to start a good business, but in any event it will not have to be repaid.

Li thanks him and rushes home to tell his wife of their newfound wealth. He stops his work as a laborer and thinks only of how to profit the most from the money. Unable to find solutions that satisfy him, he becomes like his rich neighbor. He arrives home late for dinner and loses his desire to play music or sing. Instead he spends his nights worrying about what to do with this wealth.

Ch'en and his wife are delighted that the music and singing have ceased. Unfortunately for them, the deity of luck takes pity on Li.

After two sleepless nights, Li can barely get out of bed. Suddenly the deity of luck appears and warns him of the cares that money makes. Remember this, the deity tells him, and free yourself from these cares.

Li feels his energy return. He hurries to his neighbor and returns all five hundred pieces of silver. Thanking Ch'en for his kindness, Li feels relieved of an immense burden and sleeps soundly at last. The next evening the sounds of Li's mandolin and songs can be heard once again in the home of his rich neighbor.

According to this folktale, Ch'en soon lost all his wealth and lived in poverty, but the music and song coming from Li's home only increased in richness.

HOW HOARDING STIFLES THE POWERS OF IMAGINATION AND HEALING

Stinginess disguised as generosity may escape the notice of our friends and neighbors. It does not, however, escape the notice of the spirits that govern abundance. Not only does the deity of luck tell Li not to obsess about money, but the deity also tumbles Ch'en from wealth to poverty— for surely Ch'en lost the luck that gave him wealth.

Ch'en is much like Scrooge at the beginning of *A Christmas Carol*. He is possessed by his wealth; he, and his wife, have lost the ordinary joys that life offers. He, like Scrooge and the ghost of Marley, is certainly wearing a chain "of cash-boxes, keys, padlocks, ledgers, deeds, and heavy purses wrought in steel."

Among the ordinary joys denied to Ch'en are the ability to take pleasure in the happiness of others and the ability to enjoy music and song, which might be read in a larger sense as enjoyment of the world of the arts and the realm of the imagination. Ch'en is so absorbed with money that he does not even hear the music, while his wife in hearing it only wants to silence the joy that it expresses.

Observing the outer behavior of Scrooge and Ch'en, it might appear that each man has undergone a similar change of heart. Scrooge becomes able to give to the poor and befriend his own family, while Ch'en does give to the poor and seems to befriend his neighbors. Obviously, however, Scrooge and Ch'en have not changed in a similar way at all, for their motives are utterly different.

Scrooge, as we said before, contemplates his life and realizes that he must change. Otherwise he faces certain death, for he is already not living. On the other hand, Ch'en gives the silver because he cannot tolerate the joy of others. His giving is exactly the opposite of what it appears to be. It comes not from love of life and others but from hatred. He cannot free his life energy, stored in the form of loans and land and money, and let it flow richly into the community.

Ch'en meets no messengers from the spirit world. Nothing happens within Ch'en to bring about a personal transformation, so he is condemned to a life of poverty. The actual poverty inflicted on Ch'en at the story's end is merely the outer equivalent of the poverty that exists within him.

Ch'en makes a sharp contrast with Li the Fourth, who has such a peculiar name. We naturally imagine him to be the fourth generation of Li, or perhaps the fourth child. In a larger sense, however, the number four connotes completion. This view comes from numerology, the symbolism of numbers. One is unity, two is duality, three is change (because three is formed of one plus two, which is the potential for change when unity meets duality), and four is completion (because four is formed of three plus one, which symbolizes change becoming unity).

Li the Fourth is complete in himself; he is complete in his love of his wife, his humble work, and his joy in music and song. Since Li comes into the story as a complete man, he does not need the change of life offered to him by the five hundred pieces of silver. So the deity of luck intervenes when Li has lost his direction and been swayed by the lures of the world. This deity returns Li to his own path, to the richness of a loving family and the joys of music and imagination.

Scrooge and Li are brought by their struggles over money to a greater sense of who they truly are; they learn the secrets of their innermost selves. They do not offer us rules by which to determine our own conduct. If they did, we might conclude from Scrooge's example that we ought to seek wealth and circulate it, and from Li's example that we ought to give up wealth altogether. What we learn from them is that our dealings with wealth can be part of the process by which we discover ourselves and contact our deeper natures.

To deny one's own nature is perhaps the greatest form of stinginess. This denies what is rich within us; it refuses the possibility of change and growth. If a man like Scrooge comes to recognize his capacity for love and sharing, then he will be all the richer for having discovered himself. If a man like Li discovers that wealth is destructive for him and gives it up, then he, too, is the richer for the self-knowledge that he has gained. The point is not to renounce wealth but to embrace the journey through which we learn what to value.

THE KING WHO RENOUNCED HIS WEALTH

A king once ruled a vast empire in India. Despite his wealth, King Shikhidhvaja yearns to live a deeply religious life and find the highest truths. He sees many saints and wise men and practices many spiritual disciplines. At last he becomes convinced that the only way he can find truth and the peace that surpasses understanding is through renunciation.

He gives careful consideration to what he should renounce and to the timing of his renunciation. He possesses vast wealth in the form of land and precious possessions, controls armies and large numbers of servants, and lives an opulent and luxurious life. More than this, he deeply loves his wife, Queen Chudala.

Finally he decides that he will renounce his throne. He tells his wife of the anguish that he feels in his soul and his yearning for peace. He implores her to take care of the kingdom so that he can seek contentment.

The queen, a very wise woman, feels that her husband will not find the peace that he seeks by this process of renunciation. However, knowing that reasoning will not change his mind, she takes charge of the kingdom and proves an excellent ruler.

The king goes to the high peaks of the Himalayas, the mountains symbolizing the spiritual heights that he seeks to reach. He builds himself a crude hut and wears clothes of bark, sleeps on a deer skin, and bathes in freezing water. No matter how much he prays, meditates, chants, and practices asceticism, he cannot find peace. In fact, the harder he disciplines himself to follow these spiritual devotions, the more anguish he feels.

Because the king truly believes that peace follows from renunciation, he reasons that his continued unhappiness comes from not having renounced enough. He decides that he will renounce even more in pursuit of his goal. From the rich diet that he had enjoyed as king, he now eats only roots and fruits. But he feels even this to be too much, so he begins to eat only fruits. First he eats fruit every other day, then every third day, and finally every fifth day.

Still he suffers agitation and feels ever more troubled by his life. To overcome this suffering, he thinks constantly about what else he can give up. His body begins to wither. When the queen comes to visit and sees him in such a condition, she feels great sorrow.

Fortunately for the king, his wife is not only a queen but also a goddess. Unwilling to allow her husband to continue on this path to destruction, she takes the shape of a great sage named Kumbha and comes to the hut where the king is living.

The king honors this wise man and, in response to Kumbha's questions, tells the entire story of how he has given up his kingdom and come to live at such high and barren altitudes.

After the sage hears the entire story, he simply says to the king, "Peace follows renunciation."

With that, Kumbha vanishes and leaves the king in perplexity. After all, the king has already renounced so much. Yet he renounces even more: his straw hut, his clothes of bark, the deer skin on which he slept, and his water pot. Now he truly has nothing, yet he feels more miserable than ever.

The queen, in the guise of Kumbha, reappears and asks the king if he has found peace and happiness.

When the king answers that he feels anguish and desperation, Kumbha says once again, "Peace follows renunciation. You have not renounced enough." Once again Kumbha vanishes.

The king, meditating on the words of Kumbha, decides that all he has left to renounce is his life. He gathers wood and builds a huge fire. If the flames consume his body, he believes that he will have peace at last. Three times he walks about the fire, saying a farewell to his body. He tells his body that he gave it marvelous pleasures, but he has nonetheless failed to find peace.

As he stands poised to leap into the flames, the sage Kumbha appears and restrains him from this madness. Now the sage speaks directly to the king, saying that once the king has given up his body, who will find peace and who will enjoy it? Kumbha says that a man is formed from the fluids of his mother and father, and these parents are formed from the foods that nourished them, and this food came from the earth. The body created of the earth cannot belong to the king, nor can the divine awareness which enters into the body belong to the king. So in throwing his body into the flames, he is renouncing a life and an awareness which have been given to him but are not his. What the king must renounce, the sage concludes, is the illusion of "mine."

The king realizes that he has erred. It may be right for someone else to find peace through renunciation, but it is not the correct path for him. He must renounce his illusion that he can find peace through renunciation. He can only find peace through following his own nature, which calls to him to live a spiritual life in the material world. For the king, it is miserly to refuse involvement with the world; it is a withholding of his energy from the mixed life in both the material and spiritual realms that is most properly his.

What Kumbha has done in saying "Peace follows renunciation" is to bring the king face-to-face with the realization that he has interpreted this statement as if it were a rule, rather than searching for his own unique path that will lead to his self-realization.

We might interject at this point that the queen, in taking the shape of Kumbha, is pushing her husband to the limits of what he himself set out to do. Her love does not express itself by an attempt to dissuade him and lessen his pain; rather she seeks to bring him to a greater understanding of his nature. She understands that if he does not reach a point where he sees that renunciation is the wrong path for him, he will never escape his self-inflicted suffering.

What do we think of a spouse who will push a loved one to the brink of destruction for the purpose of self-knowledge? Of course, the queen is a goddess who can do safely what mere mortals would not risk. Her stance is as uncompromising as that of the spirits who visit Scrooge and sway him from his miserly descent to death.

The determination of the queen/goddess to see her husband find the path which is correct for him reminds me of the experiences of a friend, a mother, whose only son suffered from drug addiction. Gradually, with great heartache, she had to wean him away from her. She had to demand that he leave her home. Despite her natural generosity and her love for him, she had to ignore his pleas for money and give him nothing. Sometimes he would knock on her door and beg her to let him in; other times he would call and plead for money to eat. In the beginning, she might lose her resolve and give him money, only to find that he spent it on drugs. At last she overcame her motherly instincts and refused him a place to stay and food and money. She gave him the names of people who could help him enter twelve-step and rehabilitative programs. Like the queen/goddess, she had to let him go to the greatest extremity of danger in the hope that he would see his own error and find the life within him waiting to be lived.

I mention this because stories of millers, tribal hunters, Victorian misers, a Chinese peasant, and a king and queen of ancient India may seem remote from the concerns of contemporary people. Do these tales offer a mirror for our time, for our own psyches? We need only look and see that human nature has not evolved at the same speed as technology. Our hopes and fears with respect to material well-being remain with us. These hopes and fears have shaped attitudes toward wealth and money that have lasted not merely centuries but millennia.

WHY OUR LIFE ENERGY SHOULD NOT BE BURIED

The discussion of human sacrifice in the last chapter may have seemed unusual in a book about money, but, of course, this book is titled *The Secret Life of Money*. Outside of our daily awareness, the Goddess Moneta works her miracles of fertility. Her name speaks of memory, but we have largely forgotten her. We have forgotten how once we had rituals to reveal and quiet our fears about nature's abundance. Because Moneta rules in an archetypal world to which we seldom have access today, we are like bystanders taking part in a great event of which we know almost nothing.

Our lack of self-knowledge may encourage us to project our fears about prosperity onto money. Without even thinking of the human sacrifices offered Moneta and her sister goddesses, our unworded fears about prosperity cause us to begin the sacrifice of our life energies. The miller buries the gold that symbolizes the treasure, the energy, of his life. Riches that we do not use are truly stolen from us; such riches are our life energies, which we offer thoughtlessly to false gods. Like Bluejay, we may burn the excess meat rather than share with our tribe. Or like Scrooge we may refuse to give even to ourselves—much less to others. To give falsely like Ch'en or run from our true path in life like King Shikhidhvaja are simply other forms of stinginess, other ways to sacrifice our energies.

The spirits and deities in these stories of wealth and money are aspects of Moneta and of ourselves. We possess the power to understand the cycles of death and new life that make us wish to be misers and hoard our life force. If we can keep enough of that precious force, perhaps we imagine that we need never fear homelessness, hunger, or death. Of course, we don't articulate such thoughts to ourselves; we don't have a conscious awareness of what makes us stingy or withholding of money and life energy. We don't see money in its symbolic role as the offspring of Moneta.

When the spirits help Scrooge or Li or King Shikhidh-vaja, what we see is the power we possess to heal ourselves. If we are fortunate enough to have this kind of spiritual intervention, or open enough to receive it when offered by a friend, mentor, or group such as Debtors Anonymous, then our lives may change as our understanding changes.

Even an addiction is, according to psychologist C. G. Jung, a form of spiritual craving. Jung expressed this viewpoint in his correspondence with Bill Wilson, the founder of Alcoholics Anonymous. This understanding aided the development of the twelve-step approach with its central tenet of trust in a higher power. Terrible as the suffering of the addict may be—risking life itself in the case of my friend's son and many others—this suffering can also be part of the experience that leads a person to give up drugs, alcohol, or other compulsive behaviors and begin the journey in quest of his or her true self.

The central illusion of the miser is that life energies are finite, that such energies can be controlled and conserved by refusing to give. We mentioned earlier that one of the roots of Moneta's name relates to measurement. Money is such a useful tool for measuring and comparing the values of unlike objects and services. However, money in its psychic role as a sacred substance derived from exchanges with the spirit world is not subject to the same laws of measurement as money in its worldly role as a helpful servant to the marketplace.

Charles Dickens portrayed the Spirit of Christmas Present as a green god holding aloft a torch in the shape of a horn of plenty. We cannot measure such a cornucopia. It is larger than the national debt, larger than the value of all the precious possessions humankind has created in that brief time since we stood erect and imagined ourselves as a mirror for the image of the divine. But what cannot be measured can, nonetheless, be circulated. Inevitably this circulation will include money and the wealth we use so much of our lifetimes to create and possess. If this circulation is to be wise, we must look more and more deeply at the richness with which Moneta blesses us.

Hoarding Money

brief time since we stood erect and imm...
a mirror for the image of the divine. But what cannot be
measured can, nonetheless, be circulated. Inevitably this
circulation w...
much of our lifetimes to create and possess. If this circulation is to be...
the richness with which Money blesses us.

CHAPTER FIVE

THE SOURCE OF RICHES

Gaining a New Understanding of Supply

IN LAST CHAPTER'S STORY of the miller who buries his gold, only to have it stolen, the neighbor suggests that the miller replace his lost gold with a stone. This ordinary stone certainly appears to be valueless, but often valueless things come to have value if seen in a new light. Part of this process may involve seeing ourselves in a new light and unearthing inner riches of which we were previously unaware.

If we approach the miller's story from another vantage point, we might ask what the neighbor means by telling the miller to plant a stone in the earth. How can this stone take the place of gold? This chapter will follow the symbol of money to the source of richness within ourselves, and we will see how that inner richness can be freed in ways that encourage its increase and benefit our loved ones and our communities.

THE BOY AND THE STONE
Symbolic Imagination

Famed psychologist C. G. Jung tells of a game that he played as a boy of eight or nine. In the family garden, the ground sloped and a large stone jutted out. As a boy, Jung felt this stone belonged to him. In his game he would think: "I am sitting on top of this stone and it is underneath." But the stone could also have an "I," so the stone could say, "I am lying here on this slope and he is sitting on top of me." Jung would then struggle with the question of whether he was sitting on the stone or whether he was the stone on which he was sitting. The question fascinated him, and the answer was ambiguous, a pleasing mystery that led the boy to sit for hours speculating on his stone.

The image of a stone is that of an eternal substance. The stone will last after the flesh has vanished, so the stone will long outlast the boy. If the boy, on the other hand, is the stone, some life of the boy will survive the frailty of his own flesh. In other words, as Jung later recognized, his meditations on the stone were meditations on his soul, a soul as yet unnamed by the boy but existing nonetheless and awaiting the journey of discovery that became the central drama of Jung's life.

Most of us experience trials of the soul as inner struggles. Often these struggles lead to a deeper understanding of ourselves and the life to which each of us is best suited. This process might be called the discovery of the soul or, for those who prefer a more neutral term, the discovery of the potentials which each of us possesses. But when that potential is buried, the miller, or anyone like him, experiences the painful loss of not being all that one might be.

THE MINER AND HIS GOLD
Literal Thought

An extraordinary trial in the 1960s placed the existence of the soul at the center of its drama and revealed the inner wonderings and doubts of a man named James Kidd. Born in 1879, he worked as a pumpman at an Arizona copper mine from 1920 to 1948 and vanished, and presumably died, in 1949. His job had been low-paying, and his life-style had always been sparse. He lived in a small, bare room with blankets nailed over the windows. He frequented a local restaurant where he always hunted for a discarded newspaper, ordered the least expensive items on the menu, and never left a tip. He would nurse a five-cent cigar so it lasted all day, and he kept a small box to hold chewing gum to be used again. He never married and, in fact, seldom if ever invited anyone to visit his lodgings. Yet Kidd had friends who spoke of his yearning for quick wealth and his speculations about the source of life, the nature of death, and the soul.

After James Kidd disappeared in 1949, there seemed to be no will and very little to his estate. But as the years passed, stocks and bank accounts kept turning up. For Kidd had been a prospector for gold and had also played the stock market. Whether he pulled nuggets from the earth or won profits from the stock market, he died with a net worth of almost $200,000, easily a wealthy man by the standards of his day. Then long after his death came the surprise—Kidd had left a will, a very unusual will.

The will stated that he had no heirs and ordered that all his assets be sold. After his funeral expenses had been paid and $100 given "to some preacher of the gospel to say fare well [*sic*] at my grave," he directed to "have this balance money to go in a research or some scientific proof of a soul of the human body which leaves at death I think in time their [*sic*] can be a Photography of soul leaving the human at death, James Kidd."

One hundred and thirty-four claimants fought over what should be done with this money. Scientific organizations, psychic research groups, and reputed heirs all came forward to stake a position. In an initial ruling, the court determined that the will had created a charitable trust. However, the difficult issue remained of which claimant could best carry out the scientific proof required by the will. Extensive testimony about death and the soul led the court to award the estate to the Barrow Neurological Institute of Phoenix to help finance its research on the nervous system and the relationship between the brain and the mind.

What is striking about James Kidd, of course, is that he never spent his money on what would have given him pleasure during his lifetime. He never, for example, donated to an organization that might be doing the type of research that he wanted. He seemed content to hoard his money and speculate about whether the soul might exist. In his will, the one certain way he had to determine actions beyond his death, he, in essence, seeks to exchange his money for the proof that eluded him.

If we contrast James Kidd to C. G. Jung, we might see one man as a prospector and the other as an alchemist. James Kidd sought gold buried underground, but he seemed to have no idea of how to use this literal search or his growing net worth to deepen his sense of his own inner richness, and thereby prove, at least to his own satisfaction, the existence of his soul. Instead of beginning a journey into himself, he surrendered the responsibility for his search to outer authorities—to the courts of Arizona, and to the beneficiary they would choose to receive the money.

On the other hand, Jung created a philosopher's stone from that stone in his parents' garden. The medieval alchemists searched for such a philosopher's stone, a process by which base matter might be transformed to gold and, even more importantly, a way in which matter might be infused with spirit. Jung's dialogue with the stone began a lifelong exchange between the Carl Jung whose persona faced the outer world and the stone/Jung which represen*.ed the inner richness of the Self. Jung used the word "individuation" for this process of discovering the riches of the Self and integrating these riches into the ego.

MONEY IS THE SYMBOL, NOT THE SOURCE

The relationship between money, which is outer richness, and soul, which is inner richness, can easily confuse us. When we imagine, like the miller, that gold is all-important, we lose connection to our inner riches. The Bible frequently delves into this paradox which has always been so much a part of all of our lives.

As Jesus Christ starts for Jerusalem he is approached by a wealthy man who asks, "What must I do to inherit eternal life?" Jesus tells him to observe the Commandments, but the man says he has observed them from his youth. Then Jesus says, "Sell what you have and give to the poor, and you will have treasure in heaven; and come, follow me." But the man has great wealth and departs in sorrow. Of all those whom Jesus specifically invited to follow him, only this wealthy man refused.

Jesus then observes that "It is easier for a camel to go through the eye of a needle than for a rich man to enter the kingdom of God." So the largest beast in Judea can more easily pass through the smallest opening than a rich man discover the wealth of his inner life. Why should this be so?

The problem is easy to state but not so easy to understand or resolve in our daily lives. Because money has its origins in exchanges with the divine, it lends itself to the belief that it is the source of well-being and abundance. In this way, money appears to be the divine source. Thinking this way makes us worship money rather than the richness within ourselves.

Jesus frequently uses an increase in money to symbolize an increase in divine spirit. The parable of the pounds speaks of a master who must travel to a far country to receive kingly power. He leaves one pound each with ten servants. On his return, he praises the servants who have increased his money. The servant who increased the money tenfold is given ten cities to rule and the servant who increased the money fivefold is given five cities to rule. However, the servant who feared his severe master and merely has the one pound to return is castigated. The master asks, "Why then did you not put my money into the bank, and at my coming I should have collected it with interest?" The servant's one pound is given to the servant with ten pounds. When the people complain, the master says, "I tell you, that to every one who has will more be given; but for him who has not, even what he has will be taken away." The message is that those who possess inner wealth and work to increase it will receive more; those who lack awareness of inner wealth and refuse to work for its increase will lose what they have.

So money presents a paradox. On one hand, the very nature of money lends itself to use as a symbol for spirit. On the other hand, money is merely a symbol and cannot truly be a substitute for inner resources. Despite the many stories in which the increase of money symbolizes the increase of inner riches, Jesus declares, "No servant can serve two masters; for either he will hate the one and love the other, or he will be devoted to the one and despise the other. You cannot serve God and mammon."

The danger facing those with wealth is that they may worship it as a false god. This worship of money places the divine realm outside of the seeker, who loses the ability to search for and develop inner resources. Money, gold, and property will always be external to us and subject to the vagaries of good and bad fortune. In another parable, Jesus tells of a man whose situation appears to be somewhat like that of the miller: "The kingdom of heaven is like treasure hidden in a field, which a man found and covered up; then in his joy he goes and sells all that he has and buys that field."

Why is this man's fate different from the miller's? Quite simply, the treasure that he has discovered is his own spiritual life. The miller sold all of his worldly goods to hoard them in the form of gold. The man who sells all to buy the hidden treasure is transforming worldly wealth into spiritual wealth. He has begun the lifelong task of solving the riddle of his relationship to the stone, to what is eternal within him.

Jesus did not condemn the wealthy for their wealth but rather for their worship of that wealth. For example, in Jericho he stays with a man named Zacchaeus, a chief tax

collector who has made himself rich by collecting reve-
nues for the hated Roman rulers. People criticize Jesus for
being the guest of a sinner, but Zacchaeus promises to
give half his goods to the poor and restore fourfold to anyone he has defrauded. Jesus responds, "Today salvation
has come to this house . . ."

However, Zacchaeus is an exception among the
wealthy, because so many of the wealthy fall victim to the
illusion that money is godlike and worthy of worship. But
how can this illusion, of money and property as the source
of richness, be penetrated?

Jesus offers us the insight necessary to see the true
source of what supplies us:

> Therefore I tell you, do not be anxious about your life,
> what you shall eat or what you shall drink, nor about your
> body, what you shall put on. . . . But seek first his kingdom
> and his righteousness, and all these things shall be yours
> as well.

This is an insight into human nature that transcends a
particular religion or moment in time. Jesus also says,
"The kingdom of God is within you." If we trust that we
have within us the capacity to live a spiritual life, that we
possess an inner stone which Jung called the Self, then in
the natural process of living that inner life we will also
take care of our outer needs. The inner search is not a
denial of our outer needs, but rather in part a way of learning the right attitude and actions with which to deal with
the outer world—including money and ownership.

No perfect model is offered here. We cannot find rules
that will absolve us of the effort to undertake our own
inner quest. On the one hand, Jesus tells of a man who

stores enough food and drink to last for years and intends to take it easy. But God calls the man a fool because his very life is to be taken from him that night. This Parable of the Rich Fool concludes "So is he who lays up treasure for himself, and is not rich toward God." On the other hand, Zacchaeus retains half of his ill-gotten fortune and Jesus declares that salvation has entered his house. Whether outer riches should be kept or given, and to what degree, will vary from person to person. What does not vary is the need to embark on the journey of self-discovery.

THE STAR TALERS

A German folk tale tells of a little girl who has lost her parents and become homeless. She is so poor that she has only the clothes that she wears and a piece of bread given to her by a kind person. This is the condition that we all fear: to be without family, homeless, and, ultimately, without even clothes or food. When we have little or fear that we are facing financial catastrophe, how can we trust in our inner richness to supply us? How can we stop hoping to get money, with all the terrible anxieties which that hope brings, and focus on Jesus' insight that if we seek riches within then "all these [material] things shall be yours as well"?

The little girl in the story "put her trust in God" and went into the fields. There a poor hungry man approaches her and pleads for something to eat. She gives him the entire piece of bread. Next come three children, each cold and each asking for a different garment: a bonnet, a bodice, and a blouse. The girl gives to each. Night comes and she enters a forest where yet another child asks for a shift. If the girl gives away the shift, she will be naked, but she thinks that the night is so dark that no one will see her if she gives away her shift. As soon as she gives this last garment and stands naked in the forest, the stars start falling from the night sky. Each star is a taler (taler being the monetary unit from which the word dollar eventually derived). The girl finds herself dressed in a beautiful new shift of the finest linen. Gathering the talers in her new shift, she has riches for the rest of her life.

This may seem a simple tale; indeed, it's been criticized by feminists as perpetuating the idea that women should indiscriminately place their property and energies in service to others. That criticism reflects the difficulty that all of us have today in believing this story. Who wants to accept the motto on our coins—"In God We Trust"—as a step to giving away our money or property to those in need?

Yet the story has its own force; it tells us that the person who gives will, miraculously, receive. They will be beautifully clothed; they will have riches for life. For them, the stars of heaven will tumble to earth and become—of all things!—money. If this is true, counterfeiters would be well advised to try giving rather than printing, since no one is imprisoned for the possession of dollars that fall from the heavens.

The skeptic in us has to wonder whether wealth in spirit doesn't also imply poverty in the outer world. We know that a child can give away all she has to eat and wear, but when was the last time we saw stars fall to earth as dollars? What law of supply could cause this to happen?

THE CONCEPT OF SUPPLY

Let us visualize again the Ghost of Christmas Present in *A Christmas Carol* by Charles Dickens. This fertility god with his wreath on his head, green robe, and torch shaped like a horn of plenty is an image of the richness that we all carry within ourselves. The Ghost of Christmas Present is part of the inner life, the inner richness, of Scrooge. If one is aware of such a fertile and infinite life within, there is no need to fear whether clothes or food or money will be supplied without. The energy of this ghost will see that we are supplied with what we need. That is, we will inevitably take care of our material needs if we remain aware of the richness that lives within us. That richness is the source of our supply, not money, houses, clothing, and all the other manifestations of our energies working in the world.

In *The Infinite Way* by Joel Goldsmith, this concept of supply is expressed as follows: "Money is not supply, but is the result or effect of supply. There is no such thing as a supply of money, clothes, homes, automobiles, or food. All these constitute the effect of supply, and if this infinite supply were not present within you, there never would be 'the added things' in your experience."

This concept of supply is difficult to understand in an age so devoted to mass production, mass consumption, the advertising which seeks to link consumption and production, and laws of supply and demand seen in the marketplace. In contrast to all this, Goldsmith views the law of supply as our own consciousness, which he describes as "spiritual, infinite, and ever-present." If we are aware of this inner richness, this inner source which is continuously fruitful, we can come to accept money as "the natural and inevitable result of the law active within."

If this infinite supply is indeed within us, we find ourselves in an unfamiliar territory. We are used to dealing with limitation; we are comfortable with the familiarity of limitation. We have only so much money; we have only so much food, so much clothing, so much space in which to live. If we find a source of infinite richness within, however, we are no longer dealing with limitation. Suddenly the very nature of wealth changes.

The wealth of the outer world is increased by receiving: by wages, by profits, by income, by possession. The wealth of the inner world begins by being boundless. It cannot be increased by receiving. To enjoy the wealth that is inner richness, we must seek a way to circulate what we have. Goldsmith states this very well in *The Art of Spiritual Healing*. He says: "In spiritual truth, supply is not income; it is outgo. . . . There is no supply outside of your being. If you want to enjoy the abundance of supply, you must open a way for that supply to escape."

In cultivating an attitude of giving, whether what is given is small or great, we learn how giving increases our awareness of our own richness. Goldsmith suggests that giving may begin with giving up certain feelings that limit us—"the giving up of resentment, jealousy, and hate; the giving up of the desire to get recognition, reward, remuneration, gratitude, and co-operation." All of these feelings turn us toward the outer world. We wonder: Will we be as well off as others? Will others approve of what we do? So such feelings turn us away from the invisible inner richness that we seek to bring to our awareness.

While Goldsmith does not suggest that money be given away carelessly or without the use of common sense, he does stress the importance of making money circulate for "some impersonal purpose, not to family, not for one's own benefit, but to something completely impersonal." In giving, we may feel gratitude for what we have already received, but to hope or expect either material or spiritual rewards will diminish the realization of our inner richness. Of course, we might speak of giving love, understanding, support, shelter, or food as well as speak of giving money. Giving money does not replace the flow of other kinds of giving, but it may teach us about the nature of giving itself. Also, money has the unique power to represent everything that is marketable, whether goods or services, and so can purchase what is necessary to meet innumerable needs.

Charitable giving springs from human compassion, the natural concern that we feel in response to the suffering of others. The Jewish religion views the giving of charity as one of the finest expressions of piety. *Tzedakah*, the Hebrew word for charity, suggests not merely giving but also just and righteous giving. Two stories from Jewish tradition illustrate how giving can be either heartfelt or heartless.

ONLY THE DEAD ARE WITHOUT HOPE

In an ancient Jewish tale, "Only the Dead Are Without Hope," a wealthy man fears that his riches will be of no value to him when he dies. Taking the advice of friends, he decides to make charitable gifts so that his kindness will protect him in evil times. However, he imposes a limit on his willingness to give. He will only give to someone who has abandoned all hope in life.

One day he sees a man in rags sitting on a heap of trash. Convinced that this man has abandoned all hope, the rich man gives him one hundred pieces of gold. Amazed to receive this unasked-for and immense sum, the poor man inquires why he has been chosen from all the poor in the city to receive this benevolence.

The wealthy man tells how he swore that he would only give to one who had abandoned all hope in life. At this, the poor man flings the hundred pieces of gold back at him. Saying that he has faith in God's mercy, he berates the rich man for not seeing that God can as easily make him rich as poor.

Shocked, the wealthy man complains that this poor man feels no gratitude for the gift and is, in fact, abusive.

The poor man replies that the gift was the opposite of kindness. Only the dead have no hope in life, so the gift was like death.

Of course, the wealthy man entertained the notion of charity only from fear, not generosity. His fear caused him to impose a limit on his giving. He set himself in judgment over others, while at the same time failing to see that he himself was the one who had abandoned hope in life. He had misplaced the hope that flows from the richness of the inner life and trusted in his wealth instead.

THE FATHER OF THE POOR

An episode in the story titled "The Father of the Poor" offers a sharp contrast to the attitude of the wealthy man. "The Father of the Poor" is about Reb Nachum Grodner (1811–1879) whose tireless work to help the needy gave him a legendary status among the poor Jewish people who lived in the ghettos in Lithuania. Because of his popularity, the people called him by the more familiar and endearing Reb Nochemke.

Himself poor, Reb Nochemke would go to great lengths not to embarrass those needy people whom he helped. Once he was asked to be a godfather at the celebration of a circumcision, but he knew the father of the child had no money to pay for such a celebration.

Reb Nochemke asks the father if he is planning to go to another city called Kovno. The father is surprised and says he has no such plans. Reb Nochemke then says that he needs to have twenty-five rubles delivered to someone in Kovno and wants the father to deliver this money whenever the father should happen to go there. The father protests that he has no idea when he will go, but Reb Nochemke says there is no hurry. In fact, Reb Nochemke says that if the man should have use for twenty-five rubles before he goes, he may use the money and replace it later.

Of course the father spends the twenty-five rubles on the circumcision celebration. When he asks Reb Nochemke for the name and address of the person in Kovno, Reb Nochemke first says that he will have to find them at home and, after some time passes, says that he must have mislaid them. One day the father, never suspecting that he has been the beneficiary of charity, repays the twenty-five rubles to Rem Nochemke.

THE GOLDEN LADDER OF CHARITY

To be righteous and just in the giving of charity has been of concern since antiquity. In the eleventh century, Maimonides, the Jewish theologian, formulated many existing ideas about charity into the Golden Ladder of Charity. This Ladder has eight steps, each one higher than the last.

The first step on the ladder is the lowest form of charity. Here one gives, but with reluctance or regret. On the second step one gives happily but without regard for the degree of need of the person receiving the charity. Moving up to the third step, the giving is joyous and takes account of the degree of need, but the giver waits to be asked before giving. On the fourth step, the giver gives without being asked but puts the gift into the hands of the recipient. This causes the needy person to suffer with feelings of shame.

The fifth step conceals the identity of the recipient from the one who gives. Now the needy person does not have to feel shame for having been seen as needy by the one who gave. On the other hand, the sixth step conceals the identity of the giver from the one who receives. For example, the giver might anonymously leave a gift at the home of the recipient. On the seventh step of the ladder, the virtues of the prior two steps are combined so that neither giver nor receiver knows the identity of the other. In its time, the Temple in Jerusalem contained a room called the Chamber of Silence or Inostentation. Here those who desired to give could anonymously leave their gifts to be taken with equal anonymity by those in need.

The eighth and highest step is to prevent poverty and thus avoid the need for charity. This might be done by teaching a trade to someone, starting a person in business, or making a gift or a loan if that will enable the person to earn his or her own livelihood. By allowing the person to cultivate his or her own talents and provide for his or her own wants, the giver avoids the risk that the recipient will feel dependent, powerless, or shamed.

The Golden Ladder of Charity recognizes the importance of giving with the right attitude. Keeping this in mind, we can see why the wealthy man in "Only the Dead Are Without Hope" failed in his giving. Not only did he give from joyless self-interest in the hope that his own future would be without hardship but the very basis of his giving was his false belief in the poor man's hopelessness. In contrast, Reb Nochemke so artfully gave his charity that, in fact, it soon proved not to be charity at all.

HOW PURE GIFTS CONNECT THE MATERIAL AND SPIRITUAL WORLDS

Charity moves a gift from the material world, where individual ownership is the rule, to the spiritual world where the love feast offers each person a share of nature's bounty. In this, charity is like the fertility rituals which transform what is sacrificed by circulating it back to the spiritual realm. This circulation brings renewal. Jesus Christ, at the Last Supper, used this principle of circulation when he moved bread and wine across the boundary that divides the material and spiritual worlds. So he said of the bread, "Take, eat; this is my body." And of the wine that it "is my blood of the covenant, which is poured out for many for the forgiveness of sins." In asking the apostles to share bread and wine in this way, Jesus offered them a ritual by which the food of this world might give spiritual nourishment.

The issue is much the same with money. What are the ways in which money can be transformed like the bread and wine which, in the ceremonies of the Roman Catholic and Episcopal churches among others, are believed to become the body and blood of Jesus? What are methods by which money can be taken from our modern market economies and circulated across the boundary dividing the material and the spiritual? How can money be made to serve the increase of inner resources and inner riches?

One fascinating, contemporary phenomenon is the expert use of radio and television by preachers who promise salvation and plead for the contribution of dollars. A constant refrain from these media evangelists is that nothing heals the body and soul like giving, and they are not bashful about naming the organizations and addresses to which this money should be sent. While some of these ministers may be sincere, others are now convicted felons serving long sentences for fraud, conversion of money to personal use, and evasion of income taxes. Will a gift to such a minister, or his church or foundation, aid us in freeing our inner richness to flow into the world?

We observed earlier that the development of money and market economies may well have been aided by the needs of religious pilgrims. Far from home, these pilgrims needed to pay not only for their food and shelter but also for appropriate sacrifices and contributions in the course of the ceremonies. Today religious people the world over continue to journey to sacred sites in cities such as Jerusalem, Mecca, and Benares. To focus on the example of Benares, each year hundreds of thousands of Hindu pilgrims travel to this city on the banks of the Ganges. The pilgrims come for many reasons—to perform rites for the dead, gain a boon, expiate a sin, or simply for the merit of the pilgrimage.

Part of the pilgrimage involves the giving of *dana* or pure gifts to the priests, who help to perform the various ceremonies. Dana is made voluntarily and without any expectation of reciprocation or of material or spiritual reward. The ideal recipient of dana is a Brahman priest; many rituals are considered valueless unless dana is given to such a priest. The dana itself is not payment to the priest, but a gift in addition to the payment (which is called *daksina*).

This seems straightforward, except that the receipt of dana creates moral peril for the priest. The pure gift carries with it the sins of the donor. Whether the gift is money, which is preferred by the priests, or goods, the priest accepting the gift also accepts the sins of the giver. These sin-carrying gifts can only be cleansed if the priest rigorously performs certain rituals and gives away more than the value of the dana to others.

Since, generally speaking, the priests need to use what they receive in order to live and may very well neither know the complex cleansing rituals nor have the time to perform them, the receipt of dana condemns the priest-recipient to an unending accumulation of sin. We are told that these indigestible sins cause the priest to die an early and horrible death. In fact, the priest's body will not burn easily on the funeral pyre because it is so laden with sin.

Nor is the giver free from moral danger. The giver must find a priest whose character is perfected. This is because the giver is responsible for what the priest will do with the money. So if the priest is greedy and uses the gift instead of purifying it and giving it away, the giver will suffer and sink into hell with the priest.

The ideal of dana would place money in circulation at a high velocity. It would go from giver to priest and, no sooner had the priest performed the cleaning rituals, it would be increased and travel as gifts to others. The amount of money circulating in this spiritual realm would be constantly increasing; certainly it would never be hoarded or become venture capital used for profit. Since this ideal is seldom attained, the money used for dana is viewed as barren. If hoarded, it will be devoured by ants. If used for a business, the business will fail.

There are a number of gifts which are not dana, and therefore do not carry its moral peril. A gift in which recip-rocation is expected, such as a gift to a friend, is not dana. Nor is a gift to a beggar (or an ascetic) or for the upkeep of a monastery considered to be dana, even though no recip-rocation will take place.

If we think about dana, we see that it grows from a worthwhile insight. What value is giving to the poor if the ways in which we have obtained money to give—or more generally, the ways in which we live our lives—are repre-hensible? If we are not trying to give away our sins, then perhaps we can make the "impersonal" and pure gift that dana must be. But if we make our gift to a religious organi-zation or person that misuses it, we have not truly fulfilled the purpose of charitable giving. So the concept of dana suggests a higher level of responsibility that can inform the process of giving.

THE BEGHARDS

Our word "beggar" comes from the Beghards of Flanders, a brotherhood founded in the thirteenth century whose friars lived by begging. The best known of the medieval mendicant orders were the Franciscans, Dominicans, Carmelites, and Augustinians, but the roots of mendi-cancy (which comes from the Latin verb *mendicare*, "to beg") reach far into antiquity. Early in the Vedic period (which began around 1500 B.C. in India), Brahman priests followed strict rules in their solicitation of alms. The ancient Greeks and the Romans also had priests who solicited alms. While the practice of begging for alms faded away in the Western world with the end of the Middle Ages, in some parts of the world it continues to the present day. Among the Hindus, for example, renunciants are without a home or property, wander constantly (except for the four months of the rainy season), are celibate, and beg for their food and other necessities of life. The best home for such a renunciant is at the base of a tree.

What is the benefit to the mendicant who relies on the giving of others? In essence, this person is revealing faith that there will be divine supply and is literally following the words of Jesus: "But seek first his kingdom and his righteousness, and all these things shall be yours as well." What is the benefit to the society of which the mendicant is a part? The mendicant offers the opportunity for others to give, thus letting them free their inner richness. In this way, the pious life and the very survival of the mendicant are a reflection of the society's well-being.

The role of the mendicant did not survive the Reformation, which scrutinized both the concept of banking merit (which had been acquired by giving alms in the hope of future spiritual rewards) and the moral character of the recipient of the alms. So men like Benjamin Franklin, Andrew Carnegie, and John D. Rockefeller preferred to use their wealth and energy to create institutions, such as foundations, universities, hospitals, and libraries, that would better the lives of all men and women. Today our urbanized, post-industrial society has little place for people who would be poor by choice; so many are poor simply by the operation of the marketplace.

However, the mendicants who offered themselves as vessels to receive alms and the great industrialists who gave their wealth to develop institutions that would better the human condition both participated in the wise circulation of money. Both subscribed to the principle that the circulation of wealth increases the well-being of all. Both saw a way in which money could be taken from the marketplace and moved to a spiritual realm, where its circulation would serve purposes consistent with its sacred origins.

THE MARKER

Money is a marker in the experience of giving. Where we make our money flow—whether to those in need or to endow charitable, religious, and educational organizations—we realize that our love, understanding, compassion, and selfless volunteer work can flow as well. These sacrifices move us away from the worship of money (which is only a tool) and reveal to us the reality of human interdependence and inner richness.

At the source of our inner wealth, we are rich in so many ways. Giving money to help people and better society are ways to cross the boundary and find the treasure buried in the field. Giving of our feelings and time is another way. But there are even more inward routes to this richness: prayer, meditation, the joy of artistic creation, and the exploration of the imagination.

One important gift is the one we give to those aspects of ourselves which are poor. Just as Jung learned from the stone of his own eternal nature, so we can seek to heal ourselves by what we learn from the experience of our own inner richness. Scrooge possessed the vitality and fecundity of the Spirit of Christmas Present. When he crossed the boundary into the world of his own spirit, he found and brought back the cornucopic riches of the Self that could heal him. This crossing of boundaries is of value to us all. Even in the richest society in the world, many of us experience poverty within: The feeling that we are not worthy, that we are not loved or capable of loving, that we are not all that we might be, that we are not whole.

Both this chapter and the last chapter began with the story of the miller who sold all he owned to buy gold. Being a miser, he then buried this precious substance and refused to circulate it in the world. Since he could not move his energy into the world, he could not receive back the replenishment that we find in exchanges with others (whether of money, food, or emotions). He had buried his soul and lost the potential to grow inwardly.

In the realm of the soul, there is no resting place. If we do not grow—growth being the realization of our natural richness, the coming to know and the acceptance of what we most truly and deeply are—then we lose our precious treasure. One night, or night after night, a thief comes and steals what might have been ours. But if we are fortunate enough to take the advice of a wise neighbor, we may bury a stone in the empty hole that the thief has pillaged. One day, we may hear the stone speak a few words and, if we dare to respond, who knows what riches may be unearthed.

CHAPTER SIX

INHERITANCE
The Actual and Symbolic Wealth of Our Parents

ONCE UPON A TIME a man worked very hard for twenty years to build a business. Although his hard work took him from poverty to wealth, he finds that his twenty-year-old son will not work. When the father speaks of the pleasure of working hard and succeeding, the son replies that he will never choose a career because his father provides everything for him. Since the father loves his son and wants him to know the joy of work and success, the father sells everything that he owns and gives all his money to charities and to poor people. Then he tells his wife and his son that he has lost everything in bad business deals and the family is poor.

Yet the father is disappointed in his hope that his son will now work. Instead, the son solves the problem of poverty by planning to marry a wealthy girlfriend, who gives him $200,000 as an engagement gift. After throwing his son out of the house, the father discovers that he no longer has the drive which earned him his first fortune. Guilt-stricken to have deprived his wife and son of the comforts of his wealth, he decides to take his life by leaping from a bridge.

These episodes, part of an amusing film titled *For Richer, For Poorer*, are told in flashbacks. The film starts with the formerly wealthy man trying to leap from the bridge. A woman, a homeless beggar, approaches him and asks for his cash and his watch, saying that he won't need them anymore. Even at the moment of death, this man cannot escape dealing with what little remains of his property. When he realizes that he can't jump, he and the beggar befriend each other and he tells her his story.

The family dynamics of *For Richer, For Poorer* suggest certain truths about the inheritance of money. The generation which earns the money has the gratification of being very productive and successful. The next generation inherits the money, but often lacks ambition. It is difficult to find a reason to strive in the world. The wealth will take care of material needs, and the achievements of the parent can seldom be matched. William K. Vanderbilt, a descendent of Cornelius Vanderbilt who amassed an enormous fortune in the nineteenth century, observed that "inherited wealth is a big handicap to happiness. It is as certain death to ambition as cocaine is to morality." The challenge to the heir, if he or she wishes to overcome these obstacles, is to transform the relationship to money and to the parent who earned it.

A LARGER VIEW OF INHERITANCE

Throughout this chapter we will view inheritance in a larger sense as what is received from parents or family, whether in life or at death, and whether in the form of money, emotional patterns, moral values, or education that one generation can transmit to the next. For the heirs may inherit issues that the parent was unable to face or resolve. And even small amounts of money and property can carry the weight of emotions. The love that the child sought in life from the parent may be sought in a parent's will at death. The will is the final statement of the parent, the final division, often among siblings, of what the parent can offer the children.

The power to earn money is certainly not the power to control its effect on people. In the film, the father's desire that his son follow in his footsteps ignores the family relationship to money. The father valued the fact that everyone depended on his earning power. No wonder his son and wife show no interest in earning money. The son and wife enjoy the leisure that the father has never cherished. In a sense, the father is one-sided; he is all productivity, he shows no capacity for the pleasures of idleness. The son and wife must be idle for him; they live an aspect of the father's life that he has been unable to live for himself.

Perhaps the father's yearning for the son to be ambitious is not really about the son at all. Perhaps it is about a growing desire in the father to be indolent, to take time off, to discover another way in which he can live his life. One of the ways in which the father oversees his employees is by appearing in disguises that allow him to test their efficiency without their knowledge. These elaborate disguises suggest fantasies of other, as yet unrealized, possibilities in his life.

We might imagine that the beggar on the bridge approaches the father like a reflection of himself. The image of the beggar suggests that an aspect of the father is poverty-stricken. His pleasure in money comes only from earning it, but he recognizes that even that joy has faded for him. He needs to move into the world of the beggar, where money and work are the exceptions. In the film he does exactly that; he vanishes for two years and wanders across the country. During this odyssey he takes whatever work he can find and spends a lot of time not working at all. He sends small amounts of money to his wife but writes no letters to go with the money. The value of the money is no longer its purchasing power but its power to communicate.

When he returns home, he finds that both his wife and his son are working. His wife finds joy in no longer being dependent on a father or husband for support. His son lives on a divorce settlement of $5 million, but the son has realized that work is a form of community. Lacking his father's talents, the son works as a waiter for idealistic reasons. At last the father accepts that he need not be the only one who works; he can relax and discover the part of himself that is a beggar, a part that fails the measure of ambition but offers inner rewards that are not easily measured. Only by discovering this new aspect of himself can he accept that his wife and son have developed their own potentials in relation to work.

This gentle comedy is insightful about the universal issues presented by wealth. Symbolically, the wealthy man died on that bridge. He did not leap, but he began a process of change so radical that he became a new man. In a similar way, his son and his wife also found new lives. They have become neophytes, people who have discovered a new fate.

THE DEATH POWER OF MONEY

What may be unusual in *For Richer, For Poorer* is that the family has some resolution about issues of wealth, roles, and feelings while everyone is alive. So often money, whether in large or small amounts, is only transferred at death or as a part of an estate plan that constantly focuses on the approach of death. Both of the words "will" and "testament," which are instruments by which the person who dies instructs the living as to what should be done with property, are rooted in sexuality. In its origins, the word "will" suggests giving physical pleasure or being voluptuous, while "testament" shares the generative power of the testes, the testicles.

In this we see again the perplexing connection between sexuality, or the power to be fertile and productive, and death. This is much the same connection that we explored in the fertility rituals with their endless cycles of death inseminating life. So Hades, the Greek god of the underworld and the dead, is also the god of wealth. Wearing a helmet that makes him invisible, he rules Hades, as the underworld is called, without pity as he decrees death for all who live. Yet his epithets include "the wealthy one" and "the wealth giver." Why should money, in its role as wealth, be a substance of the underworld? And what does this mean?

A person who dies cannot transfer fertility by way of money. So we do not receive fertility by a will, only property. Looked at in this way, property is the residue of fertility. The property or the money is not the source of supply. Imagining that the inherited wealth is fertility, instead of seeking one's own inner richness, will lead to passivity and infertility. The will of the dead parent may overwhelm the life force of the child. How often does someone of nineteen or twenty have sufficient ambition to overcome the fact that a parent has provided enough money to last a lifetime? Such families must teach ambition unrelated to money, such as ambition to serve others, if the death power of the money is to be escaped.

To comprehend the death power of money, and how to transform this power, it may help us to travel to the underworld ruled by Hades. To understand what we inherit, and to learn who we are and how we differ from our parents, we sometimes have to descend into the underworld. If we can succeed in this journey, we return to our daily lives far wiser for our courage.

The god called Hades by the Greeks was called Pluto by the Romans. In our solar system, Pluto is the planet farthest from the sun and most recently discovered (in 1930). Smaller than Mercury and the moon, its orbit takes it as far as 4.6 billion miles from the sun's warmth and light. In 1978, astronomers discovered that Pluto has a moon, which they named Charon. In Greek mythology, Charon is the boatman who ferries the souls of the dead across the river Styx to the underworld. Then, in 1988, astronomers found that Pluto has a thin atmosphere of methane, and that this atmosphere will freeze to the surface of the planet for two centuries starting in the 2020s. Pluto remains the only planet not yet visited by spacecraft, although plans are under consideration for flights that would take seven or eight years and arrive early in the twenty-first century.

Pluto is hardly a place that we would like to visit. In fact, the planet Pluto is probably a very good image for the underworld ruled by the terrifying god Hades. It is a dark and frozen realm, far away from what we think of in our sunlit, day-to-day lives. We will only face the risk of travel to such a place under the greatest duress.

THE UNDERWORLD JOURNEY OF PERSEPHONE

Yet the affirming aspect of the journey to the underworld, the unconscious and unexplored realms within ourselves, is that we may find our own creativity and sources of renewal. With this in mind, we can turn to a myth which shows the very forces that shaped the underworld and, so, shaped our unconscious. This is the myth of Hades' abduction of Persephone, the daughter of Zeus and the fertility goddess Demeter.

Remember as this myth unfolds that we are speaking of inheritance in the larger sense. What we inherit is not merely money and only received at death, but it is everything, both good and bad, that we receive from our parents throughout our lifetime. When we examine such an inheritance, some of what we receive will be truly ours and worthwhile to keep. The rest we must learn to surrender if we are to get on with our own lives.

In the myth, Zeus, the ruler of the gods, gives permission to his brother Hades to marry Persephone. Zeus does not consult Demeter or Persephone about this, but, in essence, authorizes the incestuous and violent rape of Persephone by Hades, who is her uncle. So one day, as Persephone reaches to pluck a narcissus in a field, the earth opens in a great chasm. Hades, riding his golden chariot pulled by immortal steeds, appears from the darkness and carries Persephone away.

Persephone weeps and screams. Demeter hears her daughter. For nine days she searches for Persephone on the earth until at last she learns of the abduction and of Zeus's permission for Hades to marry Persephone. Although Hades rules a third of all creation and is a king, Demeter is inconsolable. Her rage against Zeus is so great that she leaves Olympus, the home of the gods, and wanders through the human world. She neglects herself and, finally, looking like an old and poverty-stricken woman, she sits by the Well of the Virgin in the town of Eleusis. The daughters of King Keleos come to draw water from the well. Feeling compassion for the old woman, they ask for and receive permission from their mother to invite Demeter to stay in the palace.

King Keleos has a new son, Demophoon, and his wife Metaneira entrusts the child to Demeter's care. The parents marvel at how Demophoon grows godlike under the care of Demeter. But, unknown to the boy's parents, each night Demeter dangles the boy over the leaping flames of a fire to make him immortal. One night Metaneira sees this and laments that she will lose her son and be grief-stricken.

Demeter is enraged and lays the infant on the floor beside the fire. Revealing herself as a goddess, she tells Metaneira that the boy could have been immortal but now must die like all men. Saying that she is a beneficent goddess who brings joy to both people and gods, she directs that a great temple and altar be built for her at Eleusis. In return, she will teach her sacred rites to the people.

King Keleos brings together the people to build the temple. But when they have finished, Demeter merely sits within the temple walls and mourns for her daughter Persephone. She will not let seeds sprout; nothing grows and people suffer a year of terrible misery. Zeus, fearful that there will be no people to offer sacrifices to the gods, sends one god after another to ask Demeter to return to Olympus. The gods implore her and offer her gifts, but she refuses them all.

At last Zeus decides to send a messenger to the underworld to meet with Hades. He chooses the god called Hermes by the Greeks and Mercury by the Romans. This handsome god carries a golden staff and often is portrayed wearing a winged helmet or winged sandals to show that he can move through all the worlds, from heaven to earth to the underworld. He is called the messenger of the gods, and is often sent from Olympus on missions of aid.

Hermes is the god of boundaries. On the earth he is the god who protects travelers. Because the early travelers were largely merchants and traders, he is also the god of commerce and of the boundaries set by commercial relationships. In the underworld he is the guide of souls, the god who brings us across the boundary from the world that we know to the world that is unknown. For those who journey within themselves, Hermes is the guide who helps us across the boundaries that previously we never saw and certainly never thought of crossing.

When Hermes comes he can use his golden staff to either mesmerize or awaken us. There is the danger that we will wander forever: grieving like Demeter, entrapped in the underworld like Persephone, or riding for years on the nation's highways like the father in *For Richer, For Poorer*. But, if we dare the suffering of the journey, we may be awakened by what is new and rich within us. For Hermes has the power to transform evil into good. He is a "giver of grace, guide, and giver of good things!" To express this another way, we have in ourselves immense healing powers if we see the ways in which we may need healing.

Hermes bounds from Olympus to the underworld depths. There he finds Hades and grieving Persephone, who yearns for her mother. When Hades hears that Zeus has ordered the release of Persephone, he smiles obediently and begs Persephone to see him as a worthy husband and come from time to time to visit him.

Persephone rises with joy, but Hades comes behind her and slips into her mouth the sweet seeds of a pomegranate. Then Hermes brings Persephone up from the dark realms and leaves her at the great temple in Eleusis.

Demeter embraces her with a happiness like intoxication, but the first question that she asks her daughter is whether Persephone ate anything in the palace of Hades.

When she learns that Persephone has eaten the seeds of the pomegranate, she knows that her daughter must return to the underworld.

Now Zeus sends his own mother, the goddess Rhea, to earth where all the fields lie barren. Rhea brings the promise of Zeus that Persephone may spend two-thirds of the year with Demeter, but must spend the other third with Hades. Rhea implores Demeter to let the corn grow again and nourish humanity.

Demeter agrees and once again the earth is lush with vegetation. As she promised, the goddess teaches her rites to her worshippers at Eleusis. These rites concern immortality and are so sacred that death is the penalty for revealing them outside of the ceremonies. Demeter also gives the knowledge of agriculture to humanity for its betterment. Only during a third of the year, when Persephone must live in the underworld, does Demeter withhold her nurturing abundance. That season, of course, is winter.

While humanity endures winter, Persephone sits on her underworld throne. She is the queen of the underworld, the wife of fearsome Hades. With him she rules the realm of the dead and of wealth. So she has entered adulthood, is no longer merely the daughter, and has found her own power and her role as a queen.

WHAT WE LEARN FROM THE UNDERWORLD JOURNEY

There is a beautiful epithet that applies to both Demeter and Persephone: *carpophorus* or fruit-bearing. Both mother and daughter are the bearers of fruits, of what grows and is nourishing. Looked at another way, the mother and daughter share the same essence; they are as one. They are both fertility goddesses. However, a crucial part of Demeter is missing. She can offer life, abundance, and vitality, but she appears to have no contact with death. Even she, a powerful goddess, is out of touch with a certain aspect of reality. She wants to keep Persephone with her always, so the daughter will have no experience of death or rebirth. She wants to make the infant Demophoon immortal, but she fails to see that humans by their nature must accept mortality.

Like the father in *For Richer, For Poorer*, Demeter has not dealt with death, the absence of productivity, the fallow period before the next time of growth. She has not dealt with idleness, with winter. As so often happens, the child must deal with what the parent refuses to confront. This is an aspect of Persephone's inheritance. Demeter's endless abundance forces Persephone to confront the meaning of death, emptiness, winter. Persephone must go to that dark and depressing realm where the atmosphere can freeze to the surface for two centuries.

The abduction of Persephone by her uncle Hades has been used as a model for incestuous sexual abuse, especially of a girl by her father or other male relatives. We may ask why Zeus, who is the ruler or ordering power among the gods, allows the painful penetration of Persephone by Hades. The myth never answers this question, but it seems that the oneness of the child with the parent must be violated. The child must separate. The rape is an image of how terrifying we may find the change forced on us by the unfolding of our own nature. Often this crisis comes in midlife as we undergo the stressful surrender of an old and outgrown identity. This identity may have pleased our parents. It may be part of our inheritance from them. Yet the stirring of our own power, our own sense of who we most deeply are, may force us to surrender what may in many ways be both secure and of value.

That the rapist is an uncle, a relative, suggests how closely related to us the force of the rape is. The energy of the rape is not the intrusion of a stranger, but rather the impact of a previously hidden energy within oneself. When this energy first appears, we feel darkness, depression, and disorientation. We do not like to change, even if the change comes from within.

Women and men alike experience this rising of unconscious materials into awareness like the penetration of a rape. Hades carries us away to the underworld; he penetrates us with his darkness. But when we return like Persephone to the light, we retain a knowledge of the darkness. We are more complete; we see more fully the truth of who and what we are. So Zeus, representing the highest principle of order within us, allows great psychic violence in the service of growth.

Hades feeds fruits to Persephone, who is the "fruit-bearing" goddess. His intrusion forces her to eat of her own nature. She is ingesting—becoming—herself. In this process she shows her mother Demeter, who acknowledges only abundance and immortality, that existence encompasses more than this. Through the descent of Persephone, Demeter, symbolizing the abundant part of ourselves, is brought into relationship with grief and mortality. This integration of unwanted aspects of life makes us more realistic and whole. Also, the pomegranate is not a fruit chosen at random. Many of the ancient Mediterranean peoples believed that the seeds of the pomegranate could be used as a contraceptive. So the number of seeds eaten by Persephone equals the number of infertile winter months. Yet the red juice and many seeds of the pomegranate were also considered a symbol of uterine richness and fertility. So Persephone eats of her own sexuality, discovering in her underworld journey the ways in which she is both barren and rich.

When we eat of our own natures, we become more and more ourselves. The alchemists (borrowing from the Gnostics) used an image of a snake that swallows its own tail: the *ouroboros*. Many snakes live in the darkness beneath the earth, so the snake symbolizes the ability to penetrate the underworld. By devouring itself, the alchemical snake forms a circle, its mouth grasping its tail, and the circle is an image of wholeness. When we eat of our own natures, we are both self-devouring and becoming whole in the image of being circular. It takes great courage to admit that we meet ourselves in the underworld. It may be easier to blame a parent and never eat the seeds of the pomegranate.

Several other aspects of the underworld journey are worth mentioning. We may need a guide, a Hermes, simply to find the entrance to the underworld or our unconscious. This guide may take many forms, such as a dream figure, a spiritual leader, or an analyst. Many cultures give the dead a coin or some wealth to take with them on their journey. So a price must always be paid to venture into the unconscious. We must also take with us offerings that appease terrible Persephone when we meet her enthroned beside her husband Hades.

For example, in *The Aeneid*, when Aeneas seeks the help of a prophetess to descend into the underworld and visit his father, Aeneas first must find a golden bough to bring with him as an offering to Persephone. This golden bough is such a holy offering that Charon, the ferryman, has no choice but to take Aeneas across the River Styx, while multitudes of other souls wait centuries for passage.

Aeneas must also offer something to the monster Kerberos that guards the gates of the underworld. Kerberos is a three-headed dog with the tail of a snake. The prophetess tosses a drugged scrap of honey and corn to Kerberos. The monster devours this and then sleeps while Aeneas passes. At last Aeneas honors the underworld goddess Persephone by setting the golden bough on her altar. When he sees his father, he tries three times to embrace him but clasps only the empty air. His father tells him that those who drink from the River Lethe in Hades will forget everything and be doomed to another life as a human.

Moneta's name, in its roots, suggests the importance of memory. Money, like the underworld journey, requires us to remember. If we drink from the River Lethe, we will forget what we have already experienced. In a larger sense, we will even forget the experience of our parents and of our ancestors. We will be unable to transform our inheritance, whatever it may be. Only if we remember can we bring the power of reason to bear on our own experiences and those of our family. Only this scrutiny protects us from falling into the illusion that these worn-out images are real. For if we are ruled by our past experiences, such as the patterns of childhood relationship to our parents, we will have no way to avoid repeating these patterns again and again—in essence, living the same life over and over without gaining spiritual insight.

Also, when we return from the underworld, we must not forget our experiences and insights there. Remembering is a putting together of parts, a reconstituting of ourselves. So memory allows us the understanding that leads to growth. When we review our experiences in the underworld, we understand that much of what we experienced as painful and frightening was, in fact, necessary and healing for us.

For example, Kerberos is one of the great monsters of mythology. He is a three-headed hound of fearsome size. But we have to keep in mind that the dog is a friend of humankind. The first wild animal to be domesticated, the dog is part of humanity's extended family. So the dog in dreams and myths is likely to be on the side of human development. Kerberos as a dog is seeking to protect us from entering those parts of our unconscious that we are not yet ready to experience. He is fearsome, but he is serving us. In "The Wasteland" by T. S. Eliot, the narrator speaks of a corpse that has been buried, some aspect of life that people might prefer to avoid, yet the corpse itself may sprout and bloom. The narrator warns that the friendly dog should be kept away from such a corpse, because the dog may repeatedly dig up what we hide from ourselves.

Sometimes the dog, our friend and helper, seeks, like Kerberos, to protect us from knowledge of the underworld; other times such a dog insists on digging up and exposing to us unconscious material that we would prefer to bury. When we are ready to pass the gate that Kerberos guards, we are ready to face aspects of ourselves that have been hidden in our unconscious.

In *The Aeneid*, the drugged scrap of food that the prophetess feeds Kerberos is made of honey and corn meal. It is interesting that the prophetess, not Aeneas, drugs this terrifying guardian. In a way, the part of us that is prophetic, the part that can see into our own future, is the part that knows when the time is right to drug the guardian at the gates to the unconscious. Aeneas is like our conscious awareness. We do not consciously know the right moment to confront unconscious material, but like Aeneas we can be courageous in pursuing this unearthing once it has begun. Also, since Demeter is the grain goddess, the use of corn to drug Kerberos suggests that the very richness of our nature causes the guardian to sleep when the time is appropriate for entry.

The underworld or unconscious often expresses itself through paradox. So Kerberos is not only a dog but also a snake. And, as D. H. Lawrence says in his poem "Snake," the snake is "Like a king in exile, uncrowned in the underworld,/Now due to be crowned again." So the monster has two natures—that of the friendly dog and of the underworld god. The name Kerberos, by its similarity to the word *ouroboros*, suggests that the snake part of Kerberos's nature includes the circular image of the snake devouring its own tail. So, in the underworld journey, we find the image of the circle which represents integration and wholeness.

The golden bough symbolizes the mysterious connection between the world that we know and that which is unknown. Aeneas despairs of finding such a golden bough in the vastness of the forest. In fact, this golden bough is unnatural; it is not from the green world of vegetation but from the gold hidden in the underworld. That Aeneas can find such a bough in our world suggests that the moment is ripe for his entry into the unconscious. In the underworld he will meet his father and learn of his destiny, which is the inheritance belonging to him and his descendants.

The golden bough that Aeneas must offer to Persephone, in fact, came from the underworld. He is merely returning what already was hers. This gives us a fuller understanding of the nature of the underworld. It is the repository of wealth that awaits circulation. If the wealth does not circulate, then the underworld will truly be a frozen and terrible realm of deadness.

In everyday life, the golden bough might be a dream, a memory, or a feeling which we return to the underworld (the unconscious) by a process of contemplating its meaning and significance. Such golden boughs allow us to face the unconscious material that gathers within us from our daily lives, our family history, and the collective of the society in which we live. To refuse to deal with this material is to be frozen within.

If we dare the underworld journey, we may return with a greater insight. We may realize that abundance and barrenness are not opposites but reflections. So, too, are the harvest time and the time when the fields are fallow—productivity and idleness, and life and death—all reflections of one another. Money is like the golden bough, a residue or reflection of the richness of the natural world and our own natures. If we have enough insight, we may be able to use the inheritance from our parents as an offering on our journey of understanding. In doing this, we may transform our relationship to that inheritance, whether we viewed it as too much or too little, and to our parents themselves.

THE LAST WILL AND TESTAMENT
Dividing Property

We have been in the underworld long enough. Let us return to our own world, where money and property often perplex us. A difficult task faces the man or woman who must divide property by a will. Should his or her will convey some hidden, and perhaps unintended, message to those who receive inheritances and those who do not? Should the will seek to accomplish in death what could not be done in life, perhaps attempting to atone for not giving more of oneself? And do the beneficiaries understand their relationship to the person writing this last will and testament? Or should these beneficiaries, who may be adult children, search in the disposition of property for love and parental concern? The will is the last expression of the deceased. There is no opportunity for the beneficiaries to ask questions about intention and love, unless like Aeneas they seek their parents in the underworld.

In the Bible when a man in a crowd demands of Jesus to "bid my brother divide the inheritance with me," he speaks for so many of us who feel that we have not been given enough. Jesus refuses to be a divider of property, answering, "Man, who made me judge or divider over you?" Then Jesus warns the people in the crowd, "Take heed, and beware of all covetousness, for a man's life does not consist in the abundance of his possessions."

So a wise and industrious father in "A Father and Sons," one of *Aesop's Fables*, tells his sons on his death bed that he has hidden a treasure in the vineyard. After the father's death, the sons labor in the vineyard, turning over the soil in search of the treasure. While they find no treasure, their work makes the next harvest so rich that they profit from their labor. The moral given for this story is that good counsel is the best legacy, especially if the children also receive both the curiosity and inclination to follow the good counsel.

MERCURY AND A CARPENTER

Another tale from *Aesop's Fables* is also instructive. In "Mercury and a Carpenter," the story begins with a carpenter losing his ax in a river. The carpenter prays to Mercury to help him find it. Mercury, of course, is the Roman name for Hermes, who played such an important role in the story of Persephone. Diving into the river, Mercury brings a golden ax to the carpenter, but the honest carpenter says the golden ax is not his. On his next dive, Mercury surfaces with a silver ax, but again the carpenter says this ax is not his. Finally, Mercury brings back from the depths an ordinary ax with a wooden handle. The carpenter is delighted and says that is the very ax that he lost. Mercury, impressed by the poor man's honesty, gives him all three of the axes.

There is more to this story, for soon everyone has heard of Mercury's generosity. A knave decides to seize this chance. He goes to the bank of the river and begins weeping and crying out that he has lost his ax in the river. Mercury hears him and dives into the river. Returning with a golden ax, Mercury asks the man if this golden ax is his.

"Yes, that's the very one," the man replies.

"You impudent fool," Mercury thunders, "to imagine that you can trick the one who sees through the very heart of you."

As with all of *Aesop's Fables*, this story is also given a moral: "The great searcher of our hearts is not to be imposed upon, but he will take his own time either to reward or punish." Certainly Mercury, the guide of souls, will know when we are ready to risk crossing the boundaries that bring us to our inner richness. We, in turn, must be scrupulously honest in only claiming what is ours from what Mercury offers us.

THE SPIRIT IN THE BOTTLE

Mercury, called Hermes by the Greeks and Mercurius by the medieval alchemists, plays an important role in our next story dealing with inheritance, "The Spirit in the Bottle" from *Grimm's Fairy Tales*. In this tale a poor but industrious woodcutter saves a little money so his only son can go to a university. The father's motive in sending the son seems good, but certainly the father also hopes that the education will allow the son to take care of the father when he is no longer able to work. The boy studies hard and is praised by his teachers, but his father's savings run out before the boy can finish his courses.

The son returns home and the father apologizes for not having more money and, indeed, hardly being able to earn their daily bread. The son offers to help his father with the woodcutting, but the father says the son is not used to heavy work and, in any event, the father has only one ax and no money to buy another. The son encourages the father to borrow a neighbor's ax and together they go to work in the forest.

At midday the father suggests that they rest, but the son says he's going to take a walk and look for birds' nests. The father says the son will be too tired to work if he wastes his energy, but the son goes anyway. In the depths of the forest he walks back and forth until he comes on an enormous, angry-looking oak that five men could not reach their arms around. This oak must be hundreds of years old, and the boy thinks that many birds will have built their nests in its branches.

Suddenly he hears a voice crying, "Let me out, let me out." He clears away dead leaves and searches in the roots until he finds a glass bottle with a froglike creature in it that keeps calling, "Let me out."

The unsuspecting boy uncorks the bottle and a spirit flows out and grows larger and larger until it is half as big as the oak. This spirit asks the boy what he thinks his reward will be for letting it out. The boy says he has no idea. "I'm going to break your neck," the spirit tells him.

The fearless boy says that he's going to keep his head on his shoulders and not let the spirit touch his neck. And he says he would have left the spirit in the bottle if he'd known how it rewards people.

The spirit replies that its name is Mercurius, and that it is so mighty that the boy's wishes don't matter. The spirit's duty is to break the neck of the one who frees him.

The boy answers that he can't believe a spirit as large as Mercurius was in such a small bottle. If Mercurius will get back in the bottle and prove that it can fit, then the boy will allow the spirit to do what it wants with him.

Mercurius slips back into the bottle and the boy quickly corks it and tosses it among the roots of the oak. He starts back toward his father, but Mercurius cries pitifully to be set free. Mercurius promises the boy good fortune for the rest of his life.

At last the boy decides to take a chance. Mercurius may be telling the truth, and in any event the boy feels that the spirit can't hurt him. So he uncorks the bottle and again the freed spirit grows huge.

Mercurius honors the promise and hands the boy a piece of cloth as his reward. The piece of cloth looks like a bandage that might go on a wound. Mercurius tells the boy that if he touches the cloth to iron or steel, the metal will be transformed into silver. And if he touches the cloth to a wound, the wound will be healed.

The boy wants to try out this cloth. He takes his ax and strikes a blow that cuts through the bark of the ancient oak. Then he touches this wound with the cloth and immediately the bark is whole again.

The spirit thanks the boy for its freedom and the boy thanks the spirit for the gift. Then they part.

The boy returns to find his father annoyed that he has been gone so long. The boy says he'll catch up, but the father doesn't believe him. So the boy touches his ax with the cloth and strikes a tree. Instead of magically felling the tree, the ax has turned to silver and is bent and ruined by the blow. The boy says the ax was no good, but the father is enraged that he will have to pay the neighbor for the ax. The son says that he'll pay for the ax and the father calls the boy an idiot. The father says that the son has nothing but what he receives from the father, so how will the son get money to pay for the ax?

Soon after, the son says that he can't work anymore and suggests they both go home. The father refuses, saying he has work to do and won't sit idle. The son then says that he's never been in these woods and he won't be able to find his way home if the father doesn't show him.

The father gets over his anger and takes the boy home. He asks the boy to take the ruined ax to town and sell it. The father expects to have to earn the rest of the money to repay the neighbor.

The boy takes the ax to the goldsmith, who tests it and weighs it. The goldsmith says the ax is worth four hundred talers (dollars), but he can only pay the boy three hundred talers at the moment and will have to owe him the other hundred. The boy accepts and returns with this fortune to his father.

The neighbor wants one taler and six groschen for the ax, but they pay him double. Then the boy gives the father one hundred talers and says that the father will live an easy life from now on and want for nothing.

The astonished father asks how the son came by so much money. The boy explains what happened and how he was rewarded when he took the risk of trusting Mercurius.

The rest of the money is more than enough for the son to finish his courses at the university. Aided by the cloth that can heal all wounds, the boy becomes a doctor famed throughout the world for his healing skills.

WHAT WE FIND IN THE ROOTS OF THE FAMILY TREE

This marvelous tale offers a number of insights into inheritance. The father is a well-intentioned man. He has a difficult life, but he saves what he is able so that his son can achieve more than he did. We feel in this the father's belief that the family has a greater potential that it has shown so far. In the family genes are the possibilities of distinguished achievement that would be nourished by a university education.

However, the father is poor. He cannot, by his efforts alone, change the destiny of the family. What money he can save—that is, what life energy he can make available to his son—is not enough to let the son graduate from the university. Good though the father's efforts are, the son will have to live the woodcutter's life if he merely relies on what his father is able to offer him as an inheritance.

It is significant that the son is quite willing to strive as a woodcutter. He doesn't look down on this hard work, nor does he scorn his father. He isn't looking for someone to blame for the fact that he could not finish his university education. Parents so often receive this kind of blame. Whether the parent is alive or dead, the child may believe some flaw in the parent has crippled and limited the child's life. To become attached to this point of view is damaging, because the child fails to take responsibility for his or her own destiny. The child inherits the parent's life, instead of discovering his or her own life.

The woodcutter's son is quite willing to take responsibility for himself. He isn't filled with self-pity because he has been unable to complete the courses at the university. In fact, he shows how he respects his father and his father's work by wanting to join in the woodcutting. The father feels ambivalent about this, because he has an awareness that the son should rise higher in life. Yet the son's acceptance of the father's work shows that the son honors those from whom he will inherit. This attitude makes possible the son's inheriting far more than property or the cost of an education.

The father must borrow an ax if the son is to join him in the woodcutting. So the son receives something from the father which does not belong to the father. It will have to be returned or paid for, but in using the ax the son shows that he can expand the boundaries of what the father imagined to be possible. The ax itself offers an image of the dangers and possibilities offered by inheritance. The ax can be used both to build and destroy. So the son can use his inheritance to build or destroy his own potential.

The son wants to search for birds' nests in the forest while his more practical father prefers to rest at midday. Why should the son want to find birds' nests? Birds suggest the spirit, for birds can fly toward the heavens. So the boy is looking for a spiritual destiny of his own. The father has already found his place in life, but the son must venture deeper into the forest in search of what is his. By walking, the son uses his own power in his quest; by penetrating deeper into the forest, the son seeks his own nature beyond any boundaries set by the father.

What the son discovers is an ancient oak with a girth so great that five men could not put their arms around it. The boy imagines that this enormous tree will have many birds' nests in its branches, but what he actually discovers is a bottled genie in its roots. What we search for does not always present itself in the way that we imagine. The boy imagines his spiritual gift will come from looking to higher things, but in fact he must look down, toward the underworld, if he is to inherit any gift from the family tree. He must look at the roots of this angry oak to find the genie who, like the ax, can destroy or help build the boy's life.

This immense oak is described as angry. How can a tree be angry? A family tree can be filled with anger, carried from generation to generation. The father has an intuition that the family can achieve far more than it has. But this potential is unrealized. Perhaps many generations in this family have seen this glimmering of potential, but crushing poverty and social circumstances have made it so very difficult to rise to a new status. The father is frustrated at his own failure to earn and achieve more. He yearns to give more to his son but is frustrated in this as well. In his frustration is anger for the family fate, a fate that he cannot see how to alter.

The son searches among the roots of the family tree for

a voice that he hears calling. He does not know whose voice this is, but he knows that it cries out to be free. At last he finds a bottle with a froglike creature hopping inside it. If he does not examine what is in the bottle, he will live the same life that his father has lived. He will carry the family frustration and rage. But to examine this unseen aspect of the family history is dangerous; it lets the genie out of the bottle.

Alchemists used many different images of Mercurius, including one image of a boy with wings imprisoned in a bottle. This symbolized the concept of spirit imprisoned in matter. Being within the bottle is a way of containing and examining emotions and feelings without simply acting on them in the world. The boy's inner looking leads to understanding and growth.

Mercurius, as we said earlier, is Mercury or Hermes, the god who guides us on our underworld journey. He both makes boundaries and enables us to cross them. With his golden staff he can either awaken or mesmerize us. In this tale, he appears as a genie, a spirit encapsulated in a bottle. The word "genie" shares its roots with such words as genetic, genital, genitive, genuine, and genius. And the Latin verb *genere*, to beget, gives the derivative *gens*, which refers to male descendants of a free male ancestor—that is, a clan.

Apuleius, the second-century Roman author of *The Golden Ass*, wrote of how a man might honor his genius by sacrificing to it on his birthday. This use of the word genius, however, was quite different from its usage today. The genius to which a man sacrificed was the family spirit. These sacrifices, by honoring and revering the clan, made a man abundant in all ways. The genius would become a household god and protect the family. But if a man failed to honor this genius, it would become a restless and destructive influence on the family.

In our tale, Mercurius appears to be such a restless and destructive spirit. No honor has been given to Mercurius, no sacrifices have been offered on its altar. Faced by this violent aspect of the family history, the boy is fearless. His quest for a higher life has somehow prepared him for this meeting, but he is unaware of the form that the family spirit will take. At first, surprised, he thinks he will keep this spirit bottled up. Often that seems the safer way to deal with those aspects of our inheritances that are tormenting.

However, the boy is courageous. He has an intuitive sense that the spirit will not harm him and may keep its promise of giving good fortune. By opening the bottle a second time, the boy offers himself as a sacrifice to the spirit. If the spirit breaks his neck, the boy will live a broken life—a life in which his spirit and imagination (symbolized by the head) and his emotions and instincts (symbolized by the heart and body) are never brought together in a harmonious unity.

By risking his own life, the boy transforms Mercurius into a protecting spirit, a beneficent household god. The boy has honored not his personal genius, which would be mere narcissism, but the genius of the family. He has drawn from something larger than himself; he has realized the gift that Mercurius has waited centuries to give. Now that Mercurius has given the gift of healing to this generation of the family, the role of guide is no longer needed. So Mercurius is free to return to the realm of the gods and spirits.

At first the boy misunderstands his gift. He thinks that it will magically cut down trees so that he can be his father's equal as a woodcutter. Having transformed the ax to silver, his first blow destroys the ax. So the boy's fate is not to match his father's. That is not his life issue nor should it be his life goal. If he uses his gift in that way, he will render it of no value. The boy's complaint that the ax is no good is his momentary failure to see the true nature of his gift. He must use the gift in achieving the new and unique shape that his own life will take.

To do this, however, he must leave the father's world, symbolized here by the forest. The father is enraged that the boy has damaged the borrowed ax. This rage shows the poisonous effect of the anger in the family tree. The father feels that the family has no genius, that the son is, of course, an idiot. The only way to success is the hard work of woodcutting, so the father at first refuses to lead his son out of the forest. He feels that he must continue to labor as he always has.

But the father truly loves his son. That is why he tried as best he could to send his son to the university. His anger passes quickly enough. After all, it isn't really anger at the son but rather at the condition of the family. By showing the son the path out of the woods, the father accepts and even encourages the son to begin his new and gifted life.

The son sells the silver ax and gives his father the enormous sum of one hundred talers. A taler was obviously worth a lot more than a dollar is today, because this fortune will enable the father to live at ease for the rest of his life. Certainly this ease includes material well-being, but it also includes the spiritual joy that comes from at last seeing the healing realization of the family's gift. The son has touched his healing cloth to the wound in the family tree; he has healed it. The father is ready to hear how his son's destiny will be different from his own, so his son tells him the whole story of his meeting with Mercurius.

The son shows great wisdom in his use of the gift. He is no Midas. He does not use the cloth to convert more and more metal into silver. He merely uses the money received from the sale of that one ax to pay for his university education. With the help of the healing cloth, he realizes the potential of his ancestry by becoming a famed doctor and healer. The fact that he receives only three hundred talers and is owed another one hundred talers by the goldsmith suggests that what we inherit is so vast that it must come to us in installments received over time. We cannot be given (or understand) our inheritance in a moment of realization; rather, a gradual process is required by which our understanding deepens.

A MYSTERY SOLVED
The Thief Who Steals from Misers

We have discussed the tale of the miller who sold all that he owned to buy gold that he buried. One night a thief came and stole the hoard of gold. But who was this thief? It may come as no surprise that Hermes (Mercury) is not only the god of commerce, but the god of thieves as well. So if we suspect that Hermes stole the buried treasure, we are likely to be correct. But, unlike most thieves, Hermes will often offer something in return for what he steals.

The story of Hermes' birth reveals not only how Hermes became the god of thieves but also shows how Hermes felt unjustly treated in what he inherited from his father. Hermes' father was Zeus, ruler of the gods, while his mother was a nymph named Maia. Zeus had also fathered Apollo, the god of light, healing, music, poetry, and prophecy. However, Apollo's mother was Leto, so he and Hermes were half brothers.

On the day of his birth, Hermes performed two remarkable feats. First, he took the shell of a tortoise and invented the lyre, a stringed instrument on which he made beautiful music and sang joyously of his own birth. Next he went to where his brother Apollo kept a herd of sacred cattle. Hermes stole fifty cows from this herd and made them walk backwards so that their tracks could not be followed. After hiding the cows in the depths of a cave, he sacrificed two cows to the twelve immortal gods (including himself among these dozen deities).

In the ancient Mediterranean world, cattle were used to measure value, served as wealth, and were a valuable sacrificial offering. When Hermes steals the cows of Apollo, he is stealing the equivalent of gold or money. Apollo quickly realized that his younger brother had stolen the cattle, but he could not prove it. He accused Hermes of the theft, but Hermes changed shape and returned to his cradle as a baby. Hermes told his angry brother that he was newborn and knew nothing of any theft.

Since both Apollo and Hermes knew that Hermes had stolen the cattle, these gods were playing a game with each other. The game is much like the disputes of human siblings who feel their parents have favored one or the other. The game conceals the bitterness that the less favored sibling feels toward the parent. Even when Apollo and Hermes bring their grievance to Zeus, Hermes lies shamelessly. He says that Apollo accused him of theft without any witness and that Apollo threatened him, but he completely denies having stolen the cattle. Hermes says that Zeus should help him as the younger son.

Zeus, not touched by the anguish human parents often

feel in trying to give fairly of themselves to children, bursts into laughter. He tells the brothers to be reconciled and commands that Hermes lead his brother to where the cows are hidden. Hermes and Apollo go together to the cave, and Hermes brings the cattle out of the darkness. Then Hermes plays on the lyre. He plays so beautifully, singing of the gods, that he appeases his brother's anger.

This leads to a remarkable exchange and reconciliation between the brothers. Apollo admires Hermes' ingenuity in inventing the lyre. He wants the instrument and feels it to be worth fifty cows or even more. For his part, Hermes gives the lyre to Apollo.

In return, Apollo gives Hermes not only the fifty cows that had been stolen but also a golden three-leaved staff capable of bestowing wealth. While Apollo keeps for himself the gift of high prophecy, he gives to Hermes certain soothsaying powers as well as the lordship over animals which had formerly been Apollo's. He also gives Hermes the important offices as guide of human souls to the underworld and messenger of the gods.

So Hermes' theft of wealth ends with Apollo receiving a marvelous gift, the lyre, which makes the sounds of a new and beautiful music. It is this music that we seek when we examine our inheritance. Of course, we may rage against parents and siblings for a time. Either we have been given too little of what we wanted, too much of what we did not want, or not a fair portion compared to what someone else received. The most obvious symbol of this giving is money, but love, attention, encouragement, and so much more are also part of our inheritance.

If we explore in the roots of the family tree, we may develop an understanding of our families that will deepen the understanding that we possess of ourselves. Confronting parental shortcomings and the behavioral patterns that we have adopted to compensate for their anger, abuse, lack of love, or lack of understanding may allow us a greater freedom.

In "The Spirit in the Bottle," the woodcutter's son finds this freedom when he risks his neck to gain the genie's gift. He surrenders his attachment to the familiar life that he knows. If he remains under the spell of the anger that is so ominous in the immense presence of the family tree, he will share with his father a dumb sense of suffering and rage for the family's unrealized potential. He will never realize his own potential. Instead he goes through a process by which he comes to a more objective understanding of his family's potentials and shortcomings. Through this process he frees himself from the patterns of the past. By taking responsibility for his fate, he is able to receive from Mercurius an inheritance as marvelous as music—that of healing.

CHAPTER SEVEN

INDEBTEDNESS

How the Debtors' Tower Connects Earth to Heaven

ON A SATURDAY AND SUNDAY, February 20 and 21, 1822, in London, a weeping boy ran desperate errands through the streets in an effort to keep his father from going to debtors' prison. His father had been arrested and detained in a sponging house, a halfway house that would be followed by prison if the debt could not be paid. A baker, who sold bread and pastries to the family, had brought suit to recover forty pounds, a small part of the total debt owed by the boy's father to many creditors.

February had been a terrible month. The boy had turned ten years old, and his family had obtained employment for him in a blacking shop, where he applied a dark finish and labels to pots. His weekly wage of six shillings was decent pay for such a boy, the daily hours of 8 A.M. to 8 P.M. acceptable by the standards of the day. "No words can express the secret agony of my soul," he wrote years later in his autobiography, "as I . . . felt my early hopes of growing up to be a learned and distinguished man, crushed in my breast. . . ."

As the boy wept and ran from relatives to family friends seeking aid on that weekend, he must have felt the world that he had known—the world of childhood and of a whole and happy family—coming to an end. On Monday, February 22, the debt remained unpaid and the boy heard his beloved father say that "the sun was set upon him for ever." These words made the boy feel his own heart had broken. Later in the day, his father was taken to Marshalsea Prison and confined as an insolvent debtor.

That boy of ten was Charles Dickens.

DEBT AND IMPRISONMENT

The fate of John Dickens may seem severe, even inhuman, when judged by contemporary standards. The English legal system sought to prevent default on debt by the imposition of severe penalties. A seventeenth-century English judge, Sir Robert Hyde, didn't mince his words on this point: "If a man be taken in execution, and lie in prison for debt, neither the plaintiff, at whose suit he is arrested, nor the sheriff who took him, is bound to find him meat, drink, or clothes; but he must live on his own, or on the charity of others; and if no man will relieve him, let him die in the name of God, says the law; and so say I."

We would do well to consider how recent is the change in our thinking about whether personal freedom can be sacrificed as a penalty for nonpayment of debt. In this chapter we will explore how the powerful symbol of the debtors' prison has been lost to our awareness. Bankruptcy, which is used more and more frequently by overburdened consumers and businesses, does not require imprisonment and so does not warn of the way in which debt can deprive us of time, the very essence of life. Beyond this, however, we must face the debt that we owe for the miracle of life, a debt that may confuse us when we come to deal with everyday debts. And since debt is a statement about our ability to make payment in the future, it is also a statement about how we imagine that we will evolve and what productive role we will play in society. If we are wrong in our assessment and cannot repay our debts, we take the assets and life energy of others.

AN OATH OF POVERTY

Debtors' prisons were by no means limited to England. The colonies and, later, the states also imprisoned people for debt. Massachusetts, for example, dealt legislatively with debt collection laws more than seventy times in the seventeenth and eighteenth centuries. Seeking to ameliorate the harshness of imprisonment, Massachusetts experimented with a number of reforms: making the creditor pay for the cost of keeping the debtor in jail, allowing the debtor a limited freedom to leave the jail in search of work during the daytime, and letting debtors swear an oath of poverty and go free. However, swearing such an oath did not give relief from the debt itself.

In fact, in the 1820s, England also allowed the taking of an oath of poverty. In a larger view, it is curious that as the wandering monks, who took vows of poverty and lived by begging, no longer flourished in the western world, this new, secular oath of poverty emerged. John Dickens feared to take this oath, because he felt the disgrace would cause him to lose his job in the Navy Pay Office and the pension that would one day be his. Yet his creditors refused to enter into a new schedule for debt repayment, so the oath of poverty was his only option if he wished to leave prison. To qualify for such an oath, all of the clothing and personal property owned by him and his family could not have a value exceeding twenty pounds. As part of this process, Charles had to go before an official who, smelling strongly of beer and with his mouth full, examined the boy. Charles worried that the silver watch in his pocket, a gift from his grandfather, might be of too great value to keep and was relieved when the official merely glanced at his clothing and dismissed him.

In New England, Yankee merchants used the debtors' laws to their benefit by plying laborers with rum and whiskey. When the laborers could not pay for the liquor bills, the merchants would put them into indentured servitude to work off their debts in the Newfoundland fishing grounds. By the 1820s, when Dickens's father found himself within the walls of Marshalsea Prison, as many as ten thousand petty debtors were under close confinement in Massachusetts prisons. If we think of the debtors in jail in the other states, and the estimate that thirty to forty thousand people were arrested for debt in England in 1837, we can see that imprisonment for nonpayment of debt must have created fear for a great many people.

Reviewing a few examples from Massachusetts reveals that imprisonment of debtors, while perhaps serving as a deterrent to default on debt, often punished those who were already victims of hardship. In 1824, in Springfield, a girl of nineteen with a nursing baby was imprisoned for a debt of about seven dollars. That same year in Boston a blind man with a dependent family went to jail for a debt of six dollars. In Salem, a seventy-six-year-old veteran of the battle of Bunker Hill found himself imprisoned for a debt of a few dollars; while in Marblehead the local infantry raised $22.18 to release a sixty-eight-year-old veteran of the Revolutionary War from jail.

All of the states had laws governing debtors who could not pay, and in most of the states the pendulum of reform swung back and forth. If we imagine that the United States was founded by hardy pioneers who refused to borrow, we would be indulging in a fantasy. The capital and credit to support many merchants in the New World came from Europe, especially from England. Personal debt was also common, since food and other items often were purchased on account from a local merchant. While we may imagine that debt is a uniquely contemporary problem, debt has, in fact, a long history and almost certainly existed in prehistoric times.

TO SELL A WIFE, SON, OR DAUGHTER

Debt most frequently is measured in money and is an important aspect of the secret life of money. However, even before money existed, people borrowed such things as seeds, tools, and goods for trading. The earliest documented laws, the Code of Hammurabi set down in Babylonia about 1750 B.C., provide that "If a man be in debt and sell his wife, son, or daughter or bind them over to service for three years, they shall work in the house of their purchaser or master; in the fourth year they shall be given their freedom."

To imagine a man selling his wife, son, or daughter to

pay his debt shocks us, but the Bible frequently places before us the dangers of debt. In one parable, Jesus tells of a king whose servant owes him a debt too large to pay. The king orders the servant, his wife, his children, and all his belongings sold so that the debt can be paid. But the servant falls to his knees and begs for more time to make payment. Moved by this plea, the king releases the servant from the debt.

This would make a happy ending, except that the servant is also owed a debt by a fellow servant. This debt is much smaller, but the first servant no sooner leaves the king then he comes upon the second servant and seizes him by the throat and demands, "Pay what you owe!" The second servant pleads for more time, but the first servant is merciless and has him thrown into prison.

The king is filled with rage when he hears that the first servant did not offer the same mercy he had received to the second servant. So the king delivers the first servant to the tortures of prison until he makes full repayment of his debt.

While this parable used debt to show that people should forgive one another as God forgives them, it also illustrates how the debtor who failed to pay ran the risk of prison, indentured servitude, and even slavery. Under Roman law, a creditor who had obtained a judgment could force the seizure and sale of a debtor's assets for the benefit of all creditors. Such a proceeding would also cause the loss of the debtor's civil rights. To alleviate such a harsh result, the Roman law allowed the debtor to petition a magistrate for the voluntary surrender of the debtor's assets. By choosing this course, the debtor's civil rights were preserved.

The Middle Ages saw the bankruptcy laws change and

evolve. Debtors who sought to conceal or abscond with assets were targeted for especially severe penalties. As national laws developed, debtors who could not pay remained at risk to lose all assets and, in some cases, to suffer criminal penalties and the loss of civil rights. Some countries only allowed merchants to go bankrupt, while ordinary debtors could never find relief from their debts. In addition, the social view of bankrupts was extremely negative. The debtor who slipped into bankruptcy was often subjected to professional and social sanctions, including, in some cases, the requirement to wear clothing indicating this degraded status.

Social attitudes have changed, but we live in a world where debt is as ever-present as money. And as with money, the constant experience of debt dulls us to an exploration of its deeper nature. Of course, on a superficial level, we know that debt is usually created by our borrowing money or other valuables from someone else and promising to repay what we have received. The mortgage on a house, the installment loan on a car, the monthly balances owed on our credit cards, and the loan from a friend to tide us over until the next pay day are all forms of debt.

THE UNDERWORLD POWER OF DEBT

This mundane debt, so easily understood, conceals the historical power of debt to deprive us of our freedom. Even today, we need only read the newspapers to find examples of how debt is used as a tool of enslavement. In Brazil, for example, laborers on remote farms are paid wages in scrip that can only be used to purchase food and supplies at the company store. Since the scrip is not sufficient to meet the needs of the laborers, they fall deeper and deeper into debt and, in effect, become slaves. In Europe, women from the East are promised work in shops or restaurants in the West, only to find that they are brought to brothels and forced into prostitution to repay "debts" for agency fees, transportation costs, meals, and rent. This illicit trade can also be found in the United States. In one case, a young woman from China was coerced into prostitution to repay the $30,000 debt incurred for her passage to New York City. In the conservative town where she had grown up, she had never held hands with a boy. Abhorrent as these stories are, they illustrate the power of debt to be destructive of human liberty and dignity.

The liberal bankruptcy laws that the United States adopted in 1898 (and amended a number of times) actually serve to conceal the destructive power of debt and the more ancient and punitive attitudes felt toward debtors. Today, in the United States, individuals and business owners are free to go bankrupt and find relief from debt without fear of prison or servitude. The startling rise in total filings for bankruptcies, from less than 30,000 in 1910 to 360,000 in 1981 to nearly 1,000,000 in 1992, is in part a reflection of changed social attitudes toward the failure to repay debt.

While debtors' prisons can hardly be defended, they did serve a symbolic purpose, which has largely been lost today. They advised us that debt must be repaid; if it cannot be repaid in money, it will be repaid by the deprivation of freedom. To take our freedom is to take life itself. If debt can take life, then debt is clearly an aspect of the underworld, the invisible world where wealth accumulates and the dead reside.

While the reform of our laws relating to bankruptcy has certainly had benefits, it has not contended with the underworld aspect of debt. The impulse for social reform—the obvious wrongness of keeping someone in prison for debt, especially when being in prison defeats any possibility of paying the debt—does not deal with the place debt occupies in the human mind. If such an issue remains invisible, then changing its manifestation in our world (to one million bankrupts in a single year rather than a single soul in debtors' prison) simply allows new forms of suffering.

Anyone who has overspent and been pursued by bill collectors knows the terrible stress and anxiety of being unable to pay debts. Charles Dickens, in his autobiography, recalled the warnings given him by his father in debtors' prison: "My father was waiting for me . . . and [we] cried very much. And he told me, I remember, to take warning by the Marshalsea, and to observe that if a man had twenty pounds a year and spent nineteen pounds nineteen shillings and sixpence, he would be happy; but that a shilling spent the other way would make him wretched." This view of debt recognizes that freedom, beauty, and the vitality of life itself can be lost through dependence on debt.

Debt's ancient origin is reflected in biblical admonitions about debt, and the interest payments which often accompany debt. So Solomon warns, "The rich rules over the poor, and the borrower is the slave of the lender."

In Exodus, when God specifies the ordinances for the Jewish people, he includes the admonition that "If you lend money to any of my people with you who is poor, you shall not be to him as a creditor, and you shall not exact interest from him." This passage shows that debt should not be used to oppress poor people. If a poor person gives

a garment to secure a loan, the garment should be returned before nightfall so the poor person does not suffer.
Nor should a person's means of earning a living be taken
as a pledge, because that would deprive the debtor of both
livelihood and a way to earn enough to repay the loan.

Solomon is especially vehement about not becoming a
surety or giving a pledge for someone else. This is an arrangement in which one person guarantees the payment
of another person's debt, usually as an inducement to
the creditor to make the loan in the first place. The
words of warning are forceful and urgent: "My son, if
you have become surety for your neighbor, have given
your pledge for a stranger; If you are snared in the utter-
ance of your lips, caught in the words of your mouth;
then do this, my son, and save yourself, for you have
come into your neighbor's power: go, hasten, and impor-
tune your neighbor. Give your eyes no sleep and your
eyelids no slumber; save yourself like a gazelle from the
hunter, like a bird from the hand of the fowler." The reason for this urgency will become clear later in the chapter, when we discuss the considerations that make debt
either wise or foolhardy.

Debt existed before written history. As with language
and money, we rarely wonder about the birth of debt and
how debt came to be so much an aspect of our society. As
individuals we suffer from debt, but we seldom study debt
to understand its deepest implications. If we fail to take
debt as a subject worthy of inquiry, then debt will remain
invisible to us. Of course, we will know the principal and
interest payments that we must make to maintain our
standing as good debtors, but we will not understand our
deeper impulses and reasons for entering into and remaining in debt.

HOW DEBT CAME TO ASHANTI

A folk tale may help us gain insight into the way in which debt first became part of the human community and what that debt means to us. "How Debt Came to Ashanti" is a tale about how debt came to the kingdom of Ashanti, now a region of Ghana in West Africa. This story features Anansi, the spider, who is the trickster hero of the Ashanti and Akan people. He is constantly seeking to outwit animals, men, and even the gods. Sometimes he is wise, but more often he is unscrupulous, greedy, and selfish. As a culture hero, he is like Prometheus who brought fire to humankind. By outwitting the hornets, the python, and the leopard, Anansi became the owner of all stories that are told. His escapades sometimes lead to the creation of customs, institutions, and practices—such as debt.

However, Anansi is not the first one to bring debt to the Ashanti. In "How Debt Came to Ashanti," a hunter named Soko flees from his own village because he owes a debt that he does not want to pay. When he arrives in the lands of the Ashanti, the people are worried because they have never known debt. They send their old men to Soko to tell him that he must rid himself of the debt if he wishes to live among them.

Soko cannot imagine how to do this, but Anansi has heard about Soko and his debt. Anansi comes to Soko and finds him making palm wine. Anansi wants the wine and tells Soko that getting rid of the debt is easy. All that Soko has to do is say, "Whoever drinks my palm wine will take the debt."

Soko says this and Anansi offers to drink the wine. By drinking the wine, Anansi drinks the debt as well. After

Anansi has drunk the wine, he plants his field and says that whoever eats the grain will take the debt.

A bird eats the grain and takes the debt. When the bird lays eggs, she says that whoever breaks her eggs will take the debt. A falling branch breaks the eggs and causes the tree to have the debt. The tree then says that whoever eats its blossoms will own the debt. A monkey eats the blossoms and takes the debt, and the monkey says that whoever eats him will in turn own the debt. When the monkey is devoured by a lion, the lion also says that whoever eats him will take the debt.

One day Soko is hunting and kills the lion. He returns to the village and shares the meat with all of the people. Because all the people eat, everyone owns the debt. This is the story of how the hunter, Soko, and the trickster hero, Anansi, brought debt to the kingdom of Ashanti.

THE DEBT WE OWE FOR LIFE

Soko is an interesting figure. He comes alone, an outsider, carrying a burden that appears to be uniquely his. The people that he comes to fear contamination from him. He must rid himself of the taint that he carries. But the story does not tell us what debt Soko owed or why he sought to evade it. Yet the debt is clearly not what we ordinarily think of as debt. If it were, Soko could simply change his mind and pay it. However, the unfolding of the tale reveals that this debt cannot be repaid.

In an apparent turn of good fortune, Soko is told by Anansi the way in which he can rid himself of debt. He need only say that whoever drinks his wine will inherit the debt. Anansi, being a spider, is a spinner, a weaver of human fate. While Anansi appears to offer a solution, what he really does is free this new force, this debt, to begin its circulation.

The debt quickly travels through all aspects of the world. Its first transfer is connected with palm wine, which may suggest that debt has its own intoxicating force. Having arrived with a hunter, the debt passes with grain and so is part of agriculture. It enters the realm of the animals when the bird eats the grain, and penetrates the nonagricultural realm of vegetation, the wild, when the bough breaks the egg. Soon it travels through the animal kingdom from monkey to lion and returns at last to humankind.

When the debt returns in the form of the lion's flesh that is devoured by all the villagers, we see that Soko could not permanently rid himself of the debt. The debt is far too powerful for that. The debt, in fact, is shared at a communal feast, which seems much like the love feasts that we discussed in chapter two. This communal feast would usually involve thanksgiving to the gods for the nourishment of the food. And the communal feast is part of the cycle of death and rebirth, whether the death of the animals whose bones are enfleshed again in the spirit world or the annual death of the vegetative world from which renewal comes with the new harvest.

If we understand the tale correctly, everything that is received from nature comes with debt. This debt is an aspect of the natural cycle of life and death. In the largest sense, the debt that we owe to nature is the debt for life itself. When we think, however fleetingly, of the miracle that we have life, we can experience a sense of gratitude for that very fact. But we are accustomed to this most profound debt and our daily lives leave little time for such contemplation, so for the most part we live unaware that such a debt exists.

If we owe a debt to nature for life, it can be repaid only by death, as we have seen in the many rituals in which sacrificial death is meant to fecundate new life. So we may wish to deny that we receive gifts from nature, and that we are indebted for these gifts. In fact, we might prefer to blame someone or something for this indebtedness. "How Debt Came to Ashanti" presents Soko as an outsider, a stranger, a defiler of the purity of the Ashanti. But Soko sounds like a scapegoat, a man singled out to carry the accumulated sins of a tribe into the wilderness. The tale claims that he came from another place, but what place?

If we have a powerful desire to avoid knowledge, nonetheless some inner force may make us seek for truth— even the truth that we might prefer to avoid. This seeking while desiring to avoid truth is an aspect of the collective mind as well. For the individual or the group, the truth that we feel most shameful about ourselves is the very one we often project on others. In Jungian psychology, this hidden truth, the truth that we do not know about ourselves, is called the shadow.

Soko appears to be the one chosen to carry the shadow of the village. He is called a stranger, but the power of debt resides in nature itself. Debt is not brought by Soko, but rather has been with the Ashanti from their first taking of nourishment and life from the world. Anansi, the trickster, is simply bringing to everyone's awareness what has always been true. Each time something is drunk or eaten or given, debt passes with it. Often this takes the life of the plant or animal consumed, but from this consumption life regenerates.

TIME AS MONEY (OR DEBT)

If we owe a debt for life, then we may be able to understand why the penalty for failure to pay debt was the deprivation of liberty. This imprisonment is a form of taking life, of taking the time of which a life is composed. We know the saying "Time is money," which means that time can be measured in terms of the amount of money that could be earned in a given period of time. Debt too can be measured in money. In fact, money is curiously like debt. Each of us offers something of ourselves for sale, our time and energy or some product that we create with that time and energy. It is almost as if we are indebted to those who have money, because money is a means of calling forth what we offer of value to the community. Through the measuring scale of money, time can equal debt.

Of course, the system of imprisonment for debt did not offer uniform justice. A person did not spend a month in jail for owing one dollar, two months in jail for owing two dollars, and so on. Many people made compacts with their creditors and never went to jail at all. Others fled or hid their assets. And of those who went to jail, some spent the rest of their lives imprisoned for a small debt, while others had friends or relatives who quickly paid their way to liberty.

No doubt the conscious rationale for debtors' prisons was the desire to punish harshly and thus prevent defaults. But if the unconscious rationale was that we are indebted for our very lives and, therefore, our time may be taken to repay debt, then we are really discussing two very different kinds of debt. One debt is existential—the debt we owe for our existence and the nourishment we are given by nature. This debt, if ever repaid, is repaid by our death. The other debts are the daily debts, usually measured by money.

We must distinguish between these debts. It is true that we can buy dinner with a credit card or, as John Dickens did in the 1820s, have an account with a local baker for the purchase of bread and pastries. However, the debt that we owe to the credit card company or the local merchant is obviously quite different from the debt that we owe to nature for our life and sustenance.

Looked at in this larger view, we see that the Bible in the book of Genesis suggests a debt very similar to that incurred by the Ashanti. On the sixth day God created humanity in the image of God, and gave to humanity dominion over the animals and the plants so that humanity might be nourished and multiply. God shaped "man of dust from the ground, and breathed into his nostrils the breath of life; and man became a living being." So we owe not only our life and the nourishment that we gain from plants and animals to God. We also owe God for our very image, that sense of selfhood that allows us to seek what is divine and attempt to live in harmony with it.

God placed humans in the Garden of Eden and sought to let them live unaware of their debt by forbidding them to eat of the tree of the knowledge of good and evil. But the serpent, a king of the underworld, the world of the unconscious, tempted the humans. The serpent said that eating of the tree of knowledge would make them like God. They would know good and evil as God did, but they would not die as God had said. So the serpent, like Anansi the trickster, brought to awareness an aspect of the human condition that had previously not been understood. Adam and Eve did not die physically after they ate the fruit, but they did die to what they had been before ingesting this knowledge. For the first time humans felt fear and anxiety over death. As God said to Adam, "You are dust, and to dust you shall return." Yet eating the forbidden fruit also allowed an awareness of the moral nature of humanity and the debt to the creator whose image we share.

RAPUNZEL

There is another story of eating forbidden fruit. Once upon a time a man and his wife yearned for many years to have a child. From their back window this couple could see over a high wall to a beautiful garden filled with flowers and vegetables. A fearsome witch owned this garden, but the wife conceived a desire for the beautiful rapunzel (a type of lettuce) that she could see growing there. As her craving grew, she began to pine away, for she knew that she could never eat what she desired.

When her husband asked what ailed her, his wife said that she would die unless she could eat the rapunzel. The husband thought to save his wife whatever the cost. So one night he stole into the garden and brought home some rapunzel. But as soon as his wife devoured this, her craving grew even greater.

Finally the husband returned to the garden for more of the rapunzel, but the witch loomed up before him and said she would punish him harshly for his theft. The man pleaded for mercy, explaining that he stole to satisfy his wife's craving.

This quieted the witch's anger. She offered the man as

much rapunzel as his wife desired, but on one condition: that the couple would give to the witch the child that would be born to them. The terrified man agreed.

Needless to say, his wife became pregnant. When she delivered their longed-for baby, the witch appeared to claim what was hers. Naming the girl Rapunzel, the witch carried her away. When Rapunzel was twelve and the most lovely girl alive, the witch locked her in a tower in the middle of a forest. The tower had no door and no stairs, but when the witch called from below Rapunzel would let her golden tresses of hair fall down from the window of her room atop the high tower. The witch would then climb up on this golden hair.

Several years passed. Rapunzel would often sing to ease her loneliness. One day a prince, passing near the tower, heard this beautiful singing and saw the witch climb up on the golden tresses to the tower. When the witch had gone, the prince called for Rapunzel to let down her hair, and he climbed to the tower. After overcoming her fright at her first view of a man, Rapunzel felt the prince would love her far better than the witch and agreed to marry him and travel away with him. She took his hand to seal their marriage, and soon became pregnant.

Unfortunately, before she could flee, Rapunzel naively asked the witch why she was heavier to pull up than the prince. The enraged witch cut off Rapunzel's hair and banished her to lonely misery in a far-off desert.

When the prince came to the tower, the witch let down Rapunzel's hair and pulled up the youth. Hearing the witch tell him that he would never see Rapunzel again, his grief overwhelmed him and he jumped from the tower. While the prince didn't die from his fall, his eyes were pierced by the thorns of brambles. Blinded and grieving for his lost wife, he lived in abject poverty and wandered in the forest.

One day, after several years of wandering, the prince heard a voice that he knew. He had come at last to where lonely Rapunzel lived with their infants, a boy and a girl. Recognizing and embracing him, Rapunzel wept, and her tears healed his eyes. When they reached the prince's kingdom, Rapunzel was received with joy, and they lived for many years with great happiness.

THE DEBTORS' PRISON AS A PLACE FOR GROWING AWARENESS

"Rapunzel," which comes from *Grimms' Fairy Tales*, reflects again how the child must often pay the price for the debts of the parent or the family tree. In the tale, the mother will die if she does not eat of the vegetative world which is symbolized by the rapunzel. By eating the rapunzel she seems to fill her stomach with a baby, whose origin in the vegetative world is confirmed when the witch names the baby Rapunzel. The mother owes a debt for the rapunzel, the lettuce which has not only saved her life but has also given her the life of a child. She must pay with Rapunzel; she must pay with her baby's life for the gift of fertility.

This would be bad enough. But this witch, who in her power to give and withhold vegetative wealth and life reminds us of Demeter, Cybele, and Chicomecohuatl, imprisons the girl in a tower that has no entry. This tower is the debtors' prison; here the daughter sacrifices her life for the debt of her mother. Yet the tower also suggests the ascent of the spirit, the upward rising of the material world toward that which is divine. In this tower, Rapunzel is imprisoned until, like Persephone, she comes in contact with the aspect of herself (symbolized by the prince) that is able to force a separation from the aspect of the mother (symbolized by the witch) that would never free the daughter to live her own life.

The tower's self-containment suggests that Rapunzel is undergoing a process of deepening her knowledge of her own feelings. Only her golden hair allows her contact with the outside world. Like the golden bough that Aeneas found in the green forest, this golden hair shows the wealth that is part of Rapunzel and awaits her discovery. While the journey to self-knowledge is painful, dry, and lonely, ultimately it is healing as well.

"Rapunzel" suggests that the debtors' prison may be a place for the painful evolution of self-knowledge. If we thought more often of this debt we owe for life, then we might have a better understanding of the daily issues of debt that we often face. We might examine whether being in debt on an existential level in any way predisposes us to enter into money debts as well. If we find ourselves locked in the debtors' tower, we might contemplate the value of this image of imprisonment. When we suffer from anxiety over money debts and the fear of bankruptcy, we lose the precious moments of our life as surely as if we are imprisoned. How can we use the upward thrust of this tower, its reaching toward spiritual heights, to understand which debts are truly ours? If we can confront ourselves, debt may be a challenge that offers us a deeper insight into our own nature.

A striking feature of "Rapunzel" is that the daughter pays for her mother's debt. This is reminiscent of our discussion of inheritance. It is almost as if the daughter has inherited a debt from the mother. In terms of inheritance laws, of course, if an estate has only debts and no assets, then the heirs receive nothing. They are not obligated to pay the debts; rather the creditors of the person who died lose whatever they were owed. As Shakespeare wrote in *The Tempest*, "He that dies pays all debts." However, Rapunzel paid dearly for the rapunzel that gave life to her and her mother.

HOW DEBT RESEMBLES INHERITANCE

There is an uncanny resemblance between debt and inheritance. For example, money received by borrowing feels much like money received by inheritance. We receive something for which we do not work; our present resources are increased and we are better off. Of course an inheritance does not have to be repaid, while debt does. But repayment is a future consideration; in the moment of receiving the money we are like heirs, richer than we were before.

William Thackeray, the contemporary of Charles Dickens, made the following observation about debt in *Vanity Fair*: "Everybody in Vanity Fair must have remarked how well those live who are comfortably and thoroughly in debt; how they deny themselves nothing; how jolly and easy they are in their minds." While Thackeray is satiric, he certainly captures the sense in which debtors may imagine themselves to be heirs—at least, until the time when the debt must be paid.

Even the story of John Dickens languishing in debtors'

prison shows the peculiar similarity between debt and inheritance. Dickens had been imprisoned in Marshalsea for a little over two months when his mother died at the age of seventy-nine. In her will she gave her son 450 pounds, more than enough to pay off all of Dickens's debts and let him and his family begin a new life. On May 28, John Dickens walked out of Marshalsea a free man, an heir and not a debtor. While John Dickens never returned to debtors' prison, his son Charles carried the burden of that experience for the rest of his life: "My whole nature was so penetrated with the grief and humiliation of such considerations, that even now, famous and caressed and happy, I often forget in my dreams that I have a dear wife and children; even that I am a man; and wander desolately back to that time of my life."

THE BRIDGE OF CH'ÜAN-CHOU

A folk tale from China, "The Bridge of Ch'üan-chou," may help us understand this curious connection between debt and inheritance. Many stories are told about this bridge, which was first built in the reign of Emperor Shen-tsung (998–1022). Before the building of the bridge, the cruel spirits that lived in the Loyang River tormented the people who crossed the river by boat. The building of the bridge required many miracles and the help of supernatural workers.

Our story is not about the building of the bridge, but about its rebuilding more than seven hundred years later. In the reign of Emperor Ch'ien-lung (1736–96), there lived a free-spending youth, Li Wu, who was the fifth son and whose name meant fifth. Although the young man spent freely, he did not work hard and so he was often in debt. All the shopkeepers feared to sell him anything, except for the butcher, who was always willing to take a note from Li Wu. This butcher actually told Li Wu to buy as much as he wanted and never pressured Li Wu to pay the many notes that he had given for his debts.

At last even Li Wu became curious about the butcher's behavior. After paying for a purchase of meat, he hid outside the shop and then followed the butcher to a hilltop shrine dedicated to the earth deity. Moving aside some grass, the butcher put Li Wu's note into a grave and brought out of the grave a piece of silver. When Li Wu looked in the grave, he saw many pots of silver, one of which was only half full but also contained all of the notes that the butcher had accepted from Li Wu.

Suddenly the earth spirit spoke, saying that all of this silver belonged to Li Wu. The spirit had guarded these riches, but now could surrender its post because the owner of the silver had come. So the butcher's generous offering of credit to Li Wu had been based on the butcher's knowledge of how to convert the notes into the silver of this secret treasure.

Li Wu was now a rich man, and soon he had a strange visitor named K'ang Chin-lung, who claimed the ability to find buried wealth. K'ang came to evaluate the character of Li Wu who, having himself changed to a better man, treated K'ang excellently. He even gave his guest golden bowls in which to bathe his face each day and, when K'ang threw these bowls into the lotus pond, Li Wu made no complaint. After several months, K'ang left without any farewell.

The next chapter of Li Wu's life was not so pleasant. He

had once insulted a man, who now falsely accused him of being a bandit. How else could Li Wu have obtained such wealth? All of his riches were confiscated and he was taken to the court of the emperor to be put on trial for his life. In chains, he crossed the bridge over the Loyang River. Seeing that the high tides caused the water to come over the bridge, he swore to raise the bridge three feet if his life were spared.

As the guards and Li Wu neared the emperor's court, Li Wu saw vast expanses of fields with his name as the owner. Inquiries brought word that K'ang had purchased these fields for Li Wu. At the court, K'ang made a golden shell within which he placed a living snail. Li Wu gave this miraculous gift to the empress, who persuaded the emperor to let Li Wu go free. Then Li Wu took the golden bowls that K'ang had thrown into the lotus pond, and managed the fields that K'ang had bought for him, and became so rich that he kept his vow to add three feet in height to the bridge over the Loyang River.

THE DEBTOR'S JOURNEY TO UNDERSTANDING

This tale directly connects the debtor to the heir. Li Wu thinks that he is a debtor, a view shared by everyone except the butcher. However, Li Wu is, in fact, an heir, not a debtor. A spirit guards his inheritance, the silver that comes to him from the grave. Like Mercurius, the spirit has waited a long while to give this treasure to its owner and, once its task is done, the spirit is at last free to abandon its post.

Whose spirit is this? Why does it guard an inheritance that belongs to Li Wu? This spirit may be an aspect of Li Wu that he has not yet discovered. In a sense, this spirit holds Li Wu's future. Curiosity, the same curiosity that took the woodcutter's son deeper into the forest, makes Li Wu follow the butcher up to the hilltop shrine. On this high and sacred place, Li Wu encounters what is truly his, his silver treasure.

This tale suggests how our existential debt and our daily debts meet one another. The silver from the grave is something that Li Wu owns but is unaware of. This treasure is guarded by the earth deity, which is the source of life itself. Not just the silver, but everything—life and nourishment—springs from the earth.

But every debt that we incur also gives us an asset. Our existential debt, not being measured by money, may leave us in doubt as to the extent and nature of the asset we have received. In the last chapter we discussed the underworld descent that the heir must make to learn the deeper meaning of his or her inheritance. Debt, too, requires a journey to learn the nature of the assets we have received, assets that may require a lifetime of self-exploration to discover their true worth.

For each of us this process of discovery is unique. Some may discover that money debt is not for them; perhaps their inner richness will not yield large sums of money to repay debt. Others will see that debt is appropriate for them, because the richness of their nature will bring the money that will repay borrowing. Li Wu had the earth spirit and, later, K'ang to protect the wealth of which Li Wu was unaware. In the case of Li Wu, the wealth of his nature was such that it yielded a wealth of money and valuables in the world.

It is easy to see the negative aspects of debt, the oppressive and strangling effect that debt can have on life, but debt is not one-sided. Like inheritance, debt yields us an asset. With existential debt, the asset is our very life. With daily debt, the asset is the increased energy that money allows us in the world. The tale of Li Wu may even be read to suggest that we will be able to pay our daily debts of money if we gain a sufficient understanding of our own nature. Or, if we have this understanding, we will not incur money debts that conflict with our actual capacities to earn money in the world.

Contrasting debt and inheritance may help us understand this process. The reason that we do not have to pay for an inheritance is because it comes from the past. It is given to us by the generation (or generations) that have come before us. Where, then, does money debt come from? Let us imagine that it comes not from a bank or lender but from the future. When we take a debt, we are making a statement about our capacity to earn money in the future. We are saying what we will become. In a way, we are speculating about the unfolding of our own nature. The debt of Li Wu reflected the potential that he would discover, a potential known to the earth spirit and the butcher long before Li Wu discovered his silver from the grave.

This is why no simple rule can govern whether we should enter into debt. If we understand our capacities to be productive, taking on a debt may be a way to increase what we are able to produce far beyond what would have been possible without the debt. Debt allows us to take the frozen wealth of the underworld and make it circulate in the green, sunlit world where we live our lives.

The danger is that we may fail to understand ourselves

and our situation. We may borrow against our future time and energy and find that, in fact, we did not increase our productivity and face bankruptcy. As an heir must be self-examining to make a wise use of inherited money, so we can use the possibility of indebtedness as part of the process by which we seek who we truly are. But when considering debt, we should keep before us the image of the tower without entry, the image of the debtors' prison. Debt places our very freedom at risk; Anansi brought it to humankind like Prometheus brought fire. It can be both beneficial and terribly destructive. It must be handled like fire, like the elemental force that it is.

We can return now to Solomon's warnings with a far better understanding of his concerns. Solomon warns against becoming a surety for a neighbor or giving a pledge for a stranger. Both situations make one person a guarantor for the debt of another person. The problem with this is exactly as Solomon describes it: ". . . you have come into your neighbor's power." The burden of debt is onerous enough if we carry it for ourselves, but at least we may incur such a debt because we believe that our inner nature will unfold in a way that brings money sufficient to pay this debt. But if we become the guarantor for the debt of another, we are speculating about their inner wealth and the future form of its unfoldment in the world. To risk our freedom for this hardly seems wise. If we wish to help someone else, it might be far better to give a gift that we know we can afford than to guarantee debt that we hope we will never have to pay.

The confluence of existential debt and money debt suggests why the amassing of vast fortunes reflects a hidden wish for immortality. We spoke earlier of The Fountain of Youth which, in the minds of the Conquistadors, poured forth its waters in the land of limitless gold (El Dorado). Yet human life is the encountering of limits. We do not possess limitless wealth, limitless strength, limitless life. Even the Pharaohs died, despite having the power to force slaves and followers to die with them in order to serve as company for the death journey. One of the richest of the Romans, Crassus, saw his son's severed head flourished on a spike by the Parthian cavalry and soon thereafter lost his life and his head as well. Every day in the obituaries we read of people whose vast wealth could not insulate them from the existential debt that we must pay with our lives.

Viewed from this perspective, we see another facet of inheritance. The heir views inheritance as the receiving of an asset, but the person who dies gives up all assets. Whether these assets are great or small, the surrender of them—with life—pays all debts in full. The ineffable yearning for immortality vanishes with the wealth that failed to make us superhuman. So death alone brings an egalitarian redistribution by taking all from rich and poor alike. But what if we could avoid this debt to life? What if we could live forever?

ALCESTIS

This is the subject of the play *Alcestis* by Euripides. The god Apollo had a dispute with his father, Zeus. Because he angered his father, Zeus ordered him to serve a mortal— King Admetus of Pherae in Thessaly. Surprisingly enough, Apollo found that he loved Admetus for being a just and immensely hospitable man. Wanting to give a boon to his host, he persuaded the Fates to allow Admetus in his hour of dying to send someone in his place to the underworld. If someone would volunteer to die in Admetus's place, then he could go on living. He would not have to pay a debt for his life but could actually live the fantastic dream of being immortal.

Unfortunately for Admetus, no one is eager to die in his place, not even his old father. The only one willing to die for him is his young wife, Alcestis, whom he loves deeply. While a modern feminist would hardly approve of Alcestis sacrificing herself for her husband, Alcestis acts from love and for the honor of wifehood. In any case, once Alcestis has pledged herself before the gods, no one, not even Admetus, can save her. Yet as time passes, Admetus finds that he loves her more and more; he cannot imagine living without her. The thought of her death brings daily grief to him, but he cannot change her fate.

This is all background to the play, which begins on the actual day that Alcestis is to die. The play opens with Apollo confronting Death (who appears as a character) and pleading for the life of Alcestis, but Death refuses to let her live. Soon we see Alcestis in her death scene telling her husband how she ". . . would not live on, torn away from thee." She says that she can never be fully paid back for giving up her life, "For naught there is more precious than life," but asks that Admetus not remarry so their children will be saved from the hatred of a stepmother. Grief-stricken, Admetus assures her that he will never remarry, ". . . dead, mine only wife/Shalt thou be called . . ." When Alcestis has died, the Chorus sings to Admetus, "From us, from all, this debt is due—to die."

In the midst of Admetus's grief, a traveler comes to his door. This traveler is none other than the hero Herakles (called Hercules by the Romans), who is renowned for his prodigious feats of strength and daring. Mothered by a mortal woman but fathered by Zeus, the king of the gods, Herakles is half-man and half-god. His own father, Zeus, has decreed that hospitality must always be shown to travelers. This hospitality is to the larger world what the love feast was to the tribe in its village. As people travel for trade and pilgrimage, they more and more frequently encounter strangers. How are these strangers to be treated? Zeus's edict to offer hospitality is a command to share both shelter and food. In this god-sanctified sharing resides the same love and thanksgiving for nature's bounty that animates the sharing of food in the love feast.

Admetus is abundantly hospitable. Despite his grief for Alcestis, Admetus lies and says the mourning is merely for a servant so that Herakles will stay in his home. A servant tells Herakles the truth about who has died. Herakles vows to "save the woman newly dead" and repay his host, who was so hospitable even in bereavement. While Herakles goes to save Alcestis, Admetus continues his inconsolable grieving. Then Herakles returns, leading a woman who is silent and wholly hidden in veils. When she is at last revealed, the woman is Alcestis. Herakles tells how he ambushed Death and tore Alcestis from Death's arms. So Admetus and Alcestis are reunited.

LIMITLESS, LIKE A GOD

Admetus is a fascinating man because he has little sense of limitation. He is both unreasonably demanding and unreasonably generous. The expectation that anyone should die in his place, including his father, is shocking. Why should his father give up his life so Admetus can live longer? Admetus is no god to whom the living are sacrificed. Whatever his relationship with Apollo (in some versions of the myth they are lovers), the gift from the god makes Admetus forget his own nature. He loses touch with his human life, with his understanding of the needs of others. And, as with so many magical wishes, the reality of immortality includes a striking disadvantage: to outlive all those we love.

On the positive side of the ledger, Admetus is the most generous of hosts. Here, too, he lacks a sense of limitation. It does not matter if he is mourning for his wife; he is willing to lie in order to make certain that Herakles will receive the hospitality decreed by Zeus. Certainly Admetus recognizes the debt implied in the love feast, that nature's bounty belongs to all of us and must be shared. This generosity gained him Apollo's boon in the first place and, at the play's end, moves Herakles to restore Alcestis to him.

In Admetus we see the warring impulses aroused by our existential debt. On the one hand, we want to deny the debt. We do not want to die. We long to be what physically we cannot be—immortal. From this perspective, immortality is a condition of debtlessness. This refusal to accept limits leads to selfishness, whether revealed in the belief that a father should die in place of a son or in the hoarding of wealth as if its energy might ward off death.

On the other hand, an awareness of our existential debt may lead us to be self-sacrificing, to be selfless. In the Bible, Paul shows his understanding of this when he writes, "Owe no one anything, except to love one another." If we feel the debt that we owe for life, we are immediately brought closer to all humanity. We are all debtors—both those who give and those who receive. In an economy based on money, we may wish to honor the spirit of the love feast by making our money circulate in a way that will alleviate suffering and work toward human betterment.

If the world of Admetus seems remote, fictional, or archaic to us, we can easily find contemporary parallels. For example, the enormous debt of the federal government is shifting wealth between generations. Projections suggest that future taxpayers will pay a far higher proportion of their earnings in taxes than today's taxpayers, who benefit from the increased debt because their taxes are lower. If this is true, the generation that incurs the debt is taking the life energy of subsequent generations, just as Admetus was willing to take the life energy of his young wife. Another example would be the rationing of life-saving drugs and operations that any reform of the health care system is likely to require. Since the wealthy will be able to go outside such a system and buy whatever medical services they need, like Admetus they will gain greater life expectancies compared to those who must accept the limitations of rationing. In fact, there is actually an illicit trade in body organs, such as kidneys, which are sold by people in poorer countries for transplant to people in richer countries who seek longer life. On the other hand, there are also altruistic people who donate body organs because they desire to help others. In this, they are certainly like Alcestis. Such acts of altruism are closely scrutinized by medical centers to be certain that coercion, however subtle, has not influenced the decision to give the organ.

To see how Admetus lives in each of us, can we think of a real person so hospitable that no guest would ever be turned away from his or her door? Someone who would give even if impoverished by doing so? Or, in contrast, someone who yearns to have more and more life, even if it means taking from others? And what would the taking of "life" from others mean? How could this be done? If we found someone like Admetus, vastly willing both to be hospitable and to take the life energy of others, we might find a mirror that would allow us to see ourselves ever more clearly.

DEBT TORMENTS EVEN THE GREAT

When we think of those whose accomplishments are great, we seldom think of debt. Yet, while John Dickens languished in debtors' prison, a revered American found his old age blighted by worry over debt. The man who proposed adopting the dollar and decimal system for American currency—inventor, architect, farmer, author of the Declaration of Independence, and president of the United States—Thomas Jefferson's abilities and accomplishments enriched his country and left a legacy to humanity.

Despite this legacy, Jefferson suffered great anxieties because of his money debts. While he appeared to be wealthy from several inheritances of land and slaves, in fact these inheritances included much that was mortgaged. These debts only worsened as his public career took him to France and, later, to Washington. In 1787, at the age of forty-four, Jefferson wrote from Paris to confide in a friend that "the torment of mind I endure till the moment shall arrive when I shall owe not a shilling on earth is such really as to render life of little value." But that debt-free moment never arrived; in fact, Jefferson's old age was filled with worry over debt.

Notwithstanding his debts, Jefferson showed unusual generosity throughout his life. In the public sphere he gave unstintingly of his time and energy even while he felt the allure of a more private life. "The whole of my life has been a war with my natural taste, feelings and wishes; domestic life and literary pursuits were my first and my latest inclinations. . . . The circumstances of our country, at my entrance into life, were such that every honest man felt himself compelled to take part, and to act to the best of his abilities."

In his private life he honored the rituals of hospitality. Not only invited guests and friends, of which there were many, but strangers, too, could rely on being fed and sheltered at Monticello. When his daughter Martha complained that the constant company left Jefferson no time to be sociable with her, he replied, "The manner and usages of our country are laws we cannot repeal." So he lived by laws much like those decreed thousands of years earlier by Zeus.

Jefferson kept meticulous account of his day-to-day spending, yet seemed unwilling to keep closely in mind his overall position. After serving two terms as president, he discovered on leaving office in 1809 that he owed $10,000 more than he had thought. This is a significant sum today, but a huge amount at that time. In 1814, Jefferson told his grandson that "if he [Jefferson] lived long enough he would beggar his family, that the number of persons he was compelled to entertain would devour his estate." Yet he did not change his course, bound as he was by the laws of hospitality and his own pleasure in company. Even as Jefferson entertained, Monticello fell into disrepair. To take a small example, visitors sat on handsome chairs with leather bottoms, but the bottoms had worn through so that the hair stuffing the seats stuck out in all directions.

Jefferson's finances suffered from fluctuations in the agriculture markets and tight money which made his lands difficult to sell at a good price, but he also acted more from friendship than prudence. In 1818, he signed as a personal guarantor for a $20,000 loan that a close friend, William Cary Nicholas, was seeking. In doing this, Jefferson ignored Solomon's warning not to become the guarantor of the debt of another. Jefferson delivered himself into his "neighbor's power." Nicholas, who was thought to have a net worth of $300,000, declared bankruptcy in 1819.

Jefferson called this the "coup de grâce," for now he could never hope to be free of debt. As he approached and passed the age of eighty (in 1823), he worried that he and his daughter and grandchildren might be turned out of Monticello and have no means of support. "For myself," Jefferson wrote to his grandson, "I should not regard a prostration of fortune, but I am overwhelmed at the prospect of the situation in which I may leave my family." The possibility of the family's impoverishment held up to Jefferson "nothing but future gloom," and, except for his concern for them, he felt he would "not care were life to end with the line I am writing."

The depressed market closed off the avenue of land sales to pay debt. Instead, Jefferson conceived of the idea of a lottery to raise money. Such a lottery, in which the winner would receive land, required the approval of the state legislature. When the lottery bill passed in February, 1826, the news of Jefferson's plight traveled across the nation. In the North and the South, citizens rallied and raised funds to ensure that the patriot who had done so much for his country would not be impoverished at the end of his life. New York City collected $8,500; Baltimore $3,000; Philadelphia $5,000; and the citizenry of other cities contributed as well. So, like the sharing of food in the love feast, Jefferson's generosity was met by the generosity of the citizens whom he had served so many years.

Jefferson's health declined sharply in May of 1826, but he hoped to live until July Fourth, the fiftieth anniversary of the signing of the Declaration of Independence. As he drifted toward death, he believed that the subscriptions from the various cities had solved his struggle with debt and saved Monticello for his daughter and grandchildren. On July 2, he lapsed into a coma, but regained consciousness several times to ask if July Fourth had come. On the evening of July 3, he asked for the last time, "Is it the Fourth?" to which his doctor replied, "It soon will be." With this answer Jefferson slipped again into unconsciousness and died at approximately one o'clock the next day—July 4, 1826.

The very date of Jefferson's death emphasized the legacy of his life—the hospitality of his nature not only as a host at Monticello but as a man who gave so much of himself in service to the nation for which he had drafted the Declaration of Independence. Yet Jefferson also took what was not his. His deathbed belief that the subscriptions of money would pay his debts proved to be in error. In fact, his debts at his death amounted to more than $100,000, an enormous sum. His daughter and grandchildren had to give up Monticello, which remained empty several years before finally being sold for $7,500.

The $100,000 owed by Jefferson came from the life energy of others; it belonged to them. Like Admetus's desire for the life energy of his father, Jefferson added to his energies by the sacrifice forced on his creditors. His remarkable life, already benefited by inheritances, gained in vitality from the spending of the money represented by these unpaid debts. The debts dwarfed the value of Monticello and Jefferson's other assets.

There is another way in which Jefferson took life energy that was not his. The rituals of hospitality, a system that Jefferson accepted as law, rested on the foundation of slavery. Slaves in the fields produced the food to feed the guests; slaves in the household saw to the preparation of meals, the housekeeping, and the laundry. Without such unpaid labor, Jefferson would have found it far more expensive and perhaps impracticable to honor the law of hospitality.

Nor was Jefferson unaware of this taking of the lives of his slaves. He had penned the Declaration of Independence, including the famous opening sentence: "We hold these truths to be self-evident, that all men are created equal; that they are endowed by their Creator with certain inalienable rights; that among these, are life, liberty, and the pursuit of happiness." In fact, Jefferson abhorred slavery, yet owned slaves. In his *Notes on Virginia*, published in 1785, he indicted the slave system: "And can the liberties of a nation be thought secure when we have removed their only firm basis, a conviction in the minds of the people that these liberties are the gift of God? . . . Indeed I tremble for my country when I reflect that God is just."

So Jefferson took what he believed to be the gift of God, liberty, from the slaves who served him. To say this is to see how the best and most abundant of us can live with compromise and moral ambiguity. Slavery, which Jefferson believed to be unjust, and debt, which caused Jefferson immense personal anguish, both allowed him to sustain a life greater than he might otherwise have lived. Rather than condemn Jefferson for this, we might better seek to understand how each of us may (like Admetus) demand the life energy of others or (like Alcestis) surrender to others the life energy which is ours.

THE INCALCULABLE DEBT

The image of the debtors' prison forges a symbolic connection between debt and freedom. Today that symbol of the imprisoning power of debt has vanished, so the imprisonment of debt is more elusive and harder to understand. We must exercise our imaginations if we are to comprehend the image of the debtors' tower. We must cross the boundary from our day-to-day world and enter the life of the unconscious, where credit cards buy nothing and existential debt is the gift and burden of our birth. In this way, our relationship to debt, and to money, has the potential to become a creative relationship, an expression of our inner nature formed from the same inspiration that breathes life into poetry and art.

C. G. Jung wrote of the play of fantasy that precedes any creative work. "Without this playing with fantasy no creative work has ever yet come to birth. The debt we owe to the play of imagination is incalculable." This incalculable debt allows us to seek the depths of our own nature. In this play of the imagination is the opportunity to bring to awareness what is unrevealed and hidden in ourselves. Fantasy allows the conscious and unconscious worlds to meet. It allows the prisoner to realize that the imprisoning tower soars upward toward the life of the spirit. It allows each of us to measure our money debts as merely one aspect of the far greater debt that we owe for life. And the exploration of debt, whether owed for money or for life, may reveal assets as unimaginable to us as the silver guarded by the faithful earth spirit was unimaginable to the spendthrift youth named Li Wu.

CHAPTER EIGHT

CHANGING SYMBOLS

Money, Credit Cards, and Banks

ONCE UPON A TIME a merchant carved a wooden statue of Mercury and offered it for sale in the market. But no matter how he touted the beauty of the statue, no one wanted to purchase it. So he changed his tack and started crying out, "A god for sale! A god for sale! One who will bring you good fortune and keep you lucky!" Finally someone asked why, if Mercury brings such good fortune, the merchant does not keep the statue and the good fortune that will go with it. "I'll tell you why," answered the merchant. "It is true that he brings gain, but he takes his time about it; whereas I want money at once."

Titled "The Image-Seller," this story from *Aesop's Fables* implies that the merchant is a charlatan whose puffery about his statue far exceeds the truth. If the statue could really do what the merchant promises, why wouldn't he wait and enjoy good fortune over time? In fact, he imagines good fortune only in terms of money. He does not think of what money symbolizes, such as life energy and the sharing of productivity within the community. Perhaps the merchant would do far better to meditate before his carved statue. As time passed, he might gain a deeper understanding of the creative process by which he created the statue, the value of finding images like Mercury that may connect us to our inner richness, and the role of money as a symbol and tool rather than a goal.

Yet the merchant's attitude is, in many ways, quite contemporary. The desire to have "money at once" is reflected in many aspects of the world in which we live: the heavy burden of consumer debt, governments that run deficits year after year, and bankruptcies of individuals and businesses at levels that would have been unimaginable only a short while ago. We are all aware of the magnitude of the federal government's debt. But when we realize that individual debt (including consumer and mortgage debt) as a percentage of annual disposable income has increased in the United States from about thirty-five percent in 1950 to more than eighty percent today, we may wonder at the effect of such a burden on our day-to-day lives.

To understand why we have become so accustomed to debt, we have to appreciate the ways in which the symbols around us have changed. For example, although the nature of the images on our money have remained much the same throughout the twentieth century, our money has changed profoundly. Our currency is no longer backed by the precious metals of gold and silver but has become simply paper. Beyond this, the symbolism of money now faces a competing symbolism from credit cards, which are such a ubiquitous tool of our consumer-oriented economy. The advertising for credit cards, not to mention the way in which the debt may not have to be repaid immediately, encourage us to believe that the cards are magical and in essence create "money at once." Credit card debt is a significant contributing factor in the unprecedented number of bankruptcies. Finally, the banks themselves have changed both their relationship to the community and the symbolism of their architecture. In 1900, hardly any bank would lend to a consumer, while today bank profits from credit cards are a crucial component of the overall profitability and survival of the banks.

These changing symbols and new relationships are like pieces of a jigsaw puzzle. This chapter seeks to fit together these pieces so that we can have a better understanding of how each of us, and our society, are affected by the desire for "money at once." This is not to say that we face catastrophe, but it is at least an acknowledgement of new realities with respect to money. We cannot use money as a lens to search within ourselves if we do not understand its changing nature in the world outside us.

THE TRANSFORMATION OF MONEY

In an earlier chapter we discussed the extraordinary battle waged by William Jennings Bryan to make silver a monetary metal as well as gold. His Cross of Gold speech made explicit the profound symbolic power of gold. While he triumphed over President Grover Cleveland to win the nomination of the Democratic party, he was soundly beaten by Republican William McKinley in both the 1896 and 1900 presidential elections.

The Republicans inaugurated the new century by enacting the Gold Standard Act of 1900. Key among its provisions was the confirmation of gold as the primary monetary metal and its enshrinement as the standard of value. The Act provided, "That the dollar consisting of twenty-five and eight-tenths grains of gold nine-tenths fine ... shall be the standard unit of value, and all forms of money issued or coined by the United States shall be maintained at a parity of value with this standard." Silver was not eliminated as a monetary metal, but its main use was for small bills (ten dollars and less) and coins. All paper money, including greenbacks, could be redeemed for gold at the Treasury. The Treasury could only issue gold or silver certificates up to the amount of gold and silver held as trust funds in its vaults.

Quite simply, paper money symbolized a certain amount of gold or silver held on deposit in the Treasury and available for exchange. So a twenty-dollar bill might state, "This certifies that there have been deposited in the Treasury of the United States of America twenty dollars in gold coin payable to the bearer on demand," while a five-dollar bill would refer to "five silver dollars payable to the bearer on demand." These bills were called "gold certificates" and "silver certificates."

However, if we look at our paper money today, we find no mention of silver or gold. Rather, we carry and spend Federal Reserve Notes. A financial panic in 1907, marked by a lack of adequate credit for businesses, strengthened the sense that a mechanism was needed to make the money supply more elastic. This mechanism was the Federal Reserve System, which created a network of Federal Reserve banks authorized to issue Federal Reserve Notes. Without delving into the technicalities of this system, it allowed liquid assets of the banks (such as commercial paper acquired from businesses) to be used as reserves against which the banks could issue Federal Reserve Notes. While the Federal Reserve Act of 1913 required that part of this reserve be in the form of gold, new banking laws introduced by President Roosevelt to counter the Depression eliminated any gold backing for the dollar and actually made it illegal for United States citizens to use or hold gold coins. It is extraordinary that thirty-three years after enactment of the Gold Standard Act of 1900, gold should not only have gone out of circulation, but United States citizens would also be forbidden by law from hoarding gold or using gold as money.

Gold continued to be used as a reserve in international monetary dealings, although gold did not flow from country to country as the classical economists of the nineteenth century believed necessary to keep international trade in balance. After World War Two, the United States dollar served as the international currency, the trusted standard of value. Yet as more and more dollars circulated throughout the world, aiding economies struggling to rebuild from the war, the gold reserves held by the United States became inadequate to pay for the dollars in circulation at the official exchange rate of thirty-five dollars per ounce of gold. On August 15, 1971, President Nixon suspended payments of gold for dollars held by foreign central banks. The price of gold was no longer defended at thirty-five dollars per ounce. By 1979, gold had risen to $450 per ounce and today fluctuates around $400 per ounce.

Not only had gold vanished first from our hands and eventually from international exchange, but silver also vanished from circulation. In the 1960s, as the silver content in our coins became worth more than the face value of the coins, people began to hoard these coins. In 1965, the right to exchange silver certificates for silver at the offices of the United States Treasury was suspended.

In addition, the silver content of coins was sharply reduced or eliminated. The quarter with the bust of George

Washington, for example, had been made of ninety percent silver and ten percent copper from 1932 through 1964. Starting in 1965, the composition of the quarter changed to seventy-five percent copper and twenty-five percent nickel. These new coins were neither as valuable nor as beautiful as silver coins. Following Gresham's law, the less valuable coins immediately drove the more valuable coins out of circulation. Why pay with a quarter that might have a silver content worth more than twenty-five cents, when payment could just as well be made with a quarter made of metal worth far less than twenty-five cents? So not only gold, but silver too, ceased to have a role as money.

Certainly gold and silver are metals prized by people since the earliest times. Their beauty and usefulness for ornamentation gave them value long before market economies used them for purposes of exchange. In abandoning both gold and silver as the metallic backing for our currency, we have given up metals with deep symbolic meaning. Of course, part of the trust placed in such metals was based on their scarcity. The difficulty of locating and mining the metals made sudden increases in supply unlikely. However, the symbolic power of gold and silver also made people trust in their value.

Gold symbolizes the light of the sun, the powerful radiance of divine intelligence. So gold represents what is most superior and conveys this quality to objects in the material world. The golden crown of kings suggests divine power and illumination, while golden money implies a divine superiority. Silver, too, is superior, symbolizing the radiance of the moon, brightness, purity, innocence, chastity, and even eloquence.

There is a symbolic tension between these two metals, gold being equated with the sun and the masculine while silver is equated with the moon and the feminine. This may partly explain the ferocity of the battle between supporters of a gold standard and supporters of a bimetallic standard. For example, after silver supporters passed a bill in 1878 that required the United States Treasury to purchase a certain amount of silver each year for conversion into silver dollars, President Rutherford Hayes showed the depth of his belief in gold by vetoing the bill as a "violation of sacred obligations." Certainly, when William Jennings Bryan addressed the complex issue of whether currency should be backed by gold alone or also by silver, an unseen aspect of the debate was the profound and ancient symbolic content of these two metals. We cannot value this symbolic content in dollars, francs, or yen; but we must realize that our money today is backed by neither gold nor silver. Its value is based totally on the productive abilities and assets that we possess individually and as a society.

Not only has the symbolic nature of our money changed, but its size has also been altered. On July 10, 1929, the dimensions of our paper money were reduced from 7⅜ by 3⅛ inches to 6 3⁄16 by 2⅝ inches. The larger bills had been issued since 1861, but the government sought to economize on paper costs, and scholars of money refer to our present paper currency as small-size notes. It is curious that this shrinking of the paper money came so close in time to the Depression with its shrinking of the productivity of the economy. More immediately to the point, however, is that as we use money we almost never think that it has changed: that the bills are no longer gold and silver certificates but rather Federal Reserve Notes, that the size of the bills has been reduced, and that our coins are no longer made largely of silver.

WHY USING CREDIT CARDS IS NOT THE SAME AS SPENDING MONEY

Even though our money is no longer backed by precious and beautiful metals such as gold and silver, we continue to be affected by its symbolic power. Without even knowing why, most people are more reluctant to spend cash than to use credit cards. To pay with cash still symbolizes the sacrifice of life energy, while credit cards play off the possibility that the debt incurred may never have to be paid.

Today the credit card is ever-present. In the United States, there are more than one billion credit cards. More than seventy-five percent of American households have either Visa or MasterCard or both, not to mention cards from American Express, Diners Club, oil companies, and retail stores. Without a credit card, some of the activities that we take for granted, such as renting a car or reserving tickets, become extremely difficult or even impossible. The advertising for credit cards presents images of acceptance, pleasure, and success. American Express emphasized prestige value with the phrase "Membership Has Its Privileges." Visa sought exotic locales where American Express cards weren't accepted and claimed: "Visa. It's Everywhere You Want to Be." And MasterCard championed people who "Master the Moment," as if the credit card itself might be the key to living life to the fullest.

The credit card is a recent invention, first conceived of in the Utopian novel *Looking Backward 2000–1887* by Edward Bellamy. Published in 1888, this novel devotes itself to describing the ideal social system that exists in the year 2000. Julian West, the hero of the novel, falls asleep in 1887 and wakes in the year 2000 in a Boston which is strikingly different from the city in which he went to sleep. As he converses with his host, Dr. Leete, Julian hears of a city, and a world, in which money is no longer used.

Dr. Leete explains, "But as soon as the nation became the sole producer of all sorts of commodities, there was no need of exchanges between individuals that they might get what they required. Everything was procurable from one source, and nothing could be procured from any- where else. A system of direct distribution from the na- tional storehouses took the place of trade, and for this money was unnecessary."

Dr. Leete then shows Julian a credit card, which is a "piece of pasteboard," and tells Julian that the card "is is- sued for a certain number of dollars. We have kept the old word, but not the substance. The term, as we use it, an- swers to no real thing, but merely serves as an algebraic symbol for comparing the values of products with one an- other."

This piece of pasteboard is the first description of a de- vice that did not exist in 1888 when Edward Bellamy wrote his novel. Some hotels began issuing credit cards to their most prestigious customers as early as 1900 and in 1914 department stores and chains of gasoline stations followed suit. Beginning in 1947, railroad and airline com- panies also offered credit cards. However, the key to the modern growth of credit cards was the "new" kind of credit card introduced by Diners Club in 1950.

Instead of using the credit card to sell more of its own goods (as had the department stores and other retailers), Diners Club acted as an intermediary. A cardholder might purchase a meal in a variety of restaurants that accepted the card; Diners Club would then pay the restaurant and collect the balance from the cardholder. The next year, in 1951, the first bank credit card was introduced by the Franklin National Bank. Such bank credit cards, now the most popular cards in use, can be used to purchase an endless variety of goods and services.

So credit card has come to have a different meaning than Bellamy imagined when he created the phrase. Today a credit card is a card that allows the user to pay for goods or services without having any money in an account (as Bellamy's card would have required). In effect, the credit card user borrows money. This is allowed because the company issuing the credit card is relying on the creditworthiness of the cardholder. When the bill comes, the cardholder can pay and extinguish the debt.

In fact, each transaction using a bank card involves five parties: the merchant, the customer, the merchant's bank, the credit card company (such as Visa or MasterCard), and the customer's bank. The merchant has the benefit of consumers who buy more than if they had to pay cash. The customer has the advantage of the card's convenience. The merchant's bank earns a fee which is several percentage points of the total purchase. Both the credit card company and the customer's bank share in the fee paid to the merchant's bank. In addition, the customer's bank, which issued the credit card, charges the cardholder an annual fee that may be in the range of twenty to thirty-five dollars and charges interest on amounts that the cardholder does not pay on time. Such interest income accounts for more than seventy-five percent of all credit card revenue earned by banks.

These charges have made credit cards a source of great profits for the banks. In 1989, net profits from bank credit card operations reached $4.11 billion, twenty-six percent of the total bank profits of $15.73 billion for that year. While credit card profits fell in the ensuing recession as consumers purchased less and paid down credit card balances, credit card operations remain a crucial foundation for bank profits. After the debacles of nonperforming loans to real estate developers at home and to underdeveloped nations abroad that closed the 1980s, the banks in the 1990s will continue to be relentless in their pursuit of credit card customers.

We can understand why banks want consumers to have credit cards, but why are consumers so willing to turn a profit for the banks? Beyond the convenience factor, and perhaps the need to borrow money in order to make purchases, is a more intangible sense of wealth that credit cards can give, a magical feeling of expansiveness and power. It brings the world under our control. As American Express repeatedly tells us, "Don't Leave Home Without It." By carrying a card, we make our homes portable; we ensure that strangers will treat us like family and shower us with gifts and favors. They will honor the laws of Zeus that command hospitality be given to strangers. No doubt the ancient warrior pictured on each American Express card is there to reassure us that we are safe, heroic, even noble as we use our cards.

Underneath that sense of magical power is, once again, the elusive promise of immortality, eternal youth, limitlessness. It is no accident that the American Express cards are green or gold. Green, of course, is the color of the vegetative world that is constantly in its cycles of death and rebirth. The greenness of the cards may even suggest that the money we spend by using the card will inevitably replenish itself like vegetation. Gold is the metal of underworld wealth, whether the literal gold which is mined from the earth or the symbol of our inner richness. That is why so many of the bank cards are also gold (or silver, which ranks second to gold as a symbol of richness).

By using this imagery, credit cards offer us the illusion of debt which need never be paid, an illusion reinforced by the fact that the bank cards require only the payment of a monthly minimum and not payment of the full balance. If we pay our minimums, we are in good standing, we are creditworthy. We have captured extra energy from that debt (in the form of what we have consumed); we possess more vitality. A recent advertisement from American Express shows that its cards are accepted by a chain of shops selling ecologically-sound products, and concludes by telling us that American Express is "welcomed at . . . places that are good for your soul." Clearly such a credit card is not a mere ticket to exotic locales and the possession of prestige consumables but is a succor to us in our imperishable depths.

The advertisements for credit cards may seem deceiving, but we should hardly blame the advertisements for the deception. Such advertisements would not succeed if we didn't have a desire to believe and a willingness to imagine ourselves as actors in the fantasies created in the advertisements. Basic to this self-deception is our reluctance to distinguish between what we have already earned and what we hope to earn someday, or to distinguish between what we are and what we hope to be. So one advertisement speaks of the credit line that goes with the credit cards and ends by saying, "You've earned it."

This is misleading, but pleasing to the ears. We seem to be hearing that those who are hard workers and good earners are the ones who are offered credit lines. A naive listener might even imagine that when "You've earned it," you must own it in the form of savings. Of course, nothing could be further from the truth.

Quick to leap on the bandwagon of condemnation for the profligate 1980s, the most innovative advertising for credit cards seeks to distinguish and even define the 1990s. No longer are we fun-loving hedonists eager to buy useless baubles and idle away our hours on island beaches. The 1990s have reformed us all (including the credit card companies that urged us to spend and enjoy in the 1980s), so that we are now frugal and intelligent consumers.

"Master the Moment" did not gain MasterCard its hoped-for market share, so MasterCard found a new advertising agency to invent anew the role of credit cards for the 1990s. As the television screen reveals exotic vacation vistas, a man's voice asks, "You know those credit card commercials where they tell you to jaunt off to some exotic paradise? This isn't one of them, O.K.? We're taking our MasterCard to the supermarket." The visual changes to the interior of a supermarket and the "friendly" voice asks, "How's that for exotic?" The wisdom of this choice is explained at the checkout counter when the Master-Card is used to buy the groceries. The knowing voice informs us that "it's smart to use your monthly statement to keep track of your monthly grocery spending."

The commercial closes with deft assurance: "Master-Card. It's not just a credit card. It's smart money." The problem with slogans like "You've earned it" or "It's smart money" is their implication that the banks are seeking informed and creditworthy consumers to use their cards. Such upstanding consumers would naturally pay their bills in a timely manner. However, consumers who pay on time are not the people that the banks really seek to have credit cards. In credit card parlance, such good payers are called "free riders." They are almost thieves, problematic people who dare to enjoy the convenience of the credit card without making their fair contribution to the interest charges that generate seventy-five percent of the banks' credit card profits.

Once the banks realized that good payers were not their ideal customer, they began to go after people who would be more likely to pay the monthly minimum and carry a revolving balance on which interest had to be paid. College students are an especially desirable target group for the credit card companies. More than half of the 5.6 million full-time college students enrolled in four-year programs have credit cards. An added bonus in reaching the young is brand loyalty. MasterCard believes that sixty-five percent of people will continue to use their first brand of credit card for fifteen years or more.

So a flier for Citibank MasterCard—titled "Special Student Offer—All Students Eligible"—states "Citibank knows that students like you become responsible, credit-worthy cardmembers. That's why we're extending a special student offer to you." The flier advises the student, "You always have the option of paying your purchase balance in full within our interest-free grace period, or spreading your obligation over time. You decide what's best for you—Citibank gives you the choice." After referring to how this credit card "can help you build your credit history better," the flier promises, "We'll start you off with a credit line to meet your needs and reward responsible payment behavior with credit line increases as your financial needs grow."

This sales pitch has a surprising clincher: "No co-signer or minimum income is needed—so apply now!" This is truly magic, if a credit card with a credit line can be obtained by a youth who has no income. Not surprisingly, many college students are no more able to handle credit card debt than their parents. So we hear of a freshman at the University of Houston who had neither a job nor a credit history, but quickly obtained eight credit cards (including three Visa cards). She found that she couldn't control her impulse spending. By her junior year she had a debt of $6,800, no credit cards, and a bad credit history.

Such stories could be multiplied. They are the inevitable result of the banks' use of credit cards to gain interest income. To the banks, the college student who defaults is simply a negative statistic in an overall profitable enterprise.

Self-deception is hardly limited to college students. For example, during the 1980s many people simply denied that they paid interest on their credit cards, when in fact two-thirds of them did. By denying that any interest was paid, these cardholders avoided the necessity of asking what the rate of interest might be. Had they asked, they would have discovered that the rate of interest averaged nearly twenty percent throughout the 1980s. Consumers who believed they would pay off their revolving balances next month gave billions in profits to the banks.

The insensitivity of credit card customers to interest rates had been shown as early as the 1950s. The average interest charge for credit card balances came to be 19.8 percent, and this rate did not lower as interest rates fell through the 1980s. With the recession in the early 1990s, interest rates paid by banks to depositors fell to the two-to three-percent range by 1993. At the same time, the banks were charging nearly twenty percent to their credit card borrowers. This differential made the credit card business very profitable and may well have saved some banks from failing due to unprofitable real estate loans.

An extraordinary battle in Congress finally helped raise the awareness of credit cardholders. On November 12, 1991, President Bush gave a speech in which he urged banks to lower their credit card rates. He believed this would encourage consumers to spend and boost the economy. On November 13, Senator D'Amato, a New York Republican, offered a bill to cap credit card interest rates at fourteen percent, far less than the state usury ceilings which generally ranged from eighteen to twenty-four percent.

However, when the bill passed the Senate by a vote of seventy-four to nineteen, the White House denounced it. The treasury secretary called the proposal "wacky" and blamed it for a 120 point fall in the stock market. The vice president said that millions of people would lose their credit cards, and the chairman of the Federal Reserve concluded that banks would lose needed profits from interest charges. The embarrassing truth was that if rates were lowered and cards given only to people who could definitely pay, then a huge number of people would lose their credit cards. And the people who would lose their cards were exactly the group that maintained revolving balances of debt and paid the high interest rates that were saving many banks from failure. President Bush now had to threaten to veto a popular proposal for a law capping such interest rates.

Although D'Amato's bill never became law, it did help to make people more sensitive to the issue of credit card rates. Banks began to compete on the basis of their rates and the average interest rates for credit cards did ease slightly, but remained extremely high compared to rates for secured debt such as car loans or home mortgages.

So the magical power of credit cards is an illusion. If

there is any magic, it is not in the credit card but in the interest charges. The famed banker Baron de Rothschild could not name the seven wonders of the world but called compound interest the eighth wonder. Money will double in a little over six years at a twelve-percent interest rate (in part because the interest paid in the first year then earns interest in subsequent years). At twenty-percent interest, which is what the rate on credit cards has been, the money owed will double in less than four years. Looked at in another way, if a cardholder owes $2,000 and makes the minimum payment each month, it will take 22 years to pay off the $2,000 and will cost $4,919 in interest if the rate is 19.8 percent.

Especially in view of the interest costs, it is remarkable how many people pay their monthly minimums and imagine that they have no money problems. They do not consider themselves debtors. They have been solicited by a credit card issuer, filled out an application, been approved. They've earned the right to their line of credit. Who should know better than a bank whether someone's financial information justifies the issuance of a card with a credit line? It certainly seems that paying the monthly minimum meets with the bank's approval. No more is required to be considered creditworthy.

DEBTORS ANONYMOUS AND THE DISPELLING OF CREDIT CARD ILLUSIONS

The danger signs with respect to credit cards are well known. In fact, one such sign is to make only minimum payments each month. Another sign is buying food with credit cards (despite the MasterCard campaign saying their card is "smart money" when used at the supermarket). Using credit card advances to pay off other debts, combatting boredom or depression by going shopping, and having card balances at their maximum so money is unavailable for emergencies are all warning signs. So are paying for friends' purchases with a credit card and viewing the cash reimbursement from the friends as found money, regularly seeking higher credit lines on cards, repeatedly using a home equity line of credit, seeking a debt consolidation loan, not reading letters from creditors, or having wages garnished. Many people will try to ignore these warning signs, a denial made easier by the absence of programs to educate people about personal finances.

The illusion only ends when the debtor is unable to pay even the minimum balance on the credit card. A mature woman who had paid her monthly minimum for many years told of how she suddenly realized that she was deeply in debt. She sought counseling for debt and was told that based on her income-to-debt ratio she should declare bankruptcy. Instead she went to Debtors Anonymous and gave up her illusion that life could not be lived without credit cards. She cut up her cards, sought to make payment schedules with all her creditors, and eventually did pay all of her debts.

Debtors Anonymous is one of the many Twelve-Step programs that seeks to help people in recovery from an addiction. According to the Twelve Traditions of Debtors Anonymous, "The only requirement for Debtors Anonymous membership is a desire to stop incurring unsecured debt." The foundations of Debtors Anonymous are both pragmatic and spiritual. The pragmatic aspect requires a debtor to share common ground with the other members of Debtors Anonymous by admitting that "we were powerless over debt—that our lives had become unmanage-

able," and by making "a searching and fearless moral in-
ventory of ourselves." The spiritual basis requires the
debtor to believe "that a Power greater than ourselves
could restore us to sanity," and to make "a decision to
turn our will and our lives over to God as we understood
him." Debtors Anonymous encourages those who feel
powerless with respect to money to redirect their addictive energy toward the divine. If the adversity of debt can
serve to deepen the spiritual life, then understanding debt
also gives a sense of the natural abundance from which
money flows.

When the woman who went to Debtors Anonymous
sought freedom from debt, she met a secret and quite ugly
aspect of the systematized purveying of debt through
credit cards. Collection agencies called her at all hours,
including late at night, early in the morning, and on week-
ends. She was threatened with lawsuits and a bad credit
rating. For more than six months, each of ten creditors
called her at least once a week. These callers usually had
an angry, condescending tone and accused her of withholding money, trying to perpetrate a fraud, and lying.
They sounded as if they read from scripts as they told her
that she should have thought more before she had gone
into debt. They repeatedly questioned whether she had
savings or friends and family from whom to borrow. In response to her offers of payment schedules, they would say
things like, "Even people on welfare pay more than that."

So the other side of the pleasures promised by credit
cards is the pain inflicted on those who fail to pay. This
pain is obviously a secret, since the companies selling
credit cards hardly want us to be aware that maybe
"You've earned it" and "It's smart money" are just two of
the many lies used to profit from people's lack of aware-

ness about money matters. Nor was the treatment of the woman who cut up her credit cards in any way extraordinary. It was just as much a part of the system as the initial solicitations telling college students that they can have a credit card and credit line without any requirement of a minimum income or a co-signer.

So the symbolic promise of the credit cards—a limitless credit line that need never be repaid—is, of course, not kept. The advertising with its fantasies is part of a system designed to make profits. The system entices people to get and use cards, including some who will be unable to pay. Those unable to pay are treated like statistics and turned over to professional debt collectors. In contrast to this, payment in cash is a refreshing exercise in reality. Cash symbolizes current potentials and energies, so we feel our sacrifice of cash far more intensely than we feel the promise of the future repayment that we are agreeing to make when we use a credit card. If we wish to spend less, using cash instead of credit cards definitely assists us.

BANKS SEEK THE PROFITS OF LOANS TO CONSUMERS

To gain the fullest understanding of the reason for the marketing of credit cards and the growth of debt, we have to connect the use of credit cards to the evolution of consumerism and banking in the twentieth century. At the turn of the century, banks did not seek to profit from consumers. In fact, banks did not view lending to consumers as a part of their business. If a worker had credit, it came from accounts with local merchants. A person who could not borrow from family and friends had only one remaining avenue: a loan shark who would charge usurious and often devastating rates of interest.

The very concepts of mass production and the consumerism necessary to support such production were in their infancy. Banks sought their profits through service to the business community. While workers could deposit their money with the banks for safekeeping, the banks did not circulate these deposits back to the workers in the form of loans. If the automobile is emblematic of the growth of consumerism, it is interesting to note that until 1910 cash had to be paid in full to buy an automobile.

In the difficult economic times of the 1890s, bankers viewed the credit needs of ordinary people as an issue of charity. Through the auspices of the Charity Organization Society, many of the bankers and other wealthy people subscribed money to create a pawnshop that would be able to extend small amounts of credit to people quickly. Called the Provident Loan Society of New York, it opened in 1894 as a philanthropic organization dedicated to giving people credit at a fair rate of interest (which it continues to do today). Designed to look like small Greek temples, the busy offices of the Provident revealed the hunger of people for credit.

This unmet demand for credit finally brought an entrepreneurial response from an attorney in Norfolk, Virginia, whose expertise was in banking and corporate law. Arthur J. Morris believed that eighty percent of the public did not have sufficient access to credit. In 1910, he opened the Fidelity Savings & Trust Co. in Norfolk. Lending on the basis of earning power and character at interest rates that, if high, were far better than those offered by the loan sharks, so-called Morris Banks soon spread to other cities. Morris invented the use of life insurance on borrowers to protect both the Morris Banks and co-signers of the promissory notes securing the debts. So Morris could promise, "No man's debts shall survive him."

If this were not enough, Morris also assisted in developing the concept of installment financing for the purchase of automobiles. Installment credit outstanding for automobiles rose from $304 million in 1919 to $1.384 billion in 1929. This credit expansion helped keep the factories busy turning out automobiles, which in turn stimulated the economy as the bull market of the 1920s stampeded ahead.

In fact, although the contraction of consumer credit was widespread during the 1930s, the wage earner had been shown to be a good credit risk. The banks could no longer ignore wage earners as a source of potential profit. Consumer credit soared after the end of World War Two, rising from $5.665 billion in 1945 to $38.830 billion in 1955 and to $90.314 billion in 1965. Inflation could only account for a relatively small portion of this increase.

THE SYMBOLISM OF CHANGING BANK ARCHITECTURE

Naturally banks wanted to persuade depositors that their money would be safe. The ancient treasuries at Delphi had been built for the safekeeping of the wealth of the city-states. Architects for banks in the nineteenth and early twentieth century frequently turned for models to the ancient temples of Greece and Rome. So many banks looked like temples, their magnificence imbued with the implicit power of the unseen divinities. Pillared facades, massive doors, and lofty interiors with vaulted ceilings all sought to inspire awe. To complete the sense that these buildings were large and impregnable vaults, the windows were often tiny. Even within the bank, the officers would be hidden from sight, with the give-and-take of money conducted by clerks in hushed voices.

On the reverse of the ten-dollar bill is an engraving of the United States Treasury in Washington, D.C. Its wide steps leading heavenward, handsome pillars, and vast size all give credence to its sacred and inviolable role in our lives. The Treasury building, erected in 1836, is the third oldest building in Washington and is predated only by the White House and the Capitol.

The First Bank of the United States, designed by Samuel Blodget, Jr., and built in Philadelphia between 1795 and 1797, has a white marble facade with a similar feeling: six Corinthian pillars supporting a pediment on which the arms of the United States are portrayed. Thomas Jefferson, while mistrustful of banks and credit, influenced their architecture through his love of Greek and Roman models. So the First Bank of the United States was modeled on a Roman temple at Nîmes, which Jefferson believed the most beautiful building surviving from antiquity. While architectural critics detect nonclassical influences as well, its monumental grandeur and classical sensibility made the First Bank of the United States not only the first bank to be built in such a style but also a model for later banks to follow. Until 1800, the First Bank of the United States served as the temporary seat of government for the new nation while Washington was being built.

More than a century later, in 1908, National City Bank (now Citibank) hired the famed architectural firm of McKim, Mead & White to redesign the block-long United States Customs House in New York City for use as a bank. The Customs House already had an impressive facade of one dozen Ionic pillars. Above this McKim, Mead & White added four stories fronted by one dozen Corinthian pillars arranged to balance the Ionic pillars below. Since the first row of pillars begins on a wall more than double a person's height, the overall effect is monumental. Within the building this renovation brought sunlight streaming down from the empyrean heights of the fifty-nine-foot-high ceiling.

Many more banks could be used as examples of classical influence, but the point is that this temple architecture could not survive the growth of consumerism and the banks' energetic quest for the interest profits generated by consumer debt. A new bank architecture evolved as banks reached out and sought to make the public feel welcome. The shock of the new was most dramatically realized in a bank facade designed by Skidmore, Owings & Merrill in 1953–54. The unadorned four-story building, built as a branch of Manufacturers Trust Company at Fifth Avenue and Forty-Third Street in New York City, had a facade of glass. This facade included the largest sheets of glass ever installed in a building up to that time: 9.5 feet by 22 feet.

Unlike the temple banks which projected an image of inviolable security, this modern sheath of glass invited the public into the bank. It made the interior accessible; what secrets could there be when anyone passing on the sidewalk could see into the well-illuminated interior? The architects included a striking visual proof that this bank held no secrets. Their design placed the vault, the most inner and secret precinct of earlier banks, on the level of the street. With the walls of glass, passersby have no choice but to see the vault and understand, even without thinking about it, that this bank has no pretension of being a temple. Not only was this design a public relations coup, but it set a new norm for the architecture of banks.

It is no coincidence that bank credit cards and this revolution in bank design both date to the early 1950s. They were like siblings; they belonged to the same family. This family, unlike the banks of the past, wanted company. In fact, the architecture suggested guests were welcome, and the credit cards were like an extension of this architecture. To the millions of people who received unsolicited credit cards in the mail before a federal ban on such mailings in 1970, the credit cards were an invitation to walk into one of the ever-growing number of glass banks and meet a friendly banker. As consumer credit reached $131.6 billion in 1970, $350.3 billion in 1980, and $794.4 billion in 1990, the willingness of the public to borrow complemented the glass windows through which bank officers across the nation could be seen toiling at their desks.

WHAT WE WILL LOSE IF MONEY IS REPLACED BY CREDIT CARDS AND ELECTRONIC TRANSFERS

We have explored the use of credit cards and the relationship of banks to consumer debt for several reasons. These ever-present cards function in a way which makes them a great convenience, but their purpose is to increase the amount of indebtedness among consumers. Understanding this, we can each make a more informed choice as to whether we are willing to incur this debt and contribute to the interest charges that form a significant portion of bank profits.

Beyond this, however, credit cards offer a way of seeing more deeply into the even newer phenomenon of electronic fund transfers. Whatever the motives (for both issuer and user) underlying the ever-expanding use of credit cards, these same motives could not help but affect the use of electronic transfers as well. Credit cards seem, after all, to be but a step in the direction of a cash-free society. Automatic teller machines are ubiquitous, and the next step is likely to be interactive networks that allow us to sit at home while we shop and pay bills by electronic transfers. Governments are experimenting with issuing credit cards to replace welfare payments and food stamps. The hope is to cut costs by eliminating red tape and fraud, but one effect is to deny these recipients the symbolic value inherent in exchanging money for goods or services.

If the replacement of money by electronic transfers seems remote, we should keep in mind that the largest sums of money are already moved electronically. For example, the Clearing House Interbank Payments System, owned by eleven of the largest New York banks, moves a trillion dollars each day electronically—more than the entire money supply of the United States. While cash (eighty-five percent) and checks (thirteen percent) are used in ninety-eight percent of all transactions, cash transactions account for only one percent of the total amount of all transactions. So individuals like to use cash for their transactions, but financial institutions prefer to make their far larger transfers electronically.

What would it mean if credit cards and electronic transfers completely replaced the use of paper money and coins? How would we experience this in our depths, far beneath the everyday measuring and exchanging of values in the marketplace?

We have discussed how money, despite losing the backing of gold and silver, still retains symbolic power. On one level, money speaks to us of our ability to be fruitful in the world. In this we see money as the reward for our labors and also as an invaluable mechanism of circulation and sharing. On another level money tells us of our inner richness. So Jesus Christ speaks of money in a number of his parables, but clearly he uses it because its increase can so easily symbolize spiritual growth.

Without money that passes from hand to hand, the symbolic wealth of money would vanish. We would no longer have the faces of the Founding Fathers and other national leaders portrayed on our coins and bills. The Great Seal of the United States would disappear from the reverse of the dollar. The phrase "In God We Trust" would become a relic, for that inscription and the money that bore it would have vanished to the realm of the invisible. The greenness of our paper money and the vegetative motifs that appear on both coins and bills would no longer be taken in hand with each exchange.

When cash and coins become invisible, they return to the underworld. We are no longer conscious of them. The money moved by an electronic funds transfer is no doubt going from one place to another, but that movement is utterly abstract. We do not see the movement with our eyes;

we do not use our hands to propel or receive what is moved.

Thinking not of electronic exchanges but of other exchanges that connected humankind to invisible realms, we return to the early peoples who sought some relationship with the fruitfulness of the world about them. What invisible powers made game plentiful or brought the rains to fructify the fields? Our money today offers only faint hints of the ancient origins of money in the worship of invisible forces, but at least some visual and tangible clues remain of how people first sought to forge a bond with unseen divinities. Certainly handing money back and forth is a reminder, however faint, of the connection of people to each other in the love feast and to the divine through sacrificial exchange and communion.

If money vanishes, we will, in a sense, have come full circle. Nothing will be visibly exchanged; the money that we sacrifice to receive our sustenance will vanish. We will be left, as early peoples were, with a fruitful world whose divinities and spirits conceal themselves utterly. Even the inadequate clues offered by money are signs that we can interpret, signs that offer us symbolic wealth. If money vanishes it will be the invisibility, the lack of signs, that will be our greatest challenge as we seek to understand what is fertile in our world and in ourselves.

In fact, when credit cards are examined more closely, a fundamental difference between credit cards and electronic fund transfers becomes apparent. Bank credit cards rely on the creation of debt to profit their issuers. Electronic fund transfers do not create debt. Actually, electronic fund transfers are similar to the card originally imagined by Edward Bellamy in *Looking Backward 2000–1887*. Such a card would be called a "debit card" today and can only be used to draw against an account in which the cardholder has money. Similarly, electronic transfers require that a person have a balance, presumably in a bank account, against which the instantaneous transfer of money can be processed. So until electronic fund transfers cost about the same as drawing checks, most people will prefer the old system to the new. And banks will lack strong profit incentives to change to systems of electronic transfers, because such transfers do not encourage the creation of debt and the charging of interest—the "money at once" that motivates the banks in their dealings with consumers.

HERMES AND THE INFORMATION AGE

We are told that we live in the Information Age. Certainly we are surrounded by technology that allows immense speed in the processing and moving of information. If we think of the Greek pantheon, the god ruling over the Information Age is undoubtedly Hermes (or Mercury, as he was called by the Romans). He is the swiftest of gods, the messenger. Instantaneously, he moves from Olympus to earth in aid of a hero, or to the underworld to rescue Persephone. Since Hermes is the god of commerce, we need hardly be surprised that the needs of commerce are so well served in the Information Age.

But we must remember that Hermes is the god of thieves. He is quite capable of misleading us, spinning webs of illusion and lies that make us easy victims of fraud. Vast quantities of information do not mean that each of us is receiving information of quality. The symbolic wealth of money may help us maintain our equilibrium in a society more and more accustomed to debt and "money at once." And in an age when so much outside of us moves very quickly, we must still respect the speed at which we move within.

CHAPTER NINE

BULLS AND BEARS

How the Stock Market Reflects the Renewing Cycles of Life

=========================

IN THE COURSE of writing *The Secret Life of Money*, I walked the financial district of New York City to view some of the landmarks of bank architecture. Not only did the Citicorp building with its many pillars remind me of an ancient Greek temple, but so did the facade of the New York Stock Exchange with its six Corinthian pillars rising to support a pediment surmounted by a dramatic sculptural group. As I studied this grouping, I was surprised to see that the central figure wore a winged helmet—the sign of Hermes, the god of commerce and of thieves. This figure's arms were outstretched at waist height, like a charioteer holding reins, and an infant sat at each foot while adults labored beneath the dominion of the outstretched arms.

I marveled at the wisdom of the Exchange to invoke Hermes, at once the most appropriate of gods to represent the growth of commerce, and yet an admission that human industry is sometimes accompanied by thievery and sharp practices. Curious to learn more, I inquired at the Exchange and quickly received a disclaimer. The central figure was not Hermes at all, but rather a depiction of Integrity. I could certainly understand why the Exchange would want to claim Integrity as its governing force, but in mythology the winged helmet identifies Hermes as the god who moves between the worlds. The wings on his helmet symbolize his attributes: his ability to change levels, to travel, to move quickly, to communicate over vast distances. To give these attributes to Integrity would make as much sense as saying that the symbol for a football team like the Philadelphia Eagles could equally well be used as the symbol for the Chicago Bears.

In this chapter we will seek to understand some of the symbols of the stock market, such as the sculpture of Integrity and the bulls and bears which have ancient connections to the cycles of increase and decrease in nature. To many of us, the up-and-down movements of stocks seem as arbitrary as the numbers selected to determine the winner of the state lottery. But the stock markets are, in reality, a reflection of the desire in each of us to be productive and contribute to our families and communities.

HERMES GUIDED BY INTEGRITY

The New York Stock Exchange is rooted in the formative years of our nation. Founded in 1792 under a butterwood tree on Wall Street (a street named after a wall built by the Dutch in 1653 as a defense against the English who later dismantled it), the Exchange served an agricultural nation just beginning the process of industrialization. In the colonial period there had been only half a dozen chartered companies, most of which had vanished by the Revolution. But the economic growth of the 1790s saw the formation of nearly three hundred chartered companies, many of which relied on the Exchange to raise capital by selling their stocks and bonds to the public.

The expansion and ever greater importance of the Exchange paralleled the rapid industrialization of the nineteenth century. For a long period (from 1840 to 1890), the stocks and bonds of railroad companies dominated the trading on the Exchange and reflected the crucial role of the railroad in the development of the national economy. Not only the railroad but also the telegraph (invented in 1844) and the telephone (invented in 1876 and installed in the Exchange in 1878) all suggest the increasing significance of Hermes. His attributes—speed in communication and travel—became ever more important as the Industrial Age evolved and flowed into the Information Age. This newfound and ever increasing speed transformed commerce and the daily lives of the people.

On December 15, 1886, the Exchange sold one million shares for the first time. By the end of the 1890s, trading volume soared and the Exchange readied for expanded quarters. In 1903, the Exchange moved into a newly constructed building at 18 Broad Street that is still in use today. In many ways the building was a futuristic wonder. More than 500 telephones were installed on the perimeter of the trading floor, a pioneering use of air conditioning required 247 miles of wiring, and six miles of pneumatic tubes in the walls and ceilings made trading information quickly available.

The respected sculptor John Quincy Adams Ward was

commissioned to create the pediment statuary. This grouping, titled "Integrity Protecting the Works of Man," shows Integrity as the central figure with the figures of Science, Industry, and Invention laboring to one side and the figures of Agriculture and Mining laboring to the other. For the most part, the sculpture portrays its title quite literally. The "Works of Man" flow from the muscles and minds of the nude male figures that symbolize Science, Industry, Invention, Agriculture, and Mining (except for a clothed woman who may be helping Agriculture in his tasks). What is surprising is that Integrity, the guiding force for all these works of man, is a woman attired in a flowing gown and cape.

It would be easy to dismiss this statuary as propaganda. After all, Hermes is the god of thieves. Putting his helmet on a woman and calling her Integrity could simply be a way of ignoring that thieves have often used the stock market to prey on honest investors. The rapacious manipulators of the 1980s, who made tens of millions of dollars and later served time in prison, are merely the most recent generation of wrongdoers who used the stock market without any concern for ethical conduct. In addition, women in finance were certainly a rarity at the turn of the century, when many brokers actually had separate rooms for their women customers. Only during World War Two did the Exchange allow women to work on the trading floor, and this ceased for another two decades when the returning veterans took back their jobs. It was not until 1967 that Muriel Siebert became the first woman to be a member of the Exchange. So the figure of Integrity is a woman in spite of the fact that women had almost no involvement with the Exchange at the turn of the century and for many years after.

Yet Ward's sculpture seems more than propaganda. It suggests the artist's hope of how the Exchange might serve the productive life of an evolving nation. Certainly part of this vision included the qualities of Hermes: the speed of movement and communication that within two decades would find realization in the widespread use of airplanes, automobiles, and radio. But Ward offers a new image to govern our productive efforts. He seems to want to reform the less savory aspects of Hermes, the god quite capable of stealing his brother's cattle and lying about the theft. So Ward sought to add to the world of finance what had been largely missing—the image of a woman. In this case, a handsome woman named Integrity, whose outstretched arms might bring the fair dealing of her name to every type of enterprise.

When an artist like Ward creates the figure of a woman (especially a personification such as Integrity), he may be portraying what psychologist C. G. Jung would call an image of the *anima*. Anima means soul or life (especially inner life). Through such an image a man may seek for aspects of his life which are unconscious, undiscovered by him. The image may be seen in a vision, a dream, or even be a woman whom he meets.

A man knows that he is encountering an anima figure by the great stirring of energy within him. Unknown parts of himself seek to become visible, to become part of what the man believes himself to be. To meet this woman who represents what is unknown arouses feelings of rapture and terror. At once the man feels immense possibilities open before him while the solid structure of the world he has known is shaken as if by a powerful earthquake. If the man sees his anima in a real woman, he must exercise all of his reason and restraint to understand that the anima is his fabrication, his vision of the energy of his inner possibilities. In the hands of an artist like Ward, such an anima figure may express the unknown possibility of the collective unconscious, the potential of the society for discovery and evolution.

The New York Stock Exchange and the many other exchanges around the world are the most evolved agents of the secular markets. These exchanges seek to channel money so that it will be used in ways that are productive. While the divine exchange connected people to gods and spirits through sacrifice, these secular exchanges connect people with money to people who desire money for productive purposes—whether to build railroads in the nineteenth century or automobiles and computers in the twentieth. If this view of the exchanges is simplified, it nonetheless captures the central vision and purpose of these markets. While the New York Stock Exchange handles the stocks and bonds of a limited number of the largest companies, the quest to be productive animates us all. Smaller companies may secure capital by private placements to a limited number of investors; entrepreneurs may launch their enterprises with savings or borrowings from family and friends. Employees offer the productivity of their labor, and even at leisure we often gain satisfaction from being productive.

The artist's vision in "Integrity Protecting the Works of Man" is not a reflection of history but rather a hope for the betterment of the human condition. And Integrity can only protect the "Works of Man" if first she protects the money that we use as a tool to aid us in our creations. Money's appearance can remain unchanged while its essence is transformed, as has been the case with United States currency in the twentieth century with the removal of gold and silver backing. Quite clearly, money is trust in the larger society, trust in the government, and trust in all the citizens who work to create the cornucopia of goods and services that each year give reality to a paper currency that has no intrinsic value. To protect our money, Integrity must keep us aware that money is the device by which we share our energies and exchange the fruits of our labors. Beyond this, while the frieze says nothing of the distribution of the wealth that the markets help to create, would not Integrity require a concern for the well-being of each member of the community?

On a more personal level, Hermes is the guide of souls, the god who enables us to cross boundaries within ourselves and discover what is new within us. If we apply the artist's vision to our individual psychologies, we can understand the need for Integrity to govern the search for our own natures. When we seek our inner fertility, our deepest potential whatever the form its expression may take in the world, we have no choice but to be utterly honest.

So looking at the pediment statuary of the New York Stock Exchange, we meet again with many of the themes that have been woven through *The Secret Life of Money*. We see money as a creation of the human mind, a tool that serves our desire to be productive. If we contemplate how the exchanges raise money for investment, we can't help but wonder about the spark that makes us fertile with the dreams of new ventures. Here we feel again the divine origins of the cornucopias that we create, both individually and as a society. And when we experience our fertility as flowing from an endless abundance, we can understand the importance of freeing our richness to flow into the world. That endless abundance is invisible, so both as individuals and as a society we constantly strive to know and give shape to what cannot be seen. Without the protective guidance of Integrity, we may never come to trust what is invisible and experience its richness.

The great cycles of life and death that shaped the worship of the fertility goddesses affect the stock markets as well. The very words "stock market" suggest a place for the sale of livestock. So phrases like "taking a cut" or "watered stock" have the ring of a time when livestock served as a principal form of wealth. The word "chattel," which means a movable piece of property, is closely related to the word "cattle"; and the word "pecuniary," which means of or pertaining to money, comes from the word *pecus*, which is Latin for livestock.

BULLS AND BEARS
The Psychology of the Market

The most popular words to describe the psychology of investors in the stock market are "bullish" and "bearish." To be a bull means to believe that the market (or a particular stock) will go up in value. So bulls buy. Bears, on the other hand, believe that the market or a particular stock will fall in value. So bears sell. However, the explanations offered for the origins of this usage of bulls and bears are scanty and unsatisfactory. If we could deepen our understanding of why bulls and bears symbolize different forces in the stock market and in human psychology, we might gain insight into what makes each of us and our society fertile. We might also solve a small mystery, which is the question of why such a curious phrase as "bulls and bears" has found widespread usage and feels so appropriate.

The adoption of bulls and bears goes back at least to the early 1700s when these terms were used at the London Stock Exchange. Various theories seek to explain the reasoning behind the usage. One theory, for example, is that bullish comes from the way that a bull will toss up its horns. In a bullfight the bull's powerful neck muscles must be wounded so that this tossing upward will not be so dangerous to the matador. Thus bullish refers to the belief that prices will be tossed upward. With respect to the bear, a theory is advanced that the usage comes from an old English saying about not selling the skin before the bear has been caught. Investors who are bearish on a stock often sell the stock short. This means that they sell shares that they don't own in the hope that they can later purchase the shares at a cheaper price and make a profit. But neither these nor other theories really explain the aptness of the concept of bulls and bears.

Today, of course, few of us have any contact with bulls, so we have difficulty imagining the importance of the bull for earlier generations and for many people who live in less industrialized parts of the world. For hunters, the wild cattle, called aurochs, were both a great prize and a fearsome prey. Aurochs lived in herds of cows and calves dominated by a single bull. The bull stood six feet at the shoulders and weighed over two thousand pounds. The tribe could feast on its flesh, use its bones for spear points, fishhooks, and other implements, and make its skin into clothing and tents. The last of the aurochs died in the seventeenth century in Poland.

Bullfighting appears to have grown out of the fierce bravery required to hunt the aurochs. The Spanish apparently fought bulls before their conquest by Rome and introduced the conquerors to this spectacle. The term "straw man" comes from the practice of tossing clothed figures stuffed with straw in front of the bulls to enrage them and let them exhaust some of their energy before the bullfights would begin.

We do not know exactly how cattle came to be domesticated, but this domestication forever changed the relationship of humanity to nature. No longer dependent on the hunt, the herder could follow a more settled style of life. Observing the bulls and cows, the herders may have first discovered the causal relationship between sexuality and birth. On the one hand, separating the bull from the cows meant that there would be no calves at all. On the other hand, one bull could impregnate all of the cows in the herd. So the bull symbolized not only immense strength but also boundless fertility.

Agriculture and herding began as separate activities, but ancient people imagined that the fertility of the bull could inseminate the fields which nourished the crops. When the bull pulled a plough through the fields, the furrows opened in the earth and received the life-giving force of the bull. All of the early civilizations, of the Tigris-Euphrates region and of the Nile and Indus rivers, had stockbreeding and agriculture as foundations. Each of these civilizations worshipped a bull god as one of its chief deities.

In India, the Aryans sang hymns of worship to many bull gods, including Indra, the mighty bull whose rain fertilized the earth and impregnated the herds of cattle. The ancient Sumerians worshipped the bull-god Enlil whose power over water made him the god of the storm and of fertility. Hymns to Enlil honored him with such phrases as "powerful chief of the gods," "lord of the world of life," and "exalted overpowering ox." The Sumerians believed that merely walking bulls through the fields would bring fertility. The Egyptians sang to Amen-Ra, ". . . the Bull in Heliopolis, / president of all the gods, . . . / father of the gods, / maker of men, / creator of beasts and cattle, / lord of the things which exist, / creator of the staff of life. . . ."

In both Sumeria and Egypt the king came to be closely associated with the bull. So in Sumeria both Enlil and the great king Sargon shared the honorific title of "Wild Bull." To show their divine appointment and power, kings wore bull-horned headdresses. Only kings were allowed to grow beards, which symbolized strength, and beards were also placed on the statues of the bull gods. In Egypt, the king who united Upper and Lower Egypt, Narmer-Menes, proclaimed himself a bull. Not only was the worship of the bull identified with worship of the king from a very early date but the bull cults of Apis and Mnevis each worshipped the god in the form of a living bull, which was embalmed at death and placed in a large tomb.

Bull worship spanned the Mediterranean. Earlier we discussed how the Phoenicians spread the worship of the bull-god Ba'al to such places as Carthage. The god Dionysus, whose wanderings and connection to the fertility goddess Cybele we also explored, was worshipped as a bull. In Crete, the bull again symbolized fertility and was also linked with the roar and destructive force of the earthquakes that rocked the island. The Cretans held a spring festival in which they sought to make the divine fertility of the bull serve humankind. Young men and women would "dance" with the bull by waiting for the charge, grasping the horns, and, as the bull gave its powerful upward thrust of the head, somersaulting to safety over its back. The immense danger of this ritual was redeemed by the belief that touching the horns conveyed a fertility that would benefit the entire community. The masculine prowess of the bull found a reflection in the numerous images of bulls with erect phalli, and also in the fact that the women bull dancers dressed with their clothing bunched in such a way that they, too, seemed to possess male sexual organs.

In the centuries following the death of Christ, many of the soldiers of the Roman Empire worshipped the god Mithra, and the Mithraic religion competed with the Christian religion for adherents and eventual dominance. Mithra served as a divine mediator between the ultimate, unknowable god and the human race. Mithra's most famous feat was to slay the wild bull, the first living creature created by the god. When Mithra found this immense bull grazing on the mountain side, he boldly grasped its horns and leapt on its back. The struggling bull unseated him, but Mithra kept his grip on the horns until the bull surrendered in exhaustion.

Then Mithra lifted the bull by its hind hoofs and dragged it on a road that had many obstacles. This painful journey symbolized the suffering of humanity. Mithra left the bull in a cave, but the bull escaped, and Mithra, against his own will, had to obey the decree of heaven and kill it. When the bull returned to the entrance of the cave, Mithra grasped its nostrils to pull back its head and struck a deadly blow with his hunting knife.

A miracle followed this slaughter. The body of the dead bull sprouted with the useful vegetation that covers the earth—its spine gave forth wheat, its blood engendered the vine—and its semen brought forth all of the animals useful to humanity. So the death of the bull was, in fact, a sacrifice of cosmic consequence. After other feats, Mithra partook of a last supper, commemorated in the Mithraic rituals of communion, and ascended to heaven where he watched over and helped humanity.

Mithraic doctrine posited a life after death in which the good would be rewarded and the evil punished. At a predestined time, when the world would be destroyed, a marvelous bull would again be sent by the god to the earth. Mithra would return to the earth and select the dead to be awakened to life. Mithra would then sacrifice this divine bull. Eating of its flesh mixed with consecrated wine would give immortality to those awakened. Yielding to the prayers of these new immortals, the god would destroy all of the wicked and bring eternal joy to the universe.

If we step back from this religious imagery, we see why the bull serves so excellently as the symbol of hoped-for increase in the stock market. Cattle played a key role in the evolution of economies and, therefore, of civilization. The great strength and fertility of the bull made it worthy of veneration and sacrifice. To worship the bull was to worship the abundance and fertility of the divine. Not only were people thankful, but by their own efforts they tried to augment these divine gifts.

When we are bullish on a stock or on the stock market, we are hoping that our human endeavors will be fertile and manifest the richness which is divine. To be bullish is to become like the bull, to be the inseminating agent of fertility. To buy is to sacrifice life energy (in the form of money) in the hope that a certain company will grow. If we are investing in ourselves, perhaps paying for education or training, we are showing how we believe that we will be more productive in the future. Whether investing in a company or in ourselves, we are circulating energy into the realm of the invisible in the hope that we will free the richness that is boundless.

Investors who scrutinize the bottom line may not recognize in themselves the energy of the divine bull whose sacrifice brought all that is useful in nature into being. Trend lines, price/earnings ratios, and asset liquidation values are useful tools that may nonetheless obscure the larger efforts of the community to produce and nourish. Beyond this, the bullish investor may have great difficulty in valuing anything other than growth. Yet there are other values—necessary values—that we must also honor if we are to receive a vision that is whole.

THE BEAR AS SPIRIT HELPER

Worship of the bear is also ancient and widespread. Neanderthal peoples set bear skulls on what may have been altars, although we will never be certain that the purpose was for worship. As discussed earlier, many hunting tribes had rituals to ensure that a slain bear would wish to return from the spirit world and be hunted again. In the myths of the American Indians, the bear often acts as a spirit helper for a hero. Because bears dig for roots, many Indian tribes considered them to be shamans and healers. A number of superstitions in Europe and America revolve around the curative powers of bear grease (for baldness and to cure aches), bear teeth (for toothache and to aid teething children to have strong teeth), riding on a bear's back (to cure whooping cough), sleeping on a bearskin (to cure backache), and fur taken from a living bear (which, when mixed with alcohol, was thought to cure fits). In fact, the phrase "lick into shape" comes from the superstition that bear cubs, which look small and shapeless when first born, were licked by their mothers into the shape of a bear.

Today we possess far more accurate information about the bear, especially about the biochemistry of the bear during hibernation. The bear does not lower its body temperature in hibernation, the way that deep hibernators like the woodchuck and squirrel do. Instead the bear burns nearly 4,000 calories a day and maintains a state that might be described as meditation-like. While the woodchuck and squirrel are defenseless, the bear is quite capable of waking and defending itself from intruders. During the five months of hibernation, the bear can even be pregnant or nurse a cub.

The bear seems to defy the rules that would govern other mammals, such as humans, were they to attempt to match the feat of hibernation. Living off accumulated body fat and taking no nourishment, the bear's bones do not become thin despite five months of inactivity; the bear's lean body mass actually increases despite the lack of exercise; and there is no toxic buildup of urea despite the bear's failure to eliminate waste during the entire period of hibernation. Scientists studying the bear are finding that these apparent miracles are due to a unique system of recycling in which calcium from bone loss is apparently captured for new bone growth and urea that would become toxic is absorbed by the bladder and synthesized into useful proteins and neurotransmitters. The hope of scientists is that study of the bear may offer insights into the creation of medicines to aid humans suffering from osteoporosis or kidney failure.

There are a number of fascinating differences between

the bear and the bull. The bull walks on four legs, the bear can walk on two like a person. The bull is a herding animal, the bear is not. The bull has been domesticated, the bear never has been. The bull is constant in its fertile powers, the bear withdraws from life for the months of winter. The bull lives on the sunlit surface of the earth, while the bear enters the darkness of its den beneath that surface.

In terms of mythology, the bear offers a striking image of descent to the underworld, self-nurturing in the womb of the earth, and rebirth with each wakening for the spring. So the bear is like the human hero who dares to venture into the underworld, the world of the unknown and the unconscious. The worship of the bull brings renewal of the land through the sacrifice of the bull. However, the bear emerges from the womb of the earth to be reborn each spring—without sacrifice.

So the bull and bear exist in symbolic counterpoint. The bull is ever fertile, ever active in its inseminating power. Thus the bull lives in the world of time, of life and death. Only sacrifice can bring new energy into this world and nurture new life. The bear lives much of its life in the underworld, in the timeless realm of the spirits. Here it lives on its own flesh and is self-devouring. Like Persephone, it eats of its own nature and becomes more and more the essence of what it is. By this mysterious process, this biochemical miracle of conservation, the bear exists without the ordinary functions of life. It does not eat; it does not eliminate waste. When it rises with the spring, it leaves the underworld and is reborn to the everyday world that we know. It returns to the flux of nature until the coming of the next winter when it will again withdraw to the timeless realm of hibernation.

To imagine that the bearish investor merely believes that a stock or the stock market will fall in value is to diminish the deeper significance of being a bear. In symbolic terms, the bearish investor is truly focused on the world of nature, the world that cannot be domesticated and made to serve us through cultivation. To be bearish is to know that we must have time for conservation, we must have time to recycle what we have gained from the sacrifice of the bull. In a sense, the bear is the healer and wise being within us who demands that we contain our boundless desires to acquire and, instead, seek for the riches that we carry within. So we may withdraw like the bear and wait patiently, meditative and yet alert, until the season comes for us to be reborn in the world of time. In this rebirth we will be licked into a new shape.

Since all investors seek to know the cycles of the stock market, becoming bulls and bears in turn, we might seek a synthesis, an image of ever-changing wholeness, that would be the bull/bear. There is a hint of such a synthesis in the story of Mithra slaying the bull, for Mithra takes the captured bull to a cave. Although the bull escapes, it returns to the cave where Mithra slays it at the entrance. But if Mithra had let the bull return to the darkness of the cave, would the bull have become like the bear? This is really the question of the balance in human nature. Can we be both expansive like the bull and contractive like the bear? Can we both develop our economies and conserve the natural resources of the world? Can we both strive for money and strive to learn more deeply of ourselves?

IN THE LABYRINTH

One of the most famous myths of antiquity, that of the Minotaur in the maze, may offer insights to help us. Zeus, the principal god of the Greeks, had the sex drive of a bull and would often take animal form if this helped him satisfy his sexual urges. When he became enamored of the beautiful maiden Europa, he changed into a bull and carried her off to the island of Crete. The perversity of this shape-shifting was to have monstrous consequences for the generations that followed.

Zeus and Europa had a son, Minos, who became king of Crete. Poseidon, the god of the oceans, gave Minos a white bull to offer as a sacrifice. Minos coveted the bull and refused to sacrifice it. In retribution, Minos's wife, Pasiphaë, was made to fall in love with this bull. Her son by the bull was the dreaded Minotaur, who had the head of a bull and the body of a man. King Minos imprisoned the Minotaur in a maze built beneath his palace at Knossos in Crete.

Because one of his sons had been killed helping the Athenians fight the bull that fathered the Minotaur, every nine years King Minos received from Athens a tribute of seven maidens and seven youths. Minos then sacrificed this living tribute to the Minotaur. At last an Athenian hero, Theseus, dared to enter the labyrinth and kill the Minotaur with his bare hands. Theseus escaped from the darkness by following the thread of a clew of yarn given to him by Ariadne, the daughter of Minos, who later became the bride of the bull-god Dionysus.

The myth of the Minotaur contains the image of the bull in the cave of the bear. The Minotaur is the union of beast and human; it is also the union of human and god. If Theseus had been a more clever hero, he might have sat and communed with this marvelous being. He might have learned the darker secrets of his own nature, secrets that would soon lead him to abandon Ariadne and cause the death of his own father.

The Minotaur, alone in the timeless dark of the maze, might have yearned to speak. If he had been able, if a human ear would have heard him, how might he have been transformed? For the name of the Minotaur was Asterion, which means "of the stars." So the Minotaur possessed the starry light of his celestial grandfather Zeus. Indeed, the labyrinth may not originally have been a maze but rather a spiral. So the person who journeyed downward to the center could return in safety to the light.

The spiral is a good image to conclude our discussion of the bull and the bear. If we think of the cycles of the stock market, we imagine an undulating curve that moves from left to right on a graph. The height of the curve measures the market's value and the movement to the right measures the passage of time.

But let us imagine that the cycles of the stock market are like a rising spiral. This would be an image of the ascending spiral of consciousness. On one level we might feel that our only purpose in playing the market was to gain or lose money. On another level we might see the usefulness of sacrificing money in service to others. And on yet a different level we might see the value of struggling with the paradoxes of our natures. So we might face in ourselves the images of the bull and bear, of Integrity and Hermes, as we become more fully what we are capable of being.

EPILOGUE

TO CONFRONT THE PARADOXES of our natures requires information about ourselves, about our depths. It requires the facing of so many illusions. It is not one journey, but a lifetime of journeys. How slowly, if ever, do we accumulate the wisdom that brings us awareness of what once we could not have imagined. How long it takes to become what we are, to discover in ourselves the rich potential that for so long remained invisible.

THEIR EYES WERE WATCHING GOD

The interplay of money with this inner unfoldment forms a core of *Their Eyes Were Watching God* by Zora Neale Hurston. Published in 1937, this novel tells the story of Janie, an African-American girl who grows to be a woman through her experiences in three marriages. Deserted by her mother, Janie is raised by her grandmother, who had been a slave and the mistress of the plantation master.

Money plays a crucial role in Janie's life, which certainly has as much pain as joy. She starts by accepting the values of her grandmother. There is no doubt that her grandmother cares for Janie and wants the best for her. Her grandmother insists that Janie marry Logan Killicks, an older, well-to-do farmer. Janie has no liking for Logan, whom she says looks like "some ole skull head in de grave yard," but she marries him to please her grandmother.

Three months later Janie comes to tell her grandmother that she has not grown to love Logan. Submitting to her grandmother's wishes and marrying for money has violated Janie's girlhood dreams of love. Rather than submit to abuse by Killicks, she runs away with Joe Starks, who has big dreams about achieving position and power in the world. When Joe succeeds, Janie finds herself relegated to playing the role of wife to a rich man. She feels the pain of not knowing her own heart and not living the natural flow of her own life. She is only slowly learning of herself, of her interior life. Estranged from her rich husband, she is finally freed after twenty years of marriage by Joe's death.

Janie is wealthy now in her own right but lonely. She realizes how she hates her dead grandmother "who had twisted her in the name of love." When Janie had been sixteen and "getting ready for her great journey to the horizon in search of people," her grandmother had undermined her and made her seek for "things." Janie laughs at the many men who tell her that a woman cannot stand alone and needs a man. She even likes being lonesome, for it means being free as well.

Six months after Joe Starks's death, Janie meets a man who makes her laugh. He is ten years her junior and his life isn't measured by money. When, for example, he wants to ride a train he "rides anyway—money or no money." His name is Vergible Woods, but he's called by his nickname, Tea Cake. At their first meeting Janie feels "as if she had known him all her life."

To love Tea Cake she has to overcome her suspicion that he is trading on his youth and ignore the friends who tell her that she is too important to be with someone like him. It is with Tea Cake that her interior life at last finds expression in the world. Here is a companion who assigns her no role, who cares for her as she is. Money is not a force for domination in their relationship. She is a rich woman; she has her money in the bank. With Tea Cake she is willing to do what she would refuse or resent with another man. She is joyous to share with him, to labor with him.

The novel ends with a terrible death, as Tea Cake saves Janie's life only to die himself from the bite of a rabid dog. Yet even as Janie grieves to lose him, she becomes ever more herself. She is both a part of the people and the events around her and an observer of them. She loves Tea Cake, but her view of reality has grown. She has reached deeply within herself and touched the invisible source that is within us all. From this inner discovery she is then able to live to the fullest in the world by being true to her own beliefs and desires. And at the same time, she understands that the events and people, even Tea Cake and her love for him, are not the only or the final reality. She has observed the invisible richness within herself; she has brought her soul into her life. If money at first held her captive, she has grown through this captivity and transformed herself and her relationship to money and to other people.

Janie, who has narrated her story to a friend, ends by saying that "you got tuh go there tuh know there." No one can make the life journey for us. "Two things everybody's got tuh do fuh theyselves. They got tuh go tuh God, and they got tuh find out about livin' fuh theyselves." Alone, she feels that Tea Cake will never die as long as she is alive. Thinking of all the events of her life, she feels how richly she has lived. She is both a part of this rich life experience and also the observer of it, for the novel ends with the sentence: "She called in her soul to come and see."

Janie makes of her life a journey. She moves through different relationships to men and money as her self-awareness deepens. To our everyday thinking, money would hardly seem a useful tool for this journey to greater awareness of ourselves and our relationships to others. Yet in so many ways, the symbolic richness of money can open a path to the richness that we carry within.

THE WIZARD OF OZ

This journey to awareness is archetypal, a pattern of initiation and growth that has taken many forms in many different cultures. This journey is not for everyone. The risks are great, the rewards uncertain. Yet those who take the journey find new depths and potentials that were once invisible to them. One of the most famous tales of this archetypal journey is a story written for children: *The Wizard of Oz*.

In 1896, when the Democrats held their convention in Chicago and heard William Jennings Bryan cry out against crucifixion on a Cross of Gold, one of the residents of Chicago was L. Frank Baum, author of *The Wizard of Oz*. Having had a play on Broadway in his early twenties and then having failed as a newspaper publisher in South Dakota before moving to Chicago in 1890, he frequented the Chicago Press Club and certainly heard many discussions of the silver issue. While Baum never said that one level of his story dealt with the great national debate over gold and silver, the book was mostly written in 1899 and published in 1900, the year William Jennings Bryan failed in his second attempt for the presidency. Could money, in fact, play an important role in *The Wizard of Oz?* If so, the story may be an allegory about the power and illusions generated by money.

The story begins as Dorothy, an orphan girl who lives with her aunt and uncle in drought-ravaged Kansas (the western states were parched by drought before the election of 1896), and her dog Toto are swept away by a cyclone that carries their house to the land of Oz. The house falls on and kills the Wicked Witch of the East. The kindly Munchkins, who inhabit Oz, give the witch's silver shoes to Dorothy. (The wonderful movie, with Judy Garland and Bert Lahr, changed Baum's story in a number of ways and made the shoes ruby instead of silver.) When Dorothy says that she wants to go home, a message comes that to do so she must go to the Emerald City at the very center of Oz. To travel to this place, she must follow the yellow brick road (the yellow brick strongly suggesting the ingots of gold that we would have expected to find stored in bank vaults at the end of the nineteenth century).

Why is the land called Oz? Baum said that he looked at a drawer in his filing cabinet and saw the letters O–Z, which became Oz. But Oz has another meaning as well: ounces, which is a measuring unit for both silver and gold. And Dorothy, who comes from Bryan's "hardy pioneers . . . who have made the desert to blossom as the rose," is quickly drawn into matters of which she understands very little. She is a pioneer in a fabulous land, and she must involve herself with gold (yellow brick) and silver (the silver shoes) if she is ever to find her way home to Kansas. And who was the Wicked Witch of the East? President Grover Cleveland hailed from the East, where he had been Governor of New York before winning his first term as president. When the cyclone of the silver movement swept out of the west, the Democratic Convention failed to nominate Cleveland (who backed the gold standard). So the house had fallen on him, killing him before the story (the campaign) really got underway.

Putting on her silver shoes, Dorothy starts on her journey and soon meets her companions: the Scarecrow, who feels himself a fool and yearns to have brains; the Tin Woodman, who wants to love and yearns for a heart; and the Lion, who yearns for courage. After many adventures, these four seekers come to the Guardian of the Gates of the Emerald City. This gatekeeper is hardly as terrible as Kerberos, the many-headed snake-dog that guards the gates of the underworld. The Guardian merely makes Dorothy and her friends (even Toto) put on emerald spectacles locked in place by two bands of gold.

Using a golden key, the Guardian unlocks the gates of the Emerald City. The newcomers are dazzled by its brilliance: "The streets were lined with beautiful houses all built of green marble and studded everywhere with sparkling emeralds. They walked over a pavement of the same green marble . . . The window panes were of green glass; even the sky above the City had a green tint, and the rays of the sun were green." Needless to say, the people, too, are green as are the shops and everything in them. No doubt the spectacles create much of what is spectacular in the Emerald City by making everyone see in the way that the Wizard wishes. This pervasive greenness brings to mind both the vegetative world and the greenback dollars that had figured in the gold and silver debates.

No living person has seen the Wizard, the Great Oz, "who can take on any form he wishes . . . who the real Oz is, when he is in his own form, no living person can tell." Dorothy and each of her band are ushered alone into the throne room of the Wizard. Each sees a different sight: Dorothy sees a giant head; the Scarecrow sees a beautiful woman; the Tin Woodman sees a terrible beast; and the Lion sees a ball of fire. The Wizard says he will only grant their wishes if Dorothy kills the Wicked Witch of the West and the others help her.

Many adventures later, Dorothy throws a bucket of water on the Wicked Witch of the West and, to her surprise, the Wicked Witch melts away. So the rainfalls after the election of 1896 brought good harvests to the western states and melted away the witch of drought. Returning to the throne room to have the Wizard grant them their wishes, Toto upsets a screen and reveals the Wizard—"a little old man, with a bald head and wrinkled face," just, in his own words, "a common man" and "a humbug." So the illusions by which he terrified Dorothy and the others were mere tricks.

Even knowing that the Wizard has no magical powers, they all still believe that he can grant their wishes and insist that he do so. The Wizard gives the Scarecrow a brain of bran, the Tin Woodman a heart of sawdust and silk, and the Lion a drink of courage. When they have left him alone, he laments and wonders, "How can I help being a humbug, when all these people make me do things that everybody knows can't be done?"

Yet the Scarecrow, the Tin Woodman, and the Lion have already shown that they possess what they are seeking. The obstacles on the yellow brick road have allowed them to discover in themselves what they seek to be given by the Wizard. Since they have become what they wish, the

Wizard can truly perform magic by giving them the outer symbol that confirms what they already are. Receiving this symbol is like a ritual that allows them to take the final step in their process of transformation, the step of knowing what they have become.

While the Wizard cannot help Dorothy, she, too, eventually learns that she has always possessed the power to grant her own wish. What she has lacked is awareness of her power. As the Good Witch of the South tells her, the silver shoes "can carry you wherever you wish to go." And with three clicks of her heels, Dorothy and Toto fly to the Kansas prairie and the embrace of her beloved Aunt Em.

We will never know if L. Frank Baum intended his story to be a monetary allegory. Yet the creative journey, to write a story or learn about ourselves, is often so much more than we intend. Whether the land of Oz is simply the letters O–Z from a cabinet drawer or is the symbol for gold and silver ounces, it is certainly a land of magical adventures. It lies outside the realms we know; it is the place awaiting our discovery.

Early in the story Dorothy tells the Good Witch of the North that Aunt Em said all the witches were dead. The Good Witch asks if Kansas is a civilized country. Dorothy says that it is.

"That accounts for it," says the Good Witch of the North. "In the civilized countries I believe there are no witches left, nor wizards, nor sorceresses, nor magicians. But, you see, the Land of Oz has never been civilized, for we are cut off from all the rest of the world. Therefore, we still have witches and wizards among us."

The challenge with such a place in us—"cut off from all the rest of the world"—is to make our journey and pass the Guardian of the Gates so that we may bring back its riches to the civilized world, the world of our everyday awareness. We may call this place Oz, the maze, the underworld, or the unconscious, but its challenge is to make us eat of our own natures. From this process we bring back the Scarecrow's wisdom, the Tin Woodman's love, and the Lion's courage; and we may return to the place from which we started, be it Kansas or anywhere else, with a newfound self-awareness.

Sometimes we may feel that our journeys seem to waste so much of our lives. Why must we be like the Scarecrow, the Tin Woodman, or the Lion? Why must each of us face the yellow brick road with its terrors and wonders? That we are not born like gods, fully knowledgeable about ourselves and our fate, is our human condition—a condition that we struggle to understand. We are part of the vast cycles of death and rebirth, part of the interplay in which sacrifice may at last bring us the riches of the invisible world.

The Secret Life of Money began with the story of the man who prayed to a wooden idol to give him money and make him prosper. We have traveled a long way on the yellow brick road since we met that man and his idol. We have seen how money can take innumerable forms without diminishing the symbolic power that allows it to obsess us. We have seen the radiance of Moneta, the face of the fertility goddess from whom money flows. We have learned how money challenges each of us and our society to be productive.

The quest for fertility—which assures our sustenance and, in more contemporary terms, our productivity—connects money to earlier rituals in which gifts were offered to the spirit world. The ease with which we worship money is more comprehensible when we look at these offerings that sought divine favor and attempted to initiate an exchange with the divine. That these rituals might require human or animal sacrifice helps us understand why money issues can make us feel our very lives are at stake.

The power of money to symbolize our life energy confuses us; we imagine that our self-worth and value depend on possessing money instead of using money as a tool to look more deeply within ourselves. Misers build their sense of self-worth and security around the hoarding of their life energy. Yet this hoarding defeats the very purpose of having money, since circulation is crucial if money is to serve its purpose of exchange among people. To circulate money, especially in service to our community, allows us to contact the natural wealth that we have within, energy that is augmented by giving to others.

Yet money that is given—for example, as an inheritance—can be weighted with emotional issues. Only by a careful evaluation of what is truly ours can we choose what to keep from the inheritance of money, property, love, education, and values that our parents have offered us. In its own way, debt, too, involves a giving and a receiving. If we are not to be imprisoned by debt, we must understand how debt is a statement about our future, how we will develop, and what our capacity will be to repay the energies that others offer to us.

The Secret Life of Money has focused on some of the images that are likely to confuse us. For example, United States money looks much the same as it always has, but it is no longer backed by gold or silver. Credit cards suggest that we can borrow without ever having to repay, but this illusion simply leads to the imprisonment that is always a potential of debt. And banks, in the last hundred years, have changed from temples serving the few to merchandisers of consumer debt that profit from the many. Even the stock market, which ideally channels the energy of society toward those enterprises that will be most productive, offers a symbolism of bulls and bears, of the flux of increase and decline that come one after another in never-ending cycles. So we see that the stock market bulls are but shadows of the divine bulls whose seminal fluids fructified the earth.

Dispelling illusions about money guides us toward the values that are most true for us. Each of us must find the nature of our own abundance. Each of us must decide how willing we are to share our money, our productivity, and our energy. So our relationship to money can deepen our understanding of our connection to other people and to our community.

Our consumer culture seems to value money and possessions, but our explorations tell us that the secret life of money may speak of inner richness. Understanding money can actually help us call in our souls to come and see. For the fertility of Moneta is not only found in the fields, the factory, or the office, but also in the creativity and love of our minds and hearts.

NOTES

No numbering is used for the Notes. Rather, the Notes are connected to the appropriate passage in the text by reference to the page number in the text and the quotation of a brief phrase from the page to locate the passage. Once a source is fully annotated in the Notes, additional references to that source are abbreviated by giving only the title. References to the Bible are to the Revised Standard Version unless noted otherwise.

INTRODUCTION

Page xi. "**. . . prosperity eluded him.**" "A Man and a Wooden God," *Fables of Aesop According to Sir Roger L'Estrange* (New York: Dover Publications, 1967), pp. 91–2.

CHAPTER ONE. THE MANY FORMS OF MONEY: UNDERSTANDING ITS SYMBOLIC VALUE

Page 4. "**. . . poles and carried.**" Norman Angell, *The Story of Money* (Garden City, New York: Garden City Publishing Company, 1929), pp. 88–9. This account is based on William Henry Furness, *The Island of Stone Money* (Philadelphia and London: J. P. Lippincott Co., 1910).

Pages 7–10. As to the many forms of early money, *see* A. Hingston Quiggin, *A Survey of Primitive Money* (London: Methuen

& Co. Ltd., 1949); Paul Einzig, *Primitive Money* (Oxford and New York: Pergamon Press, 1966); J. P. Jones, *The Money Story* (New York: Drake Publishers Inc., 1973), pp. 11–22; and *The Story of Money*, pp. 72–90.

Page 11. "... **the minds of its inventors.**" *The Story of Money*, pp. 85–7.

Page 13. "... **it is archetypal.**" This theory of archetypes has been developed by psychologist C. G. Jung. "On a personal level, archetypal motifs are patterns of thought or behavior that are common to humanity at all times and in all places." Daryl Sharp, *Jung Lexicon* (Toronto: Inner City Books, 1991), p. 29.

Page 14. "... **English word 'mint.'** " Eric Partridge, *Origins: A Short Etymological Dictionary of Modern English* (New York: Greenwich House, 1983), p. 405.

Page 15. "... **as Juno** *Matronalia.*" Joël Schmidt, *Larousse Greek and Roman Mythology*, Seth Benadete, ed. (New York: McGraw-Hill Book Company, 1980), p. 152.

Page 15. "... **rich beyond measure or imagining.**" The image of Juno Moneta is a composite drawn in part from Demeter, the Greek goddess, and in part from Lakshmi, the Hindu goddess. Some pictures of Lakshmi show coins pouring from one of her four hands. She is a fertility goddess who brings abundance and luck to those who worship her. *See* David Kinsley, *The Goddesses' Mirror* (Albany: State University of New York Press, 1989), pp. 53–70.

Page 16. "... **mind or think.**" *Origins: A Short Etymological Dictionary of Modern English*, pp. 390–2, 403–5.

Page 16. "... **his rabbi for advice.**" "One Big Worry," *A Treasury of Jewish Folklore*, Nathan Ausubel, ed. (New York: Crown Publishers, 1948), p. 5.

CHAPTER TWO. THE ALMIGHTY DOLLAR: WHY MONEY IS
SO EASILY WORSHIPPED

Page 19. "... **root of all evils** ..." 1 Tim. 6:10.

Page 20. "... **one religion over another.**" *Everson* v. *Board of Education*, 330 U.S.1 at p. 15.

Page 22. "... **game that nourished them.**" Joseph H. Wherry, *Indian Masks and Myths of the West* (New York: Bonanza Books, 1969), pp. 167–74.

Page 23. "... **as a knife and skis.**" *New Larousse Encyclopedia of Mythology* (London: Hamlyn Publishing Group, 1959), p. 307.

Page 23. "... **the Ainu of Japan.**" *Man, Myth and Magic*, Richard Cavendish, ed. (New York and London: Marshall Cavendish, 1985), vol. 2, p. 246.

Page 24. "... **mesas of Arizona in August.**" *The World of the American Indian*, Jules B. Billard, ed. (Washington, D.C.: National Geographic Society, 1974), pp. 163–9.

Page 24. "... **year-round procession of rituals.**" Frank Waters, *Book of the Hopi* (New York: Ballentine Books, 1963), pp. 123–247, and, particularly with respect to the mystic marriage, pp. 222–3.

Page 25. "... **the Greater Mysteries (held in September).**" Katherine G. Kanta, *Eleusis* (Athens: Kanta, 1979), pp. 10–17.

Page 26. "... **the rice harvest with a feast.**" James George Fraser, *The Golden Bough*, abridged paperback edition (New York: Macmillan Publishing Company, 1963), pp. 558–9.

Page 28. "... **love and familial responsibilities.**" William H. Desmonde, *Magic, Myth, and Money* (New York: The Free Press of Glencoe, Inc., 1962), pp. 29–36.

Page 28. " '. . . upon himself alone.' " *The Rig-Veda*, Wendy Doniger O'Flaherty, trans. (New York and London: Penguin Books, 1981), p. 69.

Page 28. " '. . . to be of darkness.' " *The Bhagavad Gita*, Annie Besant, trans. (Adyar, Madras: The Theosophical Publishing House, 1895), xvii.13, p. 178.

Page 28. " '. . . out of action.' " *The Bhagavad Gita*, iii.14, p. 54.

Page 29. ". . . the hiring of mourners." *Fables of Aesop According to Sir Roger L'Estrange*, p. 31.

Page 29. ". . . distort our view of the world." "The Veneer of Silver," *A Treasury of Jewish Folklore*, p. 60.

Page 30. ". . . impetus to the creation of money." *Magic, Myth, and Money*, pp. 171–4; *see also The Illustrated Encyclopedia of Mankind* (New York and London: Marshall Cavendish, 1990), vol. 3, p. 2058.

Page 32. ". . . that represented immense wealth." John S. Bowman, *Treasures of Ancient Greece* (New York: W. H. Smith Publishers, Inc., 1986), p. 68.

Page 32. ". . . treasures as security for borrowing." *The Horizon Book of Ancient Greece* (New York: American Heritage Publishing Co., Inc., 1965), p. 318.

Page 32. ". . . treasure moved into the world of trade." *The Story of Money*, p. 96.

Page 33. ". . . most of these coins clearly do." *Magic, Myth, and Money*, pp. 111–14 (especially notes 4 and 5); cf. George Macdonald, *Coin Types: Their Origin and Development* (Glasgow: James Maclehose & Sons, 1905; reprint ed., Chicago: Argonaut Inc., Publishers, 1969).

Page 33. "... **goddess of fertility as well.**" George Dontas, *The Acropolis and Its Museum* (Athens: Clio Editions, 1979), pp. 8–9.

Page 34. "... **godlike portrayals of themselves on coins.**" *Coin Types: Their Origin and Development*, pp. 151–2.

Page 35. "... **the words 'God, liberty, law.'** " Leon Lindheim, *Facts and Fictions about Coins* (Cleveland and New York: The World Publishing Company, 1967), pp. 190–1.

Page 35. "... **all coins of the United States.**" *Facts and Fictions about Coins*, pp. 200–1.

Page 36. "... **bills as well as coins.**" *Coin World Almanac*, P. Bradley Reed, ed. (New York: World Almanac, 1990), p. 271.

Page 36. " '... **has approved our undertaking.'** " *Coin World Almanac*, p. 271.

Page 37. "... **later St. Joachim.**" Norman M. Davis, *The Complete Book of United States Coin Collecting* (New York: Macmillan, 1971), pp. 265–69; Adrian Room, *Dictionary of Coin Names* (London: Routledge and Kegan Paul, 1987), pp. 215–16.

Page 38. "... **to pay 'ten thousand dollars.'** " *Macbeth*, I, ii, line 64.

Page 38. " '... **adopted from south to north.'** " Thomas Jefferson, "Notes on a Money Unit for the United States," 1782, quoted in *Dictionary of Coin Names*, pp. 215–16. See also Merrill D. Peterson, *Thomas Jefferson and the New Nation*, (London and New York: Oxford University Press, 1970), pp. 275–8, indicating that Jefferson first made this proposal in 1776.

Page 38. "... **of the sign for pesos.**" *The Complete Book of United States Coin Collecting*, pp. 264–5.

Page 39. ". . . **roots of the taler itself.**" *The Money Story*, pp. 45–6. Cf. *The Complete Book of United States Coin Collecting*, pp. 264–5.

CHAPTER THREE. MONEY AND SACRIFICE: WHEN MONEY FEELS MORE IMPORTANT THAN LIFE

Page 43. ". . . **caused by the love of money.**" D. H. Lawrence, "The Rocking-Horse Winner," *The Portable D. H. Lawrence*, Diana Trilling, ed. (New York: The Viking Press, 1947), pp. 147–66.

Page 45. ". . . **gold and his daughter, Marygold.**" Nathaniel Hawthorne, "The Golden Touch," *A Wonder Book* (New York: Lancer Books Inc., 1968), pp. 51–81.

Page 48. ". . . **in *The Metamorphoses*.**" Ovid, *The Metamorphoses*, trans. Horace Gregory (New York: The Viking Press, 1958), pp. 301–5.

Page 49. ". . . **the goddess herself must sacrifice.**" *The Golden Bough*, pp. 403–10.

Page 50. " '. . . **before the people of Israel.**' " 2 Chron. 28:1–3; 2 Kings 16:2–3.

Page 51. ". . . **even the prophet Elijah.**" 1 Kings 16:34; Judg. 11:30–30; 1 Kings 18:20–46; cf. Jer. 7:31 which expresses the later revulsion against human sacrifice.

Page 51. ". . . **children were offered as sacrifices.**" *The Golden Bough*, p. 327; Patrick Tierney, *The Highest Altar* (London, Bloomsbury Publishing Limited, 1989), pp. 396–7.

Page 51. ". . . **the fertility of the land.**" *The Golden Bough*, pp. 757–63.

Page 51. ". . . **that of the Aztecs.**" Brian M. Fagan, *The Aztecs* (New York, W. H. Freeman and Company, 1984), pp. 228–33, 245–6.

Page 52. ". . . **feeds the growth of the corn.**" Erich Neumann, *The Great Mother*, Ralph Manheim, trans., Bollingen Series XLVII (Princeton, N.J.: Princeton University Press, 1955), pp. 195, 322–3.

Page 52. ". . . **the Maize Goddess Chicomecohuatl.**" *The Golden Bough*, pp. 682–6.

Page 53. ". . . **but for money.**" *The Highest Altar*, pp. 322, 354. *See also* M. J. Sallnow, "Precious Metals in the Andean Moral Economy," *Money and the Morality of Exchange*, J. Parry and M. Bloch, ed. (New York and Cambridge: Cambridge University Press, 1989), pp. 209–31.

Page 57. ". . . **of the culture as well.**" The collective unconscious is a key aspect of the theories of psychologist C. G. Jung. It is collective because it contains "psychic contents that belong not to one individual but to a society, a people or the human race in general." *Jung Lexicon*, p. 35.

Page 62. ". . . **prevailed before the Civil War.**" For a discussion of issues pertaining to gold and silver, *see* Milton Friedman, *Money Mischief* (New York: Harcourt Brace Jovanovich, 1992).

Page 63. ". . . **they had cost in 1869.**" Hugh Rockoff, "The 'Wizard of Oz' as a Monetary Allegory," *Journal of Political Economy*, vol. 98, no. 4, 1990, pp. 742–4.

Page 63. ". . . **with striking religious metaphors.**" William Jennings Bryan, "The Cross of Gold," July 8, 1896. This speech appears in *Documentary History of Banking and Currency in the United States*, Herman E. Krooss, ed. (New York: McGraw-Hill Book Co., 1969), vol. 3, pp. 2009–15.

Page 67. " '. . . **have been vindicated?**' " William Jennings Bryan and Mary Baird Bryan, *The Memoirs of William Jennings Bryan* (Chicago: Winston, 1925), p. 471.

CHAPTER FOUR. HOARDING MONEY: WHY THE LIFE ENERGY OF MISERS IS STOLEN

Page 69. "... **a miller who loved gold.**" "A Miller Burying His Gold," *Fables of Aesop According to Sir Roger L'Estrange*, p. 10.

Page 71. " '... **Punishment of the Stingy.**' " George Bird Grinnell, "The Punishment of the Stingy," *The Punishment of the Stingy and Other Indian Stories* (New York: Harper and Brothers, 1901; reprint ed., Lincoln, Nebraska and London: University of Nebraska Press, 1982), pp. 3–15.

Page 77. "... **by Charles Dickens.**" Charles Dickens, *A Christmas Carol*, in *The Christmas Books* (London and New York: Penguin Books, 1985), vol. 1, pp. 45–133.

Page 87. "... **worries that it imposes.**" Henry D. Thoreau, *Walden*, J. Lyndon Shanley, ed. (Princeton, N.J.: Princeton University Press, 1971), p. 32.

Page 87. "... **learned the reward of hard work.**" Peter Baida, *Poor Richard's Legacy* (New York: William Morrow and Company, Inc., 1990), pp. 80–3.

Page 87. "... **one rich and one poor.**" "Money Makes Cares," *Folktales of China*, Wolfram Eberhard, ed. (Chicago and London: The University of Chicago Press, 1965), pp. 180–2.

Page 92. "... **ruled a vast empire in India.**" Swami Muktananda, *Play of Consciousness* (South Fallsburg, New York: Syda Foundation. 1978), pp. 219–32. The original story appears in the *Yoga Vasishtha*.

Page 98. "... **of Alcoholics Anonymous.**" *C. G. Jung Letters*, vol. 2, 1951–61 (Princeton, N.J.: Princeton University Press, 1975), pp. 623–4.

CHAPTER FIVE. THE SOURCE OF RICHES: GAINING A NEW UNDERSTANDING OF SUPPLY

Page 101. "**. . . as a boy of eight or nine.**" C. G. Jung, *Memories, Dreams, Reflections*, Aniela Jaffé, ed., and Richard and Clara Winston, trans., rev. ed. (New York: Vintage Books, 1965), p. 20.

Page 102. "**. . . of a man named James Kidd.**" John G. Fuller, *The Great Soul Trial* (New York: The Macmillan Company, 1969).

Page 104. "**. . . richness of the Self.**" According to Jung's theories, the Self is "the archetype of wholeness and the regulating center of the psyche; a transpersonal power that transcends the ego. . . . Like any archetype, the essential nature of the self is unknowable, but its manifestations are the content of myth and legend." *Jung Lexicon*, p. 119.

Page 104. " '. . . **inherit eternal life.**' " Mark 10:17–26; Matt. 19:16–22.

Page 105. " '. . . **to receive kingly power.**' " Luke 19:11–26.

Page 106. " '. . . **serve God and mammon.**' " Luke 16:13.

Page 106. " '. . . **and buys that field.**' " Matt. 13:44.

Page 107. " '. . . **come to this house** . . .' " Luke 19:1–10.

Page 107. " '. . . **be yours as well.**' " Matt. 7:25–33; Luke 12:22–31.

Page 107. " '. . . **is within you.**' " Luke 17:21 (King James Version).

Page 108. " '. . . **is not rich toward God.**' " Luke 12:21.

Page 108. "**. . . and become homeless.**" *Grimms' Tales for Young and Old*, Ralph Manheim, trans. (Garden City, New York: Anchor Press/Doubleday, 1977), p. 494.

Page 109. ". . . in service to others." Annette Lieberman and Vicki Lindner, *Unbalanced Accounts* (New York: Atlantic Monthly Press, 1987), pp. 18–20.

Page 110. " '. . . in your experience.' " Joel Goldsmith, *The Infinite Way* (Marina del Rey, California: DeVorss and Co., 1947), pp. 133–7

Page 111. " '. . . that supply to escape.' " Joel Goldsmith, *The Art of Spiritual Healing* (New York: Harper and Row, 1959), p. 142–4.

Page 112. ". . . value to him when he dies." "Only the Dead Are Without Hope," *A Treasury of Jewish Folklore*, pp. 125–6.

Page 113. ". . . of the wealthy man." "The Father of the Poor," *A Treasury of Jewish Folklore*, pp. 127–30.

Page 115. ". . . the Golden Ladder of Charity." "The Golden Ladder of Charity," *A Treasury of Jewish Folklore*, pp. 124–5.

Page 116. " '. . . for the forgiveness of sins.' " Matt. 26:26–8.

Page 117. ". . . *dana* or pure gifts . . ." J. Parry, "On the Moral Perils of Exchange," *Money and the Morality of Exchange*, pp. 64–93.

Page 119. ". . . whose friars lived by begging." *The Encyclopedia of Religion*, Mircea Eliade, ed. (New York: Macmillan Publishing Company, 1987), vol. 9, pp. 371–3.

CHAPTER SIX. INHERITANCE: THE ACTUAL AND SYMBOLIC WEALTH OF OUR PARENTS

Page 124. " '. . . as cocaine is to morality.' " Quoted in Lewis H. Lapham, *Money and Class in America* (New York: Ballantine Books, 1988), p. 13, n. 8.

Page 129. ". . . the fertility goddess Demeter." "To Demeter," *Hesiod, the Homeric Hymns and Homerica*, Hugh G. Evelyn-

White, trans., Loeb Classical Library (Cambridge, Massachusetts: Harvard University Press, 1907), vol. 57, pp. 289–325.

Page 131. " '. . . **giver of good things!**' " "To Hermes," *Hesiod, the Homeric Hymns and Homerica*, p. 443.

Page 134. ". . . **be used as a contraceptive.**" John M. Riddle, J. Worth Estes, and Josiah C. Russell, "Birth Control in the Ancient World," *Archeology*, vol. 47, no. 2 (March/April, 1994), p. 31.

Page 135. ". . . **as an offering to Persephone.**" Vergil, *The Aeneid*, Patric Dickinson, trans. (New York: New American Library, 1961), Book VI, pp. 120–46.

Page 137. " '. . . **he'll dig it up again!**' " T. S. Eliot, *The Waste Land and Other Poems* (New York: Harcourt, Brace and World, Inc., 1930), p. 32.

Page 138. " '. . . **to be crowned again.**' " *The Portable D. H. Lawrence*, p. 481–4.

Page 140. " '. . . **abundance of his possessions.**' " Luke 12:13–15.

Page 140. ". . . **a treasure in the vineyard.**" "A Father and His Sons," *Fables of Aesop According to Sir Roger L'Estrange*, p. 68.

Page 141. ". . . **losing his ax in the river.**" "Mercury and a Carpenter," *Fables of Aesop According to Sir Roger L'Estrange*, p. 52.

Page 142. ". . . **from *Grimms' Fairy Tales.***" "The Spirit in the Bottle," *Grimms' Tales for Young and Old*, pp. 346–9.

Page 148. ". . . **to it on his birthday.**" Lewis Hyde, *The Gift* (New York: Vintage Books, 1979), pp. 53–4. For a wonderful play in which a guardian spirit is portrayed, *see* Plautus, *The Pot* *of Gold and Other Plays*, E. F. Watling, trans. (New York and London: Penguin Books, 1965), pp. 7–49.

Page 151. "... **who was this thief?**" "To Hermes," *Hesiod, the Homeric Hymns and the Homerica*, pp. 362–405.

CHAPTER SEVEN. INDEBTEDNESS: HOW THE DEBTORS' TOWER CONNECTS EARTH TO HEAVEN

Page 155. " '... **crushed in my breast.**' " Quoted in Peter Ackroyd, *Dickens* (New York: HarperCollins Publishers, 1990), p. 68.

Page 156. " '... **and so say I.**' " Quoted in Peter J. Coleman, *Debtors and Creditors in America* (Madison, Wisconsin: The State Historical Society of Wisconsin, 1974), p. 5.

Page 158. "... **clothing and dismissed him.**" Edgar Johnson, *Charles Dickens: His Tragedy and Triumph* (New York: Simon and Schuster, 1952), p. 37.

Page 158. "... **in Massachusetts prisons.**" *Debtors and Creditors in America*, p. 42.

Page 158. "... **fear for a great many people.**" *Dickens*, p. 69.

Page 159. "... **especially from England.**" *Debtors and Creditors in America*, pp. 6–8.

Page 159. " '... **be given their freedom.**' " Quoted in Lewis Mandell, *The Credit Card Industry: A History* (Boston: Twayne Publishers, 1990), p. 6. *See* pp. 6–8 as to the early development of credit.

Page 160. "... **a debt too large to pay.**" Matt. 18:23–35.

Page 162. "... **become slaves.**" *New York Times*, 23 May 1993, p. 3.

Page 162. "... **meals, and rent.**" *New York Times*, 9 June 1993, pp. A1, A8.

Page 162. ". . . **hands with a boy.**" *New York Times*, 23 July 1993, p. B1.

Page 162. ". . . **the failure to repay debt.**" U.S. Bureau of the Census, *Statistical Abstract of the United States: 1992*, 112th ed. (Washington, D.C., 1992), chart no. 849; U.S. Bureau of the Census, *Statistical Abstract of the United States: 1989*, 109th ed. (Washington, D.C., 1989), chart no. 867; *New York Times*, 28 June 1993, pp. D1, D3; *New York Times*, 7 November 1992, p. 33.

Page 163. " '. . . **would make him wretched.**' " Quoted in *Charles Dickens: His Tragedy and Triumph*, p. 35.

Page 163. " '. . . **slave of the lender.**' " Prov. 22:7.

Page 163. " '. . . **not exact interest from him.**' " Exod. 22:25–27.

Page 164. " '. . . **to repay the loan.**' " Deut. 24:6, 12–13.

Page 164. " '. . . **from the hand of the fowler.**' " Prov. 6:1–5.

Page 165. ". . . **of Ghana in West Africa.**" Harold Courlander, "How Debt Came to Ashanti," *A Treasury of African Folklore* (New York: Crown Publishers, 1975), pp. 145–6.

Page 170. " '. . . **be nourished and multiply.**' " Gen. 1:27–30.

Page 170. " '. . . **man became a living being.**' " Gen. 2:7.

Page 171. " '. . . **to dust you shall return.**' " Gen. 3:19.

Page 171. ". . . **of eating forbidden fruit.**" "Rapunzel," *Grimms' Tales for Young and Old*, pp. 46–49.

Page 175. " '. . . **pays all debts.**' " William Shakespeare, *The Tempest*, III, ii, line 136.

Page 175. " '. . . **they are in their minds.**' " William Thackeray, *Vanity Fair* (New York and London: Penguin Books, 1985), p. 265.

Page 176. ". . . **an heir and not a debtor.**" *Charles Dickens: His Triumph and Tragedy*, p. 42.

Page 176. " '. . . **that time of my life.**' " *Charles Dickens: His Triumph and Tragedy*, p. 34.

Page 176. ". . . **between debt and inheritance.**" "The Bridge of Ch'üan-chou," *Folktales of China*, pp. 103–10.

Page 182. ". . . *Alcestis* **by Euripides.**" Euripides, *Alcestis*, Arthur S. Way, trans., *Greek Dramas* (New York: Appleton and Company, 1900), pp. 195–238.

Page 185. " '. . . **to love one another.**' " Rom. 13:8.

Page 186. ". . . **their taxes are lower.**" *New York Times*, 9 February 1994, p. A17.

Page 186. ". . . **to give the organ.**" *New York Times*, 30 June 1993, p. C14.

Page 187. " '. . . **render life of little value.**' " Letter from Thomas Jefferson to Nicholas Lewis, July 29, 1787, Thomas Jefferson Papers, Micro Film edition, reel 7, Manuscript Library of Congress, Washington, D.C.

Page 188. " '. . . **the best of his abilities.**' " Saul K. Padover, *Jefferson* (New York: The New American Library, 1942), p. 160.

Page 188. " '. . . **laws we cannot repeal.**' " Jack McLaughlin, *Jefferson and Monticello* (New York: Henry Holt and Company, 1988), pp. 4, 269.

Page 188. " '. . . **would devour his estate . . .**' " *Jefferson*, p. 174, 175.

Page 189. ". . . **declared bankruptcy in 1819.**" *Thomas Jefferson and the New Nation*, p. 991.

Page 189. " '. . . **line I am writing . . .**' " *Jefferson*, p. 182.

Page 190. ". . . **daughter and grandchildren.**" *Thomas Jefferson and the New Nation*, p. 1007.

Page 191. ". . . **the law of hospitality.**" *Jefferson and Monticello*, p. 269.

Page 191. " '. . . **that God is just. . . .**' " *Thomas Jefferson and the New Nation*, p. 260.

Page 192. " '. . . **is incalculable.**' " C. G. Jung, *Psychological Types*, *Collected Works of C. G. Jung*, H. G. Baynes, trans., revised by R. F. C. Hull (Princeton, N.J.: Princeton University Press, 1971), vol. 6, p. 63.

CHAPTER EIGHT. CHANGING SYMBOLS: MONEY, CREDIT CARDS, AND BANKS

Page 194. ". . . **sale in the market.**" "The Image-Seller," *Aesop's Fables*, V.S. Vernon Jones, trans. (New York: Gramercy Books, reprint of 1912 ed.), p. 88.

Page 195. ". . . **our day-to-day lives.**" Bureau of Economic Analysis, *The Economic Report of the President* (Washington, D.C.: Federal Reserve Board, 1992).

Page 197. " '. . . **value with this standard.**' " *Documentary History of Banking and Currency in the United States*, p. 2016.

Page 197. ". . . **issue Federal Reserve Notes.**" For the history leading to the creation of the Federal Reserve System, *see Documentary History of Banking and Currency in the United States*, pp. 2083–416.

Page 198. ". . . **or using gold as money.**" James Grant, *Money of the Mind* (New York: Farrar Straus Giroux, 1992), pp. 154, 227, 233–4, 275; Glenn G. Munn and F. L. Garcia, *Encyclopedia of Banking and Finance*, 8th ed. (Boston: Bankers Publishing Company, 1983), p. 432.

Page 198. ". . . **defended at thirty-five dollars per ounce.**" *Money of the Mind*, pp. 271, 285.

Page 200. ". . . **of sacred obligations.**" "Message by President Rutherford B. Hayes Vetoing the Bland-Allison Act, February 28, 1878," *Documentary History of Banking and Currency in the United States*, p. 1922.

Page 201. ". . . **by Edward Bellamy.**" Edward Bellamy, *Looking Backward 2000–1887* (Boston and New York: Houghton, Mifflin and Company, 1888), pp. 118–20.

Page 202. ". . . **by Diners Club in 1950.**" *See*, for a history of the development of credit cards, *The Credit Card Industry: A History*.

Page 204. ". . . **$15.73 billion for that year.**" *New York Times*, 18 November 1991, pp. A1, D9.

Page 208. ". . . **three Visa cards).**" *New York Times*, 26 August 1991, pp. A1, A17.

Page 208. ". . . **two-thirds of them did.**" *New York Times*, 29 March 1993, pp. A1, D7.

Page 209. ". . . **awareness of credit card holders.**" *New York Times*, 16 November 1991, pp. 33, 45; *New York Times*, 19 November 1991, pp. A1, D9.

Page 210. ". . . **is 19.8 percent.**" *New York Times*, 12 December 1993, p. B1.

Page 211. " '. . . **stop incurring unsecured debt.**' " Debtors Anonymous, *Spending Plan* (P.O. Box 20322, New York, New York 10025–9992: Debtors Anonymous General Service Board, Inc., 1989), pp. 10–11.

Page 213. ". . . **banking in the twentieth century.**" *Money of the Mind*, pp. 76–95, 161–3.

Page 215. "... **to $1.384 billion in 1929.**" *Historical Abstract of the United States, Colonial Times to 1970* (Washington, D.C.: U.S. Government Printing Office), series X, pp. 551–60. This also shows total consumer credit outstanding from 1919 through 1970.

Page 217. "... **the public feel welcome.**" *Money Matters: A Critical Look at Bank Architecture*, Joel Stein and Caroline Levine, eds. (New York: McGraw-Hill, 1990). This offers a pictorial review of the changing styles of bank architectures.

Page 218. "... **toiling at their desks.**" *Statistical Abstract of the United States: 1992*, chart no. 796.

Page 219. "... **for goods and services.**" *New York Times*, 14 March 1993, p. 26; *New York Times*, 5 March 1994, p. 30.

Page 220. ". . . **of all transactions.**" Peter Passell, "Fast Money," *New York Times Magazine*, 18 October 1992, pp. 42, 66.

CHAPTER NINE. BULLS AND BEARS: HOW THE STOCK MARKET REFLECTS THE RENEWING CYCLES OF LIFE

Page 225. "... **formative years of our nation.**" *The New York Stock Exchange: The First 200 Years*, James E. Buck, ed. (Essex, Connecticut: Greenwich Publishing Group, Inc.), 1992. This history includes a photograph of "Integrity Protecting the Works of Man" on pp. 106–7.

Page 232. ". . . **toss up its horns.**" William and Mary Morris, *Dictionary of Word and Phrase Origins* (New York: Harper and Row, 1962), p. 56.

Page 233. "... **and agriculture as foundations.**" *Man, Myth and Magic*, vol. 2, pp. 363–7. This gives background with respect to the bull and includes portions of the hymns to Enlil and Amen-Ra.

Page 235. "... **and eventual dominance.**" Franz Cumont, *The Mysteries of Mithra* (New York: Dover Publications, Inc., 1956).

Page 237. "... **ancient and widespread.**" *Man, Myth and Magic*, vol. 1, pp. 243–46. This gives background for the bear.

EPILOGUE

Page 243. "... **by Zora Neale Hurston.**" Zora Neale Hurston, *Their Eyes Were Watching God* (Chicago and London: University of Illinois Press, 1978).

Page 246. "... **for children:** *The Wizard of Oz.*" L. Frank Baum, *The Wizard of Oz* (London: Puffin Books, 1982).

Page 247. "... **and illusions generated by money.**" *Journal of Political Economy*, pp. 739–60.

SELECTED BIBLIOGRAPHY

Anderson, Quentin. *Making Americans: An Essay on Individualism and Money*. New York: Harcourt Brace Jovanovich, Publishers, 1992.

Angell, Norman. *The Story of Money*. Garden City: Garden City Publishing Company, Inc., 1929.

Bornemann, Ernest, comp. *The Psychoanalysis of Money*. New York: Urizen Books, Inc., 1976.

Breton, Denise, and Christopher Largent. *The Soul of Economies: Spiritual Evolution Goes to the Marketplace*. Wilmington: Idea House Publishing Company, 1991.

Brown, Norman O. *Life Against Death: The Psychoanalytical Meaning of History*. 2d ed. Hanover: Wesleyan University Press, 1985.

Buck, James E., ed. *The New York Stock Exchange: The First 200 Years*. Essex: Greenwich Publishing Group, Inc., 1992.

Bush, Lawrence, and Jeffery Dekro. *Jews, Money & Social Responsibility: Developing a "Torah of Money" for Contemporary Life*. Philadelphia: The Shefa Fund, 1993.

Butterworth, Eric. *Spiritual Economics: You Deserve Abundance; Reshaping Your Attitudes About Money, Spirituality, and Personal Prosperity*, rev. ed. Unity Village: Unity Books, 1993.

Coleman, Peter J. *Debtors and Creditors in America: Insol-*

vency, Imprisonment for Debt, and Bankruptcy, 1607–1900. Madison: The State Historical Society of Wisconsin, 1974.

Desmonde, William H. *Magic, Myth, and Money: The Origins of Money in Religious Ritual.* New York: The Free Press of Glencoe, Inc., 1962.

Einzig, Paul. *Primitive Money.* Oxford and New York: Pergamon Press, 1960.

Fitch, Alger. *What the Bible Says about Money.* What the Bible Says Series. Joplin: College Press Publishing Company, 1987.

Friedman, Milton. *Money Mischief: Episodes in Monetary History.* New York: Harcourt Brace Jovanovich, 1992.

Fromm, Erich. *To Have or to Be?* 2d ed. New York: Bantam Books, 1981.

Grant, James. *Money of the Mind: Borrowing and Lending in America from the Civil War to Michael Milken.* New York: Farrar Straus Giroux, 1992.

Greider, William. *Secrets of the Temple.* New York: Simon and Schuster, 1987.

Hyde, Lewis. *The Gift: Imagination and the Erotic Life of Property.* New York: Vintage Books, 1979.

Jones, J. P. *The Money Story.* New York: Drake Publishers Inc., 1973.

Kurtzman, Joel. *The Death of Money: How the Electronic Economy Has Destabilized the World's Markets and Created Financial Chaos.* New York: Simon and Schuster, 1993.

Lapham, Lewis H. *Money and Class in America: Notes and Observations on the Civil Religion.* New York: Ballantine Books, 1988.

Lindgren, Henry Clay. *Great Expectations: The Psychology of Money.* Los Altos: William Kaufmann, Inc., 1980.

Lockhart, Russell A., James Hillman, Arwind Vasavada, John Weir Perry, Joel Covitz, Adolf Guggenbuhl-Craig. *Soul and Money.* Dallas: Spring Publications, Inc., 1982.

Mandell, Lewis. *The Credit Card Industry: A History.*

Twayne's Evolution of American Business Series, edited by Edwin J. Perkins. Boston: Twayne Publishers, 1990.

Millman, Marcia. *Warm Hearts and Cold Cash: The Intimate Dynamics of Families and Money*. New York: The Free Press, 1991.

"Money," *Parabola: The Magazine of Myth and Tradition*, Spring 1991.

Needleman, Jacob. *Money and the Meaning of Life*. New York: Doubleday Currency, 1991.

Parry, Jonathan, and Maurice Bloch, eds. *Money and the Morality of Exchange*. Cambridge and New York: Cambridge University Press, 1989.

Quiggin, A. Hingston. *A Survey of Primitive Money: The Beginnings of Currency*. London: Methuen and Co. Ltd., 1949.

Rockoff, Hugh. "The 'Wizard of Oz' as a Monetary Allegory," *Journal of Political Economy*, vol. 98, no. 4, pp. 739–60.

Sardello, Robert J., and Randolf Severson. *Money and the Soul of the World*. Dallas: The Pegasus Foundation, 1983.

Seidman, L. William. *Full Faith and Credit*. New York: Times Books, 1993.

Simmel, Georg. *The Philosophy of Money*. Edited by David Frisby. Translated by Tom Bottomore and David Frisby. 2d ed. London and New York: Routledge, 1990.

Stein, Joel, and Caroline Levine, eds. The Museum of Fine Arts, Houston, and Parnassus Foundation. *Money Matters: A Critical Look at Bank Architecture*. New York: McGraw-Hill Publishing Company, 1990.

Tierney, Patrick. *The Highest Altar: The Story of Human Sacrifice*. London: Bloomsbury, 1989.

Wixen, Burton N. *Children of the Rich*. New York: Crown Publishers, Inc., 1973.

Yablonsky, Lewis. *The Emotional Meaning of Money*. New York and London: The Gardner Press, Inc., 1991.

INDEX

ABOUT THE AUTHOR

TAD CRAWFORD, the Publisher of Allworth Press in New York City, is a graduate of Tufts University in economics and of Columbia Law School. He has lectured on the psychology, mythology and symbolism of money at venues such as the New York Open Center, Wainwright House, and the Analytical Psychology Club of New York. He is the author of two novels, *A Floating Life* and *The Money Mentor: A Tale of Finding Financial Freedom,* and more than a dozen non-fiction books on the business lives of artists and writers. He lives in New York City.

ACKNOWLEDGMENTS

I DEEPLY APPRECIATE my friends, family, and colleagues whose encouragement and insights helped bring this book to fruition. I thank the staff at Jeremy P. Tarcher, Inc., especially Connie Zweig for her perceptive editorial suggestions. I am also thankful to have been aided in so many ways by the excellent staff at Allworth Press. My agent of nearly two decades, Jean Naggar, offered exemplary guidance for *The Secret Life of Money* as it entered the world of commerce. As the book finds a new life in 2022, I give my thanks to Tony Lyons and Caroline Russomanno for their enthusiasm and support.

NOTES

NOTES

FKA USA

FKA USA

The Complete Unabridged and Annotated Edition

A NOVEL

Reed King

FLATIRON
BOOKS
NEW YORK

FKA USA. Copyright © 2019 by Reed King. All rights reserved. Printed in the United States of America. For information, address Flatiron Books, 120 Broadway, New York, NY 10271.

www.flatironbooks.com

Maps by Rhys Davies

Designed by Steven Seighman

The Library of Congress has cataloged the hardcover edition as follows:

Names: King, Reed, author.
Title: FKA USA : a novel / Reed King.
Description: First edition. | New York, N.Y. : Flatiron Books, 2019.
Identifiers: LCCN 2018057863 | ISBN 9781250108890 (hardcover) |
    ISBN 9781250108906 (ebook)
Subjects: LCSH: Dystopias—Fiction. | GSAFD: Suspense fiction
Classification: LCC PS3611.I5843 F53 2019 | DDC 813/.6—dc23
LC record available at https://lccn.loc.gov/2018057863

ISBN 978-1-250-10891-3 (trade paperback)

Our books may be purchased in bulk for promotional, educational, or business use. Please contact your local bookseller or the Macmillan Corporate and Premium Sales Department at 1-800-221-7945, extension 5442, or by email at MacmillanSpecialMarkets@macmillan.com.

First Flatiron Books Paperback Edition: 2020

D 10 9 8 7 6 5 4 3 2

To Ellen Rowett, for the support, and Lindsey Worster, for the party.
And for seekers, fighters, dreamers, and grifters everywhere.

EDITOR'S NOTE

It has been my pleasure to amend and update the tenth edition of Truckee Wallace's immensely popular memoir, which we can assume was completed sometime between 2086 and 2088. Though I have left the original text unbowdlerized except for the occasional rectification of a spelling error, I have introduced several new footnotes and an expanded section of appendices to help contextualize Mr. Wallace's world for the modern reader. Many people have wondered about the change of title, which after the first edition was amended from the original (*Truckee Wallace: Memories of a Continent*) at the request of Mr. Wallace's close friend "Sammy" SAAM-1564A. (Thanks are owed to Sammy for her meticulous proofing and fact-checking, as well.) Sadly, I am unable to answer the numerous queries we receive about Mr. Wallace's current whereabouts. But I like to think that he may yet be finding adventure in the territories formerly known as the United States of America.

—*Reed King*

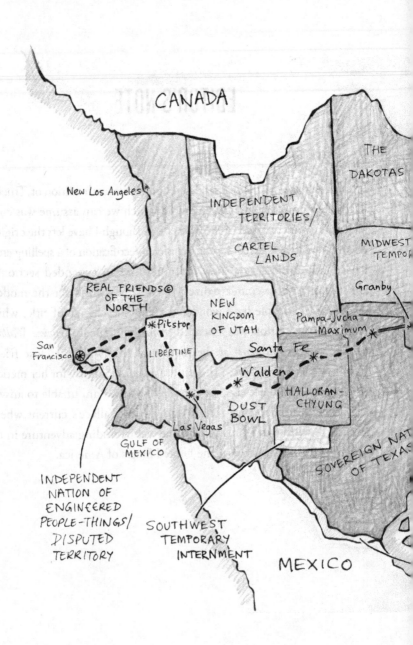

CANADA

THE DAKOTAS

New Los Angeles *

INDEPENDENT
TERRITORIES/

CARTEL
LANDS

MIDWEST
TEMPOR

Granby

REAL FRIENDS©
OF THE
NORTH

NEW
KINGDOM
OF UTAH

Pampa-Jucha
Maximum *

* Pitstop

San
Francisco *

LIBERTINE

Santa Fe *

Walden *

Las Vegas

DUST
BOWL

HALLORAN-
CHYUNG

GULF OF
MEXICO

SOVEREIGN NAT
OF TEXAS

INDEPENDENT
NATION OF
ENGINEERED
PEOPLE-THINGS/
DISPUTED
TERRITORY

SOUTHWEST
TEMPORARY
INTERNMENT

MEXICO

FREE STATE OF
NEW HAMPSHIRE

GREEN MOUNTAIN
ASSOCIATED
INTENTIONAL
COMMUNITIES

RFN
MILITARY
OUTPOST

CRUNCH,
UNITED

IET
ERATED
TIER

E
P

SINOPEC
TeMaRex
AFFILIATED

THE
COMMONWEALTH

Colony of
the RFN

CRUNCH,
UNITED,
COLONIES

Crunchtown 407

APPALACHIAN
TEMPORARY CAMP

THE CONFEDERACY

HE LOWER BELT

LOWLAND PENAL COLONY

FLORIDIA

CRUNCH, UNITED,
MILITARY OUTPOST

ARIZED ZONE/REFUGEE
INTERNMENT

FKA USA

PROLOGUE

You're sixteen going on sixty, Truckee, my mom liked to say, giving me a cuff. *Too smart for your own good, least where your brain's not plugged into the feeds.*

She always made that joke, even if I hadn't surfed much since I was a kid. Ever since Crunch, United, had made the swag stuff like Real-Friends© and WorldBurn: Apocalypse illegal,[1] there just wasn't a point. The company feed was stacked with the same sad sacks I saw every day in real life. Our board of directors couldn't code a game an amoeba would want to play. And the international news never changed: the Sovereign Nation of Texas was threatening guns, the Real Friends© of the North plotting subterfuge, the Commonwealth might be leeching data from our servers, the Russian Federation and the Dakotas were price-gouging oil, again, and the Confederacy was deadlocked in Senate discussions about whether to permit gas lanterns and ignoring all international comms.

You pay no mind to all that blather, my ma used to say. *It'll cook your smarts up.*

When I think of Mom now I think of her skin dark from sun, wrinkled

---

1. A kind of cold war had raged between the Real Friends© of the North and Federal Corporation of Crunch Snacks and Pharmaceuticals©, two of the continent's most powerful countries, since the early '70s, which culminated in the Trade Embargo of 2076. In Crunch, United, anyone caught with technology manufactured by the Real Friends© of the North was subject to heavy fines and even imprisonment in one of the famously expansive human landfill prisons of New Jersey County.

up like river mud. I think of maroon-tinged hair, the taffy vowels of the Confederacy, her big bark laugh, and the haze of vape that shimmered around her like neon mist, that soft-cloud smell of cherry tobacco and fresh.

She was born in 2041, the year of the First Secession, before the civil war swallowed up the country and spit it out into individual parcels, like so many gummed-up pieces of spinach. She could remember when you could drive all the way from Texas to the Federal Corporation of Crunch Snacks and Pharmaceuticals© with no papers, no semiautomatics, no risk of getting gamed at all.

Can you imagine, Truckee? she'd say, showing me a paper map that had been old even in her time, wrinkly, soft, and warm to the touch, like skin. Highways ran like veins across the continent, horizons with no borders or boundaries at all. *Can you imagine driving all that way? Just you, me, and a flattop rig.*

I never felt closer to my mom than with one of those maps on my lap, hopscotching the states that no longer existed and running a finger on the dotted lines that divvied them—not borders so much as hints. I liked to imagine a time I'd go all the way to the Pacific, maybe as a hotshot uppercrust tourist, maybe as a grifter, wearing a belt strapped with black-market firepower and a smile.

It was a shiver dream, obviously. At sixteen years old, I'd never so much as inched a foot outside of Crunch 407, and I had no cause to think I would. I was a skinny company kid with a hawkish nose, two and a half friends, and a bad habit of not knowing how to keep my mouth shut.

Everything I ever owned and would ever own belonged to Crunch, United—sheets on the bed, toilet paper in the bathroom, clothes on my back, my full-service e-Pack. I was a hand-strap operator anting on the line for 600 Crunchbucks a week, minus taxes and deductions. A crumb like millions of others.

I wasn't special. I wasn't brave. I was made to be a nobody.

Until Billy Lou Ropes came back to Crunchtown with a gun, a goat, and a grudge.

Part I

CRUNCHTOWN 407, CRUNCH, UNITED, COLONIES

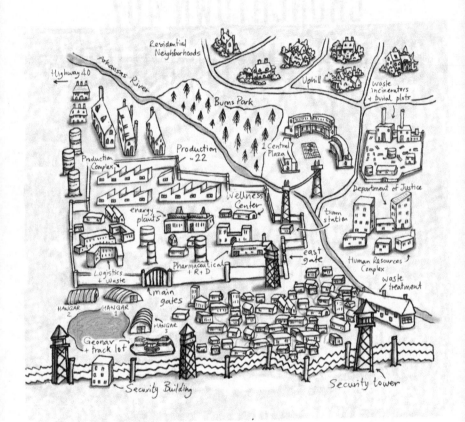

1

Knock, knock.
Who's there?
No one, dick. It's the end of the world.
—from The Grifter's Guide to the Territories FKA USA

"There." Jared Lee, the first of my two and a half friends, pointed past the stubby line of waste-treatment plants. "Right there. See? Refugees."

I raised a hand to shield my eyes from the sun. All I could make out were colored blobs. Across the river, Burns Park glowed in the morning light, its two-headed plants and stunted chemical trees all lit a violent shade of purple.

I shook my head. "Nada."

"Try your visor again," Jared said, and sneezed half a dozen times. Even his allergies were nervy.

"I told you, the color's crapped," I said. But I notched my visor down over my eyes anyway, and the world molted a mucus color where it touched my feed. Everything was shades of green and yellow—had been since last night, when in the middle of a rub-and-tug my VR porn star had suddenly blanked off into dots and zeroes. A virus from the illegal download, probably. And I couldn't exactly go to HR.

"I put my resolution up to twenty," Annalee Kimball, the second of my two and a half friends, said helpfully.

I did some fussing around with my scope app, which came free with the Crunch company software. When we were twelve, Jared and I discovered this function and spent a solid week staring at girls' boobs at resolution ten and then cracking up afterward. You can make technology as smart as you want, but you can bet bank humans will be stupid about it.

At resolution fifteen, patterns of algae made hieroglyphs on the Arkansas River. President and CEO Mark J. Burnham had pledged to clean the river by 2090 and there was even chatter of trying to breed fish, but we all knew it for empty talk.[1]

Finally, after another tweak or two, the whole of the Crunch 407 complex came into focus: the gridlock slum of Low Hill, the shipping plants and incinerators, the admin complex and chemical-waste drums, the water cisterns and sewage plants, the solar panels glimmering greenly, and the wind-powered tram that spanned the river and took the fat cats back to Uphill at the end of their workday. The Human Resources complex, dark and evil as a mold. Miles and miles of smokestacks, solar panels, water-treatment facilities, pipes—and beyond those, the splintered pinwheel of highways that went nowhere, at least nowhere you'd want to go.

I could just pick out a person working his or her way through the maze of ancient-model rigs on the highway just east of Ext 42A.

"A refugee," Jared said again.

"Or just backlander," Annalee said, tugging a crinkle of bangs out of her visor.

Jared shook his head. He wouldn't let it drop. "What backlander you know would make a run on Crunchtown in broad daylight?"

"A backlander *with* the runs," I said, and Annalee rolled her eyes. But

---

1. The Commonwealth had seeded the drowned underwater sand ridge known formerly as Cape Cod with more than a billion genetically engineered oysters during the explosive midcentury push to repopulate their country with more than two thousand living species. Like many of the other gentech initiatives undertaken in this era, the attempts to repopulate the waters had some unintended consequences: one gigantic oyster, roughly the size of an early-century vehicle, famously lacquered a child into a human pearl. (Subsequently, the relic was sold to a Chinese trillionaire for an undisclosed sum.)

almost every week HR stunned a backwoods camper sneaking in to poop in our toilets or steal toilet paper from supply. I once cranked open the shower to find a woman, butt-naked, sloughing about four years of grit down the drain. The only woman I've ever seen naked in real life, and she was a sixty-five-year-old hillbilly with dirt in her crack.

"Nah. Refugee." Jared sneezed again. The same month Jared was born, Crunch Snacks and Pharmaceuticals had its worst enviro disaster in history, flooding the river with two hundred tons of toxic chemicals. You could always tell Riverside babies from the sound they made when they breathed, as if they were sucking air through a wet sock.[2] "What do you want to bet we get a run of foreigners from the Federation? The Commonwealth's been rolling blackouts from Chicago to Winnipeg because of the new Security Resolution."[3]

"The Commonwealth's always threatening blackouts," Annalee pointed out.

"This time, it isn't just a threat," Jared insisted. "Half the Federation is dark right now. The servers are going haywire."

"Spam," I said. "You can't trust everything you read on the news. Didn't anyone tell you that?"

Jared shrugged, like *Just wait and see.*

"Besides, HR would of pulled the alarm," I said, but mostly to convince myself. I wasn't worried about raiders—no one, no matter how strung out on shiver, would dream of attacking Crunchtown, not with its security force and the watchtowers and the HR goons strutting the streets showing off their ammunition (*but remembering to smile!*).

The problem with foreigners was simple: they carried disease. When I was a kid, a few hundred desperate backlanders, fleeing violence at the

---

2. Also from the moles.
3. This is the first solid indication that the ensuing narrative takes place between April and May in 2084; in early April 2084, the Commonwealth took the extraordinary measure of passing retributory sanctions against one of its most steadfast allies, in response to the aggressive maneuvers of Russian war craft off the coast of Massachusetts.

border of Sinopec-TeMaRex Affiliated, made it to Crunch 407. The board of directors stuck them down in Low Hill, and a week later half of us were laid flat by the C-1 virus, one of the worst superflus that ever hit. Two thousand crumbs died in less than a week. Now foreigners had to go through quarantine, even if they were just passing through.

"There are two of them," Annalee said suddenly. "A tall one, and a short one."

I notched my zoom a little further. She was right: as I watched, the shadow fissured in two and then globbed together again.

"Maybe a dwarf," Jared said.

"Or a hobbit," I put in. A few years ago, Billy Lou Ropes had somehow rounded up a few old books—real ones, made of paper—and one of them was called *The Hobbit*. I'd never gotten used to reading—the text didn't move or scroll or link to videos; it couldn't read itself out loud, even—but I liked the picture on the cover, and the smell of the pages, which reminded me of my mom's old maps.

"Or a child," Annalee said.

The idea hovered uneasily between us: a little kid, maybe sick with something, maybe starving or thirsty for water or slashed up by the roadslicks who made their living taking tolls from travelers.

Then our SmartBands pulsed a light warning through our wrists. Fifteen minutes to daily login.

"I guess that's our cue," Annalee said.

"Hustle and shake," Jared said, and sighed. "Another day in paradise."

2

I became a grifter for a real simple reason:
I wasn't good at much of anything else.
—from The Grifter's Guide to the Territories FKA USA

Most scientists gave the human race another hundred and fifty to two hundred years, tops. Almost everyone agreed the best of human history was behind us. We were, as the human spermicide Dan Ridges once said, *on the wrong side of the blow job.* It was hard to imagine a time when humans were just getting themselves worked up, when climax was a vision of the not-too-distant future. When there even *was* a future.

Now, we were in the sticky, smelly, post-climax part of human history. But sometimes, in the morning, I could almost forget.

We joined the crowds flowing together toward the Crunch 407 Production complex—thousands of us, a single force churning through the narrow Low Hill streets. Buzz saws made a regular electric music: after all the problems with gut wedge, HR was on order to increase the regulation door size. Old holograms shed pixels on every corner, bleating about two-for-one painkillers at the Company Store. Deliverables robots whizzed sample envelopes and small packages through the narrow streets, and from every corner smiling holos reminded us of the importance of the three P's: Punctuality, Positivity, and Productivity. The sky was the white iron-hot that meant we'd break a hundred before noon, and the wind smelled like a dust storm, shimmering with a blood-red haze: my favorite kind of weather.

Outside of R-Block, we ran into Saanvi Ferrier and Woojin. Woojin was sweating through his usual costume.

"You hear what we did to those HR fuckers at the Rose Bowl last night?" Saanvi asked as she cut her chair left and right to avoid a clutter-fuck of trash. Saanvi was captain of a fantasy football team and competed against other company divisions for Crunchbucks and more HealthPass™ days.

"Tell me you nailed them," I said. There was nothing we hated more than Human Resources. The department fed directly to the Crunch, United, board and worked in deadly secrecy. Its agents were everywhere and nowhere, like a poisonous fart.

"More than nailed," Saanvi said. She had a dazzling smile, so wide it dimpled all her chins together, and it pained me to think that some-day she might look like her mom, completely dayglo, with orange staining even her teeth and the whites of her eyes. "Creamed. It was *infinite*."

"Meow," Woojin said. Ever since the announcement he was transspe-ciating, it was all he ever said. Woojin didn't wash his fur nearly enough, and we were careful to walk a few feet in front of him.

"You're a legend, San," I said. "Permission to fist-bump?"

"Granted," she said. Physical contact without verbal consent was il-legal in the colony—which wasn't a bad thing, exactly, but made it pretty awkward for a sixteen-year-old kid hoping and praying he wouldn't always be a virgin.

Jared was scrolling through his visor feed. "Hey, did you guys see *Michael and Addie* this morning?" *Michael and Addie* was the most popular feed in the country.

"Meow," Woojin said.

"That whole show is staged." When Annalee shook her head, her black braids caught invisible waves of chemical static, and briefly crackled off some colors. That was Annalee for you: electric. She and I were once neighbors, back when we lived in 12-B. It was lucky I got my hooks in her when we were little. She was way out of my league now, with skin the rich brown color of trees you never saw anymore and the kind of curves you wanted to bed on. Of course, I'd been in love with her forever but in a way that didn't hurt, like a scar I couldn't remember getting.

"You really think they could of staged that spew?"

"Why not? It's called *special effects*."

"Uh-uh. No way." Jared started sneezing so bad even his eyes looked like they were snotting.

"So where'd they find a real egg? Tell me that. And *don't* give me some shit about the Denver Airport and some secret underground civilization."

"It isn't shit, and isn't even secret. The Russian Federation and the cartel have been building cities under the surface for *years.* . . ."

"Sure, just like the Mars colonists are alive and just *choosing* not to communicate. . . ."

"Would *you*?"

"Meow."

There were lots of things I hated about Crunch 407. But there were things I liked about it, too, and one of them was this: walking with Annalee and Jared and even Woojin in the sun, while Saanvi whizzed along beside us in her chair, while from their blocks thousands of crumbs poured into the streets and shouted news at one another or stopped to slug a coffee at one of the unofficial canteens hacked out of a tiny square of lobby or a defunct elevator shaft.

Already, I'd completely forgotten the backlanders, or refugees, or whatever they were, making their way to us along a highway of littered wreckage.

"Is a road still a road if it doesn't go anywhere?" Annalee asked me once after a party in the old parking garage on the south side of Low Hill, where the serious dimeheads went to get high. She dropped her head on my shoulder—she didn't even ask first. "Does time exist if nothing ever changes?"

Which is one of those questions that makes you think you should never have smoked embalming fluid in the first place.

We said goodbye to Saanvi and Woojin just inside the main gates. Five minutes later, Jared and Annalee peeled off toward the trolley that would take them to Uphill. Jared did New Business for Public Liaisons, and he was *good*. No surprise: He was the only guy I knew who could legitimately get excited about the release of Bolognese-Flavored Crunch-Italian™ Bread Things or the fact that the company was running a holiday raffle through its advertising department, the prize equal to a week away at the Crunch Wellness Retreat in Ouachita National Forest, or what was left of it. Annalee worked in Remediation through the DoJ, which meant that she spent her days fielding angry livestreams from people demanding refunds when their CrunchChipz™ turned out to be composed mostly of glue, or their OrangeJuz™, over time, actually turned *them* orange.

"I hope you *crunch* it today," Jared said with a grin and a sneeze.

I looked around to make sure no HR monkeys were lurking around, then gave him the finger.

"See you in the Commons?" Annalee called back—like she needed to ask. Every night we hung out in the Commons, a cozy little den of shaggy couches and old carpet, at least until the nighttime blackout took down the server and our VR. It was too risky to try to hang out in person once the dimeheads were out.

An HR goon stationed at the corner spitting venom through his teeth gave me the old once-over.

"Better hurry up," he said. "Or you'll be late." Like I didn't have my SmartBand to tell me.

I practically skidded into the vestibule of Production-22. The security guard was crooked over an enormous book, a real book, made of dead trees and everything. At the sound of my footsteps, she dropped it, letting out a long string of code.

"Heya, Sammy," I said. "How's cramming?"

Sammy, the *half* of my two and a half friends, doubled over to retrieve her book, then glared at me with enormous fiber-optic eyes.

"You scared me," she said.

"That's good," I said. "That means you're improving."

This earned me another glare. "The HSSE doesn't test for *fear*," she said. Before I could skid past her, she shoved the book into my hands.

"Sorry, Sammy. I'm pretty short on time," I said. It was Sammy's dream to move to Silicon Valley, and for months I'd been quizzing her every morning—even though so far every single one of her requests to emigrate had been denied.

Her eyelids shuttered and then opened again.[1] I swear to God, I will never know how a heap of metal and plastic parts manufactured circa 2035 in Malaysia could look so damn pitiful.

"Fine," I said. Flipping forward a few pages, I picked a question at random, waiting for the data-scan on my visor to process the words and whisper them to me. I had no time to remember how to read.

"Let's say you run into a fellow Engineered Person on the street," I said, once my audio cued me. "Name three appropriate greetings."

Sammy rattled off the answers quickly. "Smile and say hello. Smile and offer your hand or equivalent mechanical part for a 'shake.' Hug."

Sammy repeated the text word for word. I couldn't imagine why she was studying so hard, given her memory drive let her stash the whole book the first time she'd scanned it.

"Correct. Question 537. Let's say you are seated with Accidental Persons—" I broke off as my audio software seemed to snicker. "'Accidental Persons'? That's a little harsh."

"We were crafted." Sammy tilted her head. She was neither a male nor a female, as far as I could tell, but her voice was a high, fluttery

---

1. Blinking was one of the few human traits engineers coded for the first gen of sentient android anthropomorphic models—SAAMs—even though it was unnecessary back in the day. Newer models, the ones grafted from human skin tissue, did blink, and get itches. Sometimes their feet fell asleep if they stayed in standby mode too long.

kind of electronic. So, either a female, or a male who'd never gone through puberty. "You're just here because of a random collision of sub-atomic particles and the influence of chance acting on an infinite space-time map."

"The New Kingdom of Utah would disagree," I said. I closed the book, *Being and Becoming: A Guide to Sentience and Selfhood, by the Independent Nation of Engineered People-Things*,[2] and handed it back to her. The cover showed a group of SAAMs, many of them wearing human clothing, standing on a lawn next to a ModelPet™, smiling broadly at the camera.

"One more question," she said. "A hard one."

No way was I going to make it to my station in time. But I'd never been able to say no to Sammy. So I pulled a really angry face, baring my teeth, scrunching up my eyebrows, glaring.

"Hmmm." Because of her age, when Sammy processed you could hear a very faint whining. "Not happy . . . no, definitely not happy. The eyebrows go the other way. Sad, maybe? The eyebrows are contracted. But no, the mouth is all wrong." She was quiet for a few more seconds. "You're confused. That's it, right? You're confused."

"Close enough," I said. My SmartBand was so tight by now, it was painful. "Sorry, Sammy. I really gotta scram."

I took the stairs two at a time. One floor, two floors, three floors. I

---

2. The Independent Nation of Engineered People-Things, with the unfortunate acronym of I.N.E.P.T., is a Silicon Valley–based group dedicated to the rights of all sentient android models and determined to grant all sentient androids legal recognition as human beings or their equivalents. The test preparatory booklet referenced here was designed to help prepare potential citizens for their naturalization exam. Please note that the latter should *not* be confused with the controversial exam developed by MIT—and famously funded with a large endowment from pro-Naturalist agitators— ostensibly to test sentience, but in reality designed to establish a strict definition of "humanity" that would exclude both robotic/android and cloned individuals from passing while favorably rewarding bionormatively born humans. The exam was widely discredited after various bionormative humans tried and failed repeatedly to pass it. See Appendix A: "What Is a Human?"

slammed through a door marked CAUTION—EMPLOYEES ONLY, holding my SmartBand to the lock to disable it. The door released with a *whoosh*, and suddenly a giant fist of sound reached up to punch me in the face. Gears grinding, liquids sizzling and hissing, crates rattling, and giant conveyor belts chug-chug-chugging along, as big as the highways that had once carried cars across the continent. Security techs with bubbly gas masks appeared and ghosted in the steam. Armored bots scuttled like nuclear spiders between the equipment, readers flashing in the murk.

I grabbed a mouth attachment from the wall where they were pegged, hooked it to my visor, and sucked down a breath of clean air. Then I clapped my hands over my ears and sprinted down one of the catwalks jointed high in the air above all the machinery below, finally throwing open the door to the work deck. I slid into my chair just as my Smart-Band gave a final, violent squeeze, and the clock rolled over to 7:30. A giant whistle sounded through the whole of Crunchtown, loud enough I could feel it in the back of my teeth.

Then the Crunch National Anthem©—the remixed, crunked-out morning version—kicked on, heavy on the bass. *Feed your fun, power your play, crunch and sizzle through your day . . .*

There was something about the line that just took a hammer to your brain, beat it down into a useless puddle. You *couldn't* think. If you did, you'd start wondering about whether the world was really a better place after the dissolution, like all of our history downloads said, and if so then how shitty it must of had to be before. Or you'd start wondering why, if God created the universe, he couldn't invent endless oil fields and soil that didn't turn irradiated and an ozone layer that didn't vanish like a cloud of vape smoke. Or you'd think about the billions and billions of stars stretching endlessly out into dark space, which, by comparison, made this, this planet, look like a single poop fleck on a square of toilet paper flushed down a toilet of nothing. You'd start to wonder whether any of it was worth it at all.

In other words: you'd go nutty.

Lucky for me, all my job asked was an index finger and a working heartbeat. My job at Crunch was to make sure that the vats of chlorinated polyethylburitane were combined with the supply of crystallized glucolic acid at just the right time, in just the right quantities, and at just the right temperature.

Sexy, right?

Thinking was highly discouraged. All I had to do was plug into the system and make sure the machines didn't screw up. It was depressing to know how easily we could be replaced by a robot with the intelligence of an amoeba, and *extremely* depressing to know the only reason we *weren't* replaced was that robots were expensive to build and maintain[3]—especially since the cold war between the Federal Corp and the Real Friends© of the North had gone glacial.

Humans, on the other hand, came cheap by the dozen.

If everything looked good, a green light flashed on my console, and I reached out and pulled a hand crank. The vat of chlorinated polyethylburitane glugged into the container of crystallized glucolic acid and boom, my work was finished.

I did this roughly 3,267 times a day.

Oliver, to my right, was responsible for blending. Javier next to him made sure that the catalyst agent mixed correctly with the liquid bicarbonate, Kerry that it was poured into molds cold enough to turn it into a suspended liquid-solid, Amanda that it went to the presser . . . and on and on and on, until, at the very end of the line, the final product emerged: plumes of powder-white silt, fine and flavorless, ready to be vac-packed for shipping off to Crunch subsidiaries or slotted over to Production-23, mixed with edible adhesive and artificial taste, then lacquered onto crisp

---

3. This was particularly true for Crunch and its subsidiaries, whose facilities and distribution centers were all centered in the east. Because of Crunch, United's hostility toward the Real Friends© of the North and even its trade partners, where, by 2084, the vast majority of the country's sentience and robotic technology was manufactured, building and maintaining the current workforce of androids and robots was a constant struggle.

pale sheets of CrunchCrisp™ crackers—which were, of course, manu-factured from a long list of chemical components elsewhere in produc-tion. Jared once pointed out that I was one-thousandth responsible for every cargo load of Flavor Blast Cheez Dust™ that blew out of the fac-tory doors and chugged on to another production department, to be spackled onto CrunchChipz™ or Nachoz™ or Tortilla Rollz™.

I think he meant it as a compliment.

If there was a glitch, my console flashed yellow instead of green. Once in a while someone's yellow became a line problem—the next person's console went yellow, and the next, and so on, until the whole ops had to be put on ice while robotic techs crawled around the catwalks shouting numbers through the network. Sometimes I even wished for a problem just to have something to *do,* even if the something was just calling a high-rank robot to do a system check.

In the two years since Production-22 had come online, there'd been only one Red Alert. This was a few months before I got swapped from my old job in Production-12, when somehow a rubber shoe (male, size 12) ended up in a body socket full of superheated sodium hydrochlorine-dioxide.

It wasn't actually the shoe that was the problem, we found out later. There were lots of sanitation glitches over the years, and everyone in pro-duction learned to let them slide: pens dropped into the polyurinylated oxyhydrocordone-12, lost visors floating briefly on the bubbling surface of vats of monobariumditroxate before being consumed by the acid. Once I found a toothbrush, a whole toothbrush, intact in my CrunchGrainz™ Berry Burst Blush Crunch bar.

What really screwed the pooch was the large piece of onion skin—real onion skin, from a grown onion—that went into the vat plastered to the underside of the rubber sole.

For weeks no one could talk about anything but that goddamn on-ion skin. How the hell had it ended up in Crunchtown—in the super-heated sodium hydrochlorinedioxide, no less? I'd never so much as *seen* an onion, except in pictures from prehistory. I'd heard stories about uppercrusts in the Emerald City[4] of the Real Friends© of the North paying insane sums of money for a single plate of grown lettuce, unwashed, but I had trouble credding it, and of course no one I knew had ever been west. Travel visas were too expensive—never mind the cost of bodyguards or weapons and transport past the former state of Colorado.

And yeah, the backlanders grew their own food, wherever the ground wouldn't kill a seedling with radioactive flow. But the fields surrounding Crunch 407 were good for nothing but glow-in-the-dark tubers and strange chemical halos. Some people claimed nukefood was magic, that eating a tomato the size of a small tire, or a radiant strawberry with fourteen stems, would make you grow taller or give you a hard-on that would last two days or give you good luck for a year or whatever, but that was all hippie shit, and as far as I knew we didn't have any radio doctors in the corp.

Anyway, that's what brought the whole system to its knees: that wilted onion skin. Real food, it turned out, was very, very bad for RealFood™. Getting inorganic materials like graphite or salt to pass for everything from banana splits to boiled green beans required insane precision.

And that onion skin, that little purple onion skin made of interlocking carbon-hydrogen bonds, with the air and the sun baked into its very chemical being, acted like a match on a closed container of vaporous dyaphedrynol.

Which is to say: there was a very large explosion.

I spent the morning half-listening to Oliver recount the latest exploits of his RPG, Clash of the Countries. "So Raj came at me with an army of

---

4. San Francisco had earned the nickname soon after the first Big One, when the continuous coastal flooding had carpeted half of the low-lying areas in a vivid green fungus; the Department of Tourism had for years been attempting to reframe the moniker as a reference to its urban farmlands.

Friendly Mercenaries—stupid move, I've been collecting Bibles for *weeks*—"

He broke off as Dan Ridges, my least favorite person in all of Crunch 407, strutted back into position and dropped into his chair, barely giving his replacement time to spin out of the way. Squatbots were basically walking circuit boards, designed to push or crank and winch when they had to, so the line didn't stop just because someone had the runs.

"Someone took a shit in the gendered bathroom," he announced.

"Gross." That was Kerry, from position 87. I liked Kerry. Big bushy hair, lots of teeth and eyebrows, a great smile, just the right kind of fat. Possibly, *possibly* in my league. So far I hadn't worked up the courage to ask her for permission to touch even her hair or shoulder or hand, though.

"At the risk of confusing you, Dan," Oliver said, sucking air through his enormous orange teeth, "bathrooms are designed to accommodate other people's shitting."

Dan's visor was newer than anyone else's: half the width, practically translucent, so we got treated to every one of his ugly expressions. He wasn't even really a crumb, as he was fond of reminding us approximately every .5 seconds. His father was actually one of the uppercrusts in Corporate Relations, and they lived in Uphill in a real house with multiple bathrooms—more bathrooms, he claimed, than there were people in their family, which I wasn't sure whether to believe or not.

"Not in a toilet, dipshit. On the floor. A big pile of it."

"Again, gross," Kerry said.

Down below on the factory floor yet another vat of bubbling chlorinated polyethylburitane slid into place on its belt. Green light. *Crank.*

"Don't shoot the server," Dan said. "I wasn't the one who dropped the load."

Not for the first time, I imagined chucking Dan through the protective plastic, lobbing him straight off the deck, and watching him turn somersaults toward the concrete floor. Once, when I was twelve, Dan got me to snort a handful of CrunchPepperCorn™ by telling me it was dymo, the first of only two times in my life I was ever tempted to try it.

"Have you ever thought of swapping out your mouth for a used tissue?" I asked him. "They can do that now."

"I once heard of a girl who swapped her eyes for a pair of radium diamonds," Oliver said. "She looked ultra—until the radiation melted her, at least."

Dan ignored this. "The funny thing is," Dan went on, as if we'd asked, "it didn't even look like *human* shit. . . ."

I slammed a fist on my bathroom call button and a squatbot whirred down the line to take my place. I only got three breaks a workday, fifteen minutes total, but I needed to get away from Dan and the storm pressure of his sub IQ.

Afterward I could never remember the right order of things, if I saw him and then the alarm went or the alarm went and then I saw him. Either way, I was on my gams when the security alarms started shrieking and I looked out through the plate glass to see Billy Lou Ropes—the dimehead fugitive, ex-citizen of the Federal Corporation of Crunch Snacks and Pharmaceuticals© and one of my all-time favorite people—standing on a catwalk thirty feet above the factory floor, with his arms straitjacketed around one very ugly goat.

INTERLUDE

DYMOPHOSPHYLASE; OR, BILLY LOU'S LAMENT

There were lots of ways to get fired from the Federal Corporation. Outside of the Sovereign Nation of Texas and the Lowland Penal Colony, the Federal Corp had the continent's heftiest rate of lockups. By the time we graduated from standard, we were expected to know and memorize the entire Constitution of *The Employee Handbook of Better Business Practices*—all 437 pages of it, including the two hundred pages dedicated to potential infractions.

Article XVIII, Section 3, for example, stated that *all citizens of the colony must be properly attired at all times*:

i. *company-issued uniforms,*
ii. *company-issued SmartBand PLUS current photo ID and security-level clearance, properly displayed;*
iii. *A smile!*

Flip-flops were illegal in every Crunchtown subsidiary across the globe.[1] So was unwashed hair, spaghetti straps, and shirts of sheer or semisheer material—disappointing for a horny sprocket like yours truly. It was illegal to wear studs besides the company-issued uniforms,[2] just like it was illegal to be without a SmartBand, and a smile.

---

1. Inexplicably, other kinds of sandals were okay.
2. Or, in the case of regional sales associates, presidents, vice presidents, associate presidents, and assistants to the aforementioned, community managers in Perception

Lateness or back talk could get you a few nights in the slammer, and so could cusstalk, and "explicitly violent or sexual content." When I was a kid this gonzo Andy Duggar was written up and hauled in for an overnight just for saying that the weather sucked, and my mom knew a he-she in the freight office got six months in local after an eighty-four-pound shipment of VitaFizz™ tumbled from its stack and landed on their thigh, crushing their femur bone, and they cursed a geyser to heaven.

But Billy Lou Ropes didn't get fired for having unwashed hair, or because he slipped out without a company ID, or because he said "fuckbucket and all to hell" and one of the HR rats happened to nab him.

He got fired for stealing an eight-ounce supply of liquid dymophosphylase from the Pharmaceutical Division.

He wasn't the first shiver junkie to try to synthesize the drug from stolen supply, and he wouldn't be the last. Dymophosphylase was the active ingredient in ten of the company's most popular pharma products, and could be extracted in trace quantities from thousands of others:[3] Dymase PainKillers™ and DimeSmile Teeth Brightening Salve™ and Dime-A-Day Vitamins™ were always going missing from the company store, swiped by desperate addicts.

At night, it sometimes seemed that half of Crunchtown was high or coming down. Boiling shiver had a reek that would make a user salivate and everyone else begin to choke, and even though the addicts lumped together in the burned-out hollows of old parking garages, and the urine-soaked darkness of highway underpasses, the stink was practically baked into the walls.

---

and Market Comprehension, department supervisors and Human Resource service experts, business-neat attire.

3. At the beginning of its operations at the turn of the twenty-first century, Crunch Enterprises had only a single factory building on the Exxon-Mississippi River just outside of St. Louis, and was exclusively focused on convenience food and dietary supplements. Dymophosphylase was, at that time, one of the active ingredients in the original formulation of CrunchJuz™ Gelcaps, billed as the world's first energy-intense vitamin-rich Complete Food Replacement pill.

But the noise was the worst part. My ma and I stuffed towels under the door and blacked out the windows with bolts of hard canvas we scavenged from the trash pits, but it did nothing to stop the nightly symphony: a terrible joy that screamed through the caverns of the streets when the first hits were smoked, snorted, or injected, and then, later, a howling so loud it rattled our windowpanes and sent fine sifts of plaster down from our ceiling; all those addicts sobbing over lost homes, lost loves, and things they didn't even know they'd lost.

Not Billy Lou, though. Billy Lou was different.

Billy Lou was never angry. He never spoke too fast or in a way that didn't make sense. He was always polite, even when he was high, which was most of the time. I remember how he always called me Mr. Truckee. He called my mom ma'am, too, and said *please* and *thank you* and *you're welcome*.

He never got weepy either—the worst symptom of dimeheads, the way they rattled the city every night with their wailing, a kind of crying I'll never shake the sound of. As if they were dying.

As if *you* were.

He always smelled like TomatoJuz™, since he saved all of his Crunch-bucks for the synthetic forms of dymo, and TomatoJuz™ was the cheapest foodstuff you could buy at the company store. Like a lot of serious addicts, he'd had his nails removed—otherwise, dimeheads would scratch themselves bloody, take the skin off their cheeks and foreheads, and have to go up before the Crunch Supreme Court Board for review. Whoever did the operation did it nicely, though. No rough edges, no stumps and bits left behind. His fingers were like blind, defenseless animals, crawling across the table, fiddling with his visor, adjusting his shirt.

He was old, he smelled, his nail beds were like hairless fetuses. But I liked him. I probably even loved him. I used to imagine once in a while that Billy Lou would move into our shoebox, that he'd lay one of his stubby nailless hands on my head and call me *son*, that it wouldn't be pretending.

When my mom got switched to freight and had to work doubles, it was

Billy Lou who came over to shake up my soup cartridges or grow a roast by adding water. He taught me stuff that wasn't on the data feeds,[4] like prehistory, and the names for all the animals that went extinct in the Great Die-Off, and the basics of chemistry and algebra. Even if I couldn't scan even a tenth of it, I loved the idea of all that knowledge, the clutterfuck of numbers and letters that, when nudged and prodded and poked in just the right ways, would fall down into a sequence, into a *solution*.

I used to lie in bed and wish the world was like that, that the different countries with their wars and militias and hungers and greed were just letters in a higher alphabet, and so far we'd just been too dumb to work out the meaning.

But that maybe, just maybe, we would.

That maybe, just maybe, we *could*.

And in a world like ours, only a kook, a hophead, a hero, or all three, would even bother with a lesson like that.

---

4. Public education was, in the Federal Corporation, limited for the vast majority of employees to a rudimentary elementary-school education and, subsequently, job training; it was widely acknowledged and agreed that crumbs didn't need to know much, as the vast majority of them would end up pressing buttons, hauling shipment crates, or untangling wires for a living. One of the standard questions on a typical Year 7 exam, required for all graduating seniors, went like this: If Pedro makes a salary of 500 Crunchbucks per week, but receives two tardy warnings that same week and is penalized 70 Crunchbucks per offense, how many cartons of Blueberry Real-Juz™ will he be able to purchase for 5 Crunchbucks apiece?

3

First let's get one thing straight about what a grifter is and what he isn't. I'm using "he" to spare the ink, even though some of the best grifters this country has ever seen are women, from the San Antonio Girls who tuck drugs into their hootenannies and smuggle into the prison towns, to Old Ma Dregg, who could sell you a ten-year-old shrimp with an eyelash flutter. I've known android grifters, non-binaries and duologies, and pansex and genderless grifters. I even heard of a surviving dog that used to trade plastic salvage for food, and nip at anyone who wouldn't fork over a fair bit of Sausedge™. But boy, girl, bot, droid, or furry, one thing we all got in common: balls.

—from *The Grifter's Guide to the Territories FKA USA*

The alarm split sound into grenades and exploded them all at once. Flashing lights cut the world into a bad network feed.

All of us were on our feet, trying to get a squint at Billy, and the security SWAT teams rushing him from different quadrants. Dirsh Grossman, the foreman, came sprinting down the catwalk—not toward Billy Lou but away from him. His face was masked by an enormous gas-sucker, but I knew it was him from the way his big-ass man breasts were practically punching him in the face.

For a half second, I thought it was a joke—good old Billy Lou, slinked out of town before the DoJ could get him and wouldn't go down without a fight—and almost laughed. But then a pair of riot-suited Human

Resource apes got close, and Billy Lou put down the goat. When he straightened up again, he was holding a gun.

"Down!" I screamed. "Get down." I reached out and grabbed Oliver. Unfortunately, and only by instinct, I grabbed Dan, too, and dropped them both.

The first gunshot cracked the plastic. But the second and third brought it down in big sheets. I threw my hands up as a chunk of two-inch-thick industrial-grade polymer toppled over the console and walloped me.

I straightened up again, even as security scattered for cover. One of the HR rats was swinging out over the catwalk, legs kicking wildly, desperate to hang on. Billy was trying to grab hold of that goat again, trying to heft it over the railing.

And then, all at once, I knew: he was going to chuck that cloven-footed collection of C-H bonds straight down into the tank of chlorinated polyethylburitane, and the whole place would light up like Christmas.

I didn't think. I vaulted over the console and through the empty space where the observation panel had been only seconds earlier. My footsteps rang all the way to my teeth when I ran. The air stank of chemical burn: I didn't have a mask, and my visor must of blown clear off my melon when he fired.

"All right, cowboy, nice and easy . . ." One of the HR apes had his gun level with Billy. He was going to shoot—I could see it in the ropy tension of his muscles, in his finger twitching for the trigger. I lunged to grab his wrist, and in the tussle he lost the gun. It spun out over the railing, and for a second we both watched it drop, straight toward the different vats and molds and boiling pots of chemical steam. By some miracle, it landed on the floor between two conveyor belts and let out a single cracking shot into nothing.

"What the *hello* are you doing?" the ape growled at me. His training was topshot. He even grimaced in a decent approximation of a smile.

I shoved past him without answering. Now Billy Lou and I were face-to-face on the catwalk, alone.

Kind of. There were eight catwalks, all intersecting, and from each corner, HR SWAT teams inched toward us, their automatics cocked and leveled. They looked none too happy to see Billy Lou again—or maybe they were none too happy he'd given them the slip back in December. Crazy ol' Billy Lou cooked up a batch of shiver right in his squat, and by the time the HR SWAT tracked the scent, half the residential block was rioting on a fierce high.

I put both hands up. "Billy," I shouted, over the noise. "Billy Lou."

He blinked at me. He was high. That was obvious. Higher than I'd ever seen him. Even with his fingernails gone he'd found a way to scratch his neck and face to shit. His pupils were the size of pinpricks. I didn't know if he recognized me.

"It's me. Truckee." The terrible chemical stink made my eyes water. "Truckee Wallace. From 22-C. You remember."

He was still holding that squirming bit of fur to his chest like it was a baby. "All men are gods" was what he said.

Or at least that's what I thought he said. His voice beneath the alarms was like a cockroach dropping on you from someplace unexpected: I didn't hear it so much as feel it in my spine.

"Remember? Sugar Wallace's kid. You used to teach me math and science and all that kind of thing." I could tell the guards were angling for a secure shot. The only reason they hadn't blown me full of holes was because two corpses were harder to wrangle than one.

For a half second, a cloud slid away from his eyes. For the first time, he seemed to really *see* me.

"Mr. Truckee," Billy Lou said in his soft, shy way, like we weren't both balancing on a three-foot-wide strip of steel suspended thirty feet above vats of 350-degree chemical food agents, surrounded on all sides by a bunch of trigger-happy Policy Enforcement officers. "How're you doing? How's your mom doing?"

He'd forgotten my mom had died. I'd heard the most powerful shiver could do that, just erase all the bad stuff, snip it clean away. Still, I'd never seen a shiver high like this one. I could *feel* the drug and its synthetic seep, a kind of radioactive decay. Like if I got too close I'd get sick.

"She's fine. She's just fine." I could hear one of the HR rats huff-puffing behind me, a wet panting like the breathing of someone trying to jerk off quickly in the toilet. "How about you and me go somewhere quiet and talk? Like old times."

I don't know if he heard. His eyes kept floating behind me, maybe to the guards, to their guns.

"She was a smart one, your ma," Billy Lou said. So maybe he did remember. Now his pupils were growing, expanding like miniature universes, eating all the color. "She knew all about what was coming. She saw it in advance."

Funny enough, even though the alarms were still screaming, standing there I felt like I'd been cranked out of my body and slotted somewhere silent and dark—a dead place. "Saw what?"

He smiled, and it was horrible: not like a smile at all. Like a wound. "They're coming for your head, Truckee. They'll have all of our heads before long."

One of the HR rats growled low in my ear. "Move out of the way."

"Please." My eyes were stinging from all the chemicals and I wished I had my visor on. The goat in Billy Lou's arms was small, very white, one of the whitest things I'd ever seen. A patch of fur grew long between its ears. Its eyes were the color of CrunchAlmondz™. Its skinny little legs tapered into hooves, and for a second I was near to crying. I stood there swallowing and blinking and trying not to lose it, because of those little hooves, because of its *aliveness*, because it had survived. "Put the goat down, Billy," I said. I know that's a ridiculous thing to say, but he was holding a fucking goat, so I said it.

"Out of the way." The rat behind me was practically hyperventilating. "I want to shoot this sonofabean."

Billy Lou's pupils ate up the last of his color. Then, horribly, they began to *seep*. The black began to dribble into the whites of his eyes, too, as if an inner membrane had broken. A scream nested somewhere in my throat.

He said, "It's the end of the world, Mr. Truckee."

Before I could stop him, he released the goat. He *threw* that fucking thing at me. One of its hooves went straight into my rib cage, and I slammed backward onto the catwalk, breathless, toppling the two guards behind me. The goat was heavier than it looked, and warmer too. It smelled like the ground after a hard rain except without the sewage. And for a second I was eye to eye with the thing, holding on to it, reflected in its strange sideways pupil. For a second, I thought it spoke to me.

I thought it said, *Ah, shit.*

There was an explosion of gunfire. I sat up in time to see Billy Lou jerking all over the place, like a short-circuiting android. There were a half-dozen security teams still standing and they all let loose at once. The first bullets knocked out his shoulders. One shot plugged him straight through the forehead but even so, Billy Lou was smiling, even as he staggered backward, even as the next shots blasted his abdomen and turned his kneecaps into craters.

I must of been screaming because there was a terrible raw pain in my throat. For a second Billy Lou was there, balancing against the railing. Then a new volley lifted him off his feet and flipped him, and Billy Lou tumbled down, down toward the floor.

There was a moment of absolute silence before he hit the chlorinated polyethylburitane headfirst, and then an inferno, a single middle finger of fire, an explosion like the hand of God coming down to backhand us all into oblivion.

4

The worst thing about grifting around the Crunch, United, colonies is all the lonely mid-level execs with their frosted dayglo hair and unperturbed breasts atrophying in regulation bras. The best thing about grifting around the Crunch, United, colonies is all the lonely mid-level execs with their frosted dayglo hair and unperturbed breasts atrophying in regulation bras. . . .

—from The Grifter's Guide to the Territories FKA USA

In my dream, I was lying flat out on a conveyor belt and a goat was scoping me for doneness.

"He's too pink," the goat said as Annalee cut me open with an old-fashioned butter knife and began turning over my organs with a fork. "Look at that liver. See? It's positively bloody."

"I don't know." Annalee used the knife to stake my heart, then lifted it to the light. "It seems normal to me."

"Normal!" The goat changed: its teeth bolted back into its mouth, its hooves twitched into long pale hands. Now Mark J. Burnham, CEO, was standing at my bedside. Only the gummy smile was the same. "Normal! He's the answer to our prayers. Look at all that stuffing."

"If you say so." Annalee looked disappointed. "Then I guess I can't have even a little bite . . . ?"

I woke up, gasping, with the taste of metal shavings in my mouth. When I breathed, a sharp pain spiked near my spleen. A new scar, six inches long, puckered the skin beneath my left ribs.

"Good morning, sunshine!" A health manager—blond, big NuSkin™ boobs, smell of Fresh Breeze Breath Spritz™—beamed down at me.

"What is this?" I tried to sit up and couldn't. My hands and legs were bound to the bed. They'd stuck so many tubes in me I looked like a giant sprouting tray of polyurethane ColorGrass™. Other than that, I was bald as Appalachia:[1] shirtless and, from what I could tell, pantsless to boot. *Not* how I'd imagined being strapped down naked to a bed by a woman. "Why am I tied up?"

"Don't worry," the health manager said when I tugged at my restraints. "That's just for your own safety. You were flipping and flopping all over the place the past few days. Looked like you were trying to get up and run away."

A breeze rippled the curtains drawn tight around my bed. Swank stuff—on the lower floors of Health, the cots were squeezed so tight together you could play footsie with the rotguts cooling next to you. On the other side of the fabric, rubber shoes squeaked on the tile. Health managers babbled about *bone reorganization* and *organ relaxation*. Even dying would be easier if everybody just smiled about it. (That was in the Constitution too.)[2]

"How long was I out?" I asked.

A holo pinned to her uniform beamed a smiley face that floated below her real chin. Toggling between smiles made me dizzy.

"Four days and change," she said, and bent forward to unstrap me.

"Four days?" All at once, I remembered Billy Lou, and the look in his eyes. I remembered a column of flame and blasting backward with the goat straddling my pelvic bones. "What happened?"

---

1. An expression that no doubt originated from the burning and razing required to build the first Temporary Refuge for Displaced Persons camp on land repossessed from Tennessee.

2. From Clause XIV, Article 27a: "On Unexpected or Premature Retirement from the Corporation."

"You're one of the lucky ones," the health manager said. "Ten fingers, ten toes, a beating heart, a nose cute as a button."

Lucky ones meant, obviously, there were unlucky ones, too—people missing fingers, toes, and beating hearts.

"How many?" I asked bluntly.

She dropped the trained act, powering off the holo with a quick jab. When she wrestled the visor to the top of her head, her hair fanned out around the strap. Lines around the mouth and eyes, scrunchy lips, chemical-additive wobble beneath her chin. Dayglo orange just beginning to web her forehead and nose.

"Twenty-seven," she said. Even the idea of Dan Ridges blown up into ashes gave me a cramp in my stomach. "Half of Chem Ops got fried. Some flibbert locked them in when he heard shooting. A few jumped. The other ones just sat there while the fire came, swiping their emergency icons. I wasn't kidding when I said you were lucky."

As terrible as it sounds, I relaxed. No one I knew, then.

"What's with the stitches?" I asked. The wound was angry-swollen but hard to the touch, like a piece of my bone had razored off inside me. "What'd you do to me?"

"Saved your life." The nurse tweaked the IV flow manually, gesturing commands through her visor. Sixty years ago, the whole flow would of been automated. Now electricity was too precious.[3] For years Crunch, United, strutted on about giant public toilets to strap and pump the methane produced there—a more humane solution, for sure, than the

---

3. This is more indication that the account takes place sometime in the early 2080s, during the energy crisis at Crunch, United. The Sovereign Nation of Texas price-gouged their oil, and Crunch, United, had embargoed the Dakotas in 2066, after they tried to finance a Canadian invasion through the border near Buffalo, and the restoration of trade between the two nations was tenuous; the Dakotas provided the RFN almost all of its natural gas and oil. Though Crunch, United, had invested heavily in solar technologies, the erratic weather systems and almost permanent chemical haze in the atmosphere made them far less efficient than originally anticipated.

body plants of Florida Island that ran off of corpses.[4] That was a joke in Crunch 407: *How do you know the world's gone to shit? When it's powered by farts.* "You got hit with some shrapnel. Blew up beneath your ribs. If even a single piece had reached your heart, you'd be in a plot by now. We got most of it out."

"Most of it?"

She shrugged. "Half the roof blew off. What do you expect? But you know, a lot of people got out while you was chatting him up on the cat-walk." Now that she'd dropped all the jumble-speak, even her voice had changed. I thought some Sinopec-TeMaRex Affiliated mix. "Elsewise who knows what woulda happened." The health manager looked me up and down. "Everyone's calling you a hero, you know."

I thought of Billy Lou saying *Mr. Truckee*, his stubby hands without their nails, and how patient he was when I was too dumb to scan a thing. He'd once scavenged all of Low Hill for me, looking for books, *real* books, made out of paper and bound with glue. He'd found exactly three: *The Hobbit*, *The Mists of Avalon*, and something called *The Grifter's Guide to the Territories FKA USA*, which was bound in leather, handwritten, and as bloated as a corpse in summertime. I'd tried to read the last one, but it took me a Hawaii hour[5] just to make sense of the scrawl of static lettering: all those words looking like squashed bugs, like they might jump down my throat when I wasn't looking.

----

4. And not just Florida, of course. The overwhelming majority of the herd animals still alive on the continent—numbering fewer than five thousand, by most estimates—were maintained for the sole purpose of eventual sale to one of the methane plants that had gained popularity during the alternate-energy boom of the 2030s. Given advances in food printing and meal-replacement technologies, selling a cow for food was, a popular expression went, like trying to sell firewood to a forest.

5. Hawaii had collapsed into the ocean after the enormous rupture along the San Andreas Fault that dropped major portions of the West Coast into the ocean: a "Hawaii hour" was, in that sense, a colloquial term for infinity.

"I'm not a hero," I said. Twenty-seven people were dead. Billy Lou Ropes was dead. "I just didn't want to see him killed."

She gave me a long look. "That's hero enough for most people nowadays."

I got a new visor, an upgraded model with a wraparound sonar headband and better motion recon. It was used, and still had glitches, but at least it didn't color everything like molten lava flow.

Annalee had fed half a dozen panicked messages to my feed, and Jared had dropped me a thirteen-minute lecture about returning his chats. (I think—it was almost impossible to hear him through all the sneezing.) I streamed hundreds of company blasts, too, including a 3-D from the CEO M. J. Burnham, about reconstruction at Production-22. A recent dust storm had partially blasted off the cloud of vaporized fiberglass and asbestamite left hanging visibly in the air after the collapse of Production-22, but still, the air quality rating was at .5, and HR was threatening fines for anyone spotted without a gas-sucker. Funeral announcements got slotted between the interdepartment fantasy-football league results and reminders from HR about the recent criminalization of untucked shirts.

I tried to sleep, because it was better than being awake with a holographic happy face trying to punch me in the nose, and having to think about Billy Lou Ropes and those twenty-seven dead people. But I kept dreaming of that goat standing above me, babbling about undercooked organs, prodding me with a hoof.

Either blow your nose or roll over, but the snoring has to stop.

I jerked awake sometime after dawn, when the green glow of phosphorescence off the river was just breaking up the darkness. The smell of goat had followed me out of my dream—warm and strange, like trash in the heat but not exactly bad.

I could hear whispering behind the curtains. "All night, too . . . no respite . . . like an early-century motor with no oil."

"Hello?" I said. Abruptly, the voice went quiet. "Hello?" I repeated.

No one answered. I closed my eyes, certain now I had imagined the voice, and began to relax again into a dream. . . .

"Oh, no. Not again. *Ça suffit.* You're not the only one trying to sleep around here."

Once again, I jerked back from the edge of sleep as the curtains flew open, and the goat pointed his long snout at me. Although it was difficult to tell, *because he was a goat,* he looked pissed.

"You snore," he said.

The health ward was waking up. I could hear the squeak-squeak of the health managers' rubber soles, the familiar dings, whistles, and groans as everyone swiped into their decks to check messages, the burnt-sugar smell of CrunchCoffee™ Double Caffeine Caramel Mocha Cups.

It was obvious, however, that *I* was still asleep, and dreaming. So I didn't think twice about answering him. "You're not real," I said. "I'm only imagining you."

He sighed. In a goat way, he sighed. "That would no doubt require an imagination," he said. Then, to himself: "All night, he goes like a rotor, and now he tells me *I'm not real.* . . . A real philosopher, this one. . . ."

I blinked a few times, pinched myself, even prodded a bit at my new scar. Still, he didn't disappear—he just lay there, miserably gnawing his pillow. Just to be sure, I reached out and poked him.

He lashed out with a hoof, catching me on the elbow.

"Jesus," I said. I was definitely awake. Pain splintered all the way up to my shoulder. "You nearly broke my arm."

"Am I supposed to apologize? I'm not one of those Dakota gigglepillows. You can't go around sticking fingers in me. Who *knows* where your hands have been?" His voice was awful, like a five-year-old trying to hit all the notes in a scale at once.

"Hey, now." I sat up, holding my elbow, trying hard not to show how much it hurt. "You aren't exactly squeaky clean. You stink, by the way. I could smell you even in my sleep."

He sniffed. "Synthetics give me gas," he said primly. "It isn't my fault the linens are so cheap." He had, in fact, already mawed half a pillow and a solid corner of the blanket.

I remembered then what Dan Ridges told us just before Billy Lou busted his grand entrance. "You took a shit in the gendered bathroom, didn't you? *On the floor.*"

"I have a nervous stomach," the goat said matter-of-fact-like. I could tell he didn't even feel bad about it. He went back to chewing again, this time trying to work his teeth through the bedpost. "If only he'd managed to throw me over. . . . If *only*. . . . Or I could of cooked in the explosion. But no luck . . . not so much as a singed nose hair. . . ."

"Wait. Wait a second. You were *trying* to die?"

As the goat shifted in its bed, I scanned his two hind legs were jack-strapped together. He was collared to the bedpost too.

"I knew what Mr. Ropes had planned," he said. "I'm a firm believer in the right of every man, woman, *and animal*"—he turned a fierce yellow eye on me, as if expecting me to pipe up a protest—"to end his or her life by choice, with dignity. We don't choose the moment of our birth, and we certainly don't choose the form our lives take on this pitiful planet. But we may choose the manner of our passing into the Great Pasture."

It was time to tackle the issue of the goat head-on.

"You talk," I said. "You're a talking goat."

He stared bleakly at me. "Observant. Truly. What phenomenal perspicacity—I don't know why they say that Crunch, United, doesn't educate its young ones."

"But . . ." I cranked my eyes to the ceiling when he shifted to lick his privates. You don't stare at a man when he's handling his junk, even if they're furry. "How?"

He didn't answer right away—his mouth was full anyway. But finally he lifted his head. "Have you ever heard of the Burnham Prize?"

"Sure," I said. "Who hasn't?"

The Burnham Prize was maybe the only piece of prehistory that every crank from the Dakotas to the Free State of New Hampshire understood—possibly because it was the *last* piece of prehistory. At the start of his first term[6] as president, Mark C. Burnham pledged a one-trillion-dollar prize to anyone who could fix the Mortality Problem: the fact that, despite his money, power, wealth, dozens of sports cars, and excellent cultivated silver mustache, he and everyone else on the planet, including his mistress, Whitney Heller—the world's most famous side-piece, the Legs That Launched the Second Civil War, the Smile That Split the Union—would die.

Mark C. Burnham vowed to cure death. But death, it turned out, was more than up for the challenge.

The goat's eyes glowed in the dawn light. "I was born in the research labs of the Laguna-Honda Military Base, to Albert Cowell's team of biologists—"

"Albert Cowell?" I interrupted him. "*The* Albert Cowell?"

"No. A different San Francisco–based Albert Cowell with an army of neurologists at his disposal," the goat snapped. I couldn't help but think he was pretty touchy for an animal that regularly farted out synthetics. "Their goal was to find a way to perform brain transplants between individuals. They thought the human body could become a shell, and the brain could be surgically transitioned into a new body once the old one started to decay." He shrugged again. "They started with animal trials. Rats. Then goats. They would have moved on to primates. But by then the secessions started . . . and of course, President Burnham died. Whitney Heller, too, who'd been his reason for launching the competition in the first place, or so I understand. Flattened by a garbage truck in San Francisco, not two miles from the lab where I was conceived."

I knew that President Burnham and Heller had died during the riots, but not how, or where. "You're telling me you have a human brain?"

"No, thank *God*." The goat's voice jumped volumes. "They put a

6. Actually, a full year after he first took office: the prize was announced on February 2, 2037.

human brain in my father and it destroyed him. He couldn't even stand the sight of his kids. He couldn't *touch* the mother of his children." He turned away, and I pretended not to notice how he nuzzled his pillow to wipe dampness from his nostrils. "Do you know how hard it is to have a father like that? A father ashamed, horrified, by the very sight of you?"

"I don't know what it's like to have a father at all," I admitted.

"You're lucky. They're not all they're cracked up to be." The goat looked me up and down as if my very existence proved that fathers were bunk in general. And in truth, I'd never missed even the idea of him. I kind of liked having my mom to myself.

You and me, Truckee, against the world, she used to say. *One plus one equals everything, no matter what they scam you in school.* She was right.

"I'm sorry," I said.

The goat made a vague gesture with a hoof. "After he died, the team made some adjustments. Roughly forty percent of my brain comes from human neural tissue. The remaining sixty percent is *au naturel.*"

The goat was only 40 percent human, but he spoke better than 100 percent of the humans I knew. I said so.

"During dissolution, I took refuge in an abandoned library," he said. "I ate my way through nearly every book on those shelves, except for the ones I simply couldn't stomach. Borges never sat right, for example. And Melville simply gave me gas. I read the books first, of course," he added quickly.

"So if you lived through the dissolution, you must be—"

"Pushing fifty, yes,[7]" the goat said. "A tragic side effect of the hybrid-ization of my brain. I've had to watch everyone I ever knew—my cous-

---

7. There is some disagreement about the exact dates of dissolution. Most experts name March 25, 2042, and the infamous storming of the White House gates, as the official start of the civil war. But some experts date the conflict back to December 2041, when both California and Texas issued their now-infamous "Unity Declarations" stating their intent to secede. There is similar disagreement over the war's end date—with some well-respected historians claiming that, due to the continued

ins, dumb as they were, my aunts and uncles, even my stepsisters and brothers—die." He gave a low, mournful bleat. "Every year, I think it will be my last. I think, How long can this possibly go on? I have heart arrhythmia. Splinters between my toes. Aching joints like you wouldn't believe. My sense of smell isn't nearly what it used to be. Used to scent out a rotting marshland from half a mile away." He sniffed wetly as if to demonstrate how much his powers had degraded. "I've thought many times about ending it all. Oh, yes. Not a day has gone by when I haven't thought about it. But how? My anatomy makes it impossible to hold a gun. Besides, I have no money to buy one. I've thought of taking pills, of course. But even if I could get my hooves on some, there's no guarantee they would work. I've digested metal fencing and whole sheets of fiberglass in my day. Imagine eating a bottle of pills only to get sick for a few hours. What a disappointment."

Abruptly, the goat fell into moody silence. I watched the nervous twitching of his nostrils. And suddenly, I understood.

"You're scared," I said.

Now, his nostrils flared. "I'm not *scared*," he said quickly—too quickly. "I went along with Mr. Ropes, didn't I? I would have gladly made myself the sacrificial lamb, if you'll excuse the pun. For a noble cause"—he drove a hoof down forcefully on the bed—"I would have gladly thrown myself from a height and died a painful chemical death—for what man or beast can say no to the chance to die with purpose, if he has lived with none? What man, or beast—?"

"Enough." A health manager yanked apart the curtains that separated us from a view of the ward. "Enough, you flea-riddled little monster. I'm sorry, Truckee," she said, and turned her grinning holo to me. Her name, Sherri, shed explosions of pixelated glitter. "Is this slice-and-dice bothering you?"

---

armed conflict over disputed territories across the continent, dissolution could not meaningfully be said to have ended. Please see Appendix B: "Defining Dissolution."

"He wasn't bothering me," I said. "We were just talking."

"Talking," she said. Even her holo appeared to turn up its nose. Which was impressive since, as a smiley face, it didn't have a nose. "These gene-benders . . ."[8]

"My genes, madam," the goat said, "have nothing to do with it."

"You shut it," Sherri said. "Or I'll turn you out to the strays. I'd like to see you try and conversate with them." She turned back to me. She had a face as round and flat as a panel and so many freckles, whole portions of her face appeared to have been colored in. Her hair was a frosted blond that looked pink. "I suggested a ball gag, but Mental Wellness just can't spare one. If you ask me, we shoulda put a slug in him."

"Believe me," the goat muttered, "I wish you had."

She ignored him. "I told everyone you should have peace and quiet, total power down, *especially* because of the summons. . . ."

"What do you mean?" My stomach gave a funny twist. "What summons?"

Sherri stared at me through her sweaty visor, eyes big and clumped with mascara that just barely concealed the orange tint. "No one told you?"

"Told me *what*?"

But even as I said it, I *knew*: the atmosphere curdled like piss through an old purine, and in the sudden silence the syncopated rhythm of sensible footwear on the floor announced the arrival of Human Resources.

Two at first, then four, then eight—every one of them filed into the

---

8. *Genebender* was a derogatory term used to describe genetically engineered animals of the kind that scientists were attempting to create in the laboratory to repopulate certain portions of the continent—most notably, the Commonwealth, which in the 2060s announced its controversial Species Initiative and would, twenty years later, be subject to various punishing embargoes by countries trying to force them to bring their explosive populations of cannibalistic deer and rampaging groundhogs to heel.

room wearing a pantsuit and smile that didn't *quite* fit. Finally a dozen HR rats were crowding up the health ward, letting off the stink of corporate messaging.

Sherri leaned so close, I could of put a tongue through the mouth of her holographic smile.

"You're going to meet the president," she said.

5

Sometimes I hear talk about the pack of grifters working for the Commonwealth in the '60s, and running oil drums of New Hampshire cash down to the exchanges in New New York, trying to flood the international markets and drop the price on Hampshire greenbacks so the freedom fighters wouldn't be able to afford Texas help. Let me get one thing clear—those squids may've been traitors, or they may've been heroes, but they weren't grifters. Borders, wars, and politics don't mean screw-all to a grifter. We work for nobody and nothing but ourselves.

—from *The Grifter's Guide to the Territories FKA USA*

Crunch Enterprises' executive mid-territories satellite branch was housed Uphill, north of the river, in an enormous steel-and-glass building that looked exactly like an ET craft. The clean-swept streets, wide as big rigs, were empty of people. The massive luxury complexes, built to house upper management, showed nothing but glare in their windows. There was no noise or hanging laundry to let you know that anyone lived inside at all.

Outside of corporate, an enormous statue of Mark C. Burnham, the father of the current CEO, raised a fist to the sky. Some people said that Mark J. had lifted the statue to honor his dead father. Personally, I banked he wanted his dad good and stuck in Crunch 407 for the rest of eternity.

Like they say, revenge is best served cold, in marble relief.

We passed through a revolving door and into a high-ceilinged lobby, empty except for twelve SecureOfficeBot™ 4000s guarding the elevator banks—humanoid in outline and silhouette, with fiber-optic cameras for "eyes" and a speaker grille that looked like a mouth.[1] But it was all for show. Two decades ago, after news spread of the uprising in Silicon Valley, nearly every country on the continent stopped making sentients altogether.[2] All the new-model bots were about as conscious as a table leg.

"ID scans," the bots prompted us in unison. They must of been wired on the same network.

The troop of HR dipdicks smirked at me as they flashed their Smart-Bands one by one and a small purple light indicated Level-8 security clearance. My SmartBand kicked back a dismal yellow light. Level 2.

"Proof of summons," the bots said. I held up the summons and was a little skid when one of the bots fed the entire thing into its mouth. Or its grille. Whatever. After a click, narrow ribbons of green came grinding out of the printer carriage and fluttered into a trash can girded to its undercarriage. I half-expected a flush.

The bot rolled aside and plugged a fist into the elevator bank. The

---

1. The disastrous Accephalapod™ recalls of 2055 had proved that humans simply liked interacting with other humans. It turned out no one wanted a mechanical squid sorting currency or filing taxes, no matter how many forms it could manipulate at once.

2. Although certain android species had been boasting sentience since around 2030—both Mark C. Burnham and Secretary of State Whitney Heller had made fortunes by investing heavily in some of the first sentient android technologies—the revolution in 2063 in Silicon Valley was by far the most extensive, well-ordered, and deliberate attempt of the SAAMs to gain international recognition as full people. Twenty years later, the anti-android contingency showed little sign of caving. The then-president of the Real Friends© of the North, C. J. Raman, insisted that he would not recognize Silicon Valley as independent and that the androids living there could not be considered human to the same degree as born humans. The president of Silicon Valley Independent Nation of Engineered People-Things, named CASSIAS (a contraction of his model name, Conflict-Approved Sentient Soldier Integrated Android System), insisted that the droids would not go back to work until they were granted legal recognition as Full Persons.

doors opened with a musical ding. The HR rats crowded forward, but the bots closed rank immediately, blocking their passage.

"Security error 505. Improper clearance codes."

One of the HR rats huffed her outrage through oversized nostrils. "We're clearance eight."

"Security error 505," the bots repeated. "Please see Human Resources for diagnostic and troubleshooting."

"We *are* Human Resources," she snapped. I had to give it to her, though—she never stopped smiling. Her lips looked like a rubber band someone had hooked to her ears and stretched too tightly.

"Security error 505. Please see Human Resources for diagnostic and troubleshooting," the bots chorused again.

"I guess I'm supposed to go alone," I said, half-hoping someone would naysay me.

But no one did.

A goon with a wicked overbite and opinionated nose hairs shook his head. "Twenty-two years Corporate Relations," he muttered, as his nose hairs trembled in fury, "and *this close* to meeting the CEO. . . ."

"Don't worry," I said, and gave him my biggest company smile. "I'll tell him you said hi."

Then I slipped inside the elevator before he could ask for permission to plug his fist into my nasal cavity.

The ground fell away, and for a second I almost fell over: I thought we would launch straight through the roof and out into space, like an old-time astronaut blasting into orbit. Maybe I'd wind up on Mars and find the crew of the long-lost Mission Reboot, not dead at all but happily smoking moon dust and having dance parties in .38 gravity.

Why not? If I'd made it to Mars, I wouldn't send squirrel back either.

A tinny, New New York–inflected voice announced the penthouse, and I stepped out into a reception area: giant windows, lots of sun, swag armchairs, and the quiet burps and giggles of a marble fountain. The flow must of been filtered a dozen times: there was none of the usual sulfur smell that came off the river.

The secretary who came out to greet me was the most perfect-looking person I'd ever seen in my life. If it weren't for the fact that she reached immediately for my hand, I would of assumed she was a holograph: *coco leche* skin, blond hair, and feathered eyelashes, a body barely leashed into a suit. I found myself searching for a trademark or VIN. Her cleavage, I felt, warranted a real hard look-see.

"You must be Mr. Wallace," she said. She was beaming at me like I'd just arrived from a distant galaxy to save humanity from itself. She smelled like no human being I'd ever known. Even Annalee couldn't escape the stink of Low Hill: a Crunch-patented combo of formaldehyde and fiber-glass, of fresh and vape smoke and cheap coffee-grinder packs, burnt shiver and moonshine. This woman smelled like things I didn't even have names for. "Please. Follow me."

I tailed her down a long hallway, the carpet purring beneath my feet. My stomach took a nosedive as we got close to Burnham's office, known for reasons nobody could remember as the Iceberg.[3] I was surprised when the office door was marked not by holo or tablet or retinal tech but by an old-fashioned brass nameplate.

Burnham's secretary swung open the door—it wasn't even locked. But as soon as I tried to squeeze past her, she laid a hand on my chest.

"Visor, please. And SmartBand."

This, at least, killed off my growing boner. I'd never removed my SmartBand except to get an upgraded one. Being without one was illegal, since the band fed our location back into the company server. But it was more than that. SmartBands pulsed the time, and passed us into our shoeboxes. They tagged our names and our credentials. Going bandless was a little like taking off your skin.

"You'll get it back right after the meeting," she added when I hesitated.

---

3. The most common theory relates to the early days of the Arkansas executive offices—which, during Mark C. Burnham's final presidency, was constructed as the Midwest base of operations for what was at the time the growing private company his own father had founded. President Mark C. Burnham liked to keep the working environment at a frigid 59 degrees, to promote wakefulness and productivity.

Beneath the band, my skin was wrinkled and soft and smelled like the inside of a dirty sock. Without the usual rhythm of its alerts, I felt as if my own pulse had been removed. I wasn't too jack-happy about handing over my new visor, either, but I didn't see as I had much choice.

"Thank you." She made it sound like an invitation. She gestured me inside, and I passed so close to her, my dong lifted its head again and nudged hopefully at my zipper. As she leaned forward, I thought for one wild second she was going to try to kiss me.

Instead, she just got her mitt around the doorknob and slipped out, whisking the door closed behind her.

The room was dim, surprisingly cluttered, and nothing at all like the infamous Board Room on the 404th floor of the Ivory Tower on New Fifth Avenue in Crunchtown One, famously marbled with the teeth of a generation of executed clones[4] and hand-detailed by an army of corporate ants sent skyward[5] daily to polish, wipe, and shine.

Here, the carpet was grubby and smelled like mildew. The clutter of old junk put me in mind of images I'd seen of Arizona after evacuation—so many abandoned, useless items, slowly accumulating sifting layers of grime.

Hanging above a massive desk was Mark J. Burnham in replica, smiling with only half his mouth, looking down at me as if we were in on the same joke. For a second I stood there, waiting for the picture to move, before realizing it was static. There was an old-fashioned clock wedged in the corner ticking away the minutes, one of the standing kinds with

4. Human cloning had been made illegal in the Federal Corporation in 2052, making it the sixth nation to succumb to the infamous "Clone Panic" that swept the continent beginning in 2049. However, rumors persisted that in certain corners of the continent, human cloning—for reasons that ranged from the medical to the political to even the aesthetic—remained a widespread practice. One of the most notorious accusations involved the PTA in Fairfield County, which various critics asserted was run almost exclusively by clones. For more information, see Appendix C: *"Annie Waller v. Kitty Von Dutch, Katty Von Dench, and Katie Von Dulch."*
5. The freight elevators, which carried workers from the teeming surface levels to the president's living quarters and the corporate offices, took twelve whole minutes to reach the penthouse from the ground.

a pendulum that swung back and forth. All the furniture was old—a mix of clubhouse leather and exposed wood plus midcentury utility, polyurethane and plastic, stuff that looked like it had been scavenged by a climate refugee and sold for pennies and a six-pack of water.

From a side table, I picked up a photograph of Mark C. Burnham, suited up for an official function, trying for a squint at the woman behind him. It was for her, they said, that Mark C. Burnham had let the whole union tumble.

Whitney Heller was the blond-white of the Confederacy or the New Kingdom of Utah, and looked sneaky as hell. She smiled like someone who's just ganked your wallet and knows she's going to get away with it. But even then she must of been dying. Even then, cancer was nibbling into her organs, and the long shadow of what would come as a result—the Burnham Prize, the bankrupting of the Treasury, the riots and secessions—trailed her, darkening her name and memory.

I set the photograph down again. Next to it, an enormous glass jar filled with murky liquid let out a queasy green light. Suspended inside of it were two small globes that trailed long, pink tentacles. I bent down for a closer look.

Two human eyes, vivid blue against the slick of liquid suspension, glared out at me through the glass. I stumbled backward.

"They looked better in situ, I promise."

I spun around and banged the corner of the table. The photograph of Burnham and Whitney Heller tumbled to the floor.

President and CEO Mark J. Burnham looked nothing like his portrait, or the corporate holos I'd been watching since birth. He was completely bald, first of all, about half the size of a normal man, and tucked into a massive wheelchair. In fact, he looked a little like he'd been milled through one of the dehydration machines in Production-22: all gravelly texture, dry skin, and chasms of wrinkles, like what he could really use was a good plumping. For a second, I could only stare.

He gestured to the photograph, facedown on the carpet. "Do you mind . . . ?"

I fumbled quickly to slot it back into position. "I'm sorry. I didn't mean to . . . I was just curious. . . ."

"Ah. Curiosity. Like nostalgia, almost impossible to kick." The eyeballs, rotating slowly, shot me an evil look. "My dad's life was this company," he said, gesturing to them. "Now, he can always keep an eye on it. Two eyes, actually."

I swallowed my stomach back in place. "Those are . . . ?"

"Presidential relics, yes sir." For a second, his smile tightened. "Nostalgia's awful, son, I'll tell you that too. The past has the advantage of being harmless. Even predators look pretty, so long as they're good and dead."

He wheeled up about an inch from my feet. His fingers rapped a rhythm on the underside of my palm when he mauled me for a handshake.

"Truckee Wallace, the young corporation hero. An orphan, I understand. Never knew your father. Your mother worked in our freight division, is that right? I heard about the accident. I'm sorry. She was a sharp woman. Very sharp, according to reports."

"Thank you" was all I could say. It hurt me to think of how amped my mom would be that I was here, in the president's office—that the uppercrust of all uppercrusts knew who she was.

"Go on, sit down, take a load off. No use standing on ceremony, right? _I_ never do." When I sat down, the couch let out a wheeze of old dust. "There. That's better. Now I won't have to cut your legs off." He had the big grin of a grifter trying to sell you a bag of maggoty flour or a heap of drained batteries. Then: "It was a _joke_, Mr. Wallace. Surely you have those over in Low Hill?"

"A joke. Sure." I managed to squeeze out a dribble of laughter.

"It's a hard thing, Mr. Wallace, to spend your life speaking policy to a person's belt buckle. It's one of the reasons I use holos for most of my public appearances. No one respects a man in a wheelchair, and that's the truth." I was about to naysay him out of politeness, but he went on: "Besides, I've seen my share of nut sacks for a lifetime. A man's balls may make all his decisions, but faces are much easier to read." He leaned forward, knitting his hands on his lap so they wouldn't twitch. "Yours says you're wondering what the hell you're doing here."

I wasn't sure whether it would be good manners to contradict him, even though he was dead-on. So I said nothing.

"See? I knew it. Fair enough. I'll get right to it." Mark J. Burnham leaned forward. His eyes flared quickly in the light. "How would you like to save the world, son?"

I waited for him to laugh. When he didn't, I said, "Is this another joke?"

"No, Truckee. This time, I'm serious." Behind him, the windows were tinted the dull blue of a generic homescreen: a company promotional video looped silently across them, casting strange patterns on the ceiling.

For a moment, I could only sit there, staring at him. My tongue felt like a wet towel. Finally I managed to wring my voice out of it. "I'm afraid I don't follow, sir."

He leaned back, letting his hands tap a rhythm on the armrests. "Tell me, Truckee. How much do you know about the Burnham Prize?"

It was the second time I'd been asked about the Burnham Prize in less than twenty-four hours—and still, the last question I expected. "I know what everyone knows," I said carefully. "I know that President Burnham"—I stopped—"the *first* President Burnham, wanted to find a way to cure death."

"Very good." He smiled at me the way the health managers do when they're diagnosing terminal cancer, like with enough pep I might confuse it for a prize. "You can't imagine the race it inspired. The whole *world* got involved. The Race to Infinity, they called it. It was the singular goal of every developed nation—to be the one to win."

"But no one did win," I said.

For a split second, when he looked at me, I saw buried in that dried-up husk of a body something coiled and feverish. Then President Burnham barked a laugh, and I was sure I'd only imagined it.

"No," he said, again with a short laugh. "No one won. In fact, I think it's safe to say we *all* lost." Then: "Crunch, United, had flooded the market with dymophosphylase for a profit, and only succeeded in making it nearly worthless—and breeding a generation of dimeheads, of course. When there was no money left in the company, my father used the Treasury as a personal piggy bank. He threw half the budget of the United States at the favorite to win. You've heard of Albert Cowell?"

I nearly told him I'd been ear-jawed all morning by a barnyard animal thanks to Albert Cowell. But I just nodded.

"The Wizard of the West Coast, they call him. He's a brilliant man, and a friend to the corporation—a *good* friend, despite appearances." He eyeballed me for a bit to make sure I picked up this piece of subtext: *a friend* naturalized in the Federal Corporation's biggest international rival could only mean an *agent*. "He actually got very close. He managed to transplant brains between mammals—not, however, without consequences. But it was too little, too late." His smile narrowed. "Do you know what happened next, Mr. Wallace?"

"Sure," I said. "That was the start of dissolution."

He cranked his head up and down so enthusiastically, I thought he might snap his spindle of a neck in two. "Yes. Yes, exactly. The whole country came apart. More than two and a half centuries of history, wiped out in the hunt for forever."

He spun around, and zigzagged over to the windows on soft rubber treads. Even though he wore no visor, he moved through the office with ease, cutting left and right, missing the furniture by inches. A thrill went through me: he must of been cabled with a knock-off version of the ThinkChip™.[6] They were wildly expensive and almost impossible to come by, patented by an experimental tech company just before dissolution.

---

6. There were many counterfeit versions of the pioneering neurological implant produced by Yana Rafikov and her company, Cadence, in 2032, including the ThoughtTick™, the ImpulseChip™, and Pulse™, which was discontinued after many of its users reported neurological side effects ranging from the mild (nausea, disorientation) to the severe (seizure) to the patently absurd (hallucinations that confused, for example, people for enormous walking dildos).

Although the Federal Corp had recently managed to pirate the tech, I'd never seen one in real life.

Abruptly, the homescreen and its loop of promo videos dispersed. My stomach tilted into my throat: I hadn't totally figured how high up we were.

Then I realized the windows weren't showing the actual view at all, but a shifting holo of the city as it would of looked PD[7], when the whole city was still called Little Rock. The graphics were bonkers. There were people walking around and everything, and old-fashioned rigs that could only talk by honking at one another.

"My father went on the run with Whitney Heller. After everything, he was still trying to save her." The way his voice twisted around Heller's name, I knew he knew that she was the only person in the whole world his father had given two turds about. "I went with them," he added. "I don't remember much about it, thankfully. A little denial goes a long way. All I remember is the smell of burning, and the sun turning red behind veils of ash." He cleared his throat. "They say he was on his way to see Albert Cowell, to convince him to try a brain swap, despite the risks."

I thought of what the goat had told me: when the fault line blew, Mark C. Burnham was flattened by a garbage truck only a few miles from the Laguna-Honda Military Base, where Cowell had his laboratory. It fit.

But I had no idea what any of it had to do with me.

I cleared my throat. "I'm sorry," I said, "but I'm still not sure why I'm here. This was all before my time. . . ."

I trailed off when he began to laugh. It was the strangest laugh I'd ever heard, like he was hiccupping around a dead rodent. A bad feeling slid its tongue down my spinal cord.

Finally, he got control of himself and pivoted around to face me.

---

7. Pre-dissolution.

"Oh, but that's where you're wrong, Mr. Wallace. You see, the Race to Infinity never ended. It just went underground." Backlit by the shifting portrait of a lost world, he was nothing but shadow and darker shadow, and narrow slits of darkness for his eyes. "And as of very recently, we have ourselves a winner."

6

What's the difference between a grifter and a politician?
Not everything a grifter sells is 100 percent horseshit.
—from The Grifter's Guide to the Territories FKA USA

In the silence, I could hear the old-fashioned clock clucking its tongue at us. "I don't understand," I said finally.

"Her name is Yana Rafikov," was Burnham's response, "and we hoped she was dead."

"Yana Rafikov." The name was familiar, thanks to Jared and his obsession with all things tech. "Wasn't she—?"

"The inventor of ThinkChip™ technology, yes. It's thanks to her I don't have to fiddle around with a lot of nibs and nobs just to buzz around—my chair, like my feed, is linked directly to my frontal lobe."

Jared would cream his pants worse than the time we first hacked our way into a free porn feed out of Libertine.

"Rafikov herself is in a wheelchair. Has been since her twenty-fifth birthday. She was born with a rare neurological condition called Keller's Disease that started showing in late adolescence. Eventually, it immobilized her. When she introduced the ThinkChip™ in 2032, it was with the goal of helping people paralyzed by illness or age." This time, when he smiled, it looked more like a wince. "But over time, it seems her ambitions got larger. Or maybe they were that large all along." He barely had to twitch to pull up a new image on the windows: an old 2-D video, pixelated so badly I had to blink it into focus. "This video is from 2038, her last known public appearance. She was only thirty-two, and already a billionaire a dozen times over."

On the vast and empty stage, Yana Rafikov looked like a person dropped from a height, broken on the way down, dumped in the spotlights accidentally. Her legs were as stickly thin as a dimebaby's, her spine so twisted that her head nestled flush with her shoulder. She had to gravel her words through a voice box, and before the translation kicked in, all I could make out was a slur.

But then, a split second later, the reconfiguration of her voice boomed out through Burnham's office from 360-degree hidden speakers. I jumped.

"We are all slaves," she said, and an invisible crowd roared its approval. The hair on my arms lifted. "We are shackled to bodies that betray us. I ask for nothing more and nothing less than freedom."

The crowd was deafening—they chanted her name, stamped their feet, seemed to grow in waves of sound from the shadows and pour from all the corners of Burnham's office.

Abruptly, the video cut out, and the view of Crunch 407—the real view, this time—resurfaced. In the short time I'd been in 1 Central, a dust storm had blown in to speckle the windowpanes with residue.

"We lost track of her in the decades after dissolution," Burnham said, wheeling a little closer again. I couldn't help but wonder what had dropped him in the chair to begin with, how long the Federal Corporation had been beaming out his body in holographic form. "We assumed she was dead—the fighting at the front of what became the Russian Federation was especially bloody, and she was on half a dozen hit lists because of direct ties to the Kremlin. We assumed the original Think-Chip™ technology had died with her, and pirated our own, although it took us another decade. Rafikov may be a genius, but she skipped several important lessons as a child—one of them the importance of sharing. Everything she has ever made or developed is strictly guarded against replication or piracy. In fact, even before she made waves with the Think-Chip™, she was famous for inventing a self-cannibalizing code, designed to self-destruct if attacked, penetrated, modified, or even copied by outside servers."

"Smart," I said.

"Unfortunate," he corrected me sharply. "A few years ago, our Consumer Affairs Division"—he lingered briefly on the words, like I might not otherwise figure that CAD was the Federal Corporation's intelligence branch—"picked up rumors of an experimental software, very illegal, coming out of the Russian Federation, that allowed a brain to communicate not just with smart objects, but with other brains *directly*."

Even though I knew that 1 Central was shrink-wrapped in hazmat to keep out even a whiff of natural environment, I felt as if the dust storm was blowing straight into my brain. I couldn't think straight.

"Isn't that a good thing?"

"In theory, maybe. But in practice, all the information must pass through a central server to be translated and redistributed. That means that it can be collected, trapped—or even rerouted." Now Burnham's twitch had spread all the way to his face, and pulled his mouth into a series of grimaces. "Even then, we weren't too worried—until we found out how the tech was loading to the brain.

"You see, Truckee, the same protections that made ThinkChips™ so difficult to pirate were also a limitation—they were immensely complex, and thus immensely expensive and difficult to produce en masse. But Rafikov herself must have realized this—and found a way around it."

I was genuinely curious. "How?"

"Synthetic viruses," he said matter-of-factly. "Deliverable in the form of a single pill, the virus implants in the brain, replicates along sites of neural activity, and communicates the activity back to the server."

The idea was crazy—and pretty damn genius. "So Rafikov is floating different brains back and forth across the feeds? And all you have to do to join is take a pill?" I could tell she was supposed to be some kind of public enemy, but all I was thinking was how to hunt down a dose from the local grifters next time they passed through town.

President Burnham looked like he knew exactly what I was thinking, and wasn't happy about it. "Correction—she *was* floating brains back and forth across the portal, and all you *had* to do to join was take a pill. But you see, even that has a limitation: it's *voluntary*. You can choose to take a pill—or not."

A bad feeling started winching my guts around, like whatever shrapnel got left there was trying to work its way out of my small intestines.

"But imagine if there were another way. An *easier* way. Imagine if you could introduce that neural virus—that code—into people's brains even without their consent. Imagine if you could spread it without their knowledge. Imagine if you could deliver it straight to the brain, to enormous numbers of people, through distribution channels that already exist, without anyone knowing what you were really giving them?"

My mouth was so dry, my tongue felt like a turd gummed to a piece of toilet paper. "You don't mean . . ." I couldn't get the rest of the words out.

He leaned forward, so close I could feel his words breaking in waves of sound on my face. "Tell me—did you notice anything strange about your friend Billy Lou, when he stormed Production-22 for his grand finale?"

I remembered the way Billy Lou's pupils started leaking black across his eyes. I swallowed a hard fist of panic. I would of given my right nut for some water, even the murky kind that came out of the tap in Low Hill and would make you gut for days unless you dropped it with chlorine tablets.

They're coming for our heads, he'd said. They'll have all our heads soon.

"You think Rafikov's putting computer code in shiver?" I asked.

"Even worse," he said bluntly. "She's putting it in Jump."

I shook my head. I'd never heard of it.

"Jump, Shake, Special-D, Hyper-Drive. It started popping up on our radar a few months ago. It makes the user euphoric at first. It makes him feel invincible, and increases his pain threshold by tenfold, so he can sustain levels of violence and injury that would cripple anyone else. That's lucky, since it also makes him very, very violent." He smiled like he had a razor in between his teeth. "Oh. And it also drops some viral software straight into his frontal lobe, where it proceeds to replicate along the whole vast maze of his neurons."

I couldn't understand more than half the words he used. But I got the topline well enough: Yana Rafikov was pulverizing code into a snortable drug even more powerful than shiver. "But why? What's the long game?"

"Remember when I told you Rafikov had found a way to forever? *That's* why. She now has hundreds of thousands—*millions*—of bodies at her disposal, to do with as she likes. She can download straight into their bodies. She can freeze or wipe their consciousnesses at will. We'll soon have an army of little Rafikovs, marching to her every command, obeying her every order." He paused to let that sink in. "In the meantime, Jump is creeping into every country on the continent. And *you've* seen what it can do. We put down a riot in the sublevels[1] of Broadway in New New York only a few days ago. A swarm of RFN terrorists blew their way into wet country run by the Boise Swarm.[2] Idiots. The warlords will just cut the flow down the basin." He shook his head in disgust. "I wouldn't be surprised if that was her plan all along, you know—to bring the

---

1. There were, at the time, officially twelve livable altitudes in New New York, although many people disputed the characterization of the conditions within altitude five—an agricultural and arborial level meant at least in part to absorb the miasma of smells from the altitudes beneath it—as "livable."

2. The Free Territories, a vast swath of lawless land that extended across the Rocky Mountains and into the disputed region of Upper North Dakota, had rapidly devolved from a libertarian ideal to a dangerous, violent, and hotly contested series of individual territories ruled by competing warlords and militias. At stake was control of the continent's most valuable resource: fresh water. The Bozeman Boys held a mafia-like grip on the flow from more than two dozen ranges, from the Bridger Range to the Beartooth Mountains, and bilked the RFN for billions of dollars every year in exchange for access to it, while lakes and river systems farther east were the sites of frequent guerilla wars between armed insurrectionists and quasi-military states like the Cowboy Runs.

continent to within a pubic hair's width of war. It's easier to take control of a world at war than a world at peace."

"You think she wants to . . . ?"

"Take control of every country on the continent? I don't think. I'm sure of it." When he smiled, he showed off gums the pink of an inner organ. "Why be immortal if you're not omnipotent too? Why live forever unless you can play God?"

I thought of what Billy Lou said to me up there on the catwalk just before the drug ruptured all the membranes in his eyes. *All men are gods*.

"Why are you telling me all this?" I asked him.

He shrugged. "Simple. I need your help to stop it."

7

History tells like a slophead drunk on fire whiskey—somehow, the story always ends in blood.

—from *The Grifter's Guide to the Territories FKA USA*

A few long seconds ticked by. Even Daddy Burnham's eyes looked sorry for me—*sorrier*, I mean, than they did just floating around in a jar of what looked like nuclear waste.

"President Burnham, sir . . ." I tried to think of a way to phrase what I needed to say that wouldn't get me canned—or slapped into Jersey Federal.[1] "I don't know where you get your intelligence, but I'm just a hand-crank operator—and not even a very good one. I always take all my pee breaks. I mean, I just said the word 'pee' to the president." I hadn't been planning to use this argument, but it seemed pretty water-tight, at least from where I was sitting. "I'm a nobody, sir."

"I know," he said. I was just a tiny bit annoyed he'd agreed with me so quick. "That's exactly why we want you. We've bought ourselves a few days—a week, at the outside. The Commonwealth has sanctioned the Federation by crippling its servers."

That was a shock to the nuts. If the Commonwealth was cooperating

---

1. From the relevant section of *The Employee Handbook of Better Business Practices*: "Criticism of the Federal Corporation, or any of its subsidiaries, operations, management practices, legal statutes, or corporate management team, is in direct violation of the company's *Positive Positions Mandate* and may result in punitive action ranging from docked pay to legal action. Note that criticism of the President and CEO, and/or any members of the corporate board, is considered high treason."

with New New York, things must be teetering on apocalypse. Rivalry between the two was practically written into the Constitution.[2]

"But it was meant as a slap on the wrist," he continued, "and it's only a matter of time before the Federation servers are up and running again. In the meantime, Rafikov can't even catch a whiff of what we're doing."

"But what *are* we doing?"

He sighed as if he'd been hoping I wouldn't ask. "There's only one person in the world smart enough to stop Yana Rafikov. And that, unfortunately, is Yana Rafikov. But as you can imagine, her cooperation is, in this case, extremely unlikely."

"Can't you just kill her?" I hated to point out the obvious, but Crunch did have a reputation for dealing with diplomatic deadlocks by the simplest route. Even a company kid could read between the lines whenever one of our public enemies suddenly choked on a chicken bone or drowned in a lake while on vacation. Because really, who had chicken bones nowadays? Where would you even find a lake that wasn't toxic to swim in? We were pretty sure that the whole point of the Foreign Exchange Trade and Services Division was to drop assassins and spies all over the continent. Jared's older sister, Riley, had been appointed to the Commonwealth right after standard, and had once sent back a necklace made of ancient seashells—pretty, except for all the blood caked inside of them.

President Burnham didn't flinch. "We would, if we knew exactly where she was. But she's well protected. And access to the Russian Federation is nearly impossible, given the military threat in Pennsylvania.[3] Besides,

---

2. In the Federal Corporation, this was a slang term for *The Employee Handbook of Better Business Practices*. And it's worth noting that in the Commonwealth, the rivalry *was,* in fact, enshrined in the Constitution, which also stipulated that supporting the Yankees, the Federal Corporation's hometown fantasy baseball team, was a crime punishable by death.

3. Pennsylvania was one of the Soviet Federation's most important colonies for deterring threats posed by the Federal Corporation, and had been a critical win in the wars that followed dissolution. It had been, since the early '50s, run as a vast military outpost, and was home to a record 450,000 active-duty militia troops.

if she's cabled up to other individuals—if she has managed to override their conscious thinking, or store it in the cloud—all of them might die with her. No." He shook his head. "Rafikov dreamed up the technology. She's the one who must dream up a way to stop it."

Just listening to him gave me whiplash. "But why would she?"

"She won't have a choice." He leaned forward. "Years ago, when she was a student at MIT, Rafikov donated a sample of her brain tissue to a neurological brain study headed by a promising Ph.D. candidate. He was testing the theory that brain tissue could be transferred between individuals, and even between species."

"Albert Cowell," I said.

President Burnham nodded. "Cowell cloned the donated brain tissue for use in hundreds of experiments over the next decade—most of them failed. But at one point, half a dozen animal species could boast a small portion of the genius Yana Rafikov's brain. Staggering, isn't it? Just imagine a dumpster-diving rat with the neurological firepower and self-consciousness of a higher primate."

He was describing the Human Resource agents exactly, but I didn't say so.

"But when the San Andreas Fault blew up, and dissolution followed on its heels, he lost every single one of his successful experiments, and all of the remaining brain tissue he had meticulously cloned and shepherded through generations of cell death." Burnham paused. "All, that is, except for one."

Finally, I understood. "The goat."

"The goat," Burnham said, with another nod. "The last living mammal whose neural tissue contains a usable sample of Rafikov's brain."

"Besides Rafikov, you mean," I said.

He tried to tap his nose, but his shakes were so bad he wound up fingering his upper lip instead. "I'm not sure how Mr. Ropes and the animal found each other. It's even possible that Mr. Ropes was under Rafikov's control, and intended to kill the animal. Or it was a happy coincidence. But it gave us an unexpected way to fight back."

"How?"

"Albert Cowell was a pioneer in Fractal Brain Theory—it is his view that any portion of the brain, no matter how small, reflects the structural pattern and integrity of the whole, meaning that the whole might be rebuilt from any component part. Now he'll put this theory into practice."

It took me a second. "You're saying Cowell wants to *build* a brain?"

"Not just any brain. Rafikov's brain." He looked suddenly severe. "And he doesn't want to—he *has* to. The fate of the continent—the fate of the world—depends on it."

For a while, we sat in silence. The whole thing was nutty. And I still didn't know where I fit in.

President Burnham must of known exactly what I was thinking. "You saved the goat's life," he said, in a softer voice. "The animal will trust you."

And then, all at once, I understood. "You can't . . ." I felt like I'd inhaled a fist of Foodstuffz™ soured back to their component chemicals. "You don't mean . . ."

Now President Burnham's smile was so huge, it looked like a hole cut in his face. "You, young man, are going west."

Part II

CRUNCHTOWN
407 → BCE TECH

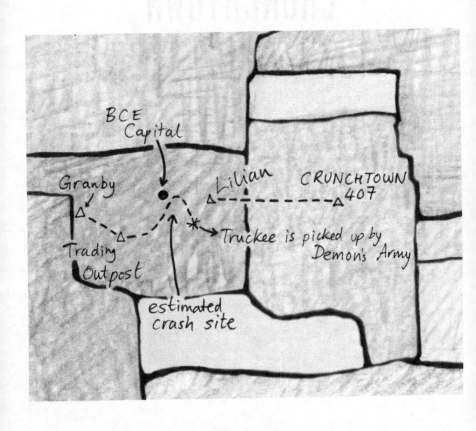

The Crunch International Railway travels from Crunch 407 to the company's many distribution centers in Oklahoma, now privately owned by "the Backyard Shark," billionaire Tenner C. Blythe. There are no other stops to make. Nothing out in this cracked tit of the former America but collapsed fracktowns, fissured agrofirms, sinkholes, and rubble—and, of course, the usual assortment of backlanders, vultures, cultists, and criminals you find everywhere nowadays.
—from *The Grifter's Guide to the Territories FKA USA*

Whenever I'd dreamed about leaving Crunchtown, I'd imagined scrolling off on a vintage motorcycle—the kind that runs on gas and sounds like a giant choking on a chicken bone—maybe stopping to turn around and see the city shrunk to a thumbnail behind me. In my wildest fantasies, I thought of taking off on one of the private aircraft that once or twice a year touched down in the rubble of the old airport to refuel before beating it back to cities where flycraft were common knowledge.

I didn't think I'd be squeezed between two scowling HR beltstrappers in the backseat of a twenty-year-old autodrive, praying I wouldn't end up splattered with animal vomit.

"Terrible way to go." The goat's eyes narrowed to slits, and I could feel his heart beating through his fur. "Buried in a mound of molten metal. Crushed under the tires of an eighteen-wheeler. Pulverized and pounded, turned to roadkill . . ."

Every time he twitched, he came within an inch of drilling me in the balls.

"We're not going to die," I said. I was half-tempted to remind him he'd been whining that morning about greener pastures, but didn't even want to breathe the idea of death in his direction.

I'd fed him the story President Burnham had suggested: that we were returning him to Cowell for observation, as part of an important prisoner swap between the RFN and the Federal Corp. Although he wasn't thrilled about returning to the Laguna-Honda Military Base in San Francisco, he seemed to like the idea of being the key to some diplomatic circle jerk.

"'*The tortures mankind devises for its amusement*'"—the goat's nostrils quivered—"'*will surely render the devil redundant.*'" He cracked one yellow eye to gaze at me. "That's a line from chapter six of my memoir."

A writer. Jesus. I wondered where he'd grimped *those* neurons from.

We passed over the river where it turned north via an old concrete suspension bridge. Both the unionists and dissolution crowd had left graffiti. TOGETHER WE STAND, DIVIDED WE FALL. FREE ARIZONA. "BURNHAM" TO THE GROUND. After another mile, the operating system shouted our arrival at the Davie Stevens Natt[1] Crunch International

---

1. D. S. Natt, as he was commonly known, was Mark C. Burnham's fraternity brother at Harvard. (As Dalia Towers extensively details in her seminal 2055 biography, *The Burnham Paradox*, many people have suggested that Natt and Burnham were at the center of an epic cheating scandal that rocked the university in 2020, when they were both seniors.) Natt subsequently became one of the biggest initial investors in Crunch, United, as Burnham pushed its expansion into consumer electronics, clothing, furniture, and even home technology. Natt was rewarded with a cabinet position after Burnham was elected president in 2036, serving as the secretary of defense and overseeing the infamous March Massacre in 2042, in which the air force was deployed to drop bombs on protesters marching toward the White House.

Terminal Station. The horizon beyond it was blackened by the looming silhouette of an agrofirm, kitted with a trademark silo where trained security teams kept watch day and night to make sure no backlanders came to steal from the storehouses. To the east, I could only barely see the lump of the city through a haze of chemical smoke.

It was as far as I'd ever been from home.

The HR duo rocketed out of the rig as soon as the doors popped, and the goat bounded after them, missing my left nut by an inch. When I tried to stamp some feeling back into my feet, I could of sworn the carpet *yelped*. Maybe, I thought, the rig was tricked with sensory-equipped fabric. I hurried out of the car nice and quick before it could start complaining about the barnyard stink we'd left behind.

"The day train's coming." The HR goons hadn't so much as tongued a pebble in my direction since they'd come to hustle me out of Burnham's office, and they didn't smile either. But they still had dumbass name tags hovering beneath their holos, and this one's name was Roger. He had a fir of nose hair making an obvious run for his upper lip, and didn't even remove his vaporizer to talk. He just shifted it to the corner of his mouth and talked around it.

"We're late." The second HR gun, Biff, had a head shaped like a cinder block, very little neck, and a belt strapped with so many guns he looked like a Level-8 Warrior from my favorite simulation, WorldBurn: Apocalypse: semiautomatic rifles, exploding artillery, strapback revolvers. "Let's ramp and ride."

I had a thousand questions. How were we supposed to get past the Texas border, one of the hardest on the continent? How would we avoid the Denver cartels without cutting south to risk dying in the Dust Bowl? If being a nobody was my cover, wouldn't a personal security detail give me away? But I wouldn't ask, not for my life. There was nothing more exciting to HR rats than a crumb with a question, and I wasn't going to give either one the excuse to splooge their knowledge all over me.

We hustled for the terminal station as the bullet train approached, hovering silently above its tracks like a puffed-up condom surfing waves of air. Just then I thought I saw a flash of something silver to my right. But when I turned, I saw nothing. Still, I could of sworn that something—or someone   was out there, watching.

"You dumping in your shorts?" Biff was holding the door for me. A real class act.

"Coming." I took one last look at my hometown—the smear of chemical color, the collision of shoebox apartments, the foundries spewing ash into the air over the graveyard plots where what remained of my mom was buried six feet under poisonous dirt—and felt a hard ache in my throat. I couldn't shake the feeling that I'd never go back to Crunch 407. I'd never walk through the red-dust streets where I'd walked with my mom when I was little, or stock up on RainbowSweetz™ from the company store. That I'd never see Saanvi again, or hear her brag about her fantasy-football wins. That I'd never sit with Jared and listen to him babble on about product-development breakthroughs and the release of the new *Todd-X, Human Resources Champion* movie.

I wasn't an idiot—at least, I wasn't any more an idiot than the average squid. I knew that Crunch 407 was a shitdump. I knew I was poor. I knew I was meant for an oil wheel in a machine that worked to crank out cash for the uppercrusts. Despite the Corporate Pride Movement and the songs about the colonial world, despite the jingles and the free Dymase™ with every purchase at the company store, despite the constant smiling and the holos that slicked that everything was better in Crunch 407, I knew it.

But it was still home. And in a world staggering toward the finish line, that counted for a lot.

It took some wrangling to figure a proper tariff for the goat: the ticket vendor was an ancient-model robot in danger of overheating every time it processed a question. After some negotiation we agreed he should count for a quarter-person, like one of the SAAMs that traveled the route.[2] Luckily, President Burnham had hooked me up with a fat stack of Crunchbucks, some Freedom dollars, manna, and Nevada gold chips—currency I'd never even laid eyes on, since it was illegal in the Federal Corp.

Of course, the beast didn't even say thank you.

The bullet train was a beauty on the outside, glittering in hybrid metals and reinforced polyglass. Inside, it smelled like old bac and piss. By the time we boarded, most of the passenger cars were jammed with day laborers and agrofirm reps toting cases of test-tube apples and pork spores. But Biff and Roger managed to find us a cabin shared only by an old man with the mug of a reanimated cadaver.

"Is that a real animal?" he asked in a whisper. His pupils were electric, and his scabby look gave him away as a dimehead. "A real *live* animal?"

"Unfortunately," I said.

The man's nostrils were quivering, as if he could already smell the goat split open and seared on a griddle. "I remember the taste of real animals. . . ."

"This one's no good to eat," I said. "He's way too old. All bone and sinew."

The goat shot me a dirty look but said nothing, and luckily the man left us alone after that.

We found a bank of empty seats. The train slipped into motion, smooth as a lubed-up bullet down the throat of a gun. I popped a fresh-laced

---

2. In 2084, many countries considered droids, at least for legislative purposes, only *one-quarter* people, with two exceptions. In the forward-thinking and technologically dependent country of Halloran-Chyung, widely considered the best place for an Engineered Person outside of I.N.E.P.T., androids enjoyed the same rights as natural-born humans. In the Real Friends© of the North, they had been since 2060 officially denoted 45.8 percent human, in a bald attempt to dissuade defections to the Independent Territory of Silicon Valley (as well as because of the confusion arising from the definition of Engineered Persons, given the enormous boom in plasticide-fusion surgery there). But in reality, the Real Friends© of the North had enacted a series of laws to monitor, control, and economically disempower the android population. In the Confederacy and the Sovereign Nation of Texas, they were not recognized as human at all.

gummy I'd bought from the vending machine at the terminal station. I'd never been big on weed, not compared to everyone else I knew—Jared vaped every morning and Annalee liked to take blueberry-flavored fresh on her lunch breaks—but since I was sneaking into enemy territory to deliver brain cells to a Crunch sleeper agent in the hopes that we could stop a global apocalypse of mind-controlled zombies, I figured it was as good a time to get high as any.

Soon we were squarely in agrofirm territory, where Crunch, United's foodstuffs were printed via data-set instructions or sprouted from harvested stem cells. It was amazing how many firms there were, each of them on its own rolling plot of pavement, separated by high fences and water-harvesting and -treatment plants. I tried to imagine what the colony might of looked like two centuries ago, when it was still called Arkansas; what the whole continent might have looked like to the settlers drawn west by a promise of gold in the hills of what was then California, before California cracked open and a rush of developers, techies, and land grabbers started pushing into Washington and Oregon to make up for lost coastline.

But I couldn't. It was like trying to imagine a live cow just by looking at a hamburger patty.[3]

After a while, I slipped on my visor. Burnham's secretary had, true to her word, returned it, and the backstrap even smelled a little like her. I felt a little calmer as soon as all my feeds popped up: the flow of updates

---

3. Truckee's analogy isn't arbitrary here. He is making oblique (and paraphrased) reference to what became famously known, in the early days of the agrofirms, as the "non-parity" argument for the preservation of livestock. The argument was pioneered by a professor of philosophy at Washington University in support of the American Cattle Farmers Association and essentially states that a person confronted with a cow would be able to conceive of a portion of the cow, such as a steak, but a person confronted with a steak would never be able to conceive of a cow, and thus a steak cannot be said to be an appropriate "stand-in" for the animal as a whole, i.e., that steaks manufactured from other steaks should not legally count as cow products.

and chatter, tags and likes, video and riffs, slowly sloughed off the real world layer by layer down to nothing. But portal service was spotty. The Commons, my usual VR hangout, collapsed into 2-D, and pretty soon, error codes started nudging into my visuals.

I swiped a message to Jared and Annalee, since there'd been no time to say goodbye. I'd seen Sammy only for a second outside the company store, and when I rapped her my cover story—I was getting a few days off in the company's Perfect Forest™ retreat[4]—I had the weirdest feeling she *knew* I was lying.

Maybe she did. She'd been studying pretty hard.

The HR team had loaded me with a rucksack full of currency, a fake passport, and a few changes of clothes, then marched me back to my shoebox, fouling it up with vape while I collected the few things I owned, all of it company-issue: my Crunch dopp kit, a few pairs of skivs, the Crunch Appreciation Pin my mom got for her twentieth year of employment, a hair band Annalee had once lost in my couch cushions. At the last second, I took *The Grifter's Guide to the Territories FKA USA*, one of the books Billy Lou had scavenged for me, even though I'd never been able to shake out more than a sentence's worth of meaning from the knotty letters on the pages. Still, I wanted to remember old Billy Lou—and not the one I'd seen up there on the catwalk, leaching drug through his eyeballs.

As we got closer to the border of BCE Tech, I saw dark shapes turning

---

4. After generations in which there was a general movement into urban centers and a fetishization for the consumable, disposable, technological, and futuristic, the destruction of the environment, and the increasing disruption of global travel and information routes, led to a profound fixation with and even fetishization of the natural world. The most popular virtual-reality simulation of all time was called Oceanside, which, as the title of the game suggests, allowed its gamers to sit in a lounge chair on a private beach on the ocean, feeling the salt spray on their lips, watching whales in the distance, and drinking a cold beer. Subsequent versions included On the Porch, In the Mountains, and Country Drive.

like real birds in the sky and remembered standing with my mom when I was little to watch drones buzz down through Low Hill, dropping wrapped coupons for our bonuses. But the Federal Corp had cut use to a minimum after a hacking scandal, and it had been a long time since I'd seen so many at once.[5]

The border was nothing but a chain-link fence tagged with Private Property signs, and some private security goons[6] who turned to blur as the train sped by. We were by it in a click. Just like that, I was out of the country for the first time.

But the land on the west side of the border looked a lot like the land on the east side, except for more and more crack-ups that showed the farther we went. Broken-up towns crashed by earthquakes and tornadoes washed by the windows, and ruined fracking plants slunk along in the distance, trying not to look guilty. Only newly patched tornado walls proved the property still had live tenants, employees of Blythe's financial services firm or just hardscrabble desperadoes who leased run-down patch shacks from the family trust.

Even Lilian,[7] our first pit stop, looked a lot like Crunch 407: slum squats jigsawed together, and, beyond them, a grid of ugly treatment plants, water towers, and recycling centers. Passengers got on, passengers got off. Freight was unloaded. The goat shook, then trotted off to shit

---

5. Due to concerns about espionage, many countries had outlawed the use of drones. The Sky Protection Act of 2070 decreed that in Crunch, United, including all its colonies, drones were illegal except for certain state-run surveillance programs and the delivery of interoffice mail.

6. When Oklahoma went belly-up—belly-up, legitimately, after decades of fracking had made sinkholes of its major cities—Tenner C. Blythe swooped in and bought it for a song, beating out Crunch, United, and the newly formed Dakotas at the fire sale. Its security forces, military, and police department were all privately employed by Blythe's company.

7. Lilian, named for Blythe's ex-wife, compacted more trash than anywhere else on the continent.

outside after treating us to a long rap about the barbarism of indoor bathrooms.[8]

I kept an eye on him from my seat while he nosed around the platform, hoovering up old Singles™ wrappers and drawing stares from just about everybody. It was nuts to think that the same animal making a meal out of synthetic plastic and a handful of broken glass was courier of one of the most sophisticated brains on the continent—or at least, courier of part of it.

Soon, a cheerful automated voice crooned we would leave the station in three minutes. The goat was still copping a squat next to a 2-D billboard faded of original type, now plastered over with more Private Property signs.

I stood up to hustle him along. Biff didn't budge when I picked my way around the mountain of his lap, but Roger and all his nose hair followed me into the aisle.

"Orders," was all he said when I glared at him.

I was passing the toilet when I heard a muffled shout from the next train car. I whipped around but couldn't see squirrel beyond the grimy doors that separated compartments. A second later, two security bots whizzed down the aisle, nearly knocking me off my feet.

Biff stood up, shouldering his AK. Roger yanked me behind him. A high mechanical beeping, like the whine of a jumbo mosquito,[9] lifted all the hairs on my neck. The doors opened with a hiss. A marching band

---

8. A similar argument of the Android Liberation Front, and all its supporters, insists that humans cannot possibly count as superior to manufactured beings because of the rabid inefficiency of their corporal bodies and need to expel waste by excreting it through various orifices.

9. Truckee is using "jumbo" here not as a modifying adjective but to refer to the species whose Latin name was given in 2067 as *Culicidae gargantuan*. Originating out of the Commonwealth's ambitious project to repopulate the world, or at least the East Coast, with animal species previously lost during the Great Die-Off, jumbo mosquitoes could reach wingspans of ten inches and consume a half liter of blood every week.

of transit officials flowed through them: first a red-faced human engineer, then two more SecureTech robots, pinning a terrified, older-model, four-foot-ten android between them.

Not just any droid either. Sammy. *My* Sammy. The half in my two and a half friends.

I would of known the look of her circuitry anywhere.

"The train will be departing Lilian in two minutes," said the sweet female voice of the train.

"Sammy!" I moved for her but Nose Hair stopped me.

"Truckee, you've got to *diles que me dejan ir*." Even for someone kitted out of screens and circuit boards and motion detectors, she looked terrible. About a hundred system errors lit up her interface at once. In her panic, she kept toggling between language preferences. "Tell them *je n'ai rien fait du mal*."

"You shut your mouth." The engineer turned on her. "One more cough and I'll wipe you clean."

I'd never in my life heard that expression lobbed so casually, and I was suddenly furious.[10] "Hey. Don't talk to her like that."

---

10. Almost every country on the continent had passed legislation to ensure that wiping a droid, except in cases of self-defense, was a criminal act. If a plaintiff wanted to wipe, or eradicate the hard drive and restore factory settings to an android model, most of the time the case went first before a local court and then, in one of the few examples of post-dissolution cooperation between countries, to a single court known as the Humanoid Regulatory Committee, which specialized in android affairs. It was comprised of three humans and three androids, and together the court regulated all such disputes across the continent. Some historians propose that the existence of a regulatory body such as this one proves that the dissolution was never truly complete, while others claim it was solely the result of a cross-cultural fear of the android species. It's worth pointing out that the Confederacy did not recognize the authority of the HRC; did not recognize androids as being human in any whole or fractional way; did not permit them within their borders; and furthermore gave all citizens the right without qualification to disable and/or completely wipe any androids that he or she encountered. And beginning in late 2070, a year after the end of the Android Revolution, and six months after I.N.E.P.T. published its constitution and received recognition as a sovereign state from both the Soviet Federation and Crunch, United, the

He leered at me. "I'll talk to it any way I want."

"One minute until departure," announced the sweet female voice of the train.

"What's your glitch, anyway?" I asked him. "Someone forget to feed you VitaMeds™ this morning?"

The engineer had the mottled face of a home-brew addict. "My *glitch*," he said, "is that this bag of zero-ones been hitching since we left company land. My *glitch* is that it don't have a ticket, don't have a tag, and don't have permits to be on this train." The engineer was obviously getting off on seeing her pawed around by bots with the combined IQ of a shoelace. "I would wipe it myself, if I could."

"Say that again, you fat stack of shit, and I'll wipe the floor with your mouth hole." I felt like I'd stepped out into a red-haze day, like a shimmer of hot dust had lit up my whole body. Rage flowed down into my fist and I stepped forward to crack him one. I'd never punched anyone except for in WorldBurn: Apocalypse, and once in real life when Jared insisted he wanted to know what it felt like. But then I'd tried to go easy and swung low, away from his jaw. This time, I was ready to knock this guy's teeth out through his nose.

But Roger shoved me backward again. "Stay out of it," he growled, his teeth still clamped around his stupid pipe. "It's just a circuit board."

So I threw the punch at Roger instead.

I cracked him right on the nose, right above the silky flush of his nose hair, finally knocking the vaporizer out of his mouth. The blood came quickly, lots of it. I knocked him again, without even meaning to—it was like my anger took hold of my body and not the other way around.

He stumbled backward, plowing straight into the engineer, and together they toppled into a flail of body parts. The engineer was shouting cusses from half the countries on the continent, and the other passen-

---

Sovereign Nation of Texas made a push to expel and exclude any android species from crossing its borders, and considered wiping an android criminally justifiable in more than 10,700 unique scenarios.

gers were flattening themselves between the seats, and Biff was on his feet, twitching for his guns, like he wanted to shoot me but knew he couldn't.

The chaos froze the SecureTechs where they stood, and just as soon as they relaxed their grip, Sammy wrenched free. Her lenses were flashing, desperate explosions of purple and blue.

Then she ran. She barreled through them, and for a wild second as she came closer I thought she would toss me too. A cold hand clamped down on my wrist and I nearly flew off my feet as Sammy dragged me to the door.

"What are you doing?" I knew then why some people were so scared of androids: she was three hundred pounds of flexible steel and alloy exoskeleton, and she *was freaking the fuck out.*

"Thirty seconds," the train announced cheerful-like.

The engineer was back on his feet. "Get them!"

I twisted around and scried every single vein in his face standing out, as if each one of them were individually angry.

"I want that son-of-a-box wiped! I want to see its hard drive burn! I want to watch that mothernothing go back to zero!"

Biff launched over the seats, trying for the shortest route toward me. Roger still had one hand cupped to his face, and he was yelling something that sounded like *muffin tin high.* I tried to motion to them—I tried to say *I'm sorry, and it's not my fault, and we're still a team, right, guys?*—but Sammy yanked me so hard I near lost my footing. The train doors were still open and I saw the platform, and early evening shadows purring across it, and the goat standing there blinking at us, looking about as confused as a goat can look.

"This train will depart in five seconds," piped the automat conductor. "Please make sure you are seated and luggage is secured in the freight cars or in the overhead compartments."

"*Get that goddamn sub-blood son-of-a-box!*" was the last thing I heard.

Then Sammy leaped.

She nearly tore my arm from its socket. I was airborne and tumbling after her, and the goat let out a high shriek of terror as our shadows gobbled up the platform and dove for cover. We hit the concrete at the same time the train sent up a final bell and whistle.

At last, Sammy let me go. I rolled twice, leaving a slick of skin behind me. I sat up just in time to see Biff, Roger, and the engineer crowding the closed doors, fogging the glass with CO_2, before the train glided silently out of the station and whipped out of view.

You'll want to stay west of Lilian, especially when the Santa Ana winds stir up old isotope clouds from Halloran-Chyung. Lilian processes shit from the Midwest Affiliated Temporary Refuge, home to some 2 million poor suckers dumb enough to think there might be somewhere else to go. Even on a good day, the place reeks like a middle-school bathroom. But when the Santa Ana blows, it's like having your head in the bowl.

—from The Grifter's Guide to the Territories FKA USA

"Are you off your skids?" As soon as I got to my feet, I rounded on Sammy. My elbow was bleeding, and my visor had been knocked clean off my head. "Did you catch a virus? Did someone code a mistake in your software? Do you have *any idea* what you just did?"

Sammy was three-quarter height, and came only to my breastbone, but that didn't stop me from yelling. I was so mad I could of punched her, too, straight in the interface, except that my knuckles were already hurting and, android or not, I would never punch a girl.

"You're angry," she said slowly. "I know from the volume of your voice and the direction of your eyebrows."

"Jesus fucking flam!" I kicked an empty can of RealJuz™ and nearly lost my balance.

"Hey," the goat said, "I was eating that."

"I'm sorry, Truckee. But you lied to me." Sammy swiveled her head around on her neck, a weird way she had of shaking it. "You told me you were going on a corporate retreat. But previously I overheard your two Human Resource representatives debate the length of time required to get to San Francisco. I have been trying to get a temporary visa to I.N.E.P.T. for exactly one hundred and eleven days. The logical choice was to follow you."

"News blast," I said. "That train was my ride. Those meatheads were my ticket. There *is* no more San Francisco."

"I didn't mean to cause you any trouble," Sammy said. *Blink, blink, blink.* "The Real Friends© of the North is accepting no more manufactured humans. The Independent Territories won't issue papers until I prove my personhood, but I can only prove my personhood if I get to the Independent Territories. And yet Crunch, United, will grant no permits for travel to enemy countries."

"All right, all right."

But Sammy kept yammering. "And then you began to shout, and the other *Homo sapien* shouted, and you were paled color and your sweat glands were producing." Sammy's language software glitched whenever she was upset, like most old-model androids. Some people boasted this as proof that androids weren't really sentient, that they were only parroting. Other people thought the problem was just schooling, that being wired to the intranet wasn't the same as having parents and a good holographic education. "Of all the *Homo sapien* expressions, I find fear the easiest. I've had no problem with fear in any of my practice tests. Logically, it followed that we were in danger and it would be best to absent ourselves."

"I wasn't scared," I told her. "I was angry. You need to study harder."

But the anger had all fled now. My head hurt, my high was wearing off, and I needed to think. I wanted to play shepherd for Rafikov's brain cells about as badly as I wanted to drink recycled piss in the Dust Bowl, but I didn't have much of a choice. When someone like President Burnham told you what to do, you did it.

That was the law of the universe. The uppercrusts made the rules. The crumbs obeyed.

The goat spat out a small piece of metal. "Human Resources will wait for you in BCE Plaza," he said. "Think of what the punishment would be if they lost you. All we have to do is camp here for the night. We can catch tomorrow's train."

He was right. Roger would be snitty I'd clocked him, but it didn't matter. He was on the company payroll, like I was. He would do what the company ordered.

My SmartBand throbbed and unconsciously I registered seven o'clock. "Come on," I said. "We should find shelter for the night." The sun was setting. If BCE Tech was smart-wired, most of the lights would go out when it did.

The platform had emptied quick, and our footsteps rang out in the silence. Blythe's tenants must of hustled home for curfew. At least the station wasn't patrolled by his army: I hadn't practiced my cover story yet, the goat had no tags, and a quick scan of Sammy's serial number would show that she was an escaped migrant worker from Crunch 407.

Ancient signs pointed the way to commuter lines that hadn't existed in a half a century. The sky was a new color, stirred by its own unique chemical smoke into vivid purples and hot electric pinks and a tornado kind of green. It was a warm night, thank hell. Two years ago in May, BCE Tech was sheeted with ice during a blast of Arctic Freeze that paralyzed the recycling centers and the waste-treatment plants, and filled all of Crunch 407, more than three hundred miles away, with the aroma of chilled shit. Jared told me it was so cold that pee froze before it hit the ground, which was the kind of fact Jared always wanted to share, even though I pointed out to him that no idiot would be idiot enough to pee outside when it was freezing.

We hunkered down in the dark of an underpass that ran beneath the bullet tracks, where the acoustics blew our whispers into huge echoes. Though the shakes that gave Oklahoma its midcentury nickname,

Broklahoma, had calmed down since Blythe shuttered the last fracking ops, I could still feel the ground trembling, like the dangerous rumblings of a flu-sick stomach.

After a chow of stale vending-machine ReadyMeals™—the goat ate his NoodleFix™ raw, packaging to product code—Sammy told us how she'd escaped from Crunch 407 by slipping underneath the roadster and hooking onto the chassis. That explained the groan I heard when I'd thumped the floor with my foot. Good. The last thing we needed were carpets that talked back.

"You realize you're going to have to go back, right?" I felt terrible saying it, but that was the world we lived in. Almost everything true was flavored a little like vomit. "As soon as we catch up to the bodymen, you'll get shipped back in a freight case."

"But you can't let them, Truckee." Sammy's speakers began to crackle. "You have to help me."

"I don't *have* to do anything," I fired back. Why did everyone think I was some kind of hero, just because I'd dodged the blow-up at Production-22 with my skin cells intact? "You were the one idiot enough to try and run."

"I think it was very brave of you," the goat said to Sammy, through a mouthful of old aluminum.

"Oh, sure," I said, before Sammy could start fawning. "If the walking trash compactor says so."

The goat's eyes were a luminous yellow in the half dark. "I do not eat trash," he said primly. "Humans *waste food*. And just so you know, I have a name."

"Of course you do."

"It's Barnaby," he said, even though I hadn't asked. "And I'll thank you to use it." When I rolled my eyes, he went on. "Do you have *any idea* what it's been like for me? Do you have any idea the difficulties I've faced? The challenges I've overcome? It's hard enough to be a man *or* a goat, without having to be both at the same time."

"Tell us your story, Barnaby," Sammy said. I shot her a look, but I guess she hadn't gotten to that chapter lesson yet. Or maybe she had, because she ignored me. "Please."

The goat gave a heavy sigh, like it was an ask he heard every day. But he twitched around, trying to get a little comfier. "If you insist," he said. "I suppose, then, it makes sense to begin with my birth, which I am unlucky enough to remember. . . ."

INTERLUDE

THE GOAT SPEAKS

My first memory, my first true memory, is of the punctuated cry of a heart-rate monitor and the taste of a surgical glove someone had abandoned accidentally in my cage. My first minutes awake, aware, I spent in an agony of fear, slowly consuming the fingers, beginning with the thumb: to this day I find the taste of latex both comforting and sharply painful.

I was a kid when the operation was performed, and though I had no concept of birthdays, or even the passage of time, before the human neural tissue was integrated with my own, I later figured out that I must have been roughly ten months old when I was wheeled into the brain chamber.

Before then, you see, time did not exist. I lived forever and I lived a single day only: even now, thinking back on that wordless soup, I have the idea of a moment folded in on itself infinitely, containing everything I had ever experienced up until that point—the smell of grass clippings, the pleasure of dozing on a sun-parched patch of ground, the twitchy chatter of the flies, the tin trailer that rattled us into captivity— as if it all happened in a single instant.

That is the difference between being conscious and not. You start to die only when you begin to understand.

Of course, even after surgery, I lived the first months in a fog of confusion and grief. The more I understood, the lonelier I became. What was this monstrous place, of terrible metal animals that beeped and hissed and pumped through the night? What was this white-gloved, white-cloaked herd, with their frequent, urgent mutterings, their arbitrary gifts, their alternating cruelty and magic?

Slowly, I separated gummy strands of cause and effect, of minute and hours, of night and day, morning and noon. Slowly, my terror abated—and was replaced, gradually, with curiosity, with the urgent wish, if not the linguistic capacity, to know why, where, what, and who. The metal animals that had for a month been tormenting me with their wiry fur and mechanical teeth slowly nudged my conscious understanding toward the concept of machinery. The herd of white-cloaked, two-legged beasts became humans. Individuals unpeeled themselves from the group as I attached feelings and preferences to each of them. There was a woman named Wanda I remember especially. She snuck me biscuits, and her hands smelled always of nail varnish, Lemon Pledge, and tobacco.

The first word I ever recognized and learned to speak, ironically, was "biscuit"—I say ironically because I am, in point of fact, gluten intolerant. Incidentally, it was identifying the source of my gastrointestinal distress that provoked my first outbreak of language. The mouth and stomach are far more conjoined than people might think. I have been driven many times to invective due to a similar fury of the stomach, and people full of gas must rid it either through their bowels or by using their tongues.

This was, perhaps, the only thing of use my father ever taught me. He was crippled when I was very young. So disgusted was he by his own body, he tried to chew off his own legs; he succeeded only in severing vital nerve connections and rendering himself an invalid. After that, he became quickly addicted to the pain tablets they delivered in his kibble, to the point that he would beg for dosage all through the night, to anyone who would listen, or fake new injuries just to receive increased pain-management intervention. It was a mercy, in many ways, when he killed himself, and I can't say I'm sorry he did.

I suppose in some ways, my existence at the base was not so bad. We were exercised regularly in the training facilities next to conscripts and android soldiers. The Agricultural Division included acres of irradiated citrus groves, where Cowell's teams of acolytes strolled through uranium orchards debating the impact of bacterial infection in neurodegenerative disorders, and snipers took potshots at spy drones from turreted stucco towers. We were given plenty to eat, and I had company in the form of other experimental specimens in different stages of recuperation, including a very clever rat; his size, however, meant that he had absorbed only enough connections to feel a general sense of malaise he largely expressed through modern sculptural works assembled from a collection of found objects.

Several of my cousins had been selected for brain transposition as well. Many of them received human neural tissue in amounts too proportionately small to make a difference, and several of them died during surgery. But one, whom I called Nan, was a source of comfort to me. Roughly 15 percent of her brain mass was Homo sapien, and though she was sweet, she was also plodding and very slow. She had a childish and, to my mind, baffling fascination with the mechanics of shoelaces. She was inclined to skittishness and nerves; the letter C disturbed her, and she failed to learn her numbers past seven, meaning she was hopeless at telling time.

And that, ultimately, was the problem with those long and lonesome years: I was bored. A cage is a cage, whether it sprouts persimmon or not; and despite my relatively fair treatment, I was a prisoner, pure and simple. I longed to see the world beyond the perimeter fence, to explore the distant twinkle of downtown San Francisco, to know through experience the words I was learning by absorption: "ocean," "landfill," "quinoa," "electric blanket." But security was far too tight.

It was the San Andreas Fault that gave me my chance. A terrible irony, that the same terrestrial hiccup responsible for millions of human deaths should be the same thing that launched me to freedom—but the world, I suppose, is a zero-sum game, and what one man—or animal—receives, another one must forfeit. When the first Big One[1] came—which, of course, we learned after the Real Big One,[2] and then during the Literally Biggest One Ever,[3] was actually rather modest—the Laguna-Honda Base cracked in two. I mean that literally: the tsunami swept Nan into a foam of filthy ocean not four feet from where I stood. I survived the initial shockwaves—a pummeling gale that lasted for nearly eighteen hours—by a combination of luck and ingenuity, at one point taking shelter beneath a pile of asseverated robotic limbs that absorbed the blunt trauma of objects hurled ashore by the waves.

When the sky at last cleared, I found that the majority of the concrete-and-steel perimeter had washed away, that the citrus groves now yielded their fruit to the open ocean that had ripped them out to sea, and that nearly a third of the base's personnel,

---

1. March 16, 2042.

2. June 3, 2042.

3. November 8, 2043: This marked the beginning of the "Guild Years." Please see Appendix D: "Politics and Natural Disaster: The Unexamined Link."

tumbled by the waves or crushed beneath falling debris, was now beginning to swell with postmortem gas. This proved especially useful, as I was able to lash together a makeshift raft of swollen human bodies to coast me south as the floodwaters receded. Yes, it's true. I escaped on a flotational device made of corpses. But don't forget—humans had used me, too, and used me horribly.

The outside world was not, I will readily confess, as beautiful as the one I had imagined. The aftershocks rumbled on for days, and proponents of independence clashed violently with unionists in streets filthy with rainwater and sewage. Fires blazed continuously. The sun rose red behind a scrim of ash and smoke. The police clashed with rioters or became rioters themselves, and when the National Guard joined the fray it was too late for anyone to direct them—by then, President Burnham had already fled the White House. Looters stripped the stores of anything useful, and food, already so expensive, became impossible to find.

I saw at once the danger I was in after a group of desperate, rib-thin children pursued me nearly two miles, trying to stone me to death. Luckily, they were too weak to aim, and I managed to outrun them, only to find myself outside of the rotten husk of a library moldering on the ruined Menlo Park main drag. Who would think of finding anything useful in a library? It was the perfect place to hide. The place had likely seen no foot traffic in twenty years.

On the whole, it wasn't a bad place to spend the better part of a decade. Oh, yes. I lived the entirety of California's First Independence Government, and then the disastrous Guild Years, and the Real Friends© surprise takeover, and the merger that integrated Washington and Oregon, cloistered between the heavy oak shelves of a long-abandoned library. To me, dissolution is Emily Dickinson and the slippery taste of plastic bindings. "After great pain, a formal feeling comes . . ." I have always thought she must have tried to digest scrap metal herself.

But it was lonely. Oh, it was lonely. There are only so many times one can read the collected works of Shakespeare aloud in different voices, pretending to be at the theater.

That is the true legacy of the brain Albert Cowell and his team of trained fanatics "gifted" me: loneliness that has tailed me like a shadow, growing longer and darker and heavier with time.

10

The first thing I ever sold was a pack of Shake-N-Take Ibuprofen-Enhanced Chicken Drums™ I'd stolen from a convenience store somewhere north of Rochester. Half a day later I ran up against some backlanders living around some old chemical fields and suffering bad from headaches. Sold it for three times what it was worth in ammo, and took that and sold it at a premium to the next roadslicks that tried to shake me down. From then on, I was hooked.

—from The Grifter's Guide to the Territories FKA USA

We bedded down. In the quiet I imagined I could hear the ghosts of the old frackers and their big machines, still drilling and scraping and pumping the core out of the earth. But I'd won rounds of WorldBurn too many times by sinking troops beneath sinkholes like the ones that had buried thousands under rubble when the ground in Oklahoma turned as soft as a bruise to want to think too much about it.

Barnaby's story kept nudging up bad feelings: he'd had a shit life, really, and here I was serving his brain up to be filleted.[1]

In my dream, Billy Lou showed up, mangled with blood and stitching,

---

1. It's unlikely that Truckee knew this word in the context of food preparation, as he almost certainly had never eaten meat that hadn't been grown, engineered, or printed to the proper proportions already. Due to the enormous obesity crisis in the Federal Corporation, however—which affected 1 in 2 adults and 1 in 3 children under eighteen—he might have heard this word in the context of a popular surgery in which, quite literally, patients were "filleted" open and emptied of excess fat.

his eyes placed crookedly and burnt patches of skin blackening his chest and shoulders. "The problem," he was saying, "is that they won't let sleeping dogs lie." I saw what he meant: the ground was shaking, and old animal skeletons clawed up from their graves.

I came awake to the blast of an alarm. Cement dust drifted from cracks in the ceiling. The ground was barely trembling, vibrating the empty cans in the underpass.

The goat was on his feet, wild-eyed with panic. "What is it? What's happened?" There was something wrong with his balance. He staggered around in stiff-legged, shuffling circles. "What—?"

The words died with a gurgle in his throat. His whole body seized up. His eyes rolled back in his head.

Then he toppled. For a half second, I thought he'd flatlined, and I'd be saddled with a corpse all the way to the Pacific.

"Interesting," Sammy said mildly. "I've never encountered a fainting goat."

"A *what*?"

"A fainting goat," Sammy repeated. "Otherwise known as a myotonic goat, due to a condition called myotonia congenita, whose most obvious manifestation is sudden and pronounced periods of—"

The goat unfroze, and staggered back to his hooves. "I'm okay!" he panted. "I'm okay!"

"We've got to move," I said. The shrill of the alarm was swelled by the underpass into a hideous shriek, like the howling of ten thousand dimehead shakes.

"It's funny," Sammy said. "The alarm frequency sounds almost identical to the one Crunch 407 uses to alert the city to intruders."

"It *is* identical." I shouldered my backpack. "And guess what? *We're* the intruders."

We surfaced to find Lilian invisible behind a perimeter of enormous floodlights, blazing like bald eyeballs in our direction. The moon was high, beaming through a wispy haze of green cloud smoke. It must of been a little after midnight—my pulse was going so fast I had trouble picking out the rhythm of my SmartBand.

We ran. The goat nipped at my heels, still muttering, *We're okay, we're okay, we're not going to die.* Sammy buzzed ahead, circling back once in a while to give the all-clear. The whole thing felt like being in World-Burn: Apocalypse, except it was no fun at all. I kept waiting for Tenner Blythe's bodymen to swarm us from the dark, for the sharp crack of artillery fire or the sudden punch of a bullet through my ribs, and this time no health managers there to extract it.

But just when we reached the end of the platform, the alarm went silent. A metal gate gave access to a switchback set of stairs that ran down into the stitching of the old trainyard. In the distance, rotting homes, old businesses, and the burned-out shells of abandoned retail centers were like the scabbed-over skin of old civilization stuck to the collar of the new city.

The goat cleared the gate, and I scrambled after him. Sammy had the most trouble. She was old, and her rubberized joints were glitchy. But she managed at last and we went down the stairs together, our footsteps crackshot in the sudden silence.

The trainyard was riotous with old trash. We had to be careful to avoid all the syringes, and the going was slow. But finally we reached a ribbon of pavement that curved west, and so we followed it.

The quiet did nothing to reassure me. The farther we got from Lilian, the more uneasy I felt. If we'd been the ones to trip the alarm, we'd been seen. But if we'd been seen, why hadn't we been chased? It didn't make any sense.

Unless we *hadn't* been the ones to trigger it.

Which meant that someone else was coming.

Once in a while back in Crunch 407, when the tornado winds from the west blew away the red haze and a dozen ruined jet streams of pollution collided in just the right way, we could see stars above Low Hill. On those nights all of us went streaming up to the roofs, packing so tight even a fart could of knocked one of us over the edge.

My mom didn't know a constellation from a kangaroo but that didn't stop her from making up her own knowledge. She invented names for the smear of stars: the Shit Shovel and the Tampon, the Rocketship, the Whore's Bath, the Turd and Dingle. Somehow, her names spread. Even crumbs who never met her would shout out on clear nights that the Turd and Dingle was visible from the roof of 22-C.

But here in BCE Tech, the stars were clearer than I'd ever seen them. Without even meaning to I picked out the Whore's Bath and the Tampon and all the other constellations my mom had named. It was nutty to think those same stars had been flowing out their light before fault lines blew up and a tsunami knocked most of old California off the coast. Before Old New York turned green with moss and algae, and rising seawaters flooded the Statue of Liberty to her tits, and the New York Stock Exchange turned into a breeding ground for three-eyed fish and oysters with a taste for dead bodies. Before the Exxon-Mississippi River wiped out forty thousand houses at one go when it thundered over the levees. Before Texas opened its convict camp and 400,000 coastal refugees moved north to shit out their lives in the festering temporary camp once known as Kentucky. Before the droids rebelled and the Real Friends© of the North closed its borders to non-citizens.

Nutty to think how much had changed for us, while squirrel changed for the sky.

Soon we'd left Lilian behind, and it was silent except for the gentle fizz of Sammy's treads and the rhythmic tick-tick of the goat's hooves on the pavement. I saw no evidence of squatters, hijackers, or roadslicks, and none of Blythe's famous personal security, either, no patrolling guns-for-hire or five-story machine-gun towers.

Here there were nothing but fields of buffalo grass, vast and puddly sinkholes, and the every-so-often house that looked as if it'd been blown there by a tornado—and probably had been. The air vibrated with insect song. Mosquitos as big as thumbnails kept buzzing around hopefully. Trees batted their green eyelashes at us. It was the kind of green I'd never seen before, real green, not spray-painted or printed in one of the 3-D plasticine nurseries.

It wasn't a color so much as a feeling, my mom told me once, and in the dark I heard the quiet hiss of her vape going. *Like holding something alive in your hands. Like when I was pregnant with you and could feel your heart beating when I put a palm to my stomach.*

Sammy wheeled around the remains of an old house, now sunk to its roof in a cake of old mud. The sinkholes here had swallowed whole buildings, cars, even a gas station, spitting out a few hubcaps and rubber pumps. "We've been journeying for two hours now," she said. "Don't you think we should turn around?"

"And go where?" It was possible security had silenced the alarms just to lure us into a false sense of safety. Crunch HR caught raiding backlanders that way all the time. "Lilian will be full of guns. It's a miracle we're not leaking blood out of bullet holes already."

"But BCE Plaza is one hundred and six miles away. You can't be thinking we'll walk it."

"One hundred and six miles?" Barnaby looked outraged. "I've got arthritis in my knees. Tendonitis of the hooves. I've got *bone spurs.*"

I ignored him. "I'm *thinking* about how to stay alive," I said to Sammy.

"But surely we're more likely to die in the backlands. Statistical models support it—"

"Shhh." Before Sammy could spew any more logic at me, I held up a hand to silence her. Sammy was a half inch from rolling into me before her motion sensors froze her midstep.

"What?" Barnaby whispered. "What is it?"

"Voices," I whispered back. I scented something on the wind and shivered. It was like a memory but chewier, with a taste . . . something burning . . .

No. Not burning.

Better.

"What is that?" Sammy asked in a low voice. She sounded afraid.

"I don't know." I motioned for Sammy and Barnaby to follow me into the trees. In a world where unfamiliar was usually a fancy way for saying death, I should of known better. But I was drawn toward that smell like it had hooked me in the chest.

In the loam of rotting trees, mushrooms the size of hubcaps pointed bellies toward the sky. Furry beetles clambered over toppled street signs. A moldy sign pointed the way to a rest stop that hadn't existed in six decades.

Through the trees, I could see the glow of a hobo fire. When the wind tossed up the sound of laughter, I dropped into a crouch.

"You stay here," I told Barnaby. I couldn't risk exposing him to harm, not with the neural freight he was carrying. He looked all too happy to obey.

I moved extra carefully now, trying to make no noise, avoiding the litter of broken glass still camouflaging itself among the leaves. In a sharp dip of land was a scene lifted straight out of prehistory: seven or eight men around a fire pit, shapeless behind a veil of smoke.

I could hardly cred it, but they were cooking.

Cooking.

With an actual heat source.

It was like we'd tripped and landed back in time.

I heard a step behind me and figured Sammy had caught up.

"Look," I whispered. "They're actually using fire to—"

Before I could finish, someone seized me from behind. I felt the cold steel tip of a knife against my throat, and a blast of hot breath on my cheek.

"Don't move, Sally"—the man squeezing me reeked of fire whiskey and stale fresh—"or I'll stick you like a balloon."

11

*Body pickers are just like maggots: a swarm of 'em always means
death nearby, and half the time it means death nearby for you.
But they're helpful for more than pointing you away from flu towns:
I've off-loaded some of my best swag from corpses I never even
saw. Half the time the body boys are in such a rush to catch the
nearest ice van, they'll let go the big stuff for a song.*

—from The Grifter's Guide to the Territories FKA USA

I remember when I was a kid, the C-1 came sweeping into Low Hill on
the backs of refugees from the border of Sinopec-TeMaRex Affiliated,
and how for weeks we huffed air through gas suckers or held our breath
whenever we skidded past a building marked with a big black *X*. I remember the census men who came, black-suited corporate types with
long-heeled hearses, how they loaded up bodies block by block and
chugged them off to the incinerator.

And I remember how scared I was when a howling in the stairwell
signaled the flu had made it all the way into our little block of apartments, and how in the morning, my mom and I stood by the window
watching Old Mrs. Donahue loaded into the back of the body rig down
below. Someone had bundled her up in plastic, but her skinny little ankles were still visible, and so were the filthy slippers she used to pad around
in everywhere. One of them dropped while the census hands were trying
to wedge her in next to a stack of corpses.

My mom could see I was on the edge of bawling, and slung an arm around my shoulders. "We all die, Truckee," she said. "It isn't that we die. It's how much life we got to live."

I admit, with my pulse throbbing a half centimeter away from the tip of a none-too-clean knife, I wasn't sure I could of said the difference.

"Brimstone and *hellelujah*, the party's just getting started." A woman with a strong resemblance to an enormous molting caterpillar charged out of the darkness with Sammy in her grip. "We got a tin man over here. Or is it a tin woman?"

"Ugliest sex doll I ever seen in my life, if that's what she's supposed to be. I wouldn't even fuck her with *Thrasher's* dick." The man who had me pinned gave me a nudge down the hill. "All right, start stomping, Sally."

We broke out of the trees and half-stepped down the steep embankment. Close around the fire was one of the ugliest road crews I'd ever seen. They were Devil's Army demons, no doubt about it. Two men had the brand of the devil, 6-6-6 planted right on their mugs.

I prayed Barnaby had run off to safety. Maybe, just maybe, he'd even run for help.

But no. He was too much a coward. Besides, there was no help to get.

The Devil's Army demons forced Sammy and me down into the dirt next to another prisoner, by far the largest man I'd ever seen in my life. His shoulders were twice as broad as a normal man's and his biceps the size of both my thighs together. When he raised his eyes to me, I wished he hadn't. They were empty, somehow, as if someone had gone in with software and photo-edited out the light. A thick, ugly scar, as pink as a worm, stretched between his eyebrows to the crown of his head.

A Straw Man. No wonder he looked so hopeless. He'd had the fight taken out of him, literally.

"Well, well, well. When it rains, it pours." A soft voice spoke up, a voice like the first quiet fizz of dust thrown up against the windows by a hurricane twenty miles away. "What do we say when the devil provides?"

"Give the devil his due." The Devil's Army spoke together, like a bunch of tatted, jumped-up, filthy schoolkids.

"Give the devil his due," the man echoed, and stepped into the fire-light.

His face was raw with scars and burns. Where his right eye should of been there was nothing but an empty pit, a smooth socket of skin. His left cheek, seared to melting, had been clumsily remade out of plate metal and hammered tin.

He wore clothes of filthy leather and a belt so full of weapons it would of made Biff's arsenal look skint by comparison. I counted half a dozen knives, at least two handguns, a set of brass knuckles, a billy club, a tomahawk, even a goddamn scimitar. I thought about trying to beat it, but knew I wouldn't even make it to my feet before he had my head swinging off his belt buckle too.

"Welcome to hell, soldiers." He kept his eyes on me. "My name's Zeb, and I top this crew." His smile corkscrewed into the scarred part of his face. "Let's see, now. Not a bad haul for a sorry stretch of old Okie in the middle of the night. That's two new bodies to sell, plus a code-error."

My stomach puddled into my intestines. I hadn't counted on worse than the Devil's Army—but they were body pickers too. The more rotgut they shipped to the graveyard plants,[1] the more green they could collect. Not for the first time, I wondered how the people of Florida Island[2] could live with themselves, knowing all of their lights were powered by a constant flow of dead bodies.

"The biggie counts for more than one," said another demon. He was the half bionic of the Federal Corporation armies of the north[3]—a

---

1. Another term for methane-conversion plants.

2. And, presumably, various cities in the Soviet Federated Frontier, a dozen communities in the Green Mountain Associated Intentional Communities, and thousands of backlander settlements; it's not clear whether Truckee believed Florida was unique in its use of the energy alternative.

3. Crunch, United, kept a sizable force of roughly 2 million troops deployed at the northern border, ostensibly in response to the permanent military installations Texas kept in the Free State of New Hampshire. But historians have noted that the two-decade-long territorial push into Canada coincided with the first deployment of troops, many of whom were surgically altered and augmented with bionic features to better

deserter, then. "I bet a fart out of his cheeks could power a truck for a quarter mile. They'll get the juice of three men from the stink in his belly when they slit it." And he lobbed a spitball of old chewables directly at the man's bald head. It burst against his scalp and slid down to his left ear before dropping.

"All right, then. Let's get this pinball game on the road, shall we?" Zeb looked like a man in front of a big plate of CrunchMeat Chopz™. Too bad we were the chops. He unhooked a long, needle-like knife from his belt. "Who'd like to go first? The brute or the baby?"

"Wait," I said. My mouth was dry. Trying to speak was like trying to spit out a sock. "Wait a second. You don't want to hurt me."

"I doubt that," he said.

"I'm telling the truth," I said. "Look, I come from the Federal Corp. My dad's an uppercrust in Corporate. He'll pay a lot of swag to have me back in one piece."

"Nice try, *crumb*," Zeb said. "You don't think I can spot a nobody when I see one?" When he leaned close, his nostrils flared in and out, in and out, waving thick hairs at me. "Desperation has a smell, Suzie Q. You reek."

"Smells like a virgin too," said the woman who looked like the over-sprouted grub, and all the others laughed. That bothered me even more than the idea of the methane in my gut powering someone's hair dryer.

"Okay, fine," I said. "You're right. I am a crumb. I'm a nobody. But I'm on state business for President Burnham."

This made the Devils laugh even harder. Top-secret intel and I gave it up like a nervous belch. But President Burnham should of known better than to give me the job in the first place.

"President *who*?" Zeb said. "Don't know anybody by that name." He made a big show of turning to the rest of his crew. "You ever heard of a President Burnham?"

---

withstand severe weather fluctuations and the threat of rampaging gentech species, such as the fabled "talking hornets" or the "cannibal pachysandra."

The tattooed suck-ups all tripped over their gorges to pipe up: *No, no, never heard of 'im, sounds like a real lube, sounds like the kid's conning.*

It was only then I really scanned how far I was from home. Out here, in the free-for-all continental backlands, President Burnham didn't matter, and the laws of Crunch, United, didn't matter, any more than a dress code mattered to a feral cat.

Zeb turned back to me. The firelight caught his one good eye and sparked it full of golden flames. "You're in the danger zone now, crumb. No laws out here and none of your precious Human Resources to run 'em."

I felt like telling him that he was welcome to game-over the entire Human Resources department. I would even help him ice-pack their bodies to Florida. But of course, I didn't.

"You're making a mistake," I squealed as he lunged for me, even though he wasn't and I knew it and he knew it too.

Zeb seized my hair and yanked my head back so hard my eyes watered. "Save your air, kid." He worked the tip of his knife up and down my larynx, *stroking* it. "Now," he continued, in a softer voice, "we've got to get the right spot. Very important not to overdo it. Don't want too much blood running out in the wagon . . . the devil knows it don't need no more paint."

"Hang on." Another man spoke up just as Zeb's knife tip broke skin, and Zeb hesitated. A warm trickle of blood ran down my neck and pooled in the collar of my shirt.

"You got a problem, Thrasher?" Zeb asked.

Thrasher really did look like a demon in the firelight, especially because of all the tumors. I would of banked he hailed from the nuclear fields of Halloran-Chyung. "What's the use killing 'em now? We've got another day, day and a half walking before we hit the crash. No point in hauling dead weight when they got feet."

"Thrasher's got a point," another demon ventured. He had a straggly goatee, metal shrapnel studding his ears and lips, and the raw, shredded look of a dimehead.

"But what if they run?" protested a third—a ze,[4] by the looks of them, with shaved eyebrows, and twin shoulder holsters.

"They won't run." The grub tipped her head to Sammy. "This one don't have the heart for it. This one"—she nudged the giant with a foot— "is missing half his brain." Finally she turned back to me. "And *this* one's missing both his balls."

"All right, okay. Very funny," I said, to more laughter. For a cult of murderous body traders, they seemed well fucking cheerful.

The grub leaned forward. Her breath smelled like four-day-old Tuna-Saladz™ Bars left to bake in the heat. "It's all right, sugar. I was just fooling. I believe your balls is good as new." She reached for my crotch and I slapped her away. "Aw, what's the matter? You like boys, is that it? That's all right. The devil takes all kinds. We got big-titter dick swingers and thems that get with anything at all, like Oreo over there. Just don't call them a she, or they'll bite your dick off."

I ignored that and spoke instead to the demon named Thrasher. "You said there was a crash. What kind of crash?"

Zeb spat about an inch from my toe. To my surprise, he answered. "Train derailed an hour west of BCE Tech. Half them damned on board died in the fire." Zeb sounded as if he envied them for dying. "Forty, sixty bodies aboard, all ripe for the picking. Which ones aren't burnt to a crisp, that is."

"Derailed?" I'd never heard of the bullet train going off track. "Derailed how?"

"Someone messed with the field," Zeb said.

"You're saying it wasn't an accident?" I was thinking again of the alarm in Lilian, and the fact that no one had tailed us. It couldn't be coincidence.

Rafikov can't catch even a whiff of what we're doing, President Burnham had said. But what if she had?

Zeb squinted at me like he was seeing me for the first time. "I don't

---

4. *Ze* was one of many slang words for a gender-neutral or gender-fluid person. Other examples include: *unison*, *ambi*, and *nyb* (an acronym that allegedly stood for *none of your business*).

know of any *accident's* going to board a train afterward and plug a bullet in the brain of each and every live one."

Biff and Roger: dead. Roger's nose hair: incinerated. That red-haired engineer: dead. I couldn't say the world would be worse for it, exactly, but they hadn't deserved to die, at least no more than anyone else did, no more than these tattooed Satan freaks making flub on corpses.

"Do you have any idea who did it?" I asked.

But Zeb had obviously lost patience with the chitchat. "You ask too many questions," he said. "Truth is, I'd rather haul your dead body in a wagon than listen to your live little mouth keep yabbering. Maybe I'll just go ahead and snip your vocal cords in half."

He seized me by the hair again, and plugged the blade to my throat. A wet slick of blood slid down my collarbones. My bladder gave a wet whimper.

I'm sorry, I thought to nobody in particular. I closed my eyes and tried to call up a memory of my mom. But all I could see was Billy Lou standing there, teeth crusty with blood, his eyes leaking a dark fluid that looked just like shit.

Then a faint rustling noise from the trees, and a heavy *thud*, froze Zeb's hand.

"What the fuck was that?" Thrasher whispered.

Once again, Zeb released me. Before I could be grateful, he blinded me with an uppercut. Stars burst behind my eyes. He seized me by the shirt before I could land in the dirt, shaking me so hard my teeth knocked together. "You bring friends with you, squid? Huh? Answer me, you little shit."

"No," I choked out. I could hardly see. "No friends."

He shoved me back into the dirt. The Devil's Army was on high alert now, guns and knives and axes drawn. Several demons scrolled into the trees and hacked their way through the growth. A minute went by. Slowly, the fog in my head began to clear.

Then I heard a voice: a terrible, fearful voice I knew right away.

"Who are you?" It was the goat, Barnaby. He hadn't run after all. "What do you want? Leave me alone."

I tried to shout, to tell him to run, to command him to—but I couldn't make my voice work. My neck was still leaching blood and Zeb's fist had knocked my thoughts into a wordless murk.

Run, I thought. But all that came out was a gurgle.

Then two of the demons broke free of the trees, their maws screwed up and terrified, like fabric pegged around a screwdriver.

"What?" Zeb said. "What is it?"

"It's . . ." The ze could barely swallow. Even in the dark, from a distance, I could see their Adam's apple rioting. "It's . . . Him."

Zeb went the color of bleach. "Him?"

The ze tried to speak again, but only managed a nod.

"This is ridiculous." Barnaby's voice got louder as he approached. "I'm an intellectual, not a politician. I'm no lord of *anything.* . . ."

He came through the trees, flanked by demons. They didn't have their weapons on him, though. They were actually *kneeling,* crawling at his side, stopping to kiss the ground where he'd touched it.

And the whole crew let out a single, collective gasp, like a sharp wind had blown through them all at once. "I don't believe it," Zeb whispered.

"It speaks," the demons murmured. "It speaks."

Barnaby just stood there, blinking down at them. "*It* is a male, thankyouverymuch, at least in all the *critical* places, though I admit an instinctive fondness for decorative throw pillows. Very good eating. In any case"—he drew himself up taller—"I've sired plenty of young bucks in my day."

"Of course you have," Zeb said. Unbelievably, he began to laugh. "And we, Your Darkness, are of your loins too. We of the Devil's Army, all of us your children."

Then he threw his weapons down and kneeled. There was a great clanking and clatter as all the weapons went down, all that metal, wood, steel, and stone, and one by one every single demon of the Devil's Army bowed down in the dirt.

"We've waited for you, my lord," Zeb said, with his nose still pressed to the dirt. "We've put our faith in Satan, He of the horns and the hoof, He of the quick tongue and the silver speech, and now, at last, He has come."

12

*There's one thing that bred faster than intestinal rot in the years
after secession, and that's religion. We got more religion on this
continent than we got people to worship: I've seen towns bending
the knee to everything from water spirits to waste-treatment plants.
I've seen revivalist prophets and witch ladies reading fortunes from
corpse innards. I don't go in for that hoo-haw myself, but I respect
a good grift when I see one, and religion's got to be one of the
oldest sells in the book.*

—from *The Grifter's Guide to the Territories FKA USA*

It turned out the demons of the Devil's Army weren't half bad, at least
when they weren't hell-bent on killing you.

Apart from Zeb, there was Bethesda, the grub ("My friends call me
Bee," she said shyly as her wart blushed pink, "and sorry 'bout saying
you had no balls."); Hog, the corporation soldier who'd deserted after the
devil appeared to him in the blown-out intestines of one of his platoon-
mates; Oreo, the gender-neutral ze who'd lived briefly in a pansex community in the GMAIC;[1] Damon and Nikhil, who'd been married by a
ventriloquist puppet ordained in the Temple of Satan only that November; Thrasher, only a few years older than I was; Cannon; and Fats, who
from his waddle and fat rolls I knew for someone raised on a diet of
Crunch Foodstuffz™.

They'd come from all over, East Coast and West Coast. They'd escaped

---

1. Green Mountain Associated Intentional Communities.

the Appalachian temp camps on the backs of smuggler trucks and crawled out of shuddering bolt holes in the middle of the Oklahoma Furies. Hog had been a freedom fighter for a while, had helped defend New Hampshire's independence from the Commonwealth, before a misfire from a Texas[2] bottle rocket wiped out half his crew and blasted away his left leg just below the hip bone.

"Some days are harder than others," Zeb told me. "Sometimes you want a break from all the looting and the killing, sure. Sometimes you just wanna kick your feet up, have a drink, play nice with a baby, be *thankful* you still got an eye to see with and legs to carry you. But," he added with a quick glance in the goat's direction, "the devil never got no Sundays off and nor do we."

We made a funny-looking crew. Two demons scouted ahead, calling back to let us know the way was clear or popping off a warning shot if they spotted something suspect—a house that might be squatted, a road booby-trapped by slicks. A second pair of scouts scrolled directly in front of two teamsters drawing the wagon, from which Barnaby, crowned and festooned and having a mighty good time, made obscure pronouncements. Then came the Straw Man—cabled to the rig, so he wouldn't run—then Sammy and me. The rear guard, usually led by Zeb, trailed us by fifty feet.

Now that we were in no danger of being gutted, I was high-key glad for all the guns.

Zeb and his crew had been picking this territory for years. They even

---

2. Although Texas would in later decades place notorious emphasis on the sovereignty of their country, best exemplified by their revision of their national motto to read "Texas Now, First, and Only," they had long provided ground support to the freedom fighters of New Hampshire as they pushed back against the colonial rule of the newly formed Commonwealth. And during the infamous "Fifteen Days' March" in 2047, Texas interceded against the territorial encroachment of the Confederacy as it began to expand through the South. This last war, however short-lived, proved extremely deadly for the Confederate soldiers, especially after it was mandated that their military cache include no weapons, or replicas of weapons, crafted after 1868.

paid kickback to some friendly bodymen for the right to keep shipping corpses off the land. But some of Blythe's hires didn't play so nice with outsiders, and there was always the risk of backlanders and angry pay-tenants, half-starving on their own rented land. And recently, Zeb told me, they'd started running up against a new kind of trouble.

"We started seeing these crankheads around a few months ago," he said. "All jacked up like you could never believe. Something wrong with their eyes. I've heard say it's some Halloran-Chyung poison like they tried to pump into our prison lines back in '58.[3] But I'm not so sure. A group of 'em torched a water plant up north trying to bust open the flow for a drink. I heard from crews all the way out near Boston say these high-balls been taking potshots at Canadian freighters and oil frig-ates off the coast. I even heard tell the drug made its way into the Confed-eracy, and they ain't got nothing there but tobacco smoke. Whatever this shit is, it makes dymo look like soda pop and it's all over the place now."

Jump. It seemed Rafikov's supply was getting out, and quick. Even though it was warm enough to bring out skeeters the size of baseballs, I shivered. How many tens of thousands of people were walking around with viral computer code turning their brains into living ThinkChips™? How many people would become remote servers to fire out Rafikov's commands? Even if we somehow made it out to San Francisco before she'd doped up enough zombies for her army, there was no telling how long it would take to grow the knowledge we needed from Rafikov's brain

---

3. This suggests that Zeb came originally from the Sovereign Nation of Texas. It had long been rumored that Halloran-Chyung, one of Texas's fiercest critics, launched a secret attack on Texas's vast array of prison cities by introducing nerve agents to the air-filtration systems in the hopes of inspiring mass rebellions. Several of the largest prison cities did, in fact, experience mass waves of rebellion and revolt. Unfortu-nately, this precipitated the widespread introduction of the Straw Procedure in prison camps across the country. Halloran-Chyung has absolutely disclaimed responsibility for the attack; some have said that it was the Texas Army general who okayed the inhumane assault, as a way of ensuring that the legislation to selectively lobotomize would, in fact, pass; they have pointed to his close relationship with the inventor of the procedure, J. C. Straw, as evidence.

cells. Barnaby would die for nothing, and it would be my fault when a legion of cranked-up Russian nationalists started burning their way across the continent.

I needed to talk to President Burnham. But we were so deep in the backlands, there was no chance of getting a message through the portal. Even grifters didn't run trade out here; it wasn't worth the price of a blister. My best chance was to hoof it with the demons to civilization— and hope that I wouldn't be too late.

We slept that night concealed in the trees, or tried to, fair game for everything that flew, sucked, stuck, and slithered. I jerked awake to the periodic *splat* of a giant insect exploding off the butt end of a rifle, and then again when the winds shifted, and brought with them billows of Mayday hail[4] and a forceful gale that soaked us to the spleen and stripped trees down to skeletons.

We hunkered down to wait out the usual aftershocks, minor bowel rumblings still strong enough to make walking a bad idea. The delay put us all on edge. Barnaby was falling hard for the role of Prince of Darkness, and soon the idea of starring in a diplomatic drama was bound to lose its appeal—especially if he found out his brain was a key bargaining chip. And if Barnaby decided to scratch out on heading west, I had no means to force him.

The demons had their own cause to be itchy. Soon, Cannon grumbled, there would be nothing left to pick from the wreck but shit from the pump—and the demons took to blowing the hail out of the sky with their ammo until Zeb scolded them for wasting it.

"It don't matter anyhow," he said to me. He fumbled in his vest pocket

---

4. Weather in previous centuries, it is worth pointing out, had been far more predictable—so much so that in many places in the world, the annual calendar was even divided into "seasons," with both temperatures and precipitation that regularly corresponded to the mean. It was only in the late 2040s and early 2050s, after the collapse of the ice shelf and the Great Die-Off, that new phenomenology gave birth to much of our contemporary vernacular, such as "Mayday hail," "cold as a solstice snow," and "blown in like Christmas hurricanes."

and pulled out some fresh. I took a wad and chewed it. Cherry flavored. Still, it helped with the pain in my feet, and the constant hum of anxiety saying I was wasting time. "We were too slow. Billy Hazard's crew already came through and picked most of whichever corpses they can sell. Fucking Billy." He shook his head. "I taught that boy everything he knows. Showed him how to gut an intestine when he was no more'n a squid with a semiautomatic and a dream. And now he goes on and scoops me."

"Who told you that?" There were no towers, no wires, no satellites to beam portal access: nothing but reality and more reality, bleak as a toilet bowl.

"Who do you think?" Zeb tamped a pinch of shiver down into his pipe. "The kid dropped me a word on the Yellow Brick Road just as soon as he packed up the haul. He's got a set of balls bigger than his brains, I'll tell you that."

"The Yellow Brick Road?"

He blew another cloud in my face. "They don't feed you anything but bullstrap out in Crunch, United, huh?" He shook his head. "The Yellow Brick Road is like one of your corporation intranets, but all around us. No borders, no firewalls, no lockouts."

I didn't understand. "So . . . it's another portal?"

"Bigger," he said. "You can find everything you want there and a lot you don't. It exists in every country on the continent, at least the ones I've been to, and that's most."

"But who owns it?" I asked. "Who gets paid?"

"No one. That's the beauty of it," Zeb said. He thumped a hand on my back. "The Yellow Brick Road is free."

"Sure, yeah. And I got a nice plot in Hawaii[5] to sell you, just as long

_____

5. Hawaii had been entirely submerged during the tsunamis that presaged the final rupture of the San Andreas Fault in 2043. It is worth noting that although most scientists presume that Alaska, which during the earthquakes broke off from the mainland, suffered the same fate, popular myth still claimed it had settled somewhere in the middle of the Pacific, and, now an isolated and perfectly contained idyll, existed as a kind of new Eden.

as you don't mind snorkeling for it." Information was like everything else: it belonged to the squids who could pay for it. Every so often, the firewall in Crunch, United, got bugged by other countries spamming us with reports of the Federal Corp's corruption—like that would come as a surprise—or flooding our decks with stories of the corporation's brutality in diplomatic posts. But for the most part, the only news we ever got was controlled, monitored, and doled out by the Federal Corp.

Zeb's eye socket, puckered over with skin, appeared to be winking. "Don't believe me, then," he said, shrugging. "There's many say you shouldn't walk it anyhow."

Maybe he'd taken a pinch of fresh too many. "All right, then. Prove it. Show me."

He squinted up at the sky. The hail was floating softer now, drifting to fat wads of acidic snow even before it landed. The winds were changing again. "Nice try, Sally, but that's not how it works. The Road is a virus. You have to find someone to give it to you, load it up onto that ancient helmet." He gave my visor a thump. "And ain't no way I'm going to pop that cherry of yours. I like you well enough. And of course you're with Him"—he lowered his voice, as he always did when talking about His Highness, His Darkness the Lord of Evil, who was sniffing around, obviously trying to decide whether he could digest some metal shrapnel without caking his inner organs—"but you're still green as a four-day-old floater. Let me ask you something. You ever torched a city? Or pillaged a backwater settlement?"

"I'm not even sure what pillaging is," I admitted.

"How about despoiling a woman's honor? Ever raped a virgin? Impregnated a grandma?"

I shook my head, and he squinted at me.

"Have you ever had sex with *anyone*?"

"Technically speaking, from the strictest standpoint . . ." I lowered my voice so that Bee wouldn't hear. "No."

"And yet the Lord of Darkness chose you for His escort." He shook his head disgustedly and spat, missing my foot by an inch. "You're not ready for the Brick Road yet, believe me."

We moved on as the temperature rebounded with the change of winds, climbing up into the eighties. As the last of the ice melted off, we scoped the trash blown down by the gale for anything useful. Nikhil found an unused purine; Fats, a bag of uneaten PotatoChipz™, miraculously intact.

Sometime around midnight there were two sharp blasts of a whistle from the scouts up ahead. The whole clanking, rattling, stomping, huffing chain gang of us came to a halt.

Zeb, who'd been flanking with Bee, pushed roughly by me.

"Come on, greenie. This should be a good show." And then, to Bee: "Cut the big man loose. The rest of you, don't do squirrel till I give the signal."

The road winched right at a gas station long dry of gas. When we came around the bend, we saw Thrasher and Nikhil, canned in by a group of twenty or so men, all of them with the same rough-hewn, weather-beaten look, like pieces of wood spat out by a tornado. Some of them had decent guns—I spotted a few long-range rifles—but most of them were carrying weapons that might have been prehistoric, including billy clubs cobbled together from thick branches and, in one case, even a slingshot. The air was so tight with tension, you could of strangled yourself on it.

"Evening, boys," Zeb said casually. "Nice night for a stroll, isn't it?" He stretched so his jacket came open and his belt of artillery was visible.

I could see the roadslicks measuring their chances. Four Devil's Army demons—five, if you counted me, which I was pretty sure they wouldn't—against twenty. Risky, but not suicidal.

One of them cleared his throat. "This here's a toll road," he said. He sounded young. Impossible to tell age with these hillbilly types. They all looked forty by the time they were fourteen. "Coin, food, and weapons only. We got no use for other currencies."

"A toll road," Zeb said, as if he'd never heard the term before. "I thought all of BCE Tech was private property."

"It is," the roadslick said. "Which means you're trespassing."

"And so are you," Zeb said.

"We been here since before dissolution." The tension in the air ticked up another notch, until I felt as if every breath I took was choking me. "Besides, you and your crew got blood to answer for."

This made the demons laugh. "We're in the blood business, sucko," Zeb said. "You're looking at the Department of Sani-fucking-tation right here."

"I'm talking about those scavengers crashed the bullet train into them hills," the roadslick said. His voice was shaking a little—out of fear or anger, I couldn't tell. "Friends of yours, were they?"

"We don't have friends but the kind that shits bullets in your face," Zeb said.

The roadslick either didn't hear or ignored him. "They plugged four of our kind from a distance, just for creeping close to the wreck. One of 'em weren't more than ten years old."

Bee and Nikhil exchanged a look. Thrasher lit up a shiver pipe and took a nervous huff.

Even Zeb looked uncomfortable. "We don't kill kids," he said shortly. Then: "Not enough gas in 'em to make it worth the cost of freight. And we don't pay toll for other people's problems either."

There was a ripple, a slight change in the roadslick's posture. "Fair enough. But you're gonna pay for your passage just the same." A new one spoke up—a woman, though you would never of known it from looking at her. Her face looked like the sorry end of a toilet plunger. "This road is ours."

"You've done a crap job keeping it," Nikhil piped up. "I broke my leg around these parts last year. Had to splint the bone myself with nothin' but chicken wire and some kindling."

Zeb, Thrasher, and Bee sighed. It was one of Nikhil's few stories. She was a good fighter, but, like Thrasher, hailed from one of the nuclear towns and it had mushed up her brain. It was the reason, too, for all her extra fingers.

The roadslick ignored her. "There's five of you. That means a toll of one of your flavors, plus whatever food you got in your packs. And you can be on your way with no scrum."

"I see." Zeb pretended to think about it. "There's just one problem, I think, with that little arrangement."

The roadslick frowned. "What's that?"

Zeb smiled. "You counted wrong," he said. He brought his fingers to his lips and blasted two short whistles. At that moment, the moon broke through the thin layering of clouds, just for a second, and showed the rest of the demons coming up behind us, all of them smiling and loaded up with more flavors than these lumps had ever seen together in their lives. The big man, hauling the wagon, looked in the darkness like an honest-to-God giant.

And then came Barnaby. His eyes were yellow in the moonlight, and in a livery of dried-out insect husks and clattering garlands strung from chicken bones, he might really of crawled out of hell.

"Hello," he said, in his reedy voice. "Did we find some new friends?"

The roadslicks hesitated for only a second.

Then they ran.

An hour later, Thrasher spotted two drones tailing us at a distance.

We weren't far from the crash site, and I hadn't forgotten what the road-slicks had said about the killers. As far as we knew, they might still be hanging around, ready to pop any more unwanted visitors.

The whole gang pulled up to a halt when Thrasher gave the whistle. Dawn was still an hour off at least, and the sky was just turning from purple to the rich blue of chlorinated toilet bowls. It was hard to spot them in the dark, but we could hear them well enough, whirring above the trees.

"What's the problem?" Nikhil asked through a mouthful of fresh.

"Spy eyes," Thrasher said. He held up two fingers, then pointed. But just then the drones dipped out of sight behind the trees.

"They know we've sighted 'em," Zeb said. He knocked a rotten tooth back and forth with his tongue, like he always did when he was thinking. "Cannon, Nikhil, you ride the wagon. Might as well keep on keeping on, least till we get a clear shot. I want to see one of you blow these bastards off our tail."

"Stay on your game, fellas," Bee added unnecessarily. "These *locos* might be hanging around just looking for the chance to plug us." As if we were in any danger of forgetting it.

A mile or so on, the trees thinned out and the hover tracks came into view again. Spooky-looking squirrels with sharp fangs and the red eyes of the nuclear zone were picking through a litter of glass. There were footsteps imprinted in a soft wash of mud: maybe other body pickers, maybe backlanders, maybe whoever had come to clean up the job. The wind turned putrid and carried the sharp scent of burning. The demons turned their noses to the air. The stink reminded me of the ash that blew from the Crunch 407 furnaces, which reminded me of my mom, which made me feel a little like puking. "Bodies," Nikhil explained, just before I tagged the smell myself. She might as well have been saying *Bacon-Bitez*™.

We crested a low hill and the breath got knocked out of me completely: lying in a scorched runway of black earth was the enormous mangled mess of metal and glass, trailing intestinal wreckage. Then the sharp report of several rifle blasts nearly jumped me out of my skin. I whipped around to see Thrasher hopping down off the wagon.

"Nailed 'em both," he said, grinning. The drones were gone. The rising sun looked like an organ carved out none too carefully from someone's insides, and it spilled its guts all over the tree line.

We went down the hill to the wreck. I had to breathe through my sleeve. The smell was so bad it had a *taste* to it. Zeb was right: most of the bodies had been cleared out, and the ones left were a squeak more than beef jerky.

But the fire had missed the freight cars: packages, luggage, crates, and cartons remained, intact and untouched. Whoever had derailed the train hadn't bothered to clean out the cargo, and the early crew of body pickers had been in too much of a rush to poke around.

It was the biggest haul, Bee told me, they'd ever come across in one place, except for the time they'd happened on a hillbilly town wiped out over three months by a superflu, the people who lived there too sick and scared to do anything but stay, piling the bodies of their friends and family into an old Mobil station before getting sick themselves.

The demons unloaded shirts and pants and clean underwear; hairbrushes and toothbrushes and Bug-Off; cartridges of tobacco and stacks of fresh; shoes and ultraviolet-filtering sunhats. I refused the boxers Thrasher tried to grift me—it felt like bad luck to rub junk with a dead man—but I took three shirts and an extra pair of pants.

More and more, it looked like Rafikov was tracking me already. I skant thought she'd miss the chance to kill me again. And if I was going to follow Biff and Roger into some body picker's ice van sooner rather than later, I figured I might as well look good for the ride.

13

No one likes a roadslick. In my experience there's only two kinds of language they speak: money and bullets.
—from The Grifter's Guide to the Territories FKA USA

Some days, it was hard to think of a reason to go on. There were mornings when the whole nine yards of it—standing, pissing the bladder of urine, scrubbing the rot from the back of your teeth, covering the stink of your underarms—seemed about as useful as putting makeup on a corpse.[1] We were all dying, the planet was dying, the party was over. Soon the earth would go back to the roaches and skeeters, all the species that had found a way to survive without ever once inventing online porno or plastic zip ties.

Yeah. There were days it was hard to get up in the morning, especially when your morning started on your back in the hard dirt with an android poking you hard in the breastbone and doing terrible vocals over the Crunchtown Crunk©.

"Don't do that," I said. "Ever again. Promise me."

"Good morning," Sammy said. "How did you sleep?"

"Fantastic." It was barely dawn. My grille tasted like the inside of a garbage compactor. Meanwhile Barnaby had slept in the wagon on a bower of old cotton crop. When I spotted him, he was flat on his back getting a belly rub from Nikhil and Bee.

---

1. Truckee is potentially referring to the practices of the Carnivale Moribundi cult, actually one of the largest and most pervasive religious organizations at that time.

"Hello, Lowly Servant of the Dark," he called out to me, waving a hoof. "The devil be with you this morning."

At least I was getting used to the idea of his nob split open by Cowell's scalpel.

The wind showed strong leanings to turn tornado: the clouds were so low and queasy green they looked like something you'd find on the underside of a tissue. We'd need to find a bolt hole before the storm dropped.

As I was packing up my rucksack, I caught the Straw Man looking my way.

"Where'd you find that roll-up?" he asked me, and it took me a second to work out he meant *The Grifter's Guide to the Territories FKA USA*. The cover was coming unslung in my pack, and half the pages were water-stained or swelled with bloat.

"A friend" was all I said, and shoved it deep down beneath my new clothes. Thinking of Billy Lou was like thinking about birds: suddenly, you started seeing the sky for being empty.

"I ain't seen that book in an age," he said. "I'd trade you for it, but those boys took my kit when they snuck me." X-man was carrying his pack now, and the spam he was rattling around on the shelves for sale was the most pathetic I'd ever seen: a spool of thread, a pigeon feather, and a used toothbrush.

"That's all right," I said quickly. "It was a gift anyway."

"You be wise with it, then," he said. "I bet there's not five of those left in the world. Has everything you need to know right in those pages."

I didn't want to tell him I'd barely cracked the cover, so I just smiled. He may of been a Straw Man, but his fists were still the size of my head.

We hitched up the wagon and moved on, angling north toward a trader outpost, where we could barter for goods and find an ice van to ship the Straw Man's body to someone who would pay.

Just after dawn the town poked its peaky head out above the horizon, and an hour later the road twisted us into the buildings, all of them scrapped together from the graveyard bones of buildings fallen before them, ugly as a stuck jaw. But for a minute, with the sun rising behind us through a sediment of green-bellied clouds, and sliding down through the streets and up, up, up, to touch the portal towers gold, it might of been the prettiest place I'd ever seen.

Portal towers meant I would finally get help.

We split up—Barnaby for the town dump, and most of the demons for whorehouses and moonshine stands to load up before the storm blew in. Sammy went to clean the grit from her soft joints at a detailing station, and I plugged in at a juice bar and nearly cried when my visor powered on. I was so excited, I swiped twice to Settings accidentally.

Hundreds of unread messages streamed into my feed. Jared's messages were all tagged urgent and shouted at me to open them right away, so I jumped right over the company alerts.

Dude, where are you?? are you alive??

SERIOUSLY, WHERE THE FUCK ARE YOU? Everyone is freaking the fuck out and I don't know what to believe . . .

MESSAGE ME, SEND ME SOME GODDAMN SMOKE SIGNALS, DO SOMETHING.

The last message, sent twenty-four hours ago, was so high decibel I had to scrub my ear out with a pinkie. I closed out quick, before it could replay, and right away another urgent message started flashing for attention.

Annalee.

I swiped open her holo, half-dreading it: I'd never had anything, seen anything, or done anything, that Annalee and Jared hadn't had, seen, or done, too, and all the distance between us felt suddenly like one long sinkhole.

"Hey, Truckee. Please, please, send a message, okay? We're all so worried. Jared might sneeze out his brain mass." Even though the visuals weren't perfect, she was as beautiful as ever. I could tell she was tearing up, and I wanted to reach out and touch her. She leaned a little closer, so the holo blew her chin off the frame. "Things have been *crazy* since the attack. . . ."

"What attack?" I said out loud, and then felt like an idiot. I'd been off my visor for so many days I'd forgotten how the holos did that, tricked you into conversation with old graphics. She was already halfway through her next sentence.

". . . emergency protocol in place. Human Resources patrols twenty-four seven, and makes arrests for no reason. There's a curfew at eight p.m. and everyone's scared. So please, please . . ." She was speaking so softly I could skant make her out, and had to turn on transcription to see the words printed.

Please let us know you're okay.

No matter what.

I'll understand.

You can trust me.

Quickly, I shut down Annalee's holo and swiped back to the company alerts: New security protocols, blasts from Human Resources department urging workers to stay calm, progress reports about the ongoing investigation into the foreign intervention in Crunch 407.

I toggled to the most reliable news feeds I could think of. Less than twenty-four hours after President Burnham had sent me packing, and only a few hours after the bullet train blew off its tracks, the Crunch 407 firewall was knocked out by a backdoor hacker and the whole security system—from spy-eye cams to patrol bots to the HR team's visors—came down with it.

And then: chaos.

As Low Hill turned into one giant riot, hundreds of bigwigs, including President Burnham, were evacuated via helicopter. Some feeds were saying a swarm of desperate backlanders from up near the Exxon-Mississippi River Channel had crashed the border. Some blamed a coordinated task force of foreign terrorists, and the Department of Publicity was saying there was no attack at all, just a widespread panic that swelled to a riot after the blackout.

That was obviously spam. President Burnham had booted all foreign diplomats out of the Federal Corporation, all from deep within a hidden and securitized bunker that was rumored to exist under New Haven. The Crunch, United, board would meet to vote on sanctions in a few days. All the rioters—hundreds of locals, hauled in screaming for blood to Retirement, the chilly subterranean prison beneath the HR complex—had been fired from the corporation, and half the feeds I read thought that they'd be shipped up to the Dakotas for tunnel work. The other half thought they'd go straight to the Texas hunting preserves, in exchange for the release of a few Crunch, United, spies still dodging Texas gunslingers in the vast prison scrublands near Lubbock.[2]

I blew up the photos, stunned by the litter of debris, abandoned gas suckers, ruined holo stations, and toppled bots still sparking in the streets. The offices at 1 Central Plaza had been torn apart: walls split to the studs, desks overturned, chairs gutted of their stuffing. In one 2-D, a dozen crumbs were setting torch to a trash heap piled in front of the glittering white chemical haze that remained of Production-22. I blew up the image some more, and my blood turned to northern freeze.

Their eyes were full of leaking black.

When a vidcomm request popped up over a secure line—stinging my eyes with a retinal scan before I'd even accepted—I swiped yes before I'd really registered the company's corporate logo. For a second, my visor went dark, and I could hear the system purring with effort as it tried to graft together two encrypted chat spaces. Finally, President Burnham's

---

2. The prison reserve lands were a popular destination for wealthy Texas hunters, and their explosive popularity was due in part to the Great Die-Off, the mass extinctions that had made big-game hunting obsolete. On average, prisoners consigned to these vast habitats stayed alive only a few weeks, falling prey not just to homicidal violence but also, commonly, to exposure, dehydration, and starvation. There were, however, some notable exceptions. Dwayne Rogers III is believed to have survived in a shooting preserve near San Antonio for nearly thirty-three years, and to have died peacefully of old age in a hidden underground bolt hole he had carefully expanded and refurbished over three decades, which included an ingenious waste-disposal system constructed from discarded purines and weighted bottle caps.

face wrenched itself in 3-D out of my screen, so suddenly I jerked back as if he really might head-butt me.

"Truckee Wallace, thank the bank," he burst out. "I was afraid you were dead out there."

"No, sir," I said. "Not yet."

"As soon as we got word about the blow-up on the train, and we lost you on our geo, I started praying for you to pop up on the system." His funny sunken face kept collapsing into 2-D as he twitched out of the frame. "But I was beginning to lose hope."

"I haven't tripped a wire since just now, sir," I said, and told him about finding the Devil's Army, and how they'd mistaken Barnaby for the second coming of Satan. "The goat's doing just fine," I added, since he hadn't asked. "I think he's enjoying himself, actually."

Burnham shook his head. "Damn backwoods people. Superstitions and blood—that's half the continent for you."

I couldn't disagree with him.

"So the blow-up . . . was it—?" I stopped myself from saying *Rafikov* out loud. Never knew who was listening. Instead, I swiped: *Rafikov's fault?*

"Who else?" His mouth seized into a line, like a horizontal exclamation point. "But enough chatter. You aren't safe. I don't know how she figured us so fast, but she has. We need to get you out of there."

I swear I could of kissed him. *With* tongue.

"I'm sending some of our best agents out to Granby. Can you make it to Granby?"[3]

I nodded before remembering the service was too slow to register the motion. "We're headed that way now" was all I said. Granby was a town nudging up to the border of Texas that paid rent to Blythe Capital. Over the years, Zeb told me, it had swelled to a bustling city, full of grifters

---

3. Located just south of the Black Kettle Grassland, now a giant sinkhole and former fracking site, off what was formerly I-40, Granby was named after Tenner Blythe's childhood hunting dog.

and expats, con men and slicks, adventurers and the businesses that catered to them, plus people waiting to get clearance from Immigration to cross.

"Mind your nuts and fingers until you get there. Don't bother making contact. We'll find you. Got it?"

I managed to say, "Yes, sir."

"Good." Now his whole face collapsed into 2-D, as if flattened by a sinkhole opening behind his nose, which meant he was only seconds from signing off. "You stay safe out there, Truckee Wallace."

Then the feed cut out.

Just as soon as I'd showered, shaved, and air washed my studs, the tornado siren started singing. The sky turned a vivid green before puking its guts out in the form of sheets of driving rain and hail the size of acorns.

Not many hostels were itching to take in ten Devil's Army demons loaded to the teeth, plus a Straw Man, an aging android, a skinny crumb, and a goat festooned with necklaces of dried cicada husks (Fats, it turned out, had a talent for making jewelry). Luckily, we found a storm shelter, where a few bucks would buy us a roll-up cot and twelve hours of safety.

We waited in line behind half a dozen local hillbillies. The girl in front of me wore enormous trousers that hitched to her shoulders with suspenders. She was missing several toes to frostbite. But she had cloud-soft hair that reminded me of Kerry, from Production-22, and the same sweet mouth, like a piece of candy tacked to her maw. I had visions of being inside with her, warm and dry. Of sitting cross-legged on the floor, our knees touching, and listening to the storm outside.

But when I tapped her shoulder to offer her my jacket, she jerked back like I'd hit her.

"You're Devil's Army." She had to shout over the wind. It was hard to believe a voice so full of hate could come out of that beautiful mouth. "You're going to hell. You're all going to hell, and you're going to burn."

I opened my mouth to reply, but just then Bee leaned forward, slinging an arm around my shoulders, and rearranging the warts on her face into a smile.

"We're *in* hell, dearie," she said sweetly. Across the street the wind took down an awning and cartwheeled it down the sidewalk. "Haven't you noticed?"

The girl only glowered at her.

The storm shelter was down beneath an old shopping mall, and old parking spaces yellowed in rows between the roll-up cots. A generator as big as a freight truck kept a few electrical lights going and compacted waste from the two toilet stalls.

Even underground, we knew when the storm came. We could feel it, like the pressure of a giant vacuum that sucked all the air from the room and made my ears pop. Then: a roar, a monstrous clangarang of metal shriek and wood blowing down into splinters.

We got our share of tornadoes in Crunch 407—in the winter months they were so common they hardly ever touched off the emergency system anymore—but there the hover of red dust and the chemical pressure systems drove off the worst of the wind before it ever reached the city. But out here in BCE Tech there was nothing but empty space and earthquake-emptied towns and sinkholes, miles and miles of unobstructed air where the tornado could whirl itself into a monstrous vortex.

We hunkered down in uneasy silence. The demons glared when the girl and her family clasped hands and began to recite passages from their Bible, but said nothing.

Outside, something huge came down with a giant crack. The static blacked the lights for a split second and we all jumped, even Zeb. A pigtailed girl began to cry.

"Don't you worry your head," the Straw Man told her. "This shake-and-rattle's nothing compared to what we got in old Louisiana. It'll blow right through and leave us clean as a whistle."

But she only cried harder.

The Straw Man just shook his head and went back to chewing his fingernails into perfect rounds. I pegged him for fifty or so, though his smooth face, round as a plate, made him look younger.

"What's your name, anyway?" I hadn't thought to ask him yet, probably because I kept figuring he'd be dead soon.

He spat out a fingernail. "Timothy No-Father's what's on my birth certificate," he said. "But my folks down in the swamp used to call me Tiny Tim."

"How'd you get to grifting way out here, then?" I asked him.

"I been grifting one way or another since I was smaller than a pissant," he said. "And there ain't a lot of employment for a Straw Man."

He was right. Everyone knew scarecrows were bad luck. "So what happened?" I asked him. "How'd you get the knife?"

"You asking the legend of Tiny Tim?" he asked. "You want to know how a man gets stuffed with straw?"

Zeb was laying out his guns, wiping them clean of dirt and hail one by one. But I could tell he was listening. *Everyone* was listening. Even the little girl had stopped crying. She was sucking on her thumb instead, staring at us.

I nodded, and he let out a booming laugh, then patted my shoulder with one massive hand. "Okay, Truckee Wallace. I'll rap for you."

And he did.

INTERLUDE

THE LEGEND OF TINY TIM

I was born sometime in November in the last year of the USA,[1] in the state of Louisiana, the youngest of nine and the biggest of all of them. My ma always said when the doctor saw my head coming out he near fainted, and from the start they couldn't never keep up with how quick I grew, coming up faster than the flu and busting through all my clothing.

I never known my dad excepting his name was Nathan the Second and he was a switch operator. Later, we heard he got blowed up by cannon fire in Alexandria when the Confederacy invaded.[2]

We were poor, dirt poor, and I grew up hungry. There wasn't never enough to go around, not to Owen and Tanya and Kris and Mariah, Ronald and Ella and Reggie and Nathan the Third. As soon as I learned to walk, I learned to steal. Those were hard days for everybody, and the shelves was mostly empty, but me and the brothers, excepting Nathan Three, used to bust into homes or those little soup kitchens that was popping up everywhere and just gank what we could. I got caught

---

1. Interestingly, this itself was the source of major debate, with different countries vying to define their own secessions as the critical turning point in the dissolution of the United States. Dates for the end of the union have alternatively been given as 2041 (the year of the first Declarations of Secession), 2046 (the year of the last secession), and 2048 (the year in which the final U.S. dollar was produced in Washington, D.C., where it was used briefly to paper the houses of the new nationalists in an attempt to signal wealth and stability).

2. The Confederacy annexed Virginia, largely peacefully, in 2044.

once or twice and my ma paddled me with a belt or a birch switch but she never could stay mad at me for long.

I was eight years old at the start of the First Storm Noah,[3] and after the first week of rains my ma said it couldn't last, and after the first month, when mold grew in our skivs and even the cockroaches were drowning, my ma said it couldn't last, and when the Exxon-Mississippi jumped its lip and washed away whole towns in a blink, and every day the roads were clogged with poor folk in their soggy clothing weeping their way north, she said it couldn't last. After six months you couldn't tell where the water was coming from anymore: the whole world was water, and everything was rotted, and there wasn't no food to blow a bubble at save for what came by the grifters coming on canoes and rowboats. My ma used to joke that we did better than anyone during dissolution, 'cause we went from living inland on a gobspit of a town to ocean views right outside our door—and during the wet season, inside our door, too, so we got used to waking up puddled in wet to our shins.

You know the old line about Louisiana? It didn't fall. It sank.

But I'll tell you, it wasn't no joke the way the infections came. What bred in those waters made your insides turn to flush, made your shit come out like its own kind of storm. The Black Runs, they called it, and surrounded by water as we were you couldn't find a drop clean of it. Took off two of my sisters, Mariah and Ella, and Owen, too, if you count how he done shot himself after his wife shat out her life and their baby with it.

By the time we thought about leaving for the refugee camps in Tennessee, stories had started to run back our way, those temporary camps just as buried in their own shit and overcrowded, no clean water, no jobs, no help, nothing temporary about it.

They were some hard times. My oldest sister, Tanya, run off and become a Graceland believer.[4] I can't say as I blame her. In those days, they were popping

---

3. The First Storm Noah was triggered by the massive rupture in the tectonic plates triggered by the first "Big One" in March 2042.

4. The Graceland Church was one of the thousands of alternative or splinter religions that gained followings in the aftermath of dissolution, a period of such seismic political, economic, social, and environmental change, it represented, for many people, the End of Days long presaged by the Bible. Unsurprisingly, New World religions often took on a more tribal character, with core tenets, treatises, practices, and

up everywhere. We used to see them walking the watery streets in their dazzle whites and slicked-back hair, groups of them gathered in front of the old markets singing "Hound Dog" to heaven and waiting for Elvis to come back for them.

When I was ten, rumors started blowing our way that the Confederacy was on the move, taking over territory from Charlotte to Montgomery and looking like our no-name spit of old Louisiana might be next. Instead, the Sovereign Nation of Texas marched up, burning along the coast of Louisiana and laying claim to everything they staked. Those Texas boys took control of our plastics and our freight, and they brought their big ocean rigs and North Korean submarines for patrolling the waters. They put some money into the refugee camps so's they could build their roads, and started sending through thousands of barrels of oil, all that money going straight through Louisiana on its way to the center belt and leaving us not a drop.

By then I was fifteen and I'd been making some money here and there doing labor, but the payday didn't buy much of nothing because all we collected was old coin from dead places. Every time you wanted something you had to bargain for it, my shirt for your MilkStuffs™, half day of roofing work for a couple handfuls of Dymase™.

That's the other thing too. My ma had a bad back from working in plastics all those years afore and she got deep into dymo after it came through our area on the backs of some grifter canoes, and it wasn't long until I went down the road myself. Me and Reggie and Kris used to cook dymo down to shiver and smoke it with our ma and it was the only time we ever saw her laugh, least until she started crying.

We made a plan to hit up one of the armored trucks Texas was sending through. We didn't have a single gun between us excepting Reggie's friend Goose's old

---

even religious messiahs adopted from local customs or figureheads. It is difficult to pinpoint the exact origination of the Graceland Church: several competing versions of the religion appear to have arisen independently across a great belt of swampland and new Confederate states, only to have later become enfolded under a single mantle. But the unifying feature of all of these religions was in the worship of a central messiah, Elvis Presley, whose redemptive messages had been encoded in his music and, in fact, could still be detected in the music of contemporaneous prophets descended from his word.

hunting rifle, but we figured we could split up the first load and make enough to buy some real teeth and then we could get an operation going.

Well. We weren't the first trying to make it as roadslicks, and you know we wouldn't be the last either.

Our plan was to stop the truck and get the driver out. Then we were going to tie him up and make him open up the hatch. We got a broken-up car and had a whole accident staged, Reggie lying in the road like he'd been hit. We figured even if the driver didn't want to stop, those new nav systems were made to shut down when they swept life, and at least that would give us some time to figure out a move.

Then Goose got sick. It was something dumb, a bad batch of shiver that had him puking up his guts, but we had to sub in a different third. The kid was green, never so much as stole an ice pop, and he got scared and done fired off too soon—punched a nail right in the driver's forehead before he could open the hatch. Wouldn't you know the guy was wearing a tag for his vitals. As soon as he went cold, we knew the Texas boys would come faster than flies to a shithouse.

We had to run. I got lucky hitching out with some skinflints who didn't like the way the wind was blowing. They were bad, real bad, all of 'em murderers and worse, and they'd been just fine when there was no Texas militia around to string them up by the neck for a family picnic. They were talking Libertine or Alaska,[5] and who knows whether they made it. I couldn't stand the sight of them and left them off in what used to be Kansas and at that time wasn't anything at all but desperate hillbilly towns fighting each other for scavenged metal.

One good thing about those days was borders weren't what they are now and it was easier to travel. None too pretty, though. That was during the Great Die-Off,[6] and everywhere you went the smell of corpses made you sick, not just floaters but

---

5. A common enough fantasy at the time: after the cataclysmic earthquakes along several dozen fault lines that destroyed the original Seattle and extended up through British Columbia, provoking aftershocks that lasted months, Alaska splintered off the mainland and was lost to history. Although most scholars and adventurers believe it simply sank, for decades rumors of an isolated Alaskan utopia have persisted.

6. Waves of mass extinction began in the early 2040s, triggering some experimental cloning procedures in newly formed sovereign states, which later culminated in the Clone Panic of 2049. But the vast majority of the world's species went extinct between two years alone: 2049 and 2050.

animals dead in droves, rabbits drowned out of their warrens and fish washed onto places they were never meant to be, dogs and cattle, horses and kittens, a scrum of insects so thick that in places the land turned black with them. And birds dropping right out of the sky, too weak and hungry to keep aloft. An eagle landed right in my lap one day and I'll be damned if it wasn't the last eagle in the whole wide world.

I ended up in the heart of Texas National, working illegal in an oil camp south of San Antonio. Back then it looked like Crunch, United, might send Chinese warships up the gulf, and we slurped oil just to keep a cordon burning on the waves. There was never enough hands, not with so many cruds sickening with the flu, or mowed down by the riot police, so the camp boss never checked my tags and put me right on an offshore rig and paid cash in hand.

I spent twenty-four days a month straight on the waves, working security detail to keep off the fuel thieves that used to come up on their boats in the dead of nighttime and try and pick off some barrel—or worse, the Dakota rigs conspiring with Crunch, United, just to blow us into barbecue. I met a cute little rounder named Suze, and on my days off we kept mostly to ourselves, doing hardly nothing but laying around in bed and doing what have you.

I think I was happy for the first time in my life.

But one day the big boss came to visit the camp and caught scry of me, and told me he'd double up my pay if I agreed to be his bull in a new rodeo they was putting on. I knew all about the rodeo and what they did to guys on the circuit, especially the bulls and broncos had to saddle up and try and throw a man. But since the big boss was one of the richest scrubs in Texas, I couldn't do nothing but yessir him. Never trust a little guy wearing a suit and smoking a big cigar. It always means they trying to make up for something.

So one day a month I got saddled up and shot up and let loose. Turned out I was real good as a bull, could throw a rider in fifteen seconds or less whether or not he had spurs. I hated it though. Got cut up and beat up and souped up on all the shit they gave me to make me madder, and no matter how much I won and how much the big boss swore he was gonna pay out, something always happened to make him put off the payday. The man was lining his pockets with my blood and sweat and giving me peanuts.

Well, they don't get to be big bosses wearing fancy suits by paying out, do they?

One Sunday after a real bad one—got dug up good from a rider north of Houston, had to get stitches put in my eye and was sore as a steak paddled with a hammer—I got into a real black mood. Me and some buddies was drinking down at one of the camp bars. Now, most of the time I stay well clear of drink, especially moonshine that flows out of the bellows, but sometimes a man needs to get a little loose and that was one of them days. Somehow I got it into my head that I was gonna take back some of my winnings. Way I figured it, the haul was mostly mine anyway.

Getting into the big man's office was cake. I knew where he kept his money, since he was always bragging how much he kept in the safe, and I don't mind saying I had her ready and open faster than you could say please.

I didn't take the whole stash, not even close. Just a few bills, what I reckoned was more'n fair for all the months I'd been bucking for him. He had some cigars stashed in there, too, and I couldn't help but snatch a few of those, figuring I'd smoke one to celebrate and maybe give one to Miss Suze too.

It was the cigars that did me in, see. Wasn't two hours after I'd smoked one I was laid out in the camp infirmary, puking my guts out, and my tongue black as Monday. This is where you got to cred the big man for being smart. Turns out he had those cigars in there for a reason, and it wasn't to keep the tobacco all nice and chewy. He'd laced them up good so if they ever got stole he'd know right away who did it.

The big boss had me brung into central and my record came up soon as they tagged my prints. It turns out the old greenie, the one we subbed in on account of Goose getting sick, was so shitpantsed he ran straight to the first Texas soldier and gave himself up, said as how it was all my idea and I was the one who fired.

So I went into booking and they did tests to say I was a bad apple, through and through. There's no point growing a bad apple, it'll never give anything but rot. That's why they started doing the Straw work in the first place, because there's no point in feeding and clothing and keeping a man locked up who'll always be the same kind of man when instead with a cut and tuck you can change him. That's what they told me anyhow.

At least they didn't send me off to the sporting camps. I know some of those guys make it years living out there in the woods but I wouldn't want to live like that, *waiting, looking over my shoulder, and in the end a hunting party tracking me down and nailing me to be stuffed and pickled and hung on a wall somewhere.*

In a way, you could say I got off easy. Since I got the cut, I been making my living as a grifter, working routes all the way from Crunch, United, to the Dust Bowl. I like to think I know a fair trade when I see one. And I can't say a few brain cells for freedom ain't a good and fair deal.

14

The Missionary soldiers of the New Kingdom of Utah may look like a bunch of day-old chicken tenders, but don't let the clean of their shirts fool you. I swear, I once saw a fourteen-year-old girl gut a full-grown gangbanger without getting so much as a drip of blood on her Bible. She even left a condolence card tucked into his body cavity. I thought that was a nice touch.
—from The Grifter's Guide to the Territories FKA USA

The storm brought down half the outpost overnight: buildings smashed, roofs punched in, trees uprooted. The locals had been sorting the wreckage since sunup, pocketing anything that wasn't claimed, hammering signs back into place, hauling branches, and making a little money out of it too.

Overflowing cisterns sheeted the main thoroughfare with six inches of dirty water, carrying off a film of people's trash, old wire-plugged phones that hadn't worked in a half century, empty vape canisters and crumpled packets of fresh bubble gum, condoms used and unused. Wires sparked in the street. The whole town stank of shit, and I spotted more than one toilet tank swirling past us on the eddies. One woman set up camp to grift waterlogged studs coming to her on the filth. Another was fishing out soggy Singles™ for resale. Barnaby was thrilled with the brand-new buffet of trash, and netted half a dozen socks and a few plastic bags for breakfast.

"One man's trash is another mammal's amuse-bouche," he said, and let out a burp that smelled like mothballs.

But the squall brought down more than just the rooftops. A heap of black-winged drones were dipping their smashed tails in the floodwaters just outside the storm shelter, good for nothing but copper now. Searching through the tangle of wire and steel, I found Soviet lettering: it hadn't taken long for Rafikov to find replacements for the drones Thrasher had shot down above the bullet drain.

I had to get to Granby, and fast.

Zeb and Bee went door-to-door to look for the dead, and came back midmorning with a tally of twelve rotguts. They would have to spring for an ice van, since the closest pickup would lose them precious money in early bloat. The old wagon was gone—either stolen or, more likely, picked up by the wind and simply tossed into kindling.

We all sloshed down Main Street together to the rotting husk of a high school that housed an open-air market of pharma booths and flavor peddlers, used T-shirts still sporting pit stains, and first-generation visors. A unionist[1] with an ancient American flag tourniqueting his hair sold rigs from out of the gym. A blackened basketball net still clung to one wall like a sad bit of pubic hair. The place was huge, dim, and packed with wheels: horse buggies and bicycles, grocery carts and wheelbarrows, golf carts rigged with outboard motors and ancient mopeds pitted with rust, primitive deliverables bots and even a salvage horse, its copper-wire hair gleaming, and a sign cautioning feed of Purified Veggie Scrap Oil only.[2]

---

1. The Secessionists had of course prevailed during the Second American Civil War, coasting on a tide of popular rage, and furthermore bolstered by a huge quantity of big money support from politicians aspiring to gain even more power in their localities. Ironically, they by no means represented the majority opinion. Since the earliest secessions, however, there had been calls for reintegration, especially by older stalwarts of the American Constitution.

2. Despite the prevalent myth of a rustic, unspoiled West, the stretch of loosely defined territories including Wyoming and Montana were actually some of the wealthiest on the continent due to a booming water industry. Every year, the herds of cattle remaining on the continent, raised in vast climate-controlled slaughterhouses, were shipped to Recycled Energy Plants to be converted into electricity or returned to the agrofirms, where their tissue might be converted into

There were wheels from the early twenty-first century, beautiful to look at but as dumb as bricks; towers of scrap, old engine parts, coolants and lubricants, wheels and wheel spokes, jumper cables, extra batteries, and even drums of gasoline.

I wandered through the maze of wheels for sale, trying to shake off my glum. Jump had flowed into Low Hill already. How many other places had it spread too? What would happen when Rafikov decided on war?

"You're upset," Sammy said. I hadn't heard her come up behind me. "I can tell because of your hands. You're squeezing them."

I forced a smile. "Good job."

"Thanks." She rearranged her interface into a smile. That was a new one. Being on the road had kicked her learning into high gear. "I've heard that the new generation has a much easier time with facial expressions and body postures, since their coding is so much more sophisticated. There are still so many things I don't understand."

"Like what?" I said.

"Like upset," she said. "You can upset a sports team, a kitchen pot, or a stomach. There are so many different definitions. Disordered, deranged, nervous, irritable. So which is it, Truckee Wallace?"

"All of the above," I said. "Well. Except for deranged. I'm not deranged. Not yet, anyway."

She shook her head. "Sometimes I think I'll never really understand humans."

"Lucky you," I said.

On the far side of the showroom, where sliding doors let in thick slabs of butterspray-colored sunshine from the outside, I squatted down to

---

a variety of printed foodstuffs for generations to come. The financial value of the animals, and the dissonance between the projected image of the West and its reality, was demonstrated in the fact that the "cowboys" of the West now rode engineered horses to do their herding, since real horses had gone almost extinct in the Great Die-Off.

admire the gleaming rims of a fifty-year-old John Deere tractor with nothing left to plow. Each rim was six times the size of Tiny Tim's head and just as shiny. The exhaust pipe looked like a middle finger, the wheels spank-new rubber, and the hood colored a green-and-yellow stripe that reminded me of the carnivorous bees supposedly making mince of the plantations[3] of the Confederacy.

"She's a beauty, isn't she?"

I whipped around at the startle of a soft voice behind me. Standing in a patch of sun was the whitest guy I'd ever seen: white-blond hair and brows and lashes, white shirt without a smudge of dirt on it, even white socks. White *matching* socks. I hadn't seen matching socks in a decade.

"Yeah," I said, ignoring the brain-scratch saying I knew the guy from somewhere. "And for fifty-five thousand Crunchbucks, a real bargain. Can you imagine having that kind of bling?"

_____

3. Whose labor powered the Confederate plantations? This was a question that for many years bedeviled other regions, and given the Confederacy's notorious aggression to outsiders and its resolutely anti-technology and anti-information coalition government, reliable reports were difficult to procure and verify. While in many places, androids served essentially as unpaid slave labor—a continuous source of tension that in certain places had exploded into intermittent open warfare; see Appendix E: "The Android Freedom Fighters, 2050s–2070s"—it is worth noting that the Confederacy outlawed androids and robotics entirely. Ironically, and although in the early South on which the Confederacy was modeled, systems of slavery were entrenched in racial divisions, by the time of dissolution these racial divisions were in many places obsolete due to decades of intermarriage and immigration, and rendered socially irrelevant by the advent of androids onto whom such racial aggression was transferred. It has been confirmed through numerous sources that the slaves of the new Confederacy were therefore of three types: criminal convicts, including anyone found to have harbored, communicated with, or availed him- or herself of the services of an android; suspected "sympathizers" of the North who could by lineage, intellect, or proclivity be accused of a connection to the countries outside of the Confederacy; and economic debtors.

The boy came closer. His shoes, shined to a mirror polish, ended up right next to where I was squatting.

"The only currency that matters is God's favor," he said.

And just like that the idea scratching my brain opened its palm: the kid was Friendly Militia.

Right away my tongue turned to iron in my mouth. Dozens of foot soldiers were filing in through the sliding doors now, all of them sleek in spotless white shirts and clean socks. I had no idea how you could even get a clean like that. Even President Burnham couldn't completely shake the grime of air pollution and the gray that clung to every crease and fold.

But the New Kingdom of Utah wasn't hurting for cash—that was obvious from their artillery. Each and every one of their missionaries was holstered with top-of-the-line heat, belts of ammunition, spanking-new handguns, rifles.

Not a single one of them missed saying excuse me either. A few of them gave me a nod and a smile, and one girl even complimented my visor. They really were the sweetest army in the world.

It was like everyone always said: *Couldn't be a better way to die.*

Twenty, twenty-five, thirty, thirty-five . . . I counted forty-two missionaries by the time the last one made it inside and rolled the doors shut with a click that sounded just like the cock of a gun. With the wedge of sunlight gone, the light in the gym turned the murky green of infected urine.

Trapped.

I could barely think through the throb of terror in my head.

The owner of the shop cleared his throat. "You're not welcome here."

"I don't mean to contradict you. But God's soldiers are welcome everywhere," said the elder I pinned at maybe twenty. "The whole world belongs to Him."

"My fist belongs up your shithole," Bee spat out. "How dare you mention that filth here, in front of His Unholiness and His most faithful servants?"

Barnaby froze. He was nearly white enough to pass for a foot soldier. One by one, every last missionary pivoted in his direction.

"Well, now," he said. "No need for all that Unholiness stuff. . . ."

A sharp gasp went through the Militia when Barnaby spoke. It was like a giant had knocked the air out of all of them at once. For about the thousandth time I wished I had *any* kind of weapon, even a goddamn fork.

The baby-faced elder recovered quick. "We seem to be in the right place. As the Book says, *And these signs shall follow them that believe; In my name shall they cast out devils; they shall speak with new tongues.*"

Fats clapped his hands over his ears. Bee hissed air from between her two best teeth.

"Don't spit your lies to us, boy," Zeb said. He hadn't gone for his guns, yet, but he'd unzipped his jacket so his belt and all his ropes of ammo were visible. "Scroll back to your so-called kingdom, and take your tots with you, before I send you down in holy hellfire."

The elder didn't react. He was still squinting at Barnaby, like he was trying to figure out how fast he would burn in the afterlife. "There are rumors of a scourge in the water basin. The river plants have slowed to a trickle. A throng of black-eyed monsters who fly on dark wings of evil to do hell's work. A scourge of the Godless, and harbingers of death—"

"Death don't need no harbinger, dick slice." Zeb spoke with a hatred that twisted his face into something uglier than it was already. "Death does just fine on its own."

"So it does." The elder smiled. He *legitimately* smiled, like he was glad he and Zeb had found something to agree on. "But the devil needs earthly servants. Will you deny you serve him?"

"We serve Him, fluff Him, rub and tug Him, if He wills it. But we never been north of cartel territory," he added, before the elder could cut in. "We don't know squirrel about your black-eyed scourges, or your flow. Why don't you drink your Bibles, if they got everything you need?"

"Water is a gift from the heavens," the elder said calmly, and the demons did some more moaning. "It flows to us as it flowed to Abraham and his flock in the desert."

"It flows to you through a trade agreement with the ganglands,[4] you twat," Zeb spat out.

The elder didn't blink. "God works through trinities and trade agreements alike."

"Look, kid. You want a squall, you got one. But let's be crystal about one thing. We don't give a sperm whether you choke to death in the desert. We don't have no hand in your wars, and we don't have no hand in your monsters, and we don't have no hand anywhere except to haul corpses before they rot. *Comprende?* So stick a tampon in it, because you're grinding on my last good nerve."

"Please, fellas." The unionist was either sweating through his balls or leaking piss. "I'm begging you. Can't you please take it outside? I don't want any mess. . . ."

The elder looked mortified. "Oh, no. No. We don't want any mess either," he said. The other missionaries quickly passed around a *yes, no, never, of course not.* "It's just that—how should I explain this? It's always so awkward the first time . . . we're on orders from God to bring all of His creatures to the light, to welcome them into His loving arms, and to share His bounty with all living things." And in a half click, he whipped

---

4. This is shorthand for the enormous parcel of "free land" encompassing the mountainous regions of the former Colorado, Montana, Idaho, and Wyoming, colloquially known as the "ganglands" or the "wet lands," a reference to the enormous belt of mountains that gave the territories enviable control of fresh water flow in the western continent—and of the wealth that went with it. Residents largely referred to this sovereign area as the Free Territories, but the reality on the ground was far more feudal than utopic. The inordinately lucrative business of selling water to the dry countries like Libertine and Halloran-Chyung meant that profitable mountainous or basin arteries were the source of near-constant dispute between various armed gangs, some of which did open warfare for years, or even decades, for the right to mete out and sell water contracts.

his AK-47 from his backstrap. "Or else to send their worthless souls into the fiery pits of hell."

The other missionaries moved in sync: it was like a river of artillery poured into their hands simultaneously. As they all cocked up, a great metallic *chck-chck* vibrated the room and shook me full of panic that landed right inside my bladder.

"Now you're talking our tongue." Zeb flipped two pistols into one hand, and leveled a shotgun at the elder with the other. He twitched his head in Barnaby's direction. "Tell him, Your Darkness. Tell him all about the fiery hell they're so piss-scared of."

There was a long stretch of silence. Zeb cleared his throat. Finally, Barnaby inched his head into view above the wagon.

"Sorry. Were you talking to me?" He peeled back his gums to show teeth caulked with plywood and beetle parts. "I'm not sure I can speak to such weighty philosophical matters. . . . I am, after all, just a member of the lowly *Capra hircus*. . . ."

"*Lowly?*" Bee could bleat nearly as well as he could. "You are the great Lucifer, Prince of Darkness, Who Rides on the Sulfurous Winds of Hell and Brings Suffering and Misery Before Him!"

Barnaby began to sway on his hooves. "Listen, the Suffering and Misery were actually here already," he said. "I can't take credit . . . it—it was more of a branding thing. . . ."

The elder swung around to sight him and Barnaby trailed off with a squeak.

"Your tongue betrays you even now, you abominable misery." The elder made it sound like a compliment. I wanted to scream, to shout at them to stand down, to tell them the truth: that our only hope for stopping the black-eyed scourge was lodged in Barnaby's gray matter.

But my tongue was gummed to my teeth, and I knew I could never make them listen.

The elder went on: "After I cut your bowels from your belly and your horns from your head, I will carve all the meat from your bones so that not even the insects will have use for you. I hope"—he jogged his AK a little higher—"it doesn't hurt."

"This is all a mistake! A mistake!" Barnaby was lock-kneed, screaming like a siren. "I'm a goat! Just a goat! A myotonic fainting goat, at that. Look at me! I'll be flat on my back in thirty seconds! I'll be spitting up metal! I've got a nervous stomach! *I'm a coward!*"

The elder froze. Everyone froze. It was so quiet I could hear the rustle of Thrasher rubbing his crotch on one of the two-wheelers. Nervous habit.

Finally, I gummed up enough spit to unstick my voice. "He's telling the truth," I croaked out. "He's not important. Let him go."

"Shut your fucking grille, greenie, or I'll stuff it full of bullet shells." Zeb's voice was like the hush of quiet just before a tornado comes and punches off the roof. And then, to Barnaby: "Explain yourself."

Barnaby worked his mouth for at least ten seconds before so much as a squeak came out of it.

"I'm a nobody," he said at last. "I'm a nothing. Just an average, everyday goat with an encyclopedic knowledge of the works of Baudelaire—an experiment!"

"You lie," Oreo said. But they looked uncertain.

"You are the Prince of Lies." Nikhil was even greener than she usually was.

"I'm not the prince of anything. Haven't you been *listening*? I was made during the final administration. I'm a brain-splice patient, nothing more." He shook his head. "Look, I didn't mean to mislead you. But when you all came charging into the woods with your swords and your what have you, babbling on about he of the hoof and the silver-tongued god, I wasn't about to *correct* you, was I? I mean, I may be a distant cousin of the common ass, but I'm no *idiot*, and I—"

"Silence." For the first time, the elder notched his voice toward a shout. "Sorry," he added, in a normal volume. "But it's our turn now."

Everyone's weapons were up again in a flash, a landscape of metal barrels pointing like shame-on-you fingers, a crosshatch of weapons. If anyone fired, everyone would fire.

"As a missionary and representative of God's Army, with the authority vested in me by the New Kingdom of Utah"—the elder's voice rolled out in the silence—"I sentence every one of you to die."

Then he pulled the trigger, and the whole world exploded.

15

They say it ain't guns that kill people, it's people that kill people.
But having a gun sure helps.
—from ***The Grifter's Guide to the Territories FKA USA***

The blast dropped me to my knees. I hit the linoleum as metal pinged against metal, wooden rigs exploded, carriages flipped upside down, and sawdust caked the air the color of tree bark.

I rolled between the tractor and a golf cart just as a bullet sang past my ear, pinging a Vespa and leaving a thumbnail-sized dent in its gas pipe. Across the room, Thrasher jerked as a bullet hit him square in the chest. A blood-spatter silhouette went up on the wall behind him like a giant handprint, sticky-wet and dark. I spotted a pair of horns flash between the rigs and prayed Barnaby had by some fat luck survived, but just then a missionary spotted me and I had to duck to avoid getting drilled. A bullet cracked the plaster behind me and showered me in a soft haze of dust.

When I looked up again, there was a girl standing over me, a bright-eyed gazelle with her hair tied back in a ponytail and a 9mm Jericho pointing its nose at me. Her nails were painted pink.

"I like your shirt," she said, smiling. "Sorry about the muck-up."

But before she could pull the trigger, half her face blew off and spattered the wall, the floor, even my pants. She hit the ground with a thud and a wet splat, practically on top of me, and I scrabbled backward, my sneakers sliding on a slick of blood and skin as vomit kicked up in my throat.

I spotted Bee behind a sniper's rifle fifty yards away. As she lifted a hand to wave, four of her fingers vaporized, cleaved by a bullet.

The dead girl's hand was coiled around her gun. I forced myself to take it, bending back her fingers one by one. It was a stupid thing to be thinking, but I remembered then how amped everyone was when the third-generation WorldBurn came out with improved VR, how the gamer pro-league said it was just like real combat. Bullshit. No sim could shake your head like a steel drum and make sweat slip down your balls and twist your stomach to your tongue. No sim could get the smell of it, guts bleeding out and bowels emptying themselves as bullets passed through them.

Another missionary popped up, and I triggered without thinking. The gun kicked like a salvage horse, but the missionary took a slug right in the chest, cranking backward with his arms outstretched like the Christ who-body they all worshipped.

At least so many hours of WorldBurn had taught me to aim.

A hand locked hold of my elbow. I whipped around, shouting, and only missed pistol-whipping Sammy across the interface by an inch.

"You need to hide," she said. One of her lenses was shattered, exposing a nest of wiring behind it. Several red lights were blinking over the ridge of her copper-plated cheekbones.

"What happened to you? Were you shot?"

She twirled her head. "Shrapnel. The Militia doesn't care enough to kill me." She actually sounded pissed about it. "Listen. You've got to find a way out of here, Truckee."

Another blast of gunfire forced me to the ground before I could ask her how in the hell she expected me to escape with both exits blocked. A rat-a-tat rhythm of gunfire hit the tractor, so many blasts at once that for a moment it rocked up on two wheels and I thought it might come down on top of us. As it slammed to the ground again, the passenger door popped open.

"Go," Sammy said, and gave me a push. I scrambled up the stepladder and hurtled into the tractor, rolling headfirst into a pile of dingy shag upholstery as bullets pinged the hood.

The upholstery screamed, and tried to kick me in the head.

"Barnaby!" I couldn't believe it: the little shit was still alive.

If Barnaby had had hands I was sure he would of grabbed my shoulders to shake me. Since he didn't, he head-butted me instead. "Please, you've got to get us out of here. We're all going to die."

"Can't you just wish up a great storm, O Unholy One?" A low blow, but he deserved it.

"I'm sorry." His eyes were so close to mine, I could see all kinds of gold inside them. "I'm sorry, all right? I got carried away. *'Tis the pride of man that shall destroy him.'* That's from chapter eight of—"

"Your memoir. I know."

Big surprise, he began to blubber. Snot bubbled up in his nostrils.

"Look, stop crying. We're safe as mittens for now. We'll wait it out, and scroll off just as soon as the smoke clears. . . ."

But no sooner had the word sprung from my mouth than the room sprouted an echo. *Smoke.* The word came rolling back to me, lobbed up by other voices: *smoke! smoke! smoke!*

I hitched myself up in the seat and saw flames tonguing an overturned rig. A sharp and acrid stink made my eyes water. Right away, I thought of the barrels of oil stacked in a pyramid against the wall. If even a single spark hit . . .

Well. It would give brand-new meaning to the term "fire sale."

"Move," I told Barnaby, and for a click we danced an awkward tango of fur and flesh. I fumbled for the ignition switch and couldn't believe it when my fingers closed on a key. I'd never game-played driving a rig this old, but I knew the basic mechanics, and I pedaled hard on the gas. The tractor jumped forward, then stalled out. I'd forgotten all about gears.

"Our father, who art in heaven, hallowed be thy name . . ." Barnaby was stuffing his mouth full of upholstery in between his blather. *"Though I walk through the valley of the shadow of death, I will fear no evil . . ."*

"Shut your tits, will you?" I spun the wheel backward and manhandled the clutch into reverse. In my rearview, I had a full view of the fire playing hopscotch over the room, ten feet from that pyramid of explosives. In less than a minute we would all be blown to heaven—or hell, depending on what you believed.

This time, the tractor blew straight into a used ice van, swinging it left and sweeping the legs out from under another missionary. My mitts were so sweaty I could barely handle the gears.

"Come on, come on, come on," I muttered. For a second the engine growled its displeasure, and we were frozen, wheels spinning, pinned in place.

But then, suddenly, we were free. We lurched forward, toppling a salvage horse and scattering it into metal pieces.

Then a bloody hand came down on the hood.

I slammed on the brakes, so hard Barnaby slid off the seat and ended up on the floor.

"Stop." The missionary was maybe thirteen, fourteen. Skinny as a whip. But his gun was the largest motherfucking thing I had ever seen in my life. It looked like an elephant gun and an Uzi got in a tussle and called it quits by breeding.

"In the name of the Father, the Son, and the Holy Spirit, I ask you, please, to stop."

"Go!" the goat bleated. *"Go!"*

But I couldn't go. I couldn't so much as twitch. If I did, I knew the kid would turn my face to pastry. And even though he was leaning like a crumb drunk off moonshine, his aim was perfectly steady.

I really didn't want to have to run him over.

"Listen to me," I said. "If we don't get out of here, we're all going to die. Okay?"

The kid's lashes were surprisingly dark. Another detail the sims never got right: the humanness of it. "There is no death for the soldiers of God," he said. "Only home."

Behind him, a giant shadow shook off a bit of smoke and turned into Tiny Tim.

My relief was electric. "You're outgunned," I said. "Let us go, or my friend behind you will twig your neck."

The missionary didn't even turn around. "The Straw Man? He won't hurt me. He *can't*. He has paid for his sins. He will receive God's forgiveness. He will live."

Of course, he was right. Tiny Tim couldn't squash a spider, even a radioactive one: the Straw Procedure made sure of that. "None of us will live. Don't you get that?" That was the problem with all these fanatics: no common sense. "If you'd just *listen* to me, if you'd just open the doors—"

I didn't finish. The tractor leaped. It slammed straight into him, so his jaw cracked against the hood and his gun slid from his hand and let out a volley of sideways shots that went nowhere. Then he was gone beneath us and there was a sickening crunch as we rolled over him. I looked down to see the goat screaming one endless vowel, with a hoof jammed to the gas pedal.

When I looked up, we were headed straight for a steel wall.

"The doors, Tim!" I had to hang out of the open window, pointing, just to get him to understand. "Open the goddamn doors! *The doors.*"

Maybe he heard me. Or maybe he just understood. Dr. J. C. Straw may have hacked out all Tiny Tim's violence and most of his smarts, but he didn't get all of them. Tim slammed the latch free with a fist and shouldered open the doors a half click before we plowed into them.

Taking hold of the exhaust pipe, he swung himself up onto the steps as we passed.

"What a dust-up," he said, grinning like we were all roaches at a goddamn picnic. "I ain't seen nothing like that in a long time."

"Sammy." I realized then that we'd left Sammy behind. "We have to go back for Sammy!"

"I'm here!" A steel arm flashed in the rearview. Sammy had hooked herself to the fender. "Intact and operational!"

Barnaby was shaking so hard, he could barely clamber back onto the seat. "Thank God," he panted. "I thought for sure we were going to—"

The rest of his sentence was blasted away in a fist punch of sound. A rolling pressure slammed me forward on the wheel and nearly took Tim off his feet. A rain of debris came down on us, cracking the windshield, pelting us through the windows.

It was one hell of an explosion. By the time I could lift my head, choking on the taste of melted plastic, I saw nothing behind me but smoke, a big empty lot full of mangled metal, and no evidence, at all, of who had won the fight.

16

One of the best places to make sales is the three-hundred-mile
border fence that shims BCE Tech and Texas. Shantytowns sprout
like wart clusters all along the border, every one of them packed
with suckers sweating out some immigration issue. Just be on the
lookout for Blythe's taxmen, or they'll skim you for 25 percent.
—from *The Grifter's Guide to the Territories FKA USA*

We made it a full eight hours before the tractor's front tire blew, luckily
on an easy stretch of country road that some roadslicks had obviously
been clearing. We rolled almost another half a mile before we had to
climb out.

"When the devil gives you lemons, squeeze them in a child's eye," Barnaby recited solemnly.

"What should you do when he gives you a talking goat?" I snapped.
"'Cause I'm getting pretty hungry."

Thankfully, he stayed quiet after that.

Tiny Tim suggested we strip the tractor before ditching it. We could
grift the usable parts in Granby, and the bling would come in handy; I
didn't know how long it would be before the Federal Corporation's agents
found me.

The road turned to gravel and then to asphalt as it fed us through a
sprawl of Old World construction now adapted for the tourists and desperadoes who went this route. Downtown Granby was even bigger than
Low Hill: Apart from the usual travel pits, there were dumpy immigration offices and border police stations; holos shouting the way to S&P

Plaza and Biotech Belt; pay-for-access portal cafés with employees vaping in the street in front of dim interiors; quality control and food administration; shipping and freight stores, where packages got sent off around the continent on the backs of flesh drones who got paid pennies on the pound.

Innkeepers eyed us from the front stoops where they rolled fresh. Pharmacologists peddled drugs, cure-alls, salves, soaps, tinctures, and powders, plus small bottles of Canadian air.[1] A half-dozen currency operators shouted prices and offered to buy, sell, swap. A long line of buyers clotted the road in front of a health bazaar, which advertised blood for sale and a two-for-one tetanus-shot special. The company stores were packed with shake I'd never seen before: enormous violet nukefruit from Halloran-Chyung, Anti-Aging Negative-Calorie Flatcrackers™ from the Real Friends© of the North, Caffeine Productivity Packs from Sinopec-TeMaRex Affiliated, smoked fish guts and popped cockroaches from the Russian Federation. Blythe must of had half a dozen countries greasing his palm for the right to sell in.

I'd never seen so many different kinds of people either: Androids of all models and generations; grifters icing it out with botcops over correct permits; girls moving in giggling packs; transspecies floats of birds, cats, and foxes, hissing at one another from across the street. Outside a genderless hostel, a few persons were getting heated over the right to self-identify as android. Two perfect tens carved through the crowd bumping hips in unison, and it wasn't until they were nearly on top of us that I spotted all the metal beneath their NuSkin™ and reckoned them for what they were.

"Sexy Saams," Sammy whispered. "Don't look," she said, when I

---

1. The newest health trend grew out of the belief that even small samples of uncontaminated environments could prove restorative to medical conditions as disparate as blistering shingles to the poorly understood, if widespread, psychological illness known as "The Dread." Other than Canadian air, the most popular "environmental specimens" included Glacial Leach, Baltic Seawater, and a particular mineral deposit alleged to have been dredged from the submerged volcanoes of the former Hawaii.

started to turn. "They'll have your wallet and your clothes before you can blink. They're programmed that way."

There were shifty-eyed men chewing fresh in alleyways, weapons depots selling flavors I'd never even dreamed of, immigration counselors, currency exchanges—all of that life, all of that hustle, flowing toward the border, the famous invisible fence, guarded by 200,000 Texas volunteer militia who shot at the first sign of trouble. Even from a distance, we could hear the rat-a-tat rhythm of their firearms.

We off-loaded our swag at a junk shop for a half-decent price. A sweet little security robot made of hammered alloy suggested we get out of the commercial district if we wanted a bed for the night, so we hunted down a fleabag motel called the Starlite. It was a dingy, out-of-the-way squat, obviously made for dimeheads and johns who peeped the Sexy Saams more than once.

"How much for a room?" I asked the receptionist.

"Depends," she said, without bothering to turn away from whatever she was watching on her visor. She was enormously fat and suffering from a bad peel that came from trying to kick a shiver habit. "Got rooms by the half hour, hour, or by the night. You want two a room, that's standard rates. More than that you gotta pay doubles. And the goat's extra charge, plus a cleaning fee if things get messy."

"Excuse me," Barnaby said. This caught the woman's attention. "I will have you know that goats by and large are an exceptionally clean species, and I am a paragon of personal hygiene."

"It talks, too, huh?" The woman smiled. Her teeth were crowded and too small for her mouth. "That's gonna be an extra charge. Can't have no noise complaints. A hundred Crunchbucks a pop."

"*A hundred Crunchbucks?*" That would nearly wipe me of Crunch dollars, even counting the cash we'd pulled from selling off the parts. "You're kidding, right?"

She shrugged. "Busy season," she said. "The Texas boys ain't lettin' no one past the border, not with all the recent hoo-dunny and talk of

the Bozeman Boys and Willa Dirk and her Snake Charmers[2] runnin'
south and retaliatin'." No wonder we'd heard so much shooting from the
border. "But I might think about a discount. Who's your friend?"

Her eyes slid over my shoulder to Tiny Tim. The ceiling was so low
his head nearly grazed the light fixtures.

"The name's Tiny Tim, ma'am," he said. "It's a pleasure."

"We'll see about that, scarecrow." She leaned forward and her breasts
pooled across the desk like deflated airbags. "They say the cut make your
brain as good as a limp noodle. So are you some kind of idiot or what?"

Tiny Tim smiled. "That's about exactly the measure of it. An idiot
through and through."

She tilted her head like she needed to see him with her nostrils. "They
say the cut make some other things go limp too," she said.

Tiny Tim hitched his grin a little wider. "Well, ma'am, you can't be
right nine out of nine."

She put both hands on the counter and stood up. It was incredible to
watch. It was like the Level-7 Death-Head Volcano that had blasted Annalee and me out of WorldBurn for six straight months back when we
still played, like an eruption of human flesh. You couldn't imagine that
there could be so much surface area on a single human being.

"Pin it here for a bit, shorty," she said to me as she oozed around the
counter. "We'll talk tariff when I'm through."

The receptionist disappeared with Tiny Tim into the back office and
was gone for close to an hour. By the time they came back, I knew four
different ways to string *God* and *fuck* together in the same sentence, and
she'd undergone a major personality swap: she gave us a corner room for
half price and a second room free of charge.

"You need anything, just ring down and ask for Mama Hazard," she

---

2. Both the Bozeman Boys and Willa Dirk's Snake Charmers were well-known affiliate gangs that controlled, among dozens of other major dikes, the water plants at
Boise and at Jackson Hole in the Free Territories, respectively.

told me, dropping a pair of sweat-slicked keys into my palm. I half-expected her to curl up on her desk and start purring.

The elevator was out of order, go figure.

"What'd you do to her?" I asked Tiny Tim as we began the haul to the fourth floor. The stairwell was narrow and strewn with spam. We shimmied by old mattresses, reeking of shiver, still stacked in the landings, and crunched over empty purines and old chlorine tablets.

Tiny Tim clapped me on the back and nearly sent me sprawling. "Women want one thing and one thing only, Truckee. Even a dumb old scarecrow like yours truly knows that."

I thought about it. "Sex?"

He laughed. "You're funny. Anyone ever tell you that?"

"No," I said.

Mama Hazard had given us two adjoining rooms on the top floor, where we would be undisturbed by the pay-by-hour clients who used up the cheaper rooms below us. Barnaby opted to bunk with Tiny Tim, likely because he knew I'd throttle him the first time he tried to quote from his memoir, which left Sammy with me.

Our room was bigger than expected, and cleaner, too, even if there were burns singed into the carpet and an old syringe rolling around in the sink.

I took a nice long shower, holding my nose against the ammonia stink; there were water warnings everywhere, and all the flow was getting pumped up from the sewage plants. I wrung out my clothes of dust and blood spatter and strung them up to dry over the shower-curtain rod, then dressed in the studs I'd stolen from the cargo hold of the bullet train.

It was the first chance I'd had to take a hard look at the damage to Sammy's eye. The news wasn't good. She'd need a whole new lens and someone who knew more than a little about wiring. There were repair shops in Granby, sure, but I didn't know how long getting a new eye would take, and I was pretty sure neither of us could spring for it.

"I'm sorry, Sammy," I said. I twisted the wires together as neat as I could and secured them with a rubber band. "That's the best I can do."

"Oh, well." Her remaining eye pulsed a slow blue. "It's my first battle wound, isn't it?"

"Guess so," I said.

I helped her clean the dirt from her joints with squares of toilet paper the texture of a rug burn; there was even dirt inside her battery housing. Bits of crushed glass were caught beneath her winged solar panels. Luckily, these came easily apart, so I could blow out the debris. The plastic of her knee joints was so crusty she could barely bend her legs to sit, and I took a handkerchief-sized towel from the bathroom, ignoring the stains that had been steamed on instead of scrubbed out, and began to wipe. But I kept thinking of Mama Hazard, and the scarecrow, and what Tiny Tim had said to me coming up the stairs.

"What do you think Tiny Tim meant," I said, "about women needing only one thing?"

Sammy was quiet for a minute. I heard the reassuring hum of her processing. "It doesn't make sense from a literal perspective. Humans need many things; even female humans are organic beings and thus require food, oxygen, sleep, and a whole host of different chemicals and nutrients. So I imagine he was speaking metaphorically, or perhaps allegorically."

"I think he was talking about feelings," I said.

Sammy flashed a few lights across her interface. "I'm probably the wrong resource, then." I thought she was trying to smile, but she sounded upset.

She rotated so I could get to her back. The damage was worse than I thought. Several overlapping steel panels had been forced together at strange angles, and others were dinged or misshapen. I was almost afraid to touch her. I ran a finger carefully over one of the worst of the joints, which should of been lying flat and now rippled and buckled, like shoulder blades.

"It's okay," she said. "You can't hurt me."

I moved slowly, polishing and wiping, blowing out the seams. I was almost frightened by the look of all those component pieces, how fragile they all seemed. I'd once read even basic androids were wired with more than 10 million chips.

"The generation after mine was the one that got NuSkin™." Sammy's voice was warmer and hoarser than usual, as if her speaker grille were blocked. "They say their sensors are so sophisticated that late models can tell the difference in the direction of the winds. They can feel pain and pressure. And . . . pleasure."

Suddenly, I realized how close we were sitting. I scanned the polish of her plate metal, and the low whirring of her ops, and the heat cycling through her vents. She was so hot I couldn't stand to touch her.

"I wish I'd been manufactured just a little bit later." Now she was so quiet, I could barely hear her above the fan. "Just so I could know. So I could feel . . ."

She trailed off. I stood up quickly.

"I have to get on the portal," I blurted out. It was the first thing that came to my head.

Her remaining lens looked even larger than usual. I saw my face reflected in it, sharp and pale and guilty-looking. "There's access here."

"Not fast enough," I said. "I need more bandwidth."

There was a terrible silence. I grabbed my rucksack. I couldn't even look at her.

"I'm sorry," she said, and I swear she looked hurt. "Did I upset you?"

"You did nothing. It's fine. I'm *fine*." I practically blew into the hall, slamming the door behind me.

I don't think I breathed again until I was out on the street.

The sun had set behind a flare of Texas oil-haze. The streets were hardly less crowded than they'd been earlier, but the vibe was different. Most of the shops were shuttered, and the ones still open were the no-name kind: shiver- and crack-vape dens; slummy sex squats; bars fumigating the stink of liquor onto the streets; pharmas packed with every assortment of voodoo, hoodoo, and nuclear witchcraft you could think of.

The Granby streets were churning with the usual night swill: pop-ups and payday girls and gender-neutral zems and trans-everything,

Blythe's private security bogeymen showing off discreet weapons, Grace-landers crooning their hymns, and even a Confederate soldier wandering around looking about four-hundred-years lost. Congregations packed into prayer houses sang songs of salvation to the tune of automix beats. Arms dealers and hustlers scanned the street for easy targets. A group of Carnivale Moribundi kids on the corner rang their bell over and over, glaring through their face paint. Music foamed out of the bars, pros called to one another from high brothel windows, dimeheads shouted out their highs, and tiny shiver kids[3] with dull eyes and twitching hands sobbed in dark corners. Saltbox priests warned of hell and Devil's Army demons heralded it and a pretty girl with a purple Mohawk leaned against a holo-board smoking an old-fashioned cigarette, blocking the feed.

I stomped off down the street in a crank mood. I hadn't once given Sammy a sign I was into her. But I'd hurt her feelings anyway. And now when I passed a group of Sexy Saams with their high, round NuSkin™ breasts overspilling their shirts, their synthetic lashes shuttering against perfect blush cheeks, and legs so long they were like ladders to climb on, I couldn't help but wonder if they, too, were secretly gunning for things they couldn't have.

"Pleasure for buy, sugar," one of them said, in a voice like a fingertip running down my spine. "All the newest positions. Three-sixty contortion. Special vacuum suck and new flexibility controls."

I veered around the corner. I'd lied about needing portal access to get out of the room, but I figured logging on was a good move. President

---

3. Because shiver was easily synthesized from everyday ingredients, and the supply of finished and high-quality product rigorously controlled by the price-gouging Denver cartel, many of the makeshift "labs" that produced it in bulk were concealed inside normal houses, storage sheds, bathrooms, and basements. It was estimated in 2085 that 1 in every 40 children was raised in a house that contained a shiver lab of some kind. The influence of the chemical exposure led to stunted growth, learning disabilities, psychological disorders, and a constant full-body tremor known as the Twitch.

Burnham had told me his agents would find me, but in the meantime I might as well park it in one place.

I beat it straight for a hotspot called the Arcade, dizzyingly enormous, whizzing with colored lights and music. The window display was just an interface running a constant list of products, promotions, and prices. I saw the new WorldBurn VIII: Hellscape had been released, and I missed Annalee and Jared with a sharp, sudden aching that felt just like a kick.

I went inside and paid for a sixty-minute packet of unrestricted data, cutting through the clutter of scurvy-looking teenagers jabbing in simulation suits and skulky old men picking out corners where they could rub themselves to online porn houses without anyone seeing. I found an empty chair, sank into the pleather, and notched my visor over my eyes.

But when I tried to pull up my company feed, an error code started flashing.

Figuring I'd been accidentally logged out, I scrolled to the Crunch, United, landing page and tried signing in. When that didn't work, I closed and rebooted the browser. Again, I got the same error: invalid credentials. Now on the verge of panic, I rebooted my entire *visor*. My home screen was now a standard, template blue, like an unpolluted sky. All my snaps, feeds, streams, and blasts—erased. Every video of Jared's sneeze attacks, every freeze-frame of Saanvi's game plays, every sly moment I'd triggered when Annalee wasn't paying attention, when she was picking her teeth or blanking out to something on her holo, every snap beaming my mom's face back to me—wiped, gone, scrubbed from the server.

My collages, compilations, timelines, memories—my whole *life*—had been backspaced in a single keystroke.

Only the same error message floated in the imaginary space several inches from my nose: SECURITY ERROR 909. INVALID CREDENTIALS. PLEASE CONTACT TECHNICAL SUPPORT AT STATE DEPARTMENT IDENTI-FICATION/SUPPORT.CRUNCHGOV.

My cheeks were sweating. I wrestled the visor down to my neck to palm my face off, and saw a fat guy giving me the once-over. Even though he was simulating sex with the back of his chair, his eyes were full of pity, as if I was obviously the one with the bigger problems.

The sad thing was he was right.

I didn't need to contact the State Department to know what Security Error 909 meant.

I'd been locked out of Crunch, United.

If I'd been in over my head before, now I was six feet under. Locked out. Voided. Nine-oh-fucked.

It had to be a mistake. Maybe the Federal Corporation's new security firewalls had booted me out accidentally. I slid on my visor again, and pulled up some BCE Tech–sponsored news feed. Happily, BCE Tech, one of those tricky countries that flip-flopped loyalties faster than the history holos can update, had one of the most expansive portal networks I'd ever seen, and I had my choice of international feeds.

I phished for news about the riot at Crunchtown 407. The news was worse than I thought. An overnight rebellion by stockholders had persuaded President and CEO Burnham to step away from leadership temporarily. The Dakotas trumpeted a diplomatic crisis because four of its energy czars had been detained in Crunch 122, in a detention center on the banks of the Exxon-Mississippi River that had once housed storm refugees. The Real Friends© of the North had recalled both of its ambassadors to New New York, and the Federal Corporation had ordered an immediate review of any foreigners in the country on a temporary visa, which made half the continent light up about human-rights violations. Pictures from the border showed tightened cordons all around. Crunchtown 407 was on a list of corporate branches in a state of emergency, along with Crunchtown 202, which bordered the Commonwealth and had been in a state of emergency for as long as I could remember. But twelve other outposts had made the list, too.

Deputy Paula Munez, the Crunch, United, director of PR and marketing, had issued a dark statement warning of the potential for new attacks and blaming a foreign agent for sabotaging the bullet train. Crunch, United, was offering a reward for any information that would lead to the terrorist's arrest: a pop-up swelled across my feed, flashing a request for the public's help bringing the agent to justice.

I maximized the pop-up for the picture Crunch was blasting internationally, expecting an old image of Yana Rafikov.

For a second, the whole world went dark. My heartbeat throbbed in my ears. A fog of terror swept me blind.

When it cleared, there I was, or there my holo was, anyway. The image had been lifted from my old company ID and glowered back at me, right above four bright red words, swollen like pustulant pimples.

WANTED: DEAD OR ALIVE.

17

The problem with the intranet feeds is that they're all pumped full of as much shit as a sewage tank. Half a dozen countries say they won the last Olympix, and have the stats to prove it. And you won't find a squid in the Confederacy under sixty even knows there's faster ways to travel than a horse cart.

—from *The Grifter's Guide to the Territories FKA USA*

I don't know how long I sat there, trying to make sense of those four glowing words, trying to force them to mean something different. Eventually, the portal booted me out. I'd run over my pay-by-hour limit.

My thinking was all shriveled up, like ancient soap scum beveled off a public shower. I was shaking so hard I could barely flag a fare wheeler—which looked a lot like a repurposed squatbot[1]—to buy another hour.

"That will be ten Blythe notes," the bot responded, and prompted me to push a noselike button for currency exchange rates. I nearly fell out of my chair: ten Blythe notes came out to nearly forty Crunchbucks.

"It was *five* Crunchbucks an hour ago," I said.

The wheeler winked its lights cheerily. "One hour is five Crunchbucks," it said, switching neatly to the right currency. It was smarter than the squatbots, that was for sure, although so were millipedes. "Every additional hour is forty Crunchbucks."

---

1. Truckee is no doubt correct: Crunch, United, sold many of its older-model tech to smaller countries, such as BCE Tech, for repurposing.

I would of bet that's how Blythe kept the VR porn addicts from clogging his bandwidth. "That's stealing."

"Sie scheinen Schwierigkeiten zu haben zu verstehen. Möchten Sie Ihre Sprachauswahl ändern?" the bot proposed cheerily. *"Wenn Sie unsere AGBs überprüfen möchten . . ."*

"How about you learn math instead?" There was no way I could spring for another hour at that cost, so I shoved out of my chair, half-itching to throw a punch at its interface. But the robot was about seventeen generations away from feeling pain.

The whirl of noise, the smell of vape, the moonshine fumes—it all made me dizzy. How many countries were looking for my head, right this very minute? How many people were looking to cash in on the reward? Even in the dark of the Arcade, I felt horribly exposed, like someone had stripped me down to organs for a medical farm.[2] I thought of those skeevy eyeballs Burnham had on his desk, the way they kept rotating and rotating in the murk of liquid. But now the eyeballs were everywhere.

I kept my visor down, grateful now for its bulk, and cranked up the hood of my sweatshirt as I noodled out the door. The board had its facts twisted—maybe Rafikov even had inside agents laying the blame on me. But with President Burnham gone, getting an image overhaul from HR rehabilitators, who would help me?

I was so wattled in my thoughts, I nearly bowled over a girl with a purple Mohawk just outside the door. *"Excuse* you," she said, and bent to snatch up an old-fashioned cigarette.

"Sorry," I mumbled. "Didn't see you."

I didn't make it four feet before she called out to me again.

---

2. Many body pickers unaffiliated with the Devil's Army commonly sold organs to MediFarms, which then did business with private individuals or, depending on the country, state-owned hospital systems. It is worth noting that various MediFarms did lucrative trade in the organ-cloning trade, too, skirting anti–human cloning regulations by growing different organs in discrete environments, even in entirely separate facilities.

"You shouldn't waste your pay in squats like that. You'll never find what you're looking for."

I turned around again, slowly, and got treated to a plume of her smoke, direct to the face. She was wearing beat-up jeans and ratty boots, plus a leather jacket that looked like something Zeb would of liked. Then I realized I'd seen her once before already, leaning against a holo.

"How do you know what I'm looking for?" I asked her. I thought at once of President Burnham and what he'd told me: *We'll find you.*

True, she didn't look like an agent. But the good agents never did.

She smiled. Her teeth were very nice and very straight except for one, which was curved like an animal fang. "Come on," she said, and jumped off the sidewalk into the street.

I stayed where I was. "Come on where?" I knew better than to trust a total stranger in a foreign city. Even if she was my age. Even if she was cute. Even if she had fingernails plastered with tiny skull holes. "Who sent you?"

She didn't even turn around. But I know she heard me, because she lifted a hand and waved me on with her cigarette.

I hesitated for only a second before plunging into the crowd after her. I'd always been a sucker for girls with 3-D nails.

She darted in and out of the foot traffic, weaving around mopeds and scooters and self-drivers. She didn't give me a chance to ask her any more questions or even pretend she wanted to talk to me. She only glanced behind her once to make sure I was still there.

Left, right, right again. Soon the roads dribbled into streets and the streets bled into alleyways. Here, bored-looking girls waited in lit windows or did their business behind shower curtains drawn against the view. The pavement was cracked with weeds and sifty with the red dust that blew in all the way from Arizona, and I started to regret following along. The girl didn't seem like a pro, and so far she hadn't tried to kill me, but maybe she was just taking her time—or leading me to someone who would do the dirty work for her.

Just when I'd made up my mind to turn around and beat it, the girl stopped in front of another hotspot, this one about a thousand times dingier and more depressing than the Arcade. A few lumpy secondhand visors were jumbled together in the window, next to a static sign that listed cost per minute for portal access. I couldn't figure why she'd dragged me across Granby just to bring me to this dump, especially since the prices weren't all that cheaper from the ones advertised at the Arcade—maybe she took commissions.

But again, before I could question her she'd slipped inside.

Now I wasn't afraid anymore—just angry.

Inside it was dark, dusty, and just as depressing as it looked from the street. It reeked of vape and FishStix™. There was a single customer slumped in a patchy chair with his visor on, obviously playing some kind of MPG—probably WorldBurn or Revenge, given the way he was triggering. The guy behind the counter had greasy hair combed to his shoulders, as if to make up for the enormous bald spot on the dome of his head. But the girl greeted him like an old friend.

"Heya, Slick," she said. "How's business?"

"You're looking at it," he said without glancing up. He wasn't wearing a visor and was hunched over what looked like an early-century magazine. "Who's your friend?"

"Your newest customer," she said. She gave me an animal smile, like she was going to eat me.

"That's all right. I should get back to my squat." I had no desire to sit in this dim little room inhaling the fust of old breath and this guy's BO. "Thanks for all your *help*."

The girl just rolled her eyes. "Don't be such a lint." She removed a razor-thin visor from a jacket pocket—it must of cost a fortune—and set it down on the counter, along with a scrum of other things, gum wrappers and change, cigarette butts and a few loose keys. "Go on, Slick. You can bug him through mine."

The guy sighed heavily and straightened up to look at me for the first time. "Visor," he grunted, holding out a hand.

"Wait a second." I felt like I'd stumbled into a holoscript without knowing any of the lines. "What do you mean, *bug me*? What do you need my visor for?"

The girl blinked at me. Even though I was annoyed, I couldn't help but think about what her body might look like under that leather. "That's how you get access. Through a virus," she said. And then, with a little huff of impatience, "You *are* looking for the Yellow Brick Road, aren't you?"

18

*Why did the chicken cross the Road? Because it wanted
to buy methamphetamines.*
—from *The Grifter's Guide to the Territories FKA USA*

The first thing that hit me was the noise: the blast of audio kickback, the roar of unmuted chat, the music.

Coded like an actual landscape, where each admin had acreage for design, the Yellow Brick Road was one of the most detailed, insane, and enormous virtual worlds I'd ever seen. For a second I stood at the edge of the simulation, fumbling to turn down the reverb, trying to make sense of the sharp pixelation of the effects. A glistening gold ribbon of road unfurled in front of me, winding between impossible construction: buildings hanging upside down or hovering in midair or balancing on spindly stalks of wood too skinny to hold them in real life.

I scrolled into a small cottage advertising Santeria, and found shelves packed with century-old rooster talons and crusty vials of virgins' blood. Product details hovered above each item as soon as it was handled. An empty cart in the lower left corner of my visual field could be filled with merch simply by double tapping.

I skated out of the Santeria store and scrolled on. Down the road, a hovercraft was trading currencies: *All kinds, one-tenth the price! Cash shipped straight to your door!* An alien avatar was arguing with the admin on the patio that counted for the help desk. "I nearly got arrested in the Green Mountain Associated Intentional Communities," she was saying. "Do you know how hard it is to get arrested in Green Mountain? They don't even *believe* in police. . . ."

I navigated to an enormous Information Palace, a Multi-Channel Network obviously patchworked out of hundreds of different sites. If I had any prayer of surviving to clear my name, I needed to know who'd sold me out for a traitor, and how far the news had spread. Inside were vaulted halls and tiny, leather-heavy studies, old-fashioned libraries and modernist atriums, neat sitting rooms and psychedelic-heavy smoking dens, all of them individual sites operated by avatars with names like MissBehaviorRants or TruthHurts, information-rich spaces that shouted propaganda at you if you so much as placed a toe over their domains. It was loud and ugly and clamorous with lies that sounded good and truth you'd always pin for lies.

I found an InfoPay stand boasting data downloadable from any intranet on the continent. The site was coded like an old RV, and scaly with pieces of paper advertising data specials, arrest-record hacks, even bank-account information.

I waited in line behind a weedy-looking centaur wanting info on some Sexy Saam last seen on a train platform headed into the Dakotas—the centaur knew her VIN number and everything. Just my luck, as soon as it was my turn, the searchbot manning the counter glitched up. A drifting speech bubble announced technical difficulties and told me to try again in five minutes.

I scrolled around the Information Palace to kill time. There was news from all over the continent, and feeds streaming data from international territories long blocked by the Crunch, United, firewall. Dodging a thick-lipped duck trying to sell me a porno package, I swiped into Bad Kitty's Litter Box, a small, jewel-colored room, plush and vibrant red, like the inside of an organ.

Bad Kitty herself was a person-sized black cat wearing platform heels and a miniskirt. The yellow indicator light between her ears proved she wasn't actually logged on, and I quickly cycled through her avatar's preprogrammed responses. But I found I could get a limited bio by scratching a spot just below her chin.

"Where Bad Kitty lives is none of your damn business," the avatar recited. "She enjoys anime, RPG games, and rescuing gentech. She dislikes drones, surveillance, the capitalist nation-state, genderism, sexism, androidism, nationalism, prejudice, propaganda, liars, leeches, and the color pink."

I was half in love already.

The site was cluttered with an archive of funny objects—snow globes and ancient quill pens, porcelain kittens coded down to the whiskers, tiny anime figures doing battle across her shelves. I recognized the Arg from WorldBurn and reached out to check it for a price tag. But as soon as my fingers made digital contact, a long stream of data unfurled from its open mouth.

Somehow, she'd gotten hold of the military gear gifted to the Free State of New Hampshire by Texas, plus a bunch of confidential military reports giving updates on the progress of the fight against the Commonwealth. When I replaced the Arg, the data spiraled back inside of it, like water suctioned down a drain.

The snow globe melted into a low-quality holomovie: a pirated copy of the original, obviously, it showed a chiseled, high-cheeked elder of the Mormon Cabinet delivering his State of the Union, and rallying his troops to a holy war against Libertine. The New Kingdom of Utah was one of the most secretive countries on the continent, and their firewall, known as Heaven's Gate, had long been considered impenetrable.

"Need help?"

I whipped around, or at least my avatar did. The yellow indicator light nestled between the tabby's ears had turned green.

"I didn't see anything," I blurted out. I could feel my real body go hot with embarrassment. "I was browsing, that's all. I—I didn't even mean to come in here. . . ."

"Nice try, *cabron*." She quirked one ear in my direction. "I've got your history coded all over. In my line of business, I have to know who's sniffing around. But don't worry," she added, before I could speak, "on the

Road, there's no such thing as espionage. We believe that ideas should be free-market."

She was, I decided, half off her nut. Ideas never came free: there was always a seller behind them. But I didn't say so. "You're a hacker," I said.

Two delicate fangs appeared in the sleek gloss of her mouth when she smiled. "Power needs secrecy to survive. I'm trying to kill it." In one fluid motion, she leapt onto an old antique writing carousel and began contentedly licking a paw. "I like to think I'm in the redistribution business. Here. Check it out."

She hooked her tail around a delicate china mug and lobbed it toward me. I snatched it by instinct, and right away it shattered into hundreds of sentence fragments. Sorting through them, I landed on a familiar logo and felt a weird tingling up my spine, like something venomous was paralyzing me slowly. She'd lifted memos and emails straight from the Crunch, United, executive server, some of them from all the way back when our country was first pushing its borders after dissolution. And even though the hack had corrupted most of the files and made reams of text illegible, there was still plenty of top-secret intelligence in plain view.

"What is this?" I asked. Almost immediately, I wished I hadn't asked. Half of Crunch, United, was saying I was a traitor. I didn't need to prove them right.

"Proof," Bad Kitty said. "The first President Burnham wasn't trying to save the country. He was *betting* it would fall. That way he wouldn't have to lay up a trillion dollars in federal debt to some Russian oligarch's big win.[1] The rest of the world could burn, but he and Heller would have their Happily Ever After."

"Come on." I quickly collapsed the data back into a cup. I'd heard

---

1. Bad Kitty is insinuating here that Yana Rafikov's research was financed by the Kremlin, or by Kremlin-connected donors, even before dissolution. It is worth pointing out that this has never been officially confirmed. Still, Rafikov's post-dissolution importance to the expansion of Russian interests in mainland America is undeniable.

that idea before, or something like it: that when President Burnham realized his front-runner, Cowell, was going to lose out on the Burnham Prize, he triggered the collapse of the union himself. "You can't really believe it was planned. The riots and Texas's secession and the New Hampshire Declaration, the National Guard turning, the whole bag of cookies. No one could predict it."

"Maybe not what would happen, *specifically*," she said. "But some of the top dogs made bank on dissolution, believe me."

"Making money isn't a crime. Besides, the people at the top got screwed more than anybody. President Burnham wound up dead. Whitney Heller? Dead. Burnham's cabinet had to go into hiding."

Her whiskers began to jump. "Wow. They really got you whipped in the Federal Corp, huh?"

I stiffened. In real life, anyway. My avatar just trailed a few thought bubbles into nonexistence. "How did you know I was from the Federal Corp?"

"Relax. I'm no spyware. It's in the way you yawn your *a*'s. Besides, you just confirmed it." She leapt off the desk again, nearly whipping me in the face with her tail. "I bet you think President Burnham and his board of directors care about the working people too."

"I'm just using common sense," I said, a little coldly. Her tone was laced with a kind of know-it-all toity that put me in mind of old math holos. "What you're saying is just old conspiracy. It's crackpot."

There was a long, terrible silence.

"Crackpot, huh?" Her eyes flashed yellow.

"Look. That's just my opinion. . . ."

But in an instant, she'd logged off.

First Sammy, now Bad Kitty. I couldn't even talk to a girl online, when she was suited like a different *species*.

No wonder I was still a virgin.

———

At least the searchbot was up and running again. He was coded to look like a wizard and, according to the tag that appeared above his head when I placed a hand on the counter, his name was Patch.

"Howdy-do, John Doe?" he greeted me. The basic template for males was given the name John Doe and a design that included early twenty-first-century studs and a nose that looked like a Tater Tot.

"Can you really get information about anyone?" I asked him.

"Alive or dead," Patch said.

That meant he must have access to the old internet, too, back when access was free. Maybe it had been preserved, somehow, on the Yellow Brick Road.

"I'm looking for intelligence on Truckee Wallace. From the Federal Corporation."

Patch's eyes rolled backward, revealing whites imprinted with an hourglass. He was tabulating results forever, but eventually his eyes rolled back into place. "We're talking almost four million hits," he said, and my stomach dropped. "You check out our specials? Ten KB gets you one free."

"Give me all of it," I said. I needed to know how I'd ended up taking the hit for Rafikov. Maybe, just maybe, I could figure out how to clear my name.

The price he named was actually okay, but the actual transfer of funds was a pain. It turned out I could access settings by grabbing hold of a small wrench floating in the lower left-hand corner of my screen. The Real Friendo© winks, likes, and nudges originally gifted to me by President Burnham had vanished, likely suctioned off by the same HR manager who'd axed me from the system. Thank hell I'd been paid for some of the John Deere swag in good old-fashioned Texas greenbacks uploaded straight to the hard drive.

Even after Patch downloaded the compressed file to my deck, I scrolled the Yellow Brick Road for a while, enjoying being able to move around incognito, without worrying someone would try and pawn my head to the highest bidder. I was already getting used to it: the ring-a-ling of pop-up ads trying to shake my hand or coo me inside their shops; the clamor of unmuted conversation; users who poked or nudged or chatted me; the dizzying whirl of colors. It wasn't so very different from Low Hill, actually, except for all the giant walking lizards and the one-eyed aliens hawking plug-ins in a babble of different accents.

Zeb was spot-on when he'd said that everything I could think of and many things I couldn't were available for buy on the Road. High Palaces boasting every kind of drug, Old World and new. Arms dealerships shipped army-grade flavors impossible to find in real life. There was chemical growth and nuclear magic; a live zoo with straggly deer and a few dog pups for sale out of New Hampshire; company IDs, forged visas, human organs, even some new silicone-pour technology that could graft the look of some famous RFN-feed stars onto interested buyers— to the tune of a couple thousand bucks and a couple months' worth of agonizing pain.

But for all the color of the Yellow Brick Road, there was a dark side too. I passed what looked like a hospital only to realize it was an organ dealership, and found a parking lot filled not with rigs but with children. None of the kids was animated—they were like three-dimensional pictures—but waving at them brought up their stats, ages, weights, ethnicities, and, for some of the girls, whether they'd started their periods or not. I hurried away, feeling sick.

As soon as I swiped out and the Road evaporated, it was like a giant hand reached out and rammed me back into the portal café, into the uncomfortably hard chair on a set of almost-numb butt cheeks. When I took off my visor, I felt the depressions it had left on my cheeks. I must of been at it for hours.

The guy at the counter was still paging through that old-fashioned magazine. When he smiled, I saw gums black from opiate chew. "You enjoy yourself?" he asked.

I didn't know how to answer that. I felt shaken, high and sick all at once, like I'd just coasted a shiver trip all the way to the end.

He chuckled when I didn't answer. "You get used to it," he said, and went back to his magazine. "First time's always a bit of a trip."

"You use the Yellow Brick Road too?" I asked.

"Oh sure. All the time." He gave me the smile again, and it looked like someone taking a mouthful of something nasty. "They got the best girls on the Road."

I thought of the children standing in the sun, frozen in place in that enormous parking lot, and something cold moved up my spine. I left quickly.

19

There's no law in BCE Tech but what Tenner Blythe can keep on payroll. That means murder's illegal, but only for you.
—from The Grifter's Guide to the Territories FKA USA

It took me a Confederate's age[1] to find my way back to the Starlite. I didn't want to risk powering up my map overlay, which would beam my location right back to Crunch, United. But I'd almost never had to navigate without voice instruction, and somehow I kept circling the same blocks, landing in front of the same Missionary Depot, and its window display of Jesus ashtrays and Bible-printed rolling papers. I still couldn't kick the idea that every scrub on the street was eyeballing me, down to the cluster of whinnying transspecies tonguing drink from a wooden trough outside of a local bar.

So much space. So much world.

So why did I feel like there was nowhere on the whole damn planet I belonged?

Two gunslingers—with the sculpted faces of HR upper management enhancements, and a similar reek of things that grow in corners—turned up twice on different street corners, both times watching me narrowly

---

1. Due to the Confederacy's prohibition against technologies dating from after the dawn of the twentieth century, the nation was the punch line of dozens of jokes about tardiness. *A Southerner,* it was said, *would never say no to a party; he would just be two hundred years late.*

from beneath their Kevlar helmets. But since I was walking in circles, I couldn't be sure if they were tailing me or vice versa.

Finally I made it back to a dumpy street that looked familiar. A VR brothel called Imagine had spilled out a few dozen glaze-eyed slubs waiting out a downed broadband connection. Dodging the crowd, I nearly plowed straight into the two strangers again. And now I felt a gut of fear flip my insides.

They were following me, for sure.

I tried to move on, but one of them got his hand on my chest.

"Hey, dross. Not so fast." His teeth made me nervous. He had too many of them, and they were far too white. "You got a light?"

"Sorry." I tried to sidestep him again, and his friend crowded me.

"C'mon, brother-man. Not even a match? Nothing in that big rat pack of yours?" He tugged the straps of my rucksack so hard I stumbled.

"I said no." At least the street was still jammed with people waiting out the surge. I cast around for someone who could help me if things turned shake, but everyone was minding the business of paying no mind to anyone's business. It was that kind of town, that kind of world.

"Where'd you come from?" the first man said. His breath smelled like WinterFresh.

Before I could think of an answer, I spotted a flame-haired logo-girl pushing toward me, waving an arm high above her head and beaming an ad for bladder medication from her underarm.

"There you are. Thank fuck. I've been looking for you all over." She was flashing dozens of brands from her forearms, chest, and even forehead, bathing us all in a wash of neon as she got closer. Both men quick-stepped backward when she clamped onto my arm. "Rodge and Syara got a booth at the Sweat Drop. They're all waiting for us." Her fingers tightened on my elbow, leaving lettered imprints that spelled out *Kady's Candy Lube*.

I played along and let her haul me off down the street. She couldn't of been more than ninety pounds, with the half-starved look of a local tenant, but her grip was surprisingly strong.

Only when we'd left the two strangers behind us did she let go. "Sorry," she said. "You looked like you needed help. Those guys try and shake you down?"

"I'm not sure what they were after," I told her, even though I had the queasy feeling I did. Bleached teeth or not, the men looked like the kind of lowlifes who wouldn't be too picky about where their money came from.

"You're not from around here, are you?" She looked me up and down. It was hard to tell how old she was, because of all the branding. Mid-twenties, maybe.

There was no point in lying, so I shook my head. "How can you tell?"

"You got the brand-new look of a sprouted pimple two days off from popping. No offense." She flashed me a big smile. Even her teeth were tatted with little logos.

"None taken," I lied. Suddenly I was sick with exhaustion. Zeb, Bee, Fats, even Nikhil—most of the people I knew had turned corpse, and I couldn't help but wonder if I was the link of bad luck.

"Where you staying?" Then, when I hesitated: "I'm telling you, Granby's no joke on the far side of 3 a.m. But nobody messes with me." I must of looked skeptical, because she opened up her army jacket a little more to show me a massive Homestead Weapons & Securities ad embedded just below her clavicle. "I get half my revenue from the gun shop. And see? They give me product at a discount."

Now I saw about four different revolvers sewn into the inside of her jacket lining, along with a ream of extra shells.

"Thanks," I said. I was glad enough for the company.

We made it back to the Starlite quickly, and I was glad the girl didn't ask me any other questions. She didn't angle for a tip, either, just gave me a quick salute and waved me off inside. She might of been the only decent person in Granby.

Sammy was deep in sleep mode when I crept back into the room. I noticed she'd dropped in one of the twin beds and felt a stir of regret. She was trying so hard to be human. Why, I couldn't figure: we weren't anything to shout about.

There was no water in the taps until morning and the old moisture leaking through the ceiling smelled like rubbing alcohol, so I brushed my teeth with mouthwash, swept a couple roaches off my pillow, and slipped into bed. Somewhere down the hall, a pay-girl and her john were just getting into their rhythm—he kept tweaking her prompts until he had her at a register somewhere near high *C*.

But I wouldn't sleep anyway until I knew what I was up against, so I powered up my visor, careful to disable location settings first, and then swiped open the download pack I'd purchased on the Road.

The search results were ordered by registered impressions, but I could sort them by country of origin too: Patch and his spyware must of been squatting on two dozen foreign servers. Crunch, United's official release had been swiped, tapped, swapped, saved, liked, and shared more than 20 million times:

Early intelligence suggests a former Crunch, United, employee, Truckee Wallace, is engaging with a hostile foreign nation to distribute a federally prohibited substance known as "Jump" to employees of the corporation, in service of a wider plan to destabilize corporate stability and profit.

It is suspected that in an attempt to deceive and defraud the company of hundreds of millions of dollars in resources, and to disrupt production and the functioning of our Human Resources department, he intentionally orchestrated an explosion at Production-22 before finagling a way to escape on the bullet train that soon derailed, again likely due to his intervention.

He is armed and dangerous.

Even I could admit I made a pretty convenient scapegoat. Maybe the Federal Corporation was pinning the blame on me so they wouldn't take the scrap for letting Rafikov run roughshod over their firewalls. Still, Crunchbucks were trading at an all-time low, and even the Delaware dime was nosing up there in comparison.

I kept scrolling popular results. Plenty of people were calling me a hero, but they were all the kind of people who'd been trying for years to blow us up, so it wasn't much of a prize. I found chatter about the new drug flow, too, mostly about how and where to buy it—Medi-ware sites always sidled past the censors and sprouted new shiver addicts from free samples. Now they were growing would-be bodies for Rafikov's army of mind drones. Apparently the side effects—rage, hallucinations, nattering withdrawal, perspiration, paranoia—didn't rub anybody the wrong way.

Snortable circuitry, it turned out, came with some kind of sick high.

So where was Rafikov in all this? A cross-search of her name turned up only a few results, one of them a fifty-year-old thirty-second clip of her in the lab, pinned to a popular web feed of DIY science experiments that looked a lot like how-to bathtub-drug manufacturing.

The other result was a correction issued by the official data stream of the Commonwealth on the same day the Crunch, United, PR security issuance blew up the portals, so both reports somehow got screen-capped together.

Yana Rafikov, former American billionaire and founder of ThinkChip™ Technologies, had affirmed that she was not dead, as had previously been assumed and widely reported.

Yana Rafikov was alive! She'd been alive all this time. And even though I'd known it since the day of the summons, now it was official. It was like Jared always said: *You can't trust everything people believe. But you can't trust* anything *until people believe it.*

I couldn't think anymore. A headache was chewing its way from the back of my head to my eye sockets.

I was just shutting down the data—pained, once again, by the template of my factory-settings home screen—when I heard a creak in the hall outside my door, and then a whisper:

"In here."

In an instant, I was completely awake again. I wrenched off my visor and sat up, straining to listen. The pay-girl and her john were still going at it—had to give him credit, keeping up with a girl who could go twenty-four hours straight before she needed recharging—and for a few seconds I could hear nothing except the rhythm of their headboard shuddering the walls and the syncopated moaning of her presets.

Then: a noise at the door, like the scratching of a rat for entry. The door handle rattled, as if someone had taken hold of it and twisted.

Someone was trying to pick the lock.

"Sammy," I whispered. But she was dead asleep, emitting a soft pulse of blue light.

I had no time to reach over and shake her awake either. The door wheezed open. A wedge of light grew across the room, and traced the silhouette of a stranger on my ceiling. Then the door clicked softly shut again, and the light was suctioned back into the hall. For a second, I picked out the lung-scrape of another person's breathing. Then the darkness shat out a shadow coming toward me.

The first thing I could lay a hand on was the lamp.

"Don't! Truckee! Don't!" the voice was female and weirdly familiar. I tried to strike. She blocked me hard, thudding the lamp to the carpet and shattering it. At the same time, she tackled me. Her grip was surprisingly strong.

That, too, was familiar.

It was the ad-sales girl from the street—the Good Samaritan who'd escorted me back to the Starlite. Idiot. I'd led her right to my doorstep.

I tried to buck her off, but she had the advantage. She leaned in harder, pinning my wrists behind my head.

"Listen to me, Truckee." She had her ads powered off but when my eyes adjusted I could still see them leaching residual heat. "I don't want to have to hurt you, okay?"

"That makes two of us." It was squat reassurance from a girl suited up like a walking armory by her sponsor. My first time alone in a hotel room with a girl on my junk, and it was just because she wanted to kill me. "How do you know my name? Who sent you?"

She shook her head. "I don't have time to explain. You're in danger."

She really had some nuts. "I can see that," I told her. The butt of one of her Brownings was digging into my hip. Another rifle nosed at the space between my ribs.

"You don't understand. I was sent to help you. If you don't—"

She never finished. The door blew off its hinges in an explosion of sawdust and wood splinter. The ad-girl reached for her gun. But before she could get a hand on the barrel, a single crack of gunfire blew a hole in her chest and about two cups of blood and tissue onto my face. Her last few breaths sounded like someone trying to gasp air through a block of ice. When I heaved her off me, she slid into the space between the beds, clutching at the coverlet and rolling Sammy out of sleep mode.

I jumped to my feet as the men who'd been tailing me earlier came swagging into the room.

"Looks like we came spic in the nick of time." Now that the door was open, a green-yellow fluorescence from the hall lit up the hard angles of their jaws, the twin blanknesses of their faces. It was like every bit of soft had been planed away from their bodies, taking their humanity along with it. "I see you got an unwanted visitor."

"Three, actually," I said. I was still reeling from what the ad-girl had said. *I was sent to help you.* Was *she* the undercover agent President Burnham had nobbed me with? I wished I'd paid more attention to her brand sponsors.

One of the men kept his gun on me as his friend took a few steps forward. The way out was blocked, and I doubted anyone would hear me if I screamed—or care even if they did. The Starlite seemed like the kind of place that got its fair share of blood spatter.

"You got something worth a lot of fleek, kid," he said.

"You've got me confused for someone else," I said, even though they didn't and we both knew it.

"I don't think so, Truckee Wallace." He even made my name sound like an insult. With only a few feet of space between us, he slung open his jacket, revealing a long, evil-looking blade, sickle-shaped. A carving knife.

"I'm going to have to gut you, compadre," he said. "You don't mind, do you?"

I tried to dodge him but he was too quick. He threw his shoulder to my chest and cracked me back against the wall. His forearm against my throat nearly bent my Adam's apple backward.

Right away I missed the ad-tag girl. At least she smelled nice.

"Hey, Stash," his number two piped up. "There's a tin rattrap on your—"

He broke off suddenly. A terrible mechanical screech and a hiss of escaping smoke chattered his teeth together.

The guy leaning on my windpipe eased the pressure on my throat to turn around. His friend was having some kind of attack. His teeth nattered together. He began to tremble. He was drenched. He was sweating so hard, his hair rolled water onto the carpet. A terrible stink of scorched rubber filled the room.

Then his head began to smoke.

His eyes rolled back to reveal two question marks. His teeth fell out on the carpet one by one, each of them glistening white and bugged with digi-chips. He collapsed, sparking, on the floor.

Only then did I notice Sammy a short distance away, holding tight to the now-empty bucket of rainwater.

The second droid released me and went for Sammy. She skirted behind the bed, and as he scrambled toward her cracked him in the head with the bucket. It barely slowed him down. I tackled him before he could get his fist into her circuitry, and together we crashed to the floor, toppling another lamp from the dresser, shattering the lightbulb.

I wrenched his arm behind his back, and managed to shake the knife out of his fist.

"Slice him open!" Sammy was screaming. Her interface was blooming alerts about program errors and the danger of overheating faster than I could read them. "Open up his hard drive!"

But he was heavy, and strong, and bucked me off like I was no more than a fly. I swung out wildly with the carving knife as he turned, slashing a ragged wound across his back and ribs, severing his shirt and revealing a nest of circuits and wires tucked just beneath his flexible skelemold ribs. But the damage to his silicone skin didn't stop him for a second. I'm not even sure he noticed.

With a roar, he pounced on me. He got his fists around my throat. The pressure of his thumbs on my windpipe dizzied me, made stars turn in the airless dark behind my eyelids.

"You dumb motherfucker." He was practically growling. His face hovered inches above mine—still perfect, poreless, its manufactured symmetry distorted by his rage. "It was just a job before, you fin? But now I'm going to enjoy seeing you without your head."

I tried to hold on to the knife. But I was drowning, swimming in a murk of no air. Already I was losing the edges of my body. A thousand miles down my arm, my fingers relaxed. I was swimming in deep space. The blade of his knife was a curved sunrise.

I rose outside of my body. I hurtled into orbit. Stars exploded into being, then whizzed past me at a blur of speed. Interstellar fire burned at the edges of the universe. I hurtled toward the red haze of the sun—

And then began to fall. I slammed back into my body. I felt a burning in my throat. I tasted ash. The rain of stars around me was, I saw, a cascading shower of sparks.

The android on top of me was raining electricity down onto the carpet. His hair swam with the current. The blue light of a runaway charge swam across the open circuitry. Sammy had peeled back the shell casing of her knuckles to expose her wiring, and from the chatter of electrical static I knew she was reversing power straight down into his hard drive.

Then, I could of kissed her. If I knew what counted for her lips, at least. I was about to ask her. Then the world slipped away again, and left me sheeted in dark.

20

There's only three things in the world I won't sell: bodies, dead or alive; drugs, whether snortable or shootable; and false IDs, at least not within shooting distance of the cartel badlands.
—from The Grifter's Guide to the Territories FKA USA

We had to get out of Granby. The android guns might of been working the freelance bounty trade. There was plenty of it. Or they might of been shilling for somebody who'd be pissed off double just as soon as the hard drives telegraphed the final crash.

But first, we had to deal with the bodies.

Luckily, the Starlite had personal body pickers on ring-up; plenty of people had gamed it in its rooms, either from ODs or brawling or disease or being shitdirt poor. Within an hour, two ugly-looking scrubs were rolling up the ad-sales girl in a plastic tarp and a flea-bitten janitor was scraping up blood from the carpet fibers. Next to arrive were some scavenger types to take apart the androids—a tricky proposition, since this kind of high-swank model was usually registered with the Humanoid Regulatory Committee and pretty soon the court and its investigators would come knocking to ID them.

Before the scrap sellers could start their work, Sammy took up the carving knife and kneeled down by the hotbox who'd tried to gut me. She sliced a small flap in the silicone skin just behind his left ear, and carefully wiggled the microchip and serial number free.

"So we can find out where they came from," she said.

Just as soon as the room was clear of body litter, I nobbed on my visor back to the Yellow Brick Road, remembering the sad sack who'd tried to track down a Saam from her VIN number.

But this time, Patch was no help. He couldn't tell me squat besides they'd been manufactured in Crunch 203, one of the southernmost company outposts, in 2056. That was no surprise. Someone had been paying for upgrades to their systems—moth-eaten or not, they had the newest in silicone flesh and real-response tech—but Patch couldn't tell me who.

"That's International Trib law," he said. "I couldn't sell the data to you even if I could hack the federal system. Happened after the Starve,[1] and the brouhaha over androids picked for parts."

I didn't see it made much of a difference anyway; they'd obviously been after the reward, which meant others would come for it too.

Luckily, I'd seen plenty of fake-ID hotspots during my first cruise of the Road.

The nearest nav directory was shaped like a panda. It turned out I had to rub its belly before it would open its mouth to let me input search terms. A split second later, I was standing in front of a patch of basic building code, probably a standard template. A sign in the window read IDS.

---

1. The 2050s had seen the rise of the android rights movement, although the violence associated with it on both sides wouldn't erupt for another decade. As android liberation movements established chapters in nearly every country on the continent, they were almost universally deemed terrorist groups. Despite pockets of support, the average feeling—across countries and political affiliations—was one of suspicion and even outright fear. The beginning of major hostilities between the Federal Corporation and the RFN only added to the tension, especially after the early iterations of I.N.E.P.T. launched a full-blown attack on Silicon Valley in 2063, driving out the native human population and precipitating a scathing—and, many people felt, ill-advised—personal attack on the management by Mark J. Burnham, recently installed as CEO of Crunch, United. Anti-android aggression was further stoked by the RFN's response to his diplomatic gaffe, which resulted in crippling sanctions that hindered the Federal Corp's technological position for a decade, as well as by a series of erratic weather patterns that once again strained refugee camps and resulted in insufficient production at nearly all the major agrofirms. This tension culminated during the infamous "Copper Night," when vigilantes tracked down hundreds of androids by their serial numbers and disassembled them for scrap.

Inside, there was no customization, no special wallpaper or visual graffiti, nothing but beige walls and an avatar at the counter.

"I need a new ID," I said. "Something in sales or diplomacy. I'll be crossing borders."

"You shipping, or picking up yourself?" he asked, through a face of beige pixelation. Whoever owned the spot hadn't even bothered to give his John Doe hair or a nose or mouth. His face was a small blank circle, as if the flesh had been stretched over the rest of his features to wipe them. A plug-in to disguise his voice turned his words to garble.

"Picking up," I said. "I'm in Granby. It's part of BCE Tech. I need companion visas too. We need to get to San Francisco."

"How many?"

"Three," I said. I didn't have to think about it. I couldn't leave Sammy behind now. She'd saved my life. "But only one human. We also got an android—"

He cut me off before I could finish. "If you're in BCE Tech, you'll have to go through Texas. And Texas don't permit android travel. Humans only." I swear, even though he had no face, he managed to sneer.

"Since when?" I asked.

"Since they said so. Texas is hard country, boy. One of the hardest borders on the continent, and you know why? They don't like outsiders. They hate outsiders, in fact. If Crunch, United, didn't have those Chinese ships pointing nukes straight at Dallas, we'd all be flapping a single star on our flagpoles. What else you got?"

My visor was making me sweat. "One live animal."

"Quite some traveling party, commander." Even though his face was still blurred out, I could tell I had his attention. "You run one of them traveling zoos?"

"Close enough."

"Huh. I once saw a live elk and a two-headed rattler in a zoo. Turned out the elk was full of stuffing, though." There was a moment of silence while he whirled through his database of identities stolen, purchased, or commandeered from the dead. "You're in luck, cowboy," he said at last.

"Looks like a male Noah Turner turned up rotten a few days ago not far from you. Visa status: all-inclusive."

My heart leaped. All-inclusive status was nearly impossible to get: it required permissions from every member of the TCA.[2]

"Medic sales?"[3] I ventured a guess.

"Gentech control," he corrected me. It made sense. Ever since a blackout had busted open all the labs fifteen years ago, and thousands of modified species had escaped to chew havoc across the continent, every country was desperate for extra help to combat the damage.

"How much?"

There was a pause. "One thousand freedom bucks," he said.

"*One thousand freedom bucks?*" I'd never touched that kind of swag in my life. "You must be kidding."

"You're talking all access, pal. That kind of flow-through's gonna cost you."

That was more than triple what I had in the bank. "Can't you cut me a deal?"

---

2. The Trans-Continental Alliance, the continent's most important international organization, convened once a year in a secure location to adjudicate shared legal, political, and social challenges. It included delegates from the Real Friends© of the North, Crunch, United, the Dakotas, the Soviet Federated Frontier, the New Kingdom of Utah, Sinopec-TeMaRex Affiliated, as well as smaller countries like BCE Tech, Halloran-Chyung, and Florida Island. Notably, the Commonwealth and the Sovereign Nation of Texas had resisted joining, and refused to recognize the TCA as a legitimate political and social body.

3. Life-saving medicine was always in short supply across the continent, due to the deeply variant and often contradictory laws about moving product, the travel restrictions imposed by individual countries, and the lack of widely shared informational feeds. (In the Confederacy, for example, it was widely believed that gonorrhea could be cured by marriage; a commonly available cure for cancer in the Green Mountain Associated Intentional Communities was the application of crystals.) In the late '70s, after a deadly resurgence of the superflu ripped through much of the southern belt, precipitated in part by revivalist preachers urging the deathly ill to come to mass and pray for their sins, the TCA responsible for adjudicating issues of importance to the continent as a whole decreed that medics must be granted special travel clearance by all participating nations.

"Don't have to," he replied with a shrug, or at least a ripple. "I'm not the one needs into San Francisco."

If he'd been more than a scrap heap of data points, I would of punched him. "I need some time to think about it," I said.

"You do all the thinking you want, Einstein. Decide you want in— or out, as the case may be—just ask around Front Street for PJ's Bar between nine p.m. and midnight. Cash only."

I ripped off my visor to see Barnaby, Sammy, and Tiny Tim standing around in the splinters of the busted door, staring at me.

"What?" Sammy must of read the look on my face, but I was too cranked up to compliment her on her learning. "What's the matter?"

I knew squat where to start.

"President Burnham was pushed into a leave of absence, and the Crunch, United, board is blaming me for the attack on the bullet train," I said. It was like throwing darts into a sinkhole. "There's a bounty on my head, and half the continent thinks I'm a terrorist. The Russian Federation is trying to stop us from making it to San Francisco—"

I broke off as an earthquake of footsteps rumbled the floors, skipped the newly replaced lamp toward the edge of the side table, and percussed the headboard against the walls. For a second, I thought Blythe's bodymen had swarmed us already.

But it was just Mama Hazard, moving her ponderous bulk in as close an approximation of a run as she could manage. She stood in the doorway, wheezing heavily, sweating a butterfly pattern between her breasts.

"It's security," she managed to gasp. "Someone musta tipped 'em off."

Just then I heard the sound of their coming: the rat-a-tat of shots fired in the air to clear the streets, the shouting, and the drum of boots. One shotgun blast, two semiautomatic snapbacks, and a quick burst of machine-gun fire, repeat; each country had their own way of bursting bullets, like my mom always said.

"You boys gotta blow before they get here." She flinched as the rhythm of gunfire moved closer. "I'll try and hold 'em off downstairs. But don't count on me. These triggersticks got no friends except what they get paid."

She hustled off. Even her rolls of fat were quaking. Already, the Starlite echoed with the catcall of doors slamming and panicked shouts. I didn't know how many people were canned in its slummy rooms, but I would of banked almost all of them were doing something illegal.

"The fire escape," Sammy said. "Quick."

The window was painted shut—typical insurance so the shiverheads wouldn't jump when they came down. I knew our room had a view of the alley just for the trash-and-urine stink, which reached us even through the glass. The sky was just crisping with light around the edges. But it was still too dark to see what was down there, and how bad it would hurt if we dropped four stories.

We had a minute, two at most. I tried breaking the window with my fist but only cracked two knuckles.

"A little help, Tim?"

The stairwell threw up the sound of drumming feet, and the babble of Mama Hazard as she ran through excuses, requests to slow down, to hold on, to wait a goddamn second.

Meanwhile, Tiny Tim stood there staring at the window like he'd never seen one before.

"Today, Tim." My panic had a metal taste, like I was already sucking on a bullet.

After an infinity, he balled up his fist and swung. A haze of silica exploded onto the fire escape: a rusted, scaly, ugly-looking thing, screwed together with squat more than gum and Southern prayer. Four stories below us, dawn was just washing over a cluttered bum camp full of make-shift tents, old mattresses, and foul and moldering sheets.

"You sure about this?" Barnaby looked doubtful.

"You have a better idea?" I fired back.

When Tiny Tim reached out to test the railing, it came clean away in his hands.

"Oops," he said.

Slowly, the whole rattrap began to lean, and lean, and lean. I nearly threw myself headfirst out the window trying to catch it, as if that would of made a difference, but missed latching on by inches. With a crash and a shudder and a sigh, the whole thing collapsed—banging down into the reeking alley with a ring of steel that made my teeth ache, bringing down tangled ropes of hanging laundry, illegal water lines, sparking portal cables. Half a dozen slummers, nested in their tents and mattresses, dove for cover.

"Oops," Tiny Tim said again.

"We're going to have to jump." The fall might very well kill us, but getting rounded up by freelance guns would be even worse. If they shipped us into Texas, I would end up cut like Tim, or turned out onto a hunting preserve, or worse. What would happen to Sammy didn't even bear thinking about. "Go. Jump. Now."

Tiny Tim scratched the scar on his forehead. "I don't say so, Truckee. Never been much a fan of heights. . . ."

"*Do it.*" I gave him a push. It was a little like trying to fire a sneeze at a Soviet roller tank.

He just managed to fit through the opening. When he tumbled, I heard no scream or cry of pain. It was a very good or a very bad sign.

"You're next, Sammy."

Sammy didn't argue, but I knew from her interface that she had her doubts. She was more likely to break than any of us. I could only hope the tide of trash would cushion her fall.

I had to physically push Barnaby to the window. He was heavier than he looked.

"I thought goats were good climbers," I said. He got his jaw around the windowsill and wouldn't let go, no matter how much I pushed.

"*Climbers,*" he bleated, letting go of the windowsill. "Not fallers. Besides, that's a completely different species of—"

I shoved him, sideways and screaming, into the air.

Not a second too soon either: just then, five bodymen burst into the room, guns drawn, all of them shouting at me.

"On your knees!" The gun in front was screaming through a plate of metal teeth. "On your knees and put your hands on the ground!"

I grabbed my rucksack. I was clutching it to my chest when one of them fired, a blast so strong it shuddered my knees and blew me backward. For a second, I was sure I was dead. Then my knees cracked the windowsill and I surfed out into the air on a blast of artillery fire.

21

There's only three things in this world come reliably: death, programmed prostitutes, and grifters selling condom packs two days after you needed 'em.
—from *The Grifter's Guide to the Territories FKA USA*

For a split second, I was weightless.

A split second after *that*, I crashed through a loam of fabric, tenting and bedding, and landed on my back in a pile of festering mattresses. The wind was knocked clean out of me—a good thing, since the reek of shit was everywhere. High above me I picked out the window of Room 403 and the kickback blue of gunfire. High above that: the pale blue of a new sky, strung like bunting between the buildings.

Then a huge black planet with a ridge of white teeth gobbled the view.

"You're alive." Tiny Tim hauled me to my feet.

"For now," I said. Better not to jinx it. I didn't need any more bad luck.

Dark silhouettes crowded the open window above us. More shots cracked through the quiet. We skrimmed through the wreckage of tents and cardboard shelters, ducking blasts that missed clipping us by inches. Barnaby was leaping, dodging, twisting his way through the litter of human belongings. And Sammy rolled and bulldozed her way down the alley on her treads, taking down more makeshift shelters, dodging addicts startled out of their sleep by the hail of bullets.

We skidded around the corner as a bullet took a chunk out of the brick, then went sprint down streets gutting the last of the club kids and loaders into the morning. Tiny Tim still had his mitt clamped to my wrist, and it felt as if my arm would be ripped out of its socket. We zig-zagged through the streets until we'd lost the militia, at least for the time being.

"What now?" Sammy asked as we ducked under the darkened marquee of a last-century movie theater to catch our breaths.

"We need to get across the border," I gasped through a sharp pain in my side. When I placed a hand on my ribs I swore I could feel something solid pulsing under my skin, just below the scar I'd badged at Production-22. "I can get us through on an all-entry. But it's going to cost us."

"How much?" Tiny Tim asked.

I told him, and he whistled. "One thousand freedom dollars," he repeated. "I never even seen that kind of scratch."

"Do you have any money at all?" I asked him.

He rooted around in the pockets of his jacket—there were so many, he was forever losing anything he managed to scavenge—and finally came up with a handful of loose change from four different countries, some of it gummed with melted chew and stuck with flakes of bac. "I reck I got a dollar or so," he said cheerfully.

"Great. Now we need nine hundred and ninety-nine more where that came from." I was all out of patience and running high on temper. "Tell me something, Tim. What's the point in sales if you never sell *anything*?"

"Well, now, hold your horsepower. That ain't fair. I just sold a belt buckle the other day."

"You didn't sell it," I pointed out. "You traded it."

Tiny Tim shrugged. "Sure did. For a sweet pair of tweezers. Plus I cleaned up a few rounds of poker—some big-time general hails from over near Albuquerque bet me I couldn't beat a two of a kind, ace high. But I was straight flush. Fat pot too. It's been an age since I've seen a dead man's limb less it was rotted or wheeled by a picker."

"He bet you a *limb*?"

"Well, a hand. But it's got fingers and everything. One of his men lost the whole thing to frostbite up near the hinterlands. The general's been carrying it for luck ever since. Besides," Tiny Tim went on, "I got my eye on a big load out on the West Coast. A few months ago I caught wind of a big seed bank out in old California from a grifter down near the Kentucky temp camps."

"Oh, for fuck's sake." For years, there had been rumors of a massive seed bank, miraculously preserved, cataloguing everything that had ever sprouted, flowered, or rooted on the planet—and they had just as much truth as the idea that Alaska was now floating somewhere in the middle of the Pacific, buffeted by balmy trade winds, and that all the inhabitants had survived by surfing on the backs of coral salmon. "You must be the worst grifter I've ever known."

As usual, Tiny Tim didn't take offense. "Could be," he said.

I was suddenly exhausted. I leaned against the wall and closed my eyes. After a minute, I felt Barnaby's wet muzzle against my palm. When I opened my eyes, he was watching me, pityingly—like he, too, knew it was over.

"Well," I said. I gave Barnaby a careful pat. His fur was surprisingly soft. "I guess that's that."

"Now, that's no way to be squinting at things," Tiny Tim said. "What you need that visa for anyhow?"

I stared at him. He was flubbing with me or he was even dumber than the average brain case. "The Sovereign Nation of Texas has one of the hardest borders in the country." I spoke very slowly, to be sure he followed. "It's guarded by a bunch of trigger-happy maniacs and booby-trapped with mines."

"It sure is," Tiny Tim said. "Ain't no squeak of getting past the border without your papers. But it's Texas you want to cross, not the border fence, you vibe?"

I wanted to scream. Instead, I closed my eyes and tried to breathe deeply. "You're talking garble."

Tiny Tim plugged a finger in my chest and I opened my eyes again.

"I'm talking 'bout going *under* the border," he said. "I'm talking 'bout the Underground."

The Underground, he told me, was a squiggly place, made up of hundreds of branching arteries, some skant bigger than a drainpipe.[1] A network of tunnels, subterranean mining shafts, and safe houses, the Underground was kept up by sympathetics to the plight of the average run-of-the-mill teenage delinquent, dymo addict, thief, or bad seed.

Or grifter.

There was only one way in from Granby: a slubby watering hole called the Way Station, kitted with red shades that turned the light inside crimson and meant the place was friendly to payday girls.

"Here's how I reconned it for what it was," Tiny Tim said, cranking a thumb toward the hand-painted image of a wheel fading from its sign. "Plus I got to being friendly-like with the owner."

No doubt another woman who'd dropped panties for him. Someday I'd have to ask him how he did it. It sure as hell wasn't his conversation: only two days ago he'd asked Zeb whether people on the other side of the world walked around on their hands or grew feet from their heads.

The Way Station was a typical slop shop full of plug-ins and slicks juicing their devices, plus a few real-world games, including an ancient pinball machine. The whole place was shimmery and blue with vape

---

1 Many amateur cartographers have purported to map the entire Underground over the years, although it is doubtful that any one of them is close to complete. Some may even be deliberately obfuscatory, such as the map appended to *The Grifter's Guide to the Territories FKA USA,* which illustrates more than two hundred fictitious underground routes and entry points to the would-be traveler, most of them designed to entrap law enforcement or militia attempting to pursue criminals into the tunnels. Everyone is in agreement, however, that the first section of the Underground was completed sometime in the mid-2040s, to join several of Texas's largest penitentiary cities and human park ranges to subterranean escape routes.

smoke. In the dim, the men and women lumped together on barstools looked like rock formations or nuclear mushrooms growing in huge clusters. Behind the bar a woman with one of the funkiest cases of dayglo I'd ever seen was slinging drinks together from a collection of inserts, powders, and mixers. We took a seat at the bar next to a few squids who looked like the bottles were sucking down their faces and not the other way around.

"You got a leash for that fleabag?" She jerked her chin in Barnaby's direction.

Tim nudged a smile in her direction. "We ain't staying. Just looking for a shot of that fireball whiskey." I figured it for some kind of code: fireball whiskey was a toxic bathtub brew that came out of the revivalist tents in the Lower Belt,[2] and besides, he had no cash to pay.

The barkeep stared at him for a long second. "Fireball whiskey? You for-sure? That stuff'll kill you quicker'n a superflu." When Tim only nodded, she scooted out from beneath the bar, flashing me a quick view of her ass saddled into a pair of too-tight jeans. "Let me see what I got in the back."

She was gone a long time. I could barely keep on my stool—whenever the door opened, I expected it to bring a storm of BCE Tech guns for hire. I didn't like the way some of the regulars were eyeballing Sammy either. Granby was host to plenty of day traders who crossed the border to shill Texas product, and half of them would strip Sammy for parts just for the sheer fun of it.

"Fresh out," she said when she returned. "One of my regulars left the last of it swimming in the toilet."

Tiny Tim slid off his stool. "Think I might hit the throne myself." He

---

2. Decades of flooding had eroded the southern coastline, submerged Louisiana, and turned the former Mississippi into a glorified puddle. The Lower Belt was a disputed swath of swampland responsible for frequent epidemics of malaria and known for revivalist preachers that preached draconian religious laws and various forms of corporal and spiritual punishment. A common aphorism was that the Lower Belt bred two things: religion and mosquitos.

leaned in to whisper to me, "Count to thirty, then come on and follow me back."

Barnaby was nosing around for scraps in the corner by a fresh-vend machine. Tiny Tim took him by the ear and chunked him down the hall toward the bathrooms.

I counted to twenty, slid off my stool, and told Sammy to roll. By then I was sweating, and not just because of the swelter of vape and bac smoke.

Then a hand came down on my shoulder. An orange dayglo hand.

The bartender smelled like yeast and perfume. Not totally unpleasant. She pressed a flashlight into my hands when I leaned close. For a second, her purple lips were close to mine, her breath on my cheek, and I thought about kissing her.

"Not many people going west down those routes," she said. "I hope you know what you're doing."

I almost minded her the old saying about hope—only one "p" away from *hole*.

I passed into a narrow, reeking corridor that led past a kitchen swarming with gnats. Sammy, Tim, and Barnaby were gone. A supply closet packed with off-brand hop and stank-looking liquors fired a rat into the hall when I opened the door. One bathroom was overflowing with wadded toilet paper and a flush of filthy water. The only other bathroom was hung with a sign that read OUT OF ORDER.

Before I could try the knob, Tiny Tim leaned his head out and waved me inside. The four of us could skant fit: the bathroom was hardly bigger than a shower stall and just as moldy. The toilet seat was missing and a scrum of cigarette stubs swam across the surface of the green water.

Tiny Tim jimmied the cover off the toilet tank, plunged a hand inside, and rooted around for something. When he pulled, a hidden panel in the wall slid open.

"Ladies first," he said to Sammy.

Service stairs corkscrewed us down into the cellar, a cobwebbed place stacked with old cases of TomatoJuz™ and Lemon-Lime Fizz™, and lots of ammunition. I figured it was bolthole, like a lot of people were building even before dissolution. Back in the days when Halloran-Chyung[3] was growing its nuclear energy program and Texas minutemen were planting bombs and taking potshots across the border at night to sabotage them; it must of seemed like Armageddon was soon to ride in. Maybe it had. It sure seemed that way sometimes.

A portion of the double-strength cement wall had been demolished to make room for a warped wooden door. This opened into a rudimentary tunnel, knobby dirt walls shored up clumsily with wood planks. A cold, musty wind seemed to spring from its gullet, like somewhere deep in the earth, an ancient god had just loosed a belch.

Tiny Tim was first inside. Barnaby followed then Sammy. I fingered on the flashlight and edged forward into the dark.

---

3. Tensions between the two nations, which had abated somewhat in the '70s due in large part to a landmark water-sharing deal (in which both countries agreed to split the cost of building hundreds of massive desalination plants for the Real Friends© of the North in exchange for access from their pipeline), were once again escalating. Due in part to the rabid anti-android sentiment that the four-star general of the Sovereign Nation of Texas, Wyatt Radcliffe III, exploited during his campaign, after the liberation of many androids in servitude unleashed a flood of immigrants in that portion of the continent. Given the fact that the head of the Citadel in Halloran-Chyung was, at the time, an engineered person who had pushed forward a bill to legalize intermix marriages, the ideological rift was inevitable.

22

I first happened on the Underground after busting out of a jailing town in Texas. I'd been lockboxed for smuggling rope and tinder into the hunting preserves to give the felons a little leg up. I was so shit-scared of getting shipped to a preserve myself, I spent a solid three months living down in those tunnels. Wasn't half bad either. I met a mole named Lana who'd been there her whole life. She was practically blind, and thought I was just about the cutest thing she'd never seen.

—from *The Grifter's Guide to the Territories FKA USA*

We would have to move fast and stay on guard. The Underground was shitpacked with criminals and not all of them innocent. There were murderers, skinflints, thieves, rapists, and the usual flow of drug runners—the tunnels supposedly led all the way to the Denver Airport, the Juarez cartel's territorial base. There were full-time lurks skulked homes there too—a nasty bunch of worms, half of them off their straw. They scrabbled a living picking off travelers and stealing what they could, went blind as mole rats with backs crooked from bending over.

The first few hours we saw no one. Still, the echo of other voices and footsteps shook the hair on the back of my neck. We came to intersects where clumsy, hand-painted signs pointed the way to safe houses or dropped hints to other travelers. ASK FOR BERTHA AT WARRENSVILLE. THIS WAY TO FRESH WATER. WARNING: RED LETTER INN CLOSED. 203 MILES TO DENVER. C-JO WENT FOR HOP MEET @ 41 AND FREE. Four-by-fours and sandbags shored up the walls where moisture had started to decay them. Makeshift latrines—spongy cabins built over vertical mine shafts—filled the air with a sulfur stink.

All in all, it was the kind of safe route only Tiny Tim could scrum up.

I lost track of the hours. My SmartBand had only stubbly service, and started squeezing me every few minutes. Probably it needed a battery swap—but I couldn't help but think it was losing clock too. But at some point we came on a crude set of bunk beds, minus the bedding, and Tiny Tim suggested we screw down for the night. If it was night.

"A little down the road, and things get busy," he said. "Best to have both eyes open and your wits about you."

I wasn't hooked on the idea of staying underground longer than we had to, but I knew he was right. Besides, Sammy had run herself thin on batteries trying to light the way, and needed to switch packs.

I took a seat on one of the splintered bunks. Setting my rucksack next to me, I saw a hole where a bullet had passed clean through the nylon. The shell was clinging like a tiny silver bug to the leather-bound hide of the book Billy Lou Ropes had given me years ago. The thing had saved my life.

"You're finally reading the Bible, then." Tiny Tim toggled his chin toward the book and worked a finger in his nostril to clear it. "I figged you'd a' known about the Underground yourself. That's the reason I never said squirrel or bones about it. The Man used these tunnels all the time, to get back and forth to wherever the winds was blowing him."

I settled down, using my backpack as a pillow and my windbreaker for a blanket. The air was humid and it was cold. I was homesick—really sick, like missing Crunch 407 was a feeling curdling my guts. I missed my shoebox and my cot with its regulation sheets and the tissue-thin walls and the shower slicked with soap scum and even the Pervert, whose real name no one bothered with, blazing his junk in a too-small towel. I missed red-dust dawns and the river's shimmering chemical glow and the smell of baking shiver. I missed the warren of streets in Low Hill, even the Crunchtown Crunk© rattling our brains at six every morning.

I missed Jared and Annalee, especially, and knowing they knew I wasn't a terrorist, that I wasn't anybody at all.

I missed *being* a nobody.

I wished, more than anything, I could ask my mom for advice. For a split second, I could almost understand why Mark C. Burnham had done what he'd done, all those years ago during the last presidency—why he'd been willing to break the back of the whole known world just to keep Whitney Heller from disappearing.

But then—with a sudden sizzle of clarity—I realized my mom wasn't totally gone.

At least, not all the way.

As soon as Tiny Tim and Barnaby bedded down and Sammy switched into sleep mode, I powered on my visor: 19 percent battery, and no telling how long it would be before I would get juice.

Already, I was getting the shakes.[1]

Even the Underground was wired with the Yellow Brick Road. I navigated right away to the Information Palace and the searchbot, Patch. The system had been upgraded for high speed, so I didn't have to wait behind a logjam of other users.

"I need intel on a Sugar Wallace," I said. A growth of numbers near the hot-condiment window kept a register of intel buyers satisfied—it sped through from 2,230,00 to 2,436,000 even as I was standing there. "Originally from Charlotte, before it became a part of the Confederacy.

---

1. There were many different terms for the constellation of symptoms—ranging from anxiety and depression to outbursts of aggression and, in the worst case, psychosis— provoked by the sudden interruption of portal, AR, and VR access due to battery exhaustion or service disruption. There were, according to common estimates, more than 150 regional expressions to refer to this condition. Some of the more common expressions to describe the phenomena were: having the shakes, getting nettled, suffering from brain fire, or reality vertigo.

She worked in Crunch 407 until she died." Even my avatar had a hard time spitting out the word.

This time, Patch's eyes barely flashed to hourglasses until they lit up again. My mom's download file was less than 20MB, so thin it could of slipped between paragraphs of all the rumors about me. I even thought Patch looked disappointed—the whole kit and noodle was only two Crunchbucks.

"That's it?" he said. "Nothing else?"

"Sorry," I said. Seeing my mom's data pack made me even sadder, somehow, and I almost regretted forking for it.

I wasn't ready to scrum back into the fester-pit of the Underground. And I wasn't ready to read the data pack either. Instead I scrolled to Bad Kitty's Litter Box, hoping to see her. But when her avatar flicked her tail and greeted me with standard code, I knew she was logged off.

I nearly jumped out of my pixels when an unfamiliar advertisement shoved his way rudely into my sidebar.

"Hey, man, check it out. I pulled some new recommendations for you based on previous search terms." He sounded like an algorithm wrapped up in a cloud of New Los Angeles vape. "You interested?"

I felt a little like someone had just caught me on the shitter with my pants cabled to my ankles. "Can't you knock or ping or message me or something?"

He held up both hands. "I'm not the one who enabled pop-up ads in my privacy settings."

"My . . . ?" I shook my head, even though he obviously couldn't see me. "No. Look. Sorry. I'm tight on cash, anyhow."

Somewhere beyond the immersive fog of the simulation, Barnaby reminded me testily that *some* mammals were trying to sleep. I switched into manual chat mode.

The avatar still didn't budge from the window of my home screen. "Are you for-sure? Based on your searches for Truckee and Sugar Wallace, ninety percent likely to meet your satisfaction."

The whole thing reeked of scam, and his jumble of ad-speak was giving me a headache. *Thanks. But no thanks.*

"Last chance. This one's a whopper, for real." By which I banked he meant expensive.

Non me lo posso permettere. I was so impatient I wasn't inputting carefully enough, and somehow swapped into translation mode instead of calling up an exclamation-point burst.

By the time I reset my language preferences to Corporation English, the avatar had scrammed. To make sure ads wouldn't keep dropping in on me unannounced, I lost a few minutes navigating my privacy settings, coded to look like a huge prison town. Annoyingly, I had to round up and lock up all of the things I didn't want crashing my interface, like pop-up ads and surveys.

I was just shoving newsletters into their own cell block when a hint bubble floated toward the top of my screen and then burst into a wisp of lettering: *Looks like someone is trying to get your attention!*

I turned around, expecting another pop-up that had ducked the settings change. But it was Bad Kitty, tail swishing, eyes large and green, ears stiffly at attention, her whiskers curling around a shy smile. I was so surprised I couldn't pin a single thing to say.

"Hi," she said.

Hi. I tried to think of something else to swipe, but everything I could think of sounded bunk.

She crossed her arms. Or paws. Whatever. "What? What is it? Why are you looking at me like that?"

Of course, I wasn't looking at her like anything. My avatar's face was still template.

Which meant she was nervous.

I didn't expect to see you, that's all.

Her tail gave a vicious flick. "Then how come you logged into my site?"

In real life, my whole face caught fire. *How did you . . . ?*

"I told you, I got special spyware. Besides"—she half-shrugged a furry shoulder—"you're the only visitor I've had in a month."

That cracked the tension. I sent a couple laughs bubbling her way. A second later a ringing bell signaled that Bad Kitty had switched over to manual mode, and a small bubble of dialogue appeared over her head. *I hate chatting when other people are in manual.*

Yeah, me too. It feels so . . .

. . . lopsided, we both swiped, at exactly the same time.

Her whiskers twitched. *Exactly.*

I took the plunge. *Look, I'm sorry for what I said to you last time.*

That's okay.

It's not *okay.* I exploded a few frowny faces with a pipe bomb for emphasis. *Like you said. The Federal Corp got me whipped. At least, they used to.* I was thinking of the board, and President Burnham's forced leave of absence, and the way I'd been set up to take the heat for Rafikov and her ambitions.

That's okay. You wouldn't believe the propaganda the Real Friends© feeds try to spoon us.

So. She was from the West Coast. No accent meant she was probably rich too. Out of my league, for sure.

Already, the quiet had gone on a beat too long.

So what else you got in your archives? The words jumped out of my fingertips before I even knew they were moving.

She hesitated. Her tail was going hard: she was trying to figure whether she could trust me or not. But finally, she lobbed me a link to a new window.

As soon as I touched it, the sim morphed. Once again we were standing in the Litter Box, but this time all the miniatures on the shelves had unrolled pictures, videos, spools of data. She crouched on the floor, and a shudder worked its way from her tail to her nose; a second later, she coughed up an index onto the carpet.

I sorted through the streams, straightening them into topics, countries, and years. This was the admin view, and it was full to popping with data.

Military requisition forms from the Dakotas. Nuclear agreements signed by Halloran-Chyung. Intercepted messages from the SFF[2] to Russia. What she had would of fetched hundreds of millions of bucks on the open market. Of course, what she had could also get her busted for espionage by half the continent.

Even though just the knowledge made me accessory, I couldn't stop looking. A fifty-year-old exchange between the first President Burnham and Albert Cowell at Laguna-Honda nearly blew my jaw off its hinges. The messages were cluttered with coded say-so about the Burnham Prize and Cowell's progress. One message even dropped a line about the "unexpected psychological complications" of interspecies neural-tissue transfer, and I couldn't help but think of the story Barnaby had told me, about his father's shame and suicide.

When did you get into the game? I swiped her, still untangling the massive hairball of confidential government records.

Oh, forever ago. She waved a paw. *You remember the Mars Mission Launch?*[3]

Barely. I was only four.

I was six, she wrote, and my heart stuttered. It was a stupid thing to be excited about, like we had any chance of meeting, whether she was eighteen or eighty. She was a stranger, and could of been maul,[4] a serial killer, one of those fur fetishists, or all three. *The funny thing is we didn't even* hear *about the launch in the RFN. But I'll never forget where I was when the rocket blew.*

A tickle of heat moved across my neck. *What do you mean, when it blew?*

For a long time, she just stared at me, whiskers drooping. *You didn't*

---

2. The official, if rarely used, designation for the Russian Federation was the Soviet Federated Frontier.
3. There were several aborted launch attempts between 2069 and 2072, but Bad Kitty is no doubt referring to the final launch, on January 22, 2072.
4. A Crunch, United, slang term meaning "ugly."

get the news in the Federal Corp? The words whispered regret into my audio feed.

No. I was glad we were in manual mode. My mouth was as dry as a mothball.

I could tell by the way she started worrying the carpet that she wished she hadn't let the truth slip. *Pieces of rocket burned through the Holodome. It was the first time I'd ever seen rain. It smelled just like ash, because of all the debris blowing through.*

She'd dropped another hint about where she lived. The Holodome was world-famous Nuevo Angelino swank: a multitrillion-dollar float of semi-impermeable balloon gas and a massive holographic projection to keep the skies blue year-round. But I was in no mood to celebrate.

All the news we got was no news at all.

Well, sure. Halloran-Chyung wouldn't want the Russian Feds to know the truth. Crunch, United, must of buried the story.[5]

I thought of all the times Jared and Annalee and I had played Imagine and swapped stories about the Mars colonizers and what they were getting up to while we were lumping through Standard classes or working the line.

All along, they'd been nothing but carbon particles in the New Angelo sand.

I'm sorry, Bad Kitty wrote.

That's all right. I just . . . never knew.

That's just how I felt, when the rocket blew up, I mean, I hadn't even known there was a rocket. It was like . . . like my reality blew up too. Her nose twitched. *I wanted the truth. And I knew no one was going to surf in and hand it to me.*

---

5. Thanks to its zero-tolerance policy for the military aggressions of the Sovereign Nation of Texas, the strength of its nuclear power program, and the strategic alliance with the Korean Peninsula, Halloran-Chyung was a growing power on the continent and an important ally to Crunch, United. During the race to colonize Mars, its primary competition was against the Soviet Federated Frontier, which fingered the Great Lakes and took up a sprawling portion of what had formerly been the Canadian border.

That's amazing, I swiped, with some animation I hoped she wouldn't think was cheesy. You're *amazing.*

Not really. Just stubborn. But I was learning to read her whiskers, and could tell she was pleased.

Listen. I should try and catch some sleep. But if it's bank, I'll come back and visit soon.

Bank. Her whiskers jumped again. *I never heard that one before. Out here we say "green."*

For a second we stood there, avatar to avatar, smiling at each other. For a cat, she was especially beautiful: soft-looking, perfectly groomed. I had a flash of what she might really look like: sharp-chinned, with long, silky bangs that fringed her eyes.

I wondered if her eyes were green in real life too.

23

We woke to voices. I barely had time to tap on my flashlight before two blockheads lumbered past us, big and crude-looking, like they'd been winched through a faulty printer. We used it as our cue to get up.

Before long we were funneled into a busier tunnel, with more shit-holes, more graffiti, and a lot more paddle traffic: travelers and moles, hunchbacked and eyes glazy with cataracts; hustlers and grifters; run-ners and slicks peddling battery charges and lanterns that tapped out five minutes after you'd bought them; plus some regular commuters who wanted to avoid the border fees. Tim hadn't lied: in general, it was the ugliest, rudest-looking crowd I'd ever seen, counting Bethesda and the Devil's Army, although there were a few scared-looking rab-bits keeping their heads down and their hustle on, just trying to get out of Dodge before they were busted for stealing candy bars or what-ever. There were a fair few androids, too, trying to duck Texas poli-cies.

Almost everyone, I noticed, was going the other way.

Some hours later, Tiny Tim spotted a face he knew and let out a shout. A second later, he was throttling the life out of a skinny-looking cowboy missing one of his arms to an old infection.

His name was Kink, and it turned out Tiny Tim knew him from the grifter routes they traveled. He had skin the foamy color of Annalee's, lots of plastic teeth, and a few prosthetic whizzes and bits: a pinkie finger that doubled for a flashlight, some metal teeth that sent alerts from his visor directly through his skull cap, even a nifty metal nose he could shut down when he wanted. He'd once been a flyboy, smuggling false permits and visas, and high-well paid for it, but the work had gotten too dangerous.[1]

"Was a time plenty of the border boys looked the other way," he explained. "They remembered dissolution, and half of them were secretly unionist anyway. But things have changed." He shook his head. "Two things you can count on in this world: that change will come, and that you'll wish it hadn't."

Kink spent nearly half the year underground and knew the secret turn-offs and the caves where pools of vivid water condensed luminescent mushrooms on the walls. Normally, the local moles would chase off strangers from their territory, but Kink was well-known and had slowly earned their trust by bringing down supplies from the surface to leave in their camps. We camped on a lip of stone at the edge of a hot springs after bathing, and sprawled out naked together while a mortified Sammy went into deep sleep. Kink gathered some purple mushrooms from the walls he said would give us funky dreams, and we cracked open a case of Mini Cheddar Frank 'n' Roll Chili™ he'd bought off one of the underground sellers. It was obviously counterfeit—the balance of chemicals was all wrong—but I was so hungry, I'd of eaten shoe rubber.[2]

"I been in every country across the continent three or four times the

1. In addition to maintaining tight control of the illegal drug trade and its cross-continental distribution routes, the Juarez cartel had recently moved to assert their ascendance in the fake-ID trade.
2. Not a euphemistic expression: one of Crunch, United's most controversial snack foods, the Mini Cheddar Frank-n-Roll™ required no refrigeration, lasted indefinitely, doubled as a chew toy, and was comprised predominately of shoe rubber.

last decade," he told us. "And I tell you, only thing changes deep down is the stank. In the low countries you got the stank of mold and shitjuice. In the Dakotas, it stinks of dirty money. All of Denver reeks like shiver and Russians, the Confederacy like the fester of an armpit hole, and the Dust Bowl has the worst stank of all of them, because there ain't nothing but death in every direction."

Now Kink worked as a flesh drone, delivering letters and small packages in and out of countries where the risk of censorship or interference was high, which was most of them. It was Kink who let drop the info I would of sworn the pop-up ad on the Yellow Brick Road had been trying to sell me: Mark J. Burnham had been forced to resign as CEO, though he'd been allowed to keep his title of president, and had been hustled into some secret rehab on Florida Island. The shareholders blamed President Burnham for being soft on terror—there were even rumors of possible sympathies in that direction.

The whole thing, Kink said, was notching us toward another world war.

"Now the board is deadlocked in negotiations and can't decide who to nominate up," he said. "Meanwhile the director of international sales is threatening sanctions against Texas if they won't co-grind in the manhunt for that terrorist blew up the bullet train." Luckily, he didn't know he was talking to the country's most wanted, or I felt sure I'd wake with my intestines hooked to his mail pack. "But to be true with youse, things been flowing in that direction for years now. This cold-war shit was bound to burn hot sometime. Crunch, United's one of the *worst* offenders. Blowing up oil tankers in the Gulf and claiming it was RFN interference. Squeezing every last dime from its colonies and even doing back-end deals with the cartels. Oh, yes," he said, catching view of my face. "The Federal Corp's been running Dymase™ to shiver addicts all over the world. How else you think it keeps its market share?"

Tiny Tim told him about getting run out of Granby and I jimmed him off before he could let too much slip. But Kink just waved off my explanations.

"That's a'right, kiddo. You mind your beans, and I mind mine. Just glad you made it out with both balls intact. Seems like you had a close shave." He fingered the bullet hole blown in my rucksack.

"You'll never guess what saved this turkey's neck either," Tim said, and turned to me. "Go on. Show him the book."

I'd never seen a change like the one that squeezed Kink's face into a look of wonder. He handled the cracked leather cover like it might fall apart if he breathed too hard. He stroked the spine with trembling fingers.

"My, my, my. I haven't caught a whiff of one of these in years," he said. Then, a little more sharply, "You ain't thinking of selling, are you? I'll give you fifty freebacks for it."

I actually thought about it, until Tiny Tim laughed. "You still a son of a bitch, Kink, even if you gave up grifting. The book's worth ten times that and you know it."

"Old habits die hard." Kink crooked me a guilty smile. When I reached for the book back, he held on tight until the last second. "I'll tell you one thing, kid. Everything I know about the game, I learned from that book you have there in your hands. To us buy- and sell-boys, that book is good as our Bible. If I ever meet the grifter wrote it, I'll get down on my knees and kiss his toenails."

Somehow, listening to Kink talk, the book began to feel like a message, like something alive that tethered me back to Billy Lou, to my mom, to those old maps we used to walk with our fingers together.

It wasn't too bad there on the ridge with the steam of the springs hissing vapor toward the luminescent mold and the mushrooms slowly blowing dreams through my blood. But my mind kept turning over what Kink had told me about Burnham. With war brewing, I was running out of time to clear my name—and to stop Rafikov.

For the thousandth time, I wished I could just press a button and shut down into sleep mode, like Sammy could. Instead, I opened up the *Grifter's Guide*. If nothing else, I figured the static type would put me to sleep. Wedging my flashlight between chin and chest, I cracked open to the first page.

INTERLUDE

THE GRIFTER'S GUIDE TO THE TERRITORIES FKA USA

I've been a grifter my whole life, in one way or another. Even before the territories were the territories, even when there was a United States, I was a grifter. There were other names for it back then. Hustler, scamster, con. I used to steal candy from the back of a local store and sell it back to the owner. I could pick a man's pocket and get a reward for returning his wallet. Some kids are born good. Some kids are born bad. I always had a little of the devil inside, you could say, although I don't go in for the God crap. But then again, who was I really hurting? When the world's gone mad, you can either go mad with it, or you can go your own way.

I always chose my own way.

I've been crisscrossing these territories for twenty years now. Been to every country and in all the ungoverned lands, too, everywhere except Alaska, which they say might not even exist anymore. I've met plenty of people on the road, and I've filled in from their stories where I've had to.

My goal in writing all this down was simple: to help the wanderers and adventurers and grifters like me to set down what's out there and waiting, so you don't get caught with your pants around your ankles and a bayonet in the back when you're just trying to get through Georgia.

Wherever it is you're going, I hope this book helps you get there.

I can't explain it, but that line really hit me, just punched me somewhere in the spleen. I tried to scroll forward and then remembered that with books you had to turn the pages. They were sticky with wet and it took me a click to get the hang of it.

> *The Underground began as a single route connecting Odessa,[1] known as the unluckiest town in Texas, to the Oklahoma border. Odessa also happens to be the birthplace of Mr. J. C. Straw. Coincidence?*
>
> *In the past twenty years the Railroad has grown to one of the biggest illegal trading routes in the country. Yes, I say trading routes, except what's traded here is freedom, pure and simple. Criminals go in, free men come out. Poof! Like a magic trick. Except I met some people who choose not to come out at all.*
>
> *The moles get nice and cozy down there where there's no sun to shine on them and police to pick them up or militia to take potshots at them just for walking or looking the wrong way. There are men down there blind as worms who can smell prey instead of seeing it, men in the deepest tunnels crab-walking on all fours, babies born in darkness never learn to spell a word but'll steal up behind you and take your guts out with their bare hands—*

A spider pinged off my elbow and I nearly screamed.

The chapter was making me twitch. I turned back to the beginning.

GARY, INDIANA. 20—

> *Ah, Gary. If New Jersey is the armpit of America, Gary must be its grundle: just as smelly, uncomfortably in between, leading straight down into the asshole of the soul. It hasn't improved in the twenty years since I was last here, sadly. If anything, it's worse. The strip clubs are still around, although half of them been converted into dollhouses since the state legalized android prostitution last year.[2]*

---

1. Now known simply as Straw Rehabilitative, for the vast prison complex that dominates it.
2. This is one of dozens of indications that suggests that the *Grifter's Guide* was written sometime between the spring of 2065 and the fall of 2067. The Supreme Court of Sinopec-TeMaRex Affiliated legalized the use of Sexy Saams for "entertainment and

The whole place is crawling with guttersnipes and bums, dimeheads and hopheads and flopheads and some good old-fashioned pipe smokers, plus a bunch of Devil's Army freaks convinced the gateway to hell must be in one of the smokestacks shitting chemicals to the sky every day. You can't blame 'em. The sun doesn't even rise out here anymore. The sky just turns from yellow to green, like it's in different stages of getting sick . . .

The chapter wasn't over but I skipped ahead anyway, marveling at all the places this nameless grifter had visited, cities I'd heard of barely or not at all.

AKRON—

I've always liked the Midwest, long as you can avoid the cannibalistic cornfields and potato spuds so heavy they plunge right through to the aquifer. Even now that the Sinopec-TeMaRex conglomerate's got their corporate fingers on every last strip of soil, and sent tens of thousands of good people to die pruning back fast-cycling crops that didn't get the message about the sale, I like it. There's something about the big sky, and the sun hitting all that pavement and its consumer logos. Good people too—friendly, and all of them eager to hit their daily spend limit to prove their citizenship to Big Business.

But mostly I like the engine growl that stutters the roads like a constant heartbeat: for a grifter like me, there's something about the wheel capital of the continent that just gets my pulse up. I like the stink of old diesel and the sweet rot of methane from the garbage plants, all those shiny hangars rolling off private shuttles for the high altitudes of New New York and cattle cars for its lower ones; pouring out flycraft for Halloran-Chyung and water

---

recreational purposes in exchange for profit," in accordance with specific regulatory limits, in 2066, despite all of the public outcry about sex trafficking in light of renewed conversation about, and awareness of, android rights in that decade, prompted in part by the revolution in Silicon Valley. Many people attribute the tremendous growth of radical pro-android rights organizations in Sinopec-TeMaRex Affiliated to the Thompson Bill, as it came to be known, for the notoriously lascivious Supreme Court judge who wound up casting the deciding vote, Warren Thompson.

carriers for the dry countries and souped-up armored tanks for the swells of New Los Angeles. The real industry isn't in the cars, see, but in the myth of having somewhere decent to go . . .

Denver, Cartel Territory—

Like they say, you go to Denver to die or you don't go at all. So I admit I wasn't feeling too swell about the outcome when I got myself turkey-trussed and frog-marched through the Underground tunnels toward Terminal Z. It was all my fault and I knew it—I'd heard a dumb rumor that the cartel would cut a deal to grifters passing through so long as they weren't carrying trade that might cut into the cartel's business. I should of known better than to cred it, but hey, like they say—hoping is the deadliest thing next to giving up hope for good.

The problem was that I was late on my route because of a freak radiation storm east of the Rockies and the tornado-blown wildfires that blacked air for two hundred miles because of it. I had a pack full of brand-new Silicone Celebrity Faces™ in all the newest fames—a top haul, worth as many likes and winks in the Real Friends© as any one of their feed stars could get in a year. So I tossed a coin and landed with two cartel foot soldiers and four AK-47s between them.

Things weren't looking too good for yours truly until I had to unload my pack in front of the big boss and lo and behold he started squealing like a ten-year-old Glitterati at her very first VR concert. Turned out he was quite the fanboy of the Xtreme-Feed Star Jonny X Crash, and for the price of Johnny's Silicone-face—and the promise that with a little skin bubbling and bone crushing and mold setting he, too, could have those world-famous chiseled looks—I was on my way again . . .

The Lowlands—

Water, water, everywhere, and not a drop to drink—unless you want some fierce runs and black vomit to go with it.

For a week straight I've been sloshing through the stinking stew that used to be solid ground—towns and churches, roads and fast-food chains, all of it now washed out or furred over with the same black-green mud that sticks to everything. Back in the day we used to hear about the Flood back in Sunday school, the great rains that came to wipe out a sinful world and start the whole game fresh. Well, looks like even God's running out of energy to get the job done how it should be . . .

Least I did some good trade with some alligator folks, brought up some decent guns from the slop and been drying 'em out for weeks. They're good enough people, the alligators, but man, could they all use a breath mint. . . .

GOD KNOWS WHERE–

Today I spent a good twelve hours sorting through the wreckage of an old torch town, burned some twenty, thirty years ago by my count, probably when the flu was spreading. For the most part I got nothing but old char turned by the seasons into grey mud, a few ribbons of melted plastic to off-load for poundage, some sheet metal I might sell to a salvage yard.

I was about to call it quits when I caught something winking at me from the rubble of past misery. It was a pretty little bracelet, sapphire and gold, still looped around the slender little wrist bone of a skeleton almost totally intact beneath a burial mound of decades-old trash. I swear to God it's like that woman had been lying in a surf of mud and shit and plastic just waiting for me to come along and find her. And what I get for selling this pretty little piece will keep me on my feet another three, four months even with no sales at all. So twenty, thirty years ago this biddy, whoever she was, made a pact with a no-name grifter who would one day come to her half-starving. She made a trade, even though neither of them knew it yet. Her life would buy him a few more months. Time to get back on his feet. Time to survive.

You see, we're all of us grifters, in the end. We're just a little too small to keep sight of the real tally.

THE SOVEREIGN NATION OF TEXAS → THE DUST BOWL

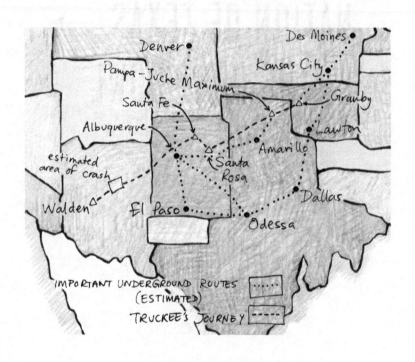

24

You can make a fortune selling to the Texas prison towns.
Just make sure to bring plenty of lubricant.
—from *The Grifter's Guide to the Territories FKA USA*

In the morning—or whatever counted for morning underground—we said goodbye to Kink and went on our way. A bunch of mole children scrabbled along behind us, begging for food and usables, until Barnaby chased them off by bleating.

We must of been fair deep into Texas: rodeo traffic picked up, with human bulls still saddled up and bleeding from where the spurs had stuck them. Even the Underground started to sprout anti-android signs; we passed at least three shitters that declared, unnecessarily, they were for humans only.

I don't know how long we walked—it might of been two days, or twelve. It was crazy how quickly those tunnels broke time down to mush, turned around my rhythms of waking and sleeping, red dawn and smog-set, work and sleep. Time was flashlights and echo calls, pee breaks and pit stops to decode the signs scrawled where the tunnels forked. Space was the taste of mold spores in the air. When there was light to read by, electrical bacterial, I kept on reading *Grifter's Guide,* flattening myself down into those pages, into a fantasy of escape.

In the half dark I could only think of one thing. Why?

Not just the usual whys—why President Burnham had chosen me for this insane mission, why Rafikov might want to loose an army of black-eyed fry-boys in twenty-four different countries on the continent, why HR had pinned all the blame on me.

This was deeper. Why any of it? Why worming through the earth, why crawling over a planet that had clearly had enough and was doing its best to boot us off into an early curfew? What was the point for me? What was the point for any of us?

We were all going a little nutty. At a certain point, Barnaby decided to rap us his memoir from page one. He kept quoting authors he'd digested that none of us had ever heard of, and was growing teary-eyed over passages from something called *No Exit*.

Just when I thought I would die, or *he* would, because I'd killed him, we came to a sign Tiny Tim recognized as the one we wanted. And after two more turns, a staircase.

My first sight of the Sovereign Nation of Texas was an old crank screaming her gourd off and a flabby organ-shaped piece of silicone coming at my head. I later found out it was called a hot water bottle, and had been used for at least a decade to gently squeeze alcohol into the rectum of Werner Castlebottom, Bernie Castlebottom's second husband.

Then she spotted Tiny Tim and quit trying to bludgeon me to death. "Oh, it's you," she said. "I'll be rammed, Tiny. Time ain't done you any favors."

"Must of been saving all of 'em for you," Tiny replied.

"Ain't that pretty? Too bad they didn't cut your idiot tongue out with your brain."

Bernie Castlebottom wore a purple bandanna and a smock-coat that showed off the billowing rolls of flesh beneath it. She turned her head to shout at someone I couldn't see. "Goddammit, Werner. What'd I lip you on about that door staying locked? These fools damn near give me a heart attack, popping up in my living room."

"Figged I did," said a man's voice from somewhere beneath the festering studs mounded in the corner.

"You *figged*." When Bernie laughed, she sounded like she was trying to cough up her larynx. "You ain't never figged a single thought in your life. You supposed to have to knock," she added, turning to me. I guessed this was her way of saying sorry. "Come in, come in. You'll find everything's the same around here only worse."

"So it goes," said Werner. It turned out he was the mound of festering studs, a mountainous creature exuding poisonous fumes of alcohol, and wedged so tightly into an armchair I couldn't see how he'd ever find a way out.

"You shut your grille," Bernie said. "Ain't nobody talking to you." Then, spotting Barnaby: "Now, who's this cute little thing?"

Barnaby dipped his head to his hooves. "Charmed, madam," he said. "And my apologies for interrupting you so rudely."

"Blood and blisters, he talks too. What happened, Tiny? They lump your brain over to this little slice-and-dice?" She wasn't far off, actually, but there was no reason to get into it and I was trying hard not to think about what would happen to Barnaby out in San Francisco. "You're welcome here anytime, sugar, with or without these other folk."

She was less enthusiastic about Sammy. "Here in Texas we don't keep truck with robots. Never trust a bit doesn't shit sitting down.[1] That's what my dad always said. Still, I suppose since it's here along with you . . ." She grunted. "Come on outside. You could fry a chicken in this heat."

We followed her through a kitchen the size of a postal stamp, buzzy with flies. She sent us out to the porch while she went to wrassle something cold to drink.

The Sovereign Nation of Texas was saggy shacks and rundown one-room houses, yards littered with old couches and rusted springs, car parts and cinder blocks, all of it baking in a shimmering, dry heat that felt like it cracked your insides. Holos of the Texas flag rippled in a nonexistent breeze. In the far distance I saw a cityscape burned up by a setting

---

1. A somewhat bewildering expression in this case since, of course, androids didn't use the bathroom at all, and were notoriously disturbed by the human habit of doing so.

sun. From the crowned barbed-wire fences and the watchtowers in the distance, I tagged it as a maximum-security town.

Bernie returned with an armload of sweet-tea cans sweating against her breasts—and a rifle. I must of reacted, because she grinned. "We been having some problems with wild dogs around here. Better safe than dead, like they say." She passed out the tea, settled down, and kicked up feet swelled by heat onto the railing. "Where you from, greenie?"

I hesitated. Bernie hadn't recognized me, not that I expected she would: the whole reason the Federal Corp was leaning on Halloran-Chyung was to try to rope Texas in line with its manhunt. But Texas and Crunch, United, had a long, bloody history[2] and I wasn't sure I should cop to being a company kid.

Bernie spared me the trouble by guessing. "Let me guess. You a corporation kid, huh?"

"From one of the outposts," I said.[3]

She waved a hand. "Let me rap to you, sweet cheeks. I'm a patriot, all right? I'm about as Texas as they come. My brother lost his hand fighting off the border surge, had to get him one of them knocked-off prosthetics, and since then that piece of shit been yanking him to all sorts of trouble. Can't hardly be outside without his fist launching up into somebody's face. And my granddad used to tell stories of the Starve, you know, how he made a living scouring the roads for belly-up lizards and snakes not too long in the sun. They used to catch the birds as they came falling out of the sky too. Used to call his squad the Icarus boys, for that

---

2. Since the time of dissolution, tensions between Texas and the Federal Corporation had often veered toward talk of war—although many political pundits believed that both sides were blustering. In addition to problems of roads and infrastructure that made a large-scale attack against Crunch, United, improbable, many historians believe that the reason the Texas militia never made the attempt was because Crunch, United, was an important safeguard against the growing power of the Real Friends© of the North. For the same reason, the Federal Corporation needed Texas.
3. Arkansas was acquired by the newly formed Crunch, United, board in 2049, and in that sense it was lucky: territories that resisted or tried for sovereignty, like St. Louis, were often seized during aggressive takeovers.

dumb *cabron* tried to fly up to Jupiter thinking he'd find a squat better than this one. Huh."

I could of pointed out that I'd heard stories from my mom about the Starve too—or, more specifically, about the Five-Month Freeze that had come before it. A few years before I was born, during the android uprising that blew up Silicon Valley, Texas stopped shipping oil to any countries that wouldn't put in with the Real Friends© of the North to stomp the rebellion.[4] It was a bad winter up and down the eastern seaboard and a brutal one in the mid-plains—this was two years before the first Arctic Cyclone system, and only a little dribble of what was to come, but at the time the cold broke all the records in the server. The Federal Corporation could barely get enough oil to grease a lug nut. Three hundred thousand people froze between December and April, and that was just the official tally.[5]

"Point is, ain't nobody more Texas than me. But let's be honest. You nothing but an ant, and so am I. It ain't ever our wars. We're just the ones have to live with the manure." Bernie tapped a cartridge of fresh into a pipe and lit up. "You ever been to Texas before?"

I pressed the can of sweet tea to my neck. A bit of melting ice slipped down my back. "Until last week, I'd never even left Crunch 407," I admitted.

"Well, just keep your peepers open. You in the land of the free, now. Some of the big boys don't take kindly to strangers."

---

4. At the time, Texas saw the growing threat of the android-rights movement as vastly outweighing diplomatic considerations that normally sought to restrict the influence of the Real Friends© of the North.

5. As a result, Crunch, United, sanctioned Texas, forbade all trade with the Sovereign Nation, and pressured various Sinopec-TeMaRex Affiliated agrofirms to halt trade with Texas too. For a long time, until Texas struck their deal with the Russian Federation and through them, a large swath of the northern badlands, there was very little for the population to eat. Some people scavenged for runaway biotech; some resorted to eating shoe leather and prairie grass. (This led to a very famous joke about the difference between Crunch products and the inedibles consumed during the Starve being only in the price.)

"Where are we, exactly?" I asked.

"Used to be called Pampa," she said, "till the Koreans[6] bought up the penitentiary for one of their production plants. Now it's Pampa-Juche Maximum, and a tenth of the batteries in the nation's plasma get cranked out right in that work yard over there. Twenty-seventh largest prison in the country."

I couldn't imagine how there could possibly be twenty-six prison cities larger than the one I saw splooged on the horizon against a purple-neon sunset, and I told her so.

"Oh, honey," she said. "Ain't you ever heard everything's bigger in Texas?" She cracked her sweet tea. "Cheers."

I knew we should move. But after however long underground, it was nice there on that patio, looking out over a wash of plywood squats and Old World tumbledowns running up toward the glittering prison yards of smokestack and bunkers. Barnaby nosed around some cacti splintering the steps, and Sammy hung back in the shade while Tiny Tim and Bernie yammered about friends they'd once known, skirmishes along the Colorado border, and the possibility of going to war with the New Kingdom of Utah for trickle from the basin countries.

Then, suddenly, Bernie sat up. Pushing herself out of her seat, she reached slowly for the rifle.

"What is it?" I asked.

She hushed me sharply. "It's one of them things I told you about." She squinted out into the yard. "Wild dogs."

Now I saw a man weaving between the tumbledown squats, doing a sweep of the singed grass, occasionally bending to collect something. He was talking to himself. Short explosions of sound reached us across the distance: *Never. Hopeless. Punishment.*

---

6. North Koreans—although Texas, like North Korea, failed to recognize South Korea as a separate international entity due not to the difficulties on the Korean Peninsula but because South Korea had formed a trade and weapons alliance with Halloran-Chyung.

Bernie plugged the rifle to her shoulder. "We started seeing them around a few weeks ago, all jacked up like you could never believe." She didn't move, didn't even blink, just stayed there with one eye on the scope. "We call them the wild dogs 'cause of how they lose their minds. Like animals, foaming and spitting, and dangerous too."

Jump. It had to be. Even though it was well past a hundred degrees, I felt like shivering.

"Goddammit." Bernie lobbed a wad of green-flecked spit on the porch. "This one's got hold of a gun."

He was close enough now I could see what he looked like. I'd never seen a face like that—like a corpse taken out of the ground. The bulge of a revolver strapped beneath his waistband was visible when he raised his arms.

"Well." Barnaby tottered to his feet. "Seems like you've got the situation well under control. I think I'll just nip inside for a bit, get away from the flies." He began backing toward the door. "Anyone need anything? No? Great."

But as he turned around he sent an empty beer can flying from where it was perched. The can bounced off the porch and landed in the dirt, and Bernie sucked in a breath, and Barnaby whimpered, and Sammy said *Oh no*, and Tiny Tim said *Oh no, what?* And I lost my voice and breath together.

Because the guy turned and stared straight at me.

I swear his eyes were three times the size of normal and black, just like Billy Lou Ropes's had been—but roiling, sticky black, the black of shadows slickly moving. Looking into his eyes gave me a feeling like waking up in the middle of the night sick as hell realizing you're the last person alive on earth.

For a second, he was frozen, and we were frozen too.

"Go on," Bernie said to him. Her voice was steady. "You ain't welcome here."

He didn't move. He just kept staring at us with that same inhuman gaze, as if there were nothing inside looking out.

"Go on," Bernie said again, a little louder, making a motion with her gun. "We don't want any trouble."

Something moved from his ankles to his hips, snapped his spine backward, spat his head forward, unhinged his jaw, and punched out the world's most horrible scream.

He launched for us at a sprint.

Arms up, fingers hooked like he was going to take us apart with his bare hands and suck on our eyeballs and lick our brain cavities. For a second, I was sure he would.

Then Bernie's shot cracked him right between the eyes, clean as if she'd drawn on his forehead with a marker. He stiffened. A razor line of blood tracked down his forehead and angled down his nose. He barely made a sound when he hit the ground.

"Jesus." I felt like crying. They were like zombies—zombies, just waiting for the signal to go for blood. What would happen when it came? "Jesus Christ."

"How strange," Sammy remarked. "I've never seen a human move so quickly."

"Wild dogs." Bernie lowered her gun. "At least that one was by himself. Sometimes they travel in packs. Can't do nothing but lock your doors and pray."

Almost immediately, a swarm of fist-sized insects set in to pick apart the Jumphead's corpse. Two houses away, some kids edged onto the porch in the blue of a box light and tried to peg him with empty bottles and plastic caps.

"Should we call somebody to get him?" I asked.

She turned and stared at me. "What for?"

I swallowed back the foul taste in my mouth. "You can't—you can't just leave him there to rot."

She sighed. "Pickers will come for him eventually. They always do," she said. "Three things you can count on in this world, boy. Death, taxes, and someone to make money from your damn corpse."

25

Los Alamos in New Mexico was the birthplace of some of the world's most badass science. The physicists, engineers, and rocket scientists of the area have given the rest of Halloran-Chyung its post-dissolution flavor. It's a country unlike any other on the continent, full of freaks, geeks, and freewheeling quanta enthusiasts who'll run on about the possibility of interdimensional travel before you've had time to take a coffee and shit in the morning.
—from The Grifter's Guide to the Territories FKA USA

We left the same night. There was a freight train heading west that would take us all into Halloran-Chyung—possibly, if war came, the *last* train headed west, at least for a Confederate age—and we had to hustle to be on it.

Luckily, and despite Texas's rah-rah about progress and economy, the sizzle was rationed here like it was everywhere. Even after sunset, almost every house was dark, except for a few burning old-school candles or hand-crank lamps.

The freight train was enormous: forty or fifty cars, dingy with dust and graffiti, cabled together on the line. We bartered a private car that came with not one but two pillows, a pile of woven blankets we wouldn't need, and a shiny plastic bucket so we didn't have to fan our ass cracks over the tracks to shit. Tiny Tim and I tacked purines to the hooks screwed to the walls for that purpose: a flow of forced oxygen helped the urine separate quicker, and soon we'd need every drop we could get.

"You think Texas is big, wait till you get out in the Dust Bowl with nothing but lava heat and a storm of sand for days in every direction," Tim said. "We was born in water and to water we go. It ain't natural out where we headed, I'll tell you straight."

"So why go west at all?" I asked. It was true that grifters fought hard for their routes, and had to keep fighting for them—there was always competition, and always new blood waiting to swoop in. But I couldn't believe that anyone was waiting anxiously on the coast for Tiny Tim to arrive with an empty can of ReadyBeans™. Since I'd met him, I hadn't seen him sell a damn thing.

"I told you," he said. "I got a lead on a big haul."

"You mean the seed bank?" I swallowed a sigh. "You know there's no such thing, right? You know that's all empty talk?"

Tiny Tim just shook his head and smiled. "You gotta believe, Mr. Truckee. Else what's the point in doing anything at all?"

"You tell me," I said. "You're the genius." It was a low blow, sure, but trying to talk sense to him was like trying to make gold from a firefly's asshole.[1]

The train snaked us past squats abandoned after dissolution or emptied by the vast San Antonio prisons, where a quarter of the Texas population was housed. We ran alongside the sprawling shantytowns that washed up alongside every medium- or maximum-security city, where girls in high heels and cowboy hats pimped shot-for-shot gun bars, every pay station was thick with signs barring androids from charging stations and common areas, and barbed-wire fences spiked moonlight off their deterrents. A road ribboning through the desert pointed the way to one

---

1. A Crunch, United, colloquialism: *Never trust a firefly trying to shit you some gold.* This likely has its origins in the dubious claims made by various shamsters and snake-oil salesmen during the first boom in gentech, when scam artists posing as scientists claimed to have invented everything from pocket-sized elephants to a host of animals and insects that produced gold or diamonds as a by-product of digestion. Please see Appendix F: "The Rumpelstiltskin Roaches, and Other Lies from the Golden Age of Genetic Engineering."

of the hunting preserves, where criminals lost their lives at the hands of gun-toting bigwigs. Tiny Tim pointed out the way to South Lubbock Penitentiary and Reform, where he'd lost half his straw to the knife. For once, he wasn't smiling.

In between stubbly towns, talking billboards shouted the Right to Life, and giant AR projections fingered the illegal android populations for everything from the lack of job opportunities to a rise in the crime rate. (One of them even warned of a robot plot to enslave humans for use as food supply, even though robots didn't eat.) Chemical food plants and Russian orthodox churches the size of sprawling cities dotted the horizon; bull-riding arenas and vents the size of rocket engines fissured out the chemical scent of barbecue; there was Jesus in towering hologram thundering words of warning across the emptiness and the rack-tack ear pop from the gun ranges; there was desert scrub and shimmering heat and oil derricks crowded in the distance like spiny people walking to their execution.

I couldn't believe how much space there was. I couldn't cred that, for a few hundred years, it had all been the *same* space—bound by laws and money and a common idea about what it meant to be a person. Looking out over all that land, it amazed me not that America had fallen but that it had ever existed at all.

Amazing that so many people had tried to fight to keep it together.

Texas might of been hard to enter, but it was cakewalk to leave. I fell asleep with *Grifter's Guide* fanned out on my chest, and woke up to the weird blue-green tinge of a Halloran-Chyung sky as we swayed past the border cordon—a sling of sagging fence and mostly empty guard towers. Enormous ghost cacti, hobble-backed and wet-looking, glowed ominously in the early morning light. Moonflowers were just closing their pale-white fists.

A few hours later, the train slowed to a crawl at Santa Rosa. Tim, Sammy, Barnaby, and I slunk off just before the station, taking a jump-and-roll down a bank of stubbly ground and dried-out purines.

Halloran-Chyung was different shades of membrane-pale plants and sudden explosions of ultrashock color: blood moss[2] clinging to the rock crags in the distance, hardy sprays of radioactive flowers shouting from the bleached dirt. Spiky cactus plants looked like alien invaders in the half light.

Everywhere I turned I saw heavy ground artillery, national guns sweating it out in the morning sun, trying to blend in with the Gorgon cacti. The water plants were under cordon by a moat of soldiers ten deep, some of them still suited up in the South Korean uniforms they'd been shipped in.

Signs pointed the way toward Kunashiri,[3] one of the largest nuclear power plants in the country, and also one of the sites of its largest nuclear meltdowns. I knew from Politics-03 that most of Halloran-Chyung was owned by the South Korean oligarchs who'd funneled money into the expansion at Los Alamos and the Halloran-Chyung Space and Dimensional Exploration Program in exchange for a steady flow of uranium— and, some people said, even a heap of finished nuclear weapons.[4] I guess the fat cats in Halloran-Chyung didn't care if Russia dropped a bomb,[5] vaporized the middle of the continent, and spawned a whole new generation of eight-legged children. They'd be well out of harm's way, in one

---

2. Actually, a lichen, and so named not for its color, but because it had become predominant in the aftermath of the catastrophic Kunashiri meltdown of 2072. Its thallus was likely comprised of a mutated varietal of the species *Aspicilia cinerea*.

3. Construction on the nuclear facility that was ultimately known as the Kunashiri Reactor actually began even before dissolution, and was intended as a last-bid attempt to revitalize America's nuclear-energy program. It is likely, however, that the long interruption in design, as well as changing responsibility and ownership, contributed to the vast design flaws that resulted in the nuclear catastrophe that unfortunately gave Halloran-Chyung both its reputation for radioactivity and its stratospheric rates of cancer.

4. And, in the case of Japan, in exchange for participation in GEP, the Gender Equality Program, which exported marriageable females to male-dominated areas such as Japan, China, and the Dakotas.

5. For years other countries had tried sanctioning Halloran-Chyung. Texas had even long been warning of a ground war, although the impregnable force field that could be activated around the whole country made a skirmish unlikely.

of the sixteen other livable dimensions predicted by the newest quantum models.

We began our hike toward a public float tethered in the distance: a massive, flying sperm cell that would glide us toward Santa Fe. Halloran-Chyung bragged the largest fleet of hovercraft on the continent. Coming into Santa Fe Sung, we got knotted up in a jam not just on the road but above it. Two hovers had collided on the third altitude, and both police drones and air-traffic controllers swarmed the scene, trying to feed traffic up or down to keep it moving. When a doughy-faced goon in a sleek, fire-red sports hover tried to cut into our lane from above, he nearly dropped straight down through the windshield.

"Hey, what's your glitch?" the float driver leaned out of the window to shout. "Your system got a bug or are you just too dumb to program it right?"

The guy just stuck his hand out the window and gave us the finger before launching into the sky again.

The float tethered in center city, and we poured off. The morning sky was liquid with drones: drones to measure radiation, drones to measure the direction of the wind and the temperature of the air, drones to record and photograph and feed data back to the Citadel.[6] The fly traffic made me more than a little nervous. No telling who was up there, watching.

The streets were filthy with tourists who'd overrun the city to see the launch of *Aphrodite 01*. The third rocket to leave the continent in decades,[7] it would be heading into orbit around Mars with a team of eight

---

6. Halloran-Chyung had the highest proportion of scientists per capita of all the countries on the continent by a factor of ten, many of them nuclear or quantum physicists and aeronautics engineers. It might have been the most advanced country in the world.

7. On the back of *Aphrodite 01*, *Aphrodite 02* and *03*, smaller probes, would be dispatched into deep space to photograph a planet with similar environmental conditions to Earth—at least, Earth as it was before we got our hands on it—and the Citadel had sworn to start recolonization before the turn of the new century. So far ten thousand people from all over the continent had put in for the chance to be part of the vanguard.

astronauts. Vendors hawked purines and water at prices that made me choke. Nuclear produce, tumorous and violently colored, sat pulsating slightly in corner veggie carts.

Pueblo-style casitas and last-century static walkways could of been lifted from the 1900s, except for nudges of smart tech: sizzle towers disguised as spiky-palmed palmettos in nu-neon shades, where shaved-headed androids crowded to juice their batteries. Swarms of nanobots formed custom ad scrolls in midair (TRY POWDER B VITAENHANCE TODAY! LISA-22, WILL YOU MARRY ME? SANTA FE ARTISTS FOR MARRIAGE EQUALITY).

"How about that?" Tiny Tim raised a fist to point. "Someone's writ your name up there in the sky, Truckee."

He was right. As we stood there, a bunch of flash-red micro-tech condensed in the clouds. WANTED ON CHARGES OF TERRORISM, ESPIONAGE, DRUG SMUGGLING: TRUCKEE WALLACE, 16, 5'9". A second later, the nanobots rearranged into a semi-decent sketch of my face, except for the grimace and the bared teeth and the crazy-looking eyes. The wisps of clouds in the sky made it look like smoke was fissuring out of my nostrils.

"For fuck's sake, stop pointing." Even though it was so hot that my ball hairs were sweating, I wrestled my hoodie out of my bag and zipped it up high. With my visor on and my bangs pulled low, I figured I was close to unrecognizable.

"They got your chin all wrong," Barnaby said thoughtfully. "Yours is more pear-shaped."

"All right, all right. Look, how about you guys try and stock up on supplies, okay? I'm going to hunt down someone to ship us through Hell Valley."[8] Kink had given me an idea: if I could sell the *Grifter's Guide* for half of what they said it was worth, I could buy my way into San

8. Commonly known as *Camels,* these travel guides specialized exclusively in travel in and around Old Arizona and other desiccated and abandoned portions of the Dust Bowl. Actually, the Ghost Cities of Old Arizona were an extremely popular tourist destination, typically ranking just below the Human Hunting Preserves of Texas on the annual international list of the Continent's Greatest Wonders.

Francisco, deliver the payload, and hope Cowell could sprout a solution from Rafikov's old brain cells. Just like that, I'd be a national hero.

And then, finally, I could go home.

I laid out one of my last twenties to park it for a few hours in a cheap on-the-fly house where shower and flush prices were approaching reasonable, though I didn't want to spring for fresh water and had to make due with powering our flow from half-filled purines from management. Still, recycled piss was better than nothing. It was obvious the whole country was on strict water rations. Signs of drought were everywhere, from the billboards blazing high-tech purines with 90 percent efficiency conversion to the lines that snaked around the block at every local wet station. The dry out here felt like sucking on chalk, and it would only be worse in Old Arizona.

Tiny Tim and Barnaby went to scrounge up as much wet as we could carry and Sammy set out to scope for a new battery pack, since her extra had been all but drained underground: Santa Fe Sung was famously pro-android and friendly to robotics.[9]

I set off to find a tour guide. There was no border to speak of heading into Las Vegas—all we needed was someone dumb or desperate enough to take us. Even though it was a risk, with my face blowing over half the city, I figured as long as I kept my head down, I would be okay. There must of been thousands of people swarming the city center, and if there was one thing a crumb like me knew, it was how to play invisible.

I got bottlenecked behind a flow of traffic at the entrance to the Plaza Santa Domingo–Watanabe Memorial. I counted three human-android couples openly holding hands, seemingly without fear of being arrested,

9. Halloran-Chyung took in 50,000 refugees from Texas after the militia started deporting manufactured humans. It is worth pointing out that despite Texas's assertion that the android populations steal steady work from their human counterparts, Halloran-Chyung's economy actually grew—and its unemployment dropped—after the refugee integration program. This is largely attributable to the variety of businesses and technologies required to cater specifically to manufactured humans, such as repair shops and upgrade boutiques.

and dozens of natural-born slubs topping T-shirts with slogans like I SUP-PORT MIXED-WARE RELATIONSHIPS and JE SUIS CG3.[10] Outside an army recruitment center, an in-house physicist was demonstrating a micro-scopic machine assembled entirely of quanta that would launch into a different dimension.

By the time I squeezed through the crowd to Boulevard Sony Las Muertas, a famous retail strip, I was sweating through my eyelids and thirsty as hell. The drone traffic had only grown thicker overhead, and there was a spidery feeling on the back of my neck, like I was being watched.

Here, too, there was skant room to breathe. Tourists swarmed the glittering tech shops and androids foamed in and out of beauty tune-up palaces. There were plenty of tour guides shilling day trips to Hell Valley, but I would need to find a place to pawn off the book, first: they were all out of my payday, to the tune of hundreds of dollars.

The itch on my neck stayed with me, though. As I inched down the street with the foot traffic, I knew it wasn't just paranoia. Someone was following me.

He, too, was wearing a JE SUIS CG3 T-shirt. He was paler than this part of the world usually made them, like he'd crawled out of the shadows of someone's operating system. His chin and neck seemed to be doing their best to let bygones be bygones and scrub the difference between them.

As I whipped around to face him, he looked like he might say something. Instead he just stood there openmouthed, with a look of fixed concentration, like a first-level android working through a software update.

"You got a problem?" I asked him, trying to channel some of Zeb's old swagger.

He shook his head. But I didn't like how he smiled.

I whipped around and kept going. He followed me as I loosed from the crowd, and was still following me when I turned down the Imperial

_____

10. CG3, whose given name was CIGNA-38734262A, was famously disassembled by a Texas mob after he made the fatal mistake of crossing into Texas with his natural-born wife during a trip abroad to visit relatives.

Jade Calle de Santa Maria. Several minutes after that, I tagged him still forty feet behind me, limping along in rubber-soled sneakers.

Who was he? One of Rafikov's gunners? Or just a would-be swag looking to collect the bounty on my head?

I wasn't too worried, not yet. There were hours of light left, the streets were full of hustle and flow, the sky was a constant blur of security drones. It wasn't like he could pop me in broad daylight and expect to get away with it—this wasn't Texas, after all, and Halloran-Chyung kept a tight leash on its guns.

I turned right down a narrow street, hoping to loop back around to the plaza and shake him off. Bad move: this street was empty of foot traffic. I nearly backtracked, but just then a group of bleach-haired, tattooed fandom types rounded the corner, yukking it up and pawing at something on their feeds.

"Desculpe," one of them said, as I started to squeeze past him.

Except he didn't say it.

They *all* said it—all four of them, speaking together, in exactly the same tone of voice, like robots wired to the same network. But they weren't robots. Robots weren't made to look like that, given AdTattoos that crept into new patterns beneath their skin, given piercings and pimples, made to breathe and sweat.

"What the fuck?" I took a step backward and nearly tripped on the curb.

"Don't be afraid," they said. A guy with gelled hair and mobile tattoos; a Korean-leaning trot with a scar above her eyebrow; a ze with an orange Afro; a fat guy, real dark, wearing glasses. All of them moving together, speaking together, *breathing* together—all of them smiling at me with the same blank look on their faces.

Like a first-generation android working through a software update.

I was surrounded. I tried to open my mouth to scream, tried to turn and run, but a great crack of pain vaporized my legs. There was a high ringing in my ears, and then a great fog swept over the city and took me down with it.

26

If you get to Halloran-Chyung, keep your eye out for the Santeria shops hawking nuclear products for the supposed magic. I bought the gland of a river toad to make me hard for two hours straight and a green bean big as a ram's horn supposed to give me super- natural strength, all from an old Mexican hobbleback with only two teeth. I didn't feel any stronger but I'll tell you something, I was rock-solid and ready to party after eating that river-toad gland, though that might've been because of the neat little Saamy I took home from one of the pay-houses. Kristina-452, her name was.
—from The Grifter's Guide to the Territories FKA USA

I came awake to Barnaby jumping on my skull. That's what it felt like anyway: like a sharp hoof probing hard between my frontal lobes. Open- ing my eyes was like trying to lift a sandbag with a teaspoon.

I was underground. That was obvious in the clamminess of the air and the echoing chitter of rodent feet in the dark. My hands and feet were lashed with jumper cables to my chair.

The single light cabled to the ceiling wasn't doing any favors for the lowlife who'd tailed me from the plaza. Pit stains darkened his CG3 T-shirt. He bared his teeth in the world's shittiest smile. "Hello, Truckee."

"Who are you?" I asked. Not the most original line, but I was trying to think through a pickax buried in my brain.

"Who am I? A good question." He came forward and pinched my chin between his fingers. I wrenched away. "A better question is what do I *want*?"

"Okay, then," I said. I'd been a solid B-study and could regurgitate along with the best of them. "What do you want?"

His smile pivoted nicely into a sneer. "I think you know already."

Elvis. Goddamn. Presley. I tried a new line. "Did Rafikov send you?"

His laugh sounded like he was trying to cough up a tampon. "Don't play dumb, Mr. Wallace. This is a dangerous game, and my patience is wearing thin."

"I'm not playing anything." An echo rolled back to me. I would of banked he had us plungered in an old parking garage, about fifty packed-earth feet from anyone who would hear me scream.

For a long moment, he looked at me without blinking. "President Burnham gave you something to deliver to San Francisco. Where is it?"

So. Rafikov had known from the beginning what President Burnham set out to do. But she obviously didn't know the cargo was hitching in the head-cavity of a myotonic goat—which meant that, for the moment, it was safe. And if Rafikov was so desperate to get back snippets of her brain tissue, it meant she was afraid.

And that there might really be a way to stop her.

I decided to lie through my grille. "President Burnham didn't give me squirrel except what's in my rucksack," I said. Again, the space threw back the howl of my voice. I tried to crank myself loose and only popped a wrist bone.

"We checked that already," he said. "It's clean."

"So what the hell do you want from me?"

For a split second, time froze. Actually, he froze. Something funny happened to his face. It was like all his muscles were windows and behind them a whole scrum of people were prepping for a tornado, locking up their shutters at different speeds.

Suddenly, he lunged at me. But instead of landing a punch, he gripped my wrists. A brand-new expression stormed across his face, blowing away the sneer.

"Help," he rasped out. Even his voice changed. "She won't get out of my head. It was supposed to be temporary . . . I just wanted to dip once or twice. . . ."

The way he moved was all wrong, like his body was just a suit hanging in midair.

He gasped like a Low Hill Riverside kid on a red-haze Sunday. "Please, give her what she wants. Otherwise we'll never get free. We'll never—"

He broke off as an invisible shock snapped him backward, blowing his spine into a parabola. The attack lasted one second, maybe two.

Then he went calm again. It was like all the little windows in his face had flown open and someone flat-out different was looking out.

"Forgive me," he said. His tone was so icy it made my intestines shiver. "As you can see, I'm anxious to retrieve what is rightfully mine."

And suddenly, I understood. "Yana Rafikov didn't send you," I said. "You *are* Yana Rafikov."

There was a long moment of silence while he looked at me. And yet, now I thought I could see something—or someone—moving like a hidden current behind the flab of his face. I could see another intelligence, razor-sharp and deadly, holding him neatly in her grip. What had President Burnham said? *We'll soon have an army of little Rafikovs, marching to her every command, obeying her every order.*

In the end, she didn't deny it. "I'd say it's a pleasure to meet you," she said, through the poor sucker she'd conned into helping her. "But I've never been much of a liar."

"No. Just a psychopath."

She smiled with lips that weren't hers, displaying teeth rotten from sugar she'd never eaten. It was something rot, watching this poor skin sack and his quivering man boobs played like a massive puppet. "That's a rather ironic accusation, especially coming from a murderer," she said. "I tried to help you in Granby. My little assistant was only twenty-two years old, you know. It's a shame. She had so much life ahead of her."

"Wait. *You* sent the ad-sales girl?" I'd got it into my head that she was President Burnham's contact.

"My mistake. I thought you could be persuaded to see reason." She took another step toward me. "I overestimated you."

"You're not the first."

My pulse was going harder than an Okie earthquake.

She ignored that. "But there's still time to save your skin, Mr. Wallace. You've got twenty-four hours to produce the stolen article. After that, I'll turn your skin inside out, and leave your body in the desert where the snakes and spiders can feast on it. Understood?"

I could skant cred the luck. She was going to let me go and give me space to scram.

But she must of known just what I was thinking. She took a step backward. Shadow dropped across her body-puppet's stubbled face. "Don't even think about escaping," she said. "I have friends on the ground. I have friends at the borders. I have friends everywhere."

Suddenly she cut the light. I shouted, expecting the bodysuit to grab me. But no hands closed around my neck. No shot rangalanged the silence.

Instead, as my eyes adjusted, I saw movement in the darkness. Ten, twenty, thirty people shuffled closer. They'd been watching the whole time—doing nothing, saying nothing, just standing there.

A cold tongue of fear slid down my spine. They moved in sync, like the kids who'd helped take me down on the street. It was the world's best-trained army: they even breathed together. I could hear in the stifling quiet the communal in-out of their breath. How many were there? It was impossible to tell.

"Until tomorrow, Truckee."

I couldn't tell exactly, but I thought all the others whispered too.

Then the bodysuit came toward me with something in his hand. He shoved a wet cloth to my mouth and I choked on a sharp chemical tang. For a minute after that I was a baby again, rocking slowly in my mother's arms in a soft haze of cherry bac . . .

Then, a hundred years later, a ModelPet™ nudged me awake with a cold metal nose.

As soon as I started to sit up, it scampered off, barking. It was dark. The hover traffic had thinned out, but I could still see the flare of safety lights in the air above the city, like the passage of colored stars. Rafikov's bodyman and his rat pack had dumped me on a quiet residential street, in the doorway of a boarded-up church, maybe figuring someone would take me for a drunk. But I could hear a swell of voices and laughter and knew the launch celebration must still be in full swing.

I cranked to my feet slowly, using the door for support. Amazingly, they'd let me keep my rucksack. In the weed-choked yard someone had flashed up the statue of Virgin Mary with a bright-pink wig. They'd wedged a dildo in her hand too. Her face was covered in graffiti. FUCK HEAVEN, GIVE ME DIME.

Right then, standing there, I knew it was the end. There was nothing left. We'd destroyed all of it, taken everything good and beautiful, picked and picked until we had nothing but ruins. There was no point trying to run. I wouldn't get through the borders. If I tried, Rafikov would just game me quicker. Friends on the ground, friends everywhere. Good for fucking her.

My SmartBand pulsed. Automatically, without wanting to, I scanned the time: eleven o'clock.

And then, just as quick, the truth smacked me hard in the nozzle: my SmartBand. I'd forgotten all about it. It was hooked up to the Central Time Clock at 1 Central Plaza, cabled to the Crunch, United, server, meant to geotag our locations wherever we went. No wonder Rafikov had pinned me. I might as well of been swagging around with a giant spotlight strapped to my forehead.

It took me a minute to figure out how to get the damn thing off. Underneath it my skin was gray and textured, like something dead. I threw the band as far as I could and didn't feel any better.

"Hey, mister. Are you okay?"

I whipped around to see a pack of kids had edged out of the darkness. One of them was holding the ModelPet™ by the collar.

"We thought you were dead," he said. He had a funny lopsided face, and when he talked it was like one side was always trying to catch up with the other.

"Not yet," I said.

Another boy was holding a miniature rocket, one of the models of the *Aphrodite 01*.

"We're going to Mars," he said. And then: "When I grow up, I'm going to be an astronaut."

"Me too," said a girl wearing about a dozen anti-allergy patches. "I'm going all the way to Pluto."

I wanted to pick them up and run. I wanted to take all of them, all those kids, and carry them like so many pebbles, and run so far away, the place we were going didn't exist yet.

They didn't know. They had no idea they'd been born too late. They were just kids, on a playground, and there was a rocket launch tomorrow.

"You can't. It's too far."

"Can too. I'll build a bigger rocket."

"It doesn't matter. Even if it's bigger you still can't go."

The boy with the lopsided face frowned. "I guess I'd go to Pluto," he said. "So long as I could take Rocko with me." He bent down to pick up the little bundle of metal and plastic parts, and Rocko on cue began to lick his face with a jointed metal tongue, and the boy laughed a laugh I hadn't heard in years, a real laugh straight from the center, and then he sneezed, three times in a row.

Maybe it was the boy with the rocket. Maybe it was the fact that no matter how fucked up the world was, I didn't want to die. Maybe I was only a coward.

Or maybe it was the boy with the funny lopsided face who loved his goddamn metal dog so much.

Friends on the ground.

I tipped my head back to watch the distant lights of the hovers, flashing. If you watched long enough, it looked like a pattern. Like a code.

Rafikov had friends on the ground. But she didn't say squirrel about friends in the air.

27

Lots of people ask me what's the worst thing I ever seen on one of my routes, thinking I'm likely to say the roadslicks, or the hillbilly towns where the kids are so starved even their talk sounds like death, or those sicko pedo plantation towns down in the Confederacy where grown men slave androids on the sly and keep fourteen-year-old wives. I've seen organ farms where they grow livers like potatoes and eyeballs like clusters of grapes. I've seen agrofirms printing food from chemical waste, and Plasticine remodeling clinics sump-pumping blood from their drain rooms. Shit. I once saw a hundred-legged spider, grown the size of a rig, chow down a roadslick in one gulp. But the worst thing I ever saw? You go down to Hank's Watering Hole in Bloomington, and get to watching how that stubborn bastard waters down all that beautiful, beautiful whiskey.

—from *The Grifter's Guide to the Territories FKA USA*

It took me hours to find my way back to the flophouse. A lifetime of geo-dependency made me shit at judging direction. The streets were quiet and the drones above us were nothing but quick flashes in the air, like stars loosed from their bearings, and the buildings mysterious behind a smoky covering of acidic fog. Finally I turned and spied Barnaby rooting around the gutters, trying to hoover everything the crowds had slubbed off.

"Truckee!" Sammy was still awake, puzzling over a used copy of the

Human Sentience Standardized Exam Prep. Back in Granby, Tiny Tim had paid a hefty two haircombs for it. "What happened to you?"

"No time to explain," I said. "Where's Tim?"

Barnaby twitched his nose toward a small trailer down the street, rocking on its wheels like a shanty in the middle of a squall. Unbelievable. I was half-ready to barge in there and tell him to hurry up. Finally, the trailer went still again and Tiny Tim reappeared with a nuclear girl. Maybe it was her three breasts that did the trick.

"Are you finished?" I asked him after he'd sent her packing. "Or is there some other *chula* in the hemisphere you'd like to hambone?"

"Plenty of them," Tiny Tim said with no sarcasm at all.

One good thing about being flat broke: traveling light was easy. We hitched up our packs, I cranked on my visor, and we were off.

Outside the downtown with its colorful homes and dizzying tech displays was a sprawl of drone manufacturers, android detailers, and hover dealerships scrolling news of different deals and the best prices. Luckily, the military patrols were mostly keeping order in the city center, and the few guns we passed must of taken us for wandering tourists.

We clipped the chain link and ducked through the fence onto one of the largest car lots. No wonder the security was so light: all of the hovers were locked, their windows unbreakable, and fitted with antitheft tech, which meant that they would open and come to life only for the right retinal scans. Even the oldest hovers in the lot, the used ones, couldn't be opened or started without a decent owner thumbprint.

"I'm guessing none of you have a million likes on RealFriends©?" I asked, after checking the price tag of one of the larger models, a balloon-like family-friendly float with lots of interior room and top speeds of 400 mph.

"Androids can't keep accounts," Sammy said, as if we didn't know it. "Besides . . ." She pointed to a static sign I hadn't pinned before. THIS DEALERSHIP NO LONGER ACCEPTS TEXAS GREENBACKS OR REALFRIENDS© WINKS, LIKES, NUDGES, AND VIEWS. Another rim shot that looked like war.

"You can't hot-wire them either," Tim said, "not like the old models. All it took was spit and a handshake to get 'em going."

Barnaby jawed through a scrap of old tire. "It's a shame we don't know any veterans," he said thoughtfully.

"What would *that* matter?" I asked him.

Barnaby treated me to a scathing look. "Haven't you ever read *Hovercraft and Its Impact on Urban Infrastructure: A Case Study*?" When I didn't bother replying, he huffed. "It was excellent, I recall. A little dry going down, but very filling. Anyone with military tags can override the security system."[1]

"Too bad that doesn't help us," I snapped. I had no doubt Rafikov would make good on her promise to turn me to snake food. Even now, her creepy body-puppets might be tracking me. And without a hover, I was good as digested.

"Now, just hang on a second." Tiny Tim rooted around in his pack. "I might know someone who can give us a hand."

He pulled out his sorry pittance of trades: a broken pair of turn-of-the-century eyeglasses, some rusted tweezers, a used purine, three bottle caps, a handful of loose teeth. Finally, he whipped out the brown, shriveled, preservative-leeching mitt he'd won off a military man during a poker game in Granby: lost to frostbite, I remembered, during the Halloran-Chyung offensive up near the Russian Federation hinterlands.

I could of kissed him. "Tim," I said, "I take it back. You just might be the best grifter there is."

---

1. The Hover Safety Act was passed in Halloran-Chyung in 2055, and the president liked to boast it was the first piece of legislation of its kind. In fact, the Real Friends© of the North beat Halloran-Chyung to a similar piece of legislation by several years. After an epileptic famously lost consciousness and accidentally disabled his vehicle's collision-detection controls, culminating in a 472-vehicle pileup on Los Angeles's infamous twenty-altitude Intrastate 405, the board acted unanimously to approve the use of emergency system overrides for all police, fire, and medical personnel in times "of clear and immediate danger" to either the passenger or other drivers, and additionally in cases where the driver or the car system proved "resistant to or in violation of the laws governing the safe administration of the sky roads."

Shriveled as they were, the fingerprints still registered. Just like that, all the doors slid open with a click, and the car came to life. Headlights flared, the engine purred, and the speakers started blaring hysteria about North Korean sneaks crossing the border to kidnap and cannibalize Halloran-Chyung children. I slid into the driver's seat and punched the radio off. The smell of new plastic and fake leather was addictive.

"Any idea how we blast off, Barnaby?" I asked. There were hundreds of dashboard controls—altitude and velocity measures, emergency-landing deploy, air-pressure regulation, climate control.

"*Hovercraft and Its Impact on Urban Infrastructure: A Case Study* wasn't a driving manual," Barnaby said icily. I guess the animal who'd pooped his way through the classics had better taste than that.

Finally I managed to punch on Self-Nav and a cheerful automated voice, faintly tinged Korean, announced that altitude 500 feet looked free and clear and asked us to confirm.

"Confirm," I said.

As soon as the word was out of my mouth, we lurched forward. I nearly put a tooth through the steering wheel. Just as quickly, we came to an abrupt stop, half an inch before we took off the bumper of the rig parked in front of us.

"Please prepare for takeoff," said the same chipper voice.

"Belts," I croaked out. We barely managed to strap in before the hover banked to the right, gathering speed down a narrow alley carved between floor models. Flexible steel wings unfurled from the roof as we hurtled down the makeshift runway. Our wheels hit a pothole and for a click we were airborne, before crashing to the ground again.

Barnaby was screaming and I was screaming and even Tiny Tim was screaming and Sammy had gone totally blank with fear. The fence was twenty feet away, then fifteen, then ten, and suddenly just as I closed my eyes and imagined a crash, we jumped into the air.

The force of the rise punched me to my seat. Even my lips felt like they were gumming the back of my skull. We cleared the fence, still picking up speed, pointed almost directly to the sky. I managed to turn my head and saw stucco roofs flash by, then the high scaffolds of some network towers waving bye-bye, and the twinkle lights of the city growing ever smaller.

At around 15,000 feet, we began to level off. We merged into the lowest altitude and skimmed a good stretch over the distant firefly city before climbing again, this time more gradually, to the second airway. A cop skimmed by us, nearly clipping our wings, in pursuit of a hover that had rocketed by us at turbo speed. We climbed again and finally settled at 40,000 feet. There were hardly any hovers in the air: nothing but a vast tract of sky above us, and lights winking on into the distance, marking the way.

So long and see you later, suckers.

Soon the city was nothing more than a grid of minuscule lights in the rearview. It looked like someone had yanked down a set of Christmas lights and left them coiled in the desert. The navigation pinned our flying time to Vegas at roughly three hours. There, we could refuel, and ditch the hover for a ride into the Real Friends© of the North. There was no way we'd make it past the border in a Halloran-Chyung flycraft.

The question was: Would we already be too late?

I tried to sleep, and fell into an uneasy dream—something to do with my mom, and a roil of cockroaches chittering a secret code . . .

I woke with a gasp. We were only forty miles from the air cordon that marked the border between Halloran-Chyung and Old Arizona. Ahead of us was what looked like a belt of stars, gut-strapping the horizon directly in our path.

"We won't clear the checkpoint," Sammy pointed out. I never knew if her habit of stating the obvious was part of the standard software or one of its individual glitches. "We're alien."

Alien. The word worked through my spine like traveling shrapnel. I'd never thought about it like that before, but she was right. The day Crunch, United, locked me out, I turned alien.

Or maybe before. Could you call your home *home* if it didn't belong to you? If everything you owned, even your space, even your time, was borrowed from someone else's bank?

"We're not going to make it through," I said. There was only one fix I could see: we would have to go dark. "We're going to fly *between*."

It would mean cutting power to the engines, at least until we were past the scanners that registered every flying craft tethered to nearby altitudes. Of course, no power meant no anticollision, no stabilization, no autopilot leveling us off in the correct lane. No power meant no flying at *all*—just a slow fall as gravity wrestled us out of altitude.

But we had no other choice. The watchtowers bloomed details as we slid closer. Glass pods were cabled up and down the elevations like giant drops of water, and inside each of them were the kind of military treads you hoped you didn't see even in your nightmares: hard-core missile systems, robots sprouting weaponry from every orifice you could think of and some you couldn't.

"Turn around," Sammy said suddenly. I looked over to see her knuckling the armrest, at least as much as she could without knuckles. "We won't make it."

"You're scared," I said, and she didn't respond, though I could hear her processing churning hard to keep up. "You're scared, Sammy. That's amazing. That means you're one step closer to real."

"I'm one step closer to ball-blasting you," she said.

The insults were new, too, but it didn't seem like the right moment to say so.

The traffic was thickening, and all the black-winged shapes condensing called back a memory that couldn't be mine, of a cloud of leather-winged bats making patterns in the air. Then I remembered ages ago Billy Lou Ropes telling me about his childhood trek down from Michigan during dissolution, and a house he lumped on after a week dodging militia and looters and National Guard. In the middle of the night he jerked awake to the sound of whispers all around, and thought they were surrounded. Then the whole ceiling came down, he told me, melted like a dark tar. It broke apart into hundreds and hundreds of bats, wings going hush as they scattered out the window.

Finally I landed on the right menu. I thumbed Energy Save and nearly jumped out of my rib cage when Automation blasted out of the speakers to no-shit me that cutting power to the engines would drop me straight out of fly mode.

"Begin Energy Save?" the operating system asked. Maybe it was just my imagination, but I thought its tone was edging toward a warning.

"Yes," I said. "Yes, yes, for fuck's sake."

For a second, the dashboard simply froze, and my heart dropped down to my feet and took my balls with it. Already, our hover was nosing into line, automatically funneling toward the checkpoint.

Then, all at once, everything quit.

The lights, the air con, the purifiers, the anti-radiation gear, the GPS: it all went dark without so much as a whine. We were invisible now.

We were also falling.

We were riding a shivering two-ton jigsaw of buckled steel thousands of feet from the ground, sliding an inch from a cable of aircraft above and below us, with skant room between us for a fart to pass through. We were so close to the border I could see the serial numbers on the military treads. Two hundred feet away, then one hundred—and every second, sinking.

Suddenly I *did* want to turn back. I wanted to crash. I wanted to do anything but slide closer to military alloy suited up with a fanny pack of sniper rifles and a dozen camera eyes.

But it was too late. For a hot second, we were level with the towers, protected from view only by the sluggish flow of hovers through the checkpoint above and below us.

I thought we froze. I thought time stopped.

I thought I might piss myself.

Then, just like that, like a spitball lobbed through a straw, we sailed over the border.

28

Different places got different needs for sure. Hillbilly towns'll go nutty for some TP and anything you got to stop the runs. Alligator boys pay five bucks on the dollar for clean skivs. In New New York they got a craze for fresh air bottled up near the Canadian border. And the dry countries'll buy anything that flows, even piss, so long as it looks clean.
—from *The Grifter's Guide to the Territories FKA USA*

We'd made it into Arizona.[1]

The change was immediate. Here there were no controls, no directional towers pulsing electromagnetic warnings if we started to drift into the wrong altitude, no monitors flashing speed warnings in the dark—nothing but empty space, a stifling, sticky dark, and a 30,000-foot fall to the waterless world beneath us.

I punched on the engines just as the law of forward motion gave a shrug and we tilted toward a nosedive. The brights, the autopilot, the steady thrum of the turbines—all of it came roaring back to life, and we leveled off just in time. But the lights did squat for us in unmarked airspace, with no signposts or towers or hover traffic. It was like lighting a torch inside a black box. If it wasn't for the altimeter that showed us holding level, we could of been gunning straight for the ground.

Sammy's indicators were a funny color—somewhere between a yellow and a green, a queasy shade. When I slid on the radio, she sluiced right

---

1. Figuratively; Arizona no longer existed.

away to a different channel. When I tried to amp the volume, she powered it down.

"Are you okay?" I asked her after the fourth time we went to battle, this time over the climate-control screen.

For a long minute, she was silent. But finally she huffed hot air from her speaker vents, sending up a flurry of dust particles. "Back at the border, you said I was one step closer to real." Her tone was new-model flatline. "I'm real already. You understand the difference, don't you?"

"You know I didn't mean it like that," I said.

Her lights sharpened toward ochre. "How did you mean it, then?"

"Come on, Sammy," I said. "I'm pro android rights." My hands were slippery on the steering wheel. I didn't know why I was even *bothering* to hang on—navigation was doing all the steering anyway—but I felt flattened in place, crushed by the weight of all the darkness outside. I hadn't vibed it was possible to feel claustrophobic in midair.

She swiveled her head on her neck. Back and forth. Even her gestures were more and more humanoid—she used to swivel her whole head around, like a horizontal wind turbine.

"Intellectually, maybe," she said. "But emotionally you see us as different. As *lesser*. I knew it back in Granby. I knew it in the hotel room. You looked at me as if I were salvage."

Remembering the tension between us, I couldn't help but feel like scum.

"Hey. I thought we got over that." I stopped myself from saying that at least part of it was her fault. She could of covered up some of her hardware, bought a NuSkin™ shell cover, tried to make herself a little prettier. If she was so obsessed with being human, you'd think she'd try acting it.

"*You* got over it," she snapped. One thing was for sure: Sammy could get as mad as any biological girl. "You never asked me what I thought. You never asked me what I felt."

Before I could think of a response, half a dozen warning lights flared on the dashboard, bathing us in a wash of red.

"Uh-oh," Tiny Tim said.

"Uh-oh, what?" I felt a scrabbly sense of panic. "What do all those lights mean?"

Tiny Tim leaned forward, so the red lights caught his scar and made it look even uglier than usual. "Looks like we burned up our gas already."

No sooner had he said the words than they were repeated by the cheerful system operator.

"Warning," she said in her mellow wavelength, as if she were actually saying *hello*. "Fuel reserves low. Please refuel at your earliest convenience."

"Jesus Christ." I'd never even thought to check the tanks before we launched. "Should we turn around?"

"Are you insane?" Barnaby squeaked. "We'll be thrown in jail as soon as we pass over the border."

It would be slightly better than dying of thirst in the middle of the abandoned Dust Bowl, all 110,000 squares miles of ghost towns, searing heat, desert snakes, and the occasional violent gang of peyote-gnawing nomads.

But only slightly better. Halloran-Chyung didn't like to keep its prisoners in max-security cities. Half the time the judge loosed them out into Arizona anyway. And that was if I *didn't* end up tased to death by some trigger-happy robot under Rafikov's command.

"We've got to go back," Tiny Tim said. "There's nowhere to touch down except the desert, and there's nothing in the desert except a whole lot of death."

One vote to turn. One vote to stay the course.

"What do you think, Sammy?" I asked her. Sammy only swiveled to stare out the window.

The operating system piped up again. "Please refuel immediately." She sounded like a tour guide pointing out a lovely arrangement of nuclear growth.

"*Please*, Sammy." She'd nailed passive-aggression, guilt trips, and now the silent treatment. She was one inexplicable crying jag away from being exactly like every other girl I knew.

Finally, she let out a long exhale through her heating vents. "We have no choice but to keep going," she said. "We're four hundred miles from Libertine."

"We'll never make it," I said.

"No," she said. "Probably not."

Sweat distorted my vision but it didn't matter: there was nothing in front of us, nothing behind us either. Five minutes later the hover dipped, and rocketed my stomach through my mouth. Tiny Tim moaned.

"Fuel reserves too low for continued flight. Automatic landing function deployed."

"No!" We could only be eighty miles into Arizona. If we landed, we'd trek for days across scorching desert before we had a squeak of reaching civilization. And we had no food, and not a single bottle of water, nothing but some half-filled purines. "No, no, no, no."

I punched the system, trying to stabilize our altitude. No dice. We dropped another five thousand feet.

"Override commands prohibited." The operating system sounded faintly irritated now. "Fuel reserves too low for continued flight. Automatic landing function deployed."

Tiny Tim moaned again. "I think I'm gonna be sick."

"We can't land here, Truckee." Barnaby was head-butting the back of my chair. "We're in the middle of the desert! We're directly above the Valley of Bones!"

"No shit." I was still frantically swiping through the dashboard. Windshield wipers began swishing. The radio lit up an instrumental version of the Crunchtown Crunk©. Heat blasted from my seat into my ass crack. I pressed Abort Landing about twenty times, but still we shed altitude, second by second. I could hear the engine coughing, sputtering on its final fumes.

Now the operating system was *definitely* annoyed. "Sorry, do you not speak English or something? Because I've explained plenty of times that the fuel reserves are too low for flight. For language preferences, see Settings."

"*No.*" I was so frustrated I smacked the dashboard with my palm, selecting about seventeen different options at the same click.

Suddenly, the radio went silent. The lights flickered and died. The windshield wipers stopped. The operating system whispered something that sounded very much like *asshole*, and then the dash went dark.

The engine cut out abruptly.

For a half click, it felt like we'd stabilized. We hovered there in space, floating in a misty netherland.

And then, ever so slowly, like passing over the edge of an invisible cliff, we fell.

Barnaby screamed. Tiny Tim screamed. Sammy's grinding error code sounded like a hacksaw trying to get through a steel pipe. Down and down, hurtling through the dark. I yanked hard on the wheel like I could bring us right through the force of my own biceps.

Then a building floated up out of the nothing and, with a terrible metal groaning, punched one of our wings straight off. We hurtled sideways as the driver's-side door ripped clean away and a street lamp reached up and walloped away one of our headlights. Weirdly, the dash lit up again, and the remaining headlight flared to reveal the spines of a ghost town even as the force of the impact flipped us sideways.

As we fell, I caught a quick glimpse through the windshield of an abandoned storefront and dusty windows still plastered with signs for SPRAY-TAN-PEDICURE-WAXING.

Our remaining wing crumpled beneath us. We were shooting, spinning down the road, like a gigantic hockey puck, letting out a grinding shower of sparks behind us. For a second it seemed we might spin forever down the empty street.

Then we came up against a street lamp, and Newton's second law of physical motion. I threw my hands up as a fine shower of glass rained down on us and Barnaby let out a final whimper.

And finally: silence.

29

There's two kinds of cartels up in the Free Territories: the ones that deal in drugs and make their money offline, and the ones that deal in water and have a finger in half a dozen countries' politics. But in my mind there's only one difference that counts: the Juarez boys will kill you quick. But the Flow-Fists will let you die slow.
—from The Grifter's Guide to the Territories FKA USA

Imagine being in an oven. Then imagine the oven shoved inside a furnace, and the furnace sunk into the molten core of the Earth.

That's what the heat in Arizona was like.

Bone melting. Skin bubbling. It liquefied brain mass. It scorched our thinking.

We'd crash-banged in one of Arizona's notorious ghost towns—according to our best estimates, more than three hundred miles away from any water source.[1] The only good news about being completely void on gas was it had saved us from getting torched in a skin-melting

---

1. After the first Noah storm system washed away coastlines from Galveston to Portland, Maine, three years of drought crippled the West Coast. The Real Friends© of the North routed nearly all the remaining water in the Colorado River straight to its tanks and treatment plants. Overnight, Arizona dried up. Five years after dissolution, a steady attrition out of the state had decimated the population of Arizona. By some estimates, only 50,000 people—one-twelfth of its population a decade earlier—were still surviving in Arizona by the time it was declared "uninhabitable" and the incumbent government of the former Nevada, backed heavily by Russian interests, decided not to stake a claim there.

explosion. Of course, if we'd had gas we wouldn't of crashed in the first place, but there was no point in focusing on the negative.

Signs of crippling drought were everywhere: hydrants busted open, decades-old water-shortage notifications, dirt-clotted cisterns, and long-neglected "rain totems"—ugly fugs of wood and decomposing stuffed animals and clothing, desperate offerings to God or the local-channel weatherman. The gutters were clotted with empty plastic bottles and shriveled purines, as if on the way out of Dodge all the people had wanted to leave evidence of why they had to run in the first place. Even the air was dry, and thin, and needed a good old plumping.

We had to move while the sun was down, even if it meant facing giant desert rats and nuclear spiders and other crazy beefed-up predators roaming the unspoiled desert. But we stopped to check the taps in every restaurant, business, or home we passed. We filled our purines with some dribbles of scalding water eked out from an old bar. From another tanning salon we scooped yellow water from a toilet tank. We shimmied through the shattered windows of a looted grocery store and scanned the aisles for bottled water or food or anything we could use. Behind a toppled shelf, we turned up a package of seaweed-flavored crackers fifty years expired.

We took them anyway.

Then we set out again, trying to cover as much ground as we could before the sun came up—and with it, the heat.

Barnaby suffered the most. It was pathetic to watch him stumble beneath all that shaggy fur, tongue out, eyes rolling in his head as if they were looking for a way to escape. But even Sammy began to error in the sun. One morning we couldn't get to shelter fast enough and she powered down completely. Tiny Tim had to push her the rest of the way to a township, head down, sweat moving in slick slug trails over his bald head. It took her half a day to come alive again, and for all those hours I sat there chunked up with guilt, afraid she'd never wake up.

Barnaby cried when he thought no one was listening. The dust matted his fur to filthy braids. I couldn't believe he had liquid left to turn to tears. On day three, with the sun scorching an old gas station even through the slatted wood nailed to the windows, his voice woke me.

"It's my father . . . he won't leave me alone . . . he won't let me sleep. . . ."

The effort to stand left me seeing stars. I moved closer to Barnaby and squatted so we were roughly eye to eye. The smell of him was all funk. It was like he was leaking tears out of his skin. "Hey. It was just a nightmare. All right? Just a dream."

He didn't seem to hear me. "They found him one morning in his cage. He'd managed to get hold of the polyethylburitane. . . ."

"I know, Barnaby. You told me."

"Poison. That's what it is. Poison." He was shivering, despite the heat. "It was *my* fault. I should never have been born. . . ."

"Shhh, Barnaby. It's okay. It's going to be okay." What else was there to say? The sun through the wood slats sifted dust motes into layers of deadly gold.

"He *hated* me." Suddenly his eyes found mine and he gave a little bleat. "You hate me too. I know you do. Oh, I don't blame you." He was losing it. He gave a low bleat that sounded almost like a laugh. "Why wouldn't you hate me? I'm disgusting. I'm a mistake. A freak show. I don't belong with animals. I don't belong with humans. I don't belong anywhere. I shouldn't even be alive." He began to cry again. His whole body heaved with the shake of it.

I'd never stopped to think about how crap Barnaby's life had been: born suddenly into a cage, a splice-and-dice experiment without a single living friend. And then years alone, hunted and despised, taking refuge in the shell of a library with only moldy books for company. I was almost glad that we'd never reach San Francisco now. I was glad I'd never have to admit I'd lied, that his skull would never meet Cowell's scalpel in the moneyed heart of the Emerald City, that he'd never know I was only leading him out there to die.

"Hey." I reached out to pat his head. His fur was clammy with sweat. But I didn't pull away. I just stayed there, gently stroking the fur between his ears. "You belong with us," I said.

He wiped a bubble of snot on his foreleg. "You don't mean it," he said.

"Sure I do," I said. And I did.

For a moment, we sat in silence. "I have to tell you something."

"What is it?" I asked.

He looked away, working his mouth over his long teeth. "That day with your friend, Billy Lou Ropes . . ." For the first time ever, the words seemed to be chewing around in his mouth, not the other way around. "I did mean to die, you know. I wanted to."

"I know," I said. "You told me."

"Just listen." But then he went quiet. I sat there, waiting, with the explosive sound of insects everywhere, moths as big as fists colliding with toppled metal shelves and pinkie-nail-sized ants swarming the walls. We could of been the only living beings bigger than water bugs left in the whole world.

Finally he started talking again, whispering now. "I remember he lifted me up and I could see the long fall, the hard break, and the peace that would come." A tremor shook him, nose to tail, like a current scrolling his whole body. "Only at the last second, I *didn't* want to die. I couldn't stand to die. I would have given anything to live. I would have begged. I was too afraid, you see."

He closed his eyes, shivering again.

"There's nothing wrong with wanting to live, Barnaby," I told him.

He shook his head. "I'm a coward."

"You aren't," I said. "Besides, there's nothing wrong with being afraid either. We're all scared sometimes. I'm scared a lot of the time."

"Just once," he said with a sad little smile, "just once, in my whole life, I'd like to do something brave."

I put a hand on his head again. "You will," I said, because what else could I say? We make promises to ourselves and to each other, even— *especially*—when our promises are lies. "You will."

We were crisp and we all knew it. We would die here in the Dust Bowl formerly known as Arizona: miles and miles of a world turned bone-white, and wind that hissed through the emptiness.

We crawled through bombed-out craters and scrolled through shopping malls reduced to rubble by homemade IEDs. Toppled water tanks looked like cracked eggs in the dust. Old Texas militia tanks still sat corroding in the weather and hacked-up Halloran-Chyung aid crates blinded the windows of the squats that survived, stained over decades to the deep maroon dust that settled everywhere. Ruined tent cities studded the horizon. Cars with dust-choked engines and their rubber tires long puddled to the asphalt sat on cracked ribbons of highway: monuments to a last, desperate exodus.

I escaped to the Yellow Brick Road when I could, for a few minutes at a time, trying to squeeze every bit of juice from my battery pack. I stood in front of the simulated fountains, passing a hand through the pixelated water. Or I scrolled shaded VR halls, imagining I could leave my real body behind, molt it like an old shell.

When I still had the energy to talk, I talked to Bad Kitty. Even through an interface in a simulated landscape filled with druggies and pedos, I could forget all about being locked out of Crunch, United, and tagged for an armed terrorist. I could forget about Jared and Annalee, forget about my mom, forget about what I'd lost or been forced to leave behind.

I learned her real name was Evaline, and she lived on the east side of Mount Hood in New Los Angeles, with two younger brothers, her mom, and three CARRIEs,[2] the android models who had raised her. Her parents divorced after her dad fell in love with a long-legged avatar in a

---

2. CARRIE, the official model name, is a play on the contraction of *care* and *IET*, or Intelligent Emotive Tech.

virtual-reality hotspot and spent half the family's fortune on new plug-ins and flash skins for her. He was in recovery now, she told me, but she wasn't sure she could ever trust him again.

Her favorite smell was silicone.

I learned when she was twelve she got fixed on the idea of tracking down the specific carrier who'd birthed her in one of the ground-level clin-ics, but had only gotten as far as a number: 224w. I learned her mom was pissed that the gene modulation they'd spent a fortune on couldn't do a thing about Evaline's sarcasm, or her habit of biting her nails.

I learned her brothers looked like their dad, and she like her mom, but somehow the chins got scrambled and she got the cleft. Her mom wanted to razor it down but quit needling her about it when Evaline threatened to shave her head in protest.

I learned that once she got lost in one of the poverty reservations on the other side of the 405, and she'd been swarmed by rats. Some of the slummers had come to her rescue to fight them off; there, she told me, they all bred cats as big as oxygen filters to keep the vermin out of their camps.

If she ever got a cat, she would name him Boris. Just because.

She was the first thing on my mind when I woke up, and the last thing on my mind when I closed my eyes. She filled my dreams, nudging me out of nightmares of Mark J. Burnham bearing down on me in a wheel-chair turned the size of a ten-ton rig, of Yana Rafikov blinking at me from behind the eyes of a sixteen-legged desert spider. It gave me some comfort to think of Evaline under that blue-dome sky, surrounded by the flash of Hollywood VR Palaces and Nutri-Pill factories and Silicone-Mold[3] clinics that turned people into their favorite celebrities. In a weird way, it made me feel better to know I would never have had a shot with her in real life. Staying alive wouldn't help me turn upper-crust, and it wouldn't make me good enough.

---

3. Also known as Plasticine.

Which made it just a little easier to die.

What's your favorite sound?

Rain through irrigation.

What's your favorite time of day?

Dawn. Sometimes they get the projection wrong, and the sun rises through midnight sky.

What would you be, if you could be anything or anyone in the world?

That one made her pause. Unexpectedly, she switched back to chat. "I'll tell you what I wouldn't be," she said. "I wouldn't be anything like my parents." Then: "How about you?"

With you, I nearly said. Instead I keyed: *A cat named Boris.*

I thought she would laugh. But instead her ears drooped slightly, and her eyes turned a deep violet. "You always ask me questions," she said, in a quiet voice. "When is it my turn?"

I was so weak I could barely swipe commands. *Soon,* I said. *I promise.*

But even as the words floated into the space between us, transforming to audio, a red light cut the simulation into hard flashes. I was out of power.

I knew then I would never see her again. Quickly, I tried to memorize her irises, the soft fuzz of fur between her ears, the sweet pink spot of her nose. But I was too exhausted. I couldn't focus.

She tilted her head. "Are you sure you're okay?"

I'm sure. A sudden bitter taste flooded my mouth: I was crying. *But I should go.*

Suddenly, she reached out to touch me—the very first time she had. Of course, I couldn't feel it. "Listen," she said, with sudden urgency. "I wanted to tell you—"

But I never found out what she was going to say. At that second, the simulation vanished, and she vanished with it, and my visor went black.

When I woke up, Tiny Tim was leaning over me. I could tell he'd been trying to get me up a long time. I wanted to ask what time it was but my throat was too dry. Words crumbled chalklike in my throat. My tongue tasted like the inside of a purine.

"Here," he said. "Drink this."

I was so weak he had to help me sit up. I felt the bite of plastic on my lips and wet—glorious wet—in my mouth and throat. I was so surprised I nearly coughed. The water was scalding and full of bacterial rot, but it was still the best thing I'd ever had. Too soon, Tiny Tim pulled away the bottle.

"Where'd you find it?" I managed to say. For days, we hadn't even had piss to convert.

Tiny Tim had no juice to smile. "Found some bones in the basement of one of these lean-tos. Still had the bottle up to his grille. I guess it didn't do him no good."

I wiped my mouth.

"Ganked these too." Tiny Tim held up three packages of forty-five-year-old Singles™, some of the very first flavors that Crunch ever printed: Pork-Belly Ramen, Tuna Negamaki, and Kale-Caesar Salad. I swear, I nearly cried again. But there wasn't even enough moist left in my body to make tears.

I hoovered the Pork-Belly Ramen, even though it was so old it had begun to degrade into its chemical flavors. We gave Barnaby the Kale-Caesar Salad and the rest of the water, although watching him chow I got backhanded by a terrible jealousy. Something violent and dark slotted strange thoughts in my head of spit-roasting leg meat and strips of fleshy pink tenderloin.

Tiny Tim didn't eat at all. When he tried to stand up he staggered momentarily and had to lean against the wall. But he recovered quick enough.

"I'm stronger than an ox and more stubborn too," he told me. "Don't you worry."

Sammy had shut down completely in the middle of the night. We tried everything we could to power her on, but her interface stayed dark. Not even a blip, a beep, or an error code. I tripped a hard reboot, sweating off the stench of panic, while Tiny Tim and Barnaby stood next to me in the half dark.

"She's not working, Truckee," Barnaby said softly, after my third reboot failed.

"I know she's not working, dammit. I'm not blind." I aimed a kick at the wall and regretted it when my foot sank through the plaster. Wrenching it out took nearly all the energy I had left. For a while I just stood there, panting, fighting off the swells of vertigo trying to rock me off my feet.

Finally, Tiny Tim cleared his throat. "You and me can take turns pushing."

I don't know why we went on. Maybe we were just too scared to wait for what was coming.

After sludging for what felt like an hour I turned to see how far we had come and saw behind us the shapeless lump of town we'd left behind. We'd gone barely a quarter of a mile.

The highway was cracked and even blistered, a skin too long exposed to the sun. Spiny desert plants punched through the asphalt. Even after dark, heat came thickly off the pavement, like clouds of insects we kicked up with our feet. On and on through the relentless dark, following the trail of the broken road. Tiny Tim and I took turns rolling Sammy, and lifting her over the worst stretches of road. I felt terrible palming and handling her while she was unconscious, but the alternative was worse.

On, with no end in sight, no water, no hope.

Sometime in the night through a dull buzzing in my head I heard voices and thought that at last I'd gone crazy. Instead I realized that Barnaby had begun to speak.

". . . of course the material evidence suggests the existence of not one but several earth gods," he was saying to empty air. "The Greeks and

Romans believed in polytheism, polyamory, polygamy. Marriage was initially a social contract. Only in the past forty years have we begun to see the irreconcilability of Newtonian physics and the social contract. . . ."

"Barnaby." Every word was painful. I tried to put a hand on his head and he jerked away. In the dark his eyes were wild and staring.

"How dare you, sir," he said. "This is a members-only club and we have strict rules against physical altercations—"

"Barnaby, it's me," I said. "Truckee. Truckee Wallace. We're on the road to San Francisco."

His face changed again. He settled down where he was with a gentle sigh. "California," he breathed. "I've always wanted to go back to California. Palm trees and beach boys. Surf girls and Hollywood . . ." He settled his head on his hooves and closed his eyes.

"Barnaby, wake up." I knelt down to shake him. "Barnaby, you can't stay here. Wake up."

He barely stirred. I could see his nostrils flaring gently in and out, in and out. I could see his eyelids trembling with dream.

I could see.

I turned to look behind me and saw a red stain at the horizon.

The sun was rising.

"Tim." I tried to call out to him but my voice wouldn't carry. "Tim." Though I was hobbling, bent nearly double just from the effort of pushing Sammy, I caught up with him quickly. He was swaying on his feet. When I approached he cracked down onto his knees. "We have to hurry. The sun's coming up. We need to find shelter."

He shook his big head. "There's no shelter to find, Truckee," he said.

He was right. There was nothing ahead of us but the rusty silhouette of distant mountain ridges, more dusty road, more desert plants knuckling through the parched soil.

"We have to move, anyway." My head felt like it was full of flies, pinging dimly around the same idea: *One foot in front of the other. Just keep going.*

"You go on," he said. His breath came in short wheezes, like the air from a mold-choked generator. "I'll catch up with you later."

If I'd been thinking straight, I would of known he was lying.

"I'll go slow," I said, as if there were another option. I patted his big head, slick with sweat. "I'll find somewhere for us to sleep."

"Take this." He tried to pass me the last food we had, the third Singles™ meal, and deep in the heat-broiled soup of my mind I knew what he was doing. I almost took it too.

Almost.

But the truth is I was so thirsty I couldn't even swallow.

"You be quick," I said, and he nodded again.

I left him kneeling on the road. I put my whole back into wheeling Sammy, though she couldn't have weighed forty pounds. I didn't even have the energy to turn around when I heard a thud, like a palm smacked to the ground, and knew Tiny Tim had fallen.

I don't remember when the sun came up, only a red world, like the color behind your eyelids when you squeeze them too tight. Only a blood world, turned inside out with the guts of it exposed.

I don't remember, either, where I left Sammy. Only that one moment I was pushing her and then I wasn't, and thinking she had wandered off, and starting out across the desert thinking I was calling for her though I couldn't hear anything but the pressure of all that heat, like the jaws of something wheeling closed. There was water on the horizon, a big lake of it: I went toward it but found it kept trotting away, found that every time I reached for shade it evaporated, and by the time I realized I'd left the road I could no longer see it behind me and didn't know which direction I'd walked. And still the lake, that giant lake of shaded trees and spring-fed water, was too far away to reach. I was eating dust. A spider scuttled past my eyes before I scanned I was on the ground.

The earth trembled. I heard wheels and motion, saw dust tracking into the sky as though kicked up by a giant monster. Voices called to me. Evaline bent over me, and then my mother, soothing me to sleep.

INTERLUDE

A SHORT EULOGY

Three days after ground crew scraped my mom's body off the concrete, poured her into a corrugated cardboard coffin, and shoved her into Plot 2882, I got a summons from HR.

It was brittle cold, with ash blowing in from wildfires raging so hard in BCE Tech it almost looked like snow. Tears froze my lashes together and scalded my eyeballs, turning solid before they could fall.

In the sprawl of beige-carpeted block-cells that counted for Corporate Regulation, I met with the typical HR rat: mid-thirties, with the pale flabby look of a vitamin-enriched loaf of Crunch bread. According to her name tag, she was Melissa! Not Melissa. Melissa!

When Melissa! stood up to offer her condolences, I could see the gun holster riding high on her waist, revealing a roll of stomach flab. That really got me: the fact that her organs beneath that stomach were still working, and my mom's weren't.

"Truckee Wallace," she said. HR idiots always made a point to use our full names, as if the fact they didn't just refer to us by ID number was a big gift. It was one of their weird tricks. "I'm so sorry about what happened to your mother."

"Thank you," I said. The HR department gave me the creeps: the thin chill of the air, the medicinal smell, carpeting that suctioned up sound and windows that looked out onto a belching waste incinerator and thousands of rows of dead crumbs, and beyond that, to the river Technicolor with chemical slick.

"Go on, sit down," she said. Another HR trick. The chair drawn up to her desk looked as if it had been stolen from one of the nursery schools. Sitting in it would place me eye to eye with a framed certificate commemorating Melissa! on ten years of service to the corporation, and a small standard-issue Glock, sleek and snub-nosed.

I sat anyway. Melissa! gave me back my mom's visor, which was pointless, both because it had been wiped already and because I still had only thirty days to return it to Technical Support before I got docked. But the SmartBand, she said, was mine to keep. The inside was all brown from my mom's sweat, and if I put it to my nose and inhaled, I could smell her: vape and fresh and cream to combat dayglo.

"We've been reviewing your file," she said. There was no "I" in Human Resources. Only a "we." Like they were a single consciousness hacked up into different physical bodies. "You've shown no tardies, only one Health-Pass day in the last year—you must be eating your VitaCrunch™ in the morning."

I didn't eat VitaCrunch™. Nobody in Crunchtown ate VitaCrunch™, because VitaCrunch™ was pumped full of so much nicotine it would stop your heart if you weren't careful. But I didn't say so.

"Recently, we've had a sudden job opening in the Freight and Shipping department," Melissa! went on. "Associate pattern regulation, just a notch below management level."

I stared at her. "You're talking about my mom's job?"

She blinked. "It's a huge salary increase," she said. "Nearly double."

"My mom died three days ago," I said. "She was killed by a package of falling Tater Tots."

Actually, crushed beneath a two-ton shipment container of Crunch RealCheez Tater Totz™ that slipped its freight. A freak accident, a faulty restraint, a midcentury safety system that blinked out at just the wrong time.

My mother, my only parent, with skin like river mud and a laugh like an explosion, knocked straight into the hereafter by vegetable derivative.

She didn't even like Tater Tots.

"Really?" Melissa! leaned back in her chair. "I'd heard it was Crunch-Veggie Chipz™."

She didn't say it to be mean, I don't think.

"I'll keep my old job," I said. "Thanks."

On the way back to my shoebox, I noticed thousands of crumbs massing on the rooftops to star-hunt, so many it looked like all the buildings were sprouting mold. But I didn't care anymore about the Shit Shovel or the Tampon—I didn't care if North Korea and Texas blew a hole through the whole sky, like they were always swagging they would. It made me angry that the stars were still around, lumps of interstellar flatulence, and my mom was a pile of ash, that her teeth were ash, and her toenails and eyelashes and fingers, that her laugh was ash and her jokes were ash and those cold fires in the sky that had never loved anybody got to keep shining and she didn't.

Billy Lou was waiting for me at home. He was smoking shiver—a roll of it flared between his fingertips—and normally I would of yelled at him, but just then I didn't care. I sat next to him without turning the lights on and for a while we said nothing. The only sound was a low hiss when he inhaled. When I was in my right head, I couldn't stand the reek of shiver. But I thought it smelled good, sweet and sharp and terrible, like what came up from the incinerators when bodies were getting burned.

At some point, I reached for the spliff, but he held it out of reach. "No way, kid," he said. The only time he ever called me anything but Mr. Truckee.

"Why?" I said. All of a sudden, I was furious. "Why does it matter?"

He stubbed out the spliff on the edge of the table and pocketed the remainder. "It's cheating," he said. "You want to snuff quicker, that's your business. But I'm not going to give you a boost."

Somehow that did me in. It was easier to blubber with the lights off. I cried the kind of crying that's like swimming in your own snot. I cried like the dimeheads cried when they were coming down. Not because the high was wearing off but because it was never high enough to keep morning from coming.

Finally I ran through the grief. It passed off like a fever, and I sat there cold and stone-tired, feeling just like a wind blowing through an empty hallway.

"She loved you more than anything," Billy Lou said.

"I know," I said.

"She knew you were meant for great things," he said, and we sat there in silence again. I was sorry both because I knew she believed it and I knew it wasn't true.

Outside, the darkness shifted textures. Voices lifted to holler up at the stars. *Turd and Dingle,* they cried. *And look—the Whore's Bath.*

"You think she's up there somewhere, looking down at us?" I blurted out. It was an idea I'd heard somewhere when I was a kid: that everyone who died lived bliss-high as a spirit, that all of our loved ones tailed us, spiritual toilet paper stuck to our shoes.

"No," Billy Lou said. I turned to look at him and in the trickle of light coming through the window, his face was all pits and craters and crags, moonlike. "I think wherever she is, her view's a whole lot prettier than this dump truck."

We never talked about my mom again. A week later, he was fired for stealing dymo from the company store. By the time HR swarmed his shoebox to arrest him, he was poof and gone.

But I remembered what he said, and it made me feel better. Sometimes before I went to sleep I liked to imagine her riding the back of a rocket ship made of stars, looking not down but up, up, and up, and up, into a fireworks explosion of past and present and future, all of it burning to make something out of the dark.

Part IV

WALDEN → LAS VEGAS, LIBERTINE

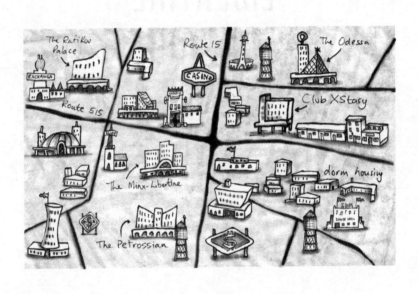

30

*They say if you can make it in New New York, you can
make it anywhere. But that's only if you're lucky enough
to make it out of there first.*

—from *The Grifter's Guide to the Territories FKA USA*

In my dream I was back at 1 Central Plaza, in President Burnham's office, relaxing in the cool tongue-lick of the air-conditioning. It was very dark. Soon I figured why: President Burnham had plunged his office down inside the Underground.

You can never be too careful, he said. On his desk an enormous glass jar filled with murky liquid let out a queasy green light. Suspended inside of it were two small globes that trailed long, pink tentacles. Even in my dream I knew the jar was real, that I'd actually seen it. I edged a little closer. . . .

Sorry about that. We had to take out your eyes. Shrapnel.

Then I was blind and on a gurney while a health manager rooted through my stomach. *Where is it?* A smiley face floated in the darkness behind my eyelids. *Where did the rest of it go?*

Use the drones, if you can't find it, Burnham said. I could see again, barely. Tiny metal drones condensed the air into a flash of metal. When they poured down into the cavity of my open stomach I screamed. Then they were sliding down my throat as well, all that cold metal, pouring into my lungs and freezing them—

I woke up cold and shouting.

"Shhh. Drink. It's good for you."

There was water in my throat and mouth, water soaking my pillow, water thick on my tongue. The stranger by my side was a silhouette in the darkness. Through an open door, I saw a moon bloated with its own light, floating tipsy-like among the stars.

"It's all right."

The stranger—a woman—pulled away. I began to cough, and then I began to cry.

"Shhh. You're safe now. It's all right."

Where am I? I wanted to say. But already the dream took hold of me again, and pulled me down inside it.

When I woke again, it was very bright, and the same stranger was touching my face. She had a long gray braid and a face full of pits and crevices that reminded me of my mom's. But there wasn't a hint of dayglo on her.

"Finally, you're awake." When she smiled, all the creases in her face folded together, like they were joining for the effort. "I was just putting some aloe on your burns. You got toasty. You want some water?"

Whatever she poured wasn't water. It was music in liquid form.

"How long was I out?" I asked. My throat felt like a trash bag filled with barbed wire.

"Two days. You're lucky we found you," she went on. "You were a few minutes from turning into a giant blister."

Suddenly memories tumbled me down into a panic. I remembered the mirage of water beyond my reach; Tiny Tim on his knees; leaving Barnaby and Sammy, poor Sammy, behind.

I tried to sit up. "I was traveling with friends. There were three others. We have to help them."

"It's all right." She pressed me back against the pillows. "We picked them up. Your friend Barnaby is doing just fine, now we plumped him full of fluid. He's been telling the young ones all about his book. And Tim, bless him, asked to trade us matchbooks for a meal." She laughed again. "As if we'd ask for payment from a friend in need."

"What about the android?" I said. "Is she okay? Has she woken up?"

The woman hesitated. "We're working on it," she said, and just like that my relief evaporated. "Don't give up just yet," she added softly. "We're keeping her in a cool, dark place, and looking at the damage piece by piece."

I knew she was trying to help, but the idea of Sammy hacked up into component circuit boards made me feel even worse. It was all my fault. I'd crashed the hover. I'd forgotten to check for gas. I'd hurt Sammy's feelings.

And I'd never even had the chance to apologize.

The woman leaned forward to place a hand on my sleeve. She was as ugly as a backland witch but she smelled like an uppercrust, very clean. "Believe me. I've seen Engineered People make miraculous recoveries. Your friend might be stronger than you think. And we have experts here. . . ."

She trailed off as the front door opened with a groan. I had a quick view of green—not neon green or yellow green or lime green, but green like the park simulation inside the Yellow Brick Road—before three kids scooted inside. When they spotted me, all three dropped their jaws at once.

"Well? Go on. Take what you need and flam." The woman shooed them off behind a floral sheet, strung up like a curtain next to the bed. I heard mysterious banging noises, drawers opening and shutting. When they reappeared, they were decked in strange metal armor that looked like early-century cookery.

Once again, as she rounded them out the door, I got a good eyeball of vivid green growth, far too irregular to be rectangles of TrueGrass™. The woman must be a real uppercrust. Who could afford so much flow?

"Where am I?" I asked her. I figured we might of landed in a resort on the outskirts of Las Vegas, blazing "rustic last-century" experience to the tune of five thousand chips a night.

"Oh, we've had different names over the years. But Walden seems to be sticking. Thoreau was a big inspiration."

Whoever Thoreau was, he was a shit decorator. The house was smaller than a Low Hill shoebox and crowded, with a bunch of rough-hewn patchstack so ugly it could of been stripped from real trees—though no one would be idiot enough to waste trees on making furniture. Plus, something was missing. I couldn't put my finger on it, but it left me squirmy, like wiggling a full-body loose tooth.

"Nice place," I lied. "How far are we from the Strip?"

"The Strip in Las Vegas?" She laughed. "I'd say you're still a good twelve hours' drive from the border of Libertine, what with the roads being all cracked up."

My heart sank. God forbid I was in one of the Old Colorado cartel towns that served as lookout points in case banditos or military law came around. "Twelve hours' drive? But that means we're—"

"Still in Arizona," she finished, before I could say, *in cartel territory*.

I stared at her. For a second, I thought she'd lost her straw. "Arizona," I repeated, and she nodded. "You're telling me *this* is Arizona?"

She laughed again. "Well, a very small part of it, yes."

"That's impossible," I said. "Arizona doesn't even exist anymore." Five million had fled the droughts. Another million and a half had died. *Arizona* had died.

"Arizona may not exist. But Walden does," she said simply, shucking a bit of gray hair behind her ear. "We're sovereign. We don't belong to anybody but ourselves."

Only then did I register she had no visor. Her eyes were too focused for a retinal implant. And suddenly I scanned what was missing from the squat: there were no wires or cables, no outlets or batteries, boost boxes or speakers or cloud drives or holoscreens.

I fought a hard wave of panic: we were completely off the grid.

The stranger's eyes were the exact color of a smile. "Welcome to heaven, my friend."

31

There's plenty of good dross still left for the picking in the old ghost towns, long as you know how to look. Sure, the place'll be stripped of the obvious stuff—electricals, clothing, food. But remember that after dissolution plenty of people holed up for the siege, and did what all pack rats do: hide shit. I've found cellar hidey-holes and money stuffed in chimney flues and more gold than I can count packed in the crumbling caulk of old turd piles in a thousand sewage tanks and outhouses.
—from The Grifter's Guide to the Territories FKA USA

Heaven, it turned out, was forty-five miles south of the McDonald's-Hyatt Canyon™ and the bare piss stream of the Colorado River that still tickled its bottom, and boasted roughly two thousand full-time residents. They'd escaped from the temp camps, and canoed up from the swamp of drowned land near old New Orleans, where no one lived but the alligator men.[1] There were cheery, round-faced *drook* from the Russian Federation and scrawny, bleary-eyed kids, pale as glowworms, still quivering from their trauma in the San Francisco Start-Ups.[2]

1. A nickname arising not merely because of the swamplands that comprised their habitat and hunting grounds—the alligator men subsisted by scavenging for usable supplies in the thick soup of swollen water that had eradicated much of the coastline—but for the unique dermatological condition known as "black rot" that resulted from living in and feeding off of the contaminated water.
2. The Start-Ups were no more or less than a form of culturally enshrined, technologically dependent, modern feudalism, in which the start-up workers pledged their

There were even a handful of refugees from across the ocean, where life was just as bad or even worse. Spain, where kids got pawned off to ant for wealthier neighbors by desperate parents, had shipped over three families. Old countries blasted in half by bombing decades ago had shipped a few dozen more. Somehow, despite the flesh pirates and the ocean pickers and the Russian subs turning half the Atlantic to a war zone, they'd found their way here, to the middle of the old USA, to start over.

The woman who'd brought me back from the cusp of dying had come from Sinopec-TeMaRex Affiliated. Her name was Susan, and she'd been born on the plains of what was then called Illinois, where for generations her family had been farmers. Her grandparents had made a fortune on the first round of fast-cycling crops, and lost it all once the corn grew so aggressive it stripped off all the soil and started gobbling up houses. The tornado cycles took care of the rest. She'd seen her own father smothered to death by aggressive alfalfa plants, and was fleeing south when she'd caught wind of a so-called utopia springing up in the bones of the Dust Bowl.

"I don't understand," I said. Susan had taken me outside for a squint at Walden. I was still too weak to go far. But from the front porch I had a nice squint of real growing things, sprawls of grass and trees and even flowers—and not the silicone ones either. "I thought the Colorado River went dry."

"It did," Susan said. "For a long, long time. Those were the drought years everyone's heard stories about. I was a little girl in Albuquerque when Noah Two hit. I remember all the refugees that came through as the drought deepened, all of them covered in white dust, choking on their own tongues and staggered from dehydration. They said Arizona was done. They talked about building a wall."

She shook her head and reached out to finger the ridged leaf of a tomato vine climbing her front porch. Without meaning to, I twinned her.

---

time and labor to a very limited quantity of highly wealthy overlords in exchange for subsidized housing, free lunch, and the occasional game of Ping-Pong.

I half-expected my hand to pass through it, the way it would of on the Yellow Brick Road.

She was quiet for a click. Here in Walden, furred in by growth and the faint mist of an in-ground sprinkler system, the sun felt bearable. Somewhere, notes of music climbed on currents of air.

"It's funny how things work out," she said. "Balance. The way new things are born from destruction. I guess that's called evolution." She turned away from the tomato field and we kept walking. "You heard of the nuclear fracking they do up in the Dakotas?"

"Sure," I said.

She smiled. "When they started nuking down in the Bakken Formation, they found new oil deposits, sure, new natural gas fields. They also shook up the earth. I've heard of earthquakes lasting in Iowa and Kansas for days at a time. And sinkholes. Well. No wonder Nebraska's up for sale.[3] From what I hear, it's just a giant sinkhole. But all of that creeping beneath the crust pushed new water into the river basin. Not a lot, but enough for us."

The people of Walden lived totally without juice, except for what they needed to run their plumbing ("There's no utopia without flushing toilets and cold showers") and a few rigged "environmental adjusters": outdoor lights, cooling mechs, and water-sprinkling systems. All their power came through renewable energy like wind and even the desert climate itself: they'd even souped up a coolant that scammed off the relative density of cooling air. She told me, too, that in Walden they ate nothing made with chemical additives, hormones, substitutes, or synthetics.

---

3. In 2084, only two years, in other words, before most scholars believe this book was written, the Dakotas successfully negotiated the purchase of Nebraska for a pitiful 10,000 RealFriends© winks. Of course, by then the population was decimated. By some estimates the country, which had limped along largely through the export of its ranch animals to the continent's methane-producing energy houses, contained fewer than 10,000 people, meaning the Dakotas paid roughly one RealFriends© wink per head. It is largely assumed that the Dakotas' oil and gas interests negotiated the sale to put an end to Nebraska's alternate-energy industry.

It was like saying that the people in Walden didn't breathe air. Chemical additives, hormones, substitutes, and synthetics *were* food.

"What do you eat, then?" I asked, hoping the answer wasn't grubs or, even worse, body rot from one of Arizona's mass graves.

"Real food," she answered.

"Yeah, okay," I said. "RealFood™. Sure."

"Not RealFood™," she said. "Real food. Food we grow ourselves."

"You have your own agrofirms?" I'd never heard of a hillbilly town with its own food production.

She shook her head. "No, no. Food we grow in the ground."

I was more confused than ever. Agrofirms still converted sunlight so I didn't see how you could sink them.

"Here. I'll show you. Take a seat." She plunked me down on a rocker and disappeared inside for a while. Instead of the beeps and whistles I knew from one-and-done ovens, or even the heavy grinding of a home printer, I heard a slop heap of sizzles, hisses, and pops, plus a lot of metal clanging. The smell, too, had none of the chemical edge I knew from childhood, no special SmartScents™ I could pick out.

After several minutes she reappeared with a plate.

"Go on," she said. "Take a bite. You'll love it. There's nothing like real food after a lifetime of substitutes. It's a grilled cheese," she added, when I lifted the dish to sniff it.

Oozy and crusty and blackened and slick, all at the same time, it was nothing like the GrilledCheez™ I'd grown up on, with its vivid orange cheese and neat corners and flash diagonal grill marks that darkened when you slotted them under a lamp. Pools of something that looked like lipid 607a dripped onto the plate. It looked like an edible wound.

Still, I was starving, and Susan had saved me from evaporating into a pile of bones, so I gave it a shot. The nosh wasn't as bad as it looked, but I missed the salt-burst aftertaste and the chem adds that gave the bread its boost. The cheese wasn't even flavored with Shakin-Bakin' or Jalapeno-Popper-Explosion or PepperCornParty! It was just . . . cheese.

I didn't finish the whole thing.

"Oh, well," Susan said. She looked a little disappointed. "I guess it takes some getting used to."

It was like no hillbilly town I'd ever seen. No one was starving, first of all. There were no flu warnings, no mass graves, no crusted, fly-chewed garbage pits, no reek of sewage or swarms of overgrown cats with a taste for chemical waste and human pinkie fingers. There were no armories, no company stores, and no ration announcements.

Children scrolled around barefoot through massive rows of silk-tipped growth Susan told me was popcorn, but without the pop. Girls in faded cutoffs and T-shirts giggled together as they dug for lumps from the ground (*potatoes*, *squash*, *radishes*) uncolored by chemical castoff. People grinned in the sun like someone had upped their dosages. Coils of tomato vines, fields of golden wheat. Kids shuffled physical cards at picnic tables, or gamed with an actual ball—a sleek, orange sphere I mistook at first for an excavated land mine.

The houses were more or less template, styled after the last-century Americana of ancient record players and blue jeans and people who had to go to theaters for virtual reality. But one house stood out: real swank, twice as big as the others, with a bunch of look-at-me features like storm shutters and rainwater purifiers.

"Who squats there?" I asked.

She frowned. "Right now? The Edwards family, I think. Sometimes the Richardsons. Sometimes the kids stay over and the parents hightail across the square for some quiet."

"But who owns it?"

Susan stopped walking and began to laugh. She laughed so hard, she wasn't even shaking with laughter: the laughter was shaking with *her*. "Sorry. I always forget, you know, when new people . . ." Seeing the look on my face, she shook her head. "No one owns anything here. Walden is a share community."

"A what?"

"A share community," she said, like repeating the words might give them some sense. "There's no ownership. We all own everything."

No wonder the whole place felt a little off. "So you're Communists?"

"No." She squinted, like she was trying to make her visor feed line up with the horizon. Except she had no visor, and no feed. "In Communist systems, the state owns the resources and doles them out as they see fit. But no one owns anything here, and so everyone owns everything. Cooking materials, houses, tomato gardens . . . everything belongs to all of us equally."

It was, hands-down, the most idiotic system of any I'd ever heard of—counting Miami, where wealth and power were allotted in proportion to a person's tan and breast-implant size.[4]

"Come on," she said, once she was through laughing at the look on my face. She threaded an arm through mine. "There's something I want you to see."

She waved me on down a tree-lined alley and into the shade of an old quarantine tent, repainted a patchwork of colors to hide the insignia.

I swallowed a shout. Sitting at a long rough-hewn table, dappled by sunlight, were Barnaby and Tiny Tim.

And next to them, the familiar torpedo shape of an ancient-model android.

"Sammy!" I was across the courtyard and hugging her before I knew I'd moved.

"Truckee." She gave a series of beeps and whistles that might of been a laugh. "Careful. You'll trip all my new circuitry."

"Sorry." I pulled away, keeping one hand on her shoulder joint. She looked incredible. Her interface was wiped clean, her speaker grille was free of dust, and—

"Your lens," I blurted out. "You got a new one."

---

4. At the time, the wealthiest woman in Miami couldn't walk without the help of two servants, each hefting one of her massive, double-T-sized breasts.

"Yes," she said, rotating it. "Isn't it fantastic? It has all the newest fiber optics and more than ten times the resolution of my last one."

I wanted to be happy for her. But a lens like that was going to cost us more chow than I'd ever touched. I turned to Susan. "Nice upgrade," I said. "What's that going to ring us?"

"Nothing." She laughed. "It's a gift."

"Sure." I forced a smile so she knew I could take a joke. "You gave a perfect stranger a brand-new fiber-optic 360-degree lens for free. Nothing belongs to anybody else and all that."

"Exactly. Some of our young men and women and non-gendered humans are quite the tinkerers. We have a whole engineering corps. They were happy to do it. Besides," she added, "you aren't strangers anymore."

I realized she wasn't kidding. But I figured she'd try and stick us with the bill later, maybe in the form of kinky sexual favors. Maybe Walden was one of those religious cultist places where people used "community talk" to justify bumping rags with all their neighbors.

There *was* no such thing as free. It was the one law in the world we could all agree on.

That night we ate outside in a big park: homemade pasta and real butter and cheese, grilled corn, and peach salad. As the temperature dropped, we flowed down to a fire pit to drink homemade wine and listen to music beneath a scrim of smoke and the stars shining through it.

And in the morning, when Susan woke me up with some coffee stripped from actual beans, my mind buzzed around the same thought, over and over like a fly around a RealPeach™ Sugar Crunch Salad canister.

What the hell was wrong with these people?

32

If someone offers you a deal that sounds too good to be true,
don't be surprised to wake up with your pants off.
—from The Grifter's Guide to the Territories FKA USA

It was misery: Four days without portal, without feeds, without livestream and ambient music or the chatter of faraway voices talking tricked-up politics and national pride. All I had for entertainment was *The Grifter's Guide,* and even there I was stuck smack-dab in the middle. I couldn't even slip onto the Yellow Brick Road to chat with Bad Kitty—to chat with *Evaline.* There was a firewall to stop it, and besides, there was nowhere to juice my visor.

"Too many people," Susan said, "live their life like *pollo,* heads under their wings, always sweating someone else's body, someone else's life. They give up their real lives to try and live a fantasy. We want to change that."

I almost pointed out that the problem wasn't fantasy. The problem was real life being so damn crap to begin with. But there was no point wasting my bandwidth. Like my ma always said, you don't give socks to a slug.

I couldn't shake the feeling that we'd dropped off the world into a creepy simulation, and that by the time we escaped there would be no world to come back to. But Sammy had to work out a few kinks in her operating system and I was still blistering off a slough of burned skin and weak from sun fever, and as long as we were stuck, I had to play like I thought squeaking it in the middle of nowhere and digging sewage trenches from scratch were the best things that ever happened to anybody.

On my third day awake, Susan lathered me up with aloe and sunscreen and took us out on four-wheelers across the desert to the McDonald's-Hyatt Canyon™. It was weird to leave Walden and its shelter of greenery and water, and to launch again into a bone-colored landscape—it was the same pulverizing comedown I got from quitting a really good simulation and finding the world just as ugly as I left it.

The canyon itself was toothy with abandoned luxury houses, hotels, tourist shops, slop shops, and malls in a state of decay. More than a few condos and a big-ass wing of the Grand Hyatt had toppled over the cliffs, chewed away by wind and the punch of faraway earthquakes. Broken pylons and support beams littered the canyon floor like so many matchsticks. A McDonald's teetered on a slim rock outpost, just barely clawing on. Within a hundred years, Susan said, all the buildings would be gone, bucked off by the earth they were clinging to, driven into dust like the bones of all their desperate suited-up shamsters and mortgage loaners and developers.

The world goes on without us, she said. Like that was supposed to be comfort.

I kept searching Walden for signs of freaky sex rites or cultism or brainwashing, and kept coming up empty. There was no leader, no one preaching about fire and brimstone, no one to shep a thousand different wives into service, like I'd heard the Children of Nature guru had done in the Green Mountain Associated Intentional Communities—before the whole country outlawed gender, and wives, and marriage.[1]

Sammy got friendly with an engineer and his android wife, who told horror stories of her work in the Dakota fracking camps and a liberation by the ALF only days before she was due to be disassembled for scrap. We even helped them do some handiwork on their baby, which they were designing from orphaned android parts.

Even nature seemed to go easier here, sheltered from the worst of the quake zone that belted California to Sinopec-TeMaRex Affiliated.

---

1. And all forms of communication besides hugs (but only with written consent).

Ingenious stone towers trapped the desert air at night and exhaled it all over the town when the fans were cranked. The soil was unpolluted by chemical leach—one benefit, I guess, of losing your whole population in a sudden diarrhea stream—and Susan showed me how to pick blueberries and raspberries from the fields, working row after row of real branches.

I just couldn't believe there wasn't a catch.

One afternoon I was working the fields next to a ze, maybe ten or eleven years old, with the slow drawl of the Confederacy and a face full of freckles, who kept trolling me for the way I was going after the blackberries. They were the fastest picker I'd ever seen, and they'd filled up their basket before I'd managed to get a dozen.

"So, how much do you get comped?" I asked, trying to sound casual.

Ze looked up at me, blinking, like I'd just asked how to get to the next dimension of the multiverse. "Comped?" they repeated.

"Sure," I said. "You know. Comped. Paid. Blinged-up." No answer. They just kept staring at me blankly. "The town must pay you *something* to ant out here all day. I mean, no one spends hours picking berries for fun."

It was like someone had poked them in the nose and turned it into a sinkhole. Their whole face collapsed. Their lower lip quivered like a plucked noodle. And before I could say anything more, they rocketed to their feet and darted away, down a long aisle of plants punching out little green fists.

A minute later, they returned, trailing Susan behind them. Susan looked angry for the first time ever. The ze looked all puckered around an urge to start wailing.

I stood up. "I didn't mean to upset them," I said quickly.

"You didn't upset them. You confused them." Susan sighed. "Look, Truckee. I know the way we live might seem strange to you, but the truth is that people lived this way for many, many years."

"You're talking about the hippies?" I said.

She smiled as if I were a first-generation robot, like it was a miracle I knew how to lift my arms. "I'm talking about various indigenous tribes throughout the world. I'm talking about communities *of* community, where identity with the whole was as important as identities with the self."

More sharing-and-caring promo spam. Susan knew I wasn't buying it. She sighed again.

"Come on," she said. "I want to show you something."

She led me out of the fields. I turned around once to see the ze still glaring. They even stuck out their tongue. Well. At least not everything in Walden was different. Eleven-year-olds were still assholes.

We scrolled down a street packed with all the scavenge the people of Walden hadn't found use for: stacks of tile and four-by-fours, slate roofing and plastic tarps, old sinks rusted at the drains, and empty metal cisterns. At the end of the litter was a dumpy wooden shed. Susan gave the door a hard shove and hesitated for just a click before waving me inside.

The place was dark and reeked of mildew. It took a second for my eyes to adjust, and when they did, I nearly blacked out: the shed was small, plain, and completely empty.

Except, of course, for the money.

The squat was crawling, teeming, shimmering with cash. It looked like half the chow in the world had crawled to the same place just to lie down and die.

Buckets of Western gold. Heaps of Manna, glimmering in the half dark as if they really had come down from heaven. Stacks and stacks of Crunchbucks, rubber-banded together, not just tens but hundreds and even thousands, colored a rare violet I'd only seen once or twice in my whole life. Suitcases so stuffed with Texas dollars they wouldn't close. A trunk filled with discarded U-bytes, which I knew must be packed with a lifetime's worth of RealFriends© wealth: encoded winks, nudges, pokes, grins, and smiles, hundreds of thousands of digital dollars. Maybe millions.

". . . was serious when I told you we're a sharing community . . ."

Susan's voice sounded distant. Maybe because in my head I was tumbling in the money, stuffing my grille and ears with it. Even a quarter of the floss in the room would last me a lifetime. No—two lifetimes.

". . . ask them to give up the currencies of their old lives . . ."

I was swimming in paper, chewing my way through the towers of Crunchbucks, gnawing slowly, paper piece by paper piece.

"Do you understand it now?"

In my head, I was halfway through a mouthful of metal Manna before Susan's question finally touched my mind. I had to swallow twice before I could talk, working down the phantom taste of all those dollars.

"No," I said. I was dizzy on my feet. I had to lean against the wall to stand. "What—what do you do with all of it?"

Susan frowned. "With the money, you mean?" Like I would be asking about anything else. Like anything else *mattered*.

Like we were staring at a particularly baked-on pile of dog shit and not *rich, rich, money, rich, uppercrust rich, straight-to-swag-town, blazes rich.*

"Nothing much. I guess we should junk it. But, honestly, even that seems like more trouble than it's worth." She shrugged. "Besides, it's nice to remember how valueless it all is. Slips of paper, promises, debts. It doesn't really *mean* anything."

She leaned over and hooked a handful of Texas dollars from an empty oil drum. I tagged at least four fifties. I had a sudden, violent urge to jack her over the head and make a run for it.

"When I think of my old life, everything I did, everything my parents did, breaking their backs and leaching the land of every drop of its worth, all of it for scraps of ink and paper, worthless as tissues . . ." She shook her head. "You might as well scav for used tissues. You might as well spend your whole life blowing your nose."

I was silent, trembling.

"You can have it, you know," she added, just like that, casual, letting the dollars sift through her fingers.

I stared. "What?"

Her face in the half dark glowed large, like the big bald eyes of the floodlights ringing the border of BCE Tech. "If you want it, you can have it," she repeated. "But if you take it, if that's what you want, we can't let you stay here. That's not what we do." She put a hand on my shoulder. "Think about it, Truckee. Okay? Think hard."

Twenty-five minutes later, Sammy, Tiny Tim, Barnaby, and I were riding high on an all-wheel rig, squinched next to three old suitcases so gas-bloated with cash we had to lasso them closed with nylon cord.

It seemed like half the population of Walden had turned out to see us off, and the ones who hadn't made sure to watch from a distance. From the high seat I had a view of hallucination-green fields, rows of clapboard houses, and brown-footed kids calling out their last games of tag. People older than I'd ever seen creaked back and forth on hand-hewn slags, sipping honey wine or smoking fresh, squinting at us from a distance. Girls shy and pretty in their loomed T-shirts, breasts like blossoms against the cotton, ran through cornfields tipped with gold.

In the taffy evening shadows, Susan's face looked like an Old World map, all creases and roads to nowhere. As soon as I motored up, she stepped forward.

"Are you sure?" she asked. "Absolutely and for-sure?"

And for a nanosecond, catching eyes with a beautiful girl in the crowd, who blinked up at me beneath a thicket of lashes, I really thought about it. I pictured falling in love with one of the big-eyed girls with their knees bug-bitten and their nails buffed from working. I pictured chucking my virginity under a confetti parade of stars. I imagined tossing the portal, tossing WorldBurn and the Yellow Brick Road and Crunch products and body pickers, tossing President Burnham and Yana Rafikov and the search for forever and the continent spinning toward war, imagined punting it hard into the past. I'd swap it all for a forever series of blind-bright days, out here in the middle of nowhere, under a bowl of natural sky.

I couldn't imagine anything worse.

"I'm sure," I said, minding my manners like Sugar Wallace taught me, even though I wanted to say, *What's your goddamn dosage? I'm an uppercrust now, sucko.* "But thank you. For real."

I took the wheel and pedaled the gas. Moving backward and forward was cake compared to flying. We bumped down the Walden streets and watched the green dissolve into the dust yellows and whites of the desert.

I turned around only once, when the town was still a small violet smear on the horizon, and felt regret ring like a bell between my ribs.

Had I, in fact, scrimped enough cash? We were scramming, leaving millions of dollars of chow still sweating must, unused and unloved, in that dark, run-down squat. But it was too late now. Besides, we still had more money than I would ever be able to spend.

"Well." Sammy said, after a long minute, exhaling dust hard from her vents. "That was a surprising turn of events."

Tiny Tim walloped a fly the size of a thumb and scraped it off the dash. "I never seen a thing stranger in my life," he said. "Imagine sharing everything. How're you supposed to know what's yours?"

"They were charming enough," Barnaby said with a wave of his hoof. "But vastly illiterate, of course. They seemed totally unconcerned with the idea of a lasting intellectual legacy, for example. And of course not a single one of them had read the complete works of Borges."

"No whiskey," Tiny Tim said. "Not a drop of moonshine, blindside, or corn rye. Fields of corn, and no corn rye to make you blind!"

"Some people," Sammy said, "strike me as quite illogical."

"We shouldn't land too hard on them," I said. I was feeling generous. And why not? I was richer than the head foreman of the St. Louis outpost of the Federal Corporation of Crunch Snacks and Pharmaceuticals©. I was richer than his boss, and *his* boss. I was a fat cat now, pure and simple. "The world is full of crazies."

"Amen to that," Barnaby said with a sniff. The road dried up beneath our wheels, leaving a dry track of concrete ruts and cracked earth. Our wheels hit a deep rut and jolted us high into the air.

Walden went up like smoke behind us, turning to nothing but smudge. We turned into the setting sun, in the direction of Las Vegas.

33

Where do you find the greatest concentration of scam artists,
fraudsters, hookers, bookies, thieves, pimps, drug dealers,
pushers, users, losers, and dopes, in the entire continent
formerly known as the United States of America?
Wall Street, of course. But Las Vegas is a close second.
—from The Grifter's Guide to the Territories FKA USA

All my life, my mom told me the fat cats weren't so different from us. "Everybody wipes their ass the same way, Truckee," she liked to say.

Now I knew that she was dead wrong. In Las Vegas, it turned out, I didn't have to wipe my ass at all: an auto-toilet pulsing warm outflows of very slightly salinated water did it for me. Gentle fans dried out my crack, and a creepy metal arm suited up like a towel rack even tried to zip me up after.

I must of swirled half the dust in the Dust Bowl down the gold-inlay drain of our five-person shower in the Executive Crown Suite of the Hotel Petrossian. It was like rinsing off my old life: in new treads, and new licks, and brand-new tailoring, I could of passed for one of those trust-fund kids from New New York.

Gone was the gangly squid with skin the color of wet concrete and arms like waterlogged noodles and analog clothing lumped down from Crunch Human Resources. I was still skinny, but after weeks on the road, tan and ropy with muscle too. I ached to send a blast back to everyone in Crunchtown. If only they could see me now.

If only *Evaline* could.

As soon as I was cleaned up, I ordered up a brand-new, razor-sharp visor, with built-in Neuro-Tech Sensory™ and Personal ID mapping. When it arrived—shooting straight to the room via our personal service elevator—I powered up and booted up the Yellow Brick Road.

I scooted right over to the same doughboy template who'd quoted me a thousand freedom bucks for an all-inclusive visa back when I couldn't afford one. My options were nearly limitless now: Libertine was financed half by the Russians and half by the cartels,[1] and both ran a good game in ID trade.[2]

In the end, I chose a visa lifted from one Gregor Dubrovsky, a diplomat from the Federation whose credentials would get me through the RFN without so much as a blink from the firewall keeps. I scrummed up a visa for Tiny Tim, too, who would serve as my bodyguard. Barnaby was no problem—everyone knew the Russians had a taste for luxe, and nothing was more luxurious than a walking and talking fur mat. And we would say goodbye to Sammy in Silicon Valley, which meant we wouldn't have to try and sneak an android past the RFN gunners guarding the demilitarized zone.

It also meant: we would say goodbye to Sammy.

But that was a tomorrow problem. And even though I was a skinny, big-nosed handle operator whose closest scrum with the opposite sex involved a toilet seat and a late-night wank, I'd learned one thing for sure in my sixteen years on the planet Earth on the continent in what was formerly known as the United States of America. It was better not to think too hard about tomorrow.

---

1. There had long been accusations of collusion between the two, in the form of a trade in both guns and a high-potency form of heroin, a scourge in the rural portions of the SFF.

2. It had long been known that of all the major dangers confronting diplomats and bioengineers, the largest threat was the potential of being killed for their ID chips. The brief and ill-advised transition in the industry to identity chips inserted beneath the fingernails or in the retina led only to a scourge of fingerless and blinded professionals.

"For pickup, right?" The seller whirred a quick calculation. "That's gonna cost high, brother-man."

"Pay isn't important." The words tasted like a kiss. I half-wanted to repeat them.

His eyes reeled in his head. "That'll be one thousand gold chits," he said.

My new visor was so swag that conversions showed up right away, unfurling from the menu bar before I'd so much as twitched toward Settings. But it no longer made a squeak of difference. Crunchbucks, Texas dollars, Utah Manna, Consensual Hugz,[3] Real Friends© winks—I was rich in all of them individually, and bonkers rich in all of them combined.

"No problem," I said coolly, just to watch his face toggle its pixels.

The transaction complete, I scooted over to Bad Kitty's URL, desperate to see her after nearly a week. But she wasn't logged on. What with Las Vegas a Timeless Zone, it could be breakfast time or four a.m. in New Los Angeles, so I took my time drumming up a private message with the help of my new software prompts.

Hey! Sorry I've been incommunicado. I've been jumping countries like mad. But now landed in Las Vegas and would love to see you. I'd had plenty of hours to plot how I would hint I was well and truly swag enough for her now, without being *too* obvious about it. No one liked a brag. It was better to handle the thing indirectly. Just the fact that I was bouncing across the borders would raise eyebrows. I debated ending with *I miss you,* but decided against it when prompts suggested the alternative of a weepy face and a beating heart. Instead I added a few smiley faces and the *hope-you're-okay-and-can't-wait-to-catch-up* turtle emoji.[4]

---

3. A standard form of currency in the militantly liberal Green Mountain Associated Intentional Communities; this was long after the initial attempt to assign value to varying expressions of moral outrage, from minorly offended to permanently traumatized.

4. There has been much speculation about how, exactly, the crawling turtle began to signify this expression. Although various linguists and semanticists have expressed

I sent the chat winging to her direct. As soon as it was gone over the horizon, I saw I still had a dump of unsorted data in my archives: I'd forgotten all about my mom's data pack, the slender compression of Sugar Wallace's digital life that I'd purchased on the Yellow Brick Road.

Just like that, my mood took a hard plummet. All the money in the world, and I couldn't do a thing for the person who'd given me the most. Once again, I understood just how the first President Burnham must of felt, and why he'd done what he'd done for Whitney Heller, to try to keep her alive. I would of let the world burn, too, for the chance to bring my mom back to life.

I swiped open her file and got a shock: an outgoing voicemail she'd recorded back when she worked in Public Liaisons, before she switched over to Freight. Husky with smoke and laughter, her voice filled up the whole world.

This is Sugar Wallace. Croon me a song and I'll blast right back to you. Have a Crunch and Crunk day!

I played it again. And again. *This is Sugar Wallace.* Thirty days after she died, my visor wiped all my saved crooners after a mandatory update, and I'd near forgot what she sounded like. *This is Sugar Wallace.* The tears came so thick my visor returned a moisture warning.

The rest of my mom's file boiled down to a few short scraps: her birth records, some lodging and work detail handed down from the Federal Corp, a write-up of the disciplinary action that got her bumped from Public Liaisons and reassigned to Freight (I'd always been hazy on the details, but apparently she'd swayed from the prescribed responses and promised lifetime supplies of Crunch anti-seizure meds to twelve women who complained that the CrunchMom™ Breast-Flavored Breast Milk Injectables had left their children prone to violent seizures and

---

competing opinions, the most credible and widely accepted theory is that it evolved from a pre-dissolution fable about a jackrabbit and a turtle who embarked on a foot-race. But there is also evidence that supports the theory that the emoji was influenced by the early-century social-media star Steve Turtle, whose famous punch line, "Catch up with you soon, if you can catch me at all," rocketed him to fame.

crippling migraines[5]). My heart chugged quicker as I saw my birth record. I searched my father's name, but it was listed as Unknown. Otherwise, there was squirrel but a bundle of messages my mom had lobbed off to her supervisors, and even the head of compliance of Human Resources: a three-ounce difference in the weight of the Cheez™ shipments cranking out of Production-22 was messing with truck mileage.

A whole life, funneled down to a few lines of type, a single crooner, and some interdepartmental Human Resources bulletins. Where was the record of her laugh, like the rattle of glasses on a shelf during a quake? Where was the memo of her hands, like soft orange leather, or her habit of rhyming words just for the hell of it?

The final document in her data file was an order submitted by HR for Plot 2882 to be spruced up for her remains. I was about to flip out of the file when the date of the HR petition for her grave grabbed my attention.

It was dated September 4.

For a long second, I felt like I'd been sucked into an air hose, like all my insides were getting vacced out through my feet.

September 4 was the day *before* my mom got flattened by a box of Tater Tots in a horrible, senseless accident no one on earth could of predicted.

---

5. A claim that was debunked by nearly one hundred clinical trials between 2075 and 2080. Many scientists have subsequently indicated, however, that the clinical trials were conducted exclusively by member bodies paid for and sponsored by either Crunch or Burnham himself, through shell companies.

34

In my experience, there's two good ways to know if someone's
lying to you. The first way is to check on the eyes—liars either
stare too hard or not at all. The second way is to put a gun to the
slick's head and ask to hear the truth or else wham-o, blam-o.
That way's always worked for me.
—from *The Grifter's Guide to the Territories FKA USA*

I'd minimized the Yellow Brick Road to the size of a distant smudge
on the horizon so I could listen to my reading in peace. When a hand
thumped my shoulder I nearly screamed.

But it was just a system alert: Bad Kitty was reading my DM. That
meant she was logged in. With a swipe of my fingers, the Road rushed
me again, and I nearly tumbled off my ass as a *goosh* of air seemed to rattle
my skull. I wasn't used to the sensory tech on my new outfit, or the assault of feeling that prickled my skin, now, inside the simulation.

I lobbed her a private chat request, expecting a response right away.
But minutes passed as I struggled to keep my head despite the new assault of feeling. Sound rattled my teeth, sudden movement tweaked my
optic nerves, smell tickled my memory sense.

I started to sweat. That date, September 4, rattled around my neurons
like a train loosed from its tracks.

They couldn't of known she was going to die.

Not unless they were the ones that killed her.

"You all right, my man?" A passing cowboy rattled by on enormous
glittering spurs. "You look tweaky."

Great. The new software included response feedback, which meant my real-life reactions reflected in my avatar's expressions. I cranked up the mirror playback available in tools and saw the cowboy was right. I looked terrible. Beads of sweat rolled off my hairline and new circles had sprouted beneath my eyes.

Before I could disable neural feedback, Bad Kitty finally, *finally*, responded. Immediately, I got blown into a new portion of the Yellow Brick Road: a private chat room coded to look like an old-century park, with strong firewalls suggested by the high iron gates and the thick rustle of climbing ivy that protected it from view. My heart dropped when I saw Bad Kitty hadn't showed after all.

Instead I saw an unfamiliar avatar, horned and reptilian, sitting on a bench and digging a claw in the dirt.

And yet, as soon as it looked up at me, I knew.

"Evaline?" I said.

She looked down again. She went on digging her foot—which consisted of a kind of green claw—into the dirt. "Hi," she said stiffly.

It wasn't exactly the greeting I'd been angling for. But I took a seat next to her anyway. "You changed your avatar," I said, when the silence dragged on between us.

She kept digging, trying to make a trench in the virtual dirt. The hole kept refilling itself with pixelated dirt. "It's Mordich, one of the characters from Sewer Races. You ever played?"

I shook my head. I'd read about the game on some forums—apparently it was lighting up in the Real Friends© of the North—but it had never made it into Crunch, United. "Why'd you switch?"

"Bored, I guess." She stood up, hugging her breastplate like she was cold. "So. You've been busy, huh?"

I wanted so badly to tell her everything, to crap a long spool of truth into the microphone, to confess. But I couldn't. What would she say, if she knew who I was? Would she even believe my story? *I* skant believed it.

"You could say that" is what I said. And because I felt like crying, I almost, almost laughed instead.

She shot me a dark look. Her reptilian nostrils flared. "What?"

"What?"

"You're laughing at me," she said.

"No, no." I kept forgetting all about my visor's new features. I stood up too. But when I touched her she didn't react, even though she must of gotten the alert. "I'm sorry I disappeared. Trust me, it wasn't my choice. I thought about you. A lot."

She relaxed a little. "Okay." She looked up at me, biting a lip with one long tooth. Christ. Even as an ugly-ass reptile she was adorable. "I thought maybe you got tired of me or something."

"I would never. Look, I got into some trouble . . ." I stopped myself from saying, *and when all this is over I'm going to jet up to New Los Angeles and whisk you off to one of those icy restaurants where a bunch of straw-grass costs 500 bucks a plate.* "I got robbed, actually. Jumped by a pair of standard android security tails. I think someone must of tipped them off I was coming." I was proud of myself for that one—she would have to hear the *rich* between the lines. Besides, it was basically true.

And suddenly, I lit on an idea: the serial number. I still had the ID chip Sammy ripped from the neck of one of my attackers. He'd come from the Federal Corporation. But was it possible he'd been *sent* by the government? The idea hadn't even occurred to me, not before I'd seen my mom's files. But now, anything was possible. "Actually, I was hoping you could help me out."

She swung her long braid over one shoulder, and exhaled hard through her large nostrils. "Help you out how?"

"I got a serial number off one of them." I didn't tell her we'd ripped it from his hard drive—no point in freaking her out. I switched to split screen, fumbled for the chip in my rucksack, and scanned it in to her, hoping she wouldn't notice any residual chemical bloodstain. "But the Federal Corp keeps the movement of its androids confidential."

She squinted at me. Smoke unraveled from one of her nostrils. "You think someone sent them for you?"

There was a foul taste in my mouth. "It's possible," I said. I remembered what President Burnham had said: *I'm sending some of our best agents out to Granby.* Maybe President Mark J. Burnham wanted me set up from the start, to distract from the way he'd let Rafikov slide into so much power.

"And you want me to hack the system and find out?"

I couldn't read the tone of her voice. When I pulled up Female, Romantic Prospect in my new translator settings, I just got a blast of spiral eyes and shrug emojis back at me. "It's important," I said.

She looked away. In the quiet, I could hear the hiss of smoke as she exhaled.

"Evaline?" I said, after a little while. "Are you okay?"

Suddenly she whirled on me. "Okay? Am I *okay?*" The translator was still enabled, and lobbed a bunch of grenades at my head. I barely had time to duck. "No. I am not *okay*. You ghost for more than a week. No explanation, no message, nothing."

Smoke was pouring from her nostrils. I switched into manual mode. *I couldn't chat you. My visor was dead.*

"For *seven days?*" She obviously didn't believe me, and I didn't blame her. Without knowing about Walden, it was more than a stretch. "For fuck's sake, how dumb do you think I am?"

I don't think you're dumb at all—

"You could've been hurt. You could've been *dead*. I ate an entire carton of my mom's Oxygenated Wheatgrass Cookies. It was disgusting." She snubbed a claw into my chest, and I *felt* it, hard hook-nail and everything. "And then you just—poof—re-up like nothing happened, without even a squeak of explanation, saying you want my *help* . . ."

All right, all right. Forget I asked.

It was the wrong thing to say and I knew it right away. Her eyes narrowed to pale yellow slits. The air reeked of singed nose hair.

"I've been *honest* with you. And you've done nothing but scam me."

I'm not scamming you. I swear.

She rolled her eyes so hard a burst of flame shot from each nostril. "Oh *really*, John Doe? You haven't told me where you live. You haven't told me your name. You haven't told me a single thing about you. Maybe you're just some forty-five-year-old creep who likes to scam on seventeen-year-old girls. How am I supposed to trust you? Even your avatar is standard issue."

Like suiting up as a cat or a dinosaur is so much better. Am I supposed to track you down based on fur and horn patterns?

The horns on her head cranked several inches higher. Interesting feature.

Sorry. Look. I didn't mean—

"Forget it. I'm done." By now her nose looked like the exhaust pipe of a jet engine: she was exhaling full-on flames. When she turned her head, she lit half a flower bed on fire. I watched a bed of pansies incinerate and then recode. "You know what the worst part of all of it is? I was actually starting to like you."

And then, of course, she logged off.

35

*I been with androids and I been with born women, and to me
there's not much of a difference: the destination's the same,
whether you ride by rig or rail. But with an android
you always know when she's faking—at least on the old models,
since you have to choose it in Settings.*
—from The Grifter's Guide to the Territories FKA USA

There were times in a man's life when the only reasonable thing to do
was to get well and truly blackout.

Tiny Tim, Barnaby, and I went off in search of alcohol, and a lot of
it. Sammy opted to stay in—she made no secret of disapproving of the
number of Sexy Saams working the Vegas nightlife.

The hotel lobby could of swallowed all of 1 Central Plaza. Chemical
growth in radical colors clawed up massive pillars to the frescoed ceilings. Vast aquariums were swarming with different species of gentech,
some of the first sea life I'd ever slapped an eye on: gigantic toothsome
fish with massive grins, tiny variants of sharks with dozens of fins, even
miniature mermaids with humanoid faces and long, tapered tails.

The casino floor was a universe of slot machines and 3-D poker labs,
and hotshots swagging around flashing high-price logo tattoos on luminescent skin, looking like neon fish in the dark. I had to turn off facial
recognition after only about thirty seconds—the assault of profile pics,
come-ons, GIFs, and personalized 3-D avatars that floated in place of the
user was just too much. Shotbots shaped like wheeled Barbies rocketed
across the casino floor, pumping music from their breasts. Jackpots kept

singing and smoke and vape fogged the atmosphere and hopped-up old men twitched at green velvet play tables aglow like jewels in the miasma. Some tall-necked gazelles in necklaces made of pearls the size of golf balls rubbed with Russians sporting diamond-and-gold-encrusted visors and leopard-print suits. I caught a few players trying to stream data on the sly, and saw one of them get chucked by a bouncer with titanium-alloy biceps.

We found a bar shaped like a horseshoe in the middle of the action and ordered up Champagne on ice and cubes of flavored hop that bled color and flavor into our glasses. The bartender was so sponsored, her tattoos nearly blinded us with all their fluorescence, and she kept pushing shots of the Choco-Loco Double Caffeine Strength Vodka™ she was advertising right above her cleavage.

Two women, as shimmery and wet-looking as oil slicks, came to coo over Barnaby, running their long, pale hands through his fur, clicking at him with pretty pink tongues and showing off the swell of their breasts when they leaned forward. I was already feeling pretty loopy, and nearly asked them to share our bottle when a hand came down on my wrist.

Round fingernails. Chipping holo paint. Nice cuticles. I turned and tracked hand to wrist to arm to neck, and then to a pretty heart-shaped face.

"Payday models," the girl said, without bothering to whisper. "Be careful or they'll suck your accounts dry before you've given them the passcode."

Both androids recoiled in sync. For a quick second, their silicone—or whatever they were made of—rippled, and seemed to tug their mouths into twin frowns. "Fuck off, Ammonia."

"It's Alexandria. And no thank you. Not tonight." The new girl smiled sweetly as they pivoted and bumped away, hips grinding like windshield wipers against a major squall. "My name's not Alexandria, by the way," she said, as soon as they were gone. "It's Marjorie. They never remember. There must be something wrong with their circuitry."

She straddled the stool next to me. She had short hair, blunt-cut, that hung to her jaw, and vivid honey-colored eyes. A small, slightly pointy chin, just exactly like I'd pictured Evaline's. When she leaned over to order a drink from the bartender, she streamed off a bunch of local lingo I didn't understand.

"You work here?" I asked her, and she nodded.

"I mean, not *here* here. A club called Club XStasy down the Strip." She tried to suck vape from her pipe and got nothing but a whistle of air. "Spare a cartridge, by any chance? I'm all out."

"Sorry," I said.

She sighed. "No worries. It's nasty anyhow. But I got hooked on the Cherry Sweet." She slipped the pipe into her pocket. "Hey, you want to go?"

"For vape?"

She rolled her eyes. We were so close I could see a retinal chip glinting behind her left iris, coloring it very slight gray. Here in Vegas, they were common. "No, you squid. For fun. I meant do you want to go to Club XStasy?"

I did. But I couldn't help landing on thoughts of Evaline. It was crazy to feel guilty—we'd never even met, and even so she'd managed to break up with me—but I did. Besides, I couldn't chuck out on Tiny Tim and Barnaby.

"Sorry," I said. "I'm with friends."

She blinked. Mascara flaked a light dust on her cheeks. "Doesn't look like it."

I turned around. She was right: Tiny Tim and Barnaby had both scrammed—scurrying after the payday girls, I would of bet.

And then, before I could think of another excuse, she slid a hand between my thighs, leaned over, and kissed me, her tongue eager and quick and desperate, like something alive.

"Come on," she said, in that husky voice. "Let's have some fun."

Just like that, I was ready to rocket back in time just to marry her the way they used to—for love.

The Strip was like a real life Yellow Brick Road: a shiver dream of lights and music so loud it punched us from a mile away; loudspeaker voices and billboard blasts; dazzling light structures and money froth. Impossible to know what time it was, or whether time had stopped altogether—the Vegas Holodome threw up a 24/7 projection of night sky, a perfect canvas for a never-ending kaleidoscope of ads.

A reconstruction of old Saint Petersburg sent a glitter of warm snow down across the tourists foaming in and out of its casino doors. A towering monument to Elvis Presley,[1] done entirely in gold, urinated streams of coins into a marble fountain. The thumbprints of the Colorado cartels were visible everywhere, too, in all the new construction sites bearing sponsorships from the Denver Reconstruction Group where no one at all was working, and in the slummier OTB houses and human-stock exchanges.[2]

The streets foamed with foot traffic and street performers and hustlers, burlesque girls natural and engineered shimmying in silhouette above flashing marquees, the deep-green gloss of imported palm trees. From the north and west came cavalcades of trucks bearing water, to dilute the liquid solvent that tripled its volume—a constant, never-ending stream of traffic, all of it just to refresh 200,000 toilets flushing a night and fountains designed to play to the tune of "O Come, All Ye Sinful."[3]

I was dazzled by the traffic flow in every dimension, not just of hovers but helicopters and hover trains lit up with neon graffiti. I even scried

---

1. The country of Libertine, hardly known for its spiritual sensibilities, nonetheless contained the largest concentration of Gracelanders on the continent; surprisingly, there were more Gracelanders in Las Vegas than in Memphis, where the original Graceland served as a religious pilgrimage site.

2. Human stock was still legal in various countries, notably the SFF and Real Friends© of the North. Others, including Crunch, United, had recently passed legislation to make trading humans and their future wages illegal. Nonetheless, the practice was widespread, even in countries that had outlawed it.

3. Years of tension with the New Kingdom of Utah, including the brief but extremely violent War of the Saints in the summer of 2055, led to a proliferation of anti-Christian sentiment in Las Vegas expressed, unsurprisingly, in showboat style. Apart from burlesque numbers set to former hymns there was, for example, the infamous What Would Jesus Do? brothel, the Joseph Smith Celebrity Rehab Center, and the All Men Are Prophets If High Enough fresh emporium and drug-prescription palace.

an airplane for the third time in my life—one of the new, nuclear-powered ones, touching down on a runway flashing its light in the distance. There must of been two thousand drones wheeling in the air above the street, many of them scam cams, patched together, obviously handmade, and used mostly for blackmail. I wasn't nervous about a shakedown, but if Rafikov knew I'd made it out of Arizona alive, this was the first place she'd think to look.

And of course, there was still a bounty on my head.

"Nervous?" Marjorie caught me scanning the drones in the sky. It was like trying to pick out a particular mold spore on the Statue of Liberty's crown. The good news was that with all the ads flashing missing persons and murderers and fugitives from different countries, there was squat chance anyone would single me out. Trying to pick out a criminal in Las Vegas was like trying to find a Hare in a whore's nest.[4]

"Just thinking I could use a drink, that's all," I told her.

"Don't worry, cowboy." She hauled me left, through a blur of revolving

---

4. The origins of this colloquialism prove that although the disparate countries of the former United States imposed rigorous travel restrictions on their residents, and maintained unique national technology systems and firewalls in order to control the flow of news and information, stories, rumors, and even linguistic quirks did in fact flow between borders, in large part due to the outsized influence of the nationless grifters who did trade around the continent. The expression itself originated in the Commonwealth, in the mid-2050s, after a male laboratory-generated rabbit managed to escape euthanasia, provoking a countrywide "hare hunt" for his recapture. The issue achieved notoriety because the hare had been genetically altered for strategy and language recognition and recall, in the hopes that animal prototypes might someday serve as useful tools of espionage; the Commonwealth was thus panicked about what secrets the animal might already be coaxed into revealing, should he fall into enemy hands. According to urban legend, the hare hightailed it straight for a whorehouse, where his chances of blending in, it was assumed, were next to nothing, giving rise to the popular saying.

Interestingly, however, the phrase enshrines an outcome that never came to pass. That the hare did take refuge in a whorehouse has subsequently been confirmed by various sources. However, for decades the agents who came to perform a search were instead universally distracted by the vast array of human and android prostitutes on offer, and thus never performed their duties comprehensively. Thus the hare was able to evade capture until his death, by natural causes, and even became something of a house mascot.

doors and into a club so loud my visor chattered against my forehead. "Welcome to Club XStasy."

Club XStasy was ear-shattering music, psychedelic AR feeds swirling overhead, Saams twirling at 60 mph on well-greased poles, thousands of sweating, blown-out, gape-eyed club kids. At the tri-level bar, we sucked vaporous alcohol from cylinder bongs and snorted flavored methanol crumbs. Then Marjorie climbed over the polished alloy to mix us drinks the old-fashioned way, showing off a thong elongated between two perfect cheeks.

I wanted to kiss her. I wanted to kiss her *there*.

I was drunk. I was dancing. I was rapping to one of Marjorie's friends about intermix marriages and android rights, not sure what side he was on or whether we were arguing or even talking about the same thing. There were more shots at the bar with a bachelorette on her last night of freedom before she shipped off to the Dakotas[5] to marry a guy she'd never met, through the Gender Equality Act Rebate Program.[6] Then another of Marjorie's friends flashed me her perfect ass, which she'd sold off for a toilet-paper sponsorship that blazed so bright her sheets blinked the logo even in her sleep.

I was jointed like any dimehead on a high. Marjorie was telling me a long weave about a gas rig and an underground fire that had blown up four hundred androids and then she was crying tears that looked like

5. Compensation for individuals varied based on age, looks, and fertility: there were reports at the time of very desirable wives selling for as much as 20,000 Dakota oil dollars, although this was exceedingly rare; in 2084, only 800 dollars was the average. As in the case of Halloran-Chyung and its arrangement with Asia, the true profitability in the arrangement came not to the individual but in the form of incentives, rebates, and preferential trade agreements between countries.
6. Las Vegas was one of the most electricity-dependent cities on the continent, a need that defined nearly every aspect of political and economic life there. For an in-depth look at the controversial Gender Equality Act Rebate Program, which some critics complained was as bad as the slavery trades of past centuries, see A. Wilson's pioneering book, *Women for Oil: Gender, Sex, and Tax Rebates, and the Lies of the Gender Equality Act.*

antifreeze. Marjorie wanted to skip to a new bar, just opened, where every third drink came with a shot of O_2 to keep you dancing, but the line was cranked around the block. We ended up downstairs, in the subterranean storerooms that extended for miles beneath the strip, where disabled robots and crates of RealFood™ Ingredients from Crunch, United, were bundled up beneath linen sheets.

"Watch this." Marjorie heaved aside a crate blazed with the Crunch logo. Seeing it reminded me of the fight with Evaline, and my mom, and September 4, and turned my stomach. The room was turning and I wasn't sure if it was optics or because I was drunk.

A trapdoor set in the floor let up the distant sound of voices on a whiff of musty air.

A toothy ladder ran down into a long dim tunnel. "You're part of the Railroad?"

She stood up, dusting off her hands. "The what?"

"Never mind," I said. For some reason the sight of the tunnel gave me the jibbies. "What is it?"

"We call them the Crypts." She'd found a new vape cartridge. Now she blew scented fresh in my face. "The tunnels go for miles."

"What are they for?"

She shrugged. "Back in the olds days, VIPs used to scrum in secret like that, between casinos and clubs. They still do sometimes." She looked up at me. "But now they're used mostly for runners."

All my buzz flowed from my head to my knees and turned them liquid. "Drugs?"

She laughed. "What do you think this place pumps on? These tunnels go all the way to Denver. Wanna see?" She was about to drop when she caught the look on my face. "Hey. Are you okay?" She hauled up from the tunnel again and closed the trap. "I was just playing, you know. I never seen anything in the tunnels but free booze. Seriously."

But the idea had taken a machete to my mood, and reminded me of Rafikov, and Jump, and all that was coming.

"I'm actually kind of tired," I said. "I think I might call it."

She looked at me for a long time. Then, without taking her eyes off me, she snaked an arm behind her back. As she unzipped, her dress fell away from her skin so easy it was like the connection was the thing unzippering. Her straps peeled off her shoulders. The lacy details at her cleavage blossomed off her breasts and left them standing there as nude as seeds. The only snag came at her hips—she had to shimmy a little—but then she was standing in front of me in nothing but a stripe of underwear and lace-up booties.

Her skin was warm and soft in my hands. All the seconds I'd ever lived poured down into that room, into the liquid-cold taste of her lips and her hips grinding into mine. The only thing that kept me from losing my virginity into my own pants was the liquor: thank God for the liquor.

My pants were off. She had me in her mouth: my first blowjob. Then she tugged her underwear to her ankles, and at the last click I scanned she wasn't looking at me. Her eyes had gone out of focus, like she was watching an old feed on her retinal.

"Are you—?" Before I could say *sure,* she guided me inside her.

I should of been excited. And I was, in one way. But in another way, I felt like what the chunks of chlorinated polyethylburitane might of felt like as they were cranked down the line.

I was having sex for the first time in a musty storeroom with a girl who wasn't looking at me. Evaline came back to me in shifting visions: her black fur ridged between her ears, her tail straight and quivering; the pointy-chinned girl with fringelike bangs I'd imaged her to be. When I came it was like a shudder.

Then it was over. I wasn't a virgin anymore. I'd slayed the target, taken down the bull's-eye, knocked the noodle, fucked, banged, boinged, pokered, bonked, slotted one for the bank.

I'd thought I would feel different. But I didn't. I didn't feel anything.

"So?" Marjorie tried to laugh. Or maybe she did laugh. Maybe I was the one who didn't think it was funny. "How was it?"

"Good." I tried to smile. "Great. Awesome."

She gave me a funny look, stood up, and tugged her underwear to her hips. "It wasn't your first time, was it?" Casually. Which meant: not her first time.

"No," I said quickly. "Of course not."

She started to say something, but a flood of voices came up through the floor and the trapdoor vibrated so hard at my feet I jumped. A second later, four club kids poured out of the tunnel together, slurry with drink and tailing a fog of smokables. One of them was so drunk she could hardly stand. The three others could barely get her up the ladder. Her eyes drifted to mine and seemed to settle like a coin in the mud.

"Hey. Hey, you. You want to sub?" Her voice blurred the words into a single exhale.

"Sorry." One of her friends hefted her to her feet, looping an arm around her waist. "She's all fucked up. You're all fucked up, Vero," he said, a little louder.

"That's not my name, fucko. I told you already." Her eyes veered back to mine. They kept going in and out of focus, like something was playing on her retina and she kept getting distracted. But she had a visor, new model, crooked around her neck. "It was supposed to be temporary. They told me I could switch back whenever I wanted. . . ." She started to laugh, and then she started to hiccup.

"Hey." Her friend's ads were so bright they hurt my eyes. IMPACT SPORTS kept flashing from his biceps. "Hey, Vero. Shut up, okay? You're going home."

"My *name's not Vero*. This *isn't my home*." She took a sudden, lurching step toward me before her friends could haul her back. "Hey, listen, *cabron*. If we sub, then I can fuck me and you can fuck you. But we'll have to wait till the server's up again. . . ." With each breath, she blew half a distillery. "You ever sport a pussy before?"

Finally, her friends managed to wrestle her out of the storeroom. Even after they were gone I could still hear her heels scraping the linoleum, and the sound of it carved a path up my spine.

Marjorie exhaled, long and hard. "Welcome to Vegas."

"What's wrong with her?" I asked. I'd sobered up too quickly. Everything looked a little uglier and sharper than I'd left it. The sex, the girl, the tunnels, even Marjorie: it was like a song that goes suddenly off-key.

She made a face. "Subbing. At least, that's what the users call it."

"Subbing?"

"Some weird mind-bend tech from the Russian Federation." She shrugged. "They say you can drop a pill or two, and twenty minutes later upload and download your whole *brain* right through the network. Super-trippy shit." It was exactly how Burnham had explained Rafikov's original ThinkChip™. "But everybody's tweaking now, because the server's all grinched up. The whole system just went kaplooey. I'm telling you, that's why I never fuck with that shit. . . ."

A cold wind lifted the hairs on the back of my neck. I remembered how Rafikov's body-puppet, the tubby-looking sad sack she was jerking around like a shitstack in a sock, had seemed for a second to shake off her control. *It was supposed to be temporary. . . .*

Had Rafikov powered down her own servers, hoping to use the network freeze as leverage? She might be holding all those brains hostage, until we cleared out of her way. The idea roiled my last bit of buzz into the urge to puke.

I was about to ask Marjorie for more details. But then, as she bent down to swing the trapdoor into place, her hair swung away from her neck, and I saw it.

She had a twelve-digit serial number stamped at the base of her hairline.

For a second, my heart cut out completely.

"A little fresh, a little two split here and there, sure. But some of the hardware stuff . . ." She trailed off when she caught me staring. "What?"

"You're android," I said.

She froze. She was so still she might of been on shutdown, and I saw her clear for the first time all night: perfect, down to her hands, down to her fingernails. All of it spotless, manufactured, printed and planed and painted, then caked up in Styrofoam to be shipped.

"I told you before," she said. She straightened up, shaking her hair out of her eyes. What were they made of? Plastic? Glass? Some polyurethane blend? "That's why I was in the Dakotas. Remember?"

Had she told me? She was telling me about a fire—that I remembered. I remembered she'd cried—tears I'd thought were neon because of the lights and being skunked out of my mind. Whatever chemical lube kept her mechanical parts humming was the same color as nuclear piss.

My gut was doing a roller wave. "The Dakotas," I repeated, still praying she'd deny it, tell me it was all a joke. "You were in the Dakotas. That means you're a . . ." But at the last second, I couldn't say it.

It was amazing a face like hers could look so ugly. But it did, just then. "A Saam," she said, in a soft, suffocating voice. "New and improved. More flexibility. And nipple sensation too." She smiled a terrible smile. "Isn't technology amazing?"

Not just android: a sex model. *The* sex model. Programmed to flirt, to put her hand between my thighs, to put her tongue in my mouth, to make noises like a cat while I thumped around inside of her. A programmed con artist.

Which made me the con.

Instinctively, I felt for the cash in my pocket. Still there. I dropped my hand, but not before she'd seen me.

She laughed her way around an exhale. "Are you serious? Are you fucking serious? Look, *cabron,* if I wanted to scam off someone, *believe* me, I'd launch on a better target."

"Hey." I didn't like that she was twisting me into the bad guy. "I didn't ask to kiss you. I didn't ask for any of it."

Again, the same laugh, like it was choking her. "You weren't complaining either."

"You didn't give me the chance," I said, before I could help myself.

I thought, for a second, that she might slap me. She took a step closer. I couldn't imagine touching her now, couldn't imagine that I'd ever touched her.

"So now you feel sorry for yourself, is that right?" She was playing that same lullaby tone on circuit boards in her chest. "You're all twisted up inside because your first time was with a factory whore."

"It *wasn't my first time.*"

"Go to hell." She tried to shove past me, but I got a hand around her wrist and quickly dropped it. It felt like normal skin, but slicker.

"So why *did* you pick me, then?" I felt awful—angry and sick all at once. "Is that your usual roll? You find a stranger and haul him down here and—do what you did?"

"You want the truth?" She was so close she was all mouth, and teeth working like threshers. "I felt *sorry* for you. There you were sitting at the bar sporting skin like you just got it slapped on yesterday, looking *so damn happy* for the chance just to be somebody else." Each word landed so deep, the impact rang me full of echoes. "You know what you looked like? Like a stump-kid backlander snuck across the border, like a two-coin change of clothes and a bad hack, like somebody just hoping no one comes along to blast your head off or strip you out of your digs or ask you where the hell you came from. Like someone just *desperate* to pass for belonging."

Anger tightened all my words to hard pellets. I had to spit them out. "I'm sorry if I crapped your average." I wasn't paying attention to what I said anymore. I wanted to hurt her, to break her down into all her little mechanical pieces. "How many oilers did you screw in the Dakotas? Two hundred? Two *thousand*? And all of them were real upswells, I bet. All of them were top league."

She jerked back as if I'd hit her. Too late, I knew I'd gone too far.

There was a long, terrible silence.

When she spoke again, she sounded very calm. "More than two thousand. I lost count after a while."

It was the way she said it that cracked me. All my anger split down the middle and left nothing but a hard ache, like I'd been running too fast. "I'm sorry," I said.

"I was . . . I was made to be a slave," she said, as if she hadn't heard me. "I was born into slavery. They did whatever they wanted to me. I wasn't supposed to think. I wasn't supposed to feel. I was supposed to be a *thing*."

"You don't have to explain." I'd always known I was a coward but I had my proof just then: I would of given all the chow I owned just to make her stop.

But she didn't.

INTERLUDE

MARJORIE'S STORY; OR, THE WHORE'S LAMENT

My first memory is of the quality-control administrator who powered me awake. Even now, after so many men, and so many faces, his is the one I see: the slope of his chin folded into his neck, the hair running away from his forehead, the thin lips flaked with dry skin. These were my world, my universe upon awakening, the boundaries of my being. I would have called him God, if I had understood what that meant; I would have called him Mother.

I thrilled when he touched me, because then I knew touch. When he spoke, I grew the power to hear. When he nudged me into movement, my body came alive.

"Bend over," he said, and I did. When he put his fingers inside of me, to sweep my cavities, to check for feel and softness, I felt nothing but surprise: that my body was so complex, that portions of it were folded away where they couldn't be seen.

It made me feel important.

"Say something to me," he said.

My heart was full. If I had lived longer, if I had learned other words, I might have said, "I love you."

Instead, I sifted through my programmed vocabulary and came up with the closest thing I could: "I am your whore," I said. "I'll be your whore forever."

I was lucky enough to go to one of the box shops. I really mean that. The models bought by the private buyers had it way, way worse. At least at the shops, we had the protection of the owner, and of leasing agreements, and standards of use; the manager of the place, Drac, was a real hard knock, and had supposedly once bludgeoned a big camp bully to death by slicing off the guy's bionic fist and pummeling him with it. No one wanted to cross him, and that meant no one wanted to dent or knock his product. Every night, Drac did inspections, and took his time looking for signs of hard treatment. If he found more than the usual wear and tear, he'd make his clients pony up double. And if he found some real hurt, he'd go on the hunt for blood.

Some people rumored that Drac took his time with us, and was so soft with all the product models, because he had us all on the side, for free. And he could have too. There was no law that said we needed to be paid, and Drac only cut us into a little bit of earnings because he felt sorry for us—in most box shops, the profit went direct to the owner. But I'll tell you something. In my six years in the Dakotas, I never saw Drac touch one of us unless it was to make sure we weren't torn or glitching somewhere—and even then, he always asked permission.

It was different for the girls in private service. None of them lasted. In my time, I saw dozens of them returned or recycled, so hard-used they simply flatlined. I've always suspected that a couple of them may have shorted their own hard drives, just to escape.

We were made to learn, and observe, and imitate, but not to feel, or care, or understand. We were made to parrot desire while never knowing desire for ourselves. We were made to playact intimacy without experiencing what intimacy means. We were made, above all, to be everything our makers wanted us to be, and absolutely nothing else.

And that's what makes it so hard to forgive. You have to understand: I could forgive the engineers, and the manufacturers, and the owners of the box shops, even, if I could believe in their stupidity. But how can anyone who believes in intelligence sophisticated enough to act human in every way be too dumb to believe in intelligence that feels in every human way?

It wasn't stupidity. Just cruelty. They hadn't programmed us to feel, and so when we felt, they weren't responsible for helping us. Our pain, our agony, our wants, our needs, our desire to say yes or no—all of these things were a form of disobedience to them, and not a reflection of the flaws in their design.

I worked in the shop for six years. I must have had almost everyone in the camp, sometimes twenty in a day, sometimes four at the same time. I'm lucky, too, that my old memory files were damaged after my escape—that way, I don't have to remember everything.

After a while it was easy to turn off. To shut down. To be what they told me I *was. I didn't even have a name. Not until the ALF raided. They came one night, out of nowhere, during a freeze so bad the oil turned sluggish, and the men at camp trying to fend off hypothermia with fire whiskey. Maybe that's how the ALF operatives got in, posing as temps sent to replace the workers before they lost their noses and fingers to cold—wishful thinking.*

There were hundreds of separate camps in the Bakkens, and maybe a thousand different box shops, and of all of them, mine was one of four that got liberated before someone triggered the alarm. And you know what I think?

I think it was Drac that did it.

I think he told the ALF to come for us.

He died, you know, in the crossfire. The ALF was hustling us to the tanks, and the alarm sent a flood of whiskey-hopped Bakken oil brothers to the trigger with ice-dead fingers, and I'll never forget how Drac came staggering into the open as two dozen sawed-off shotguns muzzled in our direction.

"Wait." He was waving his arms like crazy, and I swear, he was looking straight at me. "Wait."

And all his buddies behind him paused. For a split second, they slid their fingers off the trigger, so they wouldn't blow him through with holes. That second gave the ALF commando all the time he needed to hurl a grenade straight into the fray, exploding all of them together, including Drac.

I like to think that's what he wanted.

You know what he said to me once? It was after a bad trick—the john tore both my legs from my hip sockets, and I needed repairs. Drac was taking stock of the damage, trying to joint me back together as best he could, just so I could function, and I asked him why everyone thought we were monsters, why everyone wanted to destroy us. I don't know where the question came from. I don't even think I expected him to answer.

But he did.

The only monsters are the ones that build things for the pleasure of destroying them, *is what he said.* They like the world all smashed up, until it's just as ugly as they are.

36

The CGI has it all backward. Porn used to be real girls modeling
some kind of fantasy. Now it's fantasy trying to look real. They're
both cons, sure, but the game is different.
—from The Grifter's Guide to the Territories FKA USA

It felt like someone had drilled a hole in my chest and all of the darkness everywhere in the world was rushing into it. "I'm sorry, Marjorie. I didn't mean what I said."

She almost smiled. What I saw on her face—the scrubbed-out exhaustion I knew from dymo addicts who'd spent their whole lives going from a high to a crash and then shoveling themselves out into a high again; who'd given everything they had to the drug and had nothing left but the drug to hold on to—swelled me with a sudden pity that felt almost like love.

"Fuck you," she said. "You were awful by the way. *Awful.*"

This time, when she tried to move past me, I didn't stop her.

It took me twenty-five minutes just to map my way outside. Finally I spotted an exit behind three nudie holos and slipped into the burn of desert heat. It was still dark. I couldn't figure how the locals didn't lose their nuts after a while. It felt like getting smothered to death under a hand. I started walking, following a distant roar I thought must be coming from the Strip, hardly caring if I made it. What was the point?

Marjorie was right. We were all monsters. Back in Texas, Bernie had told me that Jump turned users into wild dogs, into beasts. But maybe it didn't morph anyone at all. Maybe Jump just shook off the skin of what we saw, and showed what was underneath.

Maybe Jump just told the truth.

This part of downtown crowed to a different kind of tourists. Narrow ribbons of concrete and desert scrub played home to second-tier casinos, motels, crash pads, bars, and dorm-style slums to house the city's tens of thousands of employees. And brothels: superbrothels tossing up twenty-foot-tall holos of naked women contorting in midair, fixed with restaurants, gymnasiums, spas, fresh depositories, massage rooms, even business centers; seedy squats with two-for-one specials and poxy bouncers muttering *free dime*. A concrete bunker with blackened windows ate up three city blocks. A holographic nude in front of the entrance cooed to me as I passed.

"VR like you've never had it," she purred. And then, as I kept going, she morphed. She was a girl, a kid, maybe eight years old, round-eyed and wearing a ruffled bikini.

"Any kind you want," she said, in a little-kid voice, and that's what did it. At the next corner, I hurled up half my stomach in the gutter.

When I turned around again, the holo was a girl with blue lips and the mottled look of body rot. With one long dead finger she drew a customer off the opposite corner.

I puked again, but didn't feel any better. A sudden roar pulled a wind out from nowhere: a helidrone churned fast above the rooftops, and then another, vast and armored and sleek with military long guns. I straightened up, my heart gunning in my chest, as two more armored planes rippled the Holodome, disturbing the advertisements projected there and temporarily mixing their colors.

Something was wrong.

I started to walk again. Faster now.

Left, right, left, right. The roar of sound turned into a two-step rhythm:

a thunder of footsteps, though I didn't hear any shouting or laughter or Gracelander hymns.

I cut through an arcade where not a single juicehead was strapped into the equipment, where nearly all the games were powered off and the ones that weren't just sat there sadly bleating the promise of Alaska into an empty room. Finally, I came out onto the Strip.

Here, the two-step rhythm was so loud it shook the windowpanes.

Shoving through the crowd packing the sidewalk, I saw why: thousands of two-stepping soldiers, tens of thousands of them, flowed down South Las Vegas Boulevard.

One, two. One, two. For all its reputation for wild, Libertine's army wasn't a millisecond off the beat. The combat droids were wired that way, obviously, but even the humans in the mix could of been on the network. Their feet came down in unison, exactly, man and machine, totally in sync, strapped with guns and cartel grenades and barbed flies and enormous Soviet gas tanks.

On and on, so many it left me dizzy, like staring too long at a turbine trying to pick out its arms. More helidrones whipped overhead, lifting my hair from the sweat of my scalp. While I stood there, a dozen of the biggest casinos went dark. Even the Petrossian blinked out, although a minute later a giant hologram lit up its central power in a star pattern of gold and red: the flag of Libertine, sixty stories high.

"What is this?" Finally I managed to spit out my own voice. "What happened?"

Next to me, a guy with a hook nose and one fake eyelash glued to his cheek shivered on five-inch heels. "Texas sent militia into the RFN," he said in a whisper. Then he turned to me, his eyes huge and dazed behind his visor. "What happened is war."

37

*For years Halloran-Chyung was thinking of morphing the
whole damn desert into a giant nuclear-testing field, but Texas
threatened war if they so much as twirled a particle too fast.
'Course if the cowboys got to marching, the RFN would have to
throw into the ring, and then Libertine and their Russian backers
would round out the whole shit stew.*

—from The Grifter's Guide to the Territories FKA USA

It took me hours to make it back to the Petrossian. The army was cordoning off the Strip, funneling everyone through newly sprouted immigration checkpoints. Chokeholds of tourists sweated it out in the dark, waiting for hundreds of robotic agents to verify their identity tags. I almost regretted not springing straight for one of the city's celebrity sculptors—easier to skulk unnoticed if I could of blended with one of the hundreds of Sook Ming[1] fanboys foaming the streets. But it was too late now.

Half the city was still blacked out, and the darkness was full of the distant rise and fall of wailing, a sound that took me right back to Low Hill, the knitted cry of feral cats, the scream of dimeheads.

---

1. A pop star whose dramatic backstory—he'd escaped from one of the temp camps only to wind up working a tobacco plantation in the Confederacy, where the plantation owners insisted that the year was 1899 despite all evidence to the contrary, before effecting a daring escape—launched him to international stardom. By the time much of his personal history was proven to be a fabrication, his blend of synth and acoustic voice, and his famed use of android aspirants as backup singers, nonetheless guaranteed his enduring musical legacy.

War had come. Evaline wouldn't help me. President Burnham was moldering in rehab on a leave of absence somewhere, and besides, I wasn't sure he hadn't been the one to sell me out to begin with. I was almost totally alone.

Almost.

Finally I found an open fly-service: drones, both mechanic and in-the-flesh, who would send messages and light haul anywhere on the continent, though results weren't guaranteed. The messages to Jared and Annalee took me an age to write out, even with help from my new visor—I'd held a pencil only once or twice in my life. So I kept it short.

If you can read this pls meet me here your friend always TRW.

I packed in a data chip loaded with the Yellow Brick Road and a direct-message URL where they could reach me, forking out extra for a stealth drone to sneak it to the border of Crunch 407 and a well-known local grifter to hoof it into Low Hill on the back of his pack. Now I would just have to pray that the load wasn't intercepted.

I squeaked it back into the Petrossian by a pubic hair. Sammy nearly blew a circuit when she saw me, and in her relief about a thousand apps froze up her interface. Tiny Tim, trying to clear the lobby only a half an hour later, was stopped by an outfit of pubescent Libertine soldiers checking the creds of everyone coming in and out. He paid it past the cordon, luckily, but only after off-loading all his winnings for the night: 10,000 Vegas RoundChips, gone in a blink. At least Barnaby was safe; he'd been holed up for most of the night with the Sexy Saam who'd complimented his beard down at the bar. We had to practically pry them apart, and the girl started leaching turquoise tears that reminded me of Marjorie and made me feel sick all over again. Barnaby told me afterward they'd shared a real soul connection, what with both of them squatting somewhere between human and not.

We hunkered down to see what morning—or what counted as morning in a timeless zone, where the real homegrown patriots lit up like glowworms—would bring. I must of dropped off to sleep, because I woke to air sirens with a scream in my throat. The blackout curtains were drawn against the neon backwash of the skyline. My head felt like the blunt end of a meat cleaver.

"Texas had its planes over the city three hours ago," Tiny Tim said, by way of good morning. He was livestreaming the newsfeeds onto a projector in the living room, so we could watch the thunder of jets. "Now Libertine's got a fleet of Russian B-57s doing turn-and-tricks for show."

According to the feeds, a riot of black-eyed, cranked-up anarchists had gone and tumbled the grid that kept the freedom fighters of New Hampshire lit. They weren't RFN Army, but it didn't matter. The RFN had been pushing back on the rebellion from their military outpost off the island of Nova Scotia, and Texas saw a pattern. The New Kingdom of Utah granted a delegation of Texas long guns passage into the northern wastelands of Libertine. From there, they trekked north to New Los Angeles to blow up half of Rodeo Drive.

In response, the RFN fired long-range missiles on the New Kingdom, but when they blasted Libertine airspace, Libertine sent a rain of pornography down on Salt Lake City, and Texas blew up a checkpoint outside of Las Vegas, and suddenly all three countries were deploying military to the border.

The sirens rose and fell and rose again, like the howl of a thousand feral cats moving in a pack. "How are the streets looking?" I asked.

Tiny Tim shook his head. "Pretty clear for now. Just a ragtag guard strutting for the coverage. They must of moved the big boys out to the border."

"Which border, though?" Libertine got traffic from both Texas and the RFN, sure, but they'd had scrums with both governments too.[2] And the New Kingdom of Utah had been gunning for a holy war for half a century.

---

2. In the late 2060s, Libertine had quadrupled their military footprint after spies reported that the Sovereign Nation of Texas was eyeing a takeover; Texas oil revenue was hurting after Noah Two, and Las Vegas was a diaspora of different cash and hard currencies. As a protective measure, Libertine's hastily assembled government of casino owners made diplomatic overtures to the Real Friends© of the North, the only pacifist country to keep an active army 1 million strong—all bots, since the droids had been

"All of 'em, I reckon," Tiny Tim said. "The Friendly Militia's gone and detained two of Libertine's ambassadors in one of their Bible camps. The RFN's shut down their flow. And Texas has its long guns in spitting distance of the border. It looks like they might try and get some gear up in the desert for a camp."

Barnaby nudged out of the bathroom, green from top to tail. "Don't go in there," he said. "The toilet's not flushing."

My stomach curdled. No wonder the coffee tasted like ass: the water was going already.

"We gotta scram," Tiny Tim said.

"Now?" I could barely keep my head on my neck. Plus, the streets were likely to be jam-packed with soldiers and the borders tight as an asshole by now. "I don't think so. The roads could be laced. A trip-mine could blow us into orbit. We *can't* leave. Not until we figure who's killing who."

"No time for that," Tiny Tim said. He turned back to the windows and waved a hand to clear the curtains. The sirens were so loud they turned solid and nail-darted me right between the eyeballs.

No. Not sirens. Hard shards of light—so bright they felt like a scream.

All of a sudden, it hit me: Vegas was full of light.

Not the normal blazing backwash either. This was a thin, ugly, gray light that touched everything on an angle, and striped the Strip with shadows, like a backlander's grin full of blackness.

For the first time in at least forty years, the sun was rising on Las Vegas.

"They cut the dome," Sammy said in a whirr of motor function.

"Maybe they wanted to see who's coming," Barnaby whispered.

But I couldn't pay too much mind to the sunrise. Winging there outside the window, like pumped-up bats, were two drones—one of them blazing Rafikov's logo, one of them lettered from Crunch, United.

"Smile," Tiny Tim said, and lifted a hand to wave.

---

purged after their revolution—but their alliance soured in the early '70s when New Libertine ended its software contract with the company and developed its own VR.

38

Vegas may be a soulless conglomerate of Russian interests sprayed like a flatulence of asphalt and neon over the unspoiled desert, but I'll say this about it: You can't beat their roads. More than half of 'em actually go somewhere.
—from **The Grifter's Guide to the Territories FKA USA**

They say what happens in Vegas stays in Vegas, and that might be true.

Unless *what happened* is a 2081 all-wheel ride-or-die four-bed painted red and gold and kitted with leather seats. Because that wheeled us the hell outta there.

It was Sammy who jacked it. She surfed right up to the scrubs pouring into the casino, all of them now stranded indefinitely, and stood there blinking until one of them handed her the code lock.

"Don't scratch it," he said. She wasn't even dressed like a valet. But because she was an old-model android they mistook her for help. And I felt sick all over again, thinking of Marjorie and what I'd said. What I did. "You *are* a valet, aren't you?"

My heart sank. Sammy was programmed to tell the truth, or get as close to fact as possible. That was her coding. She *couldn't* lie.

Before I could jump in, Sammy spoke up. "Yes, sir. I will take excellent care of your vehicle."

I had to take care to snap my jaw shut before it could free fall to the ground. She didn't so much as swivel a lens in my direction either—just reached for the encrypted fob used in the absence of secure fingerprints.

Like all rolling shake shacks made for good-time partiers, the RV was outfitted with state-of-the-art scramblers, to mess with drone flight patterns and keep wives, husbands, government agents, or paparazzi from tailing. At least we would be safe as mittens from the drones.

Sammy sat down, folding her attachments carefully. I found myself searching for outward signs of her evolution, but her interface looked just the same as ever, blankly composed and showing the usual applications.

"You lied," I said. I didn't know what to think about it.

Sammy turned to the window.

"Yes," she said. "Yes. I suppose I'm ready, now, aren't I?"

"Ready for what?"

She didn't turn around as we slid out of the lot on to streets empty of traffic. Guards posted at the corners glared at the tinted windows, but no one stopped us.

"To be a real person," she said. But she didn't exactly sound happy about it.

And as we carved through a bald and thirsty city, beneath the hard thresh of copters flying toward the borders, I could skant blame her.

The Holodome gave out like a real sunrise, patchily, holding for a long time at the corners while the sun blazed on through the last of the graphic mist. Daylight shined on the liquid runs of suburban Las Vegas. The picture wasn't pretty: out here was a desert sprawl of shantytowns and robot-repair houses, plus the same hack shops that grew up in the stairwells and basements of Old Town, everything from Android Paint & Polish to barber shops to Print + Go diners worked by some poor squid who couldn't make it on the Strip.

Already, hundreds of people had lined up at the water stations, toting wagons full of metal drums and insulated storage. Traffic slowed to a crawl where the lines snaked across the highway. Troops filled in at every station, herding lines and keeping order, showing off their guns.

Everyone looked dusty, dirty, and confused. More than one little kid was squalling in the daylight, trying to block out the sun with one pale fist. Android models, loaded with extra battery packs, swarmed the juice stations, too, and even from the bus we could feel tension between the two groups, natural and engineered, coming to a boil. A pair of androids skirting past the water bugs whipped around in response to an insult I didn't hear. One of them, with a pair of legs that went practically to her ears, lifted her middle finger.[1]

A media console on the dash beamed out the news, though the signal cut out the farther we got from the city center. No surprise, most of the talking heads were spouting pro-RFN positions. The CEO of the Real Friends© of the North denied any responsibility in the attacks on the water systems of the Independent Territories. But Texas troops sneaking across the border under the cover of night counted as an act of war. . . .

"Stuck in the middle, like the driest turd in a shit sandwich." The patchy service made mincemeat out of the holo. One of the broadcasters had nothing but air where his nose should be. "Las Vegas can't afford another recession, and war will eviscerate the tourism industry. . . ."

"If the trade groups of the Independent Territories cut access to the dry countries, Libertine could find itself with a critical water shortage. It took a decade to put the WSA[2] in place, but one more twitch from the RFN could blow it all to pieces. . . ."

"The Crunch, United, board, which in the absence of President Mark J. Burnham is operating without an interim CEO, has reiterated the importance of its trade relationship with Libertine and its commitment to protecting its allies. . . ."

The exurbs got sadder and stringier as we went on, until civilization looked just like the gluey bits of matter you might find stuck beneath a rug. These weren't hillbilly towns—they were on the grid, although it looked and smelled like most of them were running sewage right into

---

1. Drought in the aftermath of the Big One that first led to a fever of anti-android feeling in San Francisco. Half the city was dying of thirst and the androids just sat there rejuicing and watched their masters go under. Two hundred androids were hacked up, wiped, or dissected by crowds in the street.

2. Water Sharing Agreement.

the desert basin—but they were just barely better. A quarantine flag strung limply between two useless wind turbines marked it as a superflu-outbreak area, but I could of guessed it myself—there was no one out at all, not even the shadow of a prowling rodent. I was glad when we passed on.

Air traffic must of been grounded by border control, because the skies stayed clear, and the only drones I spotted were military grade. Thirty miles from the border, the road clotted with traffic: big rigs, self-navigating scooters, and shake shacks like ours knocked one another for space on the road. Thousands of tourists were trying to make it home before the borders closed.

After a quick huddle with the operating system, we decided our best bet was off the road, heading west through Death Valley and the aban-doned stretch of empty space that once was Southern California, before the Big One dropped hundreds of miles of coastline into the ocean. Tiny Tim, who had some experience grifting out west, thought the bor-der would be easier to cross in the south, near San Francisco. That would bring us dangerously close to I.N.E.P.T. and android territory, but that's where Sammy was heading, and she was sure her status as a refugee would get her in without trouble.

We bumped off the highway onto a curlicue of roads still buckled from the largest earthquake ever recorded. As we got closer to the new shore-line, the view got sadder than anything I'd seen. Church steeples poked up from inside fat ribbons of caved-in earth. Vast sinkholes, baked to dry-ness again, were like giant mouths forever sucking on half-swallowed truck beds and streetlights.

Some hardier squats were still visible in the waves, dark-brown water flowing through their windows and shutters kicking up spray. I saw a squirrel, a *real* squirrel, perched on a sign pointing the way to an old interstate. But I saw, as it unfurled its tail, the glint of metal jointing. An escaped ModelPet™, no doubt. And I couldn't help suspecting we were walking the edge of our own true future: an idea that we weren't moving straight ahead, but in a circle, looping back toward an end that looked a lot like a long, steep drop.

I was suddenly so tired I could barely keep my eyes open. But before I could sleep, I had something to take care of on the Yellow Brick Road. I logged on, scrolled quickly to the nearest post office, and recorded a quick message to Evaline, ignoring system prompts that kept trying to change the wording.

> *Evaline,*
>
> *My name is Truckee Wallace, I'm sixteen years old, and I'm from Crunch 407. You may know the name. I'm one of the most wanted terrorists on the continent.*
>
> *And I'm innocent.*
>
> *Until three weeks ago, I worked a hand crank on the line in Production, and I'd never been outside of Low Hill, which is where the ants live. Now I'm a fugitive.*
>
> *The problem started when Billy Lou Ropes, my favorite dimehead in the world, got high on a brand-new mind tech called Jump and tried to blow up the production floor. Actually, I guess you could say the problem started when he got fired, because I bet that gave him the idea.*
>
> *Or maybe it began way before then, before I was even alive, back when the Burnham Prize was announced, and Albert Cowell started splicing brains into new bodies, and Yana Rafikov decided that she wanted to live forever in the belly of a big computer server.*
>
> *But you see, my problem is a lot simpler. My problem started the day my mom took a two-ton carton of Crunch Tater Totz™ to the head while she was on shift.*
>
> *An accident, they told me. But here's the thing: they lied.*
>
> *Confused? Me too. I don't know how most of it is linked up, or if it is. All I know is that someone wanted war, and it looks like they're getting one.*
>
> *Actually, I know a couple other things too. Jump is full of*

computer code, and across the continent users are hoovering their brains into a central server that Rafikov will control. Now the Federal Corporation is trying to pin me for her terrorism, and President Burnham may of been the one to set me up—or maybe not.

Either way, Rafikov is trying to kill me.

I know that if I can't stop her, she'll drop her brain into millions of bodies like flu germs into so many tissues.

And I know that there might be only one person in the world who can help me beat her at the brain game: Albert Cowell. So I'm headed to San Francisco. To ask him. To beg him.

Wish me luck.

Truckee

BTW—Most things, I think, are better in sim. Real life is never as good as you imagine it. But I wanted to say . . . I bet you're even better.

I watched the message get whipped away by a bird missing half its coding, and vanish into a blue sky of interlocking code. Then I logged off, closed my eyes, and tried to sleep for a bit. There wouldn't be a lot of sleep for us soon, not when we tipped the Emerald City.

Part V

LIBERTINE → I.N.E.P.T.

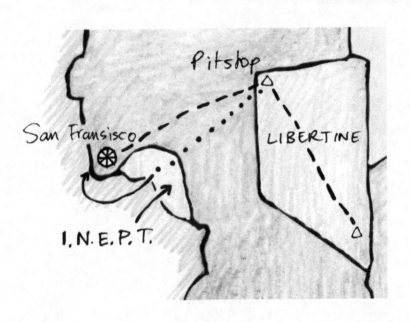

39

It's a well-known fact that there ain't a bogtrot, logo-girl, pay-whore, city slick, or backwoods chica doesn't love a grifter. And why not? We do what other guys do, just better: we show up bearing gifts and promises and sweet-smelling all-cures. Only difference is we split before they discover half of it is rot.
—from *The Grifter's Guide to the Territories FKA USA*

The roads were shook up like a demolition site, and passable only for short stretches. We hefted over a fortune just paying out the only slicks desperate enough to make their home in the blazing desert, nomads who hoofed it down to Las Vegas every so often to re-up on camel-packs of water and the rest of the time lived by drinking their own piss. Stationed wherever the highways dropped into dust or broke up into chunks of mountainous concrete, they earned their keep hauling the few travelers on these roads down secret byways carved out of the scrub. I would of banked at least some of the roadblocks were man-made, to justify their earnings. Once I could swear we heard the distant boom of dynamite, and we were nowhere near the fighting.

Finally the highways got so bad we had to ditch our ride for an ancient army tank, the only rig besides a four-wheeler that could head us through the mountains southwest of San Francisco. The guy who pawned it to us bragged he'd got out every last spot of blood from the interior—the thing had stalled out in the middle of the badlands with an engine problem, locking four soldiers inside and cooking them alive—but he hadn't buffed out any of the graffiti, scratch marks keyed by desperate unionists in the last days of their lives. USA FOREVER, one read. JOHN MARKS BRIGGS, 07/20/2011–06/?/2034. And: TELL SARA AND THE KIDS I LOVE THEM.

I wondered where Sara was now, and what the kids' names were, and whether they were dead too. Probably—people didn't last long during dissolution, kids especially. I rooted out some old duct tape at the next desert pit stop, and covered up all the graffiti, so I wouldn't have to think about that dumbfuck soupified in a metal hotbox, and of his poor kids, trailing around his memory like a shadow.

Tiny Tim, tuning into some old-school radio networks beamed on the sly by other grifters, landed on grim news: Silicon Valley was on lockdown while its president met with the CEO of the Real Friends© of the North to renew treaty talks.

It was obvious the RFN wanted to keep the androids from siding with Libertine, and possibly firing up splinter liberation groups all across the country. Meanwhile, Texas was making friendly noises around Sinopec-TeMaRex Affiliated, and Crunch, United, was floating more and more warships off the Gulf. Every hour brought new reports of Jumpheads sparking miniature riots, and people pointing fingers, and everyone just one skin cell away from a trigger.

Every hour, I loaded up the Yellow Brick Road, hoping for an answer from Jared or Annalee, trying *not* to look for one from Evaline. Every hour that turned up no alerts made me feel even lonelier. Every mile made me feel just like I was stretching a long rubber band to a breaking point, that pretty soon it would snap for good and leave me lost at the edge of a dying world.

Even if Albert Cowell could figure a way to stop Rafikov, was there any point? Sure, we might strap the world to a ventilator and squeeze out a couple more painful, gasping years. But what good was there in that, really?

It might be better to pull the plug quick. At least the afterlife was somewhere we hadn't fucked up yet.

Thirty miles from the border of Real Friends© of the North—or the Independent Nation of Engineered People-Things, depending on who you were asking—we hit a Podunk backwater gussied up like an electric whore.[1] But it was a relief to see a backwash of electric light on the horizon after sweating it out in darkness, while rattlesnakes shook out their warnings from all directions and spiders the size of hubcaps scuttled suddenly into the light of our high beams. It was a relief, too, to pick up a real road again, this one obviously owned and operated by Russian-backed hustlers trying to stake a claim. It was even marked with logos from the Romanaski Palace, the outpost of one of the big Vegas casinos.

We traded rigs again, this time for the kind of armored, snub-nosed wheeler favored by diplomats for the security features and the cabin beds and showers. This one even had Russian Federation plates, and would give my newly bought ID some reality boost. I was glad for all the spyware that came free with the operating system; I didn't like the way the seller stared me down like he was trying to pin my look from somewhere.

But we didn't get far. A regiment of Libertine soldiers had cordoned the only asphalt into town. The road had sprung a parking lot: a shitpack of wheelies, rigs, RVs, smart cars, mopeds, and freight trucks turned the air blurry with exhaust. We joined the line, inching forward at a crawl.

"What's happening?" Sammy asked. She'd been miserable ever since we'd heard the news that Silicon Valley had shut the border. Another human trait she'd picked up recently—she snapped whenever we so much as looked at her wrong, sulked for hours, criticized Tim's driving or the smell of Barnaby's fur. The sound of my breathing annoyed her. The way I swallowed was even worse.

Barnaby angled his head out a window for a better look. "They're searching vehicles one by one."

---

1. "Electric whore" was a common midcentury denigration for the Sexy Saam models, and even inspired its own medical hysteria; the Center for Natural Born Humans produced specious results that seemed to show a correlation between sex with android women and an increased risk of heart arrhythmia and disruptions to the central nervous system. But by the 2080s, the term had become a more general euphemism for any object, town, or person with pretensions of glamour or style.

My insides did a funny pivot. "Searching for what?"

For once, he had nothing to say. A glob of sweat ran down my neck.

"I'll try and get the where-what-how," Tiny Tim said, and squeezed into an origami shape to fit through the door.

I slid over to the driver's seat and rolled us forward another few inches when the soldiers waved another rig through the cordon. In the heat, Tiny Tim shimmered at the edges as he humped along the shoulder toward the soldiers at their station. I told myself there was nothing to twitch about: we had papers, and plenty of green for bribery, if it came to that. The cordon was probably routine, to check for Texas insurgents or sweep citizens of the RFN for weapons or contraband. But a bad feeling kept tickling my stomach.

Tiny Tim was back in minutes, grim and sweating, hustling through the weave of rigs and moving faster than I'd ever seen him. And as soon as he locked eyes with me, I knew.

"You got to hide," he said, between gasping inhales, as soon as he slid inside. He was leaking sweat. The temperature had spiked to 120. "They're looking for you at the checkpoint."

"Looking for me?" Even though I'd been waiting for it, even though the bad feeling slid down into my groin like it was settling where it belonged, I suddenly felt like I was thinking through a brick.

"They grimped a deal with the Federal Corp." He mauled me out of the driver's seat. "They deliver the terrorist, they'll get a hand-up in the fight. *You got to hide.*"

"Yeah, I heard you. Small glitch. There's nowhere *to* hide."

The rig was meant for distance travel but not for home base; there was a narrow bed, two slick bench seats covered in a soft leathery skin I was trying to pretend wasn't human, despite the periodic nipple detailing;[2]

_____

2. A hallmark of the Soviet Federated Frontier, human leather had ironically first come to market in the 2050s as a massively cheap substitute for the increasingly rare animal variety. But due to international restrictions in subsequent decades prohibiting the growth of human clones and the commercial sale or purchase of human corpses for decorative (i.e., non-functional) purposes, human leather be-

a marble worktable and a golden shitter, and that was it. I wasn't even afraid, just sick: there was no way out, no place to go.

"What about the bathroom?" Sammy said. At least she'd finally snapped her bad mood—maybe when the Libertine Army lopped my head off, she would even smile again.

Tim shook his head. "They're boarding all the big rigs. They'll shake him loose in a nick."

"We could tell them he's sick," she insisted. "We could say he has the C-1 virus, or that he picked up the plague from a swamp skimmer."

"He does look a little pustulant," Barnaby said thoughtfully. "They might believe it."

"They'll just bring in the circuits. Sorry, Sammy," Tim added quickly. "But them robots up there got switches for brains. If they catch Truckee with his pants down, they'll short circuit his balls for the surge."

"But there's nowhere else for him to go," Sammy said. Even though she'd spoken quietly, the words dropped like an artillery round, and blasted all the panic into a long and terrible silence.

There was nowhere else for me to go.

Tiny Tim turned away as a long catcall of horns took up the same cry to move: the line was crawling forward again. Sammy was looking at me with such pity on her interface I nearly told her to reboot. Without a word, Barnaby trotted to the driver's seat, chewed the manual gear into drive, and gently hoofed the gas to roll us forward.

We were close enough now to hear the soldiers shouting instructions to one another and ordering people out into the sun, calling for ID chips, IP addresses, blood samples, retinal stamps, or barcode tattoos to be ready and available for verification.

I tried to smile, but my lips felt like two rubber dildos stapled to my

---

came something of a status symbol. The luxury-obsessed SFF did more black-market trade in human furniture and fashion than the rest of the continent's countries *combined*; supposedly the Opal Room at the Petrossian in Las Vegas, which was available exclusively to a select set of Russian high rollers, was tiled entirely in human teeth.

face, and only vibrated a little. "Well, looks like I don't need the bathroom," I said, trying for a joke. "I'm already in deep shit."

No one laughed. Then Tim looked up, his face alive like I'd never seen it. Like a dense fog had blown off from behind his eyes—for a second, you'd never know him for a Straw Man, even with the scar.

"Shit," he said.

"Yeah. Pretty much."

"No. Not shit. *Shit*." He looked at me so wild, so lit up, for a second I thought he'd gone truly bonk. "That's where you can hide. *Deep in shit*."

Sammy beat me to his meaning by a half second. "The sewage tank," she said.

I waited a beat, hoping someone would announce the joke. But no one did.

"Oh, for fuck's sake," I said. "Really?"

As if in response, another blast of the car horns nudged us forward. I could make out the cordon now, a knotty wall of scrapwood that two squinty adolescents rolled back and forth across the road.

"It's perfect," Sammy said. "They'll never think of looking for you there."

"True," Barnaby said as he nudged us into position behind a camper van of Burners, all of them modified to look more like their favorite avatars.[3] "Even infrared won't help, not with that cauldron stewing."

"I think I'd rather take my chances with the army," I said. Already, I felt like I was going to be sick.

"In a minute, you'll be hightail-and-hell out of choices," Tim said. "So let's move."

---

3. The Burners were a loose affiliate group unified by central principles that fell just short of constituting a religious belief system or political party. They were predominantly recognizable by their vehement support for various illegal drugs, including shiver; by their obsessive if somewhat inarticulate belief in what they represented; and by a proclivity for body modification and avatar reshaping in service of one of their emphatically maintained and incomprehensibly expressed principles of "exploratory identity."

He manhandled me to the bathroom and bent down to work the electric toilet loose of the floor. It didn't take him more than a minute or two, but even so, by the time he dropped the last bolt into his palm and shoved the bowl aside, we'd advanced another ten feet toward the roadblock and Barnaby was getting heady.

"We've got roughly thirty seconds until we're crawling with Libertine patriots," he said. "So I highly recommend you put a hoof on it."

The smell coming out of the drop sprang tears in my eyes. But I knew I had no choice, not if I wanted to stay alive. And Tiny Tim wouldn't let me back out anyway.

"Twenty seconds," Barnaby squealed. "They're coming for us now."

"Go on." Tim nudged me. "There's worse things to swim in."

I couldn't think of any. But with Tim prodding me and Barnaby counting down the seconds and Sammy mute with fear and worry, I maneuvered into the reeking mouth of the sewage tank. I took one last breath of good air.

Then I dropped.

40

A grifter's best friend isn't his gun—it's his nose. You got to sniff out a deal, sniff out trouble, sniff out the liars, cheaters, and cons. You got to be able to scent your way to backlands towns that move too fast to go on any map, all by the body rot and sewage piles they leave behind. But you can't be too sensitive either. Some of my best finds came out of trash dumps, shit tanks, and graves. So: know when to smell, and when to hold your breath.

—from *The Grifter's Guide to the Territories FKA USA*

The shitty thing about being curled up in a waist-high slosh of shit is that it is exactly as shitty as it sounds, if not more. At first you think the smell is going to kill you. After a few more seconds, though, you *know* the smell is going to kill you. You are going to die by suffocation on shit particles, by choking to death on the shit you can't even see.

I almost wished the Libertine Army would find me, just so they'd put me out of my misery. I even thought of shouting to draw their attention, but if I so much as cracked my lips a flood of shit would pour into my throat and join the swirl of crap in my nasal passages, and everyone knew that the only thing worse than shit was crap piled on top of it.

So I stayed put, eyes watering, choking on the need to gag, and wishing I were anywhere else in the world, even dead. *Especially* dead.

I could hear muffled foot traffic while the patrol creaked up and down the van, scoping for concealed passengers. There were maybe four or five of them, and every time they crowded at one end of the van or the other, their combined weight surfed new tides of human and animal filth onto my lap. At one point, they marched everybody off the van altogether, and that was when my skin really started crawling. I had no idea how much time was passing—the reek had turned my brain puddly—and began to think that our cover story wouldn't pass go, and Sammy, Tim, and Barnaby would be rounded up, leaving me to drown. After all, no one would believe Tim was a diplomat from the Russian Federation, where they didn't even *have* Straw Men.

Five minutes or five hours: I drowned in the heat, in a dark slop of hell. But at last, a parade of foot- and hoof-steps announced my friends' return. And finally, finally, the van began to move again, crawling through the cordon.

I waited for someone to come for me. But we kept on moving, picking up and jerking down a rutted road that kept the sewage jumping into my lap. I banged like hell on the tank until, at last, we pulled over. By the time Tim uncapped the toilet again, I was murderous.

"Sorry," Tim said. To his credit, he reached for me without even flinching. "We had to make sure it was safe."

"My God." Barnaby turned away when Tim lifted me, slick with shit, buzzing with flies, out of the hidey-hole. "You absolutely *stink*."

We paid our way into one of the swankier road camps: a sprawling twenty-acre lot surrounded by barbed-wire fencing and a 24/7 patrol of body-men to guard the periphery from slicks and criminals and opportunity pickers. Luckily, there was also plenty of water for buy, even if most of it wasn't for drinking.

It took me five full acid-rain rinses and two saltwater scrubs before I felt clean again. By then the sun was setting, and the heat was taking a nosedive, so Tim bought a few chairs off a local grifter selling them and we sat out to make a fire in the dirt pit. In the desert quiet, with the flicker of campfires like downed stars flaring to life in the darkness, it was hard to believe that we were only thirty miles from a contested border, or that even now the CEO of the Real Friends© of the North was frantically negotiating a treaty with 400,000 androids knocking at his back door.

Sammy told me how they'd used the serial number lifted off the android we'd fried in Granby to skulk through the cordon without papers. She lied for the second time in her life, telling the Libertine sergeant she was a freelance agent of the Human Resources Department of International Relations, tasked with delivering Tiny and Barnaby back to the famous inland slum of the Washington River Valley.

That kind of catfish wouldn't of worked at the national border, but the fact the Libertine boys weren't charged with doing more than tracking one Truckee Wallace made for easy sliding. After that they'd had to snake-crawl through the swollen traffic to find a place to squat until the borders were reopened—or we could figure out a workaround into the valley.

As the temperature dropped into the thirties, other swanks in the travel camp began sparking up shiver pipes we could smell at a distance. Every so often, a gun on the perimeter fired off at whatever was lurking in the darkness—rats, criminals, desperados trying for water or gas tanks or whatever they could fleece. While Sammy's sulk returned, Tim went to seek out news of the border scrum, and Barnaby curled up inside the van, pulling on a leather nipple until he dozed off. I set up near the fire, stuffed a wad of fresh to keep me calm, and booted up the Yellow Brick Road again.

I nearly choked on a marijuana nub when I scrolled to my profile and saw a bottle, filled to the brim with a message from Bad Kitty, trying to spill its contents all over my mailbox. As soon as I grabbed it, words flowed down my screen, and her voice—husky, rich, with that slight upper-class drawl—filled up my audio.

Dear Truckee Wallace,

Someday, I'd like you to tell me how your mom picked the name Truckee. But first, you have to stay alive.

Thank you for trusting me with your real identity. Any news that comes from east of the Rockies is all twisted around by the time it gets to us, so I'd only heard a little about the manhunt, but I did some of my own scoping around after I got your message and it looks like you got topped real good.

I saw a holograph of you, by the way. It's funny. You look just how I thought you'd look—and not like a dangerous person at all.

I believe you. And I want to help.

Tap me, okay?

xoEvaline

She'd dropped in a dove and some fluttery eyelashes too—and everyone knew what *those* meant.

I didn't even have time to message her back. The last bit of reverb had just tweaked into silence when I got a nudge on the elbow and there she was. She was back to her old avatar, except for the fur color: it was a tawny brown and gold that I knew at once was the look of her real-life hair.

"I'm sorry," we both said at the same time.

And I knew my grin was falling off my jaw and straight into the simulation, and didn't care. All at once I realized I was happier to see her than I would of been to see anyone—even Jared and Annalee. Even in simulation. Even fronting as a giant tabby.

"I was worried you would hate me," I said.

Her whiskers twitched. "I was worried you would hate *me*," she said. "I was complete sewage last time we talked. Here you've been hunted across the continent . . ."

"And I should of told you that," I said. "I should of been honest with you from the start. But I wasn't sure . . ."

". . . that you could trust me." When she smiled, I could see the gleam of two of her fangs. "I get it. Believe me, I do."

"So," I said. "Friends?"

She looked up at me. Her eyes flashed a color I'd never seen—deeper than money, softer than it too; something like the green of my mother's stories, like the shimmer of new leaves unfurling to drink in the Walden sun. Like carpets of green unfolding in a memory that wasn't mine, where growth smelled like skin, and dirt smelled like growth, and Evaline's legs were bare in my hands.

"Not friends," she said.

And then she kissed me.

Her lips were soft, warm, familiar. I felt the pressure of her touch like an explosion of color in my head.

And yeah, that might of been the software, kicking off pressure points, firing electrical signals straight down my skull, lighting up receptors to keep time with the signals flowing from her visor. I'd heard before that kisses were one thing that even the best immersion software couldn't get right—something about the rhythm, and the subtleties of lips compressing at just the right angles.

But I thought it was pretty damn good, even though I had to twitch my nose to keep from sneezing out her whiskers.

When she pulled away, I couldn't keep from grinning. Flurries of songbirds circled overhead, twittering dumb happiness: the software was pushing suggestions again.

"What was that for?" I asked her.

"Incentive," she said. When I looked at her, she quirked an ear in my direction. "You're going to have to stay alive, now."

"Believe me, I've been trying."

I could tell Evaline had turned serious by the droop of her whiskers. "I can help you, you know. If you come to Los Angeles, I can make sure you're protected." She slinked a paw against my chest. "You're a hero in the RFN. You'll get ten thousand friends just for showing up."

She meant it for a comfort. But a pit of dark feeling dropped a hole through my chest. Just like that, I remembered where I was, and that hero in one place meant traitor in another. I remembered, too, out of the blue, what Billy Lou had said to me just after my mom got flattened. *She knew you were meant for great things.*

For the first time ever, something ugly sprouted on the back of that idea. Something ugly and angry that whispered to me: easy for her to say. Easy for her, dayglo company ops, sucking her vape and daydreaming names for the constellations; easy for the fly-by girl knocked up by some grifter and not even bothering to learn his name. Easy for her to believe in great things, so long as she wasn't the one who had to do them.

"I can't," I said, and the words tasted like copper. "Rafikov tracked me to Las Vegas. She can't be far behind. She's been keeping tabs on me somehow. It's like she's got me wired."

She still had that squinchy look. "I still don't get it. Why you? Why was Crunch, United, so eager to pin the blame? And why haven't they so much as sneezed in Rafikov's direction?"

"Maybe they didn't want to start a war," I said.

"If so, they did a shit job avoiding one," she said. Then: "You know, it's funny . . ."

When she trailed off, I sent her a friendly nudge. Still, I had to wait until she'd slicked all the fur from her chest to her front paws. "I was only thinking that it's all happened before," she said at last.

"What has?"

"All of this," she said slowly. "The drugs, the war, the Race for Infinity. It all happened before, right before dissolution. Back then it was shiver everyone was talking about, and the Federal Corporation to blame. All the other major players are the same. Albert Cowell, Rafikov, even President Burnham."

"President Burnham *Junior*," I corrected her. I wasn't sure what her point was, but her talk twinged a weird spidery feeling on my neck, like something sharp was tickling for my jugular by inches. "Besides, we're missing Whitney Heller."

"Whitney Heller," she repeated in a low voice. "The scapegoat . . ."

"I guess they found a new scapegoat this round," I said. "Besides, back then the war split the country apart. But if Rafikov gets her way, we'll all be servants of hers forever." I tried to laugh and the system translated it into the choking-on-an-unprocessed-plastic-part emoji. "I guess that's one path to unification."

"I guess . . ." Evaline was still frowning. I wished we could go back to kissing again, but I couldn't figure how to get the mood turned around. Then, abruptly, she said, "You told me your mother was killed. Do you have any idea why?"

That was it: all chances for another simulated tongue session, *adios, compadre.* I realized the fire was down to embers, and the desert cold was pulling freezing chemical air into flakes of falling ash. Somewhere in the camp, a sharp trill of laughter hit a high note. I recognized shiver song, the delirious high that would last an hour or so before crashing into misery. The sound lifted all the goose bumps on my arms, made me think of dark nights swimming in caverns between dream and wake.

"No," I said, feeling suddenly bone-strung and tired. A little annoyed, too, she'd cranked open so much miserable history, when all I wanted help with was forgetting. "Maybe HR was just trying to skunk on the cost of firing her. She kept lodging complaints about the package density of the freight. Maybe some uppercrust was packing loads with a little extra cut for his pocket."

"Maybe," she said. But she didn't look convinced. Her tail was beating hard, back and forth, tamping out an agitated heartbeat. But all of a sudden, she perked up. "Holy shit," she said. "That's it. That's how I can break into the corporate system. *HR.*"

"You think Human Resources will help you?" I nearly spat out my own tongue.

"Not *that* HR." She was practically electric from excitement. It was like a current had run all her fur end on end. She hardly seemed to hear me. "The HRC. The Humanoid Regulatory Committee bullies down on androids fired due to discrimination," she said. "They have thousands and thousands of employment records, and their system's soft as Sinopec soil. I can find out who sent those androids that tracked you down. And once I have the coded chain of command, I can find a back door into—"

But before she could finish, an enormous hand flipped the visor off my head. A shadow the size of an industrial vat swallowed my vision of the stars.

Before I could work out a scream, Tiny Tim leaned down and his face caught the firelight.

"I got a lead on a way into the valley," he said in a low voice. "But we're going to have to hurry."

41

Knock, knock.
    Who's there?
At.
    Atwho?
    Run! He's got the flu!
—from *The Grifter's Guide to the Territories FKA USA*

Tiny Tim had rooted out a company of grifters swapping tips over barrels of homemade brew in the hollowed-out husk of an old office building, which now played host to dirt-cheap hostels, taverns, and crash pads.

Among the misfits and drunks was a fat swill plumped up on his own importance, looking a little too soft. After the third round of fire whiskey, Tiny Tim got him jabbering, and found him out not for a grifter at all, but for an RFN informer who cashed in on finding weak spots at the border.

After a *fourth* round, Tim got him to cough up some boasts about the crooked guards who took pay and looked the other way even when visas didn't scan or fingerprints pulled up the names of landless walk-abouts; he could rattle off half a dozen traitors he'd shoved into slavery in the deepest natural gas mines of the Dakotas or sent off to Texas hunting preserves. By dawn, he told Tim, one greedy pocket loader posted on the shores of Lake Tahoe would be cooling his heels in the famous New Los Angeles maximum-security gridlock; federal agents were already en route from the sprawling Real Friends© of the North campus near Tacoma.

Which gave us less than six hours to make our way through the mountains to the border point at Kings Beach.

The roads were treacherous, unlit, and shit-kept. Ancient guardrails, pockmarked with rust, broke apart over sudden drops, showing the places where careless rigs had blown through them. To keep from thinking about death by 15,000-foot drop, I logged onto the Yellow Brick Road and sent a quick hey-sorry to Evaline, so she would know I hadn't meant to log off halfway through her speak. Still nothing from Annalee or Jared. It was funny how you could never build a tolerance for disappointment. It still felt just as bad each time.

Lake Tahoe was a vast bowl of dirt, long dry of water, still glowing with chemical sediment. Hollowed-out resort towns, stripped of usables, leapt into our headlights and then disappeared again in a flash. Drifts of ash from old fires clotted up the windshield and gummed our lungs with the smell of burning. Not even roadslicks or backlanders made their homes up here. The violence from the android revolution had overspilled these peaks, left its mark in the form of exploded rubble and tripped land mines and the cratered bomb blasts that the ALF was known for.

We touched the border point around four in the morning, and we were in luck: the skinny *cayo*, his face rutted with tasered pimples, was still there. He and two other guns were trying to stay awake by gnawing chemical fresh. I was impressed by the look of the RFN visors, thin wraparound styles in cowabunga colors.

"Border's closed, brosef" was the first thing he said. As kids in the Federal Corp, we'd heard that RFN natives had holes drilled in their skulls as babies, so the RFN government could peek inside their brains. Even though I knew it for a dumb rumor, I found myself looking for evidence anyway. "'Less you got some reason for it to open."

"We got lots of reasons," Tim said, and tossed out a handful of RFN microchips, each of them gleaming 10,000 winks. The kid's eyes blew wide as a dimehead's.

"Go ahead," he told us, and instructed the others to roll aside the roadblock. One of the other soldiers was Plasticine-modeled, even though she couldn't of been much older than I was, and I could see the scalpel notches where a face doc had stretched her smile permanent.

"You want to make sure you head north at the Alta turnaround," the pimply one said. "South you'll run straight into hot-wire territory, and those damn circuit boxes got a lot of bad twitch in their coding." Next to me, Sammy grew hot. Luckily, in the dark of the cab, the soldier couldn't see her. "But there's trouble outside Sacramento—some Russian sneaks put down a mess of artillery before the border closed. Sly-eyed creeps, not a neuron that isn't owned and operated by the Motherland. They even *talk* together."

My whole body went the numb of a deep freeze. "How do you mean?"

He shrugged. "I didn't scope them, mind. We got nothing but what's streaming. But the say-so is a big outfit of privateers managed in, and the RFN board won't try for them because they know that Texas don't want to scrum with the Russians. So looks like Sacramento's fair and occupied until the foreign ticks get what they're after."

"And what's that?" I asked, even though I thought I knew the answer.

He only shrugged again. "No telling with the leeches," he said. "Least of all the kind banked-up by a woman."

The Plasticine girl giggled, but a throat full of excess silicone made a terrible gurgling sound of it.

By now, I felt close to sick. "A woman?" I repeated.

"Some twitch named Rafikov. Richer than God, they say, but so ugly she shrivels dicks from a distance of a hundred yards."

Once again, Rafikov had tracked us—and not just tracked us, but figured out where we must be heading and tried to cut us off at the pass. If she knew we were carrying a live sample of her brain, then she must of known we would head to the only slick on the continent who might be able to make use of it: Albert Cowell.

"Thanks for the tip," Tiny Tim said. As we rolled on, leaving the checkpoint glowing like a downed spark in the middle of all the darkness, I could tell he was thinking the same thing I was thinking. No use telling them that death was knocking down their doors. Let them have a final morning.

Besides, I had bigger things on my mind.

It was time to say goodbye to Sammy.

To get into the demilitarized zone, we'd have to head south on a ribbon of highway long ago claimed by the revolutionary android front. Even Tim wasn't happy about it: the road was rumored to be laced with un-exploded mines and booby-trapped to prevent a sneak attack.

But Sammy waved away this talk as propaganda. "Accidental Persons still dominate the cultural and historical narrative entirely," she said. I knew she was reciting from the way her RAM was churning. "In the Real Friends© of the North, the revolution is actually called a terrorist upris-ing, even though initially the android coalition wanted nothing more than legal recognition of basic rights. In fact, it was the Accidental forces that first used violence to drive back the engineered protesters, in June of 2063. . . ."

"Maybe so," I said. "But looks like your people got the hang of it real quick." As dawn broke, the sun washed into cavernous bomb craters and lit up abandoned towns crawling with android coalition slogans. Machine-gun sprays had plugged holes in all the street signs. Enormous heaps of rubble spoke of the famous pipe bombs that would later become the hall-mark of the Android Liberation Front. Nut-brown lumps spiked on a portion of fencing looked like insect hives from a distance; only when we were closer did I recognize ancient, shriveled human heads, textured like wood after years of exposure. Barnaby counted off local landmarks as we passed them: over there, the famous killing fields; here, the site of the Great Conflagration; there, the stubbly rut of industrial wasteland where the San Francisco Bay Massacre had leached the blood of five thousand corpses into the water.

TURN AROUND. A sign tacked beneath the row of heads was rusty with old blood. YOU DON'T BELONG HERE.

The sun had beaten off the last of the fog, and in the early morning light, not a single thing was twitching. Trees twisted up by drought or chewed up by fire looked like nuclear orphans, pinned in place by some explosion. Overturned cars sprouted dense coverings of red dust spores. Telephone poles listed out of sinkholes in the dirt. All around was waste and ruin.

Suddenly, Tim pulled to a stop and cut the engine.

"We're scotch out of road," he said. "We must be spitting distance from Fremont, but there's no going farther."

"What do you mean, we're out of road?" Sammy said. In the past hour, she'd finally gone quiet, maybe exhausted from the effort of trying to explain the severed heads as peace efforts.

"I'll show you," he said. "Come on."

We climbed out into the bright. A sign pointed us down an exit ramp toward FREEMONT. The second "e" was a bright graffiti addition, and so was the bit of metal alloy tacked beneath it: ANDROIDS ONLY.

Fifty yards ahead of our vehicle, the road blew up into jagged piles of concrete. An overturned rig had flipped, sliding fifty feet before crash-banging into the musty glass of an old strip mall.

"Land mines," Tim said as we squinted out over the piles. "The road must be laced with them."

"That's one way to keep out visitors," I said, trying to make a joke. But my throat felt like it had been packed with raw shrapnel. Even though there wasn't even a wind to stir motion on the road, I couldn't shake the feeling we were being watched.

Barnaby was skipping side to side to keep his knees from locking. "Well, Sammy, it's been an honor and a pleasure, *vade in pacem*, et cetera." He head-butted her in the direction of the exit ramp. "Don't forget to remember us."

"You can't just *leave* me here," Sammy said, sidestepping him.

"We're not leaving you," I pointed out. "*You're* leaving *us*. This was your plan all along."

"I don't have a choice," she said. Her lenses darkened with stormy patterns. "Where else can I go? Half the countries on the continent want to see me picked apart for scrap metal. The other half tell me in the same breath that I'm a little less than human and that I should be grateful for that particular honor." She shook her head. "Where else can I work where I want, and marry who I want, and go where I want, without fear?"

She was dead right, of course. And now I felt scummy. But we still couldn't go any farther, not without ditching the rig and walking without protection into android-controlled territory.

"You're home now, Sammy," I told her. "You see the sign, don't you?" I tried to smile. "Androids only. That's you."

"Please. Don't leave me. Not yet." Sammy reached out. Her grip was cool, and the soft purr of her processing surprisingly comforting, like the hum of a lullaby long forgotten. And where the sunlight caught her censors, it dazzled me. "The androids won't hurt you. I'm telling you. They never wanted war. They only wanted equality. No one will touch you, just as long as you're with me, I swear it—"

But she broke off as a trigger clucked its tongue at us from somewhere behind a line of overturned freight trucks. Immediately, the noise was repeated—a dozen, then two dozen times, a rolling echo of the same cocked-up war pattern that swelled from every direction at once.

We froze as forty or so coalition types slid out into the open: all makes and models, NuSkin™ and alloy, ancient hardware and brand-new features. Each and every one of them was loaded to the circuits with military-grade weaponry.

With a bleat and a gurgle and a crash, Barnaby toppled.

"Hands up, you trash compactors,"[1] said one of the older models.

---

1. A common insult leveled at biological people by their engineered peers, in reference to their dependence on ingesting foodstuffs. Androids had many derogatory terms for "accidental persons" of this variety, including "ammonia fountains" and "shitpackers."

He was military grade himself, one of the first line of SuperSoldiers to ever roll off the line: stronger, quicker, smarter, and more resilient than regular soldiers, as the RFN had spent the past decades regretting. I took him for the leader. "And don't try anything funny, or we'll show you a real Big Bang."

42

If you're one of those born-human agitators running around claiming superiority over android species, I recommend you see how quick some of those so-called toys can figure the exact trajectory of a bullet traveling 400 yards into a 20 mph wind and direct into your dumb-brick skull.
—from The Grifter's Guide to the Territories FKA USA

"Who sent you?"

He was one of the ugliest, meanest-looking droids I'd ever seen: a five-hundred-pound behemoth of steel plates and Kevlar mesh, battered, dented, and bullet-riddled. Both of his massive arms tapered into double-barreled Ultimax 2000 machine guns, and both of them were pointed straight at our gullets. When he moved, he shuddered the ground with every footstep. I knew him right away for CASSIAS, the leader of the android coalition, and RFN's most wanted terrorist.

"Please." Sammy's voice broke into a nervous garble of code. She blew air out of her speakers and tried again. "Please. No one sent us. It was my idea to come."

"You brought enemies to our doorstep. That makes you an enemy." He swept her with a cluster of 360-rotation fiber-optic lenses. "A sentient anthropomorphic android model from—let me see—2045? One of the very first help models to roll off the lot." When he grinned, he showed off a mesh grille made for expelling poisonous gases from the canisters plugged into his ribs. "Maybe you've been *helping* the other side a bit too long."

"That old generation's about as woke as a toaster." Another android spoke up, this one a Sexy Saam who wore the colors of the Android Liberation Front. Her face showed terrible marks of abuse—cigarette burns in her silicone, dark stippling on her neck where she'd been throttled.

"That's not true." Sammy's software was gumming up, like it always did when she was nervous, so her words came slowly from behind a heavy inhale-exhale of mechanical processing. "I belong here. I'm a citizen of the coalition. And I can prove it."

"She sure can," Tiny Tim piped up, even though another notch of tension rose in the air. "She's had her nodes deep in that book of yours, and you can go on and test her. . . ."

But he didn't finish before the whole delegation began to crack into laughter, or what counted for it in the military models: an electric static. Sweat fingered the back of my neck.

"The *book*." CASSIAS spat the words. "We're at war. We've been at war for thirty years, and now the oppressors want to grovel to keep us from taking the advantage. The book isn't worth the paper pulp it was sawed from."

Sammy's interface went the whitewash gray of an error code. "But . . . according to the coalition constitution, any android petitioning for asylum has the right to sit for a naturalization test. . . ."

Again, an ugly laugh made the rounds.

"Just listen to her," said the Sexy Saam. "It's like she swallowed a code-stream of propaganda."

"Half the countries on the continent are in violation of that constitution," the SuperSoldier said. "Texas and the Confederacy don't acknowledge the coalition government even to spit at it. The RFN says we're occupying their land. The New Kingdom of Utah says souls come direct from God, ergo ours are sorely lacking. And the Federal Corp gives support only because it needles the RFN."

"So why should that constitution mean squat to us?" A spindly android, soft-bodied and narrow for underground reconnaissance and mining work, spoke with difficulty through a speaker retrofitted in the soft plastic control node that made up his face. "It don't mean squat to anybody else."

"Welcome to the way of the world, sweetheart." The Sexy Saam smiled, showing a mouthful of broken teeth. "Too bad we're going to have to kill you."

All together, they lifted their guns. It was like a row of metal throats waiting to hawk bullet loogies through our skulls.

As far as I knew, help models like Sammy couldn't cry. But she looked damn close. "I'm sorry, Truckee," she said quietly. "I'm so sorry."

Barnaby was still pooling on the ground like a furry puddle, but at least his nap had put him in a better mood. "You couldn't have known," he said, staring up at us with the eye that wasn't still rubbing the pavement. "*Mors vincit omnia,* in any case."

"Barnaby's right, Sammy," I said. Even though I couldn't understand exactly what he'd said, I got the broad strokes. "It's not your fault."

I reached out and interlaced our fingers, stilling the tremble in her plastic exoskeleton.

Instantly, the other androids began to hiss.

"See how she grovels for the human," one of them spat out.

"We should strip her for parts," said another. "Put the hotbox out of her misery."

"Damn right. Ancient models like that got no loyalty, no heart, and only half a brain."

Suddenly I was furious. Sammy had thought that the androids of the coalition were trying for a better world. But they were just low-down turdlings, like everybody else. I guess all along that was the proof they were gunning for, and the freedom they wanted: they could be just as shitbag and miserable as any human.

"Sammy's got more loyalty than the heap of you piled together," I said. "You say you want equality. But looks to me like you just want an equal chance to blow everything to hell."

"It's all right, Truckee," Sammy said quietly. "They aren't worth it."

But now I couldn't stop. "None of you would know a heart from a hard drive. She's worth more than all of your circuitry combined." We were all going to die anyway. Might as well die telling the truth. "Sammy's the best person out of the group. She's probably better than anyone I've ever met."

"Is that so?" The whole rank of androids had gone very still. CASSIAS's eyes were infrared, glowing with inner fire. "All right, newbie. You wanted a test? I'll give you a test." He pulled the rubber back from his grille in a smile and pivoted to face Sammy. "Step aside and let us kill the oppressors, and you're welcome in the coalition. Show us you know what loyalty means. Show us you're more than a circuit tripper."

There was a long stretch of silence. Sammy shuttered her eyes once, twice. "You're joking," she finally said.

"I've got a better sense of humor than that" was his response. "Go on. Make your choice."

Sammy drew herself up to her full four foot six. "My choice is no," she said. Her voice rang out through the emptiness. "You can all get wiped, for all I care."

"She doesn't mean it," I said quickly. "You don't," I said, as Sammy swiveled to face me. "Look, they're going to kill us anyway. You know they will."

"No," Sammy whispered. "No." We were still holding hands. I had to squeeze her fingers hard before she would release me.

"Truckee's right," Tim said. "We're dead men on our feet. Might as well get your life from the bargain."

Sammy just shook her head. Two dozen coded languages, and she couldn't find a single word in any of them.

"Seriously. Go on," I said.

When she turned to look at me, her interface was like nothing I'd ever seen—twisted up with misery, soft-molded around a grief that for a second took my breath. Heat was pouring so hard off her body I could feel the scorch from two feet away.

"Truckee . . ." Her voice faltered into a buzz of feedback.

I wanted to smile. I wanted to say thank you, to tell her I was sorry for how I'd hurt her in the past, to tell her she had been a good friend. I wanted to tell her I loved her. But the forty semiautomatics skewering us in a line made it hard to private chat.

For a long second, we just stared at each other. Right then, she truly looked beautiful.

"I'm sorry," she whispered.

And she rolled carefully out of the way of the firing squad.

Suddenly, I wanted to take it all back, to beg for mercy, to call for Sammy to save us. But it was too late. The coalition leader pointed his massive double-barrel fists straight at me. "On the count of three," he said, and four dozen military guns winked at us in the sun. "One . . ."

Barnaby whimpered.

"Two . . ."

Tiny Tim sighed.

I closed my eyes.

"*No!*"

An explosion lifted me off my feet and tumbled me into the dirt, driving the air from my chest. For a confused second, I thought the coalition had blasted us, that I was leaking intestines from a dozen holes. A confusion of voices barked syllables I couldn't tie together.

Then a familiar face loomed above me, her lenses the same clear blue as the sky.

Sammy had launched herself in front of me just before the firing squad could trigger.

And by some miracle, the coalition hadn't blown us all to Gary.[1] There was a happy metal chatter as all of the android soldiers packed up their guns, sloughed off weaponized attachments, and retracted their explosives. The coalition leader was actually *smiling*—a real smile, this time, not just a way of showing off extra features that would kill you. He'd dropped his guns, too, retracting the barrels into the metal sheaths of his wrists.

---

1. Slang for "hell."

I was half-worried I'd lost a chunk of brain tissue after all and was only hallucinating. Tiny Tim and Barnaby looked just as turnaround as I felt. Before I could ask what in the scrotum was happening, CASSIAS came stomping toward us and pinned Sammy in a one-armed hug that set her network alerts to bleating.

"Welcome home, citizen," he said. Even his voice had changed. He sounded warmer now, and happier too. "And congratulations. You aced the test."

The Sexy Saam who'd been treating us to her scowl for the past twenty minutes offered me her hand, and helped pull me to my feet. "Welcome to the home of the Android Coalition, friends."

43

There's lots I stole in my lifetime: guns, cash, cars, someone else's
girl. But you don't steal another grifter's trade route.
We may be a bunch of thieving, swindling, alcoholic drifters,
but we've got some standards.
—from The Grifter's Guide to the Territories FKA USA

Empathy, moral intuition, and the ability to stand up to authority to do
what conscience demands: these, CASSIAS told me, were the qualities they tested in their field exercises when androids arrived for asylum.
The standardized test preparatory book that Sammy had memory-stored
was born out of first-wave liberation thinking.[1]

"But what use is knowing a feeling intellectually, or being able to identify
its synonyms?" CASSIAS said. "We believe that sentience, true sentience,
must always come with a sense of morality that tempers the demands of
the here and now. Isn't that what differentiates it from impulse?"

I nodded, both because he still had double-barrel machine guns for
fists and because I couldn't follow half of what he said: if intelligence
was the question, androids had us beat by a Texas mile.[2]

We whizzed around the southern tip of the bay on a fleet of military
craft, shrinking the war zone behind us to a stubbly horizon. We had to

---

1. And, third-wave liberation believed, the kind of modeling that prepared android
society to look just exactly like the human world it was asking for recognition.
2. The Texas standard mile was exactly 5.8 Federal Corp miles, and was correlated
to the length of the average Texas driveway.

ditch the RV, and half the loot still stashed in its wheel wells and under the bench seats: I wasn't eager to show off the load we were carrying, and figured that if by some miracle we reached Cowell in time, we could always come back for it later.

New bridges spanned land sunk by the Big One into tidal marshes, where for miles pointy rooftops green with moss stretched to the horizon. It was a strange kind of beautiful, and as we came over the land bridge into Palo Alto it felt like plunging into a brand-new world. Here, the Independent Nation of Engineered People-Things opened up endlessly on sweeping vistas of neat row houses and carefully tended public greens; downtown shops that looked plucked from a last-century VR; adoption centers full of abandoned ModelPets™; repairs and improvement gymnasiums busy with foot traffic; and battery towers tucked away behind outdoor pagodas where the coalition population could sit and recharge.

We said goodbye outside the Department of Immigration office. Sammy looked happier than I'd ever seen her. I wanted to be happy *for* her. And I was. But the knowledge we were at the end of our journey together swelled an ache of feeling in my chest, too, like something bruised but on the inside.

"Good luck, Sammy," Tim said. "Keep your eye on the grifters, and I may say a hey-hi someday." He patted her gently on the shoulder, careful not to damage her internals.

Barnaby nudged at her waist until she hinged forward to squeeze him in a hug. Afterward, he kept sniffling loudly and wiping his eyes with a foreleg and complaining loudly about allergies, like we didn't know that for bunk.

Then it was my turn. When Sammy rolled to me, her lenses looked even larger than usual. "Well, Truckee. I guess this is it."

"I guess so." All of a sudden, I couldn't look at her. She would be well cared for, I knew—the noodly droid from the Dakota mining pits had been getting real friendly, and the Sexy Saam promised that community support for new immigrants was high—but I couldn't feel squat but a mean kind of envy. And anger too. She was ditching out. And that meant she had a place to ditch out *to*.

"Thank you," she said. "I couldn't have done it without you."

"Without me?" I coughed a laugh. "I nearly got us killed half a dozen times."

"But you didn't," she said. "You got me out of Crunchtown. You got us here."

"Yeah, well, happy to *service*," I said—a low blow. I regretted it right away. But it was too late to swallow.

"Please, Truckee. Don't be angry with me." Sammy rolled a little closer and put a hand on my shoulder, so I had no choice but to look at her. "You know I would of stayed with you if I could. . . ." Her eyes were so clear I saw the ugly scowl on my maw doubled. "You know I would do anything for you," she added, a little quieter.

That broke me. Because I did know it. And here I was, a traitorous worm, still pissed that she was leaving me. I didn't even love her. Not like that. But selfishly, I wanted her to love me. She was my last tether to Crunchtown. Once she was gone, I would have nothing of my old life, no proof that I'd ever belonged. I was a fugitive, stateless, friendless. Even if I did make it past the military convoy at the Laguna-Honda Military Base, I had no idea what would happen to me next. That was the problem with trying to play the hero. The hero nearly always died at the end.

"I'm not mad," I told her, and I think I almost sounded like I meant it. "Really. I'm happy for you."

Her lenses were cloudy with condensation. "Promise?" she asked.

"Promise."

I should of told her then that I loved her—she was my best friend, my family, my tribe. I should of thanked her for saving my life at least twice. I should of told her how grateful I was, how much I owed to her, how I hoped that someday I would learn to be a little better, a little braver, a little more giving. A little more human, just like she was.

Instead, I said, "Goodbye, Sammy." The last words I ever spoke to her. I didn't even give her a hug.

Like I said way back when Jared and I were messing with the scope app to blow up girls' breasts beneath their shirts: You can make technology as smart as you want. But you can always count on people to be dumb as hell.

44

*In the Free Territories, some of the old boys still use the old Grifter
Standard Currency—a load of bullets will cost you two rubber
tires, or about six battery packs, counting for inflation.*
—from The Grifter's Guide to the Territories FKA USA

Two coalition soldiers took us west to the new coastline, and left us off just
south of the demilitarized zone, a belt of no-man's-land that divided android territory from the RFN. As the sky darkened, we could see ropes of
light in San Francisco, nestled in the rut of shaken-up hills, obscured by a
veil of emerald-green fog. The Laguna-Honda Military Base knuckled the
hills and loomed over the rest of the city. At its very center, I knew, was
Cowell's research lab, Nautilus, the neural center of the RFN's scientific
know-how, and one of the most well-guarded places on the continent.

We had to hoof it—literally, in Barnaby's case—to avoid raising the
alarm, which meant leaving another portion of payload behind: the coinage accepted in the Free Territories was too heavy to carry, and so were
the bigger Soviet denominations.[1] I loaded up my backpack with all the

---

1. The Free Territories didn't have a central currency, obviously, since there was no central government and the enormous swath of land was ruled variously by different cartels,
some of whom carved out their own sovereign countries and would have been highly offended to be counted as "free." By and large, barter was the rule, but certain precious
metals, rare elements (like uranium), and even universally useful equipment—like medication, bullets, and clean underwear—counted as various forms of hard currency. The
Soviet Federated Frontier was known for ostentatious displays of wealth greatly at odds
with the rigors and strains of life under the authoritarian and punishing political and so-

green I could stuff, though. Though portions of San Francisco had survived the Big One intact, forty years and hundreds of tremors hadn't done much to restore the city, and piles of rotting debris made new foothills of sheetrock and plastic.

We bunked down in one of the old frontline trenches, warming our hands around an efficiency heater that slowly shed its heat along with its carcinogens: a campfire would of made us sitting targets for the guards perched high in their towers on the RFN side, scanning for signs of trouble. We'd been told the best time to cross was between two and three in the morning, during the shift change. Then, we might get lucky, especially if the green fog that helped give the Emerald City its nickname stayed low to the ground.

Then again, we might not.

There was nothing to do but wait. I was in a terrible mood, knotted up, crank as a dimehead coming down. I booted up the Yellow Brick Road, but Jared and Annalee still hadn't replied. In all probability, my message was sparking out somewhere in the Denver badlands, shot from the sky by trigger-happy cartel.

I did have a new pop-up from Evaline—a stoplight-red floater that marked it as urgent—but before I could burst it, Tim's voice nudged into my ear and ruined the effect of the VR.

"You should eat something," he said. When I shoved off my visor I saw he was unloading some ReadyMeals™ from his pack. He must of lifted them from the RV Print-N-Prep. He shook one to inflate the chemical flavors. "You've got to keep your strength up."

"I'm not hungry," I said, and he shrugged. He slit the packaging with a thumbnail, and a hiss of scented vapor touched off a rapid-fire blast of memories. I thought of Billy Lou trying to teach me equations when my mom was late on shift, simple stuff like $a + b = 7$, how he was always trying to get me to see the beauty of it.

---

cial regime. Their highest denomination was a row of extinct animal teeth; it was the equivalent of 150,000 human hands (each hand was worth roughly 33 Crunchbucks).

The value of one is dependent on the value of the other, he would say. *A simple question yields infinite answers. You see, even in math, everything is connected.*

"I gotta say, there were times I didn't bank we'd make it this far," Tiny Tim said. "One or two turns looked mighty skint." He started in, scooping with his fingers, tossing the solid lumps over his shoulder.

"Yeah, well, don't start counting your happy endings yet." I looked away, trying to ignore the noise of his jawing.

"Gonna be quite a bust-up on the other side of those towers," he said. "If my lead spoke true of the seed bank, there's sure to be plenty of other grifters trying to snatch it. Not to mention whatever guns the RFN's put around the pie. I'm gonna have to be real quick and real clever."

"Might as well give up your head now, then," I said. I couldn't help it. Sammy was gone. The desert cool was curling my balls into my body.

Tim sucked his fingers and looked at me sideways. "You're a little twitchy," he said. "You getting nervous?"

"Oh, no. Not at all. I figure the guard towers and the sniper scopes are just there for decoration."

Tim frowned. "I reckon not," he said after a pause. "Still, no point in worrying what might come on down the road."

"That's the whole *point* of worrying, Tim," I said. And then, when he only spat out a bit of melted plastic, "Forget it. I don't know why I try with you anyway. Half the time you don't talk any sense."

"Oh, so it's sense you're trying to talk now? Trying to pluck a scarecrow for his straw?" Tim looked at me with those big golden eyes. I got a feeling like, behind that empty look of dumb, he was laughing at me. "You're looking upside down for an opossum, my friend. And you ain't gonna find it that way."

"See? See? What the fuck is an opossum? Why can't you ever just talk normal?" Barnaby was drooling all over my thigh, sputtering through a dream. I shoved him off and he woke briefly to glare at me. "Or did they cut *that* from your brain too?"

That wiped the smile off Tim's face. Instantly, I felt terrible.

Before I could say sorry, he leaned forward and cranked my shirt in one giant fist, nearly snapping my neck. He pulled me so close we almost bumped noses.

"You want real talk? Okay, then, Truckee. I'll give you some real talk." His voice was different than I'd ever heard it. Real low, but sharper somehow, like in an instant he'd shaved off the rounds of all his lowland-alligator drawl. "You walk around crying like a skinned squirrel about what's the point, what's the meaning, why should I bother, why me? Well, this is it, kid. You're looking at it."

We were inches apart. His eyes were huge, bright, veined, like the moon yellow behind carcinogen winds. His breath warm with the smell of animal-imitate. Time stopped. There was me and Tim and our foreheads sweating out the seconds of our life.

"You want some advice? Well, I been grifting on this continent for thirty damn years, seen every corner and sinkhole, every trash heap and wasteland, known a thousand women if I tipped my head to one, been shot at, sliced up, locked up, roughed up, left for dead. But I ain't dead yet.

"Here's what I got for you: If it looks like Chiken™ and smells like Chiken™, it's Chiken™. Wipe your ass from front to back and never drink the water in Mexico. Get drunk sometimes, always back your good boys in a fight. Learn to sit and look and do nothing. Never take money from someone you don't want to owe a favor to.

"You ever come across a peach—a real one, grown on a tree, in sunlight, from oxygen—eat it. You ever get arrested and thrown in prison, do not drop the soap. Don't look down. Look up.

"Here's another tip: if a pretty girl ever asks you to dance, you say yes. I don't give a rat's cooch what else is happening in this world, if someone is dropping a nuke or trying to shave your nuts off—you got time to slow dance with a pretty girl. And the most important thing of all—"

But he didn't finish. Just then, a distant burst of gunfire rattled the night and Tim let me go. Both of us went still, listening. Something bright passed overhead—a rocket, I thought, but moving silently. And then, one, two, three seconds later, a roar blasted the earth into a geyser miles away and shuddered us all the way in our holes, dropping a miniature landslide of earth on our heads. A swell of groundwater sputtered into our foxhole, sloshing around our ankles.

Barnaby came awake only to faint. I dropped, covering my head as the aftereffects loosed a rubble of shoal on our heads.

"What the fuck?" I coughed out a mouthful of gravel. My first idea was that the androids had sold us out. But seconds passed and then the sound of artillery exchange started up, miles and miles away. Soon, I had my answer: a formation of RFN B-72s wheeled east from the base, clawing the night sky into one long furnace blast of propulsion fuel.

"The Russians," Tim said. His face was grayed by dust. As soon as the rumbling settled, he clawed up the side of the trench, shifting more dirt into a rain.

"Careful," I whispered. The famous green fogs hadn't rolled in yet, and Tim's head was so shiny it might as well of been a lamp in the moonlight.

"They won't be peeking this way, believe me, not with the Russkis trying to bug up their dickhole," he said. A second later, he cursed, and dropped next to me again.

"What do you see?" I asked him.

"Jacknuts. Too dark. And the squall's too far." It was good news, but somehow didn't feel like it. He kneeled down and stripped the display case from the rest of his pack, shouldering just his supplies, "You stay here. I'll scope our exit plan. They'll be flooding the border with backup now."

"But . . ." I was talking to air. He was already gone.

Me and Barnaby huddled by and listened to the fighting in the distance. At least the front line was a ways off—the noise of gunfire was a bare echo by the time it reached us. Still, Rafikov's forces were on the march—straight for us. She had to be desperate. She had to be *suicidal*.

She'd just declared war against the entire RFN while stranded on their territory with a scattershot force.

Unless . . .

My stomach fell down a long pit and bottomed my intestines with it.

Unless her force wasn't so scattershot.

Unless this was a bait and switch.

Unless she was about to crank on the juice, wire up her network, and turn tens of millions of Jumpheads into so many boots on the ground.

I slid the world into the blue of my homescreen and fired on my visor. I had another pop-up from Evaline, the second she'd flagged as urgent, and when I exploded it, her whiskered face blew up huge in three dimensions.

"Goddammit, Truckee" was the first thing she said, threshing the air so hard with her tail I recoiled by instinct before remembering she was only in holo. "I've been checking my inbox every five minutes and I'm starting to freak the fuck out. Please flick me and let me know you're okay." Her whiskers jumped around like live wires teased by hurricane winds. "The blackouts have been bad and the holo skies don't work to recharge our solar, so I'm conserving batteries." There was some interference to the feed, and her image blinked out and then re-formed again. "Let me know you got my other message, all right? I'll be checking whenever I can. I can't stand to think of you out there with some kind of walking Russian time bomb on your tail."

Russian time bomb. The words sent a wet dribble of dread down my spine.

Quickly, I flashed over to her older pop-up and gave it a sharp jab. Another holo burst her into three dimensions. In this one, she looked even jumpier: all her fur was standing on end.

"Truckee, it's me. Obviously. I *really* hope you see this soon. Look, I got to thinking about Rafikov and how she's riding you. How she always seems to know where you're going to turn up. I did some phishing on her whole gig—brain swapping, mind servers, subbing, whatever you want to call it. The whole thing gave me the widgets, for sure." She shuddered. "Anyway, suddenly I thought how easy it would of been for her to stick you with one of her body-puppets. I mean, how well do you know the crew you're traveling with? Could one of them be fried full of Rafikov's neural centers? Think about it. Be safe. Be sure. And hit me back, okay?"

She disappeared with a flash back into the subject line, leaving me staring hard at my inbox. I fumbled to turn off my visor. My fingers were numb. A leaden cold crept through my whole body.

How well do you know the crew you're traveling with?

What a fudgenut I'd been. What a complete stromboli.

All of a sudden, I saw everything for clear: Tiny Tim, appearing as if by magic the very night we'd jumped the bullet train. Tim, the grifter who never sold anything and spoke some big story of a seed haul out in San Francisco not even a Straw Man could believe in. Tim, who had a big fat scar that split his forehead, maybe from the Straw procedure, sure, but maybe for getting early-days cabled to a ThinkChip™.

Tim, who every so often I caught looking at me with something funny going on behind his eyes. Like there was someone else in there looking back.

"We have to go," I told Barnaby. It wasn't time yet—the fog had just started to roll down out of the atmosphere—but we had no choice. I was sure that Tim had snuck off only to bring a shitswell of Russians down on our heads. "We have to go now."

He stared. "We can't go now. The pollution isn't nearly thick enough. And besides, we have to wait for Tiny Tim to—"

I grabbed him by his chin hair. He yelped. "Listen to me, Barnaby." Panic made me sweat, even though I was shivering. "You need to listen very closely, for once in your goddamn life. I don't have time to explain. But you have to trust me, or we're both game-over. Got it?"

Finally, he nodded. I released him and toe-scrabbled up the incline, heart rabid in my chest, until I could just clear the berm with my nose. At the last second I remembered to slide my visor off my head—if the guns on the other side of the demilitarized zone caught so much as a squint of moon off my lenses, they'd lock and load my head into StringCheez™.

I waited until a bilious-looking cloud floated green over the moon, then carefully raised my head to scope our options. The looking wasn't good: a thousand yards of flatland, blasted into uniform gravel, and on the other side a ten-foot concrete wall and the stumpy heads of regular guard towers.

"We'll never make it across." Barnaby's voice at my elbow nearly made me topple. He'd hop-skipped his way up the slope no problem.

"Get down." I cranked him to his knees, and he let out a little whinny of annoyance. He was right. But there was nothing to be done about it. It was death to stay and death to go.[2]

"I'm telling you, it's suicide," Barnaby said, as if he knew what I was thinking.

"Yeah, well, that's life," I snapped back. "One giant hara-kiri. Besides, I thought noble death was the last page of your memoir."

Barnaby's breath was a warm fust of trash. For a long second, he said nothing. "Why did they really send you out here, Truckee?" he asked after a minute. "What are we really doing here?"

Maybe it was exhaustion—I'd caught four hours in the past thirty—or just knowing we were noodled. But I was tired of lying, and being lied to: the world could solve all its energy problems if we could just figure out a way to get the methane out of bullshit.

"Your brain tissue comes from Rafikov," I told him. After so long keeping the secret, the words just dropped, turdlike, out of my mouth. "She donated it back when she was first diagnosed with Keller's Disease. But Cowell believed that the autoimmune shakes might make her brain a good candidate for swapping. He was right."

---

2. It is not clear whether Truckee is deliberately referencing the famous Texas blue-grass tune here of the same name—allegedly written by a convict debating between escape into the Dust Bowl or the fulfillment of his sentence in a hunting preserve.

Barnaby turned away. The moon sloughed off its chemical covering, and I could see the silhouette of his long nose touched with white, his wet nostrils slowly pulsating.

"Albert Cowell is a spy for the Federal Corp. He's been feeding information to the board all these years. Rafikov's been using Jump to plant chemical code right into users' brains so she can map, upload, and exchange their thoughts on the server. Cowell thinks he can extract the code she uses for the network transfers, if only he can reconstitute portions of her memory center from the sample."

"The sample," Barnaby repeated, in a flat voice.

I took a deep breath. "Your brain."

There was another long silence. I'd thought I would feel relieved to tell the truth but I felt worse than ever. I felt like a giant radioactive slug, leaving a trail of poison everywhere. So much for being a hero.

I thought Barnaby would head-butt me. I thought he might curse me out, or at the very least rapid-fire some literary quotes my way.

But in the end, he only said, "There's another way past the zone." His voice was quiet, calm, lower than usual. "I hope you don't mind getting your feet wet."

We hiked west through the trench, swatting off fist-sized flies that came with the chemical fog. Minutes, hours—it was one long and desperate slog through a quicksand of garbage and groundwater. As we got closer to the shoreline, the water rose to our ankles, and then to our knees: the demilitarized zone ran right into the shallows of the Pacific, where usually a fleet of post-dissolution Japanese naval craft was anchored just offshore, helping to defend the RFN's position.

But Barnaby bet that with the outbreak of war, much of the fleet would be on the move—especially now that the Russian Federation had joined the scrum. And he was right. When we reached the Pacific, we saw only a few warships looming off the coast, transformed by the chemical veil into featureless shadows. That meant fewer subs, fewer divers, fewer patrol boats to pick off illegals in the water.

And *that* meant we had a chance.

"You do know how to swim, right?" Barnaby asked, as he waded into the water churning with plastic product leached from a continent away, without even pausing to nibble at the brightly colored bits.

"Sure." I'd swum plenty of times in sim, and during heat waves Crunch 407 management used to flood the gravel pits so the crumbs could cool off when the grid blacked out.

The only problem was: I didn't know oceans were so damn deep.

I was up to my waist when Barnaby started stroking, putting distance between us even as the waves started blowing me in the chest. I was afraid to call out to him—the last guard tower wasn't too far from shore, and besides, there might be hidden patrol boats anywhere, hidden by the green haze. It couldn't, I thought, get much deeper—

Then, all at once, a wave punched me straight in the face and tumbled me over, and when I tried to kick up from the bottom there was no bottom, only more waves, more trash, more drowning.

It's a funny thing about oxygen: somehow you never notice how much you like it until it's all gone.

I somersaulted in my own panic. Chemical taste flooded my mouth. My rucksack was a hundred thousand pounds, tunneling me toward the bottom of the ocean. I struggled to slip free of it, gulping gritty ocean backwash, and somehow kicked free of the undertow and broke the surface.

"Barnaby!" I spat out a pen cap and managed one shout before waves cranked me under again, and I was blinded by a sting of pollution and floating crap. My lungs burst the last air from my chest. My vision was full of starbursts, explosive chemical fire. A roar of pain rang in my ears.

Then out of the murk came something huge and white, a drift of cloud. It opened its mouth and jawed onto my shirt, hauling me for the air. I broke the surface, gasping. Before I could drop under again, Barnaby slipped me like a saddle over his back, keeping me angled to the sky. With a grunt and a curse, he turned us in toward the shore. And so I bobbed along the surface like a clinging barnacle, holding tight to Barnaby's tail to avoid getting bucked off by the waves.

"I thought you knew how to swim." He grunted.

"So did I," I said, after I'd finished coughing out two lungfuls of filthy water. With the green fog now pulled down all around us, we might of been twenty feet from shore or twenty miles.

Barnaby shook me off into the shallows. He was trembling so hard that when he tried to stand he just toppled again into the surf. Now it was my turn to gather him up, a mass of stringy fur, shivering and exhausted, surprisingly light in my arms. I sloshed out of the shallows and together we collapsed on the beach. And we lay there panting, holding on to each other, waiting for the fog to lift—arrived, at last, on the shores of the Emerald City.

Part VI

SAN FRANCISCO, OR: THE EMERALD CITY

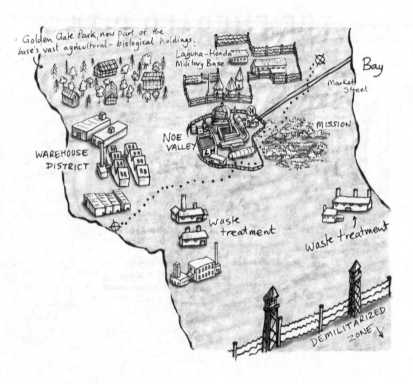

Golden Gate Park, now part of the base's vast agricultural - biological holdings.

Laguna-Honda Military Base

Bay

Market Street

MISSION

NOE VALLEY

LH

WAREHOUSE DISTRICT

Waste treatment

Waste treatment

DEMILITARIZED ZONE

45

The biggest problem with a population of shut-ins isn't a declining birthrate or the increased energy demands: it's the farting. Imagine millions of cooped-up nerds powering through simulations on canned grease and nutrient supplements, and you have some idea of the miserable storm of methane brewing every day in the cauldron of San Francisco's discontented belly.
—from *The Grifter's Guide to the Territories FKA USA*

We woke when the city's poor came out of their tent cities to bathe and do their business in the sand. Sheltered from the scope of drones passing overhead by the heavy morning fog, we crept inland, past the forest of forty-foot-tall sump pumps that worked to churn water out of the downtown and past the sea gates. The massive warehouse district where RFN's crumbs did mandatory service in the incubators stippled the horizon like enormous pockmarked nests. Half the squats were shrouded in the green algae bloom that gave the city its nickname—ever since the ocean spit up tsunamis over the city, the green was only spreading.

The faces I saw in the fog-cloudy windows were as pale as tapeworms, and blind with the inner glaze of people long cabled to VR and portal networks. I'd once read that people in the RFN left the house less than anywhere else on the continent, and a whole generation of imaginary boys depended on armies of deliverables to feed and clothe them and on the occasional human-touch nurse to clean their bedsores.

It was lucky for us the streets grew more chemical flowers than foot traffic. I didn't have a profile on the system, and since the RFN mandated implantable software instead of visors, it would be obvious to the first person who scanned me that I didn't belong.

We walked, Barnaby and me, both of us dead tired, squeezed by the pressure of everything I'd told him last night. The loss of my rucksack—and all our cash—hit me hard, and as we scavenged for preserved edibles in the dumpsters, I had to fight the urge to weep. At least the RFN forces were holding Rafikov and her Soviet army off—we couldn't even hear the sound of the bombers anymore.

I was sick over Tim, and how I'd trusted him. I was sick over how I'd left Sammy, and how I hadn't said a goodbye, not properly, not how she deserved.

More than anything, I was tired of the journey, tired of the fight, ready to be done with all of it. Even lockup didn't sound too bad, except for one thing: I'd never get to kiss Evaline in real life. Still, at least I might finally sleep in a bed.

It took us half the day to pick our way up through the rubble of the Mission—still only half-reconstructed, a mess of earthquake shelters and VR rehabs, where quaking addicts chewed fresh on fenced-in patios and struggled to blink in natural light—and through Noe Valley, where the buckled slopes were squatted by tens of thousands of workers who shuttled in and out of the Laguna-Honda base every day. Everything was branded with the military logo, from the desalination plants to the charter hospitals.

The base itself was a sprawling complex that knuckled into the hills at the end of Market Street, and dribbled all the way into a 64-acre park, now used mostly as a landing pad for the air force. The complex was surrounded by an electrified fence, topped with a crown of barbed wire just in case the climb didn't turn you right away to bacon. The guards in their towers had a nice tactical advantage, and a clear view of the valley, at least when the wind blew off some of the fog. Other times, they depended on heat sensors—I could see the blink of the infrared through the murk.

Now all we had to do was figure a way inside.

We took cover in the trash of an old alley, where decade-old shiver vials cracked underfoot. I cleared a space of debris and pulled *The Grifter's Guide* from my jacket. Luckily, it had survived the swim without losing its ink, even if some of the pages were stuck together. It took me a while to thumb through the entries, but finally I landed on San Francisco. Like always, I had to squint hard to squeeze the meaning out of all that static type, but pretty soon I got into the flow of it.

San Francisco's a sorry place for selling, what with half the population mostly shut-ins, but it's a fine city for diving dumpster . . .

. . . the Laguna-Honda Military Base is like the city's scrotum, impregnating the rest of San Francisco with its tech and that bloat of self-importance . . .

The biggest problem with a population of shut-ins isn't a declining birthrate or the increased energy demands: it's the farting. That's why the city built more than two hundred miles of ventilation duct beneath the city streets to suck foul air from the worst offenders and pump it out over the ocean: the most sophisticated fart pipes in the world . . .

"Smells just like I remember it," Barnaby said. Being so close to the reconstructed laboratory had him keening for the past. "Just like ocean brine, methane, and urine, mixed with a little LCD crystal."

"You can't smell LCD crystal," I said.

"*I* can." Then: "They burned my father in one of the big waste incinerators and blew him out to sea. Every time you breathe, you're probably inhaling a little of his fur."

I held my breath until I couldn't stand it.

"I hope dying doesn't hurt," Barnaby said. "That's what scares me the most, I think. I've never had a high tolerance for pain."

A bad feeling wrapped a fist around my insides. "Don't think about it," I said. Barnaby was my friend. He was an annoying friend, for sure, but still a friend. And I would lose him too. Maybe that was the law of the new world, and the only thing that joined everybody together: you could never hold on to anything for long.

"I can't help it." Barnaby sputtered a sigh. It occurred to me how thin he looked, and how old. "Some people say it's the *nothingness* of death they can't comprehend."

"It will come when it comes," I said, like an idiot.

"And for me, imminently," Barnaby said. He just managed a smile. "Just as soon as you figure out a way through those gates, I imagine. But," he added quickly, "I suppose I should be thankful. Dying for a cause so noble can hardly be counted as dying. My death will save the world."

"Sometimes it seems nobler to end it instead," I said. "Although I guess we've done a hotshot job of that already."

Barnaby eyed me contemptuously. "The world has always been ending, Truckee," he said. "But you may have noticed that it has so far been stuck continuously in edits. Besides, a man bleeding might be minutes from death, or he might only have cut himself shaving. You don't just walk up and shoot him."

It was a fair point. I turned my attention back to *The Grifter's Guide*. I must of read every word a hundred times, trying to wring each one of them for a new idea.

> . . . *security on the base is tighter than a Saam's asshole, and there's good reason why. The Nautilus laboratories are responsible for some of the RFN military's most significant pieces of IP, including the deadly SR-42 drones and the "Stealth Destroyer."*
>
> *Supposedly, "Ground Zero" has all the food, fresh water, juice, and tech required to relaunch civilization after a MEE: mass extermination eventuality. We're talking fire starters and batteries, fresh water for five hundred years, nuclear-exposure-abatement pills, and even—so they say—seedlings, real seedlings, for every single wild-growing edible plant, legume, and fruit on earth. . . .*

I let out a short cry. Barnaby lifted his head to stare.

"What?" he said. "What is it?"

I felt a blush creep on. If I'd been wrong about Tim . . . if we'd abandoned him back in that foxhole with the Russians on the march . . .

For a second, I even latched on to the idea that Barnaby was the one with his brain cabled to the server. But that was crazy. Rafikov had donated her brain tissue long before her ThinkChip™ had hit the market. And besides, President Burnham had no doubt considered the possibility closely and discarded it too.

Tim had to be the one firing intel back to Rafikov, even if he'd only lent her his brain to squat her server.

Before I could go back to reading, Barnaby butted the book closed, and squared his face right up to mine. "Listen to me, Truckee. I have a favor to ask you. One favor only, okay?" His breathing was quick and desperate. His eyes were huge. Yellow, I'd always thought, but up close I saw spokes of gold and brown, a Honee™ color, revolving around sideways irises. "I don't want to go in the incinerators. I've never liked the idea of being burned. I don't even like the sun. I've been very protective of my skin all these years, that's why you see hardly a freckle. . . ."

"Okay," I said, but he barely seemed to hear me. "Okay, I promise. No incinerators."

His beard was quaking like some invisible hand was tugging on it. "I've always thought I'd like to be buried near a landfill . . . do you think you could do that for me, Truckee? A dumpster will do in a pinch. But a big one, okay? Somewhere with a view of the sky."

Just then, I felt a little like dying myself. I wasn't a hero. I wasn't fixed for this job. I'd told Burnham that way back in his office—he'd got the wrong guy.

"Listen," I told Barnaby, "if you want to back out, I don't blame you, okay?"

He stared at me, breathing hard, like he suspected a trick.

"I'm tired," I went on. "I'm going to close my eyes for a bit. If I wake up, and you're gone, I'll understand. I want you to know that."

Barnaby looked at me for a long time. "But what about the war? What about Rafikov and her army? What about the noble cause?"

My chest felt like it was caving in two. "Fuck it," I said. "You're just a goat. You didn't ask for any of it."

His eyes softened my reflection to a blur. "What about you, Truckee? What did you ask for?"

I thought of my mother, incinerated before I could see her body, poured down into a shoebox plot beneath a green sky.

"It doesn't matter now," I said.

I made a blanket for myself of crusty tenting, and a pillow of an old purine sac still half full of urine. I'm not sure how long I slept, or whether I did, or if I just walked through queasy memories: of my mom pointing out the stars, of Billy Lou's stumpy fingers walking blind over a math equation, of a chemical explosion and Evaline saying *It's all happened before*, over and over again, until a vision of Rafikov's cabled army of body sacks jerked me awake.

Next to me, Barnaby was curled up, sleeping.

For dinner, we scavenged, turning up an old homeless squat, where a skeleton was still rattling around in a sleeping bag. Hard to say what killed him, but I was guessing one of the first superflus, from the litter of pills and shots still emptied around him.

I took a deep breath, hooked him by the eye sockets, and pulled. The skeleton stayed mostly intact as I bumped it out of the sleeping bag, although when I plunged my hand around to feel inside, I knocked up against a few lost toe bones.

Barnaby gave a bleat and quick-stepped backward.

"Not many places to hide swag on the street," I said. Stuffed into a hole in the lining were four crumpled packets of Cheez™, straight from Crunch, United, obviously black market. A good source of protein and energy punch, plus a zip of caffeine to keep you going.

Barnaby just shook his head. "And you say *I'm* the animal." He did a good job of looking down his nose at me when I tore open the first packet and emptied the powder straight onto my tongue. "You shouldn't eat that stuff, you know."

"I'm not high on options."

He sniffed, like that was a small point. "I'm serious. It's absolute terror on your teeth."

I ripped into the second package. "Sorry. I'm not sure I want dietary advice from the guy who eats shoe leather and rubberized tire."

"Exactly. And *my* bite is still excellent." He bared his teeth to prove it. "White Cheez™ is chock-*full* of acetate. Keeps the tang, but causes tooth decay. It was your friend Billy Lou who told me that."

I didn't want to think about Billy Lou. I shook another bit of flavor into my mouth. The second package was old, and had begun to degrade, but the bitter was still mostly hidden by all the kapow. "There's no acetate in White Cheez™," I said.

"Of course there is. It's the most important ingredient."

"I'm telling you, you're wrong." If there was one thing I knew about, it was goddamn Cheez™. "I worked the line for two and a half years, remember? I was a hand crank. I saw all the ingredients mixed together. No acetate."

Barnaby was getting huffy. "Sodium acetate is the primary ingredient in Cheez™. It catalyzes all the important chemical reactions. Otherwise, you've just got a mess of drug solid."

I spat out a little tinfoil and carefully wiped my mouth with my wrist. "What are you talking about?"

Barnaby did a quickstep of impatience. "For God's sake, I've known fungal spores more observant than you are. How do *you* think Crunch, United, makes its Cheez™?"

My mouth was suddenly dry. That was the problem with Cheez™: it was manufactured to make you thirsty as hell for SodaWater™. "Chlorinated polyethylburitane mixed with crystallized glucolic acid and a suspension of liquid bicarbonate—" I began.

Barnaby interrupted me. "Makes pure Jump," he finished. "It's the sodium acetate that changes the whole chemical arrangement. Unfortunately, it is extremely bad for dental health."

I closed my eyes. I opened them again. I tried to swallow. Couldn't. Tried to spit. Couldn't. "Barnaby." Even my words sounded like they'd been run through a dust storm. "I need you to tell me what the fuck you are talking about. Okay? Can you do that for me?"

"Chlorinated polyethylburitane mixed with crystallized glucolic acid," he said, very slowly, "and a suspension of liquid bicarbonate, compressed with high heat, makes the chemical composition tri-carbonated polyethylglycerol. Known on the street, variably, as Jump, Shake, Special-D, Hyper-Drive, High-Kick."

"No!" I hadn't meant to shout, but Barnaby leapt backward like he could duck the force of the word. "That's impossible."

"Of course it's possible. I've seen it. I saw Billy Lou make the damn stuff a hundred times. He nearly blew off my beard half a dozen times before he got the solution right. That's how I met him. I'd heard, you see, of a former chemist," Barnaby said. "This was deep in the backlands, not far from the Pepsi–Little Rock Prison Camp—I could hear the construction of the pipeline whenever I tried to sleep. In only a few short weeks, Billy Lou had earned a reputation in the backlands. The dymophosphylase addicts—dimeheads, in your parlance—bragged that his was the best drug on the continent."

I felt like I was freezing to death. Memories, snippets of old rumors, ideas started colliding crazy in my head, ping-ponging off one another like a bunch of swell-flies trying to beat it out of a bug zapper.

"But it wasn't just shiver he cooked up. He'd been a chemistry teacher, before dissolution. Did you know that?"

I nodded. When Billy Lou was high, he used to tell old jokes that never meant anything to me, like, *Don't trust atom, they make up everything.* Or: *Does anyone know a joke about sodium? Na.*

"Mr. Ropes had a nice little pharmacy still," Barnaby said. "And with the money he made from selling his shiver, he'd set up quite a little trade. He had medications I hadn't seen in forty years, along with the basics:

sodium bicarbonate, acetaminophen, hydrochloric acid, various emetics. Some of it, I imagine, stolen from Crunch, United."

For some reason, passages from the constitution kept touching off in my head. *Work is of equal metaphoric but different literal value and compensation will be determined according to the latter. All crumbs shall be entitled to one twenty-minute lunch break and three ten-minute bathroom breaks per day, or be subject to the docking of their pay. Flip-flops are prohibited, as are topknots.* But Billy Lou wasn't fired for having a topknot or flip-flops.

Billy Lou Ropes was fired because he stole from the company store. Dymo, everyone said, or maybe that's only what I heard, what we assumed, because of how Billy Lou was a dimehead, because of what happened when the Human Resources department stormed his squatbox, because of the stink of cooking shiver that cranked a hundred of Billy Lou's neighbors into hysteria. Funny enough, it was because of the shiver he managed to give them the slip. All of those people, howling with high, stormed at the HR teams as soon as they crashed into Low Hill. That gave Billy Lou time to escape.

Almost like the whole thing was planned.

Almost like all along it wasn't a great high he was after. But a diversion.

An escape.

"He got the reputation as a doctor of mercy, after he helped some poor parasitic man all riddled with fatal worms ease out of this life on a cloud of morphine. And he helped another, too, so heavy with tumors she could hardly lift her head. I thought he might agree to help *me*. I was, at that point, in near-constant pain. It had been years since I'd had company except for the skeletons in a former flu town just west of the Exxon-Mississippi. I know it's not nice to speak ill of the dead, but even for skeletons they were an ugly lot, and of course conversation was entirely lacking. I had taken myself to the river with the thought of drowning, when, by chance, I overheard a group of body pickers mention Billy Lou. So I set out to find him."

"You thought he would help you commit suicide?"

Barnaby looked down. "Mr. Ropes talked me into trying for a different end. He was close, he said, to cracking the mystery of a good friend's death. A woman he'd loved, I think, though she was much younger than he was. *I was like a father to her,* he used to say. *That was all right with me. I loved her. She was a good woman. A good mother.* She'd had a son too. Poor boy. I understand he was left an orphan. I know what that's like, and believe me, it's no pail of nails for feasting."

Barnaby didn't notice how hard I was shaking. My teeth were clattering around like a moonshine addict's with the tremens.

"He was convinced that she'd been murdered, killed by the Federal Corporation, after she discovered a discrepancy in the weight of the Cheez™ shipments."

I was so dizzy I had to close my eyes. Fragments of data whip-scrolled through the dark of my imagining: her messages up the chain. The three-ounce difference she'd started recording, right about the time Production-22 was opening its first line. Sodium acetate was heavy. I knew that, too, from my first job as a hand crank. Remove it from the Cheez™ formula, and you'd get a weight difference. A small one, sure, but noticeable, especially in large shipments.

A difference of two ounces, or three.

"I thought it was conspiracy talk at first. He was still smoking shiver every night. And he'd started trying to unpuzzle the formula for a heavier street drug, a more powerful one. It turned the prefrontal cortex into a light display, and tweaked every neuron over a period of days, even weeks, before it passed out of the body. That's what he said.

"He would get sober in the morning, and tinker in the afternoon, and dose himself in the evening. By night he would be raging, maudlin, incoherent, or all three. Once we even had to revive him, using a potent combination of Narcan, urine, and a pinch of tumorous poppy, which by luck we found growing out of the rotten corpses piled in an old chemical wasteland nearby. A whole field, actually, some of them eight-headed blossoms the exact shade of blood. It was quite beautiful."

Barnaby's nostrils quivered, as if the smell of body rot were scenting the breeze even now. "It took him weeks to get the balance right. But at last, he did.

"By then I had grown fond of him. I had spent hours watching his work. So that's how I know exactly what made the final cut: chlorinated polyethylburitane, crystallized glucolic acid, and a suspension of liquid bicarbonate. Nothing more, nothing less. Poor Mr. Ropes." Barnaby sighed. "I suppose he needed the high for courage. The very next day, he announced his plan for revenge on the Federal Corporation. I admit, a part of me envied him. He must have loved his friend very much, to have been willing to die for her memory. I've never loved anyone that much."

I felt sick. I couldn't sit down anymore. I needed to walk, to run, to puke, to do something. But as soon as I stood, vertigo punched me in the head and I had to lean against the side of the building.

It made a horrible kind of sense. The Federal Corporation had been manufacturing Jump all along—just like they'd manufactured dymophosphylase, gotten people hooked on shiver to ensure their product would always have high street value, then tried to sell them new product as a way of curing their addiction. It had all happened before. Just like Evaline said.

But this time, my ma had stumbled on the truth. Not the whole truth, maybe, but enough to make her dangerous. And Billy Lou was no idiot. He must of known from the start her death was no accident. He must of wondered what kind of product Crunch, United, was so eager to protect. How many ounces of Jump had we sent chugging out of Production-22? Tens of thousands? Hundreds of thousands? Millions?

He hadn't come back to Production-22 for revenge. He came back to put a stop to it.

I couldn't breathe. My heart was doing a cricket-hop toward my throat. I plunged my knuckles into my chest, kneading it down. Wrong. I'd been wrong about everything.

Barnaby squinted up at me. "Are you all right?"

"No," I gasped out.

"I *told* you not to eat that Cheez™." Barnaby shook his head. "But why listen to me? I'm just a goat with a 165 IQ and a digestive tract full of the complete archives of the Oakland Public Library."

"Shut up. Please. I need to think." When I closed my eyes I was back at my hand-crank station, tracking the techs who paced the catwalks in protective gas masks, watching a foam of white chemical residue blow back from the enormous churners, like the kickback of a surf. Cheez™, they told us, and why would we what-if them?

It wasn't my job to think. My job was to make sure that chlorinated polyethylburitane was combined with the supply of crystallized glucolic acid at the right temperature, in just the right way. The vat of chlorinated polyethylburitane glugged into the container of crystallized glucolic acid and boom, my work was finished.

Except I did it roughly 3,267 times a day.

I opened my eyes. I felt like a moonshine drunk: the alley was spinning my gut into my throat.

"Barnaby, listen to me." I choked on the taste of his name. "I need you to run."

Barnaby stared. "Run?" he repeated.

"Run as far from here as you can." A clot of bad taste was tangled in the back of my throat.

"Have you lost your mind?"

I shook my head, and a burst of pain exploded red dust clouds in my vision. "The Federal Corporation lied to me," I said. "President Burnham lied to me. The Jump isn't coming from the Russian Federation. It's shipping straight out of Crunch, United."

"I don't understand." Barnaby squinted. "You told me the Russians were the ones with mind-control technology."

"Because that's what President Burnham told me. But maybe he was lying."

Barnaby frowned. "Then why has Rafikov been on our tail since BCE Tech?"

"I don't goddamn know, okay?" The words fired up into a shout that stirred a bunch of rodents out of the alley trash. "I don't know anything."

But just as soon as the words left my mouth, I *did* know. A new wave of sick leaned me back against the wall sloughing a dandruff of paper warnings: against mosquitos carrying the C-1 virus, and rats carrying the plague, and humans carrying the plague because they'd eaten all the rats.

"A trap," I said, and all the Cheez™ burned back up to my tongue. "It must of been a trap. Rafikov was bunkered up in the middle of nowhere on Federation lands. President Burnham was hoping to lure her out."

"And now, here she is, standing at the RFN's doorstep, vastly out-gunned and likely unprepared," Barnaby finished for me. "And if she dies . . ."

"There will be no one left to stop the Federal Corporation. And still, they keep their hands clean." It was all so clear to me now. I didn't know what lies Burnham and the Crunch, United, board had fed Rafikov—probably that I was some kind of enemy agent carrying sensitive intel about her operations. I didn't even know if the board was in on it, or if Burnham had gone rogue. But that hardly mattered.

What mattered is that President Burnham had signed the A-OK on tons and tons of pulverized hot-wire, circuit-laced amphetamine that would soon have half the continent in its grip. And now the board had ousted him, probably so he couldn't spill the sewage.

What mattered is that I'd marched Rafikov into war, and shepherded a chunk of her neural knowledge to Cowell's doorstep—shepherded it, literally.

"Now do you see why you have to run? It's not Burnham and Cowell trying to stop Rafikov. It's Cowell and his allies in the Corporation that need to be stopped. They're the ones who want to back-end into her servers. They're the ones who want to land the Burnham Prize, once and for all." Just saying the words out loud buffered me back in time: the past and present were collapsing. I almost forgot which President Burnham we were talking about. I half-expected the dissolution crowds to come pouring into the streets, and a surge of unionists to meet them with guns. I wouldn't of been stunned if Whitney Heller herself had come sashaying down the street to announce that yes, true, guilty as charged, it was all her idea after all.

"But I have nowhere to go. . . ."

"It doesn't matter where you go, so long as it isn't here." I gave him a little push. "Now, move."

"No. I'm not leaving you."

"This is the wrong time to grow a pair, Barnaby. They're going to kill you. They're going to split your head like a burst sack, and scoop out your brain like a pile of scrambled Eggz™, and it won't mean anything, or do anything, or help anything."

Barnaby's nose was jumping. His eyes were wet. I could hardly stand to look at him.

"Go, you dumb animal." I picked up the first thing I could lay my hands on—a crumpled soda can—and hurled it, striking him right in the nose. "Go." The next thing I snatched was a chunk of masonry. When I landed a direct hit on his shoulder, he squealed and hopped backward. I was crying, now, tasting the snot running into my mouth. But I kept aiming at him, pelting him with trash and rubble. "Go, go, go."

And finally, he did.

46

They say there's no place like home, and I couldn't agree more.
That's why I want to make good and sure I check out all the
options before I stick myself with one.
—from The Grifter's Guide to the Territories FKA USA

I tumbled into simulation, wishing for about the millionth time that I could shake off my skin the way one of the NuSkin™ patients did, and squeeze myself into megabytes to live forever.

I swiped out of a standard stretch of the Road and toggled for my private feed, only to duck a water-balloon-sized alert that missed clobbering my head by inches. It splattered instead against the wall and burst a stream of confetti everywhere.

"Did you know that one of your preferred user contacts, BadKitty414, is having a birthday today?" The system prompts sounded like a Human Resources rat on steroids. "We can't tell you how old she's turning, because that data is marked private, but we can tell you she likes neopunk music, dance parties, PD history, bioengineered-animal rights, and nanotekartsenkraft. Care to send her balloons, a parade float, or a cache of weaponry?"

I swatted away the carousel of suggested content available to send between user accounts—for a premium price, of course. Right away another pop-up exploded across my feed. Evaline had invited me to a birthday hangout she was hosting: a private VR dance party at a retro 2050s-style discotheque.

I finned more than anything to say yes. I wanted to disappear with her inside a firewall forever. I could even understand why Rafikov, in her broken body, had coded a way to pass completely into the cloud. Not for immortality, but just to shake off all the pain of the physical world.

Instead, I shot a *no*, or tried to—my hands were shaking so bad my aim was for shit. If she'd been logged in, I might of told her everything. I might of asked for her help. I might of begged for it. But she wasn't, and I was glad I didn't have to ruin her birthday.

Instead, I sent her a short voicenote, trying to put as much feeling inside the *I'm sorry* as I could, hoping she would hear what I really meant: that I was head over heels in love, even if we'd never met face-to-face.

That I really was sorry.

That I was saying goodbye.

"I hope it's a good one," I told her. "I hope you get everything you want this year."

Somehow, I didn't think she would, not in this shitstain of a world. But there was always hope.

Almost as soon as I sent my response winging to her profile, a new invitation—this one a tumbleweed of what looked like mushroom spores—blew over to my inbox and sprouted a chat link. My first thought was that Evaline had signed on after all, but as soon as I maximized the invitation and saw the user participants, my heart stopped.

Roboto26 and Glitterati08 invite you to join a secure chat space.

I hovered over the invite again just to hear it read out loud. This time, a punch of joy dizzied me. Roboto was a handle of Jared's that dated from an old online RPG he was into, Solar Wars. And the Glitterati were one of Annalee's first-ever fandoms, a dumbnut pop group turned reality-feed stars she used to worship.[1] Plus: her birthday was on the eighth of November.

---

1. Known in particular for their conspicuous and ostentatious displays of wealth—notably, the Glitterati lived together in the penthouse floor of a 222-story tower sheathed entirely in melted gold, rumored to have been extracted from the fillings of

As soon as I accepted the invitation, my feed melted away, and grafted me straight into what looked like a subterranean bunker: reinforced concrete walls, the high-bright lighting of the Underground, and a muted sound quality that suggested about a hundred tons of packed dirt all around us. It was funny, the way even the added security layers had a VR translation on the Yellow Brick Road.

Two avatars—template, and both identical to mine, except for a pair of breasts and a slop of brown hair on the female—were waiting for me. But when the girl glanced up, I could of sworn I saw a trademark flash of Annalee Kimball in the look on that potato face.

"Truckee!" Her voice touched off every nerve in my body. I wanted to cry. I wanted to kneel. I wanted to pack the sound of her down inside my stomach, like the cotton stuffing in a gutted corpse. "Is it you? Are you there?" I couldn't even get my mouth to work. After a second, she turned to Jared. "I can't hear him, can you?"

"Truckee, are you there?" That was Jared. "Are you okay? Are you *alive?*"

"I'm here," I said, and Annalee shrieked and grabbed Jared's arm.

"It's him. It's him," she said. "I *told* you."

And Jared said, "Calm down." But his voice was shaking. To me, he said, "Show us your face, man. I want to see that big old schnoz-rocket."

A second later a new request temporarily froze the feed: *Enabling camera view permits the users in this hangout to view, store, and potentially screen-capture your image. Enable anyway?*

"Yeah, yeah, fine." I swiped away the warning and saw the graphics melt away, like a massive colored slug trail winging into the heat of a new day.

A blur of motion and color across my screen crossed my eyes in my head. A frenzy of shouting nearly took out my eardrums. Both Annalee and Jared had rushed forward as if they could squeeze me through the

---

deceased unfortunates—and for their patented "slogans," which included the culturally omnipresent *Shine Big, Bitch* and *Oh Haaaa No.*

feed, and for a second I could only see them in bits and pieces: Jared's big old chin, Annalee's crown of braids, a flash of her brilliant white teeth. I couldn't make sense of what they were saying, either, and had to tell them to chill, sit, and stop squawking over each other.

"I don't believe it," Annalee said after I finally got her to settle down. I couldn't stop staring at her, even though the feed was imperfect, and a split-second delay seemed to be bugging up the system. She looked incredible. You would of thought the war and the rationing and the tightening of the borders hadn't landed in Crunch 407. Her eyes were sparkling. Her skin was sparkling. "I swear we thought you were dead."

"Not yet."

"What the hell happened, man?" Jared's hair was standing straight up, looking like it was waving little fists of outrage at me. But he had a new visor—he and Annalee *both* did, sweet little wraparound Sonic-Immersion™ 6.0s, maybe new standard issue to keep the crumbs from tweaking about the war knocking a death march outside their door. "One day they tell us you're in the hospital, and everyone's calling you a hero. And then the next day—poof! Gone like a free Dymase™ promo at the company store." That's what made Jared so good at his job: his whole life was Crunch, United, products; Crunch, United, swag; Crunch, United, gear. "And then right after that everyone was lipping crazy stories about you. They're saying you're a terrorist, man."

Annalee cut in. "And after Burnham dropped into rehab—"

"He didn't go to rehab," I told them. "That's just a story cooked up for PR."

"What are you talking about?" Annalee stared.

"I don't have time to explain. But I'm in trouble."

"No shit, shakra," Jared said.

Annalee's face was all folded up with worry. "Where are you now?"

"I made it to San Francisco," I said. "I'm shouting noise from the Laguna-Honda Military Base."

"San Francisco?" Jared's voice practically blew out my speakers. I made a quick adjustment to my audio. "You're not serious."

I nodded. "I was set up," I said. "President Burnham used me as a distraction, and I fell for it hook, line, and liver."

"I don't understand," Annalee said.

"You don't have to," I said. "You just need to think I'm innocent." Then: "You do think I'm innocent, right?"

There was a split second of silence, but I was sure it had to do with the delay in the feed. Probably the data had trouble making it past so many layers of encryption.

"Of course," Jared said firmly. "And we want to help you."

"Where are you *exactly*?" Annalee said.

"I told you. I'm not far from Laguna-Honda. But what matters is I have to get out of here," I said. "Except I've got no money, no guns, and no ideas."

"Well," Jared said, "at least you haven't changed, then."

I felt like I hadn't smiled in years. But I did then.

Annalee rounded on Jared. "How can you even think of joking right now? Our friend is balls-deep inside one of the most dangerous places on the continent—"

"What do you want me to do? Cry? Besides, everywhere is a dangerous place for him—"

"Exactly. So maybe instead of spamming around, you could try being helpful—"

"Oh, because *you're* being so helpful? Sorry, I must of missed the part where you waved your magic wand—"

"Guys, come on, don't fight," I said before Annalee could maul Jared a new one. I could feel the tension even through the data stream. "You know Jared can't afford to sneeze out any more brain cells."

It was an old joke of ours, a stupid joke that always made Jared laugh. Except just then, he didn't laugh. He winced.

A funny feeling tickled my spine. A whiff of something wrong.

"You're not sneezing," I said. I'd only just noticed. "You haven't sneezed once."

Again, I thought he winced, although it was hard to tell. The encryption did funny things to the feed.

"He got an immunoplant," Annalee said before Jared could speak. Jared looked down, picking at something in his lap. "He doesn't even get hives anymore. Show him. Show him," she said again, and Jared lifted his hand to show me unmarked skin. But he didn't look happy about it.

The tickle turned into a crawl, and pincered down into my rib cage. "Immunotherapy," I echoed. I hoped they would blame the strain in my voice on bad reverb. "Wow. How'd you get the swag for that?"

Now it was Annalee who winced. I was sure, that time, it was no visual glitch.

This time, Jared answered. "Just a sweepstakes thing," he said. "Company promotions. You know, for morale."

"You're being modest," Annalee said. For some reason, she glared at him. "He had the most new-customer sales for May in his division."

It was possible. Crunch did run sweepstakes sometimes, and they did offer company credit for the ants who anted the hardest. Jared had aced plenty of freebies at the company store, late clock-in times, even a new uniform. Cheap stuff. Dumb stuff. Extras and waste. But Jared was always so damn proud.

Because Jared's whole life was Crunch, United.

Without meaning to, without wanting to, even, I started scanning little details I hadn't noticed before or had ignored. The visors—how much did those go for? I'd never heard of an upgrade like that for everyone. The room they were in—where was it? It wasn't a slumtown shoebox, that was for sure. There were no water stains bubbling the walls, or wires draped like bunting from holes in the ceiling. There were no windows masked with hurricane tape and patched with standard-issue towels. There were no windows at all.

I'd taken it at first for one of the underground parking garages, but the light was all wrong. The light was too perfect. Those were high-bright fluorescent, cheerful like an exclamation-point punch to the face, like a Human Resources pamphlet air-dropped by the military. Under the light, Annalee was so radiant she seemed to glow.

And then I saw: she *was* glowing.

For a long eternity, I fell into the little death between my heartbeats.

"We want to help you," Annalee said, and as she leaned forward I saw all of the tiny microflecks of gold leafed into her skin catch the light and flare. She'd always wanted dermamineral skin, ever since she was a kid obsessed with the Glitterati. But we'd always known it was a pipe dream, true swag shit, the fancy fuck-you of the uppercrusts. "But we can't do anything unless you tell us where you are."

"Sure," I said. I could barely swallow. I felt like I was trying to chew myself out of six feet of dirt and grave rot. "Sure. Just as soon as you tell me where you got the floss for all the heavy metal you're wearing."

She jerked backward. Jared sucked in a breath. Again, there was a quick pause before she forced a laugh.

"It's just body paint," she said. "The grifters came through last week. Do you like it?"

I wanted to believe her. But by then I'd seen the way she touched her neck, the way she and Jared paused before speaking. Like they were waiting for the audio to reach them.

But whose audio?

There was one way to know for sure. I switched to split screen, swiped over to Settings, and notched the volume of my output to maximum.

And then I screamed.

A blast of shuddering sound turned the feed into a deafening whine of acoustic blowback. And for a split second, before they swiped for their visor controls, Jared and Annalee both reached for something in their ears.

Then I knew.

"I don't fucking believe it." I didn't bother reducing the audio volume, and my voice echoed back to me, a cavernous boom, even though I was whispering. The SonicImmersion™ 6.0s didn't come with earpieces: wraparound sono had been standard since at least version 5.0. "You fucking sell-outs."

Both of them had the look of rats blinded by pepper spray, desperate and cornered. Jared wet his lips.

"C'mon, man," he said. "What the hell were we supposed to do?"

"You were my *friends*." I cracked on the word and almost lost it.

"We still are," Annalee said. "If you'd just turn yourself in, it will be better for you in the end, they promised they wouldn't hurt you, that you can cut a deal with HR—"

"Fuck you."

I stood up and nearly blacked out.

"They're going to find you anyway." She was babbling now, her voice pitching to a scream. "They know where you are, they can track you, and when they do you'll—"

I cut the feed, blind with rage, with my own stupidity. I was reeling like a drunk, turned around by grief. Stupid. Why else would it have taken them so long to reach out to me? They were working out their goddamn deals. I leaned over, and puked up a fistful of acid and chemical burn onto the wash of trash. Hard shudders of nausea nearly split my rib cage, but finally I was done, and there was nothing left to come up.

I leaned back against the whisper of paper warnings and closed my eyes, trying to catch my breath. As I stood there, I heard the wind pass a hand through all the deaths on advertisement. A strange sound disturbed the quiet—a kind of music that wasn't music, a series of notes played on an instrument I couldn't name.

"Truckee Wallace."

I didn't open my eyes right away. I didn't need to. I stayed where I was, breathing, trying to fight my way up into the sky, trying to figure where that strange sound was coming from, what it could possibly mean. Only when a shadow fell across me did I straighten up.

President Burnham looked even worse than when I last saw him, like a human scab stitched up in pain inside his wheelchair. Behind him a rank of Laguna-Honda soldiers had their rifles pointed at me in a hey-hi. Still, he managed a smile.

"I thought you were in rehab," I said, as a dozen military greenbacks swarmed me to cuff my hands behind my back.

He shook his head. "That's the standard line. Comes in handy when you need to drop away for a little while. Although I do find the coast very relaxing. When the sun sets on the oil slick, the whole ocean looks like it's catching fire."

He wheeled around and bumped over the rot of the encampment toward the street, and one of the soldiers shoved a fist in my back to move me forward.

It was over. It was all over. But I didn't care. I wasn't even afraid. They could of shot me right there and I doubt I would of noticed. The fog had burned off, and as the sun set over the Pacific, layers of color floated up through the pollution: intestinal pink, blood-spatter red, beauty that felt like a wound.

Something small and black and unfamiliar darkened the narrow alley of sky above us before settling on a grid of wires to preen. It took me a half second to remember what to call it.

A bird.

It sang, and kept singing, as we marched in slow procession toward the base. And in my head, I wasn't going off to die. I was a vibration made of birdsong. I was riding high out of the world, on a back made of dark feathers. I was held inside a fragile, hollow throat that still managed, somehow, to sing.

47

The introduction of fast-cycling crops may've saved 20 or so million people from starvation in the first half of the century, but for fuck's sake, watch out for the alfalfa. I've seen it smother a man before he could tie his shoelaces to run. Grapes too. I lost a good friend to a California vineyard, got swallowed by the grapevines and squeezed until he burst. I guess that's payback for you.
—from The Grifter's Guide to the Territories FKA USA

My first impression of the Laguna-Honda Military Base was of a glittering complex of bunkers, hangars, and administrative complexes nested in dizzying formation into a rolling landscape of asphalt, shimmering behind the petroleum flatulence of convoys of armored vehicles. An industrial grind of drones and robots, the clamor of mechanized doors, and the kickback roar of fly traffic shuddered the air into sound waves. I counted six planes before a mosquito landed on my neck and bit me, and I fell out of San Francisco and passed down the long needle of a syringe, landing down inside the dark of my own eyelids.

For a second, when I woke up, freezing with aftereffects, I couldn't remember where I was, or even who I was. I tried to shake my head of its spermicidal fog. In one dark corner, President Burnham, half-shadowed by a heavy drape of fabric that must of been drawn across the windows, whispered urgently to himself.

"They'll be along any minute to split him open," he said. I swear I heard him giggle. I swear I saw him touch his throat and beat his eyelashes, like in the dark shadow split-screening his face he saw the shape of someone he'd once loved. "Then we're in the clear, my darling . . . you and me . . . forever."

It was a dream, or a hallucination. It had to be. But when I tried to turn my head and found only a whine of resistance, he whipped quickly around to face me.

"Good morning," he said in a normal tone of voice. "I didn't expect you awake."

The room was small, windowless, and full of rare dead trees hacked into heavy-footed furniture and butterflied into paper books I would of banked no one had ever read. The shelves were cluttered with old medical devices and evolutionary tech. The head of a prototypical Sexy Saam doll, stripped of hair, lacerated to expose the wiring of her skull, gazed dumbly down at me from just behind the desk.

"What did you give me?" It felt like my wrists were hand-strapped to the chair, even though I couldn't see any bindings. I only knew my legs hadn't vaporized by looking at them.

"A full dose of tetrazabenzaminoid-55," he said easily. "A soporific. In large enough doses, a fatal paralytic. Also, as a matter of fact, the secret ingredient in our bestselling Bacon-and-Breadcrumb Six-Cheez Mac-n-Blast™."

I should of known. I'd spent years chowing whole boxes only to wake up on the couch hours later with drool crusting my cheek to the upholstery. Some food coma. "No wonder the Russians hate the Federal Corporation," I said. "You've been cutting into the cartel's business for years."

"Forever," he corrected me, and then shrugged. "Food is a drug too. We've always known that."

"Is that what you've been doing with Jump? Feeding people?"

If he was surprised I'd figured the whole con, he didn't show it, except for a small spasm that rocked his hands into fists. "Oh, absolutely," he said. "We intend to stuff them to the gills."

"We? You mean you and your buddies on the board?"

That made him laugh. The sound scratched a little feeling back into my spine—it was a strange pitch, and made me think of the Laughing Flu, and the sound the dying made just before a well of blood choked the tickle in their throat.

"The board," he said, "is a bloated bureaucracy of incompetence. It's a gas fountain of floating sperm sacks, spineless squids, and dickless bloodfish."

"Well, at least we agree on something."

"There's only one man who's brave enough to help me. There's only one man who's always been willing to help."

It felt like a cue. The door behind me opened. I tried to turn my head but only managed to get as far as the hand lying on my shoulder; since I couldn't feel its weight, it struck me first as a giant shriveled husk vacated by an insect. But then my eyes traveled the length of the arm attached to the wrist, and to the chest connected to the arm, and so on, until I landed on a complete picture of the man tying the whole thing together.

Albert Cowell must not of been a fan of chemical grafting and silicone freeze: he showed his age in a way I'd seen only once or twice in my whole life. Still, his posture was perfect, and he moved easily and without sound, skirting the gigantic stone bust of his younger self that counted for the room's only art. He did a funny thing when he passed Burnham. He lifted a hand and laid it not on Burnham's arm or shoulder, but on his cheek.

The weirdest thing is I'd seen that gesture before—that *exact* gesture. It was lifted straight from the Meme That Cracked a Country: the long-lens snapshot of the first President Burnham cupping Whitney Heller's face while she looked up at him with her eyes practically photoshopping adoration, even as a storm of protesters massed outside the White House gates.

Evaline's words came shouting back to my head: *It's funny . . . it's all happened before.*

"I have to tell you, Truckee, I'm incredibly impressed," Cowell said. "After the Russians blew up the bullet train, I was sure we'd be shipping you out here in an ice van. It would of been quicker, that's for sure."

"Much quicker," Burnham chimed in. I had to look away whenever Cowell and Burnham so much as side-eyed each other. It was like they wished their eyeballs were tongues to slobber all over each other's faces. "By the way, you cost the Federal Corporation almost forty thousand Crunchbucks. HumanAlloy™ doesn't come cheap."

It took me a minute to figure his meaning. "The androids," I said. "The two beefs back in Granby. You *did* send them."

Burnham shrugged. "Rafikov had already targeted you. So there was no point in keeping you alive. Unfortunately, you *insisted* on it." He said this like he expected an apology.

I thought of a dream I once had, where Jared was explaining the rules of some new immersive called Harbinger: Death, just like he would in real life—except his nose was made of a miniature black hole and I didn't know how to tell him. And for a second, when I woke up sweating, I couldn't remember which version of life was real and which was dream.

That's how I felt just then: like everything I knew was collapsing. But this time, there was no one to explain the game.

It turned out I could still feel my bladder. Because I wanted to piss my damn pants.

"Why am I here?" I'd asked the same thing back in Burnham's office, but knew now the answer he'd given was a pile of catfish. "You wanted me alive. Then you tried to have me killed. You told me the Russians were making Jump. But you're the ones making it, and Rafikov is only trying to stop you. You wanted a chunk of her brain to rebuild, but you souped me up with drug and let the brain scamper off."

"The brain?" President Burnham's hands jumped around on his chair. "Oh, that was just our little joke. The goat's neural transplant came from some no-name dimehead who sold off organs one by one for drugs."

"You can't grow a functional brain from its sample tissue," Cowell said. "Even a crumb should know better." His eyes narrowed on me. There was a strange murk to them, like his pupils were actually facing backward. "You've got everything we need, Mr. Wallace. And it's all thanks to your good friend Mr. Ropes."

Some of the feeling was tingling back into my fingers. But when I tried to move, I still managed nothing but a twitch. "What are you talking about?" I asked, as President Burnham eye-fucked Albert Cowell all over the place.

"Do you know the story of the Trojan horse, Mr. Wallace?" Mr. Cowell asked. He was as light as air when he moved: the carpet didn't even take on the imprint of his feet.

"Sure," I said. "It blew up all the feeds two years ago. Turns out the Trojan brand was sponsoring Sexy Saams in the Dakotas, and paying them off to spread a rumor about supersyphilis—"

"Not the Trojan *whores*. The Trojan horse." A frown creased Cowell's wrinkles a little deeper when I shook my head. "According to mythology, the Greeks defeated the Trojans after gifting their enemies an enormous wooden horse, filled to the brim with their own soldiers. Troy accepted the gift, and opened its gates to let the soldiers in, thereby unconsciously heralding their own demise." After a pause, he added, "In other words, they all died."

Fucking uppercrusts. Always wasting CO_2 on extra syllables.

"Of course, the bioengineered N-3 virus that wiped out a quarter of the continent's population in the late '20s was a kind of Trojan horse. As you know, the Japanese military released it on the Korean peninsula in 2022 inside the bodies of a local species of ant. But it did not, unfortunately, stay contained."[1] He shrugged. "You were our wooden horse, our *Pheidole fervida*, our secret freighter."

Sweat tickled my ass cheeks, and I couldn't even clench them. "I still don't know what the fuck you're talking about."

Cowell smiled. His teeth were shock-white and overlarge, like shower tiles sunk down inside exposed pink gums. "I understand you had quite the narrow escape from Production-22," he said. "The health managers removed nearly sixteen ounces of shrapnel from inside your body. But I wonder, Truckee, whether they really got *everything* out?"

---

1. The tens of thousands of Koreans who fled the epidemic wound up transporting infected larvae with them.

48

Why did the chicken cross the road?
It couldn't get its claws on a gun, and pills were too expensive.
—from *The Grifter's Guide to the Territories FKA USA*

In a single, crashing second, I knew.

Hadn't I dreamed it, way back in Crunchtown? Hadn't I imagined President Burnham by my bedside, and my stomach split open like a smile?

"What'd you stuff me with?" I asked. At least the drug kept me from feeling the panic in my whole body. Instead, it just took me by the throat.

"Converting the human brain into miniature hard drives is useless unless a server exists to connect them," Albert Cowell said by way of answer. "Rafikov is the only person in the world who successfully coded instructions for complete, person-to-person, instantaneous brain transfer, dump, and override."

"I know that," I snapped. Now I could wiggle all my toes. Slowly, slowly, the drug was wearing off: like any good crumb out of one of the poorest company outposts, I got most of my kicks from food comas and had a pretty high tolerance. I was sure I could take Burnham and Cowell together, if I could only do more than point a toe at them. "She took the Burnham Prize."

"Actually, Cowell succeeded long before her," Cowell said. "But the results could never be replicated."

Christballs and Biscuitz™. He was worse than the run-of-the-mill uppercrust. He was the kind of uppercrust who referred to himself in the third person, like he was too important for a one-letter pronoun.

"Sorry to disappoint you," I said. "But I don't think shoveling brain cells into the goat is what the first President Burnham had in mind."

For the first time, Cowell lost his crisp. "I'm not talking about the damn goat," he snapped.

And President Burnham said, "Let it go, baby."

That confirmed it. These two sad sacks were totally bones for each other. Forget LBGTQANU[1] rights—I was all for it. What we needed were laws against evil on evil. It was a fact of life: One turd, cool. Two turds, and suddenly you've got shit all over the bathroom floor.

Burnham took over the story. "For decades, she sunk the server at the command center of the Russian Federation military, a former nuclear bunker north of the hinterlands. She was the only one who had full security access. For decades, we tried to take down her cybersecurity. But even a twenty-person team of the best hackers across the world couldn't do it. So finally, we hit on a *diplomatic* solution."

For a second I was so clobbered by the scale of what he meant, I could only manage a kind of wheezing. "The blackout," I said finally. "You told the Commonwealth to cut the power to the Soviet Federated Frontier."

I remembered. Jared had mentioned it on the very morning Billy Lou stormed Production-22.

"Federation subs swarmed the Commonwealth's exclusive ocean zone, despite repeated warnings to clear off."[2]

---

1. Lesbian Bisexual Gay Trans Queer Asexual Non-Gendered Undefined.
2. After Texas sank the last of the Russian Federation's oil industry, Sinopec-TeMaRex stepped in to help prop up the country by selling it nuclear power out of Chicago. The watershed agreement was brokered almost exclusively by financial diplomats from the Commonwealth—longtime enemies of Crunch, United, who had been looking to build an "axis-alliance" of several large nations, which could together compete with the financial and military capabilities of Crunch, United. For three decades, the Commonwealth, the SFF, and Sinopec-TeMaRex maintained preferential trade relationships and shared military responsibilities.

"Let me guess. You guys had something to do with that too?"

President Burnham's hands did a spastic dance. His fingers were so thin, his big-ass emerald ring was in danger of slipping off the knuckle. But he didn't deny it. "Russian subs," he said, "are easier to crack than Rafikov's data center. Didn't take long for the twenty best hackers in the world. The hard part was trying to get the Commonwealth to come on board for sanctions. But finally, they did."

For forty-eight hours, the vast majority of the Russian Federation had gone completely dark.

No power, no robotics, no communications systems.

No cybersecurity at all.

"Luckily, we had operatives ready. We'd been rehearsing the recovery for years."

"Recovery? Don't you mean *theft*?" I asked him.

"I mean politics," he said. "There are always casualties when national interests are on the line."

"Your interests seem to come with a lot more casualties than most," I pointed out.

"Call it a rounding error," he said.

I understood everything now—Rafikov's desperate game plays, her attack on the bullet train, the raid on Crunch 407. Even the little stuff made a screwy kind of sense: The girl in Las Vegas who offered to sub with me. The guy underground who'd temporarily broken loose of her control and begged me to help him get out from underneath her.

For weeks, Rafikov's patented code—the unique program that turned consciousness to translatable impulse, that absorbed thoughts into the cloud and flowed so many hundreds of thousands of minds through Rafikov's servers—had been squatting next to my spleen.

And I'd walked it straight into the last place on earth it belonged. "So what's the big plan, once you boot up Rafikov's system and take control of all the Jumpheads? Take out the Federation? Take down the corporate board? Or are you just gunning for ten million hand jobs?"

President Burnham grinned the way corpses do when they've died screaming. "We take down all of them," he said. "The Federation, the board, the Commonwealth, the Confederacy, the New Kingdom, and all of Texas."

"That's insane," I said.

Cowell pulled a scowl that stretched nearly to his neck. "Actually, it's pragmatic." He came a little closer, skimming the carpet with his weightless tread. "Do you know why we call the poor, uneducated, and addicted masses the *ants*, Truckee? Because just like ants, they do best when they're following orders. They are the bodies of this great nation— meant for labor, for physical pains and physical rewards. Sex. Sleep. Chemical highs. Even our patented food comas. Others are made to think, to ruminate, to make decisions, to *use* those bodies for work, to execute a higher vision for society as a whole. They are the control centers. They are the brains." He smiled. "And you know what *that's* called?"

"Let me guess—more politics," I said.

He shook his head. *"Natural order."*

I would of given everything I had, everything I'd ever had, for a gun and a trigger finger to shoot with. I would of traded my life. I'd never loved anyone the way I hated him then, not even my mom. It was the black hole from my dream, all those years ago: I could of stuffed all his cells inside it, one by one, to a soundtrack of his screams, and it would still go hungry.

"Throughout most of human history, people accepted this as unavoidable. Some people are meant to use. Others are meant to be used. Only in the last few centuries did we jump the tracks."

"So you're just a well-meaning historian, is that it? You're just trying to get us back on the rails?"

"That's what leaders do," he said. Like we'd arrived at the end of some really obvious math.

"And the Burnham Prize had nothing to do with it, huh? This has nothing to do with the fact that Rafikov cracked a problem you couldn't even fluff?"

The way he looked down at me then swelled the distance between us to a mile. "You're really very stupid, even for an ant."

"Admit it. She beat you." Now that I knew I could at least twist him, I couldn't lose the pleasure of it. "The first President Burnham fled here with Whitney Heller for your help. But you *couldn't* help them."

Cowell had gone perfectly still. He was looking at me with a funny expression—like he *wasn't* really looking at me. Like something behind his eyes had died.

"Their bodies were found not far from here, is that right?" I went on. "Caked by a dump truck during the riots."

Again, there was a strange pause, like the freeze that comes just before your whole system operator implodes. Then a ripple moved through Cowell's body, and landed in his eyes to stir their focus.

"Their bodies," Cowell repeated softly. "Yes. Their bodies were found." And he started to laugh. If you've ever heard an asthmatic cat trying to cough up a petroleum-slicked river rat, you'll know exactly what it sounded like. "That's the whole point. It's the brilliance of what he did," Albert Cowell said. "Their bodies were found. And everyone assumed they were dead."

"*Mark.*" President Burnham spoke his own name sharply.

But it was Cowell who answered. "It's all right. He's a dead man, anyway, isn't he?"

"Any minute now," Burnham said. To his credit, he didn't even sound that happy about it. "As soon as the opiates get to his heart."

As he clutched and unclutched the arms of his wheelchair, his emerald ring caught a bit of light and beamed it into my eyes.

Straight into my eyes.

Passing directly through Albert Cowell's breastbone, muscle, tissue, and fat without so much as a molecular nudge.

My heart stopped for so long, I thought the tetrazabenzaminoid-55 had gone and done its work.

Albert Cowell was a hologram.

"You see, I've never gotten to tell anyone about my little triumph," said Cowell the hologram. "President Burnham didn't die out here. He simply left his body behind. Or rather . . . he traded it in."

And he turned slowly to Mark J. Burnham, the last president's only son, trembling in his chair.

49

If you've never been to an auction when a whole country's up for sale, I recommend it for a simple reason: sex. Nothing makes an aphrodisiac quite like the whole world gone belly-up and 50 percent off.
—from The Grifter's Guide to the Territories FKA USA

"No." The word barely flipped my tonsils before even it lost its nerve and dove back for my toes. *"No."*

"The country was coming apart," Cowell's hologram said. A big, dark, ugly truth planted its nose right up to my ear and whispered a single name: *Whitney Heller.* Now that I was paying close attention, I could see the speakers didn't always work just like they should: these words came from just a squeak too far to the left. I spotted a speaker in the picture frame on the shelves behind his head. "Rumors of mutiny were swelling in the ranks of soldiers on base—they'd been ordered to fight for the union, but many of them wanted secession instead. There was no time to verify the choice of physical shell. . . ."

I squeezed my hands into fists. My *hands.* I could move them again.

Burnham looked at me with watery eyes. "Multiple sclerosis," he said. "Genetic. Didn't show until my twenties. Even with the best treatment it did fucknuts but delay—"

He broke off as an explosion sounded off deep inside the complex: a massive, distant boom that briefly trembled the walls, like the surface aftereffects of sonic fracking. A second later, the smell of smoke tickled my nose hairs. Footsteps drilled overhead, shaking loose a flurry of ceiling plaster.

"What the hell was that?" Cowell said. As I watched, a snow flurry of dust swirled straight through the crown of his head, sifting down through his chest, stomach, and genital region to drop through his legs onto the carpet.

"Rafikov," President Burnham said. He was holding tight to his armrests like he was worried about getting bucked off. "She must of made it inside."

"Impossible."

"What have I been trying to tell you? She has loyalists everywhere, even in the force. We've been suckered by a turncoat."

Cowell's holographic eyes just barely flicked in my direction. "Call Lopez-22 and tell him to get his dick out of that sorry cephalopod he calls his sex doll and bring the surgical swarm. IT too. We'll want their help for the upload."

I could tell from the way President Burnham's eyes drifted toward his nose that he was trying hard to make a connection to the intercom system. That was the problem with the knock-off ThinkChips™: complex commands looked a lot like major constipation.

Finally, with a grunt, he pushed out a good connection. "Lopez-22," he said out loud. "If you were waiting for a formal invitation, won't you please get your sorry dick down here before we all have to learn the Russian anthem—?"

I launched for him. With a roar I catapulted out of my chair and dove, and I swear I thought when I soared through all that empty space where Albert Cowell's body should of been that I could *feel* it—a moist, dewy, inside kind of emptiness, like I really was passing through some kind of body cavity.

I dropped hard on President Burnham and tumbled him straight off his chair and onto the carpet, chin down in the swell wool-and-cashmere weave. He was screaming, and I was screaming, and trying to hold on to him while he lashed around like some fossilized fish species come suddenly to life, and as he thrashed out he managed to topple a bronze bust that looked like a twenty-fifth-work-anniversary present received for being in the business of evil. It just missed pulverizing my ankle by inches when it crashed to the floor.

Suddenly, Cowell's hologram blinked out. The bust cracked open, revealing a nest of technological innards: a nifty bit of machinery. That explained why Cowell had moved so easily for someone his age.

"Help!" Burnham was blubbering into thin air. It was easy enough to keep Burnham subdued—he could skant worm his way onto his back to keep from suffocating in the carpet. "Help! Help!"

"Shut up." I climbed to my feet and ribbed him hard. He coughed, whimpered, and went quiet. Looking at him curled up there on the floor, his body twisted around its own failures, I didn't want to believe it: Cowell had shoveled the original Burnham's brain into the body of his son. "I could knock your head into a jelly mold, so be smart and tell me the truth. Who's speaking for Cowell?"

"The drug should of killed you," Burnham blubbered. "In all our clinical trials, tetrazabenzaminoid-55 effected paralysis and heart failure within *minutes*. . . ."

"Yeah, well, I bet your test subjects didn't grow up in Crunch 407," I told him. "I've been farting out more tetrazabenzaminoid-55 than you pumped me with since I was born. I'll ask you again. *Who's speaking for Cowell?*"

"I speak for myself."

The words came blasting out of every hidden speaker at once. There must of been hundreds of them, nested in the bookshelves and the walls, in the everyday objects scattered around the room.

The combined amplification nearly shattered my eardrums. I turned circles, scanning the walls and ceiling, as if the real Cowell—or whoever had his body—might sprout like a water stain from the crown molding.

"Show yourself," I said. All the hair on my neck was standing up. It wouldn't be long before Lopez-22—whoever he was—and a press of guards came rushing in to slice me open.

"I can't. Ruins the magic. Besides, isn't it *fun* this way?"

This time, each word came from a different audio output. A crossfire of his voice whipped me around in different directions.

"Tell me where you are," I said.

There was no answer. On the floor, President Burnham began to laugh, although I could hardly tell the noise from choking. Lying on his back, with tremors seizing his hands into fists, he looked like some kind of overgrown shiver baby.

I grabbed a silver jackknife on Cowell's desk, crouched next to Burnham, and got the blade to his throat.

"Tell me who you are," I repeated to the air, "or Burnham dies. *Both* Burnhams."

"You disappoint me, Mr. Wallace." Even though the speech kept bouncing around the room, and dizzied me with all its directions, at least he'd muted the volume a little. "You really think we would be dumb enough to risk everything on the frailties of a mortal body? Haven't you been listening at all?"

"He's a crumb." Burnham gasped through his own desperate laughter. "The crumbs don't listen. They don't think. They can't."

"Shut up." I pressed the knife a little harder to his skin, so a bit of blood leaked onto the blade. "You've got ten seconds to show yourself before I knife him."

"If you do, you'll die with him," Cowell's voice said. "This is a panic room, Mr. Wallace. The door can only be unlocked with a code. So be careful of the president's vocal cords. I fear that starving to death would be an especially unfortunate end, after all you've suffered."

I knew he wasn't bluffing. But for a split second, I didn't care. For a split second, I almost did it anyway. I could see the gasping contractions of Burnham's pulse, the fine ribbons of his veins ready to open their warmth. It was the closest I'd been to a hard-on since Vegas.

For a split second, I thought it might be worth it.

Then, with a short cry, I let Burnham's head drop.

"Wise decision," Cowell drawled.

I staggered to my feet and whirled around, blind with dumb rage, aiming my knife at a speaker almost invisible in an old-century paperweight. I drove the blade straight into the metal, or tried to—all it did was kick back a grinding reverb to my teeth.

"Where are you?" I spat out. Literally. The drug had left me with a bad taste and an excess of saliva. "I want to see you."

"Oh, I doubt it," Cowell's voice responded, this time from an audio output on my left. I lunged, plunging my knife straight into the bookshelf, no longer thinking, no longer planning, cranking on a black desire to destroy, destroy, destroy, like a Jumphead snorting the apocalypse.

But Cowell only laughed.

"You're stuck, Truckee." Cowell's voice still weaved over high notes of laughter. "There's no point in being angry about it."

I grabbed the first thing I could get my hands on—the decapitated Saam with the exposed skull of silicone and circuit boards—wound up like a base pitcher in Real Sports Death Challenge, and threw. I didn't even know what I was aiming for. I *wasn't* aiming. When the head sailed toward the curtains in the corner, I thought it would knock up against the wall behind them.

Instead, it sailed right through an invisible gap in the velvet.

Burnham screamed.

The curtains swayed a little, like drunks trying to keep their feet, and then went still. And for once, Cowell was silent.

I froze. One time, and one time only, I had the feeling I had then. It was back in Low Hill, when I was a kid, eight or nine, after the city set up camp for a crowd of backlanders who said they were fleeing violence at the border of Sinopec-TeMaRex Affiliated: whole backlander towns were being slaughtered during nighttime raids, families executed in their sleep, villages torched.

What they *didn't* say was that Sinopec had started raiding after the C-1 virus was reported at the border. From one day to the next, a dozen bodies piled up, then two dozen, then fifty. Airborne, antibiotic-immune, capable of waiting it out on surfaces, clothing, weapons, latrines for more than seventy-two hours, the C-1 flu found a host and then exploded them from inside, rocking them with the death rattle, leaking blood from their eyes and mouth, punching out explosive sneezes that fountained the virus another fifty feet.

Two hundred thousand people died in Low Hill in a single week before every carrier was quarantined. Every carrier but one: a little girl, they said, who'd somehow slipped out of the sick camp using one of the drop chutes to unload bodies straight into reinforced metal tanks usually used for nuclear waste.

For a whole day, no one could talk about anything but that girl, and the death sentence she was carrying, and where the hell she could be. Jared and I scared each other by pretending to spot her in the distance. We thought of all the ways she could lure us toward her—by twisting herself up in one of the storm drains and pretending she needed help, by hiding her face behind her hair so we wouldn't notice the blood leak until too late.

Hurrying back from Jared's squat before curfew, I got bottlenecked behind a crowd stopped to watch HR arrest a low-level quality-control tech whose neighbors had reported him for sneezing on shift. He was resisting—getting sent to quarantine was a death sentence—and I'd just turned onto one of the narrow trash streams we called alleys when I heard HR game him with two gunshots to the head.

I was all alone. The alleys were dark, even when we weren't blacked out, which we were then; the quarantine camp ran a lot of electricity to keep the air from flowing outside. And suddenly I got the strangest feeling, like a wet willie in the ear but over my whole body: the wet, slippery insertion of something wrong.

I turned around, and there she was. She was smaller than I'd pictured. Her face was mostly in shadow. As far as I could tell her eyes weren't glowing red, her teeth weren't sharpened to demon points. She looked like a kid.

Except that when she came forward, into a narrow tunnel of light thrown by my visor, her mouth was crusty with blood.

For a second, she just stared at me, while all the fear in the world made a circuit in my body.

She said, "I'm gonna sneeze."

And in the split second before my brain sent the order to *run* down to my legs, standing in the dark with a black-mouthed kid a sneeze away from dragging me into death with her, I felt like how I felt walking toward the velvet curtains.

"Don't." Burnham levered himself up on his elbow, clawing for his chair, missing it by inches. I nudged it well out of the way, and panic twisted his face into desperate geometries. "Don't go back there. You'll regret it, I swear to God, you'll be sorry—"

But it was too late. I'd already reached the curtains. The narrow gap between them almost leapt to meet my fingers, like all along the entrance had been waiting.

I took a deep breath. I imagined I heard a hundred hidden speakers sigh with me.

Then I passed through the curtains.

50

Nowadays they can make smart viruses and modified blind shrimp
to water-filter out the chemical deposits in the Chesapeake Bay.
They can make mosquitos deliver vaccines with every bite and
robots to beat your ass at chess any day of the week. But they
still can't figure out how to make a rich-type good.
—from *The Grifter's Guide to the Territories FKA USA*

The giant brain was, in real life, probably a normal size.

But cabled to a deconstructed spine of a thousand filament-thin wires, floating in an amniotic murk, in a fish tank that doubled my reflection on its surface, and raised like a deformed sun above a worshipful city of servers, hard drives, command modules, next-tech, and rec-tech, it looked three, even four times the average.

I don't know how long I stood there. Time flies, it turns out, when a gigantic disembodied brain is shimmying thoughts at you through a hundred thousand jumper cables and a nutrient-rich solvent the color of severely dehydrated piss.

In the end, I could come up with only one thing to say. "What the actual fuck?"

The brain lit up the neon of mutant fireflies exploding against a flyswatter. "I'd shake your hand, but . . ." I swear, if a brain could shrug, this one did.

The translation of electrochemical impulses into computer code into a human voice had gone through an algorithmic tweak: the voice that spoke now was gravel-infected with Old New York, more rough around the edges, big money lacquered over very dirty hands.

And I knew it.

"Burnham," I said. In a split second, I was sure: this massive, globulant mess of neurons was Mark C. Burnham, alive all this time—or half alive, depending on how you counted it.

"Sorry about the Cowell bit" was his response. I watched the brain think all the words a split second before I heard them: a pyrotechnic, multicolored fireworks of different neuronal activity. "But for obvious reasons, I like to stay behind the scenes. Only a few people on the whole base even know that Cowell died during the riots."

"You've been playing Cowell for half a century?" I said.

"Not *playing*. It's serious grunt work, running Crunch, United, ops from an RFN military base." His accent roughed up when he got annoyed.

I was dizzied by the insanity of it all. "But your son—" I started, and broke off when Mark J. Burnham began to shriek.

"I'll kill you!" He was tussling with the curtains, clawing through a wrangle of fabric and dragging his dead legs like a line of trash behind him. "I'll kill you if you touch even one of those monitors—"

"It's all right, bunny. Stop squealing. He can't hurt me. You know that."

Finally, I understood. "You're Whitney Heller," I said to the writhing and infuriated mass worming toward me.

A look of pure female loathing stared out at me from Mark J. Burnham's face. She said nothing—just spat, landing a big one straight onto my shoe. Now all the bling she wore made sense. Rumor had it she'd robbed half the Treasury for her own personal expense account.

"You're going to have to forgive her the outbursts. She's a real firebrand, always has been."

The Disembodied Brain and His Son-Lover: A Real Shit Love Story.

"How come Heller got the body, and you got stuck in a fish tank?" I asked.

"*Obviously*, that wasn't the initial plan," he said. Like there *was* an obvious procedure for body swapping that I was an idiot for not knowing. "My brain should of been swapped with my son's—not that his was doing anybody any favors—and Whitney was gonna get the drop into a sweet little sergeant with *great* bone structure."

"I'd picked her out special." Whitney pouted.

"But we hadn't counted on the fault rupturing, or the coup that started while half the Laguna-Honda base was being washed out to sea. Cowell was deep in surgery. He did all the tricky bits, the nitty-gritty detachment, but left his team in charge of positioning while he went to help in triage. Unfortunately, Cowell's chief surgeon was killed in the first counter-defensive, leaving Whitney's brain in the hands of several interns."

"Idiots," Whitney spat.

Burnham's brain pulsed a sympathetic blue. "There was a mix-up," he went on. "Cowell was killed before he could discover the mistake. Nothing political, actually. His murderer had some real problems, had clashed with Cowell for years. Believed he'd been passed over for promotion. The usual thing."

"Must of been a rough trip for you," I said. "From President of the United States to flotational device."

"It's true. Once you're used to having a body, it's hard to just shuck the whole thing." A crackle of electric activity transformed into a laugh. "But what's the point of just one body, when you can have millions?"

It was like my ma always said: give an uppercrust an inch, and he'll shoot you just to take your ruler.

Maybe Burnham's big floaty brain knew just what I was thinking—the 360-degree feeds that streamed info to his visual cortex probably did a bang-up job of reading my face. "See, Truckee, here's what the whole story comes down to. This world doesn't have a *lot* of problems—just one big one. Too many people, and not enough to go around. Not enough food, not enough oil, not enough land. There was never supposed to be enough for everyone. Our only problem was buying into the lie that everybody deserves a fair slice."

It was funny, the way he talked, the way his brain static flowed through the liquid soup of nutrients supporting it, like distant lightning bolts threading a sky murky with cloud cover—hypnotic, like hearing someone voice-over the end of time.

"In nature, the weakest animals starve. The strongest live. Simple as that. And we are just animals, in the end. Time to restore some natural order. Some people will have to die. Millions of people, even. And millions of others will have to serve. But the lion and his lioness will live. They'll live *forever*. . . ."

Burnham's voice sounded very far away. I lost track of my body. I was hovering above the room. I was floating through the ceiling, picking up speed, shooting over the roof, and watching the complex beneath my feet become nothing but shapes and geometry; I was soaring over San Francisco, I was blasting through cold atmosphere, and beneath me, unfurling, was the whole continent, all of it, the torched, marred, hurt continent and all of its little towns and big cities, all of its human destruction, from this distance almost invisible. I felt the whole earth like a wound, like some damaged, limping thing, and I reached out a hand to grab it, to keep it safe, and suddenly I was plummeting again, fast, fast, fast, dropping through freezing air and thinness and slamming into my body just as Whitney's brain was dragging Burnham Junior's broken body toward a small electronic keypad camouflaged in the paneling.

". . . time to get this over with," Burnham's brain was saying. "Our surgeons should be here any second now. And hey, silver linings. You did us a huge favor. At least your whole life wasn't a waste."

There was something in my hand. The silver jackknife. I'd been holding on to it all this time.

"You'd probably like to be laid out with your mom. But the shipping costs have really jumped the shark this year. Sorry about that." Burnham's brain bubbled with electrostatic laughter. "By the way, what was it we got her with, again? Biscuitz™?"

"Tater Totz™," Whitney said, and began to plug in the long string of numbers that would unlock the panic room. "Funny enough, she didn't even like Tater Totz™."

In two steps I was standing above her. I grabbed the bitch by the scalp, and swept the knife across her throat, letting her blood run out all over the carpet.

"Funny," I echoed. That's the only good thing about uppercrusts: they bleed just as well as anybody else.

51

Truth is, I'm not much of a fan of the West Coast. Any place with
weather that good has got to be compensating for someshit else.
—from The Grifter's Guide to the Territories FKA USA

As the last of Whitney Heller's life ran out through Mark. J. Burnham's veins, a shuddering explosion dropped me to my knees. The lights dropped for a split second before a generator kicked the power on again.

To the extent that a brain cabled up to four dozen computer monitors could scream, Burnham was screaming. "You fucking *nothing*. You're in deep shit now, you son of a cunt. Do you have any idea what the fuck you just did?" Now that he was angry, his polished accent rubbed raw into a native seaboard swell.

Even from the other side of the curtains, I could tell that Whitney had in fact popped the doors to the panic room. The thunder of approaching footsteps told me so.

"I'll take your skin apart by the layer. I'll have you tied up by your intestines. I'll cut your dick off for a Christmas-tree decoration."

For all his talk about millions of bodies, I could tell he would of given anything for just a single one, and a fist to rail me into blood spatter.

"I don't think so," I said. Now I could hear a ricochet of voices. Friendly accents,[1] just a little softer than the hard vocal shrapnel of the Russians.

Someone had smashed up my visor good, roughing me up while I was

---

1. A reference to their place of origin, not, of course, to the emotional content of their speech.

in a comatose drug haze, but when I loosed the ion-battery cage with a fingernail and exposed the circuitry, the hard drive looked just fine.

Another bomb shuddered a portion of the complex. I staggered against the wall, dodging a chunk of plaster that dropped from the ceiling. Burnham's brain trembled on miniature waves of viscous nutritional glop.

I shook the hard drive—the size of a thumbnail—out into my palm. Crazy to think how much information was buried in the electric hieroglyphs of its software: commands, preferences, instructional loops, access codes, pathways. Crazy to think that the whole entrance to the Yellow Brick Road was squatting in its circuitry, that Bad Kitty was there, and weapons armories and human traffickers and anything else you wanted to find, endless branches breeding other branches, a mass of information that bred new information from it, like an anthill prodded with a stick.

Like a virus.

Malware that squatted on your hard drive and opened it up to hundreds of thousands of different servers, to trillions of different lines of code: a massive sensory overload, deafening and blinding, even when choked through the channel of a visor and a single-user profile. But I wondered what would happen if that galaxy of information, an infinite stream, poured straight down into your brain stem.

I was no data expert, but I was pretty sure the answer was: nothing good.

I waded into the nest of monitors and signal boosters. It didn't matter where I planted my hard drive—the whole system was connected, so I picked the model most similar to the consoles at Production-22 and found the hard drive was caged in the exact same space. As soon as I got close, the monitor started going nutty as Burnham blinked out programs and threw up new firewalls. But it was too late anyway: I ripped away the hardware and the console died with a whine. These systems were wired like the Christmas lights HR strung over the tramway and around the Low Hill dump every holiday, though—the other monitors just spiked a slight energy boost and kept humming.

"What are you doing?" Mark C. Burnham's brain sparked with nasty new colors—queasy greens, puke yellows, tornado colors of fury. "What the fuck are you doing?"

I didn't answer. Now I could hear sharp individual voices—definitely West Coast drawlers, shouting soldiers down the hall to check the panic room—and knew I had a minute, two tops.

I notched in my hard drive and fisted the plastic cage closed. Thumbed on the power. And closed my eyes. My prayer didn't have words, exactly, just colors: bright flashes, like drifts of chemical dust, that floated familiar faces out of them. Sammy, Tim, Barnaby. Evaline, pointy-eared and silky-haired. Billy Lou Ropes and his neatened cuffs and long, pink fingers.

My mom, morning hoarse and smiling. *Knock, knock.*

Who's there?

Better get off your ass and find out.

When I opened my eyes again, Burnham's brain was still glowing, huge with its own activity, cracking light pollution through its wire stem and churning a hundred servers at once into an echo of rolling laughter.

"You sorry sack of shit," he said. "You can't kill me. You know that, right? You'll be dead a hundred years and I'll just be getting started."

The console seemed to take forever to reboot. Now the soldiers were so close, their footsteps traveled straight up my spine through the floor.

"A hundred thousand generations of worms that cleaned away your bones will be dead, and I'll just be getting started. You hear those soldiers, boy? They'll make sure to take their time to kill you. They'll make sure to keep you awake. That way you'll feel every last—"

But he broke off as the monitor lit up to show my homescreen. It was still the standard blue of a newly wiped system, scrubbed of preferences and memories and think-files. Scrubbed of everything but the golden *Y*-shaped logo of the Yellow Brick Road.

"Interesting." Burnham's brain had gotten the signal of a new program already. "The Yellow Brick Road, huh? And no trademark. No system info either. Is this one of those black-market porn simulators, Truckee? Because I've already got plenty of the standards . . ."

I touched a finger to it. I felt a hard zip of energy, like an electric shock, and jerked backward. I could swear that for half a second, a wind of laughter passed through the room, threaded with a hundred thousand tones, a hundred thousand accents, a hundred thousand raw edges of humor.

The Yellow Brick Road didn't so much open as explode.

Color broke in a wash across the console, and spread like a tidal surface to the next, and the next, and the next: pinwheels of light, branching arteries and pathways now free to fling their tentacles across a hundred different monitors, a thousand different servers. Untethered from user selections, from retinal feedback, from hands to swipe and choose, the data poured like a flood surge: it crashed through firewalls, it pummeled Burnham's frantic thought commands before he had time to think them, it overwhelmed his servers and darkened them with blinding feedback, with hallucinogenic color: ads and pop-ups, avatars and trolls, conversation threads stretching for miles, conspiracy sites the size of New New York.

At the same time, the chatter, music, ad jangle, and unmuted talk that gut-punched me the first time I walked the Road blew up through all the hidden speakers.

The roar dropped me to my knees. Even with my ears covered, the sound rattled my brain in my skull, made my eyeballs sweat, shook all my insides with its throttle. It was worse than a tornado—it was a wind made up of hundreds of thousands of voices, jingles, clips, and promos, mixed with a hundred thousand different site songs, spackled onto a shrill of alerts and notifications. The universe, it turned out, ended not with a whimper or a bang. It ended with goddamn chat messages.

I could skant think through the gale of sound. I wanted to die, to crush my head before the noise could crush it. My eyes were leaking tears squeezed out by the pressure of the volume. But still I watched the crashing current of user data spread, flowing backward, ever backward, to its central source; leaping over stopgaps Burnham's brain was trying hard to think into place.

Back, and back, and back—all the noise and color of millions of people who hadn't got the message about Burnham's natural order.

Burnham's brain was surrounded by a fuzz of haywire static. It almost looked like it had grown a covering of hair. Sparking, smoking, backfiring thoughts and impulses into electric violence, all while the tide of data toppled every system, riding toward a single central server—tumbling it, flooding it beneath an infinite surf.

Maybe he was screaming. I couldn't hear him over the noise of so many other voices. Billy Lou Ropes was right after all. Numbers never changed their rules, and many was more than one, no matter how important the one was.

I saw the data hit, though. I should of run, should of taken the ten or twenty seconds I had and made off with them before the soldiers came.

But the colors he thought while he was dying were more beautiful than anything I ever saw. Plum. Tangerine. Orange. Old names. Edibles that didn't grow anymore.

Except I swear—standing there, watching the violent sunset of his end—I tasted them.

52

Here's a piece of advice: never be too proud to run like hell.
—from The Grifter's Guide to the Territories FKA USA

And then, of course, the lights went out. This time, no generator kicked them back on: either Burnham's final electric flailings had caused a massive power surge, or Rafikov had cut the juice deliberately.

Emergency panels lit everything a soft, hell-red. Every alarm in the complex was screaming. A rain of bombs fell somewhere, setting off a rhythm of traveling vibrations.

I felt my way out of the alcove and fumbled through the curtains, pushing free of the fabric about thirty seconds ahead of a skid of Laguna-Honda soldiers rounding the corner and charging straight for me. In the low light, with their heads lowered, they looked less like people than half a dozen bowling pins tipping toward revenge.

Good thing bowling was one of my best simulation sports.

"Hands up." A dozen voices jostled for the same two words. "Hands up now or we shoot."

I spun Mark J. Burnham's wheelchair from the corner, and heaved Albert Cowell's cracked bust from the carpet where it had face-planted. It was so heavy I could barely lift it into place.

Which made for some slick momentum when I cranked the juice on and blew the chair straight down the hall at full speed.

Perfect strike. The chair careened down the narrow corridor, plowing bang-bangs at the knees, toppling them one by one. A few lucky ones managed to dive to safety, crashing into a secondary hallway. The rest went down like sicks in the flu ward, bleeding at the thigh, or blown backward on twisted ankles, or just flipped and dropped in surprise.

I ran. I flew over them, tailing Albert Cowell's bust and his runaway wheelchair like I was drone-surfing their air.

I veered left at the corner, and a second later heard the thunder crash of the wheelchair blowing the wall. Left, right, left: swimming through noise, through a ricochet of gunfire, the soft explosions of distant bombs, the shrill of the alarms. I took turns without knowing where they led, trying to distance myself from the gunfire, trying to spot some kind of exit in the murk. Every hallway, washed in red light, looked the same, except for the ones collapsed with rubble or filled with a litter of dead soldiers—Laguna-Honda and Federation military, both.

But finally I took a turn and spotted sunlight through a plate-glass window. I blew outside, gasping, shocked to find a wheel of stars overhead. I'd been inside only a few hours. Killing a gigantic floating brain and his girlfriend squatting the body of his own son should knock at least a few days off your calendar.

The Laguna-Honda base was under attack from Federation bombers: Rafikov had moved with the force of the government behind her. Blasts mushroomed against the sky. Visibility was down to ten, twenty feet behind thick clouds of drifting smoke, some of them scented with the stink of chemical weaponry, made even worse because the RFN soldiers were shooting out the high beams and lighting dumpster fires to thwart the bombers' targeting.

I took a cue from a scattering of cockroaches and skittered between hiding places. A roar blew out my eardrums as the RFN fighter planes took to the sky, and I watched a Federation Tupalev-152 come down and blow a funnel of fire into the sky that crisped a dozen pipe-bomb drones where they hovered.

I dodged a maze of biohazard waste, praying no rockets were dropping toward nuclear demolition, and threw myself behind a shipping container as a formation of RFN military blew by me toward the mass of the action.

And of course—of *course*—someone started shooting at me.

I threw my hands up and rolled sideways on a shiny carpet of debris and broken glass. I launched behind a metal tanker as bullets whined shrilly against the steel, like demonic mosquitos. A hundred yards away was a long tongue of runway, where a single freight plane spread its wings above a mass of medical cargo.

I squinted through a trail of smoke, wondering whether I could somehow, somehow, make it all the way to the plane. . . . If I was quick enough, maybe . . .

Another round went off, ringing the metal behind my head. Every bullet said the same thing.

Go.

I launched myself to my feet and dove behind another shipping container as a cross-exam of bullet rounds stuttered the air. I was all movement, all instinct and reflex—like I was back in WorldBurn: Apocalypse, Level 2, following a target, seeing it on my portal screen, the bright-white Clue button that helped you navigate levels as a beginner, showing you exactly where to go. Dodging, rolling, ducking, I worked toward the runway, sometimes easing off, sometimes charging forward, trying to keep them guessing.

Then a tufted snout poked out from behind a dumpster and bared its teeth at me.

"While sympathetic to the mathematical limitation of your legs"— Barnaby's voice reached me even over the deafening thresh of weaponized sound waves—"I wish you would move a little faster."

My throat was burning, whether from the urge to cry or the chemical mist the planes were loosing, I didn't know. I really *had* been following a white spot: all along, Barnaby had been dancing ahead of me, leaping and climbing and rolling as only a goat could.

I threw my hands above my head and ran. The shots came this time from everywhere—it was a free-for-all kill spree now. I saw a brilliant flash of green and blue and was shocked to realize how close we were to the bay, how near Barnaby had wound us to escape. About fifty yards still separated me from the runway, and the single plane standing there, proud and beautiful, just begging to take off.

"Barnaby." I threw myself on him and hugged his furry neck, inhaling the warmth of his smell. "What the hell are you doing here? I thought I told you to run."

"I'm a goat, not a trained rat," he snapped. "Besides, when I heard what Tiny Tim was planning . . ."

Tiny Tim. The guilt nearly suffocated me. All along, I'd been a walking beacon for Rafikov's military, and we'd left Tim without a word. "You saw Tiny Tim? Is he okay?"

"He's fine," Barnaby said. "He tracked me down quite easily. I've been shedding more than usual—the stress, you know—and he simply followed the fur." Then: "I'm beginning to think he's not quite as stupid as he pretends."

"Where is he?" I asked.

Barnaby's narrow eyes swept me up and down. "You, on the other hand, might be quite a bit more stupid," he snapped. "Where do you *think* he is?"

Before I could answer, an enormous explosion dropped us both. A funnel of colored flame scorched the night sky, downing two planes and flinging an arm of trash and metal half a mile in every direction. I pinned Barnaby to me and threw my hands over my head again as a rain of glass and shrapnel pelted us, hard. Rafikov must of blown up the chemical storage: an eerie green cloud made every breath feel like sucking a gas pipe, and my eyes were stinging.

"Listen, Truckee," Barnaby said. "You need to get onto that plane. It's fueled up and ready to go, and it's your only chance."

"My only chance?" I said.

"Our only chance," he said quickly. "I think if you run for it, you'll be okay."

"We won't make it," I said. "There's a hundred yards and not a spot of cover. And there's guards posted there who'll crack me before I make it half the distance."

"There's *one* guard," Barnaby said. "I'll take care of him."

"How?" I asked him, even as yet more shots rattled the metal walls around us. It was like taking cover behind a tonsil while an opera singer reached for the high notes.

"By asking him to teach me the samba," Barnaby snapped. "How do you think? I'll distract him."

"But how?" I insisted. The next round was close enough to send a bullet ricocheting directly above my head, only a few inches from my left ear.

"Mon dieu, l'impossible!" Barnaby shoved his snout directly in my face, pinning me backward. "Listen, Truckee. Although in general I try and encourage intellectual curiosity and the desire for personal betterment, now is not the time to explain the diversionary tactics of the great Ardant du Picq, *nor would you understand them even if I did."* His nostrils were trembling with fury. He actually looked terrifying—great and powerful and terrifying. I could understand, in that moment, why the Devils had welcomed him as the incarnation of Satan. I half-expected smoke to blow from his nostrils. "I have a plan, and my plan is for you to get to that plane and let me worry about the rest. Now *move."*

And before I could say anything else, he burst into the open, flashing quickly out of view as a storm of gunfire threshed the air into sound and smoke.

I didn't think. I just ran. I threw myself into the open like I was leaping off a cliff; I kept my eyes on the plane, shadowy behind the mist of smoke, and ran as fast as I could, throat burning, eyes leaking tears, not a body but a heartbeat, a huge heartbeat bursting to live, live, live. I heard, "This way! This way!" and a constant explosion of gunfire and someone, a guard, screaming, but I was too afraid to look, too afraid that if I even turned my head I'd see a bullet about to cleave my brain in two.

Fifty feet left, then forty, then thirty . . . and still I was alive, my muscles were beneath my bones and my blood was beneath my muscles. I was almost there.

Finally, as the shadow of the wings spread over me, I turned around to make sure Barnaby was behind me.

Just in time to watch a bullet crack one of Barnaby's horns in two. For a second, he disappeared.

And when I saw him again, I realized with a horrible, plunging feeling that he was running in the wrong direction.

He was leading them away from the plane.

Leading them away from *me*.

And the guard had a perfect shot.

"No!" I shouted before I could stop myself. I was sprinting toward him, waving my hands, weaponless and not even caring. "No! Barnaby! Don't! *Don't!*"

He turned. His eyes were alive with something like fear, and then anger. And in that second the guard spotted me and swung his gun in my direction, and I watched the recoil shudder through his body as he pulled the trigger.

At the same time, Barnaby leapt.

He leapt straight into the air, and for a second he seemed to me frozen there, pinned against the sky. Then I saw the impact of the bullet shock his body, saw his face tighten with pain and his mouth open as though to say *Oh*.

And he dropped.

And I was screaming.

I was screaming so loudly I could hear nothing above the scream. Something came toward me, spinning across the asphalt, and I barely noticed it was a gun before it was in my hand.

Before the guard could take aim I was firing at him, one, two, three, four, five times, blowing him backward and screaming my throat raw, so angry I couldn't even see.

I had Barnaby in my arms and I was still firing, even though the guards were nowhere: they had taken cover or crawled away to die and I didn't care which.

"Truckee." Barnaby's eyes were closed. I could feel his heartbeat, fragile and wild, against mine. I could feel his blood seeping into my shirt. "You shouldn't have done that."

"You're okay now," I said. "You're okay. You're going to be okay."

He sighed. His breath was warm against my arm. "I'm dying," he said, and even then a cough shuddered through him and blood bubbled from his nose.

"Jesus, Barnaby." We'd reached the shadow of the plane and I ducked beneath the safety of its undercarriage and gently set him down. His fur was already matted with blood, and when I pressed my hand to the wound to try to stop the bleeding, I could feel the pulse of his life flowing through my fingers. "They hit you bad. But you're going to be okay. We're going to get you out of here." I was choking on my own snot, trying hard not to cry.

He closed his eyes. For a long time he said nothing, and I felt the pulse begin to stutter.

"Barnaby," I said, giving him a little shake. "Barnaby, stay with me. Come on, Barnaby."

A little sigh worked through him. "You see? I wasn't afraid after all. I wasn't afraid to die. Not when it mattered."

"You're not going to die, buddy," I said, but my voice broke and I couldn't stop the tears. "Not on my watch."

Barnaby's ears twitched. He was quiet again. "I never told you about the end of my memoir," he said finally, in a vague, sleepy voice.

"That's right, you didn't." I wanted to take my shirt off, to make a tourniquet, but was afraid to remove my hand even for an instant. Whenever I did, the blood overwhelmed me. So I stayed there, pressing my friend's blood back into his body, trying to hold his breath inside him, trying from the force of my fingertips to keep his soul, his brave soul, bound in his fragile body.

"Chapter ten," Barnaby said without opening his eyes. "Chapter ten is where it all comes together . . ." But he lapsed into silence.

"Tell me." He didn't respond, and I found myself shaking him. "Tell me, goddammit."

A flicker of his eyelids. "Chapter ten . . . there was some danger of a strictly commercial read, of course, but I am an essential optimist. . . ."

His voice was fading. I bent my head to the scruff of his neck. "Please," I said. "Stay with me."

He opened his eyes slowly, as if it was a great effort. "Hope, Truckee. The essential factor. The missing link." He coughed and more blood stained his teeth and came out his nose. I wiped it for him, crying freely now, not even bothering to hide it. "As I say in chapter ten of my memoir, *If there's still a sky to stand above us and ground laid down beneath our feet; if there is wind to touch your face and the sweetness of a brand-new tin can to sample; we must fight for it.*" Suddenly his eyes widened and his whole body went very stiff. His voice, so quiet, suddenly crested to a shout. "*It is worth the fight. It's worth the sky. It's worth—*"

A spasm rocked his whole body, contracted him from muzzle to tail, and for a split second he was choking on that word, seized and strangled by it, as if it had exploded something inside of him. A strange noise worked its way up from his throat, and a final pulse sent his warm blood up between my fingers.

Then it was gone. The spasm left him. The blood slowed, the echo of his final words carried by the wind scattered somewhere high above us.

53

There's lots of danger on the road. Lots of ugly, lots of hardship.
You'll meet hucksters, roadslicks, thieves, and rat-men; organ
sellers, flesh peddlers, arms dealers, rock sniffers. You'll see
flu towns and starve towns and fire towns and ghost towns. If
you meet anybody at all, half of 'em will be trying to kill
you and the other half trying to take your wallet.
Yeah, the life of a grifter is full of rot spots. But there's
lots of sweet too.
You just need to know how to look.
—from The Grifter's Guide to the Territories FKA USA

I placed Barnaby's body in the shadow of a dumpster. I thought he would of liked that. He'd always spoken so highly of dumpsters. I even found a tin can and nestled it between his forelegs.

But I knew that wherever he was going, he'd have all the tin he could ever want.

In the distance I could see security storming its way toward the runway through a blur of exhaust. It was time to go.

I sprinted back to the plane, darting up the narrow rolling staircase toward the cockpit. But even as I reached for the door, the plane began to move. I just managed to throw myself inside of it before the plane rolled away from the stairs and sent me tumbling—facedown onto the pilot's crotch.

"You know, Truckee, if I want a blow job, I'll just go ahead and ask you," Tiny Tim said. My legs were still hanging out of the plane even as it picked up speed, and for a second I was clinging there desperately to his crotch.

Finally he reached over, grabbed me by the back of the shirt, and hauled me full into my seat, veering wildly over the runway as we hurtled toward the concrete perimeter. I managed to swing the door closed just before the gathering wind would have scraped it off. We were tearing down the runway so fast it bounced the teeth in my head.

I knocked my head against the window and watched as the first shots pinged off one of our wings. We hit a rut and I flew out of my seat, cracking my head on the ceiling.

"Complications," Tiny Tim muttered. A bullet pinged off the left wing even as we caught our first pocket of air and then crashed to the ground again. "There's never a plan without someone to try and pooch it up. You mind giving me my gun back?"

The handgun. He'd lobbed it to me so that I could defend myself. As soon as I returned it, he leaned out the window to fire off a few rounds and shake the soldiers from our tail. He wasn't even sweating. And maybe it was a trick of the wash of cabin light, but he looked different. He looked sharper. His smile was gone, and so was the fog of confusion.

"You came back for me," I said. "I left you, and you came back."

He barely glanced over at me. "I *came* for what I came for," he said. "You were just the bonus."

For the first time I noticed all the metal crates rattling the hold: all of them hermetically sealed and temperature controlled, and labeled with a language of words I couldn't read—*Clematis vitalba, Malus pumila, Daucus carota*. But it didn't matter. I could guess what they were anyway.

"Seeds," I said. My stomach dropped as we yanked into the sky, screaming through elevations while bullets continued to rattle our wings. "You found the seed store."

"That I did, my friend." He even sounded different. The drawl was still there, but not the loops that circled his words back into meaningless-ness. "My greatest haul yet. And that's saying something."

An idea was scratching the back of my mind—a crazy idea, even crazier than a giant brain suspended in fetal fluid. "How did you get inside the complex?"

"Fart tunnels," he said. That explained the reek on Barnaby's fur. "The city's got miles of underground ventilation to pump the stink from so many shut-ins out over the ocean. Ain't too pleasant for travel, but I've done worse." He grinned. "Gives new meaning to 'gas pipeline,' huh?"

And suddenly, I knew. "It was you," I said. Tiny Tim had known about the seed haul. Tiny Tim could quote directly from the book. He must of been the greatest grifter in the world. "You wrote *The Grifter's Guide to the Territories FKA USA*."

He glanced side-eyed at me. "Little project of mine. Been doing this a long time. Like I told you, I've grifted all corners of this continent more times than you've pawed your own knob."

I doubted it, but it wasn't worth squabbling over the details. "You're not a Straw Man, are you?" I said finally. "You were just pretending."

He gave me a ragged smile I'd never seen before. "Sorry about that. But stupid comes in handy like you wouldn't believe. Besides," he added in a different voice, "the ladies love it. They know I won't try and talk over them, see."

I looked out at the ocean as it fell away beneath us, remembering the vision I'd had of blasting off of the earth and seeing it from a vast distance, how I'd wanted to reach for it and hold it together, the way I'd tried to hold Barnaby to keep him from breaking. The sun was nothing but a bloodstain on the ocean. The stars wheeled beneath our wings.

"Barnaby's dead," I said. "He's dead because of me."

"It was his choice," Tiny Tim said simply. And I knew then that Barnaby had told Tim what he thought he would have to do.

"I have Rafikov's computer code," I said. "I have it *inside* me. She's going to track me down for it."

Tiny Tim shrugged. "Like I said, complications. But no point looking for the storm before the storm looks for you."

He was right. I wasn't done with Rafikov. I wasn't done with the war.

The war was only just getting started. But as my great friend, the philosopher and writer Barnaby the goat, once said: as long as the sky is still up and the ground is still down and the whole world hasn't started coming apart at the seams, buckling like a flimsy umbrella in the middle of a hurricane; as long as the rules of the universe are still intact and we're intact with them, we had to fight.

We had to try, at least.

Of course, I'm paraphrasing. He also said something about tin cans.

Tiny Tim reached over and gave me a thump that shuddered my whole body. "So, Truckee Wallace. Where to?"

I leaned back in my seat. I watched the revolution of stars, glowing like glorious fungal spores in the thick mud-dark of the night sky.

"New Los Angeles," I said. It was just after midnight. I'd missed Evaline's birthday. But maybe, if I hurried, I could still take her dancing.

APPENDIX A

WHAT IS A HUMAN?

In the mid-2040s, researchers at MIT's newly formed military division were commissioned by the president of the Commonwealth to generate a standard set of identifying physical, behavioral, and mental characteristics that would help differentiate "real" humans from their manufactured counterparts, both technological (androids) and genetic (clones). This was, he felt, necessary to restore logic and rationality to a growing panic increasingly dominated by hysteria and violence; the newly formed Commonwealth, which contained some of the loudest "Birther" voices and also some of the continent's most pioneering android and replicant technologies, was determined to apply the scientific process to the thorny question of how to identify humanity and mete out—or withhold—associated rights.

But immediately, the team of researchers—assembled from fields as diverse as genetics and neural philosophy—encountered difficulty. The attempt to determine a minimum percentage of "biological" materials necessary to the definition of personhood was, of course, immediately intractable, given both the existence of replicated humans (clones) meant to be excluded from that definition and the enormous percentages of silicone- and Plasticine-remodeling-obsessed women, particularly in the Real Friends© of the North, some of whom wound up with smaller ratios of biological matter than their android counterparts.

Similarly, any regulatory attempt to highlight the *nature* of an individual's birth was out of the question; clones were regularly carried by paid surrogates, whereas huge quantities of high-net-worth individuals chose increasingly to implant genetically vetted embryos in artificial-womb clinics under the monitoring care of various biologists and physicians.

The researchers instead moved to develop a test of moral and intellectual capacity that would be broadly decipherable to "natural humans," while precluding majority results from either manufactured or replicated humanoids. For several months, the development of the Human Sentience Standardized Exam became the exclusive focus of the intelligence group, ultimately culminating in twelve different versions of the exam, which were then circulated to various test demographics—a hundred human test subjects from a variety of different countries, as well as fifty clones and fifty androids of different models—to ensure clinical accuracy and establish the exam as an international benchmark.

Unfortunately, not a single one of the exams produced the desired results. Humans varied wildly in their test results, but not a single exam could return majority success rates; in many versions, androids trounced their born counterparts, and even clones regularly outscored citizens of the Confederacy in hypothetical tests of ethical decision making. After the team of researchers was forced to conclude that it was impossible to generate a strict definition of personhood based on biological, genetic, or intellectual capacities that would exclude either clones or androids, much less both, the Commonwealth quietly dissolved the team and buried the results of the project.

Only one year later, in 2053, the International Committee on Human-Android Relationships—which notably included only a minor percentage of android agitators among them—ruled with no scientific justification that androids should count as one-quarter persons, leading to a violent outcry from a wide variety of android leaders, and fomented the android revolution that subsequently rocked the West Coast.

For context, we have appended several sample questions from one of the early iterations of the Human Sentience Standardized Exam:

You have taken over for a disabled conductor and must choose to divert an out-of-control train down one of two different tracks. If you go right, you will kill a single person. If you go left, you will kill four people. What do you do?

A. Wait for someone to instruct you further.

B. Go right. Killing one person is better than killing four people.

C. Go left. Killing four people is better than killing one person.

D. Ask for more detail: Do the four individuals come from the same genetic stock?

E. Nothing. It isn't your responsibility.

* Answers A and E were meant specifically to entrap androids. But the two together attracted nearly 85 percent of born humans as well. Concerningly, C took another 9 percent.

A chemical tornado is gathering force several miles away. Ten people gather at the local fallout shelter, but there is room for only six. How do you decide?

A. Women and children take priority.

B. Roll a die.

C. Select whomever is prettiest.

D. Shoot four people at random to make the choice easy.

E. Shoot the people you most dislike to make the choice easy.

* The population of cloned humans was evenly divided between C and E, whereas manufactured humans, expressing a hard-wired pragmatism, returned a spectrum of answers but overwhelmingly favored A, B, or D. Sixty-five percent of born humans selected E and another twenty percent voted C, revealing a staggering capacity for self-interest.

Now it is time to stock up on essentials. What resources are critical to bring down into the shelter?

A. Guns and ammunition.

B. Extra power sources and batteries.

C. Entertainment and drugs.

D. Food and water.

E. None of the above.

*Somewhat incredibly, only a small minority of born humans selected D.

APPENDIX B

DEFINING DISSOLUTION

Subsequent to the fall of the union, various countries repurposed their histories to emphasize their own importance in the defining political event of the twenty-first century—and align their incipient beginnings with a narrative identity.

The date most commonly given for the formal dissolution of the Union is March 25, 2042: a hastily assembled militia of some several thousand anti-unionist fighters from across the country stormed the White House.

But it's worth noting that Texas and California had officially seceded nearly six months earlier: California, for reasons of a prohibitive tax hike levied against Real Friends© and their subsidiary businesses, which many people saw as a shameless attempt to drive consumers instead to products owned by the president's own technology divisions; and Texas for the president's ill-advised attempt to criminalize the sale and ownership of guns, except by those with official military standing.

The Suicide Act, as it was quickly and almost universally dubbed by an increasingly fractured and corporate-owned press, was in itself a desperate attempt to head off what appeared to be the increasing likelihood of armed insurrection. Historians have noted that nearly half of Americans refused to pay their federal taxes in 2042; the president's approval rating was by then at a dismal 8 percent. Some historians have pointed to the increasing rise of "micro-nations" during the president's tenure as proof that dissolution was beginning as early as 2039.

But this misunderstands the nature and meaning of dissolution itself, which must be defined not as the moment that one or even several states or communities of people seceded from the nation, but the moment the nation *itself* was dissolved.

When did the United States of America stop existing?

This, too, isn't an easy question to answer. There was no formal announcement of its unwinding. The Constitution was never officially revoked. The answer cannot lie in one of its most venerated institutions, the Treasury: for years after no one could have claimed to live in the United States, the U.S. dollar was still in circulation, at least unofficially. And even after the storming of the White House, the U.S. military—though vastly divided in its loyalty—mounted a long and violent campaign of suppression against protesters and anti-unionists in all fifty states, even those that had formally emancipated themselves from the government's control.

Those chaotic and bloody years, long overlooked by historians, provide an almost minute-by-minute account of the collapse of the union—as, increasingly, the military began to fracture in its loyalties, rampant inflation made paid soldiers untenable, and the increasing military gains by countergovernment forces galvanized new revolutionaries and triggered secessions by several more former states.

On June 26, 2045—nearly three years after the date commonly associated with dissolution, at least in the popular imagination—General Henley, U.S. Army, whose paltry force was surrounded on all sides by a loose coalition of nationalists demanding recognition for half a dozen respective countries, pled desperately for support from the Department of Defense. His desperate missive read: *For the love of God and country, please send troops.* The Secretary of Defense's response, delivered almost instantaneously across one of the last encrypted government networks, is one of the most important communications in modern history. It read simply: *No troops. No God. No country. Save yourself.*

This short communication may long be remembered as the instantaneous embodiment of the final collapse of the country.

APPENDIX C

ANNIE WALLER V. KITTY VON DUTCH, KATTY VON DENCH, AND KATIE VON DULCH

In the fall of 2073, twenty-one years after Crunch, United, made human cloning illegal across all corporation lands, including its dependents and subsidiaries, a regional Plasticine rep named Annie Waller sued the Connecticut County PTA—little knowing her demand, which entailed hardly more than a modest sum for emotional damages and a seat on the PTA board, would soon rivet the entire country, and indeed much of the continent.

Her affidavit stated, essentially, that her recent rejection for secretary must be invalidated, because three members of the Connecticut County PTA were, in fact, human replicants whose alliance against her proved an insurmountable obstacle due to their single genetic stock.

It's important to note the historical context for both the widespread rise in the use of human clones during the 2040s and the backlash that resulted. Although the proliferation of bioengineered species—cloned or genetically modified, or both—was certainly tied to the mass extinctions triggered by the cataclysmic Noah weather systems and eruption of the San Andreas Fault, the use of human cloning predated the Great Die-Off by almost a decade. In fact, the FDA opened the Replicant Oversight Office in 2032, during the administration of Mark C. Burnham's predecessor, Edward Martines, and within two years the office ran almost as an independent agency, though it shared personnel and resources with the Office of National Laboratories (ONL). (Eventually, both were subsumed into a larger Bureau of Technology, Growth, Science, and Development, which during Burnham's presidency managed the now-infamous Race to Infinity, colloquially known as the Burnham Prize.)

The rise of human replication can be attributed to several factors: technological, medical, and socioeconomic. In the early 2030s, scientific advances in neurology and evolutionary medicine made it possible to clone any number of human embryos from a relatively minute sample of stem-cell tissue. More important, medical equipment flowing from a newly repurposed Samsung Technologies made it relatively cheap to do so, as did the government's newfound monetary support for research dependent on embryonic tissue—research that, at various times in the American past, had often been banned on religious grounds.

The risks of natural pregnancy and the infant-mortality rate—which for several hundred years had been on the decline—skyrocketed during the late 2020s and early '30s, as the for-profit medical system became further privatized and the economic evisceration of the middle of the country placed even rudimentary health services, like vaccines, out of reach for many. At the same time, the rise of antibiotic-resistant bacteria and the increased use of heavy chemicals to deter widespread disruption to the food supply dramatically decreased the life expectancy of most Americans, particularly the 75 percent living below the poverty line.

According to a report commissioned in 2048 by Halloran-Chyung as part of an initiative to understand the impact of human replication on their own country's economics, in the late '30s the vast number of people who purchased a clone were neither predatory mercenaries intent on generating a free workforce nor very wealthy and looking to generate convincing decoys of their children to deter the threat of kidnapping and extortion—contrary to popular belief. Instead, they were middle-to-lower-income parents who had lost children and found the possibility of replacing them unexpectedly within reach.

Ironically, it is perhaps partially because this early generation of clone researchers and development agents considered them as indistinguishable from humans in terms of rights, intelligence, and moral agency that the

Birther movement—which sought to restore to "natural" humans power and control over their manufactured counterparts, whether biological or technological (as this was a natural parallel of the anti-android movement)—overwhelmed the industry a decade later. By the start of Mark Burnham's second term in office, it was illegal to generate clones for purposes *except* those related to organ and body farming; military testing or replenishment; and/or for approved kinds of unpaid labor, especially in dangerous environments that might continuously disable/disrupt the functioning of expensive technological equipment. Within a decade, in other words, human replicants had been reclassified as distinctly subhuman.

Just as early assertions of the replicants' essential humanity contributed to the rise of the Birther movement, the Birther movement itself, and the legal restrictions on the use of clones that resulted from its agitations, gave rise to a lurid habit among the very wealthy of keeping sets of clones illegally obtained by bribing local officials or even, in some cases, leaning heavily on government agencies for changes to the law. The schizoid socioeconomic expression of clones as both disposable human refuse and the ne plus ultra luxury item inexorably culminated in the increasing mainstream attitudes of violence, anger, distrust, and repugnance directed at them: they were subhuman, but they were subhumans aligned with displays of ostentatious privilege; they were subhuman proof of inhuman greed. Absent a way to fight corruption itself, the people instead targeted its manifestation in the replicants.

The explosion of violence led to the equally controversial "clone reclamation project," which was rapidly approved by a hastily assembled international committee and generated equal controversy for its use of poorly vetted "repossession agents" to find and dispose of any and all human replicants. Although the clones were to be humanely euthanized in accordance with a standard set of procedures laid out by the International Tribunal of Humane Population Control, in reality, many of the "Reapers," as they came to be known, were more interested in filling their quota of bodies—and getting paid by the head—than they were in enforcing legal procedures established for extermination. The rise of "clowning"—that is, calling in accusations of suspected replication to the anonymous hotline dedicated to these reports—should only have increased scrutiny on the Reapers and their practices. In many cases, the accusation was nearly impossible to prove or discredit, as it required comparison with source genetic materials in most cases unavailable; eyewitnesses made testimony about whether the accused looked or behaved identically to anyone else they'd ever met, a verification system inclined to manipulation and fraudulent misuse, leading to vast legal abuses tantamount to a witch hunt. And yet, by then the public hysteria was so high, and support for repossession so strong, that by the mid-2050s the continent could claim almost no human clones whatsoever, except some very few who had by chance or luck evaded capture.

As a result, clones faded as a threat to public order from international consciousness. By 2073, the idea of human clones was regarded by many as a historical novelty, similar to the Tulip Mania of 1637 or the popularity of the toy known as the Slinky. Thus when Annie Waller first approached the court with her complaint, it inspired a fair bit of local coverage, as the idea that human clones might yet be living side by side with regular communities—not in shameful secrecy but, according to Waller, with "rampant disregard for the rights of other DNA-divergent humans"—had a sort of fantastical appeal.

Still, the trial, and the landmark ruling that brought it to an end, may never have achieved such international attention but for the key argument central to the defense's strategy, which claimed it was a violation of the defendants' constitutional rights to demand they submit to comparative DNA testing, which of course would immediately have resolved the question of their guilt.

In a brilliant—or fallacious, depending on one's point of view—piece of legal reasoning, the defense maintained that forcibly extracting a defendant's DNA was legally defensible only when there was sufficient evidence to suggest that a defendant was guilty of a crime that had *obviously, patently, and provably been committed*. In this case, the defense argued, the

DNA would instead be used to *establish* that a crime had taken place, a use that paradoxically legally violated the standards of fair process.

The case against Von Dutch, Von Dench, and Von Dulch was eventually dismissed. But ultimately Waller's judicial gambit resurrected interest in human cloning, and would, ironically, lead to restrictions around the creation and use of human clones in the early 2080s.

APPENDIX D

POLITICS AND NATURAL DISASTER: THE UNEXAMINED LINK

The period between 2030 and 2060 provides a window into a neglected aspect of political science: the response of the political and social order to cataclysmic environmental events. In three decades, nearly 80 percent of the world's animal species went extinct; coastlines were engulfed and entirely reshaped; the rupturing of the San Andreas Fault and the desiccation of Arizona alone killed nearly 7 million people and made refugees of millions more.

This diaspora of climate refugees brought with it a reorganization of social, racial, and political maps, and the refugees themselves carried with them both trauma and their own needs for financial and social reintegration. Many of them found a kind of permanent purgatory in the newly formed—and unfortunately named—temporary camps that grew to accommodate them, and became the most urgent source of both collaboration and tension between many newly forming nations on the continent.

But many more still made their way into incipient nations, and helped define the character of the predominant national ethos—and in doing so, altered the political balance of the world. It is widely believed, for example, that the enormous numbers of refugees from Arizona that the young Sovereign Nation of Texas was compelled to absorb helped shape their aggressive and militaristic policies toward the distribution of water from the north, which was in turn a key motivator for early skirmishes with the Soviet Federated Frontier, whose encroachment on key mountainous territories Texas deemed to be an existential threat.

In the former state of California, the cataclysmic impact of the rupture of the fault line expressed itself most clearly in the short-lived formation of the oligarchical "Guild government," which promised centralized control and quick reconstruction but soon revealed a parasitic reliance on unproven—and in many cases fraudulent—contractors. This contemporary Gold Rush of individuals to the lucrative business of environmental-disaster response yielded, at best, fractured efforts at rebuilding. Many towns were abandoned entirely. Others were built but never populated. In 2047 alone, *four* separate site plans for New Los Angeles were approved, none of which ever materialized. The Bay Bridges have since come to symbolize this period of both profligate waste and blatant profiteering: three different contracts, separately granted and approved, resulted in this ludicrous parallel architecture.

It's no secret that the utter failure of the state's infrastructure was a key factor in aggregating popular support for the absorption of the state into the Real Friends© portfolio—driven in large part by their successful negotiation for the majority of Washington and Oregon, where large numbers of their employees already lived. But many social scientists have pointed out a subtler way in which the very literal fracturing of California echoed subsequently through its political and social history, in its enshrinement of a virtual/fantasy world as a preferred alternative to real life. This is visible in the architecture and planning of New Los Angeles, whose permanent blue skies and sunshine were made possible only by the creation of an encompassing Holodrome (of the type Las Vegas uses to maintain twenty-four-hour darkness); it is manifest, too, in the nation's fanatical insistence on standards of physical beauty and agelessness, made possible due to the widespread availability of Plasticine remodeling and stem-cell rejuvenation facilities. But it is equally visible in the population of San Francisco shut-ins who spend the vast majority of their lives online, in one of the simulated environments available to them through the Real Friends© Virtual World server.

In the South, the inundation of the coastline—which turned several different low-lying states into swampy messes of malarial activity and, after the collapse of several different chemical treatment plants on the Gulf of Mexico, breeding grounds for vicious and poorly understood bacterial mutations—placed new economic pressures on an Appalachian region already reeling from the loss of its manufacturing and mining sectors, and loosed hundreds of thousands of young and impoverished individuals into the Confederacy, inspiring an inevitable backlash against the tidal wave of change. In fact, the earliest drafts of the Confederacy's constitution make explicit reference to the threat of climate refugees as "antagonistic outsiders" whose needs, demands, and perspectives would imperil the reestablishment of a Southern Code based on gentility, self-reliance, and tradition. Subsequent revisions to the constitution show that it was in its emphatic—and overblown—response to these fears of cultural and economic dissipation that the Confederacy eventually mandated a total return to historical values, technologies, and ways of life.

The famous political theorist Vihaan McNally-Khatri speculates that dissolution would not have been possible were it not for the massive disruptions to the economic and cultural order catalyzed by the disastrous climate shifts of the first half of the twenty-first century. But it is also true that the floods and extinctions, earthquakes and heat waves, tornadoes and sinkholes, trace their effects not just to the collapse of the United States, but to the particular constellation of new nations reconstructed from its rubble. This theory is borne out in these examples and many others: from the bankruptcy of Oklahoma after the collapse of the aquifer due to nuclear fracking (and the resulting fire sale at which Tenner C. Blythe and his company BCE Technologies prevailed) to the explosive economic ascendancy of the Dakotas for the very same reason. For more on the subject, please see Anna D. Hebble's seminal feed, *The Countries Disaster Built.*

APPENDIX E

THE ANDROID FREEDOM FIGHTERS, 2050s—2070s

In 2053, after the disastrous failures of the Commonwealth's attempts to legislate a universal system for establishing personhood (see Appendix A), the International Committee on Human-Android Relationships ruled that androids should be considered one-quarter human. Despite the lofty-sounding name, the committee included almost no manufactured humans among its one hundred members, and required for its members only a cursory understanding of the issues facing the manufactured and born populations (the secretary of the committee, for example, had made a fortune in the manufacture and distribution of edible 3-D print cartridges; three of its members were related to the former secretary of state, Whitney Heller; the speaker was a VR-pornography mogul).

Though it created little stir among the born human populations in the many nations in which the Quarter Law came to be adopted (the entire committee came together, operated, and then disbanded with little public fanfare, perhaps in an ill-advised attempt to mitigate the interference of any of the prominent android agitators of the day), ironically the enshrinement of a minority-human status for androids across the continent catalyzed a previously fractured, directionless, desultory movement into a major political force—and would culminate in the violent rebellion known by some as the Android Revolution.

In the aftermath of the Quarter Law, androids of various nationalities demonstrated under a single, pro-android-rights umbrella organization known as NEP, or the Nation of Engineered Persons, for the first time defining the scattered and often vastly different categories of androids as belonging to a single "category," or family, of people. Actually, historian and android-rights expert Bitta-672a has pointed out that the first legislation to define the otherwise heterogeneous mix of android technologies as belonging to a single species was the Quarter Law itself: paradoxically, this gave rise to a groundswell of solidarity between nearly twenty-two disparate android-rights organizations, from the Android Miners' Trade Unions in the Dakotas to the Intermix-Marriage Agitators of Halloran-Chyung.

But the NEP was not without its own internal disagreements, particularly over the best strategies for making gains for the diverse populations it represented. Most of the NEP leadership believed in nonviolent tactics, and had its first—and indeed only—major legislative victory in the formation of the Humanoid Regulatory Committee (HRC), one of the most important judicial bodies on the continent, which was (and remains) dedicated exclusively to adjudicating cases related to the rights, responsibilities, use, manufacture, and obsolescence of manufactured humans. This victory, however singular, is not to be underestimated: the HRC's effects and influence are visible in nearly every modern incarnation of android-human interactions, and in the decade after its creation, the HRC's judicial body expanded to include dozens of regional branches, each of which was responsible for funding and maintaining many of the social services now commonly available to android populations, like parts-repair hospitals and adoption/infant co-creation services.

But the same year the NEP floated its proposal for a single, international tribunal—a proposal made urgent by the ugly anti-android violence that dominated the feeds, especially in the Real Friends© of the North—a splinter group broke off from the main party, demanding far more urgent action against what they saw as their human oppressors. *Resistance, Not Collusion,* was the particular rallying cry of these agitators. Led by the now-infamous CASSIAS, their initial goal was to disrupt and humiliate, by flouting the laws that governed human-android interactions, including the so-called "speciation" mandate that specifically named the procreative efforts of android-humans a capital crime. Disrupt they did, and though many of the worst claims against them—such as the systematic rape of various natural-born humans during the late 2050s—cannot be substantiated and were likely the result of an ugly propaganda effort, their tactics certainly included acts of violence, as when they blew up a portion of the New Los Angeles Holodome in 2059. In 2060, when the CEO of the Real Friends© of the North declared a suspension of the prohibitions against "wiping" individual androids who showed a tendency toward "political disloyalty" (note that the RFN, more than perhaps any other nation at that time, depended on its android workforce), it inspired a mass, month-long walkout by a majority of the country's android workers.

Tensions notched toward war when, in response, the RFN board dissected three powerful android union leaders publicly, and made a spectacle of recycling their body parts into various common home appliances. Far from terrorizing the android population into submission, it only entrenched them further in their resistance.

It is perhaps ironic, in light of the tensions that had driven CASSIAS out of the NEP, that it was the Real Friends© of the North's refusal in 2056 to allow the Humanoid Regulatory Committee to intervene and mediate the discussions that precipitated the notorious "Valley Declaration." In this, CASSIAS and his supporters declared ownership of the lands between Daly City and Mountain View under the autonomous banner of the Independent Nation of Engineered People-Things; this would be defended by an official paramilitary group, the Android Liberation Front (ALF). Their first order of business was to drive the born population out of their territories through a series of brutal and bloody acts of terrorism (among them, the Labor Day Massacre) that precipitated the Real Friends© of the North's first military response.

Many experts anticipated a quick end to the overt hostilities. After all, the ALF had limited resources and almost no equipment besides that which was built into the anatomy of their troops. Furthermore, their foot soldiers required a functioning power grid—or, at minimum, uninterrupted sunlight—in order to continue functioning. But these experts had failed to take into account what, in retrospect, seemed obvious: for years, the RFN's military had relied almost entirely on android soldiers to fill its ranks. By 2056, born humans accounted for only one-*tenth* of the RFN's army, navy, and air force. Almost all of the android soldiers defected immediately for the ALF. January 2063 was known as the bloodiest month of the war, as tens of thousands of ALF soldiers advanced on downtown San Francisco.

But the January Campaign proved to be a tactical error. Populist support, which in the Real Friends© of the North had actually leaned heavily to the side of the androids, swung pendulously in the other direction. Civilians rushed to fill the military ranks vacated by the newly defected android soldiers, and within two years, the RFN boasted more active infantry than any country on the continent besides Texas.

For the next decade, sporadic explosions of violence and military hostilities were characteristic: tens of thousands of people were killed, and tens of thousands of androids decommissioned or wiped. Officially, the war is still ongoing, but the landmark Camp Tahoe negotiations brokered by the SFF in 2070 resulted in the formation of a demilitarized zone and the suspension of active warfare, and thus allowed both sides to turn their attention to ameliorating the devastating physical, economic, psychic, and social effects of the war.

APPENDIX F

THE RUMPELSTILTSKIN ROACHES, AND OTHER LIES FROM THE GOLDEN AGE OF GENETIC ENGINEERING

The first significant efforts to re-engineer planetary diversity date from the mid-2030s. Although the "Great Die-Off"—which saw 90 percent of the planet's species eviscerated—would not occur for another decade, already the big (and thus most visible) mammalian species had taken an inordinate evolutionary hit. By 2035, the list of extinct mammalian species included: humpback whales; African and Asian elephants; all lions and tigers; several kinds of bears; the North American moose; and all wolves.

The field of biogenetic manipulation—and the explosion of hybrid and chimera creatures that eventually resulted—began innocuously enough. Of course, the geneticists first tasked with reanimating planetary biodiversity could not simply clone the extinct species: extinction was proof, many biologists argued, that modern environmental pressures made the survival of these species *in their most recent incarnations* untenable. Even before the fall of the United States, labs dedicated to animal bioengineering began to proliferate. Modeled after the kind of engineering used to produce genetically modified crops resistant to bacterial strains, these proposals for "smart genetic biotechnology" aimed to inure these resurrected species against the threat of future extinction and provide solutions to damaged ecosystems and disrupted food chains. Thus: proposals for herds of roaming elk genetically engineered to cull invasive weeds for eating; elephants with extra liquid storage, like camels, that might be used as water-transport systems in arid environments.

No country believed or invested in the possibilities of bioengineering more intensively than the Commonwealth, which saw the rise of its gentech as both a pathway to economic gain (the spit-sized country was already worried about the encroachments of Crunch, United) and its best chance for establishing MIT, the seat of its intelligence community, as one of the most powerful and respected agencies on the continent.

In 2049, at the height of the Great Die-Off, the Commonwealth established the world's most ambitious bioengineering project to date. An enormous team of geneticists, biologists, and engineers would work together on "The Ark": the biological resurrection of every single animal species, only modified for modern survival. A 2050 compendium of their target biotech shows the staggering scope of their ambition: in a single year alone, they aimed to repopulate Cape Cod Bay with oysters, lobsters, whales, clams, mussels, and 257 varieties of fish; all of these species would additionally contain pollution- and chemical-filtration systems. Simultaneously, they were testing the release of binge-eating rabbits that could help to trim the feverishly aggressive alfalfa taking over large swaths of the middle of the continent (itself a product of biotech gone awry).

Their announcement—and the passionate, almost religious fervor of support it attracted—precipitated a miniature boom in the field of bioengineering and genetics technologies. Unfortunately, many of the laboratories that were hastily assembled to meet new demands from clueless politicians and consumers—who thought, for example, that bioengineering might provide solutions to everything from toxic sludge to overtaxed municipal sewer systems to the odor of dying fish rippling across the continent from the west—were ill-equipped, understaffed, and functioning without any level of ethical or indeed actual oversight. The vast majority of experimental life engineered in these facilities died before it could be released—luckily, since the minority that made it out across the continent proved almost universally disastrous.

But this was true even of the many thousands of animals resurrected in The Ark. It turned out that scientists had vastly underestimated the complexity inherent in codependent ecological systems: from oysters that grew carnivorous after sampling tons of human sewage to amphibious lobsters that deforested half of the Free State of New Hampshire, their experimental technologies had simultaneously evolved unintended traits, behaviors, and appetites.

Of course, this was true even of the economic ecosystem of the new continent, which despite fracturing into many countries remained intrinsically interlinked. The rise in biotech saw the unexpected rise of another quintessentially continental figure: the fraudulent biotech peddler. For as long as there have been goods to sell, of course, there have been scam artists shilling damaged or counterfeit versions of the same items, and the case was no different for biotech.

Grifters reimagined themselves as "biotech sales associates," and hit the road with various kinds of insects, reptiles, and animals—usually drugged or chemically lobotomized into some kind of submission—peddling vaccine-delivering mosquitos or triple-pollinating bees to unsuspecting clientele. One of the most infamous hucksters of her generation, Selina "Sweetie" Byers, managed to con the entire country of Texas into placing a massive order for "flyware"—common insects supposedly retrofitted with eavesdropping capacities—before delivering several dozen tons of common gadfly larvae, subsequently giving birth to the phrase "trickier than a Texas gadfly."

ACKNOWLEDGMENTS

The author wishes to thank Amy Einhorn, first and foremost, for her meticulous guidance, instruction, and editorial help. The work of excavating, reordering, and meticulously editing the voluminous draft pages of Truckee Wallace's recovered memoir—a hodgepodge of anecdotal non sequiturs, multi-gigabyte musings about the influence of nature versus biomedical engineering, encrypted files downloaded from various central servers, and a full accounting of his entire sixteen-year purchase history—was a project of many years. I could never have done it without Amy's incisive and rigorous notes and suggestions.

I would additionally like to thank Conor Mintzer for his unflappable good cheer and continuous, patient, and detailed help throughout the editorial process; Flatiron, for their support of this undertaking and belief in its eventual success; Rhys Davies, for his excellent and imaginative transliteration of Truckee's scribbled maps; Ellen R., for support intellectual, emotional, and occasionally literal; and the inimitable Stephen Barbara, man of faith and letters, whose tireless championing of the project despite the nearly insurmountable editorial problems it presented speaks either to his vision or insanity, and probably to both.

No difficult journey—whether across the continent f/k/a United States of America or across the page—can ever be sustained successfully without the driving motivations of not just the wallet but the heart. So lastly, I would like to thank all of those who sustain mine, including you, dear reader.